CASCADE-OLYMPIC NATURAL HISTORY

Daniel Mathews

Cascade-Olympic
Natural History

A Trailside Reference

Second Edition
Updated and Expanded

Raven Editions
Portland Oregon

Library of Congress Cataloging-in-Publication Data

Mathews, Daniel, 1948—
    Cascade-Olympic natural history / Daniel Mathews. -- 2nd ed.
        p.   cm.
    Includes bibliographical references (p.   ).
    ISBN 0-9620782-1-2 (alk. paper)
    1. Natural history—Cascade Range. 2. Natural history—
Washington (State)—Olympic Mountains. I. Title.
QH104.5.C3C38   1999
508.795—dc21   88-61494

Library of Congress Catalog Card Number: 99-32445

Printed in U.S.A. by Publishers Press, on acid-free paper. Book design by
John Laursen. Typeset in Minion. Cover design by Martha Gannett; photo
by Gary Braasch: Old forest, Western Cascades. Back cover inset photo by
Daniel Mathews: North Cascades in fall color.

Eating wild plants and fungi is inherently risky. Individuals vary in
their physiological reactions, and may make mistaken identifications
regardless of their level of expertise or the accuracy of printed information they read. The publisher and the author cannot accept responsibility for their health. Readers eat wild foods at their own risk.

This book is for
the fourlegged people
the standing people
the crawling people
the swimming people
the sitting people
and the flying people

that people walking
with them may know
and honor them.

Preface to the Second Edition

In the eleven years since *Cascade-Olympic Natural History* came out, more than water vapor has transpired in the Northwest woods.

Wolves returned, denning and raising pups in the North Cascades. Grizzly bears leave signs of their presence. Lyme disease, hantavirus, and *E. coli* 0157 arrived, and Stinky Bob spread. A honey mushroom clone usurped General Sherman as The World's Largest Living Thing. Cougars became more dangerous (though still far less so than, say, cars or rifles.) Spotted owls neither disappeared nor began to recover, but were joined on the political firing line by marbled murrelets and various salmon and trout. Taxol fulfilled its promise as a cancer drug, and is now synthesized from farmed yew needles, so Pacific yews are no longer imperiled by their own life-giving ability. New extractive industries bloom.

Scientific name changes affected 120 of the species in the book. I also added 34 species, 9 new sidebars, and 130 line drawings. By re-editing for terseness I held the net gain to about 10,000 words, and by reducing the type size slightly and wrapping the text around the art I kept the size and number of pages the same as before.

No Cascade volcanoes erupted. But the idea that our subduction zone produces major earthquakes grew from an intriguing hypothesis to a consensus view. Backed by several independent lines of evidence, it even has a date: the last one was a magnitude 9 (about as big as quakes get) at 9:00 p.m. on January 26, 1700.

Cascades frogs, whose decimation was a mystery ten years ago, now stand revealed as victims of stratospheric ozone depletion. Ecologists measure Cascade tree rings and find growth accelerating; is it the increased carbon dioxide, or climate change? Geologists measure the shrinkage of Cascade glaciers as an index of global warming—but this past winter's snowfall set new world records. The East Pacific Ocean warmed for several years, helping cause Northwest salmon and smelt numbers to plummet, but that climate trend may have just turned a cyclical corner.

While ancient forests continue to fall, the term "climax forest" falls further into disuse. Ever more clearly we see the ubiquitous hand of fire and random small disturbances, and the equally ubiquitous touch of symbioses that were completely unknown just a few decades ago. I see our forests as a post–Ice Age story still in, let's say, its third chapter, rather than as an eternal verity.

In a word, there's still a lot to learn. Join me…

Acknowledgements

Many people have been amazingly generous, cooperative, and interesting, in the course of putting all this information in your hands. David Perry, Lorelei Norvell, Bruce McCune, David Duncan, Ernest A. Mayer, and Jon L. Riedel reviewed portions of this edition and made helpful suggestions and corrections. That's in addition to reviewers named in the first edition. Any errors that survived are my fault entirely. Thanks again to the contributors of illustrations and photographs, and to Keith Garnett for improving the maps. Thanks to John Laursen and Martha Gannett, who fielded endless pesterings from me for design and production advice.

It has been my pleasure to work the names of several scientists into the text where I quote or paraphrase their papers. Of course, I could not name every contributor of important research without making this book itself look like an academic paper, so, to those of you whose names do not appear, my apologies. And to the many who gave their time to explain things to me over the telephone or by e-mail, my profound thanks. In particular Ken Chambers, Scott Sundberg and Bill Burley responded unstintingly to repeated inquiries.

Finally, from the heart, I thank Sabrina, Gabriel, and Margot, who generously yielded family time to allow me to reach completion.

Photography Credits

Cover by Gary Braasch. Back cover inset by the author. The author by Laura Ewig Garnier.

Plants (pages 115–46) by the author, except squawcarpet, ladies-slipper, buckbean, dogbane, woolly-sunflower, sweetpea, and yerba de selva by Julie Kierstead; and yellow pond-lily by Gordon Whitehead. Fungi and lichens (pages 483–89) by the author, except destroying angel, honey mushroom, autumn galerina, and hedgehog mushroom by Kit Scates; fly amanita and king boletus by Preston Alexander; and admirable boletus by Kent Powlowski.

Mammals by Tom and Pat Leeson, except Douglas squirrel, flying squirrel, jumping mouse, and striped skunk by Richard B. Forbes; badger and mule deer by Geoff Pampush; ground squirrel and chipmunk by Nancy A. MacDonald; red tree vole by Murray L. Johnson; marmot by Roger Baker; and vole nest, gopher cores, porcupine, mountain goat, and bear/bobcat slashings by the author.

Birds by William E. Hoffman, except osprey, red-tailed hawk, kestrel, prairie falcon, ptarmigan, and dipper by Tom and Pat Leeson; Mallard, harlequin duck, Vaux's swift, and downy woodpecker by

Richard B. Forbes; grebe, heron, vireo, and warbler by Harry Nehls; goshawk, tree swallow, and Cassin's finch by Tom Crabtree; northern flicker and western flycatcher by Nancy A. MacDonald; golden eagle and blue grouse by Geoff Pampush; Townsend's solitaire by Jeff Gilligan; song sparrow by Roy Gerig; and bald eagle by Ethel Paschal.

Amphibians and slug by Richard B. Forbes, except Larch Mountain salamander, Oregon slender salamander and roughskin newt by Alan D. St. John.

Butterflies by John Hinchliff with the author.

Rocks by Gene Pierson with the author.

Drawing Credits

Raven emblem and mosses (Chapter 6) by Barbara Stafford Wilson.

Maps by Keith Garnett, reworking originals by Kris Elkin.

Conifers and Flowering Trees and Shrubs (Chapters 2 and 3) by the U.S.D.A. Forest Service (artists not known); except yew, ponderosa pine, cottonwood, aspen, ninebark, bitterbrush, elderberries, snowberry fruit, salal and pyrola by Willis L. Jepson, courtesy of the Jepson Herbarium; and Douglas-fir, whitebark pine, cedars, hazel, Scouler willow, cascara, cinquefoil, maple-leafed currant, Oregon-boxwood, Oregon-grape, yellow heather, single delight, crowberry, and twinflower by Jeanne R. Janish, by permission of University of Washington Press.

Flowering Herbs and Ferns (Chapters 4 and 5) by Jeanne R. Janish, used by permission of University of Washington Press; except rushes, bottlebrush squirreltail, groundsel, thistle, hawkweed, lovage, cow-parsnip, poison-hemlock, and water-hemlock by Willis L. Jepson, courtesy of the Jepson Herbarium; wall lettuce from *The New Britton and Brown Illustrated Flora*, by permission of the N.Y. Botanical Garden; and meadow-rue by Barbara Stafford Wilson.

Flower parts (pages 147, 181); leaves (pages 88, 186-88); mammal tracks, antlers, and volcanoes by Kris Elkin.

Insects (Chapter 13) by Eric Eaton with Kris Elkin; bark beetle galleries (pages 458–61) by the U.S.D.A. Forest Service.

Mammals, Birds, Amphibians, and giardia by the U.S.D.A. Forest Service, except tailed frog by Pat Hansen, and great horned owl, raven, jays, and Clark's nutcracker by Sharon Torvik, all by permission of the Oregon Department of Fish and Wildlife.

Reptiles by Alan D. St. John; used by permission.

Fishes by Ron Pittard, used by permission of Ed Lusch/Windsor Publications (courtesy also of Frank Amato); except shorthead sculpin by Reeve M. Bailey, used by permission.

Contents

Organization of Chapters 2–6 (the Plants)

Cascade-Olympic Natural History

The high mountains in the neighborhood, which are for the most part covered with pines of several species, some of which grow to an enormous size, are all loaded with snow; the rainbow from the vapour of the agitated water, which rushes with furious rapidity over shattered rocks and through deep caverns produc[ing] an agreeable although at the same time a somewhat melancholy echo through the thick wooded valley; the reflections from the snow on the mountains, together with the vivid green of the gigantic pines, form a contrast of rural grandeur that can scarcely be surpassed.

—David Douglas
March 20, 1826

1

The Cascades and Olympics

This book is designed for the rucksack that can't hold a library. It treats most field guide subjects—plants, mammals, birds, lower animals, and the land itself—in a single volume. Included here are not only plants and animals you can't miss, and unseen creatures that see you, but also many equally vital, but often overlooked, smaller organisms.

Cascade-Olympic Natural History is much more than names, identifications, and pictures. It describes the behavior of living things, and their relations to each other, to habitat, and to people.

The Cascades and Olympics comprise five visibly different physiographic provinces described in this chapter. The varied landforms are unified by their inhabitants; along similar east-to-west cross-sections they support similar communities of plants and animals. Though the wet Westsides contrast dramatically with the dry Eastsides, north-to-south changes are slight and gradual between southeastern Alaska and the far tip of the Sierra Nevada.

Within that long spectrum the sharpest single vegetational shift (brought about largely by the duration of summer drought) is between Central and Southern Oregon. This book keeps its range unified by drawing a boundary at the Willamette/Umpqua divide, a common practice in Northwest plant books. That means species are included based on their prominence in "our range" rather than in the Cascade Range as a whole. And it means generalizations about "here" may not apply to the Southern Oregon and Northern

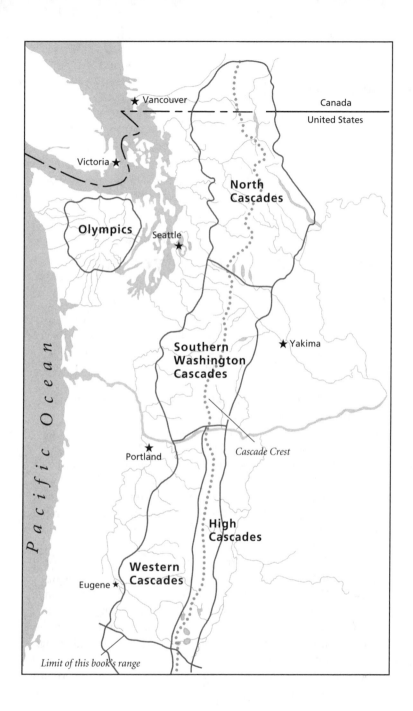

California Cascades. Nevertheless, the book can be used outside of its range, especially in the Coast and Insular Ranges of British Columbia and Southeast Alaska, and in the Oregon and Washington Coast Ranges. It should be useful also in the mountains of Northeast Washington, Southern Interior British Columbia, and adjacent Idaho and Montana.

The Olympics

The Olympics are unusual in being a nearly round mountain range. No strong grain is discernible in the layout of their peaks and ridges, and their drainage patterns are often described as "radial"— the main streams radiating from the center—suggesting that they result from the uplift of the round range, rather than predating it. This radial pattern is less clear at the center of the range than at its perimeter.

With help from a geologic map (page 550) and some imagination, you can see a deeper pattern—NW-to-SE arcs, bowed out to the northeast. The greatest of these is the Olympic Basaltic Horseshoe, a belt making up the south, east, and north flanks of the range and running WNW out to Cape Flattery. Just inside this arc lie a number of concentric arcs—ridges, valleys, faults, additional slices of basalt. Each arc includes prominent peaks, evidence of basalt's relative resistance to erosion. The rest of the rocks in the Olympics derive from marine sediments—shale, sandstone, graywacke, and their metamorphic products slate and schist.

During the last Ice Age, major ice sheet tongues grinding west through the present-day Strait of Juan de Fuca and south through Hood Canal shaved the abrupt north and east flanks of the Olympics. These megaglaciers brought huge loads of rock from Canada, leaving individual boulders as "erratics" at elevations up to 4,500' on Olympic slopes—impressive visual aids for imagining the enormity of the ice. The valleys have since been thoroughly recarved by smaller alpine glaciers, of which today's glaciers are the uppermost remnants. Lower portions of valleys were left with broad bottoms lined with outwash gravels and cobbles, and later terraced by minor glacial advances and retreats of the last 1,000 years.

The same processes worked on many Cascade valleys, but here in the western Olympics some poorly understood combination, including ocean fog and heavy selective browsing by elk, has produced a unique style of forest (see page 36). The Olympic Rain Forests are famous for huge conifers, both standing and down, and an abundance of tree-draping mosses, lichens, and ferns unequaled outside the subtropics. But in comparison to other Northwest old-growth these forests are parklike and open—to sunlight, and to people on foot.

Timberline—the transition from closed forest to meadow vegetation—begins below 4,000' in parts of the Olympics, yet a few trees grow on 6,000' crags nearby. This situation doesn't fit concepts of timberline developed in other mountain regions. Many alpine timberlines are a function of temperature; up to a certain elevation there are trees, and above that grow smaller, more cold-tolerant plants. Such a timberline would lie well above 6,000' in the Northwest. Our timberlines are low thanks to the short growing season; the sheer quantity of snow takes a long time to melt. (Annual precipitation, most of it snow, probably exceeds 240 inches—the greatest total in the lower 48 states—somewhere high on Mt. Olympus, but the difficulty of servicing snow gauges up there leaves both the location and the amount imprecise. Precipitation decreases sharply northeastward; see page 560.) Additional effects on timberlines here, especially in the western Olympics, are that they are broad elevational belts; they are continually, subtly shifting; and since they enjoy a warmer climate than subalpine areas elsewhere, their meadows are extraordinarily luxuriant.

The North Cascades

Extending from the Fraser to the Snoqualmie and Yakima Rivers, the North Cascades are the topographic *ne plus ultra* of the entire lower 48 states. Local relief, measured as the total ups and downs on, say, a fifty-mile line crossing the range, exceeds that of any comparable breadth of U.S. Rockies or Sierras, and approaches that of the Alps. The majority of the active glaciers in the lower 48 states are here; most of the remainder are on other Cascade volcanoes or Olympic peaks.

These glaciers, and the much longer, deeper incarnations of them that waxed and waned over the last two million years or so, eroded the mountain walls to their present precipitous state. Filling the stream valleys nearly brimful with ice, glaciers deepened them and reshaped them from V to U cross-sections. Heads of major valleys in the heart of the range were eroded to within 3,000' of sea level, leaving such a low gradient (slope of descent) out to sea that current stream cutting is relatively slow. With the ridgetops eroding as fast or faster than the valley bottoms, relief is about as high as it can get—until uplift speeds up or the glaciers grow down into the valleys again.

If you reach a high central viewpoint on a clear day, you can't miss the resemblance of North Cascade topography to waves on a stormy sea—wild array, whitecaps, vastness, and generally equal height. The broad equality of peak heights is attributable primarily to frost shattering (expansion of ice within cracks), which breaks down rocks most efficiently at elevations where the temperature goes from well above to well below freezing on many, many nights each year. At higher and lower elevations the freezing point is crossed less frequently.

At any rate, major peaks near the Cascade Crest from Canada to just southeast of Glacier Peak tend to be 8,000–9,000' high. To the north, south, and west of that backbone, elevations of peaks and valleys decrease together, so that local relief is scarcely less; 6,000' peaks on the Western range-front, or near Snoqualmie Pass, are nearly as impressive as 8,500' peaks on the Crest.

Eastward there is a marked decrease in ruggedness (with one dramatic exception, the 9,415' Stuart Range) even though many peaks are over 8,000'. Frost shattering and stream erosion, rather than alpine glaciers, were the chief sculptors of the eastern North Cascades, and they produce gentler topography. The rain shadow effect (pages 559–62) makes alpine glaciers relatively scarce east of the Crest. Where Ice Age glaciation had the greatest effect on eastern topography—in the Pasayten—it was more gentling than sharpening. The Okanogan Lobe of the Cordilleran Ice Sheet ground across the entire area east of Ross Lake for a few centuries just before its abrupt retreat 17,000 years ago.

The rain shadow effect also populates the East Slope with strikingly different plant and animal species. The Cascade Crest line that marks the falling off of precipitation and glaciation, and the sharpest biotic shift, diverges at its north end from the drainage crest which is marked by county lines and the Pacific Crest Trail. This true Cascade Crest runs along the Picket Range and Eldorado Peak, through the center of North Cascades National Park, before converging with the drainage crest from Boston Peak south. In this book, "Cascade Crest" and "Eastside" refer to this true, albeit nontraditional crest. In other words, Ross Lake and Granite Creek are east of the Cascade Crest.

The geology of the North Cascades is a bewildering variety of rock formations of widely differing ages. Geologists consider it a cluster of exotic terranes that has been joined to North America for only around 50 million years (see page 554). Most of its rocks are much older than that, unlike the rocks of the rest of the Cascades. Major North Cascade peaks are made of gneiss, schist, or granitic rocks, all rare in other parts of our range. Conversely, volcanic rocks, which comprise the other Cascades almost exclusively, constitute only a small portion of North Cascade rocks—two High Cascade-age volcanoes (Mt. Baker and Glacier Peak) and some residue of Western Cascade-age volcanoes in the form of sediments eroded from somewhere above the present peaks and deposited in peripheral basins. The deep roots of those long-gone volcanoes remain at today's surface in the form of granitic intrusions.

The High Cascades

The High Cascades Province includes all of Oregon's famous snow-capped volcanoes, with elevations of 7,500 to 11,235 feet. Building upon a long, 5,500-6,500' plateau consisting of overlapping volcanoes dating from the last seven million years, the conspicuous cones grew within relatively recent times—the last ¾-million years. Some will erupt again.

All but the youngest (South Sister, Bachelor) are markedly eroded by glaciers. Most have had sides of their craters breached (Hood, Jefferson, North Sister). Several are stripped down to mere cores of their former selves (Three-Fingered Jack, Washington, Thielsen), their "necks" or central magma columns remaining after much of the more fragmental flanks have eroded away.

The base plateau has been sharply incised by streams or glaciers in only a few places. It includes most of the mildest topography in our entire range, and all of our biggest high lakes.

A different High Cascades eruptive style produces basaltic cinder cones and lava flows much smaller and more numerous than the high cones. Many basaltic volcanoes, such as those of the McKenzie Pass area, appeared within the last 20,000 years.

Volcanoes of the Washington Cascades and of Southeast British Columbia and Northern California are of High Cascade age, type, and tectonic origin; they are High Cascades volcanoes, though not all in the High Cascades physiographic province. The main difference is that north of the Columbia the major peaks are isolated and surrounded by older material, rather than connected by a volcanic plateau of High Cascade age (less than seven million years).

The Western Cascades

In Oregon, the Cascades form two parallel mountain provinces—the High Cascades and the Western Cascades. Few Oregonians and fewer maps identify the two separately, but you can easily see them on a good relief map, or from several viewpoints. For much of their length they are separated by north-south stretches of the major westward-draining river valleys, the Clackamas, North Santiam, and McKenzie.

The Western Cascades are a heavily wooded jumble of 4,000-5,600' ridges left standing between valleys cut, primarily by streams, into a great mass of volcanic material. Few volcanoes as such remain; to put that another way, individual mountains were given their present locations by erosion, not by the vents their materials originally erupted from. The exceptions, like Battle Ax, are outliers of the later High Cascade volcanism. What we have here is the eroded base of an old volcanic range, originally much like the present High Cascades but larger and more prolonged in its activity. The locale of activity shifted 20 to 40 miles eastward around 7.4 million years ago, when Western Cascade volcanism gave way to High Cascades volcanism.

The Western Cascades bear no glaciers, and lie entirely below timberline—though "grass balds" and "hanging meadows" persist on many exposed, thin-soiled sites. Less spectacular than the High Cascades and with far greater timber value, they have received scant and belated protection as Wilderness Areas. On their lovely, riffled rivers, fishery and recreation values have often suffered in competition with hydroelectric potential.

The Southern Washington Cascades

Here we find the same elements as Oregon's High and Western Cascades Provinces, but not separated into two lines. The youngest and most active of our stratovolcanoes (St. Helens, less than 40,000 years old) is near the western edge. Far to the east lie the Cascade Crest and our two highest peaks (Rainier and Adams, built over the last half-million years) as well as the Goat Rocks, remnants of a huge, somewhat older volcano. Still more voluminous, though less towering, are Indian Heaven and the Simcoes, two areas of basaltic shield volcanoes southwest and southeast of Mt. Adams. All of the above are of High Cascade age—younger than seven million years.

The remainder of the province, like Oregon's Western Cascades, consists of erosional forms carved out of the base of a 35- to 8-million year-old volcanic mountain range. North Cascades-style elements also emerge toward the north end of the province, where the slightly higher latitude and altitude (5,000-7,750') produced more and bigger Ice Age glaciers, leaving as their legacy a few remnant glaciers and a great deal of glaciated topography. The old volcanic rocks around Mt. Rainier have been uplifted thousands of feet since they were formed, perhaps twice as much as the 3,000' of uplift near the southern edge of the province. The net difference in peak elevations is only a fraction of difference in uplift, since erosion accelerated as well, nearly keeping pace; but much deeper parts of the old volcanoes are now exposed here, including several granitic intrusions. If uplift continues, with its inevitably concomitant erosion, they would probably expose more granite and turn the area into an extension of the North Cascades. Some day that may well come to pass.

2

Conifers

If when you think of hiking here in the Pacific Northwest, you think of cool, dark, mysterious forests of huge conifers, you've got the right picture. The area made rainy by the Cascades, Olympics, and other Pacific coastal ranges is the Conifer Capitol of the World. This is the only large temperate-zone area where conifers utterly overwhelm their broadleaf competitors. It grows conifers bigger than anywhere else, and the resulting tonnage of biomass and square-footage of leaf area, per acre, are the world's highest, even greater than in tropical rain forests.

Our conifers don't just win growth contests against other trees when each grows in its native habitat. They also outgrow natives of similar climates when they're planted in each other's habitats. In other words, the superiority is at least partly in the trees' genes, not just in our climate and soil. Though just one small test plot has been growing long enough to demonstrate this, industry has been acting upon the assumption for a century: noble fir and Douglas-fir have been heavily planted in Europe, New Zealand, and Chile, but the Northwest's tree farmers have shown no interest in non-native trees. One possible explanation is that European conifer genes were sabotaged by ten to twenty centuries of "high-grading"—logging the best trees and leaving the rest to perpetuate the forest. (High-grading was rife here, too, but only for only a century or so.) Also, the climate here may have come up with the cream of the crop by selecting tree species able to handle both huge snow

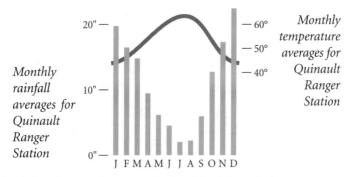

Monthly rainfall averages for Quinault Ranger Station

Monthly temperature averages for Quinault Ranger Station

loads in winter and—get ready for this—drought in summer.

It's *when* the rain falls that makes our region unique. Generally, a wet temperate climate on this planet either supplies rainfall throughout the year, or concentrates it in the warmer months. (See p 558.) Here, summer brings low humidity and frequent drought, actually so severe for weeks at a time, most summers, that conifers and broadleaf trees alike close their leaf pores, shutting down photosynthesis rather than risk serious drying through open pores.

Succession vs. Chaos

In the forest you can see a continual "succession" of slow changes—different kinds of conifers increasing or decreasing in number, stature, and health or vigor. It might look like this: deep forest; canopy foliage way up out of view; the biggest trunks mostly groove-barked Douglas-fir; a few fibrous-barked red-cedar and checkery-barked western hemlock; ground profusely littered with cones conspicuously including Douglas-fir cones with their three-pointed bracts; but the saplings are hemlock—not one Douglas-fir! If it all could age several centuries without other forces coming into play, the Doug-firs would die and hemlocks, with a few redcedars and silver firs, would replace them in succession.

This would happen because hemlocks tolerate understory conditions (primarily shade) while Douglas-firs are relatively intolerant, i.e., young Doug-firs lose their vigor, their health, their needles and usually their lives when kept in deep forest shade. In higher forests you might see Pacific silver fir saplings in deep shade, either in lieu of or along with hemlock. Western hemlock and Pacific silver fir are the most tolerant tall trees here and probably anywhere in the Temperate Zone. Old-growth forests containing a lot of them are considered "late-successional."

For a deciduous broadleaf tree, whose main life functions are confined to the half-year when it has leaves, this is a great handicap. Our evergreen conifers, in contrast, get more than half their photosynthesis done during spring, fall, and even winter, when sunlight and temperature are limiting but moisture, to say the least, is not.

Nutrient uptake during the cooler seasons is likewise crucial, since summer drought shuts down the bacterial and fungal decay activities that liberate nutrients. Evergreen conifers, though slower than flowering trees in acquiring nutrients, acquire them all year long. They also deploy them efficiently, retaining their needles rather than jettisoning them each growing season.

Our conifers' sheer size is an advantage here, providing storage space for water to tide them through summer. In many other regions, typhoons and hurricanes blow through often enough to make the genes for great height and longevity just about pointless.

The term "ancient forest" refers, of late, to the finest stands of Northwest old-growth. To earn that title, the oldest trees in the stand should be over 400 years old. That's old, no question. Yet as

Succession used to be described as a linear series with a stable end-state called a climax community; the series would reach climax if it wasn't interrupted by a "disturbance" such as a forest fire, flood, blowdown, landslide, avalanche, or logging. Today, many ecologists avoid the term "climax" (or marry it to disturbances in oxymorons like "fire climax," avalanche climax," and "disease climax") because they see disturbance as omnipresent, turning the successional ladder into a maze of feedback loops and eddies, with elements of chaos. For example:

Fungal (rot) diseases create canopy gaps *by continually killing some dominant trees. Even a hemlock will slow to negligible growth under a closed canopy, and will reach canopy stature only if a gap opens for it to grow into. Most windthrown trees (outside of windswept coastal forests) are victims of rot fungi.*

One root rot fungus *species lives and expands for well over 1000 years, very slowly killing most trees (some genera more than others) within its perimeter. The resulting patches have sparser canopies and richer understories and wildlife populations. See page 268.*

Mycorrhizal fungi *transfer photosynthetic products from big trees that produce them to little seedlings that need them. This subsidy helps*

a forest community type, these forests are barely out of diapers. They are not the product of millions of years of genetic refinement coevolving *in situ*. Before the last Ice Age ended, 14,000 years ago, our region was too cold for today's megaconifer species; it supported communities resembling those of today's northern Rockies. Before long, it was too warm for 5,000 years; much of the Westside saw frequent forest fires and supported rather sparse forests with a lot of alder. The Puget Trough had vast oak savannahs. Nor, as far as we know, did today's combination of Douglas-fir, western hemlock, and red-cedar form ancient forests in any other region nearby, ready to move here collectively as the climate shifted. The best estimate is that forests resembling today's Northwest Coast ancient forests have only existed for five or six thousand years.

Their biography isn't merely short; it also hinges on twists of climate. Stands we call ancient today mostly originated between 1448 and 1538, a period slightly colder than the twentieth century which had several really enormous fires, perhaps due to a few dry summers with prolonged strong east wind patterns. Our ancient forests rose from those ashes, and it seems reasonable to say that the

---

determine which seedlings survive long enough to take advantage of a gap and become independent.

Plants alter the soil to stabilize their own positions. Though hard to see and poorly studied, the changes are profound. They involve soil texture; acidity; beneficial mites and protozoans; beneficial fungi; antagonistic fungi; and "allelopathic" chemicals produced by plants, which are toxic to other plant species. Some kinds of disturbances totally disrupt community self-stabilization; others don't at all.

Certain understory plants can take over and prevent tree growth indefinitely. (Peat mosses, p 250; salmonberry, p 81; manzanita, p 105; snowbrush, p 102; bracken, p 239.) Chance variables determine when and where this happens. Many boreal forests, for example, tend to be replaced by treeless muskeg except to the extent that tree seedlings germinate on mineral soil raised up on the roots of windthrown trees; killing trees, paradoxically, is the only way to maintain forest there.

Plants alter climate. In our mountains, old lichen-draped trees can double local precipitation by intercepting cloud droplets; young forests are less effective at this. In the Amazon basin, rain forest doubles rainfall by recycling it through transpiration.

exact ancient forests we admire could only have been produced by that kind of century followed by several less pyrotechnic ones, at first cool and then warmer. Their opportunism and rapid development here is both encouraging and frightening to realize, when we contemplate what global warming might due to them in the century to come. (Page 571.)

"Conifer" is a common name for trees and shrubs in Phylum Coniferophyta, many (but not all) of which bear needlelike leaves and woody "cones." The largest family of conifers, the Pine family (page 16) has both needles and cones. The Yew family (page 38) has needles but carries its seeds singly, in juicy berrylike orbs. The Cypress family (page 55) has cones, but has sprays of short, crowded scalelike leaves (except for junipers, which may have either scale- or needlelike leaves) and bears dryish, several-seeded "berries" instead of woody cones. The four other conifer families are not native here. (Higher taxonomy, including this phylum, is very unsettled; the version this book follows is on page 577.)

All conifers are woody, i.e., trees or shrubs. They produce true seeds by sexual fertilization, but they lack true flowers. The young

---

Climate is always changing. It can oscillate from year to year (the El Niño/La Niña cycle); it can slide over a 50-year period or flipflop drastically in the space of a decade; changes can be regional or global, natural or human-caused (p 568-72). Northwest old-growth forests developed partly during the Little Ice Age; forests originating in the present (warmer) century will probably never duplicate them.

Browsers, grazers, and predators alter vegetation. Human actions thus pervade wilderness, as when elk hunting and wolf eradication outside Olympic National Park caused elk population swings that in turn affected seemingly pristine rain forests.

Fire-adapted forests maintain their normal healthy state with the help of frequent low-intensity fires (page 44). Without these, they develop in directions that make pest outbreaks, fungal diseases, and high-intensity fires inevitable. In general, fungal disease, insect infestations, and fires (or lack of them) can all lead directly to each other.

Feedback loops tend to involve at least three species, often from three kingdoms. Trying to study a relationship between just two species often produces an incomplete or distorted picture. Understanding ecology requires understanding whole systems.

---

cones are the female flower counterparts, receiving airborne pollen from less conspicuous male "staminate cones." Seed plants other than conifers are "flowering plants" or Angiosperms.

Confusion abounds over the many terms for conifers and flowering plants. Flowering trees and shrubs are "broadleaf" even though a few, like heather, have needle-thin leaves while some conifers, like the bunya-bunya, have rather broad ones. To a forester or a lumberman, conifers are "softwoods"—even those few that are very hard, like yew. "Evergreen" and its opposite, "deciduous," refer to whether the foliage remains alive through more than one growing season; people tend to think of them as synonymous with conifer and broadleaf, but in fact there are several deciduous conifers, like larch, and a great many broadleaf evergreens.

Conifers with single needles

Douglas-Fir

Pseudotsuga menziesii (soo-doe-**tsoo**-ga: false hemlock; men-**zee**-see-eye: after Archibald Menzies, p 97). 72" diam × 250';* needles ½–1½", varying from nearly flat-lying to almost uniformly radiating around the twig, generally with white stomatal stripes on the underside only, blunt-pointed (neither sharp to the touch nor notch-tipped nor broadly rounded); cones 2½–4" × 1½", with a paper-thin 3-pointed bract sticking out beneath each woody scale; soft young cones sometimes crimson or yellow briefly in spring; young bark gray, thin, smooth with resin blisters; mature bark dark brown, deeply grooved (up to 12" thick with grooves 8" deep), made up of alternating tan and reddish brown layers visible in cross-section slice; winter buds ¼" long, pointed, not sticky; trunk usually very straight, tapering little. Ubiquitous below 4,000'. Pinaceae (Pine family). Color p 115.

As a first rule for recognizing Northwest trees, I can propose with only slight exaggeration that if you see a big evergreen tree, it's probably a Douglas-fir. This is far and away our most abundant

---

* Dimensions given for conifers are those typical of intact mature specimens on the very best sites the species naturally occurs on.

---

and widespread tree, and one of our biggest. Economically it's the Northwest's chief crop and export. If you see a board in the Northwest, it's very likely Doug-fir. It would be a strong candidate for World's strongest, straightest, fastest-growing tree. Rarely can so many superlatives be heaped on one species.

It's also the tallest. The coast redwood's better-publicized claim to being tallest is an artifact of early logging, which went for the finest Douglas-fir stands, taking no prisoners nor measurements. One giant remained, near the Wind River, to die a natural death in 1930: it was 393 feet tall—taller than any recorded redwood, with almost twice the bulk of any of the competing Doug-fir champs of recent decades. Canadian loggers claimed to have measured a 415-footer after felling it in the Lynn Valley just outside Vancouver.

The tree is named for David Douglas, popularly but erroneously known as "the Discoverer of Douglas-fir." It is chauvinistic and silly to call any paleface the discoverer of America or of any conspicuous feature on it; but even to Western science, this species was described before Douglas was born, by another Scot, Archibald Menzies, who was surgeon and botanist on Captain Vancouver's ships in 1791. The tree didn't escape Lewis & Clark's notice either, in 1806. All that was left for Douglas to do in 1825 was to sing its praises, and ship its seeds, to a waiting England. Douglas called it a pine; later taxonomists tried out "yew-leafed-fir," "spruce," and finally "false-hemlock," while sticking with fir for the common name. In truth it is none of the above. Like our hemlocks and cedars (two more misapplied European names) it is in a Pacific Rim genus, having three congeneric species in Japan and China and one in a tiny mountainous area of Southern California. Since 1826 it has been planted abroad with great success, especially in New Zealand and Scotland; Douglas and Menzies would be pleased.

For a century, timber extraction ruled Northwest economics virtually unchallenged. Douglas-fir was the top timber species and Washington and Oregon, in succession, were the top timber states. In the 1990s, a century of overcutting finally caught up with us. Our National Forests are catching their breath while their mission gets redefined through political processes; meanwhile, private harvests are at a low while rotations planted after 1950s and 60s clearcuts are not quite ready to cut. So for a few years now, Douglas-fir has come in second (in board feet logged, if not in value) to yellow pine from plantations in the southeastern states.

Douglas-fir's commercial reputation was built upon our inheritance of old-growth fir trees, now on the verge of total depletion. Top grade fir plywood and lumber is the close-grained, almost knotfree stuff the tree makes after its first century, after the scars of self-pruned limbs heal over on the lower trunk. This part of the tree's volume is added more slowly than the wide-grained, knotty wood of its youth, so timber crop rotations of longer than 30 to 75 years don't look cost-effective to traditional timber accountants. The old dogma holds that centuries-old wood will never command a sufficient price to carry an extra 200 years of capital costs. However, at least one newer study shows that it just might, i.e. that long rotations can produce equal quantity and superior quality of wood if the forest is carefully, repeatedly thinned. More importantly, the diversity and health of the ecosystem—including the commercial timberland—requires that all ages of forest be represented throughout the region, not just in a skein of protected wilderness

David Douglas should be canonized as the patron saint of Northwest backpackers. Time and again he set off into the wilderness, usually with Indian guides or Hudson's Bay Company trappers, but also often alone. He packed a cast-iron kettle, a wool blanket, lots of tea and sugar, trade items such as tobacco and vermilion dye, his rifle and ammunition, and pen, ink, and reams of paper for wrapping plants, seeds, and skins—no shelter usually, no dry change of clothes, no waterproofing but oilcloth for the papers and tins for the tea and gunpowder. Often without food in his pack, he might eat duck, venison, woodrat, salmon, or wapato roots; other days he consoled himself with tea, and berries if he was lucky. Once while boiling "partridge" for dinner, he fell asleep exhausted and, waking at dawn to a burnt-through kettle, counted himself clever to boil up a cup of tea in his tinderbox lid.

He approached each Indian as a potential friend, accepting his dependence on Indians for food, information, or portage while also knowing some of them would rather kill him or steal than barter for his goods. "They think there are good and bad spirits, and that I belong to the latter class, in consequence of drinking boiling water and lighting my tobacco-pipe with my lens and the sun." Perhaps they didn't intend to kill Man of Grass quite as many times as he thought.

Douglas figured he walked and canoed 6,037 miles of Washington and Oregon in 1825–26. In 1827 he crossed the Canadian Rockies to along the Cascade Crest. Ancient forest sanctuaries cannot preserve anywhere near enough of the ecosystem to keep it healthy. They need lots of help from the surrounding logged forest in the form of simulations of natural forests. Until that vision has been reality for a few (human) lifetimes, clear vertical-grain Doug-fir lumber may remain exceedingly scarce.

Douglas-fir predominates in natural forests here almost as much as in managed timber. In the biggest Cascade forest population study done yet, it was the dominant tree species in two-thirds of the sample plots; in the lower-elevation half of the study, it was the only plant species found in all 202 plots. It's our only tree that's equally abundant west and east of the Cascades; it even grows down the east slope of the Rockies, and is abundant over a wider elevational range than our other trees, being uncommon only at upper and lower timberlines.

Douglas-fir moved into the Northwest fast 14,000 years ago, at

---

Hudson's Bay to catch a ship back to England. For all that, the Royal Horticultural Society paid him their standard collector's salary of £100 a year, plus £66 for expenses. His mission was to ship them seeds or cuttings to grow lucrative exotics for English gentlemen's gardens. He enjoyed minor celebrity in London at first, but soon ran into the proverbial difficulty keeping his head above water in high society.

He undertook a still more ambitious plan to trek from Northwest Mexico to Southeast Alaska and Kamchatka to Europe. He did cover central California, the Columbia region again, and the Fraser River (losing all his notes, journals, and instruments in the Fraser Gorge rapids) before sailing to Hawaii where, at the age of 34, he came to a gruesome end. Out walking alone with Billy, his faithful Scotty dog, he was gored and trampled in a pit trap for feral bulls. Did he fall, or was he pushed? Rumors that he was pushed persist to this day.

As a boy in Scotland, Douglas was too rebellious (or energetic) for school; his stonemason father took him out at age 11 to apprentice in gardening. As his interest grew, he gleaned a botanical education wherever he could, eventually auditing lectures by William J. Hooker (page 166). Hooker took young Douglas on field trips in the Highlands, was impressed with his fanatical drive and enthusiasm, and sent him off to London and fame. Despite the spotty education, Douglas wrote well, sometimes eloquently, in his journals. Their subject fascinates.

---

the end of the last glacial stage. Curiously, we don't know where it moved in from. Some areas near the Oregon-California line were probably warm enough for it, but its pollen has yet to turn up in quantity in any Ice Age pollen study. The warm era between 9,000 and 5,000 years ago established it in the Westside foothills and lower mountains. Frequent fires apparently kept the forests relatively open at that time, preventing shade-tolerant conifers from becoming abundant. Mature Doug-fir bark, thick and corky, is more fireproof than any in our region except ponderosa pine.

Douglas-fir was traditionally regarded as a climax dominant only in the Eastside parts of its range that are too dry for significant populations of more shade-tolerant species. West of the Crests it was thought of as "seral," or doomed to be shaded out of the competition sooner or later. It's true that its seedlings can't grow in the shade of a closed forest canopy, so Doug-fir numbers may trend downward, but canopies don't stay closed long enough to sweep Doug-fir off the game board. There are too many fires and other gap-forming agents, and Doug-firs live too long. Putting it purely in numbers, foresters who watched the rate of species change in a 400-year-old west-side forest for 20 years calculated that Douglas-fir would take 755 years more to disappear. When similar forests have been examined for fire history, the average return intervals for major fires range from 300 to 550 years.

The Northwest will soon have truly indigenous fine alcoholic spirits: a clear *eau de vie* turned brilliant green by infusion of young Douglas-fir branchtips. It has a touch sweetness reminiscent of the legendary "Douglas-fir sugar" exuded from Douglas-fir needles under rare weather conditions in northeastern Washington.

Other Indian uses of the tree were also minor: sap could be chewed, thick bark gathered for fuel, and the trident-bristling cones, either tossed into the fire or gently warmed next to it, fortified people's hopes for a break in the weather. Douglas-fir wood was economically unimportant until white men came with steel tools; red-cedar was much preferred, both for aesthetics and for ease of working.

The seedlings are a winter staple for deer and hares, and the seeds are eaten by small birds and rodents. Bears strip the bark to eat its succulent inner layer; this wounds the tree, often fatally, by making an opening for invasions of insect larvae or rotting fungi.

Western Hemlock

Tsuga heterophylla (**tsoo**-ga: the Japanese term; hetero-**fill**-a: varied leaves). Also **lowland hemlock**. 42" diam × 200'; needles of mixed lengths, ¼–¾", round-tipped, flat, slightly grooved on top, with white stomatal stripes underneath only, spreading in ± flat sprays; most cones just ¾–1" long, thin-scaled, pendent from branch tips; mature bark up to 1' thick, platy, checked (almost as much horizontal as vertical texture); inner bark streaked dark red/purple; branch tips and treetop leader drooping. Pinaceae.

My image of western hemlock is of a sapling's limbs, their lissome curves stippled a soft green made incandescent, in the understory dimness, by a stray swath of sunlight. While less abundant than Douglas-fir as a canopy tree, western hemlock is far and away our commonest understory sapling, owing to its efficiency at utilizing those scant filtered rays. Its hordes of saplings are the wave of the future; western hemlock is a chief late-successional tree of nearly all sites below 3,500' in and among mountains west of the Cascade Crest, and also on some Eastside slopes at around 2,600-4,000'.

Western hemlock is not only slower-growing, but also shorter-lived and hence inevitably smaller than the behemoths it replaces—Douglas-fir, Sitka spruce, and the coast redwood, *Sequoia sempervirens* in southwest Oregon. A Westside forest succeeding to hemlock may trend toward smaller stature and a younger average age. Size and longevity may impress humans, but as competitive strategies they are most useful to tree species that tend to die out in succession, and hence need old seed trees to hold out until the next postdisturbance opportunity. In contrast, hemlock's terrific shade tolerance is a slow but sure tactic assuring that forest succession will always tend to favor it.

Thanks to shade tolerance, hemlocks can share an acre of

---

sunshine among an exceptional number of individuals, leading them to a kind of speed record. Where there's plenty of moisture, as on our coastal fog-belt lowlands, a very young pure hemlock stand can produce organic tissue ("biomass") at a phenomenal rate—the fastest yet measured in the world. A densely stocked acre of mature hemlocks often yields more board feet than a like-aged stand of larger but necessarily sparser Douglas-firs. Hemlocks

Nurse Logs

The best seedbed for a NW conifer, especially a hemlock, is the rotting trunk, stump, or upended rootwad of a fallen tree. In some stands, especially in the Olympic rain forests, these "nurse logs" support hundreds of seedlings and saplings while the ground in between has none.

Buttresses, prop roots, and colonnades are typical shapes and patterns of grown trees that reveal their origins on nurse logs long after the nursing wood itself has disappeared. By age ten or sooner, a seedling extends fine rootlets down a nurse log's sides to mineral soil, even from perches 20' up on snag tops. Over the decades, the rootlets grow into sturdy root "stilts" while the nurse log slowly rots out from underneath. You can see this process at all stages; at some point the support relationship may reverse, a few chunks of rotting nurse now dangling from tree stilts. Over the course of two to six centuries, the nurse log disappears and the stilt roots fill in, remaining as buttresses on the lower trunk of a huge spruce, hemlock or Douglas-fir. (Red-cedars develop flaring buttresses without stilt root origins.) Where adjacent trees' buttresses head straight toward each other, more or less meshing, they were once stilt roots on the same nurse log. You can also infer a bygone nurse log under a row or "colonnade" of trees with aligned buttress roots.

A nurse log plainly offers great advantages to a seedling, but what these are has been the subject of a lot of speculation and some research. Here are a few hypotheses:

Water: This writer is convinced that year-round moisture is the key. Well-rotted wood stays sodden all through the summer, not only retaining rainfall but actually manufacturing water as a decomposition by-product. Water may be especially critical in deep forest because the canopy trees consume so much of it, while dim light severely slows growth of a seedling struggling to reach reliable moisture with its root.

Moss thickness: A thorough study by Mark Harmon found the species

achieve their efficiency partly by sheer leafiness—a six-inch trunk typically supports over 10,000 square feet of leaf surface area, almost twice as much as Douglas-fir. While the greater leaf area catches more light, it also loses more moisture; shade tolerance seems to be a tradeoff against drought tolerance.

Western hemlocks are prolific: notice the profusion of little hemlock cones on the forest floor, or on the tree, lending it a

---

of moss competition to be key: soil was covered with Oregon beaked moss in a 3" mat, too thick for seedlings to root through and reach secure moisture in their first summer. Nurse logs had only a 1" moss mat (a mix of other species) and first-year roots could get through that. Unfortunately, the study site was at Cascade Head, a coastal headland that soaks in cool, thick fog during summer high-pressure weather, making it one of the few sites in the Northwest with no summer soil drought—and with such uniformly thick moss mats. I am unsure how well the results apply to other forests. Even in the Hoh rain forest, summer can dry out soils, especially on well-drained cobbly river terraces.

Litter: *Dale Thornburgh found hemlock seedlings fatally flattened by tree litter coalescing within melting snow in some montane forests. Hemlock seedlings were confined to nurse logs there, and he deduced that litter sloughs harmlessly off of nurse logs.*

Mycorrhizae: *Quickly forming a mycorrhizal partnership with a fungus is crucial to conifer seedlings (page 260). While some mycorrhizal fungi specialize in rotten logs, and link up with nitrogen-fixing bacteria there, forest-floor humus appears to be at least as supportive of both these kinds of partners as logs are.*

Disease: *Nurse logs may be "pathogen-free zones." Many fungi produce chemicals toxic to competitors, including pathogenic fungi.*

Nutrients: *A young conifer inherits suitable nutrients from a conifer log, but again, they are not known to reach advantageous levels there.*

Sunlight: *A good position for catching light, up above fern, herb, and shrub competition, is an explanation often heard. This may figure in some cases, but in many groves the competition is almost entirely up on the nurse logs with the conifer seedlings. Seedlings favor Douglas-fir and spruce logs over hemlock, and half-rotted logs over either fresher or totally decayed ones; these preferences point to factors other than physical position.*

---

purplish cast in the distance. Cones are produced copiously every year—unlike most other conifers that drastically vary their seed production in order to limit the numbers of seed-eating creatures. Each year, a mature hemlock drops more than one viable seed per square inch of ground under it. Only an infinitesimal fraction, of course, will make it to tree size. More than any other species, western hemlock reproduction is confined to "nurse log" substrates—rotting logs, snags, rootwads, etc. (See page 22.)

Mature hemlocks, with thin bark and shallow roots, are frequent victims of fire or wind, and also of heart rot, the usual cause of death among aging hemlocks and the first strike against them as lumber. Hemlock wood is rather soft, weak and prone to splitting, but resilient and easily worked. It's excellent for gym floors, for example, displaying good sportsmanship under softsoled pummeling. In recent years, strips of clear, straight-grained hemlock command prices equal to clear Douglas-fir, for use as mouldings and door and window veneer; they don't need strength in those roles, after all, and they keep their pale color better than fir. But the bulk of the hemlock harvest gets pulped for paper.

Northwest tribes used tannin-rich hemlock bark to tan skins; to dye and preserve wood (sometimes mashed with salmon eggs for a yellower dye); to shrink spruce-root baskets for watertightness; to make nets invisible and even alluring to fish; and on their own skins to stop bleeding. They smeared the pitch on their faces to prevent chapping or to provide a dark sticky base for face paint.

Under the bark lies a soft layer which some tribes ate to tide them over the lean times of late winter, after the dried salmon was all eaten or putrid. Countless hemlocks (and some Sitka spruces and other trees) died, their bark stripped to keep the Indians from starving. Though edible fresh, the "slimy cambium" was preferred steamed in pits over heated rocks laden with skunk-cabbage leaves, then pressed with berries and dried in cakes for later consumption with the universal condiment, candlefish oil.

The word "hemlock" traces back to A.D. 700 as the English word for the deadly parsleys notorious for their role in Socrates' execution. The English somehow saw parsley in the lacy foliage of certain unfamiliar New England conifers; they called them hemlock spruce—later shortened to hemlock.

Mountain Hemlock

Tsuga mertensiana (mer-ten-see-**ay**-na: after Karl H. Mertens, p 110). Also **black hemlock**. 36' diam × 110" (average much smaller); needles ½–¾", bluish green with white stomatal stripes on both top and bottom sides, ± ridged, thus somewhat 3- or 4-sided, radiating from all sides of twig, or ± upward- and forward-crowding on exposed timberline sites; cones 1–2½", light (but coarser than spruce cones), often purplish, borne on upper branch tips; bark much furrowed and cracked; mature crown rather broad; also grows as prostrate shrub at highest elevs. Subalpine; abundant near and W of both Crests; lower limit 4,500–5,500'. Pinaceae.

The compact, gnarled shoulders of mountain hemlocks shrug off the heaviest snow loads in the world.* At every age, this species' form is brutally determined by snow. The seedlings and saplings are gently buried by the fall snows, then flattened when the snowpack, accumulating weight, begins to creep downslope. When tramping across the subalpine snowpack on a hot June afternoon, you can almost hear the tension underfoot of all those young trees straining to free themselves and begin their brief growing season. The stress of your foot on the surface may trip some unseen equilibrium,

---

* Paradise on Mt. Rainier is the nation's best-buried year-round weather station, averaging 626" a year. Its single-season record was broken in 1998–99 by Mt. Baker Ski Area with 1,141", or 95'. But the real snow apex (the one where no one visits daily to check and empty a snow gauge) is likely somewhere around Humes Glacier on Mt. Olympus, or possibly in Alaska's Wrangell or St. Elias Ranges. All these mountains grow mountain hemlocks at timberline. Most of the world's other snowiest places lack an annual snowmelt to equal their snowfall—an imbalance that grows glaciers, not trees.

---

snapping a hemlock top a few feet into the air. After the trees grow big enough to take a vertical stance year round, they may keep a sharp bend at the base ("pistol-butt") as a mark of their seasons of prostration. Even in maturity they may get tilted again, on sites so steep and unstable that even the soil creeps downslope. Their crowns grow ragged from limbs breaking; some, after being encased in snow the better part of the year, spend the remainder matted with a weird black fungus called snow mold, *Herpotrichia nigra* (meaning "black creeping hair," but much less hairlike than horsehair lichen, page 296). Luckily, snow mold isn't as deadly as it looks.

Mountain hemlock abounds in subalpine tree clumps and in closed subalpine forests (those just below timberline) over most of our range. More shade-tolerant than its competitors other than silver fir, it tends to become dominant in the closed forests except in areas hit by laminated root rot (page 268), which is more consistently lethal to hemlock than to true firs. Mountain and western hemlocks seldom grow in the same place; where they do, they may hybridize naturally.

Timberlines

"Timberline" (as used in this book) is not a line, but a belt encompassing three successive "lines," all of them irregular:

Forest line *is the uppermost boundary of continuous closed forest growth. Meadows enclosed by forest may also occur below forest line at any elevation, usually due to patch fires or to soil peculiarities. (****Lower timberline**** is the similar boundary on the Cascades' east slope below which forest gives way to steppe.)*

Tree line *is the upper boundary of erect tree growth.*

Scrub line *is the upper boundary of conifer species growing in the prostrate, shrubby form called krummholz ("crookedwood").*

The "subalpine zone" or parkland is the interspersed grove-and-meadow area between forest line and tree line, and the "alpine zone" is everything above tree line. Some writers divide the two at scrub line instead, but in our region krummholz associates with characteristic alpine species, so we will consider it alpine.

Timberline is a visible dynamic equilibrium between huge, often invisible forces. It responds sweepingly to slight changes in climate—but so slowly that the climate may be swinging the other way by the time tree succession gets into gear; so slowly, in fact, that timberline

---

Subalpine Fir

Abies lasiocarpa (**ay**-bih-eez: the Roman term; lazy-o-**car**-pa: shaggy fruit). 24" diam × 100'; needles ¾–1½", bluish green with one broad white stomatal stripe above and two fine stripes beneath, usually curving to densely crowd the upper side of the twig, tips variable; cones purplish gray to black, barrel- to cigar-shaped, 2½–4 × ¾–1¼", borne erect on upper branches, dropping their seeds and scales singly while the core remains on the branch; bark thin, gray, smooth exc on very old bases, without superficial resin blisters, resin in pockets throughout inner bark; upper branches very short, horizontal, lower branches at ground level, long; or shrubby, prostrate. Abundant at timberline, esp eastward; rarely down to low elevs.
Pinaceae.

soils and communities today are still recovering from the Ice Age. With glaciers in retreat this century, you can find near each glacier's toe a primary successional sequence starting from bare rock emerging from a "Little Ice Age."

Nevertheless, charcoal in meadow soil profiles reveals that most meadow areas below tree line have grown trees at least once since the Ice Age; forest is the climax vegetation for most of the subalpine zone.

Timberline successional patterns move horizontally in space, as well as in time. Once a tree gets established in the open, it's easier for others to get their start right next to it, for two reasons. First, most subalpine trees are adept at "layering," or growing a new stem where branches in contact with earth take root; the parent limb feeds the new shoot intravenously, a big advantage over growing from seed. Second, during spring thaw tree foliage, being dark, absorbs more of the sun's heat than open snow does, and melts itself a little well in the last few feet of snow. The well is a microsite with a growing season several weeks longer than the surrounding meadow—just what seedlings need. Hence trees in subalpine parkland typically grow in tight, slowly expanding clumps, often elongated downslope into a teardrop shape.

The founding mother of a tree clump is often a subalpine fir or

---

The peculiar narrow spires of subalpine firs, ubiquitous at timberline here and in the northern Rockies, stay in my mind's eye as the archetype of a subalpine tree. The upper limbs are short and stubby because, being true fir limbs, they're stiffly horizontal and brittle; if they were long, they wouldn't hold up to the snow and wind in the subalpine zone. The long lower limbs escape those stresses by spending the winter buried in the snow; their way of hugging the ground puts them where they need to be for "layering," or reproducing by sprouting new roots, and then stems, from branches in contact with soil. Subalpine fir is our best layerer, and hence our strongest species in pushing both tree line and scrub line upward. At scrub line it grows in krummholz (prostrate) form, and spreads almost exclusively by layering.

Occasionally it produces an asymmetrical, half-dead-looking, little tree with voluminous krummholz "skirts." Such trees were confined for years to the shape of the snowpack; any foliage above the snowpack was killed during winter by a combination of wind desiccation, frost rupturing, and abrasion by driven snow. This is the krummholz way of life. Then, maybe, for a couple of winters there was deeper snow, providing growing room for half a dozen little vertical shoots. The next time a normal-snowfall winter came, one of the shoots managed to survive with some needles on its downwind side—the side relatively protected from desiccation and abrasion. Even years later, the little tree is likely "flagged," its surviving limbs positioned exclusively downwind and above the snow abrasion zone (the first 8–12" above the snow/krummholz level).

whitebark pine. As the clump gets big enough to have a shaded clear floor in the center, a few mountain hemlock seedlings appear there, eventually growing to replace the oldest firs or pines. As the broader, denser hemlock crowns mature, the deepening shade favors silver fir, provided there is a mature silver fir nearby to provide seeds and a chipmunk or other animal to bring them. Subalpine fir continues expanding the clump by layering at the perimeter, often behind a vanguard of low-to-tall heath family shrubs. Eventually our typical tree clump might display in slowly expanding, roughly concentric rings, this successional sequence: red heather → black huckleberry → white rhododendron → subalpine fir → mountain hemlock → silver fir. Sometimes the pioneer trees in the center die and nothing but shrubs

Though a little bit of lasting snow may be a conifer's best friend up on windswept alpine ridges, down in the subalpine parkland the huge quantity and consequent duration of snow is the main hindrance to tree establishment. On steep meadows, tree seedlings are often wiped out by snow creep. Other hindrances include soil too sodden, arid, or shallow, or sedge turf too dense.

Also, conifers don't adapt as easily to a short growing season as do herbs and shrubs. Once the seedlings are several feet tall they can start photosynthesizing long before the snow is gone, but making it past the seedling stage in the open requires a run of longer than average snowfree seasons. Such a run between 1920 and 1945 started a generation of young trees, mostly subalpine firs, scattered in subalpine meadows. This invasive growth contrasts with the normal style of slow tree-clump expansion. (Sidebar on facing page.)

Since 1957, when the European balsam woolly aphid reached our area, subalpine fir has proven highly susceptible to it, with mortality as high as 80% in a few mid-elevation stands. You can recognize the aphid's victims (which may be any of our true fir species) by their extremely swollen branch tips.

In subalpine forests of the NE Washington and much of the Rockies, subalpine fir and Engelmann spruce are late-successional codominants, though less abundant than the fire-adapted pioneer, lodgepole pine. In our range, subalpine fir can be replaced by the more shade-tolerant hemlocks, silver and grand firs, or Douglas-fir. It reaches its lowest elevations here—3,000' or even 2,000'—in cold air pockets and scant-soil sites like lava flows and talus.

manages to grow there, leaving a hollow tree clump or "timber atoll."

Timberline species vary along our wet-to-dry west/east gradient. Whitebark pine, Engelmann spruce, and subalpine fir increase from west to east, while silver fir, Alaska-cedar, and mountain hemlock do the reverse. In the eastern North Cascades, subalpine larch as a "mother tree" enables other species to grow upright at higher elevations than they could without its protection.

Compared to other mountain ranges, ours have a wide subalpine parkland belt and only a narrow fringe of alpine vegetation. Like other peculiarities of our flora, this can be attributed to our prodigious winter precipitation, i.e., to our paradoxical combination of mild temperatures with a very brief snow-free season.

Pacific Silver Fir

Abies amabilis (a-**ma**-bil-iss: lovely). Also **lovely fir**. 40" diam × 165'; needles of two sizes: some ¾–1¼", flat-spreading, others ¼–¾", pointing forward and upward along the twig; deep glossy green on top, with two strong white stripes beneath; notch-tipped exc on cone-bearing branches; cones dense, heavy, barrel-shaped, 3–5" × 1½–2", green maturing to brown, borne erect on upper branches, dropping their seeds and scales singly while the cores remain on the branch a year or more; bark gray to silvery white, resin-blistered, smooth exc on some old trees; branches horizontal. Dense mature forests near and W of Crests, mainly 3,000-5,000'. Pinaceae.

The handsome dark needles of silver fir lie mostly in a flat plane; an additional series of shorter ones presses forward in a herringbone-like pattern that neatly hides the twig from directly above. This unique arrangement is Clue #1 both to which species this is and to what it's up to—shade tolerance. Hiding the twig from above means not letting any sunlight go to waste on a nonphotosynthesizing surface. The dark surface also maximizes light absorption.

Because it's our most shade-tolerant tree (along with western hemlock) you can expect silver fir to be a late-successional dominant everywhere you see it's saplings. The traditional silver fir vegetational zone is a Westside midslope belt—3,000-4,000' in southern Washington, a little higher in Oregon, and lower north, all the way to sea level in extreme southeast Alaska. Silver fir is uncommon in our lowlands, but oddly enough, the very finest stands, including the largest known individual (7'10" diameter by 203' tall) grow below 300' near the Olympic seashore. These stands are fog-soaked so frequently in summer that neither summer soil drought nor forest fire are factors at all; without them, silver fir can eventually encroach on the domain of lowland spruce and hemlock. At the upper extreme, it can reach tree line in the protection of other trees, but doesn't thrive in the open, being prone to windthrow and excessive transpiration. It grows only in our range and northward.

The first appearance of these forest-green saplings can bolster your sense of progress during long slow hours of switchbacking up from valley floor to high basins. Vistas unfold, even while you can't see out of the forest. The shrub layer is thinning, perhaps showing off charming montane herbs—bunchberry, bead lily, false-Solomon's-seal, coral-root and wintergreens. Or perhaps its a drier, sparser community with beargrass—spectacular in its better flowering seasons. This zone can be incredibly quiet, with only faint fricative sounds sifting up from some torrent far below. Animals are relatively scarce and mainly diurnal here. Grouse flushing under your nose may raise more adrenalin than "BOO!" in an empty house at night. Don't be alarmed if an unseen assailant high in the trees bombards you in September; it's only a Douglas squirrel harvesting big thudding silver fir cones for his winter stores.

After deep shade, late-lying deep snow is the second crucial challenge silver fir has adapted to. The dry season is often well under way before the snowpack melts from silver fir habitats; within a few weeks the meltwater is gone and the needle duff seedbed may be bone dry. Silver fir seeds germinate the moment they see the light of day after the winter chill— even though this means all too many of them germinate *on* snow and die. Luckier ones put most of their energy into their taproot for a few seasons, getting a tap on summer-long moisture. Silver firs have a first-year root length advantage over their competitors because they have bigger, richer seeds, and put relatively little of that seed energy into upward growth, raising their shoots a scant inch or so before forming fat buds well protected for winter. The shoots are relatively stiff, and less vulnerable to being squashed flat by the mat of litter that may form as the last snow melts.

Amabilis is one of several names we have from the pen of David Douglas. Travelers of his day found that, of all boughs, silver fir made the loveliest bedding. Foam pads, which are much less trouble, turned up in time for our age of low-impact camping.

Grand Fir

Abies grandis (**gran**-dis: big). Also **lowland white fir.** 44" diam × 200'; needles ¾–2", quite broad and thin, spreading in a flat plane from the twig, notch-tipped to rounded, dark green above, two white stomatal stripes beneath; (needles of topmost branches often neither flat-spreading nor esp dark); cones dense, heavy, ± cylindrical, 2½–4 × 1½", greenish, borne erect on upper branches, dropping their seeds and scales singly while the core remains; bark gray to light brown, resin-blistered, becoming ± ridged and flaky with age; branches horizontal. Common E of Cas Cr, 3,200–5,000'; scattered on W-side. Pinaceae.

The foliage on a grand fir sapling catches your eye, the tidy flat array of long, broad needles showing off the glossy green color. Flat leaf arrays (facing page) imply shade tolerance. Grand firs are only slightly less tolerant than western hemlocks and silver firs, and prefer less rainfall—30–45" per year, especially where the summer drought is ameliorated by streamside groundwater or by mountain coolness. That "either/or" preference makes the species ecologically two-faced, with two ecotypes thought to be somewhat distinct genetically as well as geographically.

"Typical" grand fir is commonest below 1,500' west of the Cascades, mostly in partially rain-shadowed areas like the northeast Olympics and the Willamette Valley. Stream bottoms with high groundwater levels make it happy.

"Montane" grand fir grows at mid elevations in the Cascades and eastward. It is the leading shade-tolerant tree for a 3,200-5,000' East Slope belt in Oregon and most of Washington. Forests of that zone are very mixed, usually including a lot of Douglas-fir and locally some subalpine fir, western hemlock, redcedar, western larch, and lodgepole and ponderosa pine. Given a natural regime of frequent low-intensity fires, the pines, larches, and Douglas-firs would typically predominate, but the thin-barked, shade-tolerant grand fir has been the chief beneficiary of Smokey's fire-fighting efforts over the past century. This has made it the group's ecological bad boy: the notoriously sick, half-dead, and conflagration-susceptible stands of the Blue Mountains are typically overly-dense grand fir stands that filled in where ponderosa pines were logged out.

South of our range, in the Klamaths and Sierra Nevada, grand fir's close relative white fir, *A. concolor*, plays similar roles. Where the two species meet they "intergrade," or hybridize in proportions that vary along a continuum. The slight differences of form between typical and montane grand firs may represent a genetic trace of white fir in the montane type—longer needles, more stomatal bloom in the upper groove, more upward curve from the twig, and less notch at the tip. Variable needles and lots of intergrading make our true firs notoriously hard to tell apart.

Why Deep-Forest Leaves Lie Flat

Flat leaf arrays, an adaptation to deep forest habitats, are conspicuous on herbs (vanillaleaf, bunchberry, twisted-stalk) and conifers (western hemlock, silver and grand firs). They make the most of weak sunlight filtering from straight above.

Knowing this helps us connect the descriptive traits of trees with their habitats. Unfortunately, it doesn't make distinguishing among the true firs or the hemlocks easy so much as it explains why it's hard. When a western hemlock grows in the open—not uncommon along Eastside streams—it adopts a round bottlebrush leaf array just like that of mountain hemlock. Luckily, we can check for the top-and-bottom stomatal bloom of mountain hemlock's needles or, better, for its much larger cones on the ground.

To identify true (Abies) firs we sometimes have to see cones, since both leaf array and stomatal bloom (our handiest identifying characters) vary not only from site to site, but from branch to branch on the same tree. Topmost branches in the forest canopy are always in full sun, and don't develop the flat leaf arrays and bottom-only stomata that typify the shade-tolerant silver and grand firs. These nondescript top branchlets are the very ones that turn up on the forest floor, since they're the ones in the wind and, more importantly, the ones bearing the cones squirrels harvest. Conversely, lower branchlets in a mature forest are way too high for us to see their stomatal bloom. We can only hope to identify a harvested cone before the squirrel collects it.

Noble Fir

Abies procera (**pross**-er-a: noble or tall). 50" diam × 210'; needles ¾–1¼", bluish to silvery green with white stomata on both upper and lower surfaces, typically* in four distinct stripes, blunt to pointed (not notch-tipped), thick, ± 4-sided, crowding and curving upward from the twig, many with a sharp "hockey-stick" curve right at the base; cones dense, heavy, nearly cylindrical, 4–7" × 1¼–2½", green maturing dark red-brown, scales almost entirely covered by papery green to straw-colored bracts with slender upcurved points; cones erect on upper branches, dropping their seeds and scales singly while the core remains; young bark gray, smooth, resin-blistered; mature bark red-brown, thin, flaking, cracked rectangularly; branches horizontal. Mostly at 3,100–4,800' on W-side, OR and S and C WA Cas. Pinaceae.

Nineteenth-century botanists gave the Pacific Coast's true firs Latin names meaning Grand, Lovely, Magnificent, and Noble—saving Noble for the largest, longest-living member of the genus. The evenly spaced annual tiers of stiffly horizontal limbs, characteristic of all true firs, are shown off best on this one. On a slope these can be seen even from a quarter-mile away as a fine horizontal lined texture. The boughs, with their balsam fragrance, are the top NW species for Christmas wreaths, one of several flourishing "special forest products." Juvenile noble firs make the most elegant Christmas trees. Due to slow juvenile growth, they cost about double Douglas-fir Christmas trees of the same size. Growth rate picks up impressively after the second decade, though, ranking among the best. Hundred-year and older noble firs are often larger than the like-aged Douglas-firs they typically grow with, and can produce even more wood volume per acre.

Noble fir is, after Douglas-fir, the tree most often planted in timberland west of the Cascades. On British tree farms it has been planted for over a century. Since its lumber is scarce here, and few

---

*One versus two topside stripes of stomata is the easy way to tell subalpine noble firs apart, but it isn't reliable. Once I picked twigs of the two species growing side by side and couldn't spot any difference in their needles, whether of stomata, color, size, curvature, or tip. Hitchcock and Cronquist supply a distinction visible in a clean cross section of a needle under 10× magnification. You can go by the resin-blistered bark of noble fir, or by its lower-elevation, more southerly and westerly range. To be more positive, you have to find cones. Noble fir cones are green to brown and they bristle with hooked bracts; subalpine fir cones are smaller, gray to black, with straight bracts that stick out only from immature cones.

buyers know how strong it is, it gets stamped "Hem-Fir" along with all the true firs and hemlocks. Earlier lumber merchants tried to raise noble fir and Doug-fir above the true-fir pack by calling them "Oregon Larch" and "Oregon Pine," respectively. Such deceptive labeling may have been warranted, but the misnomer filtered back via loggers to cartographers, and we ended up with two Larch Mountains—so named for their noble firs—near the west end of the Columbia Gorge. No larches grow there.

Noble firs are fairly shade-intolerant; they pioneer after fire, usually mixed with Douglas-firs and a few other conifers, and persist as canopy trees for many centuries. Lovely stands result, with massive straight trunks supporting a dense canopy way up somewhere above 100'. As much as three-quarters of the total height may be limbless, a sign that intolerant foliage doesn't photosynthesize efficiently enough to earn its keep after it loses its canopy position in direct sun. These stands have few shrubs and fewer saplings—mostly the shade-tolerant silver fir. The herb layer may also be impoverished, but more often it is lush, featuring vanillaleaf, dwarf raspberry, and small false-Solomon's-seal.

Noble firs' range is small. Their northern limit, near Stevens Pass, is abrupt, but they are vigorous enough there to suggest a potential range well into British Columbia. Fossil pollen shows that they grew far to the north before the Ice Age, but have yet to regain the border in following the retreat of the glaciers. Blame their slow migration on heavy seeds (poor wind carrying distance) and shade intolerance; each time the northernmost noble firs are replaced by climax silver firs, the migration is pushed back until fire clears a path again. They also failed to cross the lowlands to the Olympics, but they have reached the Oregon Coast Range.

The southern limit of noble fir is not abrupt at all: it and its closest kin, California red fir, *Abies magnifica*, hybridize and intergrade where their ranges meet. The intermediate trees, ranging roughly from the Three Sisters to Mt. Lassen, are sometimes classified as Shasta red fir, *Abies X shastensis*.

Engelmann Spruce

Picea engelmannii
(**pis**-ia: Roman term, from "pitch," for some conifer; eng-gell-**mah**-nee-eye: after George Engelmann). 40" diam × 160'; needles ¾–1¼", sharp, 4-sided, bad-smelling when crushed, crowding upward and forward from the twig or ± evenly around it, deep blue-green with stomatal stripes ± equally on all sides; young twigs usually fuzzy; cones 1½–2½", light, much like mtn hemlock cones but scales are thinner, closer, and irregularly toothed-to-wavy along outer edge; often with conelike galls from branch tips; bark thin, scaly; crown dense, narrow, with fringelike pendent branchlets; or prostrate, shrubby. 3,000–8,000' E of Cas Cr, esp in N- to E-draining ravines; rare in NE Olys. Pinaceae.

Spruces are the second most northerly conifer genus (after larches). In the Rockies, Engelmann spruce and subalpine fir dominate the higher forests. Here, this spruce specializes in cold and/or swampy Eastside sites, ranking about average in tolerance. Though it is large and distinctive among subalpine trees, its three stands in the Olympics went undiscovered until 1968. Take that as a challenge to your tree-spotting skills.

In addition to their cones, many Engelmann spruces bear curious conelike appendages — galls, or "houses" for aphid larvae (page 455). Gall tissue is secreted by a plant in response apparently to chemical stimulation, usually by a female insect laying eggs. The familiar spheres on oak twigs are galls of various creatures, especially gall wasps. The spruce gall aphid's gall terminates and envelopes new growth at the tip of a branch. The dead needles turn a tan color along with the gall; together they look much like a 1–2" cone with needle-tipped, melted-together "scales" each hooding an opening into a larval chamber. The gall may hang from the branch

---

*Engelmann spruce intergrades with white spruce, *P. glauca*, across a large area of BC and Alberta. Some taxonomists rank it as a subspecies, *P. glauca engelmannii*.

for years, long after the larvae mature and move on; other insects may colonize it. The spruce gall frustrates the growth of its branchlet, but scarcely harms the tree.

After many decades at the low end of the value scale, Engelmann spruce lumber at last found a market that appreciates it in Japan. Very white, it reminds of certain Japanese woods that are scarce now. It's logged mainly east of the Cascades, being rather scarce and inaccessible here.

Sitka Spruce

Picea sitchensis (sit-**ken**-sis: of Sitka, SE Alaska). 90" diam × 235'; needles stiff and very sharp, ± 3-sided (flat on top), ½–1" long, equally on all sides of the twig, light green with 2 stomatal stripes on top only; young twigs smooth, old defoliated twigs rough and scratchy with the peglike bases of the fallen needles; cones 2–3½" long, light, scales thin and finely, irregularly toothed; bark scaly, thin (less than ¾" even on huge trees); mature trunks very straight, round, and untapering, though often buttressed. W-side lowlands; abundant in Olys, uncommon in WA Cas and absent from OR Cas. Pinaceae.

Sitka spruce, the world's fourth-tallest species, occupies a 2,100-mile coastal strip bounded by the reach of ocean fog. The successional role of Sitka spruce is puzzling. Though measurably less shade tolerant than western hemlock and red-cedar, and considered successional to them by some ecologists, it holds its own in competition with them even in a sodden range that rarely burns. If these spruce/hemlock rain forests are not climax, then what has been disturbing them? Elk, for one thing: Olympic elk congregate in these valleys every winter, browsing hemlock seedlings and avoiding prickly spruce. Elk browsing also helps to keep the forest open, and so does each huge tree that falls; this makes shade tolerance less crucial.

The river bottoms are young soils dating from minor glacial advances, and rarely as much as a century older than the oldest spruces

---

upon them. The glaciers themselves did not reach the lower river bottoms that recently, but each time they retreated, meltwater flooded valleys downstream from the glacier snouts, dumping deep layers of cobbles and gravel. As the glaciers advanced again, the rivers cut through the "outwash fill" until the next glacial retreat, then partially refilled that cut; then began cutting again. Each new, narrower cut left a terrace. Spruce-dominated stands along the Hoh are on two terrace levels, 630 and 350 years old. Soil development may yet allow the stands to succeed to hemlock, but there is no clear evidence of that happening now. It's hard to say whether the abundance of spruce along Olympic rivers relative to similar Cascade ones owes most to elk, fog, or cobbly terrace soils.

Sitka spruce's high strength-to-weight ratio was pounced on early in the history of aviation; spruce was pronounced the ideal aircraft material. It provided nearly all the airplane frames for America's side in World War I. Sitka spruce logging peaked then at more than twice the volume of any time since—except for World War II, when planes still had a lot of spruce in their frames.

Nature Out of Balance?

Scientists increasingly see nature as full of change, chaos, and imbalance. Some nonscientists infer that scientists have no stable natural baseline with which to compare human-induced change, or that human-induced change is nothing to worry about because "nature also destroys." Nothing could be further from the truth.

It is true that in nature species do travel to new locations and sometimes take over, and other species do go extinct. But these things are happening 100 to 100,000 times faster today, from human causes, than they happen in nature. Geologists look back at extinction events that took out many species "at once;" but that's "at once" in a very geologic sense: somewhere between a hundred thousand years and over ten million. Again, that's 10,000 times slower than the extinction rate predicted for the 21st century.

Looking at our region, some say that clearcutting followed by slash burning mimics natural disturbance by fire. It does not. Forest fires leave a vital legacy of biomass, which clearcuts cannot match. Most of the wood in trees killed by fire "lives on" as wildlife snags and nurse logs. Even wood that burns up stays on the site as minerals. Stumps are no match for wildlife snags and nurse logs; on the contrary, they are

Today the arts claim the highest-grade spruce; it has the best resonance for piano sounding-boards, guitar tops, etc. Old-growth Sitka provides far and away the biggest clear, straight-grained sections. Sitka spruce also makes the best paper pulp on the West Coast. It hybridizes with white spruce, *P. glauca*, a chief lumber species up north, where their ranges meet in Alaska. The hybrid has been proposed for commercial planting in coastal Washington and Oregon, because it seems resistant to the white pine weevil, which stunts and deforms young Sitka spruces.

The long, tough, sinewy (after pounding) small roots of Sitka spruce were vital to Northwest Coast culture. They supplied most of the exquisite and highly functional basketry, and also most of the twine and rope, including whaling lines. A spruce twig stuck in the hair was a charm for whaling, while the harpoon tips were protected, and the canoes caulked, with spruce pitch. The Makah and Quinault were fond of chewing spruce pitch; it's fragrant and spicy-sweet, turning bitterish as it is chewed. Try some.

disease magnets. Clearcut sites lack the diversity of animals and fungi found after natural burns. Fires themselves are extremely diverse: hot or cool, low or high, spring or fall, huge or small. Compared to that, clearcuts are all alike. Typical logging equipment compacts soil, rips up streambeds, and greatly increases runoff and erosion. Oregon has seen clearcuts on sunny ridges refuse, decade after decade, and even with multiple replantings, to regrow forests. These were forests well adapted to fire, but they couldn't recover from clearcutting. Alteration of the balance of soil microorganisms is probably the problem.

A second-generation tree plantation in the Northwest may look a bit anemic compared to a natural forest; an eighth-generation plantation is far more so, after centuries of removing organic material, centuries without nearby old-growth to serve as a genetic lending library. Europe has many eighth-generation and older plantations; even before they started dying from air pollution and acid rain they grew feebly, compared with ones in the Northwest.

(The New Forestry of the 1990s attempts to devise cutting systems that come closer to the effects of natural disturbance. Of course, no cutting system can avoid removing a lot of organic material from the

Western Yew

Taxus brevifolia (tax-us: the Greek term; brev-if-**oh**-lia: short leaf). Also **Pacific yew**. 16" diam × 35' or (rarely) up to 80'; or sometimes a sprawling shrub; needles ½–¾", grass-green on top, paler and concave beneath, spreading flat from the twig, broad and thin, drawing abruptly to a fine point but too soft to feel prickly; new twigs green; male and female organs on separate plants; seeds single within juicy red cup-shaped fruits ¼" diam; bark thin, peeling in large purple-brown scales to reveal red to purplish, smooth inner bark; branches sparse, upper ones angled up, often much longer than the leader; trunk often crooked. Scattered below 4,500'. Taxaceae (Yew family). Color p 115.

Our yew is an anomaly from almost every point of view. It is a conifer, with evergreen needles—but without cones. Instead it bears its seeds singly (and only on female trees) cupped within succulent red seed coats loosely termed berries, but technically "arils." These are treacherously pleasant-tasting; the seeds of many yew species contain alkaloids capable of inducing abrupt cardiac arrest in humans. Attractive but poisonous fruits are few in our area, but smooth bright red berries are good ones to keep your kids away

site. The New Forestry's authors admit their humility and ignorance: they might need another fifty years of research to do the job really well, but logging rushes on, so the effort has to be made now.)

Exotic species are sometimes carried in by logging and roadbuilding equipment. (And just as many by recreationists.) Some are serious weeds. Others are deadly pathogens. Whitebark pines, western white pines, and Port Orford-cedars are likely to all but disappear from their Northwest native habitats due to exotic fungal diseases brought in the course of timber management.

Still scarier is deforestation that perpetuates itself by changing the climate. For example, new studies suggest that even the Amazon rain forest could permanently turn to shrub-steppe or semidesert if deforestation crosses a certain unknown threshold. Since half the basin's rainfall consists of previous rainfall recycled by plant transpiration, from. (Also Baneberry, page 232). Birds love yew berries, passing the toxic seeds undigested.

Woodworkers class conifers as "softwoods," by definition, but they know yew as the exception that proves the rule: it is among the hardest of woods. It can be worked with power tools, or even carved to make extraordinarily durable and beautiful utensils. The sapwood is cream, the heartwood orange to rose. Yet few have worked it. Loggers burn it with the slash, finding it hard to market such small, allegedly scarce trees. But yew is not scarce here, and often reaches marketable size by hardwood standards.

The Indians knew better. They made it into spoons, bowls, hair combs, drum frames, fishnet frames, canoe paddles, clam shovels, digging sticks, splitting wedges, war clubs, sea lion clubs, deer trap springs, arrows, and bows. (Yew species were the wood of choice for bows worldwide. The Greek name for yew, *taxos*, spawned both "toxin" and *toxon*, meaning "bow.") Prizing yew for strength, elasticity and hardness, young Swinomish men rubbed a yew's limbs on their own in the belief those qualities would rub off on them. They also sometimes added yew needles to their smoking mixtures, perhaps more for "toxins" than flavor.

Anomalous among conifer barks here, yew bark resembles the peeling bark of madroño. The smooth red underbark, tawny on madroño, can be almost cherry red on yew. In 1987, Western science suddenly wanted yew bark. An order was filled for 60,000 pounds

---

fewer trees will mean less rain. Scanty rain, no rain forest.

Whether similar things could happen here is simply unknown. (One modest parallel was found, so far, in the Cascades: Portland's municipal water supply was diminished by logging of high ridges in the watershed, because big trees there gain far more moisture by intercepting clouds than they lose through transpiration.) In any case, it's high time to lay to rest the hubristic twentieth-century fantasy that Northwest forests will just regrow, as fast as they ever grew naturally, in logging rotation after rotation as far as the eye can foresee.

In sum, there are big differences between natural instability, in which particular places may see particular species come and go, while almost always retaining organisms diverse enough to perform each of the whole system's vital functions, and anthropogenic instability which, to put it mildly, is a loose cannon.

Conifers: single needles

of bark from which to extract a tiny amount of taxol, soon dubbed the chemotherapy drug sensation of the 1990s. For a few years we feared that the species might be wiped out in its native habitat by free-lance bark strippers. Fortunately, the drug industry soon stopped buying yew bark after finding they could more reasonably extract the drug from cultivated European yew needles. A similar but potentially more effective and cheaper drug was recently isolated from a bacterium, so in another decade taxol may be all but forgotten, after serving as an example of life-saving herbal toxins to be discovered growing under our noses.

Paradoxical truths about western yew just go on and on. The largest of all yews, the smallest of our forest conifers. Typically more tree than shrub in form, in stature it ranks in the tall shrub layer. Like vine maple, it will root and start a new tree when its long limbs get pinned to the ground by branches fallen from above. Described anecdotally as a moist-site tree, in research plots it proved indifferent to climatic variation within Westside forests; yew ranked 13th of all plant species in total cover in the big survey of the H. J. Andrews Experimental Forest—astonishing, for a tree often called "scarce" or "little-known." It is also common on the Eastside below 4,000', specializing in streamsides there. It is never a canopy tree in the Cascades, but seems able to completely take over some stands in the Northern Rockies, flying in the face of a common assumption of climax community theory—that in succession, taller vegetation tends to replace shorter. (Yew would have trouble taking over, though, without fire suppression, since even low fires kill it.) Extremely shade-tolerant, it may suffer when shade is removed, turning orange all over but not necessarily dying. I know one thicket of orange-leaved yew shrubs on a steep, burningly exposed southwest slope, with no sign of ever having enjoyed shade.

Conifers with bunched needles

The needles are bunched differently in these two genera:

Pines of every species bear long evergreen needles in fascicles (bundles) bound together at the base by tiny membranous bracts. The number of needles per bundle (5, 3 or 2) is the easiest step in identifying pines; check several bundles, because individual trees may be inconsistent. Five-needle pines (pp 48–51) are loosely termed "white pines" and three-needle pines (below) are "yellow pines." The East has various two-needled "red pines," but no one calls our lodgepole a red pine. The Southwest has pinyon pines with bracted fascicles of just one needle.

Larches bear soft deciduous needles, mostly in fat false whorls of 15 to 40 needles at the tips of peglike spur twigs about ¼" long and wide. However, on this-year's twigs the needles are single, and spirally arranged. Technically, the pegs and their whorls are also twigs—very short ones, with compressed spirals of single needles—hence "false whorls." To the naked eye they are bunches.

Ponderosa Pine

Pinus ponderosa (**pie**-nus: the Roman term; ponder-**oh**-sa: massive). Also **western yellow pine.** 44" diam × 175', needles 4–10", in bunches of 3, yellowish green, clustered near branch tips; cones 3–5" × 2–3", closed and reddish until late in their second year, scales tipped with stout recurved barbs; young bark very dark brown, soon furrowing, maturing yellowish to light reddish brown and very thick, breaking up into plates and scales shaped like jigsaw puzzle pieces. Dry habitats, mostly at low elevs E-side; very few in E Olys and Willamette Valley. Pinaceae. Color p 115.

Much of ponderosa pines' charm is in the parklike grassy spacing they maintain over the centuries. It evokes the spirit of the great cowboy West, or at least the great cowboy Western. It makes you wish you were on a horse. That spacing pattern—and the prevalence of the pines and the grass underneath—result from frequent ground fires. A 316-year-old ponderosa east of Mt. Jefferson, for example, bears scars from eighteen fires. Mature ponderosas are the most fire-resistant trees in their range, thanks to thick bark and high crowns, but young ones are vulnerable. The sapling that stands a good chance of surviving fires to reach immune size is the one growing away from other trees, because the two fuels likely to bring ground fire to it are other saplings and the needle litter under big trees. Hence the parklike spacing.

As long as the stand is widely spaced, shade intolerance is no problem, but where fire-fighting and adequate moisture have allowed denser stands to grow, we find a strong successional trend away from the pine, in favor of Douglas-fir, grand fir, and incense-cedar, which are less fire-resistant but more shade-tolerant. Since ponderosa pine is a preferred lumber species in most of its range, this trend was one compelling reason for foresters to reconsider the virtues of fire. Another was the correlation of dense growth with bark beetle outbreaks (page 458). A third was that without fire, brush and dead branches build up to a point where a fire won't stay on the ground, but will ignite even the tallest pine crowns and kill them. This makes "prescribed burning" much harder and riskier than it would have been fifty years ago.

While other conifers can, in the absence of fire, crowd them out from much of their range, there is a ponderosas-only fringe of dry sites where no other large tree survives. Some irregular "lower timberlines" at this limit reflect soil texture more directly than climate; coarser soil permits easier, deeper rooting, and absorbs more of the rain or snowmelt. Central Oregon's Lost Forest is an isolated stand of ponderosas and sizable junipers neatly filling a patch of sandy soil, surrounded by 40 miles of sagebrush steppe on relatively clayey soil. It lives on 8.7" of precipitation a year—the driest climate that supports a forest anywhere in the American West.

Fire Histories

Northwest conifers may not have had very many millenia to coevolve with each other in their currently typical combinations, but they have had a great many millenia to coevolve with fire. Thanks to study of tree rings, including dozens of fire scars per tree on trees up to 1,000 years old, and to pollen studies going back 200,000 years, we know that even on the rainy Westside, forest fires prevailed throughout prehistory. The twentieth century, with its heroic but scientifically questionable fire suppression efforts, has been the one with the least fire.

East of the Cascade Crest, thickbarked ponderosa pines, Douglas-firs, and western larches easily survived fires that swept through the grasses and low shrubs every seven to forty years. Saplings were readily killed, so very few of them reached maturity; this resulted in open forests, protecting the big trees by keeping fires from climbing up to their lowest limbs. Such "frequent low-intensity" fire regimes characterize all except the moistest forests all the way east from the Cascades to the edge of the Great Plains.

Westside fire regimes varied according to latitude: the farther

Though young ponderosas have been turned into a lot of knotty pine paneling, mature wood is versatile, resembling white pine but nicely two-toned, with pale yellow to orange-brown heartwood and broad creamy sapwood. Ponderosa pine production peaked when the old-growth was being rapidly liquidated. It still ranks second (after Douglas-fir) in the West, but will continue to decline, since foresters have yet to figure out how to manage forests to grow ponderosa, even where it once dominated.

Commercial pine "nuts" come from pinyon and European stone pines, but the seeds of all pines are delicious and prized by birds and rodents, who bury countless seeds in small caches. They intend to come back for them some day but inevitably overlook some caches, which then germinate.Ponderosas evolved spines on their cones to discourage seed eating, even though it appears that pines benefit from it: it plants seeds where wind might never carry them, and plants them deeper, in mineral soil often in litter-free spots, sparing the seedlings from drought and the eventual saplings from ground fire. When you see a clump of several pine seedlings within a square half-inch or so, it's undoubtedly a forgotten cache.

---

north, the less frequent—but more deadly to trees—the fires. The Klamaths, with their unique set of broadleaf evergreen tree/shrubs that stump-sprout after fire, burned just as often as the Eastside. Many Western Cascades sites are almost as dry; fires at 20- to 100-year intervals torched and killed trees in patches, while sparing some or all of the mature trees in other patches. Today's old-growth there has scattered giant Douglas-firs of mixed ages (280 to 700 or even 900 years) and has far more Douglas-firs, and fewer hemlocks, than it would if it had not been periodically winnowed by fire. The typical southern Washington regime allowed 200 to 450 years before a stand-replacing series of fires. In northwestern Washington, fires were so few that a scrupulous statistician would not speak of a "return interval." Yet stands with no sign of a fire history are scarce. Vast areas burned either 450 to 550 years ago or around 700 years ago. Only when we reach the western Olympic coastal lowlands does fire at last yield (to windstorms) its rank as the top natural catastrophe. The essentially fire-free extreme is found in coastal B.C. and Alaska rain forests, where substantial rain falls throughout summer.

Recovery is surprisingly fast and complete even from a large fire,

---

Lodgepole Pine

Pinus contorta. 20" diam × 100'; needles in twos, 1½–2½" long, yellow-green; cones 1½–2" long, egg-shaped, point of attachment usually quite off-center, scales sharp-tipped; cones abundant, borne even on very young trees (5–20 years), persistent on the branch for many years either closed or open (empty of seeds); bark thin (less than 1"), reddish brown to gray, scaly. Common above 3,500' in E Olys and E Cas; scattered elsewhere. Pinaceae. Color p 115.

Lodgepole pines are tricksters on the ecological playing field. They don't bother to compete with our other conifers in size, longevity, shade tolerance, or fire resistance. They excel instead at profligate and gimmicky seeding habits, short-distance speed, and tolerance of poor soil.

---

if there's only one. But often, the first large fire in over a century is followed by one or two more within forty years. Subsequent fires are very hot, fueled both by dried-out victims of the first fire and by dense sapling regrowth. After three fires in a series, very little organic humus remains on the ground, the soil is compacted and drier, mycorrhizal fungi are dead, conifer seed sources are far away, and as a result succession is very slow.

The "pioneer" plants after a devastating fire either sprout from charred stumps or root crowns, or grow from seeds adapted to withstand heat or to move in abundantly from nearby. Their seedlings are quick to tap water, nutrients and light. Their shade and transpiration make new microclimates. Their roots, in symbiotic association with fungi and bacteria, work over the soil physically and chemically, depleting some nutrients and accumulating others. Many pioneers are fast-growing annuals that donate their entire corpses to the humus fund in the fall; perennials and shrubs contribute leaves. The seeds of more diverse and subtle competitors, trickling in on wind and fur and feces, soon find the environment more congenial than it was at first.

Indians set fires to improve hunting, to maintain lowland prairie, and to maintain huckleberry patches in subalpine areas. It is less likely that they ignited many big forest fires in the mountains. Legends describe a few conflagrations as fearful events perhaps torched by enemy tribes, but certainly not their own. Computer models suggest

Prolific to a fault, they produce viable seeds in huge numbers year after year (a rarity among conifers); they release some seeds at all times of year; they bear cones younger than other conifers; and their seedlings and saplings grow fastest. They unleash their most remarkable punch after a fire; some of the cones on many lodgepole pines are sealed shut by a resin with a melting point of 113°. The seeds inside, viable for decades, are protected through the fire by the closed cone. The fire kills the pines but melts their cone-sealing resin; afterward, the cone scales slowly open, shedding seeds upon a wide-open field. (These "serotinous" cones, typical of lodgepoles in the Rockies, are rare in our range.)

As in rabbits, prolificacy leads to overpopulation—a "doghair" stand stunted by intraspecific competition. In this all-too-common circumstance, the speed demon slows to a near halt, like the rabbit that lost the race with the tortoise. It looks dismal to both

---

that weather like what we see today could account for the known fire history as lightning-caused. A set of huge fire years in the Olympics — around 1310, 1450, 1510, 1670, and 1700—probably had worse weather than we usually see. They correlate with extreme low sunspot activity during a cool period, which could have brought severe spells of dry summers with strong east winds over western Washington.

Since 1950, the trend among foresters has been to view fire as our ecological friend, and to learn to use it as a management tool. Yellowstone's recovery from its 1988 conflagration lends great support to this movement. Still, it is unrealistic to think managed fire can be reapplied to Northwest forests on a grand scale. Too much smoke. Too much risk to human lives and dwellings. Too much timber revenue lost. And too much ecological risk in areas where natural fire-adapted conditions are already gone. (Out-of-control fires may nevertheless devastate large areas due to global warming and ecologically stressed forests.) We're in a tricky paradox in regard to preserving the ecosystem. We must protect most remaining ancient forest from fire as well as from logging, or we risk losing the very heart of the ecosystem. At the same time we know that due to fire exclusion they are already unnatural, and will only get more so, losing some of their unique qualities through preservation. The keystone of preservation has to be managing the unpreserved part of the National Forests to produce both valuable timber and an effective simulation of a fire history.

---

foresters and hikers, but isn't so bad in terms of species survival. In nature, the stagnant stand might well persist until fire comes and resets the stage, favoring lodgepole all over again.

Lodgepole pines are the commonest tree of the Rockies from Colorado north; in our region they are far fewer, albeit widespread, because at maturity they fall short—short-statured, short-lived, and utterly shade-intolerant. But they dominate many sites by tolerating difficult microclimates and substrates. One such habitat is frost pockets with severe temperature fluctuations, on the lower east slopes. Another is the seashore, with its unwholesome salt spray; the contorted "shore pines" that grow there are so unlodge-polelike that they were considered a distinct variety until it was found that a shore pine seedling transplanted among montane lodgepoles would grow just like them, and vice versa. A third lodgepole habitat is on chemically bizarre, sparsely vegetated soils made up of serpentine minerals (page 543). Whatcom County's Twin Sisters, a rare large block of the rock dunite, which weathers into serpentine, support an unusual krummholz form of lodgepole pine at timberline—making lodgepole the only tree found at both sea level and timberline in Oregon or Washington. The fourth, supporting the vastest stands of lodgepole in our mountains, is the poor soil of relatively recent lava flows, mudflows, and pumice deposits from Cascades volcanoes—in particular, the 100-mile stretch of Oregon's Cascade Crest and Eastside that is mantled with pumice from the huge Mt. Mazama (Crater Lake) eruption of 7,700 years ago. Mt. St. Helens' timberline was similar before 1980, and lodgepole pines are pioneering there again.

Where the Puget Ice Lobe melted away, 14,000 years ago, lodgepole pines colonized and dominated the deglaciated land for several thousand years.

Whitebark Pine

Pinus albicaulis (al-bic-**aw**-lis: white bark). 20" diam × 65'; needles in 5s, 1½–3" long, yellow-green, in tufts at branch tips; cones 1½–3" long, egg-shaped, purplish, dense, long persistent on the tree, usually falling scale by scale long after dropping the seeds; bark thin, scaly, superficially whitish or grayish. Alp/subalpine. Pinaceae. Color p 115.

With their broad crowns and tufted, paler foliage, whitebark pines are easy to tell from the other high-country conifers—subalpine fir, Engelmann spruce, and mountain hemlock. They are shade-intolerant, dry-terrain pioneers, only occasionally found west of the Cascade Crest, and very rarely in the Olympics.

Growth form varies with elevation. As krummholz (dense prostrate shrubs) whitebark pines reach the highest elevations of all our conifers—8,200' in the Stuart Range. At their lowest (5,000') they grow straight, resembling lodgepole pines. Their main range is the subalpine parkland, where they are usually contorted and multistemmed, but nevertheless erect up to 7,000'. Blue grouse find their dense crowns cozy in winter.

Whitebark pine "nuts" travel on adopted wings. Their own wings, undersized to begin with, remain stuck to the cone scales when the seeds fall out. Fat, heavy and wingless, the seeds nevertheless fly far in the beaks of Clark's nutcrackers. Most whitebark pine seedlings grow from caches buried and then forgotten by these birds; you can tell when you see pine seedlings in tiny clumps. The birds seem to like caching seeds in burned areas, enabling white-barks to quickly recolonize catastrophic burns where wind-disseminated trees can only crawl back, generation by generation, from the green periphery. The tree's black-and-gray allies may be making a critical difference in saving it from white pine blister rust (page 51). The deadly fungus kills trees from the top down, elimi-nating cone and seed production early. In heavily infected stands, nutcrackers are thus forced to find the small percentage of white-barks with rust-resistant genes. Our region very likely suffered over 50% whitebark mortality by 1950, but there seems to be a fair level of resistance in the ones we see today, both the old survivors and the younger gen-eration. They won't be able to recover ground that they lost, though, to subalpine fir, which took advantage of fire suppression while the pines died of rust.

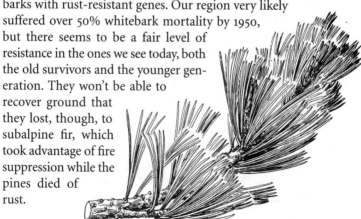

Sugar Pine

Pinus lambertiana (lam-ber-tee-**ay**-na: after Aylmer
Lambert). 50" diam × 180'; needles in 5s, 2–4" long,
blue-green with white bloom on all surfaces, sharp;
cones 10–18" × 3–6" (the largest cones anywhere)
hanging from upper branch tips by stout 1½–3"
stalks; seeds with wings 1–1½"; dark gray bark maturing rather early to reddish brown, deep-fur-
rowed and scaly. Low to mid elevs in C OR.
Pinaceae.

The biggest pine of all is this California tree,
fairly common also in Southern Oregon
but not so in our range—its northernmost
occurrence is on the upper Clackamas.
(Size does matter: its wood fetches the best
prices of any western pine.) Western white
pine, our common five-needled, big-coned
pine, overlaps sugar pine's range, so don't
think you're looking at a really big cone unless it's a foot long. If it's only 8 or 10 inches,
it's probably western white. Sugar pine is limited to hot/dry sites on the Westside, mostly
below 3,000', and (less commonly) well-wa-
tered sites on the East. Of all five-needle or
"white" pines, it is one of the most vulnerable to
white pine blister rust. (See facing page.)
    The tasty, nutritious seeds from these giant
cones are good-sized, but no larger than pine nuts
traditionally collected from small pines—pinyon
and digger pines in the southwest, and stone pines in Europe.
    David Douglas counted the sugar pine the greatest of his
Northwest discoveries. He trekked south from Fort Vancouver
specifically to find it after being shown some seeds and told of the
cones by Indians. When he found it he was alone in country almost
totally unexplored by whites, somewhere near the Umpqua Divide.
He retrieved cones by shooting them down with his rifle, leading
forthwith to what he felt was his closest brush with death at the
hands of Indians. He managed to divert them and run off with his
precious specimens. No wonder he cherished them.

Western White Pine

Pinus monticola (mon-**tic**-a-la: mtn dweller). 40" diam × 120' (larger else-where); needles in fives, 2–4" long, blue-green with white bloom on inner surfaces only, blunt-tipped; cones 6–10" × 2–4", thin-scaled and flimsy for their size, often curved, borne by a short stalk from upper branch tips; young bark greenish gray, maturing to gray with a cinnamon interior, crack-ing in squares. Widely scattered at mid elevs. Pinaceae. Color p 115.

The Latin name "mountain-dweller" notwithstand-ing, western white pine is scattered throughout the Northwest from coastal bogs to low-subalpine forests. In the mountains of Northern Idaho it grows bigger, used to dominate many forests and the lumber trade, and is the State Tree.

In our mountains, white pines were no more than a minority in any stand a hundred years ago, and they're sadly diminished today. You might walk by without noticing them, if it weren't for their outsized cones on the ground among smaller cones from larger trees. Most of the ones you see today are young, and sick. Commercial success brought them their evil fate: an introduced fungus, white pine blister rust, *Cronartium ribicola*. America's logging industry, after feasting on eastern white pine, *P. strobus*, until that species was depleted, was delighted to find a bigger white pine in the Northern Rockies. The hottest demand, oddly enough, was for wooden matches in the 1920s and '30s, the decades of peak western white pine production. As the pines were logged, demand for replanting stock grew so fast that foreign nurs-eries entered the market. A 1910 shipment of French seedlings to Vancouver brought blister rust, a European disease to which Europe's pines are resistant. Since the rust fungus requires a currant or gooseberry plant as an alternate host, currant extermination programs were carried on for several decades. They proved futile. Western white pines died off almost as inexorably as American elms and chestnuts (each with its own European fungus disease).

Natural selection should increase the proportion of pines that are rust resistant, and foresters, using nursery stock, are doing all they can to help. But lab tests show that blister rust can develop its own counter-resistance, and natural selection may spread that, too. In nature, species and their enemies coevolve over long periods, with selection eliminating genetic strains that fail to develop mutual survivability. The reason we have so many catastrophic pests (and weeds) in modern times is that all our trade and travel continually makes new bad matches between pests and hosts. When it comes to living organisms, free trade is a bad thing.

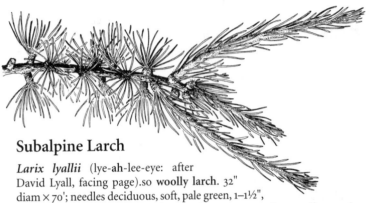

Subalpine Larch

Larix lyallii (lye-ah-lee-eye: after David Lyall, facing page).so **woolly larch.** 32" diam × 70'; needles deciduous, soft, pale green, 1–1½", 30–40 in apparent whorls on short peglike spurs, exc that needles are single and spirally arranged on this-year's twigs, and are usually evergreen on lowest branches of saplings; cones 1½–1¾", bristling with pointy bracts much longer than the scales; this-year's twigs densely, minutely woolly; bark gray, rarely more than 1" thick; tree broad-crowned, heavily branched and/or multistemmed; or occasionally a low shrub. 5,800–7,500' in the N Cas, from Mt. Stuart N and from Cas Cr E. Pinaceae. Color p 115.

A paradox: though evergreen conifers generally inhabit colder climates than broadleaf trees, the most cold-loving of all trees are deciduous conifers, the larches. They are the most northerly and the most alpine genus of trees all around the Northern Hemisphere. Where it is so cold that plants go for months without liquid water for their roots, the winter wind sucks all the moisture (even frozen) out of needles, killing them. Any foliage caught showing above the snow in midwinter gets nipped, so the outlines of evergreen krummholz show summer hikers the depth and shape of the winter snowpack. But in places we find subalpine larches standing tall above the krummholz, their bare branches relatively safe in winter from both cold desiccation and storm breakage.

Sometimes an early frost "freezes" the needles in place through the winter; they drop when they thaw in spring, and are soon replaced. While the tree's base is still deep in snow, its upper branches leaf out, providing spring's first greens—a treat for grouse that survived winter on a diet of tough old fir needles. Larch needles taste like tender young grass, with an initial spicy resinous burst. They're a visual treat, too, contrasting dramatically with other needles twice a year—bright grass-green in June, yellow in late September (or even August in dry years).

Subalpine larches keep no low limbs, a habit with one big disadvantage—they cannot layer—and one big advantage—they are relatively invulnerable to ground fires. They outlive their associates and possibly Westside cedars as well. It is no coincidence that some resemble California's bristlecone pines—another dry timberline species, which includes the world's oldest trees. Year after year, century after century, they put out a tiny bit of growth here while they die a little over there. On congenial sites they reach impressive size: the champ, in the Chelan Mountains, is 94' tall and 6'7" in diameter. Outcrops of bedrock or talus are typical sites, since this larch needs to be snowfree by July; that's on the early side for the Cascades, especially near the Crest, which is the tree's westerly limit. Subalpine larches on Luna Peak are among the botanical signs that the Picket Range, not the Skagit-Pasayten divide, is on the true Cascade Crest. (Page 7.)

David Lyall was one of the last of the rugged Scots prominent in early exploration of the Northwest. After a pioneering botanical trip to the San Juan Islands in 1853, he was appointed surgeon-naturalist to the British contingent (Canada then being a British possession) of the Northwest Boundary Survey of 1857–62. The American survey party included George Gibbs *as naturalist, geologist, and ethnographer, and Henry Custer, a topographer who was the first explorer to write passionately on the beauty of the North Cascades. The two parties did the same job separately, often coming up with different boundary locations. (The boundary was resurveyed more accurately in 1901–08.) Following an arbitrary beeline across the unknown, precipitous North Cascades was a heroic task, and they did well to find energy and enthusiasm for science along the way. Lyall published a* Botany of Northwest America *in London in 1863.*

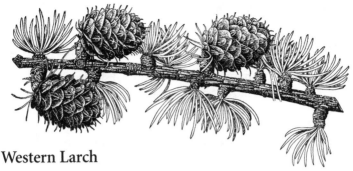

Western Larch

Larix occidentalis (**lair**-ix: the Roman term; ox-i-den-**tay**-lis:
western). Also **tamarack**. 52" diam × 170'; needles deciduous, soft, pale green,
1–1¾", 15–30 in apparent whorls on short peglike spurs, exc that needles are
single and spirally arranged on this-year's twigs, and often winter-persistent
on seedlings; cones 1–1½", often persistent, reddish until dry, bristling with
pointy bracts longer than the scales; young bark thin and gray, maturing yellowish to cinnamon brown, 3–6" thick, furrowed and flaking in curvy shapes
± like ponderosa pine bark. Scattered, on ± moist sites 2,500–5,000' E or (S
of Mt Adams) slightly W of the Cas Cr. Pinaceae. Color p 115.

A larch is something many people mistakenly think of as a contra-
diction—a deciduous conifer.* The deciduous needles always set it
off visually, even from a distance: intensely chartreuse in spring,
then a subtler but still distinctive grassy-green through summer,
smashingly yellow for a few weeks in October, and conspicuous by
their absence for a five- or six- month winter. You can tell a larch in
winter from a maple or cottonwood by its coniferous form (single,
straight trunk, and symmetrical branching) and from a dead evergreen by its warty texture (pegs on its twigs).

Ecologically too, western larch's anomalous leaf-dropping
habit sets it apart. Among big East-slope conifers, it ranks among
the fastest-growing, longest-living, most shade-intolerant, fire-
resistant, and water-demanding—an unusual combination. Since
its evergreen competitors photosynthesize through much of winter,

---

*Other deciduous conifers are the bald-cypresses, genus *Taxodium*, of
Southern swamps, and the dawn redwood, *Metasequoia glyptostroboides*.
The latter once dominated Northwest forests, judging by its fossils all over
eastern OR and WA. It was believed extinct for millions of years, with the
coast redwood its only descendent. Astonishingly, a few remnant stands
turned up in 1946 in remote mountains of central China. Since then it has
done well where planted in Northwest cities.

the larch has to make up for lost time with maximum photo-synthetic efficiency. This requires full sunlight and ample ground-water through the dry months. Deciduous needles also help larches recover from defoliating insect attacks; a larch is going to produce a whole new crop of needles every year anyway. It can likewise afford grouse eating its irresistibly tender needles.

Conifers with tiny scalelike leaves

This group consists of the Cypress family (Cupressaceae). The fo-liage is typically compressed and scalelike at maturity; most fami-ly members also have a juvenile phase of sharp, spinelike needles up to ¾" long, closely packed along the stem. These differ from other conifer needles in being arranged (like the mature scales) in oppo-site pairs or in whorls of three. In the three genera we call cedars, juvenile foliage grows only for the seedlings' first year or two, but in many junipers it continues for years—through sapling size and even into maturity on lower branches. Common juniper is includ-ed here to keep its family together; its leaves are all of the "juvenile" spinelike type, rather than scalelike.

Western Red-cedar

Thuja plicata (**thoo**-ya: a Greek term for some tree; plic-**ay**-ta: pleated). 84" diam × 200'; leaves tiny, yellowish green, in opposite pairs, tightly encasing the twig, strongly flattened, the twig (incl leaves) being 4–8 times wider than thick; foliage dies after 3–4 years, turning orange-brown but persisting several months before falling; cones about ½" long, consisting of 3 opposite pairs of seed-bearing scales, plus a narrow sterile pair at the tip and 0–2 tiny sterile pairs at the base; bark reddish, thin (up to 1"), peeling in fibrous vertical strips; leader drooping; trunk very tapered, its base fluting and buttressing with age. Moist to wet sites below 4,200'. Cupressaceae (Cypress family). Color p 115.

Our cedars are manifestly a breed apart, easily recognized (as a family) by their droopy sprays of foliage and vertical-fibrous bark. The bark is relatively clean, being too acidic to encourage lichens, fungi or moss. Though slow-growing, our cedars resist windthrow, rot and insect attack, and commonly live over 1,000 years. Western

---

red-cedars, the family's largest trees, can develop buttressed waist-lines 30 to 60 feet around.

Pure stands of red-cedar occur only on ground too wet for other big trees. Scattered individuals, though, are widespread. Once established, they are too tolerant to shade out. East of the Crests, their soil moisture requirement—about 12% through August—limits them to year-round seeps, typically in ravines. They can venture into slightly drier climates than hemlocks or silver firs, provided their roots are wet.

Red-cedar was the Northwest Indians' most important plant. The inner bark, woven after laboriously shredding with deer bone, made warm clothing. Unwoven, it was soft enough for cradle lining or menstrual pads; torn in strips and plaited, it became roofing, floor mats, hats, blankets, dishes, or ropes.

Buds, twigs, seeds, leaves and bark each had medicinal uses. Cedar charms sanctified or warded off spirits of the recently deceased. Cedar bough switches were skin scrubbers for both routine and ceremonial bathing. A Lummi boy would rub himself with cedar switches, then tie them to the top of a cedar tree, in preparation for his guardian spirit quest.

The wood was used for every purpose that didn't require hardness or great strength. Easy to work with stone tools and fire, it made up in durability and aesthetics what it lacked in strength. Structural timbers, totem poles, and dugout canoes were almost always cedar. The size of the biggest canoes—60' by 8'—enabled both trade and war to flourish along the Coast. Surprisingly, coastal cultures first put cedar to these uses only about 3.500 years ago, though they lived on the Northwest Coast for more than 10,000. The reason was availability. Fossil pollen studies show that cedar was uncommon until 5,500 years ago, when the climate shifted a couple of degrees cooler. Add 1,600 years for really big (1,600-year-old) cedars to be common, and several generations for the people to learn to reduce them to workable pieces, and you get a reasonable fit between the botany and the archaeology. (The equally culture-transforming practice of preserving salmon developed at around the same time. Coincidence?)

Cedar heartwood is warm red, weathering to silver-gray; it smells wonderful, resists rot, and splits very straight if it comes from an old, slow-grown tree. Split cedar shakes made superlative roofs in pioneer days, when most Northwest buildings had shake roofs and many had shake or shingle siding. The split surface sheds water well, having scarcely any cut-into cells or vessel ends to absorb it. In dry weather the shakes shrink, enlarging the spaces between them so that the roof breathes. High quality shake wood is a rarity today, and appearing chic is the only reason people spend big bucks for shake roofs. I know two much better reasons not to: sparing the cedar resource, and not wanting to live in a box of kindling, especially near trees.

Alaska-Cedar

Chamaecyparis nootkatensis (cam-ee-**sip**-a-ris: dwarf cypress; nootka-**ten**-sis: of Nootka, B.C.). Also **yellow-cedar**. 50" diam × 130'; leaves tiny, bluish green, encasing twig but ± divergent from it at the sharp tips, prickly-feeling, spray twig (incl leaves) from only slightly wider than thick up to twice as wide; foliage dies after 2 years, turning brown but persisting usually a year before falling; cones round, less than ½" diam, like hard green bumpy berries their first year, becoming brown and woody the second and opening into 4–8 scales like tiny shields with a central prickle; bark thin, silvery gray, red-brown inside and on saplings, flaking in thin strips but not especially easy to tear vertically; leader and branch tips drooping extremely; mature bases ± fluted. Above 3,000', esp in avalanche tracks and wet N aspects; locally abundant as alpine krummholz. Cupressaceae (Cypress family). Color p 115.

The name "weeping cedar" may not have seen print until now, but it comes quickly to mind for this lovely species. The willowy branches slough off snow when it gets too heavy. Their extreme flexibility minimizes snow breakage, whether from accumulation on the limbs, snow creep on a steep meadow, or the shock of an avalanche. Alaska-cedar is the main avalanche-track community dominant at highest elevations. Lower (often within the same track) it is far outnumbered by faster-growing Sitka alders.

A spell of sunny weather while the soil is frozen may kill upper parts of the tree, bleaching them to white "spike-tops." The tree usually survives this and other hardships—thanks to the rot resistance typical of this family—often for over 1,000 years. The maximum age may be less than the 3,500 years that some foresters have asserted, but it is probably older than any other Northwest plant.

Alaska-cedar is commonest on soggy steep north slopes with devil's club and sword ferns, but it is also found on dry, rocky, exposed ridgetops; this implies it selects not wet sites but poor ones, where its competitors are handicapped. It grows too slowly to survive vigorous competition.

The U.S. champion Alaska-cedar is in Olympic National Park, but bigger ones grow near the Campbell River on Vancouver Island. The biggest is 200' tall and 13'7" in diameter.

Little Alaska-cedar is logged here, but much is logged in coastal British Columbia and Alaska. Almost all of it, and most Port Orford-cedar (*C. lawsoniana*) is exported to Japan because of their close resemblance to *hinoki* (*C. obtusa*). The Japanese revere *hinoki*, and pay high prices to get their *Chamaecyparis* from us and save their own from the axe. Alaska-cedar wood is clear pale yellow, straight-grained, with close, faint annual rings and a heavy smell. Its great durability even when soaked led Alaskans to use it for fishing boats, Japanese for temples, Oregonians for hot tubs, and the Haida, Tlingit and Tsimshian for canoes, paddles and totem poles. (Red-cedar and Alaska-cedar shared those uses, Alaska-cedar was available to coastal peoples only in Alaska). Indians found the inner bark even softer and finer than western red-cedar's; they stripped, soaked, and pounded it for weaving and plaiting into clothing, bedding, or rope.

In alarming contrast to their general durability, millions of Alaska-cedars have died near the shores of Southeast Alaska—the

Cedar Aromatics and Misnomers

Each of our cedar woods has its own pungent smell, emitted by rot- and insect-repellent chemicals they have evolved. The traditional moth-repellent Cedar Chest is Eastern red-cedar—not a Thuja, *but a* Juniperus—*but Alaska-cedar and incense-cedar were used in similar ways in nineteenth century China.*

Human response to these smells is highly individual. Speaking for myself, I would wear Port-Orford-cedar for perfume if I could, I find it so exquisite. Red-cedar's smell is one of the beauties of cedar cabins and saunas; I poke my fire with split cedar for its smouldering fragrance. But Alaska-cedar, which charms my eye, displeases my nose. Mill-workers after eight-hour doses of Chamaecyparis *volatiles suffer everything from headaches to laxative effects to kidney complications.*

The Europeans who first named America's scaly-leaved trees

Northwest rain forest's only major case of mysterious Tree Death. No disease or pest seems to be the agent. The die-off is correlated with wet soil and with January mean temperatures close to freezing, so the leading theory is that these soils were reliably insulated by winter snowpack in the previous, cooler century, but not in this one, leaving the roots vulnerable to occasional hard freezes. If correct, the theory shows that even though Northwest conifers survived many extreme climate shifts over the last 150,000 years, fairly minor shifts may still inflict unexpected region-wide casualties. (This particular die-off began around 1880, earlier than any climate change most experts would blame on humans.)

"cedars" were either confused or at a severe loss for words. These trees resemble their relatives the cypresses, genus Cupressus, *and not the true cedars, which have long needles in whorls (like larches, only evergreen) and fat, solid, upright cones (like true firs). The true cedars (Cedrus, a Pine family genus) are much planted in Northwest cities; they are three species native to Lebanon, Israel, and the Atlas and Himalaya Mountains. Each of our "false" cedars represents a Pacific Rim genus, with other species in Northeast Asia.* Thuja *and* Chamaecyparis *each have an Eastern North American species called a "white-cedar," while "red-cedar," back East, means a juniper tree.*

Foresters and entomologists make a rule of hyphenating or compounding all common names that are taxonomically misleading. Though botanists have not adopted the rule, this book finds it a useful principle for hyphenating some other names, like wild-ginger.

Conifers: tiny scalelike leaves

Incense-cedar

Calocedrus decurrens* (cal-o-**see**-drus: beautiful cedar; de-**cur**-enz: running down). 40" diam × 140'; leaves small, average ¼" but up to ¾" on larger twigs, yellowish green, tightly encasing the twig, flattened, the twig/leaf 3–6 times wider than thick, the opposite pairs of leaves so nearly neck-and-neck as to make apparent whorls of 4; cones about 1", of apparently only 3 scales but actually of 6 (a sterile fused pair in the center flanked by an equally long fertile pair, and then by a tiny, recurved sterile pair); seeds with 2 unequal wings; bark red-brown weathering grayish, fibrous but smooth, furrowed, up to 4" thick; leader erect; crown regular, dense, narrowly conical. Sunny E-side slopes below 4,000' S of Mt. Hood; uncommonly, on W-side below 3,000'. Cupressaceae (Cypress family). Color p 115.

Incense-cedar's aroma takes some of us back to school days when we first sharpened pencils. Some wooden pencils are still made from incense-cedar. The lumber often has fine parallel, linear holes left in it by a dry-rot shelf fungus, *Tyromyces amarus*, but fashions in some decades have found this defect attractive. Most fungi and insects find this tree as repellent as our other cedars.

Outliers of a primarily Californian range, our incense-cedars grow on the hottest, driest sites in the Oregon Cascades. They are slightly more tolerant (but less fire-resistant) than Douglas-fir and Ponderosa Pine, so they tend to persevere and perhaps increase in a stand between fires.

A year-old incense-cedar seedling displays the gamut of juvenile leaf styles found in its family. First come the two cotyledons, or "seed leaves," about 1" by ⅛". Above these grow needles half as large, in whorls of four. Then, still within the first year, an incense-cedar branches and grows its first scalelike, close-packed foliage—still slightly more spreading and prickly than the mature foliage.

---

* Incense-cedar long went under the name *Libocedrus decurrens*.

Western Juniper and Rocky-Mountain Juniper

Juniperus spp. (ju-**nip**-er-us: the Roman term). 18" diam × 30'; mature leaves tiny, scalelike, yellowish green, tightly encasing the twig, not flattened; juvenile leaves (seedlings, saplings, lowest limbs of young trees) needlelike, average ¼", prickly; cones berrylike, blue to blue-black, rather dry, resinous, 1–3-seeded, ¼" diam; a few plants have only male (inconspicuous) or only female fruits; bark red-brown, fibrous, shreddy; dense small pyramidal trees with limbs nearly to the ground, or sometimes sprawling shrubs. Cupressaceae (Cypress family).

Western juniper, *J. occidentalis* (ox-i-den-**tay**-lis: western). Leaves in whorls of three, each whorl rotated 60° from the next. Dry low E-side from Mt Adams S.

Rocky Mountain juniper, *J. scopulorum* (scop-you-**lor**-um: broomy). Leaves opposite, making the stems 4-angled. Berries have heavy bluish bloom. Dry low elevs E of Cas Cr from Mt Adams N, incl upper Skagit Valley.

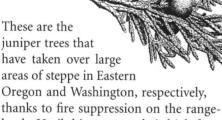

These are the juniper trees that have taken over large areas of steppe in Eastern Oregon and Washington, respectively, thanks to fire suppression on the range-lands. Until this century, their high fire susceptibility kept them confined to sites, like rimrock, with too little vegetation to spread a fire; once mature, their own shade and litter helps create a grass-free firebreak to protect them. A few slip into Eastside Cascade forests, mainly in drought-induced clearings on rocky ground. They achieve their best growth far to the south. In the Sierra Nevada stands a western juniper 14' in diameter and 87' tall, thought to be around 4,000 years old; that would place the species among the world's top five trees in longevity. A nearly equal Rocky Mountain juniper grows in Utah's Wasatch Range.

Junipers' insect-repellent and disinfectant aromatics are widely appreciated. The Swinomish boiled juniper leaves to steam sickness out of a house, or to bathe a sick person in juniper leaf tea. Back east, juniper trees called "red-cedars" (mainly *J. virginianus*) are made into moth-repellent cedar chests and closets.

Common Juniper

Juniperus communis montana (com-**you**-nis: common; mon-**tay**-na: montane). Leaves all ¼–¾", sharp, curved upward, closely packed along the twig in whorls of 3, from a ± distinct joint at each leaf base (unlike juvenile *J. occidentalis,* whose 3-whorled needles bend sharply, with no joint, to run down the twig); cones berrylike, blue-black with bloom, round and quite fleshy, ¼–⅜" diam, 1–3-seeded, resinous but sweet; bark red-brown, thin, shreddy; our variety a prostrate, mat-forming shrub. Mainly alpine here. Cupressaceae (Cypress family).

The common juniper is among the most widespread conifer species in the world. It's stature is humble but well suited to cold windswept ridges and slopes where even tall conifer species grow as low creeping krummholz. Dry alpine slopes—south-facing, rain-shadowed, rocky, almost devoid of real soil—are where we typically find common juniper around here, often with evergreen shrubs like kinnickinnick and Oregon-boxwood. All look beaten down, confined within the shape of whatever little snowbank they manage to keep through winter, for exposure to wind while frozen would dry and kill their leaves.

Junipers are anomalous among conifers in enclosing their seeds in fleshy, edible "fruits." (Yews cup—but do not enclose—their poisonous seeds in "berries.") Properly speaking, a berry is a fruit and a fruit is a thickened ovary wall, so neither junipers nor yews have true berries; a juniper berry is technically a cone of very few, fleshy, fused scales. It has a sweetish resiny flavor of suspiciously medicinal intensity. Used with restraint, they're a delicious seasoning in teas, stuffings, gin (a word derived from the French *ginevre* for juniper) or your water bottle, if your water has been tasting plasticky in hot weather. Those with inquisitive palates will try them straight off the bush. Birds love them, and disseminate the indigestible seeds.

3

Flowering Trees and Shrubs

The distinction between trees and shrubs is neither absolute nor taxonomically meaningful, but simply descriptive. Many species in this chapter grow as either trees or shrubs depending on their environment. You would be safe to call anything a tree if it has a single, woody, upright, main stem at least 4" thick or 26' tall at maturity. All shrubby plants, regardless of height, with stems more canelike or vinelike than truly woody and self-supporting, are in the "under 6 feet" category, which begins on page 82.

Trees and Shrubs: deciduous, over 6'

Bigleaf Maple

Acer macrophyllum (ay-sir: the Roman term; macro-fill-um: big leaf). 30" diam × 65'; leaves opposite, deeply 5-lobed, 5–12" wide and long, on equally long leafstalks, turning rich yellow in fall; flowers small, yellow-green, 10–50 in long pendent clusters conspicuous in Apr-May when leaves are just emerging; 1½–2" winged seeds in acute-angled Siamese-twin pairs; bark gray-brown and smooth in youth, later furrowed and often mossy; trunk and limbs ± knobby and crooked. Widespread W-side below 2,000'; less common 2,000–4,600', and in E-side Canyons. Aceraceae (Maple family).

The largest of all maples is the broadleaf tree that makes the greatest inroads into our mostly coniferous landscape. Not confined, like cottonwood and red alder, to streamsides and disturbed sites, bigleaf maple is nevertheless favored by sites where conifers have failed, for one reason or another, to form a deep shading canopy. The Olympic rain forests include prime examples. Bigleaf maples grow there on old rockslides fanned out across river terraces. Rocky soil may help answer the mystery of why these valley bottoms, which obviously grow conifers to perfection, don't grow them to maximum density. "Halls of Mosses" in these valleys are named for their extravagant raiment of epiphytic plants—lichens, club-mosses, some ferns, and higher plants, as well as mosses proper—all of which seem to find maple an ideal host. Maple's main advantages may be simply that it's big and goes naked half the year; epiphytes are photosynthetically active in late fall and early spring, and can take advantage of the brighter light when the leaves are gone. They also may like the alkalinity and porosity of maple bark, even though they rarely draw nutrients out of their tree hosts. (Drawing *no* nutrients was the doctrine on epiphytic lichens until 1988, when two research papers unmasked a common lichen as a partial parasite on oaks.)

Epiphytes do compete with trees for nutrients that come trickling down the tree trunk. Tree dripwater originates as pure rain and fog; nutrients are contributed by nitrogen-fixing lichens and by insects and mites that graze in the tree canopy. Maples, alders and cottonwoods extend small roots among the epiphytes on their own bark to catch a share of the nutrients before they reach the ground.

Deer and elk relish maple leaves when they can reach them. People relish maple syrup, which is maple sap with 98% of its water and volatiles boiled away. Bigleaf maple syrup can be made; sugar content and flavor are adequate by most accounts, and plenty of sap flows, though without the strong spring burst (following an icy winter) exploited in New England's sugar maples.

Maple wood is very hard, and makes good flooring. Some trunks near the ground develop the "curly" grain patterns prized in furniture and stringed instruments. Difficult to cut and carve without metal tools, maple wood was used in Northwest Indian culture for utensils, tools, and ornaments. The inner bark was plaited into straps or woven into baskets, and the leaves were used to line berry baskets and baking pits, or as rags for cleaning fish.

Douglas Maple

Acer glabrum douglasii (glab-rum: smooth; da-**glass**-ee-eye: after David Douglas, p 18). Also **Rocky Mountain maple**. Leaves opposite, 3- (or ± 5) lobed, toothed, red-orange in fall, 2¼–5", on equally long, often reddish leafstalks; twigs reddish; flowers small, green, in small clusters; winged seeds rarely over 1" long, straight- backed, in pairs at ± right angles; bark gray to purplish; tall shrubs or trees up to 40'. Shrub thickets and open forests E of Cas Cr; uncommon in W-side forest openings. Aceraceae (Maple family).

The common maple of eastern Washington and Oregon, Douglas maple is vital winter browse there for deer, elk, and sheep, who eat the twigs.

Vine Maple

Acer circinatum (sir-sin-**ay**-tum: round, referring to the leaf outline). Leaves opposite, 3–5", ± circular overall with fine teeth on 7 or 9 shallow pointed lobes, coloring intensely in fall or late summer, on short (1–3") reddish leaf- stalks; new twigs often deep red in sunny places; flowers small with red sepals, in small loose clusters; seeds in obtuse-angled (to 180°) "Siamese twin" pairs, each seed with a 1¼–2" wing; ± erect multistemmed shrubs to 20', or small trees to 30'. Ubiquitous below timberline on W-side. Aceraceae (Maple family).

The vine maple is Mr. Hyde to loggers, and Dr. Jekyll to landscapers and nurserymen. Loggers call it "vining maple," implying some devilish animism in its tendency to ensnare passing feet and lash at passing heads. Sunday drivers love it as our one abundant lowland source of incandescent fall color. Landscapers appreciate that being native here, it is hardier and faster-growing than Japanese maples, while rivaling them in the delicate incisions of its leaves, the contortions of its branches, and the intensity of its seasonal red. Hikers bushwhacking just have to learn to thread the thickets. Deer and elk browse it enthusiastically. The Quinault called it "basket tree," and wove long shoots of it into heavy baskets for firewood or shellfish. They swung their babies" cradles from its saplings.

Vine maples flourish indiscriminately at all forested elevations west of the Crest; they are far and away our most ubiquitous and abundant tall shrubs. At higher elevations they shy away from dry ridges that favor beargrass; in Western Olympic valleys elk browsing holds them back. For unknown reasons they have yet to invade Vancouver Island.

Maples have a lovely helicopterlike way of extending their seeds' range in a breeze. Their fruits (called samaras, or winged achenes) provide each seed with a long wing, sending it into a fast spiral for a slow fall.

Red Alder

Alnus rubra (**al**-nus: the Roman term; **roo**-bra: red). 24" diam × 110'; leaves 2–6", oval, pointed, flat green above, pale gray beneath, margins coarsely toothed, ± wavy and/or rolled under; catkins, male and female on the same tree, appear in summer and mature the next spring before leaves appear; female catkins ½–1" long, woody, like miniature spruce cones; bark ± smooth, pale lichen-coated. Abundant W-side on logged land, burns, and streamsides. Betulaceae (Birch family).

The splotchy whiteness of red alder bark, ranging from paper birch white through various pearl grays, is really a crust of lichens that the bark reliably hosts. The redness of red alder might be the gorgeous antique rose cast lent to hillsides in early spring by millions of alder catkins and buds. More likely the name refers to the deep stain that appears on freshly cut alder bark or green wood. Indians boiled, chewed, or urinated on cut bark and wood in various techniques to make dye; one use for the dye was to make nets invisible to fish. Alder's easily carved, flavor-free wood was good for spoons and dishes, and its rich, oily smoke for smoking salmon.

Northwest alders serve an invaluable role in nature: they pioneer on wet gravel exposed by retreating glaciers and by shifting, downcutting rivers. Fresh or shifting gravel bars, with little or no sand between their cobbles, support mainly willows and annuals; older, sandier bars become alder flats. Recently deglaciated terrain here is above red alder's limit (2,500') but often grows Sitka alder. Alder seedlings prefer poor mineral soil, since they don't need soil nitrogen, but do need so much water that they suffer on duff, which gets very hot and dry. They grow fast, and rapidly improve soil structure and fertility. Like legumes, alders host bacteria in nodules on their roots that convert atmospheric nitrogen for plant use, fixing some in the soil and some directly into the plant. Alder leaf litter is plentiful, fast-decomposing, and nitrogen-rich.

In nature, red alders in our region grow mainly along lowland streams and swamps; but after white settlement red alder was seen as an invader of cleared land. The better the land for timber farming, the more likely it was to be taken over by alder. "Scarifying" or scraping the earth down to mineral soil, which in theory enhances Douglas-fir seedling survival, often did the opposite by aiding alder more. Nitrogen fixation—long appreciated in legumes—went undiscovered in alders. As long as there was plenty of other wood, alder was used for little but firewood, being soft, brittle, and relatively short-fibered. For decades, a primary task of forestry in the Northwest was to find an easy way to massacre alders without harming Douglas-firs. Broadleaf herbicides were tried, but are too broadly toxic.

Fortunately, foresters are turning the ugly duckling back into a swan. A planting of alders sparsely intermixed with Douglas-firs may be an economical way of feeding firs nitrogen. Alder is planted on some of the worst disease centers of laminated root rot (page 268), to which red alder is toxic. Alder lumber, long used in lower-priced furniture, is increasingly appreciated in fine woodworking. Alder chipboard faced with Douglas-fir veneer is replacing plywood in many uses, as veneer-grade old-growth fir gets scarce. Still, three-fourths of red alder production gets pulped (and needs lots of bleach to prevent the characteristic reddening of alder chips).

Every ten years or so an outbreak of tent caterpillars (page 462) makes the region's alder stands look wretched, consuming billions of leaves down to the midvein and tenting the remains under cobwebby shelters. This stunts the alders' growth for the year, but does no lasting damage.

Sitka Alder

Alnus crispa sinuata* (sin-you-ay-ta: bent). Also **slide alder.**
Leaves 1½–4", oval, pointed, shiny, margins sharply doubly
toothed, ± wavy but not rolled under; flowers or "catkins," male
and female on same tree, appear in spring simultaneously with
the leaves; conelike woody female catkins ½–¾" long; bark gray-
green, warty-textured, often lichen-coated; erect to sprawling
shrubs 5–12', or rarely trees up to 25'. Abundant on mtn streamsides, seepy slopes, avalanche basins and tracks; rare below 2,600'.
Betulaceae (Birch family).

The Sitka alder we know best is at its worst—the downhill-
sprawling "slide alder" of avalanche tracks. What the roaring avalanche finds accommodating, the sweating bushwhacker finds
maddeningly intransigent, a tangle of springy, unstable stems always slipping us downslope like flies in the hairy throat of a
pitcher-plant. Too often, what we slip onto is a neighboring devil's
club. If, like the avalanche, we could stick to downhill travel, we
might have no problem with slide alders. Or, if we can't beat'em, we
can join'em Indian-style—by cutting a stem to wear for perfume.

A Sitka alder has the genetic information for growing upright,
as a tree, but it also knows how to flex and bow and sprawl where
its environment demands. To this yielding nature it owes its dominant position in three-fourths of the avalanche tracks and basins
in the Cascades and Olympics. Few other ranges in the world have
so much snow combined with such steep valley walls; as a result,
few have so many avalanche tracks. A typical North Cascades track
has a superficial avalanche (one just trimming the top of the
plant community) every few years, or every year
in some places. Full depth avalanches come
at 6- to 20-year intervals, snapping some of
the larger Alaska-cedars, mussing up the
Sitka alders a bit, and demolishing nearly
every other woody plant in their paths. Alaska-
cedar is the only robust tree adapted for life in
the avalanche track, and it is a slow grower, competitive
with Sitka alder only on severe, cold, high sites.

---

* Different authorities either keep the Western form as a separate species, *A.
sinuata,* or lump all North American forms into the Eurasian *A. viridis.*

Scouler Willow

Salix scouleriana (say-lix: the Roman term; scoo-ler-ee-ay-na: after John Scouler, below). Also **fire willow**. Leaves 2–4", narrowly oval, widest past midlength, typically reddish-velvety underneath, flanked at first by pairs of ¼" ear-shaped bracts; male ("pussy willows") and female catkins on separate plants, flowering very early, occasionally before snowmelt; bark bitter, bad-smelling when crushed; shrubs or small trees in clumps, 3–40'. Widespread. Salicaceae (Willow family).

Scouler willow is a pioneer on two radically different habitats. On gravel bars and banks of braided mountain rivers where little soil has accumulated, it is often the only shrub able to grow, and rarely exceeds 4' high. In clearings (such as recent burns) on the dry east slope of the Cascades, it invades along with snowbrush. Thriving independently of watercourses is unusual among willows. Umpteen species and hybrids of *Salix* line streams throughout our range; they are notoriously hard to identify. Most look a lot like Scouler willow but have narrower, pointier leaves. Two other *Salix* species (page 190) are mat-forming alpine shrubs about 4" high.

Northwest tribes all twisted willow bark into twine for many vital uses—fishnets, baskets, tumplines, even harpoon lines for sea lions. Poles were cut from willows to support fishing platforms or weirs. They would often take root where implanted in the riverbed.

John Scouler, as a Scottish lad of 19, signed on as ship's surgeon to H.M.S. William and Ann for the same 1824 sailing that brought David Douglas (page 18). Douglas was delighted, since the two had been school pals in Glasgow. Scouler spent only seven months in the Northwest, taking a few walks with Douglas, and botanizing on his own when the ship visited the San Juan, Queen Charlotte, and other Islands. The same ship and all aboard were lost entering the Columbia River a few years later, but Scouler was safely back in England, where he completed his M.D. and lived to a ripe old age.

Hazel

Corylus cornuta (cor-il-us: the Roman term; cor-new-ta: horned). Also **filbert**. Leaves 2–4", broadly oval, doubly toothed, ± minutely fuzzy all over when new; female flowers tiny buds with red stigmas, appearing very early in spring along with the male catkins; nuts much smaller than cultivated filberts, in heavy shells about ½" diam, in hairy long-necked husks; tall shrubs 4–18', rarely treelike in our mtns. Hot, dry sites (often S to W slopes) at low to mid elevs, mainly W-side. Betulaceae (Birch family).

Though our native subspecies is called *californica*, hazels belong to Oregon, which has more hazels—both this native shrub and the orchard tree derived mainly from European hazels. Accustomed to orchard nuts, we find our native nutmeats puny, albeit tasty. Lewis and Clark were more than grateful for the ones they bought from the Indians. The nuts grow in back-to-back pairs, each nutshell encased in a fuzzy leaf shaped like a fringe-topped, long-necked vase.

Quaking Aspen

Populus tremuloides (trem-you-loy-deez: trembling-). 10" diam × 40'; leaves 1–2½", broadly heart-shaped to round, point-tipped, bumpy-edged to fine-toothed, on leafstalks 1–2½" long and flattened sideways; female and male catkins on separate trees; ¼" conical seedpods, in long strings, splitting in two to release minute seeds; bark greenish white, smooth, dark and rough on old trees only. E-side streamsides and avalanche tracks. Salicaceae (Willow family).

Quaking aspen is the widest-ranging American tree, ranging from Alaska to New England and down the Rocky Mountains and Sierra Madre to Guanajuato. In the Rockies it provides most of the fall color—yellow. In the Okanogan Highlands it fills avalanche tracks, like Sitka alder. But our range, atypical as it is of North American forests, offers quaking aspen only a small role along streams east of the Crest. Wildlife, from elk and beaver to grouse and pika, make the most of it: aspen leaves and shoots are choice browse.

Aspen leaves quake or flutter in the lightest of breezes because their flat leafstalks are limp in the lateral direction only. (Try rolling one between your fingers.) This fluttering suggested the name *tremula* for the European aspen, and thence *tremuloides* for its American cousin.

Most aspen trunks grow from root suckers, a type of asexual reproduction. Whole groves are clones or genetic individuals, each with a single huge root system. An aspen clone is all of one sex, and may spread over acres and acres. (One in Utah is 106 acres — arguably the largest living thing.) A clone's extent is dramatically visible in autumn, since the timing and hue of fall color are identical throughout a clone, but vary from one clone to the next.

In most of the range, aspen reproduction from seeds just doesn't happen; in much of it, clonal reproduction isn't doing so well either. The species seems to be in precipitous decline. The current huge numbers of deer and elk are involved, and so is fire suppression; but putting the whole story together will take further scientific sleuthing. Surely aspens must have used seeds to spread out over so much of North America. How much were they aided by natives setting fires and hunting elk? Or by wolves preying on elk?

Black Cottonwood

Populus balsamifera trichocarpa * (**pop**-you-lus: the Roman term; try-ko-*car*-pa: hairy fruit). 40" diam × 150'; leaves 3–6", long-pointed, broadly round-based or somewhat heart-shaped; glossy dark green above, dull light gray beneath, coloring bright yellow in fall; leaf buds (and their fallen scales in spring) sticky and richly sweet-scented; female and male catkins on separate trees; round seed pods, in long strings, split three ways to release many tiny seeds with cottony fluff, bark gray, grooved (see below); tall, fairly straight trees with V-shaped crowns. Low to mid-elev streamsides. Salicaceae (Willow family).

The elegant trunks of black cottonwood are straight and limbfree to such a height that they often go unnoticed among red cedars and hemlocks. You spot them instantly, though, once you've learned their distinctive bark — clean pale gray with little flakiness, moss or horizontal texture, but vertically fissured with heavy, dark, rough

---

* The former *P. trichocarpa* is now a subspecies of the balsam poplar, a tallish shrub of northeastern North America. I can't imagine calling our big tree a balsam poplar as a common name.

grooves. In spring the luscious honey fragrance alone will alert you.

Black cottonwoods are easily our largest broadleaf trees and our fastest-growing trees of any kind. They can reach 100' in as little as 20 years—twice as fast as red alder and Douglas-fir. The first tree farms planted by white settlers in Oregon were of black cottonwood, but the "instant wood" made lousy lumber and worse firewood. In recent years instant wood plantations were reborn, this time with pulp for paper, or theoretically even biomass to fuel power generation, as the goal. The trees are generally all one clone, and look eerily uniform in their vast grids, thanks to identical genes and highly mechanized irrigation. They're called "hybrid poplar," but at least in the Northwest most of their genes are cottonwood.

Cottonwoods rarely grow far from water, though they can in our rainy climate. On Westside river flats they join Sitka spruces and maples in replacing red alders; they will be outlived by the spruces and eventually replaced by hemlocks. With their stout crotches 120+' above ground, they provide choice nest sites for river-fishing bald eagles and great blue herons.

Oregon White Oak

Quercus garryana (**quer**-cus: the Roman term; gary-ay-na: after Nicholas Garry). Also **Garry oak**. 36" diam × 80'; leaves 3–6", deeply pinnately blunt-lobed; male catkins on same tree with females, which are single or paired in leaf axils, each consisting of a 3-styled pistil in a cup-shaped involucre which later hardens into the cap of the acorn; acorns ¾–1½" long; bark gray, furrowed; limbs gnarly. Dry rocky spots near the Columbia River. Fagaceae (Beech family).

When white people first saw the Willamette Valley, it was a savannah of grasses and scattered, huge white oaks, thanks to centuries of prairie-burning by the natives. White settlers cleared the flats for farming, leaving the hills that dot and line the Valley to be taken over, in the absence of fire, by closed forests of relatively puny white oaks; a few scattered old giants remain. The oaks are long-lived (300 years or so) but intolerant of shade, so they are being replaced by grand fir and Douglas-fir saplings. The Puget-Willamette Trough has a much drier climate than the mountains on either side of it; residents may have a hard time believing that, but the oaks prove it. In our mountains, oaks grow only on the dry margins of pine forests near the Columbia, and on rocky slopes of the Gorge. Vast oak savannahs also grew all around Puget Sound during the warmer, drier period of 9,000–5,000 years ago; the climate must have been very much like it is in western Oregon's valleys today.

Oak galls—hard, hollow round structures on oak twigs—show that oaks are favored hosts of gall wasp larvae.

California Digger Indians who subsisted heavily on acorn meal from various oaks worked hard to leach out the tannic acid. Northwest tribes ate white oak acorns raw or cooked, usually without prior processing except sometimes burial in maple bark wrapping until rotten; presumably they ate few enough acorns for their bodies to tolerate the tannin. White people's tastes generally can't.

Cascara

*Rhamnus purshiana** (ram-nus: the Greek term; pur-she-**ay**-na: after Friedrich Pursh, p 84). Also **cascara buckthorn**. 12" diam × 35'; leaves 2–6", oval, with recessed, strikingly regular pinnate veins, dark glossy green above and sometimes rather leathery but deciduous (exc ± persistent on saplings); flowers tiny, greenish, with 4 or 5 calyx lobes and minute petals, clustered in leaf axils; berries up to ½", 1-seeded, yellow or red ripening to black; bark thin and smooth, or scaly on mature trees only, numbingly bitter; trees or shrubs. Scattered, W-side below 2,500'. Rhamnaceae (Buckthorn family).

Settlers in the Northwest learned from the natives that this tree's bark, after curing for many months, is a potent laxative. The medicine leapt to commercial success under the strangely religious name Cascara Sagrada ("Holy Bark" in Spanish, contrasting with the scatological American "chittambark") and before long the species was well-nigh endangered. Though a felled cascara regenerates luxuriantly from stump sprouts, a bark-peeled tree dies. Today the tree is far from abundant, and mature specimens are rare. The national organization United Plant Savers has cascara on their "Watch" list.

Cascara prefers south aspects with conifers, or swampy lowland clearings with alder and vine maple; it tolerates shade, unlike most broadleaf trees here. The berries are edible, nutritive, and nonlaxative, yet unliked by humans.

---

*PLANTS database calls this *Frangula purshiana* due to a genus split.

Pacific Dogwood

Cornus nuttallii (cor-nus: the Roman term, referring to "horn" due to toughness; nut-all-ee-eye: after Thos. Nuttall, below). 8" diam × 30'; leaves opposite, 3–5", bright green, elliptical, pointed, wavy-edged, with veins curving around to merge along the leaf margin; flowers tiny, greenish white, 4-merous, in a tight head surrounded by 4–7 large (1–2½") white ± parallel-veined bracts; berries bright orange-red, mealy, dry, bitter, tightly crammed hence irregular in shape; trees or tall shrubs. Scattered in lower W-side forests. Cornaceae (Dogwood family).

The function of showy petals is to provide a visible target for near-sighted insects as they buzz around gathering nectar and inadvertently strewing pollen. There is no reason this function couldn't just as well be performed by, say, leaves close to the flower; and sure enough, specialized leaves called "bracts" are the showy parts of some kinds of flowers, like paintbrush and dogwood. (On many tiny-flowered plants a chemical attractant does the job, or wind pollination obviates nectar and insects both.) The only trouble with showy bracts is that they can confuse people when they read flower descriptions; dogwoods have their flower parts in fours, but the showy bracts (which are not flower parts, and surround a head of

Thomas Nuttall probably collected and named more new species from west of the Mississippi than anyone else. He came along at the right time, after travel had become easier and safer than it had been for Douglas or Lewis and Clark, but while there were still plenty of conspicuous species left to describe. He made his reputation botanizing on the Great Plains and writing a major flora, The Genera of North American Plants *(1818). In 1834, the visionary settler/entrepreneur Nathaniel Wyeth persuaded Nuttall to quit his prestigious chair at Harvard and join an expedition to the Oregon Territory. Nuttall collected along the Columbia, then sailed to Hawaii, California, and home via Cape Horn. Having exhausted his savings on the expedition, Nuttall retired to an inherited estate in his native England.*

flowers, not a flower) are often five, six, or seven.

Dogwood leaves put on a second show in the fall, a fine painterly smear of plum, bronze, russet, and magenta. A modest batch of white-bracted blooms may appear then as well, alongside red-orange berries from the spring flowering.

Pacific dogwood can grow up to 60' tall, but is more often suppressed by the shade of conifers, joining vine maple, yew, or perhaps chinquapin, in a tall shrub understory layer.

The tough wood was used here for bows and salmon spears. Europeans used their species for mallet heads, tool handles, and weaver's shuttles.

Red-Osier Dogwood

Cornus sericea* (ser-**iss**-ia: silky). Also **creek dog-wood**. Leaves opposite, 2–5", elliptical, pointed, wavy-edged, with veins curving around to merge along the leaf margin, coloring richly but inconsistently in fall; petals 4, white, ⅛", stamens 4, as long as petals, sepals 4, minute, flowers in flat-topped clusters; berries dull pale bluish or greenish, ¼" diam, single-seeded, unpalatable; new twigs deep red or purplish; shrubs 6–16'. Widespread in wet places. Cornaceae (Dogwood family). Color p 116.

It is hard to think of this shrub as a dogwood because its flowers lack the large white bracts we think of as dogwood flowers. The tiny true flowers of all dogwoods are alike in structure, though, and red-osier and Pacific dogwoods are also alike in the outline, venation, and fall coloring of their leaves. After the leaves have fallen from this species, rich-red young stems (osiers) remain. They make the plant easy to spot in every season except summer, since it is usually found (or lost?) in swampy or streamside thickets with willows and salmonberry. "Osier" is an old word from the French, meaning a long slender new shoot, originally of willow, suitable for wicker. "Dogwood" derives from the Scandinavian *dag*, for "skewer." The Okanagan and Shuswap also used this species for skewers, roasting racks, and drying stretchers for salmon, crediting it with a nice salty flavor. Other Indian uses revolved around food, fire, or fibre—fishing weirs, sweatlodge frames, fuel to smoke fish or dry berries, and pipestems.

---

*Western red-osier dogwoods, formerly *C. stolonifera*, are now relegated to varietal status within this transcontinental species.

Elderberries

Sambucus spp. (sam-**bew**-cus: the Greek term). Also **elders**. Leaves opposite, pinnately compound or (rarely) twice-compound, 5-12" long; leaflets narrowly elliptical, pointed, fine-toothed, ± asymmetrical at base; flowers cream-white, 5-merous, tiny, in dense clusters; berries ¼" round, 3–5-seeded; stems pith-filled; shrubs or shrubby trees 3–20' tall. Roadsides, streamsides, clearings, thickets. Caprifoliaceae (Honeysuckle family).

Blue elderberry, *S. mexicana*. * Leaflets usually 7, 9, or 11; leaf undersides and twigs whitened; flowers and (later) berries in ± flat-topped clusters without a single central stem; berries blue (blue-black with a waxy bloom). Common E of Cas Cr, less so W.

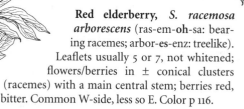

Red elderberry, *S. racemosa arborescens* (ras-em-**oh**-sa: bearing racemes; arbor-**es**-enz: treelike). Leaflets usually 5 or 7, not whitened; flowers/berries in ± conical clusters (racemes) with a main central stem; berries red, bitter. Common W-side, less so E. Color p 116.

Black elderberry, *S. racemosa melanocarpa* (melon-o-**car**-pa: black fruit). Like red elderberry, but berries black to very dark red; shrubs mostly 3–6'. E edge of Cascades; commoner farther E.

Where they grow together, red elderberry blooms, sets fruit, and ripens a good month ahead of blue elderberry. The blue berries are more popular for jelly, wine, or eating fresh than our red or black ones; legendary elderberry wine comes from an Old-World black elderberry, *S. nigra*. Ugly rumors crop up to the effect that our red elderberries are poisonous, but this is normally untrue of the fully ripe fruit. Northwest tribes ate berries of both species, fresh or more often steamed and stored until lean times. Elder bark, leaves,

---

* Until recently, this was *S. cerulea*, meaning "blue." Then a valid older description of it (from Mexico) as *mexicana* turned up in some archive. The Rules require using the oldest validly published name. Alternatively, PLANTS lumps it under the European black elder, as *S. nigra cerulea*.

---

twigs, and roots, however, have been regarded as toxic and/or medicinal. Infusions of them were used to induce perspiration, lactation, or vomiting, or alternatively to reduce swelling, infection, or diarrhea—an odd mix of prescriptions. The soft pith of elder stems was hollowed out to make "pea shooters" for little boys, drinking straws for girls during the ritual restrictions of puberty, pipestems for men, and whistles to lure elk.

Red elders are invaders of new clearings here, often shooting up to 12' in their first year. On lowland streamsides they might be confused with Oregon ash, *Fraxinus latifolia*, which barely enters our mountains. The ash's compound leaves, like elders', are opposite; ash is a bigger, sturdier tree, with more broadly oval leaflets drawing to a short point. In the mountains, the only other pointy, pinnately compound shrub leaves are on Cascades mountain-ash (page 80), which bears them alternately on the branch.

Trees and Shrubs: deciduous, over 6', many stamens

Chokecherry

Prunus virginiana (**prune**-us: the Roman term; vir-gin-ee-**ay**-na: of Virginia). Leaves 2–4", oval, pointed, fine-toothed; flowers ⅜", white, with 20-30 bright yellow stamens, very showy, in long dense racemes; cherries oval, ¼", sweetish but astringent, crimson to black; shrubs or (rarely) small trees up to 20'. Thickets and edges of clearings; common on E edge of Cas; also (subspecies *demissa*) in W-side lowlands. Rosaceae (Rose family).

The genus *Prunus* includes all cherries, prunes, and plums. Chokecherries are named for powerfully puckering the mouth and throat. Fortunately, their sweetness preserves better than their astringency; plains tribes pounded them into pemmican, settlers boiled them into jelly. Though pemmican contained quantities of pounded chokecherry pits, some modern texts advise scrupulous avoidance of all cherry, peach, and apricot pits, since they contain amygdalin which can break down into cyanide. Chokecherry leaves, though choice browse among deer and elk, have in large quantities killed cattle.

Bitter Cherry

Prunus emarginata (ee-margin-**ay**-ta: notch-tipped). Up to 18" diam × 80'; leaves 1–3", elliptical, round-tipped or occasionally pointed, fine-toothed; flowers ½", white with 20-30 yellow stamens, in loose clusters of 2–4, with several clusters grouped together; cherries ¼" round, bitter, bright translucent red, drying dark; shrubs or trees. Uncommon; moist lowland woods. Rosaceae. Color p 117.

These cherries are astringent and bitter, but somehow tasty to birds and rodents. The bark, of a lustrous bronze color, peels in horizontal strips almost like birch bark. It played a key decorative role in spruce-root basketry patterns, and was used medicinally. The wood is dark, lovely, and aromatic when split, or while burning.

Oregon Crabapple

Malus fusca* (**may**-lus: the Roman term; **fus**-ca: dusky). Leaves 1½–3", ± oval, pointed, fine-toothed, often with a small lobe on one or both sides; flowers white to pink, ½–1" diam, broad-clustered; apples ½", egg-shaped, greenish yellow to red; twigs armed with stout thornlike spur twigs; tall shrubs, or trees to 40'. Uncommon; wet W-side lowlands. Rosaceae.

Our crabapples are hard and sour, but most tribes found them sufficiently softened and sweetened to eat very happily after several months' storage; maybe that really works, as it does with Anjou pears, or maybe it's just that several months on winter rations could make anything taste sweeter. In any case, pioneer women found it more effective to cook them with lots of sugar. Crabapple bark tea was used for all kinds of stomach troubles among the Indians, and the hard, tough wood made seal harpoon points and other tools.

*Formerly included, as *Pyrus fusca*, in a genus with the pears.

Indian-Plum

Oemleria cerasiformis (ohm-**lair**-ia: after August Oemler; ser-ass-if-**or**-mis: cherry shaped). Also **osoberry**. Leaves 2–5", elliptical, smooth-edged, pointed; flowers ± white, bell-shaped, borne very early in pendent racemes below the new leaves, stamens 15 or none, since male and female flowers are on separate trees; berries ⅜" diam, 1-seeded, bitter, peach-colored ripening to blue-black; shrubs or small trees 5-15'. Low elevs W-side. Rosaceae. Color p 116.

Indian-plum's tassels of blooms below upraised sheaves of new leaves would be welcome any time of year, but are all the more so in February and early March. The cherrylike fruit is no plum; legend has it the Indians used to know where the sweet ones grow. Maybe we just never taste ripe ones, since birds eat them all first.

Serviceberry

Amelanchier alnifolia (am-el-**an**-she-er: archaic French term for a related shrub; al-nif-**oh**-lia: alder leaf). Also **saskatoon**. Leaves 1–2", broadly oval, toothed at the tip but not at the base; petals white, ½–1" long, narrow, often so widely spaced and twisted that the inflorescence of 3–15 flowers is a jumble of petals; berries ½", several-seeded, red ripening to purplish black, with bloom; low spreading shrubs to 30' trees, though rarely over 10'. Exposed slopes, esp E-side. Rosaceae. Color p 116.

Meriwether Lewis said "sarvisberry," as many Easterners still do. The word derives not from "serving" but from *Sorbus*, the Latin for mountain-ash. Serviceberry leaves look much like mountain-ash and wildrose leaflets-oval, toothed only on the outer portion—but no confusion need result. Just remember that a compound leaf (ash, rose, etc.) terminates in a leaflet, while a stem of simple leaves (serviceberry) terminates in a bud, flower(s), or a growing shoot.

The Northwestern serviceberry is another edible fruit no longer much eaten in this fussy-tongued culture of ours. Birds and bears eat them, all the Northwest tribes ate them, Lewis and Clark ate them, and traditionalists on the Plains and in the Appalachians still turn local varieties into pies and jams.

Ocean-Spray

Holodiscus discolor (ho-lo-**dis**-cus: entire disk; **dis**-color: variegated). Also **ironwood, arrowwood, creambush, rock-spiraea.** Leaves 1–2½", roughly oval, with coarse teeth and often fine teeth upon those; flowers tiny, whitish, profuse in 4–7" conical clusters; seeds single in tiny dry pods, the clusters of pods persisting in place through winter; shrubs 4–12'. Dry, exposed sites up to mid elevs. Rosaceae. Color p 117.

Blooming with masses of tiny cream-white flowers in parallel sprays, ocean-spray resembles an ocean wave breaking. "Ironwood" and "arrowwood" suggest uses Indians found for the straight branches after hardening in fire—arrows, fishing spears, digging sticks for clams and roots, roasting tongs, drum hoops, and baby's cradle hoops.

Common on both sides of the Cascades, ocean-spray on the Westside indicates hot, dry forest habitats which will shift toward hemlock dominance only at a snail's pace, if at all. On the Eastside it usually associates with ninebark.

Mountain-Ash

Sorbus spp. (**sor**-bus: the Roman term). Leaves pinnately compound, leaflets 7–13, 1¼–2½", oblong to elliptical, fine-toothed at the tip but not at the base (note similarly placed teeth on serviceberry, p 79, and wildroses, p 86); flowers white, ½" diam, in dense, flat-topped clusters 1¼–4" across, fragrant; berries red to orange, ⅜" diam, several-seeded, mealy, bitter; leaves color brightly, mostly yellow, in fall, and berries may turn purplish; dwarfed to tall shrubs or occasionally small trees. Subalpine. Rosaceae.

Sitka mountain-ash, *S. sitchensis* (sit-ken-sis: of Sitka, Alaska). Leaf tips toothed, round in outline. Common in WA. Color p 116.

Cascades mountain-ash, *S. scopulina* (scop-you-lie-na: of crags). Leaf tips toothed, pointed. Common in OR.

Mountain-ash berries offer little but fall color to humans, but are important forage for birds and subalpine small mammals, especially since they stay on through winter. Apparently they have enough sugar to ferment on the bush, judging by reports of birds flying "under the influence." A reputable wine is made from the sweeter berries of the European mountain-ash or rowan tree, *S. aucuparia*, a familiar ornamental on Northwest streets. Our two species, true to their name, are strictly montane here, ranging from timberline up to windswept ridgeline thickets.

Shrubs: deciduous, under 6', many stamens

If you don't find a plant you're looking for in this section, the next place to look would be in the preceding one (over 6') on the guess that you may have a young or environmentally suppressed specimen; categorization by size is unavoidably arbitrary. The present section begins in the middle of a continuum of larger-to-smaller Rose-family trees and shrubs.

Redstem ceanothus properly keys out to this section, but is mentioned under its close relative snowbrush, p 102.

Robust herbs sometimes mistaken at first glance for shrubs include corydalis, p 195; spreading dogbane, p 207; goatsbeard, p 218; and baneberry, p 234.

Salmonberry and Thimbleberry

Rubus spp. (**roo**-bus: the Roman term). Rosaceae.

Salmonberry, *R. spectabilis* (spec-**tab**-il-is: showy). Leaves 3-compound; leaflets 1–3", pointed/ oval, fine-toothed, often ± lobed; petals red or hot pink; fruits like large juicy raspberries in form, in mixed shades of yellow to scarlet irrespective of ripeness; stems erect, 4–10', ± woody but weak, sparsely thorny or occasionally thornless. Abundant on wet slopes and bottoms, W-side. Color p 117.

Thimbleberry, *R. parviflorus* (par-vif-**lor**-us: small- or few-flowered). Leaves 3–8", at least as broad as long, palmately 5-lobed (maplelike), fine-toothed, soft and fuzzy; petals white, ½–1", nearly round, crinkly; berries red, like thin fine-grained raspberries; stems erect, 4–7', ± woody but weak, thornless. Widespread.

A hitherto unreported controversy, apparently rooted in the collective Caucasian subconscious, concerns the palatability of salmonberries and thimbleberries. Most authors praise one or the other—but never both. I belong to the thimbleberry cult. I often try two or three salmonberries just to attune myself with the bears, or to see once again if the yellow ones are really any better than the red ones, or was it vice versa, or maybe because their peculiar vapidity challenges my powers of gastronomic recall. But thimbleberries! How anyone could call the thimbleberry "insipid" defies comprehension. Perhaps it's a kind of colorblindness of the tongue. I concede thimbleberries their grittiness, their sometimes dryness, their eventually cankering acidity, and their exasperating sparseness on the bush, yet I find in a good thimbleberry the most exquisite berry flavor on earth.

Indians ate both salmonberries and thimbleberries, of course. Also the young shoots, peeled, were a major food. Their astringent flavor cut the greasiness and fishiness of all those salmon dinners. That may be how salmonberries got their name.

Both shrubs require moisture and sun. They colonize roadsides, clearcuts, and burns west of the Cascades. In the mountains, low lobes of subalpine meadow are full of thimbleberry, fireweed, and bracken. Salmonberry prefers soggier spots—streambanks or marshy flats too saturated for full tree cover. At lower elevations it grows with red alder, and may replace it in succession. This looks like a potentially serious problem, at least in the Coast Range: forest practice laws require that streamside buffer strips be left alone during logging. But the vegetation in the second-growth forests there in this century tends to be mostly red alder with a lot of salmonberry in the understory. By prolifically sending up new canes every year, the salmonberry is able to crowd out seedlings of anything else, and may take over completely as the alders grow old and die out. The beneficial riparian characteristics which the buffer law was meant to preserve—e.g., plant species diversity for rich animal habitat, tree shade to keep the water cool for fish, and trees to fall into the stream and slow its flow—would be lost.

Fruits of the genus *Rubus* can all be classed as either raspberries or blackberries. A raspberry, when picked, is cupshaped, pulling cleanly from its receptacle, or core. A blackberry pulls its receptacle with it. Both salmonberries and thimbleberries are raspberries by this definition, but don't taste at all like a garden raspberry. Our dwarf *Rubus* berries (page 217) don't have enough little drupelets per aggregate berry to form a cup. The blackcap, *R. leucodermis*, is a bland black raspberry of lowlands peripheral to our range.

Wild Blackberry

Rubus ursinus (ur-**sigh**-nus: of bears, referring to the Bear constellations, i.e., northern). Also **dewberry**. Leaves 3- (or 5) compound, often persistent but not thick nor truly evergreen; leaflets elliptical, pointed, toothed; flowers white, usually with either stamens or pistils stunted, the functional males and females on separate plants (this species only); flowering stalks up to 16″ tall, from long trailing stems with many slender thorns. Widespread in clearings and ± sunny forest. Rosaceae.

The Northwest is famous for growing mouthwatering blackberries like weeds. They *are* weeds. The most eaten ones are exotic backyard nuisances, archetypal briarpatch—but mouthwatering. They sometimes sweeten dreary approaches over logging roads.

The Pacific "wild" blackberry, our only native blackberry, is not the sweetest but the most elegant, distinctively firm-textured, long and fine-grained. Though dwarfed and outnumbered by exotic blackberries in the towns and farms, it is the abundant species of lower mountain slope forests.

Most weed blackberries are of two species. The Himalayan blackberry, *R. armeniacus*,* came from (possibly) India via (certainly) England, where Luther Burbank refined and named it as a garden variety in 1885. The Northwest's most familiar blackberry, it combines great flavor with sleeve-shredding prolificacy. The tall (20′ or 30′, given something tall to clamber on) arching canes bear compound leaves of usually five fine-toothed oval leaflets that often persist through mild winters. This ability to photosynthesize in

winter characterizes the Northwest's most successful shrubby weeds, e.g., Scotch broom, English ivy, gorse, and these blackberries; all are European. The evergreen blackberry, *R. laciniatus* (pictured at left), often grows

---

*Most U.S. texts treat the Himalayan as *R. discolor* or *R. procerus*. European botanists have treated it as *R. armeniacus* for some time.

---

near the Himalayan. Its five dark green leaflets are deeply incised. Unlike the native wild blackberry, these exotics have bisexual flowers, robust high-climbing canes, and heavy, flattened thorns.

Bitterbrush

Purshia tridentata (**pur**-shia: after F. Pursh, below; try-den-**tay**-ta: 3-toothed). Also **antelopebrush**. Calyx funnel-shaped, fuzzy, 5-lobed, petals yellow, flat-spreading, ¾" diam, stamens protruding; capsules 1-seeded, long-pointed; leaves aromatic, ¾" long, very narrow, 3-pointed and -veined, grayish, white-woolly underneath, edges rolled under; stiff bushy shrubs 3–6' (rarely up to 10'); leaves may persist through some winters. Open forest and steppe E of Cas. Rosaceae. Color p 118.

Bitterbrush is a major shrub of the Intermountain West, thriving on sites marginal for forest growth, such as lower timberlines. On the east Cascade slope, it dominates shrub layers under ponderosa pine and over bunchgrasses. The leaves, bitter to us, are delicious and nutritious to deer, elk, and pronghorn antelope. Years of heavy browsing sometimes give the shrub a low, mounded form.

Bitterbrush shares with big sagebrush not only the specific name *tridentata* and the leaf shape it refers to, but also a fuzzy gray leaf surface and many of the same sites. Their flower structure, however, couldn't be more different, and the plants are unrelated; the leaves evolved convergently in adapting to similar habitat. (Sagebrush leaves do not roll under at the edges, and they're equally woolly on top and bottom surfaces; see page 91.)

Friedrich Pursh (also spelled Frederick), a German botanist, spent several years in the eastern U.S., where he came into possession of the prize set of hitherto unpublished plant specimens of the era—those from the Lewis and Clark Expedition. He published them in his Flora Americae Septentrionale *(1814), the first attempt at a coast-to-coast American flora. Detractors claimed he had no right to first publish these specimens, let alone to take many of them to Europe, as he did. To be fair, overacquisitiveness of this kind was rife among naturalists of that century, even some great ones, and Pursh at least did a creditable job of naming and describing. He spent twelve years on an intended second magnum opus, a flora of Canada, only to see it totally lost in a fire.*

Ninebark

Physocarpus spp. (fie-zo-**car**-pus: bladder fruit). Also **sevenbark**. Flowers small, white (stamens often pink), in dense hemispheric heads 1¼–2" diam; leaves 1–3", palmately veined and 3- (rarely 5-) lobed, coarsely toothed; bark flaking away, reddish or yellowish brown. Rosaceae.

Mallow ninebark, *P. malvaceus* (mal-**vay**-see-us: mallow—). Usually two pistils per flower, becoming two single-seeded seed pods per cluster; erect shrubs mostly 2–8' tall. E-side. Pictured.

Pacific ninebark, *P. capitatus* (cap-it-**ay**-tus: headed). 3–5 pistils; 3–5 seed pods; erect shrubs 6–13' tall. Moist sites, lower W-side. Color p 118.

Apart from stature, and which side of the mountains they grow on, these two ninebarks are much alike. On all ninebarks the bark of large stems shreds and peels in layers—but rarely, if ever, so many as nine, or even seven.

Spiraeas

Spiraea spp. (spy-**ree**-a: the Roman term). Leaves 1–3", oval, toothed on outer half only; flowers pink to white, tiny, in dense fuzzy heads, the 25–50 stamens protruding; seed pods tiny, 2- to several-seeded. Rosaceae.

Hardhack, *S. douglasii* (da-**glass**-ee-eye: after D. Douglas, p 18). Also **steeplebush**. Flowers pink, in conical to spikelike heads often over 3" tall; leggy shrubs 2–7' tall. Streamsides, marshy thickets, mainly W-side. Illustrated at right, and color p 118.

Subalpine spiraea, *S. splendens.** Flowers pink, in slightly convex-topped heads about 2" across; prostrate to low shrubs, up to 3'. Moist thickets and meadows, commonest at 3,000–5,500' W of Cas Crest. Color p 118.

Birchleaf spiraea, *S. betulifoli*a (bet-you-lif-**oh**-lia: birch leaf). Flowers white to very slightly pink; otherwise as above. Widespread on E-side only. Illustrated at left.

---

* Treated as *S. densiflora* in some texts.

Shrubby Cinquefoil

Pentaphylloides floribunda (penta-fill-**oy**-deez: cinquefoil-like; flori-**bun**-da: flowers abundant). Petals yellow, ½" long; sepals apparently 10 (5 smaller bracts alternating with 5 true sepals); compound leaves of 3, 5, or 7 leaflets, hairy, not toothed; seed pods long-haired; dense, rounded to matted shrubs 6–24" tall. Rocky alp/subalp places. Rosaceae. Color p 117.

Though shrubby cinquefoil or "yellow rose" is an alpine specialist in our area, it also grows on rocky hills all across the country and in Eurasia, and is cultivated in cities. Under the name *Potentilla fruticosa*, it was until recently the single shrub in a genus of dozens of herbs, the cinquefoils (page 218). That's one name change so plausible that few laymen would complain.

Wildroses

Rosa spp. Leaves pinnately compound; leaflets 5 to 11, oval to elliptical, toothed except at the base; flowers pink, ¾–3½"; fruit orange, turning red or purple, many-seeded, dry and sour; ± thorny shrubs 1½–8' tall, rarely climbing. Rosaceae.

Baldhip rose, *R. gymnocarpa* (gym-no-**car**-pa: naked fruit). Flowers ¾–1"; fruits ⅜", unique among our rose hips in not retaining the crown of 5 sepals—hence "bald"; plants 1½–4', bristling all over with fine thorns; common W-side; also E-side mid elevs.

Peahip rose, *R. pisocarpa* (pis-o-**car**-pa: pea fruit). Flowers (1–2") and fruits in small clusters; fruits small (¼"), pear-shaped, purplish; thorns usually few; plants up to 8'; strictly W-side, moist places.

Nootka rose, *R. nutkana* (noot-**kay**-na: of Nootka, Vancouver Island). Flowers (2¼–3½") and fruits large, single; thorns variable, typically in stout pairs at leaf nodes; plants usually 2–6'. Both sides Cas, commoner E. Color p 116.

Looking at a wildrose, one wonders whether Europe's horticultural wizards had been at work multiplying rose petals and colors before her poets ever invested The Rose with all its mythic and symbolic weight. In fact, they had. "Hundred-petaled" roses were in cultivation at least by 400 B.C. In comparison, the five-petaled wildrose ranges from unassuming to downright ragged; its virtues are humility, delicacy, and tender fragrance. Its fruit, the rose "hip" or "apple," has ruggeder qualities—perseverance on the bush, lots of vitamin C, and a reasonably pleasant flavor after a couple of frosts have broken it down. Rose hips are trailside breath fresheners, as the Indians knew, and good survival forage.

Shrubs: deciduous, under 6', 5 stamens

Currants and Gooseberries

Ribes spp. (**rye**-beez: Arabic term for rhubarb). Flowers ± tubular, the 5 sepals united about half their length; 5 petals smaller and less colorful than sepals, attached just inside calyx mouth alternately with the 5 stamens; leaves palmately lobed and -veined; weakstemmed shrubs 2–6'. Grossulariaceae (Currant family).

Red-flowering currant, *R. sanguineum* (sang-**gwin**-ee-um: bloody). Flowers ¾" long, red to pink, 10–30 in dense pendent clusters; berries black with a heavy white bloom; leaves 1½–4"; shrubs 5–12'. Lowland woods. Above, and color p 119.

Maple-leafed currant, *R. howellii* (how-el-ee-eye: after Thomas Howell). Sepal lobes flat-spreading, dull red; berries black; leaves 2–3"; shrubs 2–4'. Mid elevs to subalpine, esp in streamside thickets. Illustrated at left.

Wax currant, *R. cereum* (**see**-ree-um: wax). Flowers yellowish white, tubular, ¾" long, ending in short spreading calyx lobes; berries red; leaves grayish, ± round, ½–1¼" diam, toothed, gummy-surfaced, muskily aromatic when crushed; bushy shrubs 2-6'. Sunny slopes E of Cas Cr. Color p 119.

Swamp gooseberry, *R. lacustre* (la-**cus**-tree: of lakes). Also **prickly currant**. Flowers saucer-shaped, dull pinkish, 10–15 in pendent clusters; berries hairy, dark purple; leaves ½–2½"; stems covered with tiny prickles, larger spines whorled around stem nodes; straggly or sprawling shrubs 3–5'. Forested wet spots, esp mid elevs W-side.

The gooseberry has nothing to do with geese; the word (along with the family name) comes straight from the French *groseille*. Gooseberry plants are distinguished from currants by having prickles. All Northwest *Ribes* fruits are edible and nutritious, and most were widely eaten both fresh and dried by the Indians, but today they are recommended only to the starving or insatiably curious. Various authors suggest that certain species are worth eating, but don't agree as to which ones. Some will take your mouth to the movies, running sweet moments tightly sandwiched between sour and bitter episodes; others are only insipidly bitter. Many thickets offer side-by-side currant tastings.

All *Ribes* species prefer moist habitats, but there are as many Eastside as Westside species. All are prey to white pine blister rust, *Cronartium ribicola*, an introduced fungus that devastates western white pines (page 51). Since the fungus' life cycle alternates between *Pinus* and *Ribes* hosts, foresters used to try to eradicate currants from some prime white pine areas.

Our showiest currant is the red-flowering, which blooms deep pink profusely in early spring, when it may be the only burning color in the forest. It is an esteemed ornamental outside of the Northwest; David Douglas' original exportation of this species alone is said to have paid off his sponsors' investment in his two-year expedition. Occasional white-flowered specimens have been prized as breeding stock.

Large gooseberry thorns were used by some tribes as fishhooks and as needles for tattooing or for removing splinters. However, they inflict painful allergic reactions in some people.

Orange Honeysuckle

Lonicera ciliosa (lo-**niss**-er-a: after Adam Lonitzer; silly-**oh**-sa: fringed). Petals orange to almost red, 1–1½", fused (tubular) over ¾ their length, one petal lobe drooping ± apart from the upper 4, hairy inside tube; calyx insignificant; flowers and red ½" berries in terminal clusters ± nestled in a perfoliate leaf (see below); leaves opposite, oval, 1½–3", finely hairy-margined; perennial vines climbing 5–20'. Low-elev openings. Caprifoliaceae (Honeysuckle family). Color p 118.

This honeysuckle attracts its pollinators—hummingbirds— visually, whereas sweet-scented honeysuckles attract night-flying moths. Its flowers, long and narrow like a hummer's bill, are crammed together to make a bright orange bullseye in the center of a target comprised of the uppermost pair of opposite leaves modified into a single fused leaf—often shaped like a very full pair of lips-with the stem passing through the center. The next lower one to three pairs of leaves are decreasingly fused. Northwest tribes saw honeysuckle as women's medicine, using tea or steam from the leaves to encourage lactation, discourage conception, ease cramps, or add luster to little girls' hair. The vine occasionally clasps its host tightly enough to kill it by allowing no room for growth.

Black Twinberry

Lonicera involucrata (in-vo-lu-**cray**-ta: with involucres). Also **bush honeysuckle, inkberry**. Petals pale yellow, ½–¾", fused (tubular) over ½ their length, stamens just appearing at tube mouth, calyx tiny and scarcely lobed, flowers paired, as are the glossy black ¼" berries; leaves opposite, elliptical, pointed, 1½–5", hairy especially at margins and under veins; shrubs 3–6' (rarely to 10'). Widespread on streamsides. Caprifoliaceae (Honeysuckle family).

Northwest tribes called twinberries "crow food," Crow being the only spirit crazy and black enough to relish such bitter, black fruit. "Inkberry" juice was face paint for dolls, or dye for graying hair.

   The twinberry plant carries twinning (the opposite-leaf style) to an extreme; opposite leaf axils bear long opposite stalks, each bearing a pair of flowers between two crossed pairs of hairy bracts, two of which are two-lobed. Two or all four of the bracts (collectively an "involucre") typically turn deep magenta and reflex downward over time to better offset the paired, purplish black berries that replace the pale flowers. This display usually hides in a wet thicket.

   Purple-flowered bush honeysuckle, *L. conjugialis*, grows less abundantly, in the Oregon and Southern Washington Cascades. Its flower pairs are "conjugally" fused at the base, and produce just one, two-tipped berry from their fused ovaries. (Contrast orange honeysuckle, below, with several flowers above fused leaf-pairs.)

Snowberries

Symphoricarpos spp. (sim-for-i-**car**-pus: gathered fruit). Also **waxberries**. Flowers pinkish to white, bell-shaped, less than ¼", petals fused over ½ their length; berries pure white, tightly clustered, pulpy, 2-seeded; leaves and twigs opposite, most leaves (see text) oval to elliptical, 1" long. Caprifoliaceae (Honeysuckle family).

juvenile

mature

S. albus (**al**-bus: white). Berries ½"; shrubs 3–7' tall. Mainly E-side.

S. mollis (**mol**-iss: soft). Berries ¼"; trailing shrubs with erect stems less than 20." Mainly W-side.

I've always thought of this as "popcorn plant," which seems to capture its likeness better than "snow" or "wax," though at the risk of falsely encouraging hungry hikers. The lightweight berries are utterly unlikable as people food; Indians appreciated them ironically as "good for the kids to throw at each other." Maybe that's the mode of dissemination they evolved for. (Actually, birds and rodents eat and disseminate them.)

Our two common species differ little, aside from growth form and range. *S. albus,* a sizable bush, dominates shrubby understories with wildrose and spiraea under sparse Eastside canopies; the northeast Olympics and Puget/Willamette Trough are also dry enough for it. *S. mollis,* a trailing vine, is scattered in Westslope forests. Fast-growing juveniles of both species have highly variable leaves, sporting all numbers and sizes of odd-shaped lobes, symmetrical or not; with maturity they calm down to nondescript inch-long ovals.

Devil's Club

Oplopanax horridus (op-lo-**pan**-ux: heavily armed cure-all; **hor**-id-us: horrid). Leaves 6–15" diam, palmately 7–9-lobed, fine-toothed, all borne ± flat near the top of the stem, leafstalks and undersides of main veins densely spiny; flowers ¼", whitish, in a single erect spike up to 10" tall; berries bright glossy red, 2–3-seeded, up to ¼"; stems 3–12' tall, ½–1½" thick, punky, crooked, usually unbranched, entirely covered with yellowish tan prickles. Seeps and small creeks. Araliaceae (Ginseng family). Color p 119.

Devil's club prefers cold, shaded, sopping, "gloomy" spots; a devil's club thicket is Thorniness in the form of knobby, twisted, tangled, untapering stalks rising out of wet black earth. In summer these hide devilishly under an attractive umbrella of huge leaves. Worse, the spines inject a mild irritant. The scarlet berries, eventual centerpiece to the broad table of leaves, aren't recommended either.

Oplopanax is an oxymoron; *oplo* implies weaponry, while *panax* is a cure, as in panacea. Devil's club may seem more weapon than cure; the "cure" half of its name refers to its relative ginseng (genus *Panax*), perhaps the most crossculturally recognized of all herbal panaceas. Under devil's club thorns lies a thin bark which Puget Sound tribes used medicinally, magically, and cosmetically. It was thought to alleviate such diverse ailments as colds, rheumatism, excessive milk, amenorrhea, and bad smells. A twig on the wall was a household charm. The Lummi mixed the bark ash with bear grease to make black or sepia face paints and tattooing inks. Coastal tribes used the thorny stems as fishing snags and lures.

Big Sagebrush

Artemisia tridentata (ar-tem-**ee**-zhia: the Greek term, honoring either a goddess or a queen; try-den-**tay**-ta: 3-toothed). Composite flower heads drab yellowish, tiny, in loose spikes; leaves spicy-aromatic, grayish-woolly, wedge-shaped, ± shallowly 3-lobed at the tip (average ½" wide), tapering gradually from there to base; bark shreddy; average 2–6' tall where growing abundantly at lower timberline (and eastward *ad nauseam*); or dwarfed to 1–1½' on subalpine ridges. Asteraceae (Aster family).

Most parts of Wild Oregon that aren't covered with Douglas-fir seem to be dotted with sagebrush. Those parts lie east of the forested Cascades, however; this legendary bush could have been left out of this book but for its importance in subalpine communities on ridges east of the Crest in Washington. The form growing here is a dwarfed, more or less isolated ecotype sometimes regarded as a distinct species. Sagebrush is closely related not to culinary sage (*Salvia*, in the mint family) but to culinary tarragon and wormwood (page 188).

Poison-Oak and Poison-Ivy

Toxicodendron spp.* (toxic-oh-**den**-dron: poison
tree). Leaves compound, leaflets 3 (rarely 5), 2–5",
with highly variable lobes, the two lateral leaflets
usually less lobed on their inner edge than on either
their own outer edge or the 2 symmetrical edges of the
terminal leaflet; flowers ¼" diam, greenish white;
berries white, up to ¼", single-seeded, ± striped longitudinally. Anacardiaceae (Cashew family).

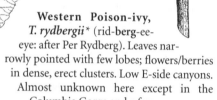

Western Poison-ivy,
T. rydbergii* (rid-**berg**-ee-
eye: after Per Rydberg). Leaves narrowly pointed with few lobes; flowers/berries
in dense, erect clusters. Low E-side canyons.
Almost unknown here except in the
Columbia Gorge and a few
hot, dry lowland sites
peripheral to the range.

Poison-oak, *T. diversilobum** (diverse-il-**oh**-bum: varied
lobes). Leaves coarsely lobed (oaklike); flowers/berries in loose
pendent strings; straggly shrubs 2-6' or sometimes climbing as
a vine up to 40' on trees. Low elevs in Columbia Gorge.
Color p 118.

Leaflets in threes almost always.

Some leaflets crimson by midsummer;
others merely yellowing just before dropping in fall.

New foliage reddish and glossy in spring;
later, foliage is not often strikingly glossy in
our region.

Translucent white berries (for mnemonic aid, think of

---

* Chalk up two for the splitters, including Per Rydberg, who have argued for
these names for at least a century. First, the "poison trees" are now a genus
apart from their less irritating relatives, the sumacs, genus *Rhus*. Second,
western poison-ivies are now a species apart from eastern ones, *T. radicans*.

---

blisters) in bunches, present by late summer and into winter, long after the leaves; many plants may fail to fruit.

Often on or near white oak, its leaflets seeming to mimic nearby oak leaves in shape, sheen, and shade.

Unlike nettle stingers—an elaborate and effective defense against browsing—poison-ivy/oak/sumac poison has little survival value to the plant. Call it an accident of biochemistry, or one of the commonest allergies in *Homo sapiens*. Other species don't seem to be susceptible; they gather the nectar, or browse the leaves with pronounced indifference. In humans, susceptibility can be acquired but rarely shed. Many people sure of their immunity have tried to show it off, only to get a rude shock a couple of days later. Apparently this never happened to Leo Hitchcock, senior author of *Flora of the Pacific Northwest,* who liked to show off by casually picking specimens with his bare hands on class field trips. Lore has it that immunity can be cultivated by eating tiny leaves over the period of their development in spring. **Don't try it.**

Symptoms usually appear, if at all, between 12 and 72 hours after contact. We often start itching within minutes of laying eyes on poison-oak, but in most people this is due to other irritants, like anxiety. If you can wash your exposed parts within ten minutes with soap and hot water (or, in the field, with Tecnu) and quarantine your exposed clothes (and dogs) until laundry, your chances of escaping are still excellent. The allergen, urushiol, is in the sap; a light brushup hardly brings any forth, and is harmless to most people. A few people, though, are alarmingly sensitive. There have been fatalities following poison-ivy smoke inhalation—drownings, technically, in a sea of blister fluid in the lungs. (The toxin is destroyed by complete burning, but smoke may carry unburned particles.)

For most of us, the only defense needed is to know when we are going into areas where poison-oak or ivy grows, and then to know the characteristics, spot the plants without fail, and circumvent them. All in all, the Olympics and Cascades are almost as good a place for staying away from poison-oak and ivy as from poisonous snakes and grizzly bears.

Huckleberries/ Blueberries

Vaccinium spp. (vac-**sin**-ium: the Roman term). Leaves elliptical; flowers pinkish, small, globular, with 5 (rarely 4) very short, bent-back corolla lobes, and similar calyx lobes on the tip of the berry. Ericaceae (Heath family). Individual species described on following pages.

This diverse and well- distributed genus has always been of intense interest to bears, birds, Indians, and hikers. Toward summer's end, bear scats are often little more than barely cemented heaps of recognizable huckleberry leaves; the cement is first to decompose, so you may wonder, a week or two later, how these heaps of dry leaves came to be so neatly molded. The bears lack the patience or the dexterity to pluck the berries singly, and who can blame them, with only a month or two left to fatten up for hibernation?

Indians used the most sophisticated known huckleberry management technique—burning—to maintain areas of berries to pick, including the 8,000-acre Twin Buttes field southwest of Mt. Adams. That particular legacy has dwindled to a mere 2,500 acres under Smokey's antifire administration. The Forest Service is now rediscovering the beauties of a low blaze; one USFS report assigned twice as high a cash value per acre per year to the berries at Twin Buttes as to the trees that have been replacing them. Maybe they never should have made Smokey out to be a bear at all, since bears no doubt preferred Native American management at Twin Buttes to the huckleberry-squelching that goes on in Smokey's name.

"Huckleberry" vs. "blueberry" is a messy issue. Around here I mostly hear the terms used for "wild" and "cultivated" *Vaccinium*, respectively, but back East a related genus (*Gaylussacia*) with seedy black berries has a prior claim on the name huckleberry. Some authors, to resolve this dilemma, try to reinstate the old English names "whortleberry" and "bilberry"; these may be a short etymological hop from "huckleberry" and "blueberry," but could you use them with a straight face? We could call them all blueberries, right down to the "red blueberries." I could get used to that. Still, there's nothing wrong with calling them huckleberries—it just risks confusing Easterners. Cranberries and lingonberries, though also in genus *Vaccinium*, are never spoken of as huckleberries.

The Northwest has twelve species of huckleberry. The following five, taken in order of descending elevation, are each important in one or more montane community types.

Cascades blueberry, *V. deliciosum*. Berries bright blue due to a heavy coating of waxy bloom; flowers spherical; leaves slightly toothed; plants 2–18" tall. Alp/ subalpine. Color p 120.

Cascades blueberries provide about 90% of the gorgeous scarlet fall color of subalpine slopes (see back cover photo), and can also be credited for a lot of excitement in the animal kingdom at that time of year. Deliciosum indeed!

On moist alpine sites, they often grow on a two- to three-inch scale that makes the berries look hugely rotund. Both there and in the subalpine zone, where they average a foot in stature, they often grow with red, yellow, or white mountain heathers. This "low heath community" is highly characteristic of our range: that is, it's ubiquitous here on suitable sites, but it's not known in the same form in mountains east or south of the Cascades. The suitable sites are next to subalpine trees or on rocky subalpine convexities, in either case getting a longer snowfree season than nearby herbaceous meadows. The low heaths are prone to takeover by trees during warm/dry decades.

Grouseberry, *V. scoparium* (sco-**pair**-ium: broom—). Berries bright red, tiny (⅛"); leaves ¼–½"; plants 4–14" tall; twigs green, with angled edges, numerous, all ± vertical. Near and E of Cas Cr in OR.

Grouseberry is locally abundant on dry habitats, often on overly drained (gravelly) volcanic soil. The fruit is scrumptious but hard to gather in quantity.

Black huckleberry, *V. membranaceum* (mem-bra-**nay**-see-um: thin). Also **thinleaf huckleberry**. Berries black to dark red; flowers much longer than broad; leaves 1–2½", thin, pointed, minutely toothed; 2–6' tall. Low subalpine.

Top huckleberry for combined availability, flavor, and texture, the black huckleberry is the main attraction of the huge wild huckleberry fields southwest of Mt. Adams. Though it grows and bears fruit most lavishly in burns and other clearings, it also dominates the shrub layer of many midmontane forests. It mingles there with the following two species, or with Cascades blueberry around timberline. Beargrass is another frequent companion.

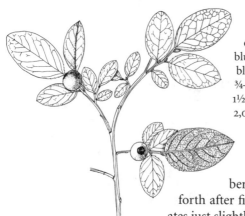

**Oval-leaved huckleberry,
V. ovalifolium ***(**o-val-if-
oh-lium: oval leaf). Berries
blue with bloom or purplish
black without bloom; leaves
¾–2½", smooth edged; shrubs
1½–5'. Abundant in forests at
2,000–5,000' elev.

Typically a straggly
understory shrub,
oval-leaved huckle-
berry is prepared to burst
forth after fire or clearcut. It tolerates just slightly less temperature and
moisture stress than black huckleberry, but for all that, produces
sparser, seedier, sourer berries.

Red huckleberry, *V. parvifolium* (par-vif-**oh**-lium: small leaf). Berries bright
red; flowers at least as broad as long; leaves ¼–1", smooth-edged; twigs squarish, angled; shrubs 3–12'. W-side.

Red huckleberry is widely scattered in lower Westside forest spots
with some warmth to them. Its berries are sparse, too; if only they
were easier to gather in quantity, the legendary red
huckleberry pie would be better known. For
eating fresh, they are juicy but sour.

White Rhododendron

Rhododendron albiflorum (roe-doe-**den**-dron:
rose tree, a doubly misleading name; al-bif-**lor**-um:
white flower). Also **Cascades azalea**. Flowers white, ¾"
diam, broadly bell-shaped, petals fused no more than ½
their length, 1–4 in clusters just below the whorllike leaf
clusters at branch tips; leaves elliptical, 2–3½", glossy,
bumpy, slightly reddish-hairy; capsules 5-celled; bark
shredding; leggy shrubs 3–6'. Locally abundant around
timberline, especially on colder sites. Ericaceae (Heath family). Color p 119.

It's hard to see these blossoms — so modest by garden "rhodie"
standards — as rhododendrons. But few who have reached timberline by foot would question their showiness.

---

*The long-standing taxonomic quandary over *V. alaskaense* is resolved (in
some texts, including this one) by lumping it into *ovalifolium.*

Fool's-Huckleberry

Menziesia ferruginea (men-**zee**-zia: after A. Menzies, below; fair-u-**jin**-ia: rust-red). Also **false-azalea, rusty-leaf.** Flowers pale rusty orange, jar-shaped, pendent on sticky-hairy pedicels, ¼", calyx and corolla shallowly 4-lobed, stamens 8; capsules 4-celled; leaves 1½–2½", elliptical, seemingly whorled near branch tips, often hairy, coloring deeply in fall; bark shreddy; leggy shrubs 3–6'. Mid elevs to subalpine. Ericaceae (Heath family). Color p 119.

This plant has no berries to tempt anyone, no matter how foolish, so I'd call it a fool's fool's huckleberry. True, on the basis of summer foliage alone it could be carelessly mistaken for its close relatives, black huckleberry and white rhododendron. More often it simply goes unnoticed among them, growing where one or both of them outnumber it. Together they make up the tall heath-shrub community ubiquitous around forest line here, possibly a successional stage leading to subalpine fir or mountain hemlock forest. Often the tall heaths encircle an expanding tree clump (see page 28) or fill in among scattered trees invading subalpine meadowland.

Menziesia's flower parts in fours are unusual in the heath family, but not unique. In the family's many 5-merous species there are often some 4-merous individuals.

Archibald Menzies was the first scientist to explore Washington or Oregon, so it's fitting that more species (six, plus this genus) in this book honor him than anyone else. After spending a month at Nootka on Vancouver Island in 1787, he was appointed surgeon-naturalist on H.M.S. Discovery *under Captain George Vancouver. Menzies' 1792 journal records the first Washington landing at Discovery Bay and the naming of many other land and water features after officers on the ship (Puget, Whidbey, Baker, Vancouver) and Englishmen the captain admired (Rainier, St. Helens, Hood). The ship's mission didn't allow Menzies time for much exploration ashore, and his live collections all died on board, but his plant descriptions and dried specimens that reached England aroused intense interest in the Northwest, eventually leading to voyages by David Douglas and others. Menzies was an old man by 1824, when young Douglas visited him for a briefing on Northwest American plants.*

Shrubs: deciduous, under 6', 8 or 10 stamens   *97*

Broadleaf evergreens are primarily a tropical and subtropical life form; where the growing season is year-round, the leaves stay put, naturally. Though our region has winters, it offers advantages to evergreen plants that can continue their life functions, even at sharply reduced rates, through the cool seasons. This is largely because our summers are dry enough to curtail warm-season photosynthesis (see page 11). Our type of broadleaf evergreens, called sclerophylls ("hardened leaves"), have adapted with heavy, rigid leaves that dry out partially in summer, reducing transpiration and conserving water, without danger of wilt damage. Most of temperate North America's sclerophylls are found in Pacific coastal forests—many here in our range, but far more in southern Oregon and northern California. Down there, wet mild marine winters like ours alternate with summers longer, dryer, and hotter than ours.

This section begins with our only reliably tree-form sclerophyll, and moves on down through the tall and medium shrubs to the dwarf and prostrate shrubs and subshrubs. The Ericaceae (Heath family) dominate this section; they share a strong family resemblance, not only in the heavy, evergreen, elliptical leaves but in their small, usually white to pink, jar-shaped flowers. While broadleaf evergreens dominate the family, it also includes deciduous shrubs, herbs, and even non-green herbs.

Evergreen blackberry, page 83, an introduced weed, is placed with the other blackberries, which are essentially deciduous despite keeping half-dead leaves on some plants through some winters.

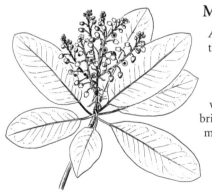

Madroño

Arbutus menziesii (ar-**bew**-tus: the Roman term; men-**zee**-zee-eye: after A. Menzies, p 99). Also **madrona, madrone, arbutus.** 24" diam × 80'; flowers small, white, jar-shaped, 5-lobed, berries bright orange, pebbly skinned, many-seeded, ¼–½" in large clusters; leaves heavy, glossy dark green above, silvery beneath, oblong, 2½–6"; bark flaking in thin sheets, very smooth and pale green when young, turning through bronze to deep red, finally becoming rough dark gray-brown, esp near base; irregularly branched trees. Sunny, rocky slopes, low E Olys and W-side Cas. Ericaceae (Heath family).

I can't stop gazing at madroño bark, can't resist touching it, only barely resist stripping it—such elegant voluptuous limbs, so smooth and richly colored. Similar limbs on a smaller scale grow on manzanitas and kinnickinnick, similar leaves on rhododendron; but of all the heath family, only *Arbutus* grows as a tree. It is by far the most northerly broadleaf evergreen tree on the continent, growing along the coast from mountains near San Diego to rocky shorelines up on the Georgia Strait. To cover that stretch it has to be indifferent to precipitation (18" to 166" a year) and temperature, requiring only that its own spot be well drained and sunny.

Around the Mediterranean grows a shrubby tree, *A. unedo*, called *arbutus* by the Romans, *madro* by the Spanish, and "strawberry tree" by the English. Spaniards in early California recognized its relative, calling it "big madro," madroño, later corrupted by Anglos into madrone or madrona (the two usual spellings today). The sweetish berries of the strawberry-tree flavor a liqueur, *crème d'arbouse*; but madroño berries are bitter and slightly narcotic. The wood is heavy, hard, strong, and beautiful, but splits badly in drying, and isn't used much. Indians made spoons and ladles from it.

Pacific Rhododendron

Rhododendron macrophyllum (roe-doe-**den**-dron: rose tree, two misleading words for this genus; macro-**fill**-um: big leaf). Flowers pink, 1–2", broadly bell-shaped, in large dense clusters, petals and sepals 5, fused at the base, 1 upper petal usually spotted; capsules woody, 5-celled, ½–¾"; leaves heavy, deep glossy green, 3–8" long, with smooth rolled-under edges; often straggly shrubs 3–15'. Abundant in some drier mid-elev forest, OR and S WA Cas, and E Olys. Ericaceae (Heath family). Color p 120.

The 600-odd species of genus *Rhododendron*—mostly Asian—have been recombined into thousands of garden "rhodies""and azaleas of all colors; they make overwhelming displays. Our native rhododendron is plain pink, spends most of its time in the shade, and runs to legginess. Still, when the woods are in bloom with them, like fat pink mirages on a gray day, or like randomly bursting fireworks in the shifting sunbeams of a sunny day, they have great power to enchant. Washington named them its State Flower, perhaps to make up for having fewer of them than Oregon.

Salal

Gaultheria shallon (galth-ee-ria: after Jean-Francois Gaultier; **shall**-on: NW tribal term). Corolla pinkish to white, bell-shaped to spherical, sepals red; flowers 6–15, pendent along a ± horizontal stalk; berries purple-black ; entire inflorescence (incl flowers and berries) minutely hairy and sticky; leaves glossy, leathery, broadly oval, pointed, 2–3½"; branches zigzagging at leaf nodes; shrubs 1–8'. Abundant W-side. Ericaceae (Heath family). Color p 120.

April 1825. Saturday the 9th in company with Mr. Scouler I went ashore on Cape Disappointment as the ship could not proceed up the river in consequence of heavy rains and thick fogs. On stepping on the shore Gaultheria shallon *was the first plant I took in my hands. So pleased was I that I could scarcely see anything but it. Mr. Menzies correctly observes that it ... would make a valuable addition to our gardens....*

(1826) Called by the natives "salal," not "shallon" as stated by Pursh... Bears abundantly, fruit good, indeed by far the best in the country...*

I wonder if David Douglas would have logged that appraisal if he had been in the mountains in huckleberry season; in any case, salal berries deserve a better reputation than they now enjoy. At their best, they rival huckleberries in flavor—less acid, with spicy resinous overtones—but their skins and seeds are a bit heavy, so they are most popular strained and made into jelly. Formerly, Northwest tribes dried huge quantities of them in big cakes or loaves, stored them wrapped in skunk-cabbage leaves, and ate them all winter long dipped in seal or candlefish oil. According to Kwakiutl protocol (among the most elaborate and stringent protocol

---

* See David Douglas, p 18, John Scouler, p 71, Archibald Menzies, p 99, and Friedrich Pursh, p 84.

ever known) pure salal cakes were exclusive fare for chiefs at feasts; the *hoi polloi* were allowed only cakes of salal berries stretched with less sweet fruit, such as red elderberries, that are barely edible by themselves. Salal was perhaps the sweetest and certainly the most available berry for coastal tribes.

As for Menzies' prediction of "a valuable addition to English gardens," it looked true enough for a century or so, but the English are starting to regard salal as weedy. Don't waste your pity on them. A majority of the Northwest's most invasive aliens—Scotch broom, gorse, English ivy, holly, blackberries, and stinky Bob—came here from the Emerald Isle, and few of them can equal salal's redeeming virtues.

Salal certainly can spread by sprouting from rhizomes. Big clonal thickets often grow in areas of poor soil. (Like others in its family, salal has a rich partnership with mycorrhizal fungi which procure ample nitrogen and phosphorus from soils deficient in same; adding fertilizer actually stunts salal's growth!) Typically, salal grows under gappy canopies. When a canopy gap closes up over salal plants, they respond by growing bigger, thinner "shade leaves," and can survive deep shade for several years waiting for the next tree death to bring back the sun flecks; then they make small (less than 2" wide) thick "sun leaves" again, even from the same twig that bore shade leaves last year. During the deep shade period, the salal thicket thins out, letting many of its stems and rhizomes die; when it finds itself in a gap again it redensifies, sending up lots of new shoots from the rhizomes.

The leaves, which live about four years, are important winter browse for deer. Salal branches for use as floral greens are a sky-rocketing "special forest product." Salal picking rights are lucrative enough that one brushpicker murdered another over them in a tragic case that echoed the several murders among matsutake mushroom pickers in the 1990s.

Two dwarf shrubs called wintergreen (page 112) are recognizable, at higher elevations, as salal's baby brothers.

Snowbrush

Ceanothus velutinus (see-an-**oath**-us: thistle, a misleading name; ve-**lu**-tin-us: velvety). Also **tobacco-
brush, cinnamon-bush, sticky-laurel.** Flowers tiny,
white, in dense fluffy ± conical 2–5" clusters; petals,
sepals, and stamens each 5; seed pods of 3 separating,
1-seeded cells; leaves 1½–3½", broadly oval, fine-toothed,
often tightly curling, heavily spicy-aromatic, shiny and sticky
above, pale-fuzzy beneath (exc ± smooth on a variety found W-side
below 2,600'), with 3 ± equally heavy main veins from base nearly to tip,
otherwise pinnate-veined; robust shrubs 2–6'. Dry, sunny clearings, abundant E-side. Rhamnaceae (Buckthorn family). Color p 120.

Snowbrush invades burns, including slashburned clearcuts. Its
seeds are activated by the heat of a fire and the increased soil
warmth of a new clearing. The young shoots grow slowly, but easily crowd out annuals like fireweed in three or four seasons. The
roots host nitrogen-fixing bacteria, a big advantage where the soil
has lost most of its organic nitrogen. Snowbrush often grows dense
enough to prevent conifer establishment, especially in southern
Oregon where it rose high on foresters' hit lists. But like the once-
maligned red alder, it should eventually aid conifer growth by
adding nitrogen. Snowbrush reproduction is largely vegetative,
while most of the seeds lie dormant and viable as long as 300 years,
waiting to be reawakened by a fire. The reappearance of a full-
blown snowbrush community centuries after snowbrush was shaded out of the forest will seem miraculous.

Some *Ceanothus* species are evergreen (e.g.,
squawcarpet, page 113) and others are not; redstem
ceanothus, *C. sanguineus*, has distinctive smooth
purple stems, but rather nondescript thin deciduous leaves — not fragrant, sticky, shiny, velvety nor
prominently three-veined. The two species are similar in stature, flowers, fruits, and habitat; both are
commoner on the Eastside. Redstem is also known as
Oregon-tea, but any tea made from its leaves would be ersatz
ersatz; the reference is to New Jersey Tea, an eastern *Ceanothus*
brewed by patriotic colonists wanting to declare their independence
from the tea taxed under the Stamp Act. The name "tobacco-brush"
comes either from snowbrush's fragrance in the afternoon sun, or
from rumored (desperate) use of the leaves as a smoking herb.

Golden Chinquapin

*Chrysolepis chrysophylla** (cris-**ahl**-ep-iss: gold scale; cris-a-**fill**-a: gold leaf). Catkins clustered ± erect at branchtips, each bearing a series of male fuzzballs, with fewer female flowers near the base of the catkin; nuts ¼–½", in very spiny hulls ¾" diam; leaves 3–6", narrow, tapering, dark glossy green above, with a rough yellow-brown ("golden") coating beneath; new twigs yellow-coated; bark white-splotched in youth, eventually thick and furrowed; shrubs or small trees (here) 10–30'. Drier forests and thickets, mainly W-side OR. Fagaceae (Beech family).

In its best range—southwestern Oregon and northwestern California—the golden chinquapin is a big tree, up to 150' by 6' diameter, which would top any of our broadleaf trees except cottonwood. But in our range we know it mainly as a tall shrub. It is easy to spot in much of Oregon's Cascades as the only big shrub with such long, narrow, evergreen leaves. It grows on dry lower-slope sites, joining rhododendron, salal and vine maple to make a very dense understory. In Washington it grows only in two places—one near the Columbia Gorge and one near the Hamma Hamma River. These small isolated, or "relict," populations are left over from the warmer era of 9,000 to 5,000 years ago, when Washington's climate was much like Oregon's is today, and chinquapins were widespread there.

Chinquapins are in a family with oak, beech, and chestnut trees. The word "chinquapin," for chestnut trees (genus *Castanea*), is originally Algonquinian. Chinquapin nuts and chestnuts are both edible and both borne one to three in a bristly hull. Fortunately for our chinquapin, no chestnuts are native to the Northwest. If they had shared any range they would probably have shared a dismal fate—the introduced blight that wiped out the American chestnut.

The wood is easily worked, and takes on a beautiful hue.

---

* *Chrysolepis* was recently split out from the genus *Castanopsis*.

Oregon-Grape

Berberis nervosa* (**ber**-ber-iss: the Arabic term; ner-vo-sa: veiny). Also **mahonia**. Flowers yellow, in a terminal group of 3–7" spikes amid a cluster of sharp ½–2" bud scales; petals/sepals in 5 concentric whorls of 3, outer whorl(s) ± green; berries ⅜", grapelike, purple with a heavy blue bloom; leaves compound, crowded at top of stem, 10–16" long; leaflets 11–21, spiny-margined (hollylike), pointed-oval, palmately veined; stems unbranched, 4–18"; inner bark yellow. W-side forests, ± ubiquitous. Berberidaceae (Barberry family). Color p 120.

Though Northwesterners today may take them for granted, David Douglas rated Oregon-grape and salal each a smashing find for the English garden. He was right, especially about Oregon-grape, which was all the rage there during Victoria's reign. Though the leaves are evergreen, a few may burst crimson at any time of year. The stamens snap inward at the lightest touch to shake their pollen onto a bee.

The berries (not grapes by a long shot) have an exquisite sourness not balanced by much sweetness. Both jelly and wine from Oregon-grapes are traditional since pioneer days, but decreasingly popular. Gourmands may gag, but those with a penchant for wild plant foods still smack their lips. They're juicy, and refreshing in their way. Indians mashed them with sweeter berries for winter storage in dry cakes. They also gathered the roots for yellow dye, and for a tea to soothe a sore throat or stomach.

This is the most ubiquitous understory plant of the western hemlock zone in Oregon; less so in Washington, it is absent from Sitka spruce bottoms in the western Olympics.

Two close relatives have leaflets with just one prominent midvein. Tall Oregon-grape, *B. aquifolium*,* the State Flower, grows on semi-open lowlands. Its leaves, rarely of more than nine leaflets, are on tall (2–10') woody stems. Creeping Oregon-grape, *B. repens*,* ranges up the Cascades' east slope to middle elevations. Its leaves of five or seven leaflets stay close (6–30") to the ground.

---

* Also known, in PLANTS database and elsewhere, as genus *Mahonia*. Taxonomists have batted Oregon-grape back and forth for ages. The Oregon Flora finds that they do belong in genus *Berberis* with the barberries.

Oregon-Boxwood

Paxistima myrsinites (pa-**kis**-tim-a: thick stigma; mir-sin-**eye**-teez: myrrh-like). Also **mountain-boxwood, myrtle-boxwood, mountain lover.** Flowers ⅛" diam, clustered in leaf axils, dark red petals and whitish stamens and sepals each 4; capsules splitting in two; leaves opposite, ½–1¼", elliptical, shallowly toothed, glossy, dark above; twigs reddish, 4-angled; dense shrubs 10–40". Mostly dry sites, mid to high elevs; locally abundant E-side under true firs or western hemlock. Celastraceae (Staff-tree family). Color p 120.

Oregon-boxwood is our only sizable evergreen shrub whose leaves are opposite. (The evergreen dwarf shrubs, pages 106–14, are mostly either opposite-leaved or indistinctly alternate-leaved; also don't mistake Oregon-grape's leaflets for opposite leaves.) Otherwise it looks much like the heath family; florists use tons of it interchangeably with evergreen blueberry sprays from the Coast, and few customers notice the difference. Definitely a "foliage plant," it has pretty flowers if you squint down close enough to make them out. Deer browse it in winter.

Manzanitas

Arctostaphylos spp. (arc-to-**staf**-il-os: bear grapes). Flowers pinkish to white, jar-shaped, 5-lobed, in small clusters; berries reddish brown, dry, mealy; leaves grayish, ± elliptical, 1–2"; twigs minutely hairy; larger branches smooth, red, with peeling flakes; dense shrubs 3–8'. Rocky exposed sites at all elevs. Ericaceae (Heath family).

Green manzanita, *A. patula* (**patch**-u-la: spreading). E-side from Mt Adams S, common on pumice. Pictured above, and color p 120.

Hairy manzanita, *A. columbiana* (co-lum-be-**ay**-na: of the Columbia River). W-side.

More than thirty species of manzanita conspire in the making of California's notorious chaparral, a dense brushfield community adapted for taking over mountain slopes after fires. Manzanita

---

seeds lie dormant in the soil until awakened by groundfire heat; between fires, the plants spread by layering. After the chaparral burns, manzanita root crowns sprout again like crazy. The finishing touch in this monopolistic strategy, according to some scientists, is an allelopathic secretion which poisons the soil against competing species.

Our manzanitas are remote outliers of the chaparral, and they lack chaparral's monopolistic success. In fact, they are probably a big help to forest recovery after fires, because heath shrubs share with conifers many of the same mycorrhizal partner species; manzanitas quickly resprout after a fire, and keep in place the mycorrhizal community which conifers will need a few years later, as their seedlings germinate. Otherwise the soil might be taken over by fungi that associate with grasses, say, or rose-family shrubs, and these are useless if not downright hostile to conifers.

Hairy manzanita, the W-side lowland species, also pioneers on lava flows in the High Cascades. In the eastern Olympics (and anywhere their ranges overlap) it hybridizes with kinnickinnick, producing a red-fruited low erect shrub popular in cultivation.

Shrubs: broadleaf evergreen, under 10"

A woody stem may be hard to detect in very small plants; the difference between subshrubs and herbs is gradual. For category purposes, we'll take evergreen leaves as proof of aboveground perennial (i.e., shrubby) parts to support them; but there seem to be almost as many cases of borderline evergreenness as of borderline shrubbiness. Many small species whose closest relatives are clearly deciduous have adapted to long-lasting snowpacks by keeping leaves in place and green through one winter, and then letting them slowly wither as they are replaced by new foliage the next summer. This way there is green foliage ready to photosynthesize, however meagerly, from the first snowfree day to the last. Alpine ecologists call foliage on this schedule "wintergreen," as opposed to "evergreen" leaves that function during more than two summers; the more usual, vaguer term is "persistent." In this book they are keyed with the herbs, according to flower structure: alpine willows, p 190; penstemons, p 195; violets, p 200; sibbaldia, p 208; sandwort, p 212; yerba de selva, p 213; partridgefoot, p 216; dwarf raspberries, p 217; kittentails, p 227; wild-ginger, p 231; lewisias, p 234.

When in doubt as to evergreenness or shrubbiness, think of other plants your specimen resembles and may be related to. This group (broadleaf evergreens under 10") has firm, dark, waxy-looking leaves; all but the final three are in the Heath family. The only plant placed elsewhere despite having dark, firm evergreen leaves is rattlesnake-plantain, p 173, which is taxonomically remote: look closely at its flowers, and you'll see they're orchids.

Kinnickinnicks

Arctostaphylos spp. (arc-tos-**taf**-il-os: bear grapes*). Flowers pinkish to white, jar-shaped, 5-lobed, clustered; berries ¼", dry and mealy, flat-tasting; leaves ½–1¼", widest past midlength; thin gray bark flaking, revealing smooth red bark underneath. Rocky, exposed sites. Ericaceae (Heath family).

Kinnickinnick, *A. uva-ursi* (**oo**-va-**ur**-sigh: grape of bears). Also **bearberry.** Berries bright red; leaf tips rounded; shrubs prostrate/ trailing, rarely over 6" off the ground. All elevs. Illustrated at right, and color p 121.

Pinemat manzanita, *A. nevadensis* (nev-a-**den**-sis: of the Sierra Nevada). Berries dull red; leaves pointed; shrubs dense, cushionlike, 4–10" tall. Above 4,000'. (Compare manzanitas, p 105.)

"Kinnickinnick" was an eastern intertribal trading word meaning "smoking-herbs;" Hudson's Bay Co. traders brought the word west and applied it to this plant the Northwest tribes taught them to smoke. Popular more for the high than the flavor, it quickly came to be viewed as a way of stretching tobacco, after the latter arrived in the Northwest. (Fur traders taught Coast Indians to cultivate tobacco even before Lewis and Clark.) The berries seem to please bears, but among Indians they were starvation fare or adulterants for sweeter berries like salal. These species are valuable pioneers on volcanic or glacial soils, and well-known ground cover ornamentals in the cities.

---

* Originally named *Uva-ursi uva-ursi;* the Latin genus name was translated into Greek after an International Rules convention banned hyphens in names of genera, but not in species names.

Pyrolas

Also **wintergreens, shinleafs.** In forest. Ericaceae (Heath family).

White-veined pyrola, *Pyrola picta* (pie-ro-la: small pear, referring to leaf shape; **pic**-ta: painted). Petals spreading, pale, greenish to purplish, style downturned; flowers 5-20 on a reddish, 4–12" stem; leaves all basal, egg-shaped, 1–3", dark green white-mottled along the ± pinnate veins (compare Rattlesnake-plantain, p 173). Commoner E-side. Pictured at left, and color p 121.

Heart-leaved pyrola, *P. asarifolia* (a-sair-if-**oh**-lia: wild-ginger leaf). Petals spreading, pink to red, style strongly downturned; flowers 8–25 on a 6–16" stalk; leaves basal, long-stalked, round to heartshaped, 1–3".

One-sided pyrola, *Orthilia secunda** (or-**thill**-ia: straight and small; se-**cun**-da: with flowers all to one side). Flowers greenish white, bell-shaped, with long straight style, 5–15 all facing ± the same way; leaves 1–2½", variably egg-shaped, running up the lower half of the 3–7" stems from rhizomes. Commoner W-side.

Single delight, *Moneses uniflora** (mo-**nee**-sees: single delight; you-nif-**lor**-a: one flower). Flowers single, ½–1", waxy-whitish, petals flat-spreading, pistil fat, straight, 5-tipped (like a chess rook); leaves oval, usually toothed, ½–1¼", from lower ¼ of 2–6" stem; often on rotting wood. Pictured at right, and color p 121.

Pyrolas are mysterious and interesting at first glance, and all the more so when you know they demonstrate a transition in the evolution of non-green plants, and in human science regarding non-green plants. (Page 177.) When the Northwest was first botanized, reports came back of totally leafless but healthy specimens otherwise resembling the familiar genus *Pyrola* (It's hard to identify pyrolas to species with-

---

*Both *Moneses* and *Orthilia* were long included in genus *Pyrola*, and their relationship to *Pyrola* is close enough to warrant keeping them all together under this common-name heading.

out benefit of leaves.). These were formally named *P. aphylla*; but later they proved to be specimens of several other pyrola species in "degenerate" form. Apparently individual pyrolas may hover at the threshold of non-greenness. As a young forest matures around one of these plants, competition for light and water intensifies; the weaker individuals die and the stronger ones jettison any leaves that aren't in a position to pull their own weight. That applies to trees, shrubs, and subshrubs alike, but for a period (foresters call it the stem exclusion phase) most of the survivors are the taller trees; the forest floor can get pretty bare, and pyrolas, small orchids, and non-green plants become conspicuous. These plants get most or all of their carbohydrates from the tree canopy via mycorrhizae in any case. To some pyrolas, apparently, it's the leaf exclusion phase: they let their leaves atrophy, and fall back on their fungal partners to deliver all the photosynthate. They can regrow leaves another year if a few trees die, bringing back better light conditions. The evolution of non-green plants may well have included a stage just like that, and then taken the next step, the genetic loss of the ability to photosynthesize.

Pipsissewas

Chimaphila spp. (kim-**af**-il-a: winter loving). Also **prince's-pine**. Stamens and pink-to-white petals flat-spreading, pistil fat, hublike; flowers ½" diam, nodding; leaves very dark, 1–3", narrowly elliptical, saw-toothed, ± whorled on lower ½ of stem. Widespread in forests. Ericaceae (Heath family).

C. umbellata (um-bel-**ay**-ta: bearing flowers in umbels). Flowers 4–12; leaves widest past mid-length; plants 4–10" tall. Pictured, and color p 122.

C. menziesii (men-**zee**-zee-eye: after Archibald Menzies, p 97). Flowers 1–3; leaves widest below or near midlength; plants 2–6".

These are among our most habitat-indifferent forest plants, growing in virtually every type of Westside forest and in closed forests on the Eastside as well. The chief difference between the two is that *menziesii*, as you might expect of a reduced version, is slightly commoner at higher elevations. (It is also confined to the Northwest, while *umbellata* is "circumboreal," or common to all northern coniferous forests.) Though widespread, neither pipsissewa is really an herb layer dominant, nor are they predictable in their occurrence. Their success under heavy shade suggests heavy dependence on mycorrhizae, which can often lead to spotty distribution. Their leaves, "*Foliachimaphilae*," used to sit on apothecary shelves as a remedy for bladderstones; herbalists still harvest them, sometimes excessively, in the Northwest.

Mountain Heathers

Cassiope and *Phyllodoce* spp. (ca-**sigh**-a-pee and fil-**od**-os-ee: characters in Greek myth). Ericaceae (Heath family). Color p 122.

White heather, *C. mertensiana* (mer-ten-zee-ay-na: after Karl H. Mertens, below). Also **moss heather.** Corolla bell-shaped, white; flowers pendent from axils near branchtips; capsules ± erect; leaves tiny (⅛"), densely packed along the stem in 4 ranks, thus square in cross-section; spreading, mat-forming shrubs 2–12". Alp/subalpine.

Pink heather, *P. empetriformis* (em-pee-trif-**or**-mis: crowberry shaped). Corolla pink, bell-shaped; flowers 5-15 in apparent terminal clusters, erect in bud, pendent in bloom, then erect again as dry capsules; leaves needlelike, ¼–½"; dense matted shrubs 4–10" or up to 15". Alp/subalpine.

*Heinrich Mertens accompanied the Russian Count **Fedor Lütke** on his globe-circling voyage of 1826–1829, when both were heir early thirties. In London in 1829 they so impressed David Douglas (page 18) that he became obsessed with completing his second trip to the Northwest by sailing from the Russian colony at Sitka to the Siberian shore. He would then have walked the length of Siberia, collecting plants.*

Mertens died the following year. His plant discoveries at Sitka, Southeast Alaska, include a half-dozen species named mertensiana *(mertensianus, mertensii) and as many more named* sitchensis *(sitchense), such as Sitka spruce, as well as the partridgefoot,* Luetkea, *but not the* Mertensia *bluebells, which were already named after his father, botany professor **Franz Karl Mertens.***

Yellow heather, *P. glanduliflora* (gland-you-lif-**lor**-a: glandular flower). As above, exc corolla cream yellow to off-white, narrow-necked jar-shaped. Alpine.

Mountain heather is an old friend, always there to welcome you back to the high country. Loosen your bootlaces, sit still, see how much you can take in. Innumerable scattered patches of pink and white heathers are a common denominator of the subalpine zone throughout the greater Northwest; both reach the alpine zone as well. Pink reaches the lowest (forest fringe) elevations, Yellow the highest and driest (rare below tree line), while White has an in-between range; all three overlap between 6,000' and 7,000' in the North Cascades.

In subalpine parkland, the mountain heather or low heath community usually grows on stony soils with fairly late snowmelt. This community is prone to tree invasion; trees encroach a few feet at a time, making the snow melt earlier with their "black body effect" (page 28). If fire in the subalpine were somehow prevented, all the heather might eventually be replaced by trees. (God forbid.) Unlike huckleberries, mountain heathers rarely persist under a tree canopy, though they often encircle tree clumps.

Cassiope (white heather) foliage is almost like clubmoss; *Phyllodoce* (pink/yellow heather) foliage is more like common juniper or crowberry; still, heathers share an obvious resemblance in their flowers and habitat.

Vast communities known as "heath" took over much of Scotland following deforestation and heavy sheep grazing hundreds of years ago. They are dominated by species of *Cassiope, Phyllodoce, Erica,* and especially *Calluna*—all called "heather" by the Scots. The "Scottish heather" of Northwest gardens is *Calluna vulgaris.*

Wintergreens

Gaultheria spp. (galth-ee-ria: after Jean-Francois Gaultier). Flowers white to pinkish, bell-shaped, about ⅛" long, from leaf axils; berries red, up to ¼", delicious; leaves oval, ± pointed; spreading shrubs 1–6" tall. Ericaceae (Heath family).

Oregon wintergreen, *G. ovatifolia* (o-vay-ti-foe-lia: oval leaf). Sepals densely hairy; leaves ¾–1¼"; mid-elev forest. At right, and color p 121.

Alpine wintergreen, *G. humifusa* (hue-mi-few-sa: trailing). Sepals and berries smooth; leaves ½–¾"; around timberline.

That these wintergreens are dwarfed versions of salal is plain to see; you might guess them to be just stunted salal until you see and taste their fruit. The common name "wintergreen" has been used for both *Gaultheria* and *Pyrola*, but oil of wintergreen indisputably comes from leaves of *Gaultheria procumbens*, similar to these sweet-fruited shrublets. Though that Eastern North American plant put "wintergreen" into common parlance, modern candy and gum makers substitute an extract of birch twigs, or a synthetic flavor.

Alpine Laurel

Kalmia microphylla * (kahl-mia: after Per Kalm; micro-fill-a: small leaf). Corolla pink, bowl-shaped, ½" diam; sepals tiny, green; flowers 3–8 in terminal clusters; capsules 5-celled, with long style; leaves opposite, ½–1" long, narrow, often with rolled-under edges; spreading subshrubs to 6". Marshy subalpine soils. Ericaceae (Heath family). Color p 121.

These profuse pink blossoms brighten up high seasonal bogs and soggy alpine slopes right after snowmelt. Look closely: ten little bumps on the odd-shaped buds hold the ten anthers (stamen tips). When the flower opens, the stamens are spring-loaded to throw their pollen on the first insect to alight.

This plant and its relatives are toxic. Laurel is a common name for *Kalmia* of all sizes, though they aren't closely related to the Laurel tree (genus *Laurus*) with which

---

* Some texts consider *microphylla* a subspecies of *K. polifolia*.

the ancient Greeks wreathed their champions. Pioneers all across North America often called rhododendrons "mountain laurel"— at Laurel Hill, for example, on the Barlow Trail over Mt. Hood.

Crowberry

Empetrum nigrum (em-**pee**-trum: on rock; **nye**-grum: black). Flowers tiny, brownish purple, in leaf axils, ± 3-merous (maximum of 3 stamens, 3 petals, 3 sepals, 3 bracts), stamens twice as long as other parts, or sometimes stamens or pistil lacking; berries blueblack, ⅛–¼", juicy, 6–9-seeded; leaves needlelike, crowded, ¼–½", with rolled edges; mat-forming prostrate shrubs, erect stems to 6". Rocky slopes, mostly 5,750–7,400'. Ericaceae (Heath family). Color p 122.

Crowberry grows in coastal bogs up north, and sometimes in Oregon and Washington, but bypasses intermediate elevations in our mountains. The berries stay fairly sweet and juicy all winter on the plant under the snow blanket, making them a crucial resource for ptarmigan, grouse, bears, and Alaskan Inuit. For my taste, they are minute, scarce, and insipid.

Squawcarpet

Ceanothus prostratus (see-an-**oath**-us: thistle, a misleading name). Also **mahala-mat**. Flowers whitish to blue, tiny, 5-merous, in round-topped clusters from leaf axils; capsules of three 1-seeded cells; leaves opposite or in pairs of opposite whorls, spiny-edged (hollylike), ½–1½"; mat-forming prostrate shrubs, freely rooting from branch nodes. E-side Cas from Mt. Adams S, uncommon in our range. Rhamnaceae (Buckthorn family). Color p 121.

Squawcarpet, an attractive ground cover in cultivation, has leaves very different from our other *Ceanothus* species (page 102).

Twinflower

Linnaea borealis (lin-**ee**-a: after Linnaeus, below; bor-ee-**ay**-lis: northern). Flowers pink to white, two per stalk, conical, pendent, ½" long, 5-lobed, stamens 4; capsules 1-seeded; leaves opposite, very shiny, dark, ¼–1"; spicy- or anise-fragrant esp in warm sun; flowering stalks 3–5", reddish, with 2–6 leaves on lower half only; from long leafy runners. Dense mature forest; abundant on W-side. Caprifoliaceae (Honeysuckle family). Color p 122.

Linnaeus, who chose the scientific names for thousands of plants, didn't name any for himself, but he is said to have asked a colleague to name this one after him. If so, the choice was devious in seeming humble: though tiny and simple, the twinflower grows throughout the cooler third of the Northern hemisphere, and is universally admired.

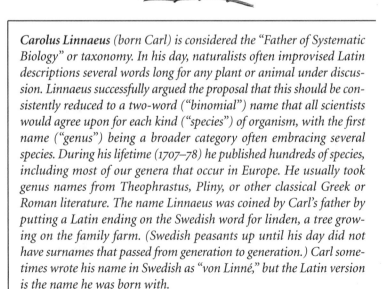

Carolus Linnaeus (born Carl) is considered the "Father of Systematic Biology" or taxonomy. In his day, naturalists often improvised Latin descriptions several words long for any plant or animal under discussion. Linnaeus successfully argued the proposal that this should be consistently reduced to a two-word ("binomial") name that all scientists would agree upon for each kind ("species") of organism, with the first name ("genus") being a broader category often embracing several species. During his lifetime (1707–78) he published hundreds of species, including most of our genera that occur in Europe. He usually took genus names from Theophrastus, Pliny, or other classical Greek or Roman literature. The name Linnaeus was coined by Carl's father by putting a Latin ending on the Swedish word for linden, a tree growing on the family farm. (Swedish peasants up until his day did not have surnames that passed from generation to generation.) Carl sometimes wrote his name in Swedish as "von Linné," but the Latin version is the name he was born with.

Douglas-fir, p 16.

Engelmann spruce, p 36.

Western larch, p52.

Western yew, p 40.

Ponderosa pine, p 43.

Lodgepole pine, p 46.

Western white pine, p 51.

Western red-cedar, p 55.

Alaska-cedar, p 57.

Incense-cedar, p 60.

Conifers

Mountain-ash, p 80.

Red elderberry, p 76.

Nootka rose, p 86.

Serviceberry, p 79.

Red-osier dogwood, p 74.

Indian-plum, p 79.

Bitter cherry, p 78.   Salmonberry, p 81.

Shrubby cinquefoil, 86.   Thimbleberry, p 81.

Pacific ninebark, p 85.   Ocean-spray, p 80.

Subalpine spiraea, p 85.

Hardhack, p 85.

Bitterbrush, p 84.

Orange honeysuckle, p 88.

Poison-oak, p 92.

White rhododendron, p 96.

Cascades blueberry, p 95.

Devil's club, p 90.

Wax currant, p 87.

Fool's huckleberry, p 97. Red-flowering currant, p 87.

Shrubs: deciduous, under 6'   *119*

Pacific rhododendron, p 99.

Snowbrush, p 102.

Salal, p 100.

Green manzanita, p 105.

Oregon-grape, p 104.

Oregon-boxwood, p 105.

Shrubs: broadleaf evergreen, over 10"

White-veined pyrola, p 108.

Kinnickinnick, p 107.

Single delight, p 108.

Squawcarpet, p 113.

Oregon wintergreen, p 112.

Alpine laurel, p 112.

Yellow heather, p 111.

Twinflower, p 114.

White heather, p 110.

Pipsissewa, p 109.

Pink heather, p 110.

Crowberry, p 113.

Shrubs: broadleaf evergreen, under 10"

Cottongrass, p 151.

Showy sedge, p 151.

Purple hairgrass, p 154.

Woodrush, p 153.

Herbs: grasslike

Avalanche lily, p 164.

Beargrass, p 169.

Skunk-cabbage, p 160.

Herbs: showy monocots

May lily, p 161.

Trillium, p 163.

False-Solomon's-seal: *S.racemosa* and *S. stellata*, p 161.

Bead lily, p 163.

Fairy-bells, p 162.

Twisted-stalk, p 162.

Twisted-stalk, p 162.

Herbs: showy monocots (lilies)   *125*

Cascades lily, p 167.

Tiger lily, p 167.

Hooker's onion, p 166.

Chocolate lily, p 167.

Camas, p 168.

Death camas, p 169.

Tofieldia, p 162.

Herbs: showy monocots (lilies)

Oregon iris, p 172.

Purple-eyed-grass, p 172.

Glacier lily, p 164.

Cat's-ears, p 165.

Corn lily, p 171.

Twayblade, p 176.

Rattlesnake-plantain, p 173.

Round-leaved
bog orchid, p 174.

Lady's slipper, p 176.

Calypso orchid, p 176.

Phantom orchid, p 177.

Western coralroot,
p 177.

Striped coralroot, p 177.

Candystick, p 178.

Pinedrops, p 179.

Indian pipe, p 180.

Pinesap, p 180.

Golden fleabane, p 182. Aster, p 183. Arnica, p 183.

Goldenrod, p 184. Balsamroot, p 184. Woolly-sunflower, p 184.

Pearly
everlasting, p 185. Yarrow, p 184. Pussytoes, p 186.

Herbs: composite flowers

Coltsfoot, p 186.

Silvercrown, p 187.

Silverback, p 187.

Wormwood, p 188.

Thistle, p 185.

Saw-wort, p 187.

Pale agoseris, p 189.

Alpine dandelion, p 189.

Hawkweed, p 189.

False-bugbane, p 191.

Arctic willow, p 190.

Nettle, p 191.

Vanillaleaf, p 190.

Hedge-nettle, p 196.

Blue-eyed Mary, p 194.

Self-heal, p 197.

Broadleaf lupine, p 198, and Mtn. daisy, p 182.

Monkshood, p 201.

Bleedingheart, p 196.

Corydalis, p 195.

Creeping penstemon, p 195.

Elephant's head, p 193.

Sickletop...

Birdbeak, and

Coiled-beak louseworts, p 193.

Menzies' larkspur, p 201.

Yellow monkeyflower, p 192.

Crazyweed, p 200.

Dwarf lupine, p 202.

Purple monkeyflower, p 192.

Sweetpea, p 199.

Foxglove, p 194.

Pussypaws, p 196.

Flett's violet, p 200.

Herbs: dicots, irregular flowers

Indian paintbrush, p 194.

Mountain-sorrel, p 196.

Youth-on-age, p 197.

Herbs: dicots, irregular flowers

Silky phacelia, p 206.

Sky pilot, p 204.

Silverleaf phacelia, p 206. Douglasia, p 204.

Alpine collomia, p 202.

Spreading phlox, p 203.

Herbs: five petals

Bluebells, p 207.

Bellflower, p 207.

Waterleaf, p 206.

Shooting star, p 205.

Skyrocket, p 203.

Buttercup, p 218, and Towhead baby, p 231.

Dogbane, p 206.

White catchfly, p 213.   Moss-campion, p 213.

Buckbean, p 207.   Wild strawberry, p 217.

Anemone, p 223.   Strawberry bramble, p 217.

Brook saxifrage, p 210.   Fringecup, p 209.   Tiarella, p 209.

Alpine saxifrage, p 210.   Partridgefoot, p 216.

Grass-of-Parnassus, p 208.   Field chickweed, p 213.

Roseroot, p 211.

Columbine, p 219.

Purple avens, p 216.

Lanceleaf stonecrop, p 211.

St.-John's-wort, p 215.

Wood-sorrel, p 212.

Yerba de selva, p 213.

Herbs: five petals   141

Goatsbeard, p 216.

American bistort, p 222.

Martindale's desert-parsley, p 224.

Miner's-lettuce, p 220.

Chocolate-tips, p 224.

Valerian, p 221.

Springbeauty, p 219.

Herbs: five petals

Alpine willow-herb, p 226.

Dwarf fireweed, p 226.

Yellow willow-herb, p 226.

Kittentails, p 227.

Veronica, p 230.

Toothwort, p 228.

Bunchberry, p 228.

Herbs: four petals

Smelowskia, p 229.

Meadow-rue, p 229.

Dirty socks, p 230.

Farewell-to-spring, p 227.

Wallflower, p 228.

Starflower, p 233.

Wild-ginger, p 231.

Herbs: dicots, four, three, or six petals

Yellow pond-lily, p 233.

Oval-leaf buckwheat, p 230.

Inside-out flower,
p 231.

Towhead baby seed heads, p 231. Flowers
shown on p 138c.

Columbia and…

Tweedy's lewisia, p 234.

Herbs: dicots, six or several petals

Baneberry, p 232.

Mountain bog gentian, p 233.

Marshmarigold, p 231.

Bitterroot, p 234.

Herbs: dicots, several petals

4

Flowering Herbs

Defined simply as seed plants without woody stems, the flowering herbs include most plants thought of as "wildflowers," as well as grasses and similar plants. Some wildflowers, even small ones, are shrubs. Since distinguishing between herbs and shrubs can be tricky, most borderline cases, or "subshrubs," have been placed in Chapter 3 if they are evergreen, and otherwise here in Chapter 4.

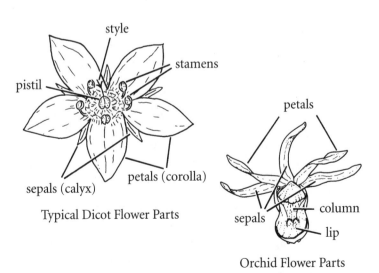

Typical Dicot Flower Parts

Orchid Flower Parts

Grasses, sedges and rushes are the three huge families of grasslike plants. Grasses proper are outnumbered by sedges above timberline here. To identify the family, roll a stem between thumb and forefinger; the rules of thumb:

sedge stems are triangular in cross-section, with V-shaped leaves in 3 ranks along the 3 edges ("Sedges have edges.")

grass stems are round and hollow, with a swollen node at the base of each leaf; and

rush stems are round and pith-filled; their leaves too are often tubular, especially near the tip; the pistils and seedpods are 3-celled.

The reminder that "sedges have edges" is clearly true throughout the genus *Carex*, which includes almost all or our sedges, but some sedges such as cottongrass (p 151) have somewhat rounded stems, often triangular only near the top.

When a *Carex* sedge blooms, straw-colored stamens adorn the sides of the (usually darker) flowering spikes, in conspicuous disarray. The units within the spike that bear stamens are male flowers, while female flowers each bear two or three barely visible threadlike stigmas. The distribution of male and female flowers on the plant is useful for identification. For an oversized illustration, picture corn, a grass: the male spikes (tassels) are all clustered terminally, while numerous stigmas (silks) show that the lateral spikes (ears) are all female. Those are unisexual spikes; bisexual spikes, in a clever twist of jargon, are either *androgyn*ous or *gynecandro*us, depending on whether males or females are on top.

Positive identification of grasslike plants requires a whole new vocabulary of grass parts (page 157 footnote), and a microscope. This book includes only a representative handful of species, out of hundreds growing here, and describes them minimally. If both habitat and description fit what you're looking at, then you have an educated guess of what it is.

Beargrass, p 169, is a lily you might mistake for a sedge when its flowers are absent, as they usually are; its leaves are V-shaped in section, dry, pale, abrasive, and robust, in abundant thick clumps. Blue-eyed-grass, p 172 , is a slender iris that blooms early and briefly, and then goes unnoticeable in grassy Eastslope meadows.

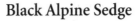

Black Alpine Sedge

Carex nigricans (**cair**-ex: the Roman term; **nye**-grik-enz: blackish). Flower-spike single, quite dark, male flowers above females; three stigmas per female flower; leaves 4–9 per stalk, ± curling; plants 2–4", turf-forming. In small hollows, alp/subalpine. Cyperaceae (Sedge family).

Dense, turfy concave beds of black alpine sedge underlie the latest-melting patches of snow around timberline. Once they dry out in late summer, they offer the perfect spot for basking, tumbling, or sleeping. What's good for you is in this instance tolerated by the flora, too, as these sedges are relatively resilient. Not even sedge turf is immune to trampling damage, though; no subalpine community should be camped on more than two nights in the same year. Camp on sedge beds only when away from trails, and pick beds unmarked by previous campers.

To suit its extremely short growing season, black alpine sedge is the speed demon among grasslike plants, setting seed as soon as 13 days after its release from snow. (Nearby subalpine plants typically take 42–56 days.) Even that is rarely quick enough, so it spreads mainly by rhizomes, producing a turfy, rather than clumpy, growth habit. The only even later-lying snowbed communities (ones that survive some dormant years when they don't melt out at all) are largely mosses and lichens; next to a black sedge bed you often see a strip of haircap moss, indicating the direction of snowbank melting.

Dunhead Sedge

Carex phaeocephala (fee-o-**sef**-a-la: dun head). Flower-spikes pale, few, small, closely clustered; spikes with female flowers above males, or sometimes all female; two stigmas per female flower; plants 2–12". Abundant in alpine tundra and rock fields. Cyperaceae (Sedge family).

Though "dun," "dusky" and *phaeo* usually mean medium-dark gray-brown in taxonomic usage, these straw-colored flowers suggest instead a dun horse—pale, washed-out.

Mertens' Sedge

Carex mertensii (mer-**ten**-zee-eye: after Karl H. Mertens, p 111). Flower spikes dense, cylindrical, ¾–1½", several; male florets (darker) take up the lower half of the terminal spike, and at most the lowest few scales of the other spikes; females have 3 stigmas; stem edges sharp and rough; leaves flat, bigger ones all at least a few inches up the stem. plants 16–40". Forest openings, low elevs to near timberline. Cyperaceae (Sedge family).

Though not abundant, Mertens' sedge is visually striking, its stems arcing gracefully under the weight of its nodding spikelets.

Elk Sedge

Carex geyeri (**guy**-er-eye: after K. A. Geyer, below). Spike single, androgynous; female flowers exceptionally few (1–3), large (¼" + 3¼" stigmas), and set off from the close-packed males; leaves about as tall as the stems; plants 6–20", in clumps. Open E-side forests. Cyperaceae (Sedge family.)

Elk sedge stands out among sedges for its form of inflorescence, its dry forest habitat, and its high forage value —equal to the better native grasses. Eastslope deer and elk rely on it briefly around snowmelt time. It grows with needlegrass and snowberry, under pine and Douglas-fir.

Karl Andreas Geyer, a German botanist, came to the Rocky Mountains with Sir William Drummond Stewart's 1843 expedition for science and pleasure. The party camped on Persian carpets under crimson canopies. Three of its botanists, perhaps succumbing to an unscientific surfeit of pleasure, collected little of note, but Geyer went on alone and made many new collections, and sailed home from Fort Vancouver.

Water Sedge

Carex aquatilis (a-qua-til-iss: of water). Spikes up to 2", terminal one male or androgynous, lateral ones female, erect; plants 16–40", rhizomatous. In water or wet soil. Cyperaceae (Sedge family).

The commonest sedge of Cascades marshes, water sedge is important waterfowl forage. You may think "marsh plant" when you hear "sedge," and many sedges are; but they grow in all but the driest moisture regimes. It seems, though, that all their environments are in some way stressful; i.e., competition from grasses is discouraged.

Showy Sedge

Carex spectabilis (spec-**tab**-il-iss: showy). Flower-spikes ½–1¼", several, the terminal one male or androgynous, lateral ones female with three stigmas; plants 8–32". Alp/subalpine meadows. Cyperaceae (Sedge family). Color p 123.

Our abundant subalpine tall sedge typifies an environmentally moderate meadow, with fairly early snowmelt and deep soil.

Cottongrass

Eriophorum polystachion * (airy-**ah**-fur-um: wool bearing; polly-**stay**-key-on: many spikes). Also **Alaska-cotton**. Spikelets 2–5, becoming white, cottony tufts ¾–1¾" long (in seed); leaves triangular near tips; stems ± round to triangular, 8–36". High bogs. Cyperaceae (Sedge family). Color p 123.

The sight of mile after mile of cottongrass blowing in a breeze, up in Alaska, is hard to forget. Here, it is a little-known plant, though not uncommon in subalpine bogs.

---

* Many authorities include these plants in a larger *E. angustifulium.*

Herbs: grasslike, with triangular stems   151

Rushes

Juncus spp. (**junk**-us: the Roman term). Flowers of 6 dry tepals + 2 outer bracts; leaf blades tubular, resembling the stems; stems dark green, tubular, pith-filled, in dense clumps. These 3 species alp/subalpine. Juncaceae (Rush family).

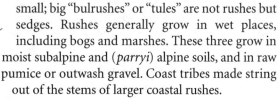

J. drummondii (dra-**mon**-dee-eye: after Thomas Drummond, p 473). Tepals ¼"; flowers green, 1–4, in an apparently lateral cluster; stems 6–14", apparently leafless because the uppermost leaf, borne just below the inflorescence, looks like a continuation of the stem, and the lower leaves are reduced to sheaths. Illustrated at right.

J. parryi (**pair**-ee-eye: after Charles Parry). As above, exc with one leaf blade ¾–3" long from the uppermost basal sheath.

J. mertensianus (mer-ten-zee-**ay**-nus: after K. H. Mertens, p 111). Flowers dark brown, tiny (⅛" long), many, in a compact rounded terminal cluster; leaves 1–4, the uppermost one angled off just below the inflorescence; stems 4–12". Illustrated below.

Rushes are tough, reedy, deep green, round-stemmed, round-leaved plants with chaffy tufts, often nearly black, for flowers. Ours are small; big "bulrushes" or "tules" are not rushes but sedges. Rushes generally grow in wet places, including bogs and marshes. These three grow in moist subalpine and (*parryi*) alpine soils, and in raw pumice or outwash gravel. Coast tribes made string out of the stems of larger coastal rushes.

Woodrushes

Luzula piperi (**luz**-you-la: light—; **pie**-per-eye: after Charles Piper), and
L. parviflora (par-vif-**lor**-a: small-flowered). Flowers tiny, dry, green to brown, with 6 tepals and 2 sepallike bracts, in a very loose, often arching inflorescence; leaves grasslike, wide, flat, finely hair-fringed, from sheathing bases without swollen nodes; plants 6–20". Abundant alp/subalpine; also scattered in montane forest. Juncaceae (Rush family). Color p 123.

Like the glacier lily, the subalpine woodrush may melt its own hole to bloom through a few inches of dwindling snowpack. Its ancient name, *gramen luzulae* or "grass of light," observed the grace of an otherwise inconspicuous plant when bearing dewdrops in the morning light. More shade-tolerant than most grasslike plants, the woodrush can indeed grow in the woods, particularly near timberline, but it's more abundant in open meadows and on moraine gravels.

The Rush family is represented in our region by two genera, rushes and woodrushes. The tight inflorescences of the three rushes above contrast with the open, delicate, spraylike ones of these two woodrush species, yet each genus includes other species with those characteristics reversed. (For example, the spiked woodrush, *L. spicata*, illustrated at right, is an alpine plant 2–16" tall with a single, usually nodding, bristly flower spike ½–1¼" long.) A stronger across-the-board distinction is that a woodrush has a three-celled seed capsule with one seed in each cell, while a *Juncus* rush has a three-celled, many-seeded capsule. Grasses and sedges have one-celled, one-seeded fruits.

Herbs: grasslike, with round, pith-filled stems

Grasses

Family Poaceae.*
Grasses Primarily of the High Country

Idaho fescue, *Festuca idahoensis* (fest-**you**-ca: the Roman term; Idaho-**en**-sis: of Idaho). Spikelets of 3–7 florets forming a 4–7" spikelike panicle, with short (⅛") awns; leaves narrow, wiry, dark green; plants 16–32". Subalpine meadows; abundant in Olys.

Green fescue, *F. viridula* (vee-**rid**-you-la: green). Plants like Idaho fescue, but without awns. Subalpine and E-side in Cas.

Alpine fescue, *F. brachyphylla* † (breaky-**fill**-a: short leaf). Spikelets of 3–4 florets forming a 1–3" spikelike panicle; awns less than ⅛"; plants 2–8". Alpine. Illustrated bottom right.

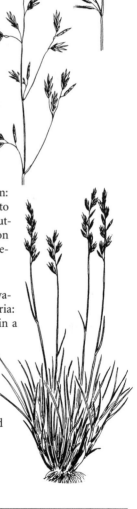

Downy oatgrass, *Trisetum spicatum* (try-**see**-tum: 3-awned; spic-**ay**-tum: spiked). Spikelets of one to three florets forming a 1–3" spike; awns ¼", bent outward; plants 4–16", ± fuzzy all over. Common on alpine ridges, sporadic elsewhere; globally widespread. Not illustrated.

Purple hairgrass, *Vahlodea atropurpurea* ‡ (va-**load**-ia: after Martin H. Vahl; at-ro-pur-**pew**-ria: black purple). Purplish spikelets of 2–3 florets in a wide, sparse panicle 2–4" tall; awns less than ⅛", bent inward, hidden within floret; leaves flat; plants 6–24". Abundant, subalpine. Color p 123. (Not illustrated this page.)

---

*The grass family was previously known for centuries as Gramineae—simply the Latin word for grasses. See footnote, p 181.

†Formerly known as *Festuca ovina* var. *brevifolia*.

‡ Formerly *Deschampsia atropurpurea*.

Grasses Primarily of the East-Side

Bluebunch wheatgrass, *Pseudoroegneria spicata**
(soo-doe-reg-**nair**-ia: after another genus; spic-**ay**-ta: spiked). Large (6–8 floret) spikelets spaced out along the stem to form a 3–6" intermittent spike; awnless and (¼–¾") long-awned types (both illustrated at right) may occur together; plants 24–40", in clumps. Pine/steppe timberline; originally the principal grass of E OR and WA, now largely displaced by weedy grasses.

Tufted hairgrass, *Deschampsia cespitosa* (desh-**amp**-sia: after J. L. A. Loiseleur-Deslongchamps; see-spit-**oh**-sa: growing in bunches). Spikelets of 2–3 florets in a wide, sparse panicle 4–10" tall; awns barely protruding from floret; leaves creased; plants 8–48". High open forests and meadows E of Cas Cr.

Western needlegrass, *Achnatherum occidentale*‡
(ac-**nath**-er-um: awned scale; ox-i-den-**tay**-lee: western). 1-floret spikelets held tightly erect against the main stem, in a 2–12" spike; awns ¾–1½" long, twice-bent, spreading at various angles; leaves often inrolled; plants 8–40". All elevs. Illustrated at right.

Pinegrass, *Calamagrostis rubescens* (cal-a-ma-**grah**-stiss: reed grass; roo-**bes**-enz: reddish). Flowering stems few or absent, the plant spreading mainly by rhizomes; 3–6" spikelike panicle of 1-floret spikelets; awns bent, barely protruding; leaves narrow, flat to inrolled (not creased), rough to touch; plants 16–40". All elevs E of Cas Cr; the dominant herb in many pine forests, often with elk sedge. Illustrated at left.

---

*Formerly included in the large and unruly genus *Agropyron*, as *A. spicatum*.

‡Formerly *Stipa occidentalis*.

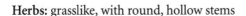

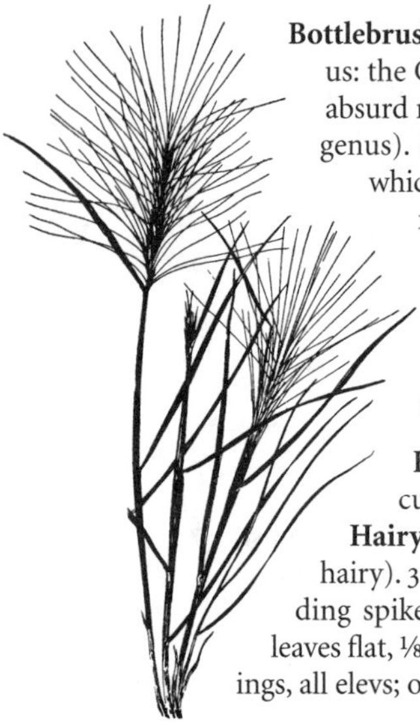

Bottlebrush squirreltail, *Elymus elymoides*[*] (el-im-us: the Greek term; el-im-**oy**-deez: like *Elymus*, an absurd name now that this species is placed in that genus). Spikelets of 2–6 florets in a 1½–6" spike which looks strikingly brushlike thanks to the many awns, ¾–4" long; plants 4–20". Pine forest with bitterbrush; also on alpine pumice. Color p 123.

Grasses Primarily of the Lowlands

Blue wildrye, *Elymus glaucus* (glaw-cus: bluish pale) illustrated at right, and **Hairy wildrye**, *E. hirsutus* (her-**sue**-tus: hairy). 3–5-floret spikelets in a 2–8", often nodding spike; awns vary from 1" long to absent; leaves flat, ⅛–½" wide; plants 16–48". W-side clearings, all elevs; often in gravelly soils, incl river bars.

Redtop, *Agrostis stolonifera*[†] (ag-**ros**-tiss: Roman term for some grass, also meaning "field"; sto-lon-**if**-er-a: with runners). Also **creeping bentgrass**. Purplish, awnless, 1-floret spikelets in a delicate, loose 2–10" panicle; plants 8–40". Lowlands, e.g., W-side Oly valleys. Introduced variety, much planted in lawns and pastures. Illustrated at bottom right.

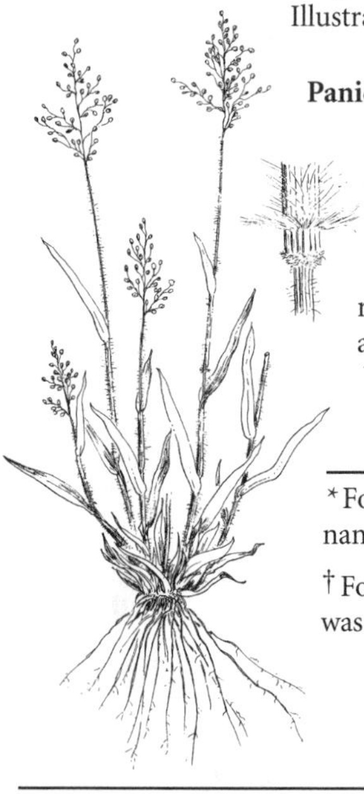

Panic grass, *Panicum acuminatum*[‡] (**pan**-ic-um: millet; ac-you-min-**ay**-tum: sharp-tipped). Seeds and florets round, like grains of millet (a relative); ½–1" tall, very sparse, wide panicle of 1–2-floret spikelets; no awns; stem usually hairy; plants 6–16". Gravel bars. Illustrated at left.

---

[*] Formerly *Sitanion hystrix*, a beautiful name I am loath to part with.

[†] Formerly *A. alba alba*, a name that was found to be incorrect.

[‡] Our populations were formerly included in *P. occidentale*.

Grasses are classically personified as humble, but in fact they're taking over the world. Going by their rate and breadth of genetic diversification in geologically recent time, you would have to call them the most successful plant family. The ascendency of grasses is reflected in, and has been magnified by, the development of agriculture, which has always focused on grains (grass seeds) and on grazing (grass-eating) mammals. Of course, wild animals also co-evolved with grasses, and make plenty of use of them, but it's we humans and our livestock that have really gone to town with them, literally and figuratively.

Few grasses like shade, so the Cascades and Olympics are not the best region for grasses. Our meadow communities are maintained typically by extreme snowiness, wetness, or infertility —and the first two conditions favor sedges and rushes more than grasses. New clearings here are mostly made by fire, and quickly reoccupied by stump-sprouting shrubs and plants with windborne or fireproof seeds. (Grasslands also excel at regenerating after fires, but the grasses have to be there before the fire to spring up after it.) This is not to say there are no grasses here, just fewer than elsewhere. Our chief grass habitats are:

open forests and steppe margins on the lower East-slope;

dry meadow types at timberline and above; and

gravel bars and river terraces at early stages of plant succession.

Periodic soil drought seems to be a factor in each.

Identification of grasses requires a special vocabulary. Keeping it to a minimum, grasses are flowering plants with simplified, undecorated, single-seeded dry flowers ("florets") each with three stamens and a usually two-styled pistil. (These sexual parts are short-lived and easily overlooked.) The florets are flanked by any number of scales or bracts.* Since the bracts are arranged alternately, in two ranks, rather than whorled, they are not sepals or tepals like the six whorled, scalelike tepals of a rush flower. In many species, certain

---

* For those interested, the bracts are a "palea" enveloping or subtending each floret; a "lemma" across from the palea and partially enfolding its base; and a pair of "glumes" at the base of each spikelet. Thus a typical single-flowered spikelet has four bracts. Additional bracts are considered to be sterile florets each consisting of one empty lemma. Most awns are on lemmas. The main stem is a "rachis"; each spikelet's stem is a "rachilla."

---

bracts bear stiff hairs ("awns") a conspicuous feature for identification. One or more florets and their bracts along a single axis make a "spikelet." Several spikelets attach to the main stalk either directly, making a "spike," or by small stalks (often branched) making a "panicle." The thirteen species descriptions above are intended to suggest educated guesses on the identity of the grasses you will see most often.

Though some grasses are annuals, the above thirteen are perennial, and several are major forage plants. Tufted hairgrass is so sought out by sheep and cattle that its presence indicates a meadow in virgin condition; once grazed out from a meadow, it returns slowly, if ever. All of the thirteen species are native except perhaps redtop, which is so thoroughly naturalized that no one is quite sure whether it was always here.

Cattails

Typha latifolia (**tie**-fa: the Greek term; lat-if-**oh**-lia: broad leaf). Flowers minute, chaffy, in a dense round smooth spike of two distinct portions, the upper (male) thicker when in flower but withering as the lower (female) thickens and turns dark brown in fruit; stalks 3–10'; leaves half as tall by ¼–¾", smooth; from rhizomes in shallow water. Typhaceae (Cattail family).

Big lowland cattail marshes are avidly sought out by migrating waterfowl and by hunters thereof. Few such marshes lie among our mountains, though; the Quinault used to travel all the way to Gray's Harbor to pick cattails. Like all Northwest tribes, they wove the stalks (never the leaves) into thick, spongy mats for mattresses, kneeling pads in canoes, packsacks, baskets, rain capes, and temporary roofs in summer. Oddly, only a few of the tribes ate cattails, though the rhizomes and inner, basal stalk portions are pretty good baked, raw, or ground as flour.

Herbs: showy monocots

Monocots and dicots are named after and defined by their respectively single or paired seed leaves, or "cotyledons" (the first green part[s] to sprout from a newly germinated seed). Since those are ephemeral, monocots are often known by two less reliable traits:

parallel-veined leaves; and

3-merous flowers (generally 3 petals and 3 sepals, though these are

---

sometimes nearly identical, in which case we call them 6 "tepals" in an inner and an outer whorl.)

The monocots on the following pages are distinguished from the grasslike monocots by (most of them) broader leaves and (all of them) moist, generally delicate flower parts evolved for visual attractiveness — in a word, showy. Most fall into the Lily, Iris, and Orchid families according to whether they have 6, 3, or 2 stamens. Three plants that don't fit those stamen numbers come first.

Very few dicots have reliably 3-merous flowers. Only three such genera are in this book, and they are easily segregated since they don't have parallel leaf veins: Inside-out flower, p 231; wild-ginger, p 231; and wild-buckwheats, p 230.

Herbs: showy monocots with 4 tepals, 4 stamens

Wapato

Sagittaria spp. (sadge-it-**air**-ia: arrow-like). Also **arrowhead**. Three petals white, spreading, nearly round, ⅜–¾"; three sepals green, pointed; many stamens; pistils on separate, ball-shaped female flowers, less showy and usually borne lower on the stem; flowers (both sexes) in whorls of three; leaf blades narrowly 3-pointed or arrow-shaped, on long leafstalks all from the base, which is usually submerged in water. Alismataceae (Water-plantain family).

S. latifolia (lat-if-**oh**-lia: wide leaf). Leaf blades 4–12" long, almost as broad. W of Cas.

S. cuneata (cue-nee-**ay**-ta: wedge-shaped). Leaf blades 1–5" long × 1–3" broad. E of Cas.

In fall the slender rhizomes produce potatolike tubers about the size and shape of hens' eggs, with a flavor a little like roasted chestnuts. Traditionally retrieved from the mud with the toes, by humans, or with the bill, by ducks, wapato roots were widely traded among the tribes of the lower Columbia, and gratefully accepted by Lewis, Clark, & Co.

Skunk-Cabbage

Lysichiton americanus (lye-zih-**kite**-on: loose tunic). Flowers greenish yellow, 4-lobed, 4-stamened, ⅛" diam, many, in a dense spike 2½–5", partly enclosed or hooded by a yellow, parallel-veined "spathe"; leaves all basal, ± net-veined, oval, eventually up to 3' × 1' or even bigger; from an enlarged fleshy vertical root, in wet ground. Araceae (Calla-lily family). Color p 124.

Many plants evolved sweet fragrances that attract sugar-loving pollinators, like bees. Others, such as the Eastern and European species of *Symplocarpus* (also called Skunk-cabbage) evolved putrid smells that attract pollinators, like some flies and beetles, that feed on, shall we say, decaying organic matter. Our skunk-cabbage lies in between, attracting bees as well as beetles, distinctly skunky to the human nose but not foul, merely rank, like long-faded skunk aroma. It releases different odors at different temperatures, each odor matched to the kind of pollinators most likely to be out and about at that temperature.

The Calla-lily family has a characteristic inflorescence called a spadix (the fleshy spike of crowded flowers) and spathe (the large bract enfolding it). These organs have an evocative, voluptuous look; Whitman named a book of suggestive poetry after a similar species, *Calamus.*

In the case of our skunk-cabbage, spathe and spadix thrust up from wet ground in early spring. Leaves come later, and keep growing all summer to reach sizes unmatched north of the banana groves; they were universally used as "Indian wax paper" to wrap camas bulbs, salal berries, and other foods for steam pit baking or for storage. The leaf bases and the roots are themselves edible after prolonged cooking or storage breaks down the intensely irritating, "hot" oxalate crystals. Some tribes ate them during the perennial hard times of late winter. Tales told that in the bad old days before Salmon came, the people had nothing to eat but skunk-cabbage roots. Anthropologists theorize, however, that food was actually easier to get in the "bad old days:" that the culture-transforming shift into a salmon-storing economy was a response to human population reaching the point of being food-limited.

Elk and bears eat them, with no complaints recorded. Food or not, skunk-cabbage was regarded as strong medicine —for example, to induce labor, either timely or abortive. Later, some white man patented and sold it under the name "Skookum."

May Lily

Maianthemum dilatatum (my-anth-ee-mum: May flower; dil-a-**tay**-tum: widened). Also **false-lily-of-the-valley.** Flowers white, ¼" diam, with 4 stamens and 4 spreading tepals in a single whorl; berries ¼", ripening red, in a 1–3" raceme; 2 (occasionally 1 or 3) leaves, 2–4", heart-shaped but distinctly parallel-veined, ± shiny dark green; plants 4–14", slender, rhizomatous. W-side forest up to 3,500', often on nurse logs. Liliaceae (Lily family). Color p 125.

The insipid berries were eaten unenthusiastically by most tribes, but in the woods you rarely see a full stalk of them even half-ripe, which shows that small mammals cherish them.

Herbs: showy monocots with 6 stamens (lilies)

False-Solomon's-Seal

Maianthemum spp.[*] Flowers white, fragrant, many, in one terminal inflorescence; berries ¼", round; leaves heavily veined, pointed, oval to narrowly elliptical, 2–7"; stems arching, unbranched, often zigzagging at leaf nodes; from horizontal rhizomes. Widespread. Liliaceae. Color p 125.

M. stellatum (stel-**ay**-tum: starry). Tepals ¼", flat-spreading; flowers 6–18; berries longitudinally striped, ripening dark red to blackish; stems 8–24".

M. racemosum (ras-em-**oh**-sum: bearing flowers in racemes, a misleading name for this plant). Tepals minute, stamens longer (⅛"); flowers in a ± conical fluffy panicle; berries speckled at first, ripening red; stems 1–3'.

False clues galore: Solomon's seal (genus *Polygonatum*) bears too little resemblance to this genus to justify "false." *Racemosa* isn't racemose, it's paniculate; but S*tellata* is racemose. I find false-Solomon's-seal berries sometimes delicious (and not purgative, as some authors report) but often insipid. Both species are locally abundant in deep W-side woods, but also look happy in clearings or even dry open slopes. Form varies with environment. In the silver fir zone, *stellata* spreads its leaves flat from a bent-over stem; on the sunny Eastside, it holds its stem upright, grows narrower leaves, angles them upward, and folds them sharply at the midvein.

---

[*] These former *Smilacina* species were found to belong in the May-lily genus.

Twisted-Stalk

Streptopus spp. (**strep**-ta-pus: twisted foot). Flowers bell-shaped, one (sometimes two) beneath each leaf axil; berries red, ¼–½", juicy, sweetish but insipid; leaves 2–5", tapered, elliptical. Liliaceae.

S. lanceolata* (lan-see-o-**lay**-ta: narrowleaved). Tepals ⅜", variably streaked rose with white, slightly reflexed at the tip; style 3-branched; flower-bearing stalklets straight to curved; stems 6–14", rarely branched, arching. Higher (3,000'+) forests. Color p 125.

S. amplexifolius (am-plex-if-**oh**-lius: clasping leaf). Tepals ½", dull white, reflexed from near midlength; style unbranched; flower stalklets with a sharp kink (illustrated); stems 12–40", much branched.

Twisted-stalk discretely hides its flowers under its leaves —quite a trick, since the the crotch *above* each leaf bears the flower. Look closely to see the flower stalk where, fused to the stem, it runs up it to the next leaf base. (The first leaf can't have a flower under it.) The berries were called "snakeberries" by the Quileute, "frogberries" by the Kwakiutl, "owl-" or "witchberries" by the Haida—and inedible by all—but Makah women chewed the roots to induce labor.

Fairy-Bells

Prosartes spp.* (pro-**sar**-teez: for use in crafts ?). Flowers bell-shaped, pendent in pairs (or occasionally 1–4) from branchtips, white; berries red, egg-shaped, ¼–½", ± edible—juicy, sweetish but insipid; leaves 2–5", long-tapered oval, wavy-edged; stems 14–40", much branched. Liliaceae.

P. hookeri (**hook**-er-eye: after Sir Joseph Hooker, p 166). Tepals ¼–½", flaring; stamens exposed. Widespread in forests. Color p 125.

P. smithii (**smith**-ee-eye: after Sir James E. Smith). Tepals ½–1", nearly straight, hiding the stamens. W-side.

Tofieldia

Tofieldia glutinosa (toe-**field**-ia: after Thomas Tofield; gluten-**oh**-sa: sticky). Also **false-asphodel**. Tepals white, ⅛–¼", persistent while the 3-styled pistil grows out past them into a fat, reddish, 3-celled capsule; flowers/fruit in a dense cluster atop an 8–20", sticky, hairy stem; 1–3 grasslike basal leaves 2–6", and sometimes 1–2 smaller stem leaves. Boggy meadows, esp subalpine. Liliaceae. Color p 126.

---

* A genus split took both of these species out of genus *Disporum*.

Trillium

Trillium ovatum (**tril**-ium: triple; oh-**vay**-tum: oval). Also **wake-robin**. Petals 1–3", white, aging through pink to maroon; sepals shorter, narrower, green; flowers single, on a 1–3" stem from the whorl of 3 leaves, 3–7", often equally broad, net-veined exc for the 5 or so ± parallel main veins; plants 6–16", rhizomatous. (Rarely with 4 or 5 leaves and/or petals and sepals, instead of 3 each.) Low forest. Liliaceae or Trilliaceae.* Color p 125.

What a pleasure, seeing the year's first trilliums in March or April, just when the winter rains feel like Forever! Quinault elders used to warn youngsters that picking trillium would bring rain —a safe bet in Quinault country at that time of year. Whites spun the less reliable tale that picking the flower will kill the plant. It merely discourages it; still, waiting to pick the seeds is a better choice. Then, with a little effort, you can have trilliums blooming year after year in a shady spot near your house. Trillium seeds require two winter chillings before producing a shoot; either use your refrigerator for one of them, before planting, or be patient. The seeds come packed in a gummy oil which ants, the usual disseminators, find tasty.

For most flowers that shift color as they age, as Trilliums do, the advantage is in using the aging blooms to help make a grander display to attract pollinators from afar, and then directing them toward the whiter blooms with more viable pollen.

Bead Lily

Clintonia uniflora (clin-**toe**-nia: after DeWitt Clinton; you-nif-**lor**-a: one flower). Also **queen's-cup, bride's-bonnet**. Flowers single, white, ± face-up, broadly bell-shaped to nearly flat-spreading; tepals ¾–1"; berry intensely blue, ⅜" diam, many-seeded, inedible; two or three leaves 3–6" × 1–2", heavy, smooth, ± shiny, basal, sheathing the 2–4" stalk; from slender rhizomes. Deep forest, mainly 2,500–5,000'. Liliaceae. Color p 125.

The beady blue berry is more striking than the formal white blossom. Though they don't look much alike once you know them, you might confuse bead lily with avalanche lily. Bead lily, common in mid-elevation dense forest, holds its flowers erect to ascending, and rarely bends its petals sharply backward. It's leaves are often minutely fuzzy, and hardly ever wavy-edged.

---

* Plants in the Lily family are not all very closely related. Some taxonomists split it, creating Trillium, Onion, and/or Mariposa-lily families.

Glacier Lily and Avalanche Lily

Erythronium spp. (air-ith-**roe**-nium: red—, the flower color of some species). Tepals 1–1½", spreading to reflexed either in an arc or from the base; flowers ± nodding, single or sometimes 2–6 on a 6–12" stalk; capsule erect, 1" tall, 3-celled and -sided; 2 leaves 4–8", basal, wavy-edged; from a scallion-like bulb. Abundant around timberline, scattered at lower elevs. Liliaceae.

Glacier lily, *E. grandiflorum* (gran-dif-**lor**-um: large-flowered). Flowers yellow. Color p 127.

Avalanche lily, *E. montanum* (mon-**tay**-num: of mtns). Flowers white with a yellow center, sometimes drying pinkish. Color p 124.

The snowy names refer to two amazing abilities of these lilies—they can generate enough heat to melt their way up and bloom through the last few inches of snow; and they proliferate into overwhelming drifts of white, or yellow. Fluttering with illusory fragility in subalpine breezes, they seem ideal vehicles for those anthropomorphic virtues we love to foist on mountain wildflowers—innocence, bravery, simplicity, perseverance, patient suffering, etc. "They toil not, neither do they spin," and they don't taste half bad either. (Bulbs, leaves, and flowers are edible, in that order, but not a good idea except when far from trails.)

Glacier lilies are far more common north of Mt. Rainier and south of Mt. Hood; avalanche lilies prevail in between, and in the Olympics. In either case, lush subalpine meadows are preferred, though glacier lilies find their way down to near sea level. Below 2,500' occur two uncommon congeners called trout or fawn lilies. Pink fawn lily, *E. revolutum*, grows in Olympic and coastal lowlands. White fawn lily, *E. oregonum*, mainly of the Puget/Willamette lowlands, has white tepals that sometimes dry pinkish. Both have brownish-mottled leaves, a clear distinction from glacier and avalanche lilies.

Common names in this genus are many. One well-known English name for the entire genus is "dogtooth-violets"; several European species are in fact violet, but resemble violets in no other way. "Adder's-tongue," another old name, is used in this genus and in unrelated genera. New-world settlers, finding new species in America with no violet hues, but with mottled leaves, came up with "fawn lily" and "trout lily." But those sweet East Coast names didn't stick when settlers in the West met our unmottled montane species. Some texts call both colors "glacier lilies," while some others call them both "avalanche lilies." This book will shore up the plurality that calls our white ones "avalanche" and our yellow ones "glacier." But *E. grandiflorum*, the glacier lily, also has a white-flowered variety in Idaho and Southeast Washington.

Cat's-Ears

Calochortus spp. (cal-o-**cor**-tus: beautiful grass). Petals ⅝–1" long, almost as broad, usually with a fine purple arc at base; sepals pointed; flowers 1 to 5+; seed pods 3-winged, with persistent 3-branched styles; the only large leaf basal, flat, grasslike; from a small bulb. Liliaceae (or Calochortaceae, see page 163 footnote).

C. subalpinus. Flowers creamy yellow; sepals have a purple dot near base; petals have long hairs over most of inner face; flowers usually all stem from one point high on the stalk; seed pods nodding; leaf taller than 3–12" stem. Subalpine in OR and S WA Cas. Color p 127.

C. lyallii (lie-**ah**-lee-eye: after David Lyall, p 53). Flowers white or pink-tinged; petals have an outer fringe of hairs, and a fringe just above the purple crescent; sepals almost as big as petals, and may also have purple crescent; seed pods erect; main leaf not as tall as the 6–18" stem. Cascades lower E slope in WA. Illustrated at right.

C. tolmiei (**tole**-me-eye: after William Tolmie, p 197). Flowers cream to purplish; sepals unspotted; petals have long hairs all over inner face; seed pods nodding; stems often branch at several points; leaf taller than 3–12" stem. Uncommon; rocky open slopes, W Cascades in OR. Illustrated at left.

"Cat's-ears" is the most pictorial of many flattering names given to these sensuous blossoms, perhaps all the more admired for being prohibitively hard to cultivate. Most members of the genus require bone dry soil before the bulb can go into healthy winter retirement. Several are desert flowers, with lavender to white flowers; many reach just the east edge of our range. Called mariposa lilies (Spanish for "butterfly") the desert species bear little resemblance to feline anatomy, their petals fringed with only a few hairs at their edges or around the basal arc. The hairs at the base can be extremely long, as in *C. longebarbatus*, which ranges from Yakima County south.

Wild Onions

Allium spp. (al-ium: the Roman term). Flowers ¼–⅜" long, several, on stalklets all from one spot between pointed, onionskinlike segments of the spathe that encased the inflorescence in bud; stems often bunching; from small onions with the trademark aroma. Liliaceae (or Alliaceae, see p 163n).

Hooker's onion, *A. acuminatum* (a-cue-min-ay-tum: pointed). Tepals pointed, purple or pink to (occasionally) white, the outer whorl ± spreading, bell-shaped, inner whorl smaller, narrowly jar-shaped; leaves 2–5, withering before flowers open, much shorter than the 4–12" tubular stem. Rocky openings, lower E Cas slopes. Color p 126.

Nodding onion, *A. cernuum* (sir-new-um: nodding). Inflorescence nodding (but often erect in fruit); tepals pink or white, oval, much shorter than stamens, all ± alike but inner and outer whorls separate; leaves several; stem 8–20". Dryish openings, W of Cas.

Olympic onion, *A. crenulatum* (cren-you-lay-tum: scalloped). Tepals pinkish, narrow, pointed, all ± alike; leaves 2, longer than the stem but not much higher, being downcurved; stem 2-angled, 2–3". Alpine gravels, WA Cas and Olys and at Jefferson Park, OR.

An onion is easy to recognize—indeed, often hard to miss—because it smells like an onion. If it doesn't, don't try a taste test; it might be death camas.

*Sir William Jackson Hooker was a great British scientist of the nineteenth century. He developed Kew Gardens into a great institution filled with plants sent from all over the world during the Era of Plant Hunters. Earlier, while professor of botany in Glasgow, he had noticed the astonishing zeal of a teenaged gardener there, and taken this David Douglas as his protege on field trips; eventually he sent him out to explore North America. Hooker catalogued and named hundreds of new plants sent in by Menzies, Douglas, Drummond, Gairdner, Tolmie, and others. The plants included Hooker's onion and Smith's—not Hooker's—fairy-bells. (Tradition forbids a namer commemorating himself in a scientific name, though his name may turn up in the common name of the species.) Hooker's fairy-bells were named after his son **Sir Joseph Hooker**, a noted plant hunter and colleague of Darwin.*

Tiger Lily

Lilium columbianum (lil-ium: the Roman term; co-lum-be-**ay**-num: of the Columbia River). Tepals orange with small maroon spots, 1½–2½" long but so strongly recurved as to make a ± full circle; capsule fleshy, 1½–2"; flowers/fruit nodding, several, on long stalks; leaves 2–4", narrow, the ones near midstalk longest and in the largest whorls; stem 2–4'; from a large, many-cloved bulb. Clearings and thickets up to timberline. Liliaceae. Color p 126.

The rather bitter bulbs were eaten by most tribes.

Cascades Lily

Lilium washingtonianum (washing-tony-**ay**-num: allegedly after Martha Washington). Tepals white, often purple-tinged or -spotted, and aging pink, 2½–3½"; flowers fragrant, bell-shaped, several, slightly nodding on short stalks all near the top of the 2–5' stem; capsules fleshy, 1"; leaves 2–4", narrow elliptical, often wavy, many of the upper ones in distinct whorls; bulbs large, many-cloved. Clearings and thickets, OR High Cas. Liliaceae. Color p 126.

Our grandest lily grows only south of the Columbia, *washingtonianum* notwithstanding.

Chocolate Lily

Fritillaria affinis* (frit-il-**air**-ia: checkered; **aff**-in-iss: related). Also **rice-root lily, mission bells, fritillary**. Tepals ¾–1½", inward-curving, brownish purple mottled with yellowish green; flowers pendent, 1–2+; capsule ¾", 6-winged; leaves 2–5", narrow, both whorled and single; stem 8–30"; from a bulb of a few large garliclike cloves with many tiny ricelike bulblets. Moist clearings up to 5,000'. Liliaceae. Color p 126.

These elegant flowers sell themselves short, with camouflage coloring and a fetid smell. The bulbs with their rice-like bulblets were universally eaten in the old days; they're too rare and too bitter to justify digging up now. When the Haida were introduced to rice, they named it "fritillary-teeth."

Yellow Bell

Fritillaria pudica (**pew**-di-ca: modest). Flowers single (or rarely up to four), yellow, pendent, narrowly bell-shaped, ⅞" long; six tepals all alike; leaves ± grasslike, either two or several; stem succulent, 4–12". Grassy ponderosa pine woods. Liliaceae.

---

*Formerly *Fritillaria lanceolata*.

Camas

Camassia quamash (ca-**mass**-ia **qua**-mosh: two versions of the Chinook Dialect term from an originally French word). Tepals blue-violet, ¾–1½", narrow, the lowermost one usually noticeably apart from the other five; inflorescence roughly conical; capsule ½–1", splitting three ways; leaves narrow, basal/sheathing, shorter than the 8–24" stem; from a deepset bulb, ½–1" diam. Seasonally moist meadows, to 4,500'. Liliaceae. Color p 126.

Camas bulbs were the prized vegetable food of most tribes of Oregon and Washington. The Nez Perce War was touched off by white settlers plowing up camas prairies for pastures. Camas cakes were second only to dried salmon in trade volume, especially northward along the British Columbia Coast, where no camas grows. In many tribes, a family would mark out, "own" and maintain a camas patch year-round for generations, weeding and burning it. This might suggest the beginnings of an agricultural economy, but it was unique to camas. Year-round tending of a patch made it possible to weed out death camas when in flower and easy to recognize; that made it safe to dig camas in spring before flowering, when the bulbs are best. Nevertheless, many people died from eating death camas. Camas bulbs are not recommended to hikers.

David Douglas described quamash cuisine: "A hole is scraped in the ground, in which are placed a number of flat stones on which the fire is placed and kept burning until sufficiently warm, when it is taken away. The cakes, which are formed by cutting or bruising the bricks and then compressing into small bricks, are placed on the stones and covered with leaves, moss, or dry grass, with a layer of earth on the outside, and left until baked or roasted, which generally takes a night. They are moist when newly taken off the stones, and are hung up to dry. Then they are placed on shelves or boxes for winter use. When warm they taste much like a baked pear. It is not improbable that a very palatable beverage might be made from them. Lewis observes that when eaten in a large quantity they occasion bowel complaints... Assuredly they produce flatulence: when in the Indian hut I was almost blown out by strength of wind."

The flatulence is attributable to inulin, an indigestible sugar that takes the place of starch in camas bulbs, Jerusalem artichokes, and a few other vegetables.

Death Camas

Zigadenus spp. (zye-ga-**dee**-nus: paired glands). Also **zygadene**. Flowers white, ± saucer-shaped, in a tall raceme, withered tepals persistent; capsules ½–¾", splitting, 3-celled, 3-styled; most leaves basal, narrow, sheathing, but often 2 or more along the 8–30" stem; bulb 1". Liliaceae.

Z. venenosus (ven-en-**oh**-sus: poisonous). Tepals less than ¼", inner ones slightly longer than outer, all with a ± oval greenish spot near base. Grassy, ± open spots.

Z. elegans (**el**-eg-enz: elegant). Tepals all alike, ⅜", with a heart-shaped greenish spot near the base; leaves, stem often with whitish coating. Mainly alp/subalpine. Color p 126.

One of these two species has earned the name "death camas." Back during camas digging days, *Z. venenosus* undoubtedly killed more people in the Northwest than any other plant ever will. Today it maintains its reputation with an occasional sheep death. No humans are known to have been killed by *Z. elegans*, which holds less toxin and sticks to elevations where edible camas is rarely found. No one would mistake the small white flowers of death camas for the big blue ones of camas, but mistakes occur when populations of the two are intermixed and both have gone to seed or withered—and camas bulbs are ripest for eating.

Beargrass

Xerophyllum tenax (zero-**fill**-um: dry leaf; **ten**-ax: holding fast). Stamens longer than tepals; flowers white, fragrant, saucer-shaped, ½" diam, numerous; inflorescence at first nippled, bulbous, 3–4" diam, slowly elongating up to 20", the lowest flowers setting seed before the highest bloom; capsules 3-celled, dry; leaves narrow, tough, dry, V-shaped, with minutely barbed edges, the basal ones largest, 8–30", in a large dense clump; stalk up to 60", covered with much smaller leaves; from rhizomes. Cas Cr and high W-side, in dry forests and clearings. Liliaceae. Color p 124.

Once you've seen beargrass in bloom you will have no trouble ever recognizing its wonderful flower heads again. But the flowering schedule is erratic. You often see only the bunched leaves. Communities of beargrass may go for years without one bloom— and then hundreds bloom at once. Like the century plant, beargrass clumps grow slowly, accumulating photosynthates for years before venturing a flowering stalk. Having flowered, the clump dies, but its accumulated nutrients are siphoned off through the rhizome to a new offset clump.

The plants are slowest to flower in closed forest, but they are no less successful for want of sexual reproduction: beargrass can monopolize the understory community on ridgetops and high south and west aspects. Most ridges in the Oregon and Southern Washington Cascades are mantled with pumice that rained down from the skies during volcanic eruptions. Though the climate is wet, the water drains so fast through young pumice soils that herbs and shrubs have a hard time. Here beargrass excels, like a dry-leafed bunchgrass transplanted from the arid steppes, except that it's willing to settle for scantier light.

Beargrass may provide part of a bear's spring diet, when there isn't much else to choose from, but the neatly clipped leaf bases you see here and there are more likely the work of a "brushpicker"—a person making a living gathering foliage for the florist trade. Beargrass was in high demand from European florists for several years before we started seeing it in wide use locally.

The wiry strong leaves made this an important plant to Northwest Indians, and one of their many incentives for trips into the mountains. They wove beargrass into all kinds of baskets, also usable as hats. As David Douglas was pleased to report, "Pursh is correct as to their making watertight baskets of its leaves. Last night my Indian friend Cockqua arrived here from his tribe on the coast, and brought me three of the hats made on the English fashion, which I ordered when there in July; the fourth, which will have some initials wrought in it, is not finished, but will be sent by the other ship. I think them a good specimen of the ingenuity of the natives and particularly also being made by a little girl, twelve years old… I paid one blanket (value 7 shillings) for them."

Douglas' imaginative biographer, William Norwood, later read between the lines of that and other journal entries to argue that Douglas, with his cavalier praise for a little girl's ingenuity, was disguising a romantic entwinement with a nubile "Chinook princess."

Corn Lily

Veratrum spp. (ver-**ay**-trum: true black). Also **false-hellebore**. Flowers saucer-shaped, numerous; styles 3, persistent on the 1"-long 3-celled capsules, but usually lacking from the (staminate) lower flowers; leaves mostly 5–12", coarsely grooved along the veins, oval, pointed; stem 3–7', from a thick black rhizome. Wet meadows, mainly subalpine. Liliaceae.

V. viride (**veer**-id-ee: green). Flowers pale green, ½–¾" diam, in a loose panicle with drooping branches. SE Alaska to N OR Cas. Color p 127.

V. californicum. Flowers dull white, or only slightly greenish, ¾–1½", in a dense panicle with ascending branches. WA Cas to S Calif. Illustrated this page.

Heavy beds of snow lying on steep meadows tend to creep downslope through the winter, scouring off all vegetation at the surface. Woody seedlings are frustrated year after year, while perennial herbs with fat storage roots and fast spring growth are favored; and so the meadow community is perpetuated. On many wet slopes, the fastest plant to thrust up from the mud as the snow recedes is the corn lily, whose clusters of blunt, wrapped shoots look so strange and rank as to suggest an imagined land like Venus. These were the only herbaceous shoots robust enough to push up through six inches of new ash near Mt. St. Helens; most herbs in the same meadows died. The big lush leaves, startlingly clean and perfect when they unclasp from the stalk, often look ragged by the time the lily flowers.

The roots and young shoots are quite toxic, and used to be ground up for a crop insecticide, by farmers, or for a sinus-clearing snuff, by several NW tribes. Virtually every tribe that had the plant used some part of it—sometimes burned as a fumigant, sometimes worn around the neck as a charm, or in other ways—to ward away evil. The toxic alkaloids must degenerate or drain from the leaves by the time they mature and are eaten by elk and insects.

Herbs: showy monocots with 6 stamens (lilies)   *171*

Irises

Iris spp. (**eye**-ris: rainbow). 3 sepals spreading, 3 petals erect, + 3 smaller petal-like parts (pistil branches) ± resting on the sepals and hiding the stamens; leaves grasslike, mostly basal; capsule 3-celled, splitting; from horizontal rhizomes. Iridaceae (Iris family).

Oregon iris, *I. tenax* (**ten**-ax: holding fast). Flower usually single, violet (or occasionally blue, white, yellow, or pinkish); stem 4–12", with one to four small stem leaves. Open woods, lower W-side. Color p 127.

Western iris, *I. missouriensis* (miz-oo-ree-en-sis: of the Missouri River). Flowers pale blue, 2 (rarely up to 4); stem 12–24", with no midstem leaves (or rarely one). Open pine woods, lower E Cas.

David Douglas found Indians braiding iris leaves into snares for large game, even elk: "It will hold the strongest bullock and is not thicker than the little finger." Such tenacity in a slender leaf suggested the name *tenax. Iris* was the Greek goddess who flashed across the sky, bearing messages—the rainbow.

Blue-Eyed-Grass and Purple-Eyed-Grass

Sisyrinchium and *Olsynium** (sis-er-**ink**-ium: the Greek term, derived obscurely from "pig snouts"; ole-**sign**-ium). 6 tepals alike, ¼–¾"; flowers 1 or a few; leaves grasslike, ± basal (exc the bracts at base of flower stalks, the longer bract looking like a continuation of the stem above the flowers) shorter than the 6–14", 2-edged stem. Dry grassy sites that are briefly moist in spring. Iridaceae (Iris family).

Blue-eyed-grass, *S. idahoense** (idaho-en-zee: of Idaho). Tepals blue with yellow base; stamens fused into a single, 3-anthered column. Sporadic.

Purple-eyed-grass, *O. douglasii* (da-**glass**-ee-eye: after David Douglas, p 18). Also **grass widows, satinflower.** Tepals magenta; stamens fused less than half their length. Mainly (here) in and near Columbia Gorge. Color p 127.

These delicate perennials complete their active season in wet soil in a few weeks of spring, then wither and die back for the rest of the year, going dormant through the long drought of summer. (See page 220 on spring ephemerals.)

---

* Formerly a *Sisyrinchium, douglasii* was moved into this S. American genus; *idahoense* was formerly included with eastern relatives in *S. angustifolium.*

The orchid's flower structure is a snap to recognize; one petal, lowermost and thrust forward, is always utterly unlike the others and usually much larger. It's called the "lip" and serves as a platform for insect pollinators. Above the lip is a combined stamen/pistil structure called the "column." Illustration on page 147.

Irregular dicots, pages 192–201, have no more than 5 petals.

Orchid flowers are among the most elaborate insect lures on earth; but while the flowers evolved outlandishly, the roots mostly degenerated: a majority of the 500 or so genera of orchids are rootless lianas living on air and dripwater in tropical rain forest canopies. Our orchids are tenuously rooted, with vestigial root systems that tap into preexisting networks of fungal hyphae.

Rattlesnake-Plantain

Goodyera oblongifolia (**good**-yer-a: after John Goodyer; oblong-gif-**oh**-lia: oblong leaf). Flowers greenish white, many, in a one-sided spike up to 5"; lip shorter than and hooded by the fused, ¼"-long upper petals, all connected to the stalk by a twisted ovary; leaves 1½–3", in a basal rosette, thick, evergreen, very dark glossy green, mottled white along the veins; stem unbranched, 10–16". Widespread in dense forest. Orchidaceae. Color p 127.

> *"The Klallam informant, who is a devout Shaker, said that since she is a Christian she should not think of such matters, but formerly women rubbed this plant on their bodies to make their husbands like them better."*
>
> —Erna Gunther

The intensity of the snakeskin pattern on the leaves varies, even among side-by-side plants. Sometimes only the midvein is white, but usually there is enough white pattern to tell these leaves from those of white-veined pyrola (page 108). This is one orchid with enough leaf area to make it nearly independent, when mature, of its mycorrhizal partners.

Ladies-Tresses

Spiranthes romanzoffiana (spy-**ranth**-eez: coil flower; roman-zof-ee-**ay**-na: after Count Rumiantzev, below). Flowers ± white, ½" long, seemingly tubular, in (usually 3) ranks in a 2–6", dense, coiled-looking spike (perhaps suggesting a 4-strand braid); leaves sheathing, mostly basal; stem up to 24"; from swollen roots in wet ground. Orchidaceae. Illustrated at right.

Bog Orchids

Platanthera spp.* (plat-**anth**-er-a: broad anther). Also **rein orchid**. Flowers in a tall spike; lip with a long downcurved spur to the rear, two sepals horizontal, the other sepal and two petals erect, hooding the column. Orchidaceae (Orchid family).

White bog orchid, *P. leucostachys* * (loo-co-**stay**-kiss: white spike). Flowers white, spicy-fragrant, in a dense 4–12" spike; stem 8–40", with many clasping leaves, the lower ones up to 10" × 2", but much smaller upward. Wet ground, often subalpine. Illustrated at left.

Round-leaved bog orchid, *P. orbiculata* (or-bic-you-**lay**-ta: circular leaf). Flowers white to greenish or yellowish, in a loose spike; stem 8–24", leafless exc for a few tiny bracts; basal leaves typically 2, broadly oval to nearly round, 2–6". Deep montane forest. Color p 128.

The distinguishing feature of bog orchids is a narrow nectar-filled pouch or "spur" projecting rearward from the lip. The spur is an element in the grand pattern of orchid evolution, which has allied each variety and species of orchid with one, or at most a very few, species of insect. The right insect is not only powerfully attracted, but also physically unable to extract nectar from two successive

---

*These orchids have also been placed in genera *Platanthera* or *Limnorchis*, and *leucostachys* is sometimes treated as a variety within species *dilatata*.

Count Nikolai Rumiantzev (or *Romanzoff*) *financed Captain Kotzebue's Russian exploration of 1815-18. Johann Friedrich von Eschscholtz and Adelbert von Chamisso were the naturalists. They collected extensively in Alaska and California, but apparently sailed right past Washington and Oregon. Chamisso, a poet from Berlin, was the primary botanist while Eschscholtz, an Estonian doctor, preferred insects.*

---

blooms without picking up pollen from the first and leaving an adequate dose of it on the stigma of the second. Inadvertently, of course. Bog orchids' devices include:

proboscis-entangling hairs to engage the insect for a little while;

adhesive discs that stick to the insect's forehead while instantly triggering the stamen sac to split open;

little stalks that each hold a cluster of pollen to the adhesive disc (now on the insect's head), at first in an erect position that keeps the pollen *away* from the stigma of that same flower, but then (when the insect flies on) drying out and deflating into the right position to push the pollen onto…

the gluey stigma of the next flower of the same species, where the insect repeats her routine exactly in order to extract more nectar.

All this just to minimize waste of pollen in the wrong places.

Several less showy bog orchids with small greenish flowers grow on wet ground, or in deep forest. The flowers are always spirally arranged on the spike, though less dramatically than in ladies' tresses. The inch-long apparent stalk between the flower and the stem is actually the flower's ovary; a 180° twist in it shows that the lip evolved from what was originally the uppermost petal.

Goals of Evolution?

The idea (expressed above in regard to orchid design) that species evolved certain traits in order to better accomplish certain functions is a timeworn misconception about evolution. A few respected scientists uphold subtle versions of this concept, but they are far outnumbered. A more accepted description is that huge numbers of new traits turn up randomly, through genetic mutation. Only a tiny proportion of them just happen to confer some advantage on individuals that happen to get them. Over time, individuals that draw the lucky straws—the advantageous traits—tend to produce more offspring than others (by surviving longer, or by attracting more mates, etc.) and those of their offspring that inherit the trait also have greater reproductive success, preserving the trait in increasing numbers of descendents, until nearly a whole species carries it. Meanwhile, some other traits appear and persist without any adaptive value whatsoever.

Since that description is so unwieldy and abstruse, I give in to the charms of the teleological fallacy—an easy-to-grasp figure of speech.

Calypso Orchid

Calypso bulbosa (ca-**lip**-so: hidden, the name of a Greek sea nymph; bulb-**oh**-sa: bulbous). Also **fairy slipper, deer's-head orchid**. Flower single, pink; lip slipper-shaped, almost white, magenta-spotted above, magenta-streaked beneath; other petals and sepals all much alike, narrow, ¾"; leaf single, basal, growing in fall, withering by early summer; stem 3–7", from a small round corm. Moist, mature forest, mainly lowland. Orchidaceae. Color p 128.

A close look reveals these little orchids to be just as voluptuously overdesigned as their corsage cousins, which evolved bigger to seduce the oversized tropical cousins of our insects. Get down onto their level to see and smell them, using a handlens if you like, but don't pick them. Their bulblike "corm" is so shallowly planted that it's almost impossible to pick them without ripping the corm's lifelines. A calypso is dependent on its fungal and plant hosts (see page 178); its single leaf withers and is gone early in the growing season. Like other orchids, it produces huge numbers of minute seeds (3,770,000 seeds were found in one tropical orchid's pod) with virtually no built-in food supply, and an abysmal germination rate. They germinate only if particular species of fungi are already there to supply nutrients. The black specks filling vanilla beans and vanilla ice creams are familiar examples of orchid seeds.

Lady's-Slipper

Cypripedium montanum (sip-rip-ee-**dium**: Venus' slipper; mon-**tay**-num: of mtns). Flowers one to three; lip 1" long, very bulbous, white with purplish veins and a yellow staminate structure at its base; upper sepal and lateral petals brownish purple, about 2" long, slender, often twisted; stem 6–24", with several broad, clasping-based, 2–6"-long leaves plus a smaller bract beneath each flower. More or less open forest, E Cas slope, or rarely W-side in OR. Orchidaceae. Color p 128.

Twayblade

Listera caurina (**lis**-ter-a: after Martin Lister; caw-**rye**-na: of the NW wind). Also **big-ears**. Flowers pale greenish, small (½"), with a flaring/rounded, ± flat lip, several, in an open, short-stalked spike; leaves 2, apparently opposite, clasping the stem at mid-height, 1½–2½", pointed but usually broad; stem unbranched, 4–12". Various habitats, mostly forested, restricted to the PNW. Orchidaceae. Color p 127.

Coralroot

Corallorhiza spp. (coral-o-**rye**-za: coral root).
Entire plant (exc lip) dull pinkish brown, or rarely
pale yellow (albino); flowers ¾–1¼" long (½ of
that being the tubular ovary), 6–30 in a loose spike;
leaves reduced to inconspicuous sheaths on the 6–20"
stem. Forest. Orchidaceae.

Spotted coralroot, *C. maculata* (mac-you-**lay**-ta: spotted). Lip usually
white, with many magenta spots (sometimes also on petals).

Western coralroot, *C. mertensiana* (mer-ten-see-**ay**-na: after
Karl Mertens, p 111). Lip redder than plant, often with one
or two spots or blotches. Color p 128.

Striped coralroot, *C. striata*
(stry-**ay**-ta: striped). All petals
and sepals brownish- to pur-
plish-striped. Color p 128.

Coralroots usually grow in forest stands with few
herbs or shrubs. They blend in with the duff and sticks
until one of those few shafts of light hits, suddenly turning luminous their eerie, translucent russet flesh. Their rhizomes do resemble coral—curly, short, knobby, and entirely enveloped in soft fungal tissue. As in other orchid genera, a seed's embryo develops only
if penetrated, nourished, and hormonally stimulated by a hypha
from a fungus in the soil; fungal hormones suppress root hair
growth and stimulate the orchid to produce mycorrhizae instead
(page 260). In the case of coralroots, no true roots or root hairs ever
form. The vestigial leaves do not photosynthesize; surprisingly, the
flowers' ovaries do, though in insignificant quantities.

Phantom Orchid

*Cephalanthera austiniae** (sef-a-**lanth**-er-a:
headlike stamen tip; aus-**tin**-ee-ee: after
Mrs. R. M. Austin). Entire plant ivory white
(aging brown) exc for a yellow spot in the lip pouch;
sepals, petals ½–¾", lip shorter; flowers 5–20; leaves mostly
just sheaths, but one or two may have blades; stem 8–20". Forests; uncommon. Orchidaceae. Color p 128.

---

*The former *Eburophyton austineae* is now included in this otherwise green-
leaved European genus.

Candystick

Allotropa virgata (a-lot-ra-pa: turned various ways; veer-**gay**-ta: striped). Also **stickcandy**. Entire plant fleshy, bright red and white; no petals, five white sepals shorter than the 10 dark red stamens and pistil; flowers many, in a ± dense spike; stem thick, 4–16", leafy, sharply striped. Uncommon, in dense lowland forest. Ericaceae (Heath family). Color p 129.

This plant bursts astonishingly, at once candylike and gothic, from the drab shady duff and litter. The genus *Allotropa* grows its only species only here. If you ever begin to get used to it, head south to find its Sierra Nevada cousin the snowplant, *Sarcodes sanguinea*, which is 100% scarlet.

Candystick and the other non-green heaths often show up during what foresters call the "stem exclusion phase"—the period in the development of a forest when competition among trees (for light and water, especially) is most intense, and in consequence very few understory plants remain and the weaker individual trees die. (I.e., many stems are excluded.) The underground community that candystick represents may never develop in forests that get thinned,

Non-Green Orchids and Heaths

Some of our most arresting and intriguing herbs are those without chlorophyll, which obtain all their nutrients from fungi. Non-green plants were once called saprophytes, meaning that they live by extracting carbohydrates from dead organic material. The saprophyte myth was first debunked in 1882, and its coffin was nailed up by various papers between 1960 and 1987, yet it pops up ghoulishly in new books, even by biologists, to this day. In fact, living green plants provide the carbohydrates, and mycorrhizal fungi (page 260) connect the green and non-green plants' roots. Efforts to coin an accurate term for non-green plants have come up with "epiparasites," or indirect parasites, and "mycotrophic achlorophyllous angiosperms," or "mycoheterotrophs" for short. "Non-green plants" should do, for our purposes.

The mycorrhizal symbiosis must have evolved because it lets fungi and plants take advantage of each other's strengths—the fungi's efficiency at getting water, phosphorus, and nitrogen, and the plants' ability to make carbohydrates through photosynthesis. Some mycorrhizal

or selectively logged from time to time, in efforts to produce both timber revenue and eventually an old-growth-like forest from the same stand. That's one of the risky unknowns of New Forestry management plans: they may lose something important if they bypass the stem exclusion phase on their way to big trees.

Matsutake mushroom pickers learned to look for dried candy-stick stalks in fall as a marker for a patch of matsutakes. A scientist then investigated whether there was a mycorrhizal association between the two, and so far he finds that, sure enough, all the mycorrhizae he looks at on candystick look much alike, and all have that unique matsutake aroma. One scientist tried doing the math, using recent prices for matsutake, and found that many Northwest forests could be managed more lucratively for special forest products than for timber.

Pinedrops

Pterospora andromedea (tair-**os**-por-a: winged seed; an-drom-ed-**ee**-a: a name from Greek myth). Entire plant gummy/sticky, monochromatically brownish red exc for the amber, 5-lobed, jar-shaped corollas; flowers many, on downcurved stalks; capsules ± pumpkin-shaped; leaves brown, small and sparse on the 12–48" stem. Lower montane forests. Ericaceae. Color p 129.

plants, it would seem, gradually contributed less and less to this exchange, and got away with it as long as there were other plants connected to the same fungus. As the freeloaders evolved, unneeded organs atrophied. They ended up with vestigial leaves, little or no chlorophyll, and no real roots—nothing but a stalk of flowers reproducing, while the trees above provide leaves and the fungi below provide both roots and lifelines to the trees.

One green species will accept dozens if not thousands of fungal species as partners. In contrast, non-greens appear to be monogamous or nearly so, and the fungi they connect to (mainly boletes and truffles) also specialize, with pine family trees their main host in our area.

The non-green plant may have some useful substance to offer on its underground market: secretions from non-green plants have been shown to stimulate growth in fungi. Some researchers call the secretions "vitaminlike," but others remind that it is common for parasites to stimulate growth in their hosts in ways that drain the host's energies, rather than augmenting them.

This year's glowing amber stalks of pinedrops, our tallest non-green species, shoot up alongside still-standing dry brown stalks from last year, and even the year before. As the name implies, they may be found under (and mycorrhizally linked to) Ponderosa pines, but also just as often under Douglas-fir and, indeed, all across the continent under many kinds of trees. As their direct partners, in contrast, they apparently accept only one species of fungus.

Indian Pipe

Monotropa uniflora (ma-**not**-ra-pa: flowers turned one way, a meaningless name for a one-flowered plant; you-nif-**lor**-a: one-flowered). Also **ghost-plant**, **corpse-plant**. Entire plant fleshy, white or pink-tinged, drying black; flower single, narrowly bell-shaped, ½–¾", mostly 5-merous (occasionally 4–6), pendent, but erect in fruit—a soft round capsule; leaves translucent, small; stems densely clustered, 2–10". In dense forest. Ericaceae (Heath family). Color p 129.

A strange plant, but a familiar one all across the continent. Mushrooms in the Russula family are the usual cosymbionts here, and Douglas-fir is often at the far end of the pipeline. Don't pick Indian pipes—they'll just turn black and ugly within hours.

Pinesap

Hypopitys monotropa* (hye-**pop**-it-iss: under pine). Entire plant fleshy, yellow (rarely red) to straw, tinged with pink, drying black; flowers narrowly bell-shaped, ⅜–¾", mostly 4-merous (rarely 5), several, initially all down-turned in one direction, but erect when fruit matures; seed capsules round, soft; leaves translucent, small; stems clustered, 2–10". In dense forest. Ericaceae (Heath family).* Color p 129.

Digging up a pinesap (Don't!) would reveal a soft mycorrhizal root-ball only a couple of inches deep. Species of *Boletus* (page 274) are common partners of this species, and a pine or other conifer is almost always hooked up to the same bolete.

---

*Generations of taxonomists have debated between this name and the reverse, *Monotropa hypopithys*, depending on how closely related this species is to Indian pipe. In the past 20 years, most books have put it in *Monotropa*. I sense the wind shifting again: DNA study found the two plants far from being each other's closest relatives. An equally hoary controversy concerns whether the non-green heaths warrant a family of their own, Monotropaceae. Dick Olmstead at U.W. studies this issue, and advocates a broad Heath family, including both non-greens and Empetrum, often put in its own family.

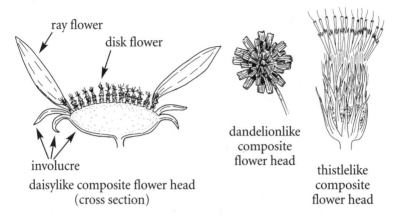

ray flower

disk flower

dandelionlike
composite
flower head

involucre

daisylike composite flower head
(cross section)

thistlelike
composite
flower head

Picture a daisy. Seeming petals radiate from a cushiony "disk" in the center. On closer examination, the base of each petal-like "ray" en-wraps a small pistil. The ray and pistil together constitute a "ray flower," not a petal; the petal-like length is an entire corolla of petals, fused then split down one side and flattened. The central disk turns out to be lots of little flowers too—"disk flowers"; each has a (usually two-branched) style poking out of a minute tube of five fused stamens, within a larger tube which is the (usually five-lobed) corolla. What we saw at first as one flower is a "composite flower head," the characteristic inflorescence of the family Aster-aceae,* or composites. "Involucral bracts" surround the head as se-pals do the flowers of other families. True sepals may also be pre-sent in the form of a "pappus"—a brush of hairs, scales or plumes that remain attached and grow as the seed forms, usually to provide mobility via wind or fur.

Some composites, dandelionlike, have only ray flowers and no disk. In these the ray flowers are bisexual, having stamen tubes as well as pistils. Other composites have only disk flowers, and some *appear* to have only disk flowers because their inner and outer

---

*This family was known for centuries as the Compositae. Recently, a new rule was passed to the effect that all families should have names formed from the name of a member genus and the suffix *-aceae*. The term "com-posite"—and the cranky epithet "D.Y.C."—are still widely used.

flower types are equally unshowy; we will call both kinds of rayless composites "thistlelike."

The tight fit of the stamen tube around the style is a mechanism that prevents self-pollination. As the pistil grows, it plunges all the pollen out of the tube; once its tip has grown free of the tube, it can split, exposing stigmas on the inner faces of its two branches.

Composite flowers excel at producing copious fat, well nourished seeds. The family's strongest tactic here is rapid invasion; year-to-year survival in severe cold is not its forte, and in shady boreal habitats even less so, so composites are fewer here than in many mountain regions. Still, they are conspicuous in our meadows, providing most of the color in late summer when most flowers have gone to seed and huckleberry foliage hasn't yet colored.

With somewhere between 15,000 and 20,000 species (several hundred in our range) the composites are even more diverse than grasses, but much less important as large-animal foods. It's notoriously hard to recognize all or even most of them. The larger genera are represented in this book by two or three species apiece.

Herbs: composites with disk and ray flowers (daisylike)

Daisies

Erigeron spp. (er-**idge**-er-un: soon aged). Also **fleabanes**. Rays 40–80; disk yellow; heads usually single; leaves narrow, mostly basal; stem leaves get smaller upwards (few and tiny on alpine plants). Asteraceae (Aster family).

Mountain daisy, *E. peregrinus* (pair-eg-**rye**-nus: wandering). Rays violet to pale blue, pink, or white, ⅜–1"; involucre uniformly woolly or sticky from top to bottom. Widespread; abundant in subalpine meadows, esp in WA.

Alice Eastwood's fleabane, *E. aliceae* (al-iss-ee). Rays ± violet, ⅜–⅝"; lower ½ of involucre white with long hairs, upper ½ sticky/fuzzy. Olys, OR Cas.

Golden fleabane, *E. aureus* (aw-ree-us: golden). Rays bright yellow, ¼"; involucre woolly; stem 2–8". Alpine. Color p 130.

Daisies generally bloom during the spring flowering rush, earlier than most composites, which could be the implication of the Latin name. Insecticidal properties implied by "fleabane" are Medieval superstition, or confusion with *Pyrethrum* daisies. The name "daisy" (originally for the English daisy, *Bellis perennis*) traces back to "day's eye" in Old English.

Asters

Aster spp. (**ast**-er: star). Rays 6–25, lavender to blue, pink or white, ¼–¾";
disk yellow. Asteraceae.

A. ledophyllus (leed-o-**fill**-us: rockrose leaf). Heads several; leaves ± elliptical, 1–3", all on the 8–30" stem. Mid to subalpine elevs. Color p 130.

A. alpigenus (al-**pidge**-en-us: alpine). Heads single; stems 1–3, 4–12", often
oblique; leaves ± linear, basal ones 2–7", stem leaves tiny. Alp/subalpine.

Asters tend to bloom later than daisies and to have fewer, broader
rays. *A. ledophyllus* joined the subalpine elite that came up in large
numbers through inches of Mt. St. Helens ash in 1980.

Arnicas

Arnica spp. (**ar**-nic-a: lambskin, referring to leaf texture). Heads entirely yellow, single to few; leaves opposite, plus some in non-flowering whorls from
the rhizome; stems 4–24". Asteraceae.

A. cordifolia (cor-dif-**oh**-lia: heart leaf). Rays 8–15, ½–1¼"; leaves ± toothed,
heart-shaped to broadly oval; lower stem leaves narrow to a stalked base.
Meadows and open forest. Color p 130.

A. latifolia (lat-if-**oh**-lia: broad leaf). As above, exc stem leaves stalkless.

A. rydbergii (rid-**berg**-ee-eye: after Per Rydberg). Rays 7–10, ½"; leaves ±
smooth-edged, narrow-elliptical, with 3–5 ± parallel main veins; stem 4–12".
Alp/subalpine.

Arnicas bloom early to mid summer. Several tribes used them as a
plaster for sore or injured muscles or joints; European herbalists
made similar use of their *Arnica montana*.

Groundsels

Senecio spp. (sen-**ee**-she-oh: old
man). Rays ¼–½", few (4–10 or
rarely none) sparse and disorder-
ly; disk yellow; heads several;
stem 1–6'. Asteraceae.

S. triangularis. Rays yellow; leaves narrow-triangular,
3–7", all on stem. In lush meadows. Illustrated this page.

S. integerrimus (in-te-**jer**-im-us: very smooth-
edged). Rays yellow to white, or lacking; leaves ±
elliptical, on long leafstalks, preponderantly basal,
smaller upwards. Mainly E-sides.

Herbs: daisylike composites

Woolly-Sunflower

Eriophyllum lanatum (area-**fill**-um: woolly leaf; lan-**ay**-tum: woolly). Leaves, stems and involucres all thickly white-woolly; rays about 13, ¾"; heads all yellow, single; leaves on stem, often narrowly 3–7-lobed; stems 10–24", many, weak, in thick clumps or sprawling mats. Dry meadows at all elevs. Asteraceae. Color p 130.

Balsamroot

Balsamorhiza sagittata (balsam-o-**rye**-za: balsam root; sadge-it-**ay**-ta: arrow-shaped). Heads all yellow, single, 2½–4" diam; leaves all basal (exc one or two small bracts on stem), triangular, 12" × 6", on long leafstalks; plant silver-velvety, esp under leaves when young, 10–30", in thick clumps. In sun, lower E-slope of Cas. Asteraceae. Color p 130.

Balsamroots are spectacular in the spring, and they are also a good food plant. Deer and elk eat the leaves, and Indians ate the young shoots, the seeds, and the fat, fragrant, slightly woody taproot.

Goldenrods

Solidago spp. (so-lid-**ay**-go: healing, a misleading name). Heads yellow, numerous, in a large fluffy inflorescence; rays 5–18, small. Asteraceae.

S. simplex nana* (**nay**-na: dwarf). Inflorescence ± round-topped, rays 5–10; leaves basally crowded, tapering to leafstalks; stem 2–18", smooth. Alp/subalpine. Color p 130.

S. multiradiata (multi-ray-dee-**ay**-ta: many-rayed). As above, but rays 10–18, and stem minutely woolly.

S. canadensis. Inflorescence pyramidal; stem 1½–6', very leafy. Widespread.

Yarrow

Achillea millefolium (ak-il-**ee**-a: after Achilles; mil-ef-**oh**-lium: thousand leaf). Rays 3–5, white (rarely pink), ⅛" long and wide; disk yellow; heads many, in a flat to convex inflorescence; leaves narrow, extremely (though variably) finely dissected, fernlike, aromatic; to 3', or dwarfed (alpine). In sun. Asteraceae. Color p 130.

Achilles, the Greek hero of the Trojan war, was taught by Chiron the Centaur to dress the wounds of battle with yarrow. Northwest Indians also used yarrow poultices, and drank yarrow tea for myriad ailments. They steamed the homes of sick people with the pungent

---

* Formerly *S. spathulata nana*.

smell of yarrow leaves—rather like rosemary and sage. In China, the yarrow stalk oracle was systematized by Confucius and his followers in the *I Ching*.

Some *Achillea* species have perfectly smooth-edged linear leaves. Our "thousand-leaf" species was once divided into several species on the basis of varying degrees of leaf dissection, but it was found that transplanted specimens would within a few years alter their leaf shape to fit their new environment, nearly matching the yarrows around them.

Herbs: composites without rays (thistlelike)

Thistles

Cirsium edule (**sir**-shium: swollen vein; **ed**-you-lee: edible), illustrated at right, and
C. brevistylum (brev-iss-**tie**-lum: short style). Flowers bright pink to purple; involucral bracts ending in long spines, cobwebby-haired at the base; leaves very spiny, pinnately lobed, up to 10" long, narrow, all on the 1½–7' stem. Widespread in sun, mainly W-side. Asteraceae. Color p 131.

These native thistles are herbaceous biennials, storing starches in their taproot their first summer, dying back to the ground, and then resprouting to flower, fruit, and die in their second year. The taproot and fat stems, peeled, are nutritious and tasty, highly rated in both ethnobotanical and survival-skills texts. Two European species are nasty weeds of Northwest lowland fields and lots.

Pearly Everlasting

Anaphalis margaritacea (an-af-a-lis: the Greek term; margarite-**ay**-see-a: pearly). Disks ± yellow, surrounded by innumerable tiny papery white bracts (not ray flowers); heads ⅜" diam, many, in a convex cluster; leaves 2–5", linear, woolly (esp underneath), all on the 8–36" stem, the lowest ones withering. Widespread on roadsides, burns and clearcuts; also alpine. Asteraceae. Color p 130.

Pearly everlasting may appear daisylike, but in fact it has no ray flowers, only dozens of dry scaly white involucral bracts which persist everlastingly—either in the field or in a vase.

Pussytoes

Antennaria spp. (an-ten-**air**-ia: antenna—). Disks ± white, soft-fuzzy, deep, surrounded by numerous scaly bracts (not ray flowers); heads several, ¼" diam; leaves woolly, mainly basal. Asteraceae.

A. lanata (lan-**ay**-ta: woolly). In clumps, occasionally broad but without runners; bracts white; basal leaves 1–6"; stems 4–12".

A. media * (**me**-dia: medium) and *A. umbrinella* (um-brin-**el**-a: brown small). Mat-forming, with leafy runners; sepallike involucral bracts dark; few leaves over 1"; stems 1–7". Color p 130.

A. rosea *(**rose**-ia: rose-colored). Mat-forming, with runners; bracts pink to white; few leaves over 1"; stems 6–18".

Alpine forms of many composites, including *umbrinella* and *rosea* pussytoes, usually reproduce asexually, the ovules maturing into seeds without being fertilized by pollen. Any given patch is likely a female clone, perhaps with interconnecting runners. These plants are adapted to a severe climate in which the blooming season all too often zips by in weather too nasty for small insects (pollinators of minute flowers like these) to be out and about.

These clone populations make lots of work for taxonomists. Since they vary from each other but are internally consistent over broad areas, many were named as species in the past. It is taking a lot of close study to weed out the many unjustified names.

Coltsfoot

Petasites frigidus [†] (pet-a-**sigh**-teez: hat-shaped). Flower heads white or pink-tinged, occasionally with a few tiny rays, many, in a ± open round cluster, vanilla-fragrant; stems 6–24", with clasping, elliptical leafy bracts 1–3" long; true leaves basal on stout 16–24" leafstalks, palmately deeply 5–9-lobed, 6–16" broad by not quite as long. Wet places, mainly W of Cas Cr. Asteraceae. Color p 131.

Fast-growing coltsfoot shoots appear very early in lower forests. The flowers wither before the leaves reach full size in midsummer. A smaller, less common high-elevation variety has shallow-lobed leaf blades somewhat longer (up to 8") than wide.

A. microphylla of Hitchcock is referred to *rosea,* and his *A. alpina* to *media.*

[†] Some authorities (but not PLANTS) treat our main variety, *palmatus,* as a separate species. In either case the high-elev type is *P. frigidus* var *nivalis.*

Saw-Wort

Saussurea americana (so-**sure**-ee-a: after Horace and Theodore Saussure). Disk flowers usually 13, dark purple, narrow-tubular, protruding haphazardly from a fluffy mass of pappus bristles; heads several, crowded; leaves ± triangular, sharply toothed, narrow, the lower ones up to 6", all on the 10–30" stem. Lower subalpine lush meadows, WA. Asteraceae. Color p 131.

Silverback

Luina hypoleuca (lu-**eye**-na: anagram of genus *Inula*; hypo-**lew**-ca: white underneath). Flower heads distinctively cream-colored, several; leaves 1–2", oval, white-woolly on both sides or just the underside, attached directly all up and down the stalk; plants 8–24" tall, in ± dense patches. Rocky sites, widely scattered at high elevs. Asteraceae. Color p 131.

Silvercrown

Cacaliopsis nardosmia * (ca-cay-lee-**op**-sis: resembling genus *Cacalia*; nar-**dos**-mia: nard aroma). Disk flowers bright yellow, large, tubular, with paired curled stigma tips protruding; heads ½–1¼" diam, several; plant 2–3½' tall, with several long-stalked basal leaves deeply palmately lobed but round in outline, 8–10" diam; + a few similar but smaller leaves on main stem. Locally abundant in meadows near and E of Cas Cr in S WA Cas; uncommon elsewhere. Asteraceae. Color p 131.

On this handsome plant, the individual flowers in the composite head are big enough for you to see them as flowers, with five petal lobes and two stigma branches.

Trail-Plant

Adenocaulon bicolor (a-den-o-**caw**-lon: gland stem; **by**-color: two color). Also **pathfinder**. Flower heads tiny, white, several, in a very sparse panicle on a 10–32" stalk; leaves all on lowest part of stem, triangular, 4–6", dark green on top, white-fuzzy underneath. W-side forest up to mid elevs. Asteraceae.

This is an unusual composite in adapting primarily to deep shade. The leaves are suitably large, thin, and flat-lying—and easy to

---

* Formerly included in genus *Luina*.

recognize by their unique shape, while the flowers are rarely noticed. (They attract small flies by their smell, not their looks.) The combination of weak leafstalks and high contrast between upper and lower leaf surfaces led to the common name; a good woodsman tracking a large animal through the woods appreciated a conspicuous series of overturned trail-plant leaves. The sticky seeds also "trail" us by adhering to our legs. And then there are the tiny circumlocuitous trails—the work of leaf-miners—etched across many trail-plant leaves by summer's end. Leaf-mining, or chewing around through the cells of a leaf between its upper and lower cuticles, provides a sheltered way of life for the larvae of certain moths, flies, beetles, and wasps. Trail-plant leaves, along with those of tiarella, aspen, and dwarf raspberries, make good "mines."

Wormwoods

Artemisia spp. (ar-tem-**ee**-zhia: the Greek term). Flower heads tiny, pale, within ⅛" diam cups of fuzzy bracts, forming tall to ± spreading inflorescences; spicy-aromatic and fuzzy-coated all over, the leaves silvery underneath, ± greener above. Asteraceae. Color p 131.

Western wormwood, *A. ludoviciana* (lu-doe-vis-ee-**ay**-na: of the Louisiana Purchase area) and **Douglas' wormwood**, *A. douglasiana* (da-glass-ee-**ay**-na: after D. Douglas, p 18). Plants 1–5' tall, leaves 1–4", most with a few irregular, fingerlike lobes. Scattered; abundant in some dense meadows. Both leaves at right.

Three-forked wormwood, *A. trifurcata* (try-fur-**cay**-ta: 3 forked). Dwarfed plants, 2–10"; similar to above exc leaves mostly basal, ½–1¼", with a few smaller leaves along stalk. Alpine, in WA.

Wormwoods are proverbial "bitter herbs," figuring in several dire biblical prophesies which seemed to come true when a town named Chernobyl ("wormwood" in Ukrainian) became synonymous with ungodly disaster. Bitter aromatic wormwoods of Europe include the intoxicating absinth and the *vermouth* ("wormwood" in German) that flavors aperitif wines. Another species is a sweet herb, French tarragon or dragon wormwood, *A. dracunculus,* which grows weedily in eastern Washington. Wormwood's flowers are nondescript but its silvery wool is striking, and its spicy fragrance more so; crush a leaf and you're perfumed for hours. Native shrubs of this genus perfume about three-fourths of the American West. You guessed it. Sagebrush (page 91).

Mountain-Dandelions

Agoseris and *Nothocalais* spp. (a-**gah**-ser-iss: goat chicory; noth-o-ca-**lay**-iss: false *Calais*). One 1"-diam flower head per stem; plants milky-juiced; leaves basal, ± linear or with a few widely spaced teeth. Asteraceae.

Alpine dandelion, *N. alpestris* (al-**pes**-tris: alpine). Rays dandelion-yellow; plants 2–10" tall. Alp/subalpine, from Mt Rainier S. Color p 131.

Pale agoseris, *A. glauca* (**glaw**-ca: silvery). Rays pale waxy yellow, drying pinkish; dwarfed (4–10") on alpine slopes, where ± common N of Mt Rainier; or 10–30" in dry meadows E of Cas. Color p 131.

Orange agoseris, *A. aurantiaca* (aw-ran-**tie**-a-ca: orange). Rays red-orange, drying purplish; 6–12". Lush high meadows.

These are closely related to true dandelions (genus *Taraxacum*, also native here) and resemble them in their seed-parachutes as well as their flower heads,which on *Agoseris* tend to close up on hot days.

Hawkweeds

Hieracium spp. (hi-er-**ay**-shium: hawk—). Flower heads ½" diam, in a sparse panicle; stems milky-juiced. In sun. Asteraceae.

H. albiflorum (al-bif-**lor**-um: white flower). Heads white to cream, several; leaves long-elliptical, hairy; stem 12–20". Forest openings. Illustrated above.

H. gracile (**grass**-il-ee: slender). Heads yellow, few or single; leaves almost basal on long leafstalks, oval, smooth; stem 2–12", fuzzy. High meadows.

H. scouleri (**scoo**-ler-eye: after John Scouler, p 69). Heads yellow, several; stems and undersides of leaves covered with long white hairs; stem 10–30"; stems and leaf veins often magenta in spring. Low to mid-elevs, esp in Columbia Gorge. Color p 131.

Wall Lettuce

Lactuca muralis (lac-**tew**-ca: Roman for lettuce, from "milk"; mew-**ray**-lis: grows on walls). Rays consistently five, resembling petals, yellow, from a tubular involucre; flower heads very sparse, blooming a few at a time; leaves coarsely pinnate-lobed, with "ears" clasping stem; plant milky-juiced, 2–3½' tall. Low forest openings; Eurasian weed. Asteraceae.

Stinging nettle has four tiny, obscure sepals, but getting close enough to see them would likely prove painful. Aside from that, "without sepals" is applied pretty strictly to this group of oddities, not to betray readers who look closely enough to see and count minute sepals.

Marginally countable sepals or petals are on mountain-sorrel, p 196; pussypaws, p 196; skunk-cabbage, p 160; bunchberry, p 228; desert-parsleys, p 224; goatsbeard, p 216; and baneberry, p 232.

Vanillaleaf

Achlys triphylla (ay-klis: a night goddess; try-**fill**-a: 3 leaf). Also **deerfoot**. Flowers cream-white, minute, without petals or sepals, in a dense spike 1–2" × ¼", on a leafless stalk a little taller (8–16") than the one that bears the uniquely shaped 3-compound, flat-lying leaf (6–10"). Abundant in W-side forest. Berberidaceae (Barberry family). Color p 132.

The vanilla fragrance is indetectable in growing leaves, but will be unmistakable and durable if you pick a few and let them dry. The odd leaf shape makes a good Rorschach pattern; where some see a deer foot, this writer sees Bullwinkle Moose.

Alpine Willows

Salix spp. (**say**-lix: the Roman term). Female and male catkins on separate plants; leaves ± elliptical; prostrate shrubs forming cushiony mats to 4" tall. Alp/subalp in WA. Salicaceae (Willow family).

Cascade willow, *S. cascadensis* (cas-ca-**den**-sis: of the Cascades). Catkins 15–25-flowered, ½–¾" long; leaves ¼–1" long. Illustrated above.

Arctic willow, *S. arctica.* Catkins 25–60-flowered, ½–2" long; leaves ½″ or ranging upto 4" and spoon-shaped toward N. Color p 132.

True willows reduced to carpet stature are fairly common in the North Cascades. But for their catkins, you might mistake them for huckleberry, which also prostrates itself under alpine conditions.

False-Bugbane

Trautvetteria caroliniensis (trout-vet-ee-ria: for Ernest Rudolf van Trautvetter; carol-in-ee-en-sis: of the Carolinas). Flowers white, in broad rough clusters, consisting mainly of many stamens (up to ¼"), the 4 (3–7) sepals falling off as the flower opens; leaves predominantly basal, 4–10" wide, deeply 5–7-lobed; 20–36". W-side streamsides; wet forest. Ranunculaceae (Buttercup family). Color p 132.

Nettle

Urtica dioica (ur-tic-a: burning; die-oy-ca: with male and female flowers on different plants, an untrue name for our nettles). Flowers 4-merous, tiny, pale green, many, in loose panicles dangling from the leaf axils, the panicles unisexual, with females higher on the plant (our varieties); leaves opposite, sawtoothed, pointed/oval, 2–6"; stem (2–6') and leaves lined with fine stinging bristles; from rhizomes. Moist, ± open lowlands, mainly W-side. Urticaceae (Nettle family). Color p 132.

Nettles are seen nowadays as something to avoid, but older traditions both here and in Europe held them the most estimable of weeds. They're food: the young plants make outstanding greens. They're fiber: the mature stems have been made into high-quality twine, cloth and paper, substituting for flax in wartime as recently as World War II, and several tribes here made nettle-twine nets for ducks and fish. They're medicine: the sting helped stoical Indian hunters stay awake through the night, and tasty nettle tea has earned medicinal reputations worldwide.

Nettle stingers are miniature hypodermic syringes, like bee and ant stingers. The bee-sting toxin, formic acid, was long but erroneously believed to be the main toxin in nettles, which inject a cocktail of acetylcholine, hydroxytryptamine, and a histamine. They evolved as a defense against browsing, but they don't save nettles from Milbert's tortoiseshell and other caterpillars. One folk remedy holds that if you pull up the nettle that bit you, you can soothe the sting by crushing juice onto it from the nettle root. Thorough steaming or drying renders nettles harmless. If you ever camp in April or May near a good bed of nettle shoots a few inches high, cook them up. Wear long sleeves and gloves (or socks) over your hands, lop them with your knife, and steam them limp in half an inch of water. (If cooked only *al dente*, they have enough bristle left to worry your lips and tongue.) Butter, sour cream, feta or bleu cheese, maybe crepes…

Irregular flowers are those in which the petals (or the sepals, if they are the showy parts) are not all alike. You might think of them as bilaterally—as opposed to radially—symmetrical, but their are exceptions; some louseworts are twisted and have no symmetry at all.

Irregular flowers display advanced specialization of form. Each species matches a particular form and size of insect, for pollination. Irregular shapes run in families: you can probably think of the three familiar shapes—orchids, sweetpeas and snapdragons—which represent our three biggest families of irregular flowers, the Orchidaceae (pp 173–77), Fabaceae (pp 198–200), and Scrophulariaceae (pp 192–95).

Flowers are not placed here if the irregularity consists only of unequal-sized, but otherwise similar, petals or lobes. For example, veronica, p 230, and kittentails, p 227, each have four small blue to lavendar petals. Cow-parsnip, p 225, has five unequal but similar two-lobed white petals, and a flat-topped Parsley-family look.

Monkeyflowers

Mimulus spp. (**mim**-you-lus: mime or clown). Flowers snapdragonlike— corolla with a long (¾–2") throat, hairy inside, and 2 upper and 3 lower lobes; calyx angularly 5-lobed; stamens 4, paired; leaves opposite; stems in dense clumps on stolons and/or rhizomes. These three species all of wet places. Scrophulariaceae (Figwort family).

Purple monkeyflower, *M. lewisii* (lew-iss-ee-eye: after Meriwether Lewis, p 234). Flowers deep pink to violet; leaves sessile, pointed, 2–3"; plants 12–36", sticky-hairy. Mid to subalpine elevs. Color p 135.

Yellow monkeyflower, *M. guttatus* (ga-**tay**-tus: spotted). Flowers yellow, throat often red-spotted; 4–30". Low to mid elevs. Color p 134.

Mountain monkeyflower, *M. tilingii* (til-**ing**-ee-eye: after Heinrich S. T. Tiling). Flowers yellow, ¾–1½", very large for a tiny plant, throat ± red-spotted; leaves ⅜–1"; plants 2–8". Subalpine. Illustrated at right.

Both "monkey" and the "mime" in Mimulus are impressions of this fat irregular blossom as a funny-face. Some other monkeyflower species here don't depend on getting wet feet, but bloom very early to compensate.

Louseworts

Pedicularis spp. (ped-ic-you-**lair**-iss: louse—). Corolla fused, with two main lips, the upper ± long-beaked, the lower usually 3-lobed; calyx irregularly 2–5-lobed; capsule also asymmetrical; leaves (exc on sickletop lousewort) fernlike, pinnately compound; flowers many, on an unbranched stem. Scrophulariaceae (Figwort family).

Sickletop lousewort, *P. racemosa* (ras-em-**oh**-sa: bearing racemes). Flowers (our variety) pale bronze-pink, beak curled strongly sideways, so inflorescence looks pinwheellike from above; leaves reddish, ± linear, fine-toothed, all on stem; 6–18". Openings near forest line; or alpine. Color p 134.

Elephant's head, *P. groenlandica* (green-**lan**-dic-a: of Greenland). Flowers purplish pink, in a dense spike, elephantlike (upcurved beak as the trunk, lateral lower lobes as the ears); leaves preponderantly basal; 8–16". Subalpine rills and boggy meadows. Color p 134.

Birdbeak lousewort, *P. ornithorhynca* (or-nith-o-**rink**-a: bird beak). Flowers purplish pink, with a thin downturned beak, few, in a short round inflorescence; leaves almost all basal; 4–7‴". Moist alp/subalpine gravels in WA Cas. Color p 134.

Bracted lousewort, *P. bracteosa* (brac-tee-**oh**-sa: with bracts). Flowers yellow (rarely purple to dark red), scarcely beaked, in a robust spike; stem leaves as big as basal ones, aging purplish; 24–36"; lush subalpine meadows.

Mt. Rainier lousewort, *P. rainierensis* (ra-near-**en**-sis: of Mt Rainier). Flowers yellow to cream, scarcely beaked, in a robust spike; stem leaves much smaller than basal ones; 6–16"; subalpine; only in Mt. Rainier vicinity.

Coiled-beak lousewort, *P. contorta.* Flowers (our variety) pale yellow to white, in a loose spike; beak semicircular, arching back into lower lip; leaves mostly basal; 8–14". Alp/subalpine turfs. Color p 134.

The louseworts are as curiously irregular and varied a genus of flowers as you could ask for, deserving their curious pictorial names. "Lousewort," however, dates from an ancient superstition that cattle got lousy by browsing louseworts. Each of the flower shapes suits the anatomy of one or more species of bumble bees—pollinators of the hundred or so species of louseworts.

Herbs: irregular dicots　　　　　　　　　　　　　*193*

Indian Paintbrush

Castilleja spp. (cas-til-**ay**-a: after Domingo Castillejo). Inflorescence most often red, varying to every shade of pink, magenta, orange, yellow, and greenish white; true flowers subtended and largely hidden by brightly colored bracts (lower bracts grading to green at their bases); calyx narrowly 4-lobed, same color as bracts; corolla a thin tube, dull green; leaves (incl the colored floral bracts) often narrowly 3-, 5-, or 7-pronged, elliptical, their main veins appearing parallel; stems usually several, unbranched, from a woody base; roots partially parasitic, esp on grasses and composites. Widespread, in sun. Scrophulariaceae (Figwort family). Color p 136.

Indian paintbrush is easily recognized as a genus, but notoriously hard to identify to species. Neither coloring nor hairiness are diagnostic, though within a small area the members of a species match up pretty closely. Our commonest species, *C. miniata* ("cinnabar-red"), ranges from the coast to subalpine meadows and sometimes a little way into the forest, throughout the montane West. It grows 8–30" tall and is usually scarlet, varying to yellow-orange. The Makah used this paintbrush as a hummingbird lure; they trapped hummers to use as charms for whaling.

Blue-Eyed Mary

Collinsia spp. (ca-**lin**-zia: after Zaccheus Collins). Also **innocence**. Corolla blue to violet, the upper two lobes fading to white; lobes seemingly 4, the fifth being the inconspicuous central lower lobe, creased shut to enclose the stamens and style; calyx 5-lobed, green; flowers in axils of upper, often whorled leaves; lower leaves opposite, ± linear; plants annual, 2–14". Sunny low to mid elevs. Scrophulariaceae (Figwort family).

C. grandiflora (gran-dif-**lor**-a: big flower). Corolla at least ½" long, bent over at right angles to the calyx. Color p 133.

C. parviflora (par-vif-**lor**-a: small flower). Corolla usually much less than ½", bent at an oblique angle to calyx.

Foxglove

Digitalis purpurea (digit-**ay**-lis: finger —; pur-**pew**-ria: purple). Corolla pink (to purplish or occasionally white) tubular, 1½–2", with five very shallow lobes; sepals 5; stamens 4, paired; flowers many, in a very showy one-sided spike; leaves oval/pointed, up to 20 × 6"; stems fuzzy and ± sticky, 2–6'; biennial. Roadsides and scarified clearcuts. Scrophulariaceae. Color p 135.

Our most beautiful European weed, foxglove is the age-old source of digitalin, used as a heart stimulant in cases of cardiac arrest. Doctors prescribe it with care and precision; foxglove can be deadly to those with previous heart disorders.

Penstemons

Penstemon spp. (**pen**-stem-un: five stamen). Also **beardtongues**. Corolla typically blue or violet to pink or sometimes yellow-white, swollen-tubular, with 5 (2 upper, 3 lower) short rounded flaring lobes, and a broad ± hairy

sterile stamen resting on the throat; fertile stamens 4, paired; sepals 5, hardly at all fused; leaves opposite, often basal-clustered in part. Rocky places and drier meadows; common. Scrophulariaceae (Figwort family).

Creeping Penstemon, *P. davidsonii* (david-**so**-nee-eye: after George Davidson). Flowers blue to lavender, ¾–1½"; stems woody, dense mat-forming, 3–6" tall. Color p 134.

Rock Penstemon, *P. rupicola* (roo-**pic**-a-la: rock dweller). As above exc more pink to red; and leaves whitish-coated. Illustrated at left.

Small-flowered Penstemon, *P. procerus* (**pross**-er-us: noble). Flowers usually blue/purple, ¼–½" long, in 1–3 apparent whorls; leaves narrowly elliptical, to 2" long; stem 4–24".

Paintbrush and penstemons are famous wildflowers of the Western National Park circuit. Both are more plentiful in the Rockies, with more numerous species, than here; you could predict that from their preference for drier than average sites here. While most penstemons range between blue and pink, a white or yellow blossom isn't necessarily a rare species: several blue species, including *procerus*, may occur in pale form.

Corydalis

Corydalis scouleri (cor-**id**-a-lis: the crested lark; **scoo**-ler-eye: after John Scouler, p 69). Flowers light pink, 15–35, variously angled in an open spike; petals 4, upper one with a rearward spur at least as long as the forward part; inner 2 ± hidden; sepals 2, falling off early; stamens 6; seedpod splits explosively to propel seeds; leaves large, much compounded, round-lobed; plants 1½–4' tall. Seeps and streambanks, lower W-side. Fumariaceae (Fumitory family). Color p 133.

A very rare aquatic corydalis, *C. aquae-gelidae*, grows near a few Cascade streams and marshes in N Oregon and S Washington.

Bleedingheart

Dicentra formosa (di-**sen**-tra: two spur; for-**mo**-sa: beautiful). Corolla pink, ¾–1" long, pendent, shaped like an elongate heart made of two fused petals, hiding a smaller pair of fused petals inside; sepals 2, falling off early; stamens 6; seed pod growing as long as 2" out through the corolla mouth; stalks several-flowered, 12–20"; leaves fernlike, compound and incised. Open spots up to mid elevs, W-side forest. Fumariaceae (Fumitory family). Color p 133.

Mountain-Sorrel

Oxyria digyna (ox-**ee**-ria: sharp —; didge-in-a: two ovaries). Flowers tiny, greenish, of 2 erect and 2 spreading lobes, 2 stigmas and 6 stamens, in rough spikelike panicles; fruit rust red, tiny, 2-winged; leaves kidney-shaped, 1–2" broad, on long basal leafstalks, coloring brilliantly in fall; stalks several, 4–18". Rocky streambanks and wet talus; alp/subalpine. Polygonaceae (Buckwheat family). Color p 135.

Mountain-sorrel leaves are sourly tasty, with ascorbic (vitamin C) oxalic, and other acids. Don't eat too much.

Pussypaws

Calyptridium umbellatum * (cal-ip-**trid**-ium:with a cap over the seed—not true of this species; um-bel-**ay**-ta: with flowers in umbels). Sepals 2, round, ⅛–⅜" diam, sandwiching and nearly hiding the 4 much smaller petals and 3 stamens; flowers rust-pink to yellowish white, in fluffy, chaffy heads on prostrate stalks radiating well past the cushion of 1–3", narrow, semisucculent basal leaves. Alp/subalpine, or dry E-side; rock crevices and ± barren gravels, esp pumice. Portulacaceae (Purslane family). Color p 135.

Hedge-Nettle

Stachys spp. (**stay**-kis: ear of grain). Corolla purplish red to pink, ½–1¼", with a round upper lip and a longer, 3-lobed lower lip; calyx 5-pointed; stamens 4, paired; flowers in an open spike of several whorls; leaves opposite, elliptical, toothed; stem square, 1–4'; fetid when bruised. Marshy places, low to mid elevs. Lamiaceae (Mint family) . Color p 132.

Like the English, Northwest Indians named this stingless plant after nettles, and sometimes mixed the two in infusions. Hedge-nettles often grow near stinging nettles, but claim mints for family relations, as evidenced by their flowers and square stems.

---

*Older texts call this *Spraguea umbellata*, and some (but not all) newer ones, including PLANTS, call it *Cistanthe umbellata*.

Self-Heal

Prunella vulgaris (pru-**nel**-a: purple, small; vul-**gair**-iss: common). Also **all-heal**. Corolla blue-purple, ¼–¾", 4-lobed; upper lobe hoodlike, lower lobe liplike, fringed; calyx half as long; stamens 4 (rarely lacking); flowers bloom sequentially upward, in a crowded broad-bracted spike of opposite pairs neatly offset 90°; leaves opposite, elliptical, 1–3"; stem squarish, 4–16" tall, or sprawling. Sporadic up to mid elevs. Lamiaceae (Mint family). Color p 133.

The mint family is loaded with medicinal, poisonous and culinary aromatic herbs, including catnip, pennyroyal, horehound, oregano, sage, savory, thyme, and of course peppermint. Europeans once believed in self-heal as a panacea; in tribal and modern herbal lore it's prescribed to heal sores, wounds, and chapped skin.

Youth-on-Age

Tolmiea menziesii (**tole**-me-a: after William Tolmie, below; men-zee-zee-eye: after Archibald Menzies, p 97). Also **piggyback plant**. Calyx purplish to brownish green, bell-shaped but cut away on one side, ½", with 3 large and 2 small lobes; petals longer, threadlike, red-brown, 4 (or 5); three stamens; flowers many, in a raceme; leaves shallowly palmate-lobed, 1½–3" broad, mostly basal on long leafstalks; stems several, 1–3', from rhizomes; entire plant hairy. Moist W-side forest. Saxifragaceae (Saxifrage family). Color p 136.

This anomalous saxifrage has several quaint names referring to its way of producing aerial offset plants from its leaf axils. These may take root when the mother stem reclines.

William Frazer Tolmie arrived at Fort Vancouver in 1833, a 21-year-old Scot fresh out of medical school and into the employ of the Hudson's Bay Company. The same year, at his suggestion, the Company established there the Northwest's first lending library. In September while waiting for a ship north out of Fort Nisqually he set off to collect alpine plants from Mt. Rainier. Ankle-deep in fresh snow on a precipice directly facing the mountain (more likely Mt. Pleasant than the present Tolmie Peak) he dropped any notion of scaling Rainier. No white man had seen it so close. He remained in the region all his life, a Company physician and later a supervisor. His son became Premier of British Columbia. Like many early naturalists, he chose to be an M.D. because it was the standard way of being a biologist; botany, zoology, physiology, and medicine were all just part of natural science.

Lupines

Lupinus spp. (lu-**pie**-nus: the Roman term). Flowers blue to purple (sometimes white), pealike, small (½"), many, in several ± conical racemes; calyx 2-lobed; pods hairy; leaves mostly basal on long leafstalks, palmately 5–9+-compound; leaflets center-folded. Fabaceae (Legume family).

Broadleaf lupine, *L. latifolius** (lat-if-**oh**-lius: broad leaf). Plant bushy, 1–3', woody-based. Subalpine, profusely abundant. Color p 133. Illustrated at left.

Dwarf lupine, *L. lepidus lobbii** (**lep**-id-us: charming; **lobb**-ee-eye: after Wm. Lobb). Plant dwarfed, semi-prostrate, the leafstalks and flower stems radiating horizontally but the racemes ± erect; leaves 1" diam. Alpine gravels and tundra. Color p 135.

Broadleaf lupine in bloom paints our bluest subalpine slopes—you can literally see it a mile off. A bumblebee in search of lupine nectar might be overwhelmed by too many choices, so the lupines help her out: the upper petal has a pair of white spots that serve as nectar guides. As a blossom ages, the spots turn magenta. Bees learn to skip those, since their nectar is often depleted. This efficiency benefits both bee and flower, by taking stale pollen out of circulation.

Both of these species were important survivors and colonizers on post-eruption Mt. St. Helens, but dwarf lupines came first—many bloomed all alone on barren areas of ash, and provided striking photos. Both species are nitrogen-fixing legumes. Both quickly send taproots to draw water from at least 10" down, and both have leaf adaptations to minimize water loss when it gets hot and dry. Broadleaf lupine draws its leaves up into a cone shape; in so doing it sacrifices much of its ability to photosynthesize on the hottest days. In contrast, dwarf lupine leaves are covered with shiny silky hairs that reflect back some of the intense light, and hold some of the drying wind away from the leaf surface. They were able to photosynthesize at temperatures up to 104°, while broadleaf lupine gave up at around 86°; botanist Jeff Braatne found this to be the key difference. Broadleaf lupines did better after more vegetation was in place to temper the heat. Dwarf lupine also turns its leaves to face

---

* *L. lepidus lobbii* is treated as *L. sellulus* in PLANTS and as *L. lyallii* in *Flora of the Olympic Peninsula*. The silky-hairy form illustrated above is subspecies *subalpinus*, variously placed in either *L. latifolius* or *L. arcticus*.

---

the morning and evening sun, maximizing photosynthesis at cooler times of day, and keeps its leaves green through winter, making the most of early- and late-season sun. Patches of it on the ash expanded each year. Individuals died after a few years, leaving a mound of improved soil that facilitated establishment of a new round of immigrants. But the patches were too small and far apart to constitute a major nitrogen source for the blast zone as a whole.

I photographed the lupine field on Old Snowy (page 133) in 1985, an outstanding year for flowers in the Goat Rocks, 41 miles downwind. It seemed that five years of snow had leached some fertilizing minerals out of the ash.

We don't know for sure why the Romans named these flowers after wolves. It may indicate an affinity they felt—remember their myth of a she-wolf as the mother, or at least the wetnurse, of Rome. Or they may have decried lupines so weedy as to seem predatory. ("Lupine" means "of wolves" or "wolflike" in English, too.)

Notice the way a little sphere of dew or rain is held on the centerpoint of each leaf.

Sweetpeas

Lathyrus spp. (**lath**-er-us: the Greek term). Petals 5, our varieties blue to violet (or sometimes albino), the upper one largest, the lower 2 partly fused, creased, enclosing the pistil and 10 stamens; calyx 5-toothed; stigma toothbrushlike—bristly on upper surface; fruit a pea pod; leaves pinnately 6–16-compound, often tendril-tipped; stems angled, climbing or (these species) ± erect, 4–32". Fabaceae (Legume family).

L. nevadensis (nev-a-**den**-sis: of the Sierra Nevada). Flowers 2–10; leaflets 8–10. Clearings up to timberline. Color p 135.

L. polyphyllus (poly-**fill**-us: many leaves). Flowers 5–15; leaflets 12–16. Drier open woods, lower W-side. Illustrated above.

Our two common sweetpeas rarely climb or clamber, unlike many of their congeners, so their tendrils are often short, straight and nonfunctional. Locoweeds and crazyweeds (below) lack tendrils altogether, the leaf terminating instead in a leaflet. Vetches (genus *Vicia*) are harder to tell from peas; their key difference is in the tiny pistil, which on a vetch is hairy near its tip on all sides—like a bottlebrush, as opposed to the toothbrush-shaped pistil on a pea.

Crazyweed

Oxytropis campestris (ox-**it**-ra-pis: sharp keel; cam-**pes**-tris: of fields). Also **stemless locoweed**. Flowers pealike, pale yellow (our variety), 8–12; calyx black-hairy; pod very thin-walled; leaves near-basal, densely silky-hairy, pinnately 13–25-compound; stalks several, 3–15". Alpine and arid meadows. Fabaceae (Legume family). Color p 135.

Crazyweeds and their close cousins the locoweeds, genus *Astragalus*, got their nasty names and ill reputes from their several rangeland species that sabotage the muscular coordination and vision of cattle that graze them in quantity. However, the many mountain goats that graze this sweet alpine variety don't appear any crazier than other mountain goats, and you'd think an uncoordinated purblind mountain goat wouldn't still be around.

Violets

Viola spp. (vie-**oh**-la: the Roman term). Petals 5, the lowest one largest, spurred behind, ± distinctively pigmented; sepals 5; stamens 5, short; flowers on long stalks; capsules split explosively to propel seeds; leaves mostly heart- to kidney-shaped. Violaceae (Violet family).

V. sempervirens (sem-per-**vee**-renz: ever green). Flowers yellow; leaves rather firm, evergreen, purple-flecked; flowers and leaves rising singly 1–4" from runners. Ubiquitous in W-side forest.

V. flettii (**flet**-ee-eye: after J. B. Flett). Flowers lavender to blue; leaves kidney-shaped, often purplish; stems clustered, 1–6". Only in Olympics; subalpine, among rocks. Color p 135.

V. adunca (a-**dunk**-a: hooked). Flowers lavender to blue; leaves heart-shaped to elliptical; stems clustered, 1–5". Scattered, esp in wet montane meadows. Illustrated at right.

V. glabella (gla-**bel**-a: smooth). Flowers yellow; several flowers and leaves borne from the upper third of each 4–12" stem. Widespread, open forest and subalpine meadow.

Our yellow violets bloom soon after the retreat of snow, often so early and chilly that the necessary pollinators are not yet on the wing. Violets respond by producing a second kind of flowers ("cleistogamous," meaning "closed marriage"): greenish, low and inconspicuous, and able to pollinate themselves without ever opening, for sure-fire seed production.

Monkshood

Aconitum columbianum (ac-o-**nigh**-tum: the Greek term; co-lum-be-**ay**-num: of the Columbia River). Sepals 5, petal-like, blue-purple (rarely greenish or albino), the upper one hooding, helmetlike; true petals apparently two, smaller, hidden under hood; flowers ¾–1½" tall, in an open raceme atop the 1–6' stem; leaves 2–5" diam, palmately deeply incised. Moist sites, mainly E of Cas Crest. Ranunculaceae (Buttercup family). Color p 133.

Most blue irregular flowers are bumble bee-pollinated. Monkshood's odd-shaped flower excludes from its nectary all insects except highly motivated, intelligent bumble bees, whose advantage to the plant is their fidelity; having been once well rewarded with monkshood nectar, they will visit only monkshoods, whose pollen will then not be squandered among a haphazard sequence of flower species. Monkshood is regarded as toxic to humans and stock; but one study found lots of it in elk scats in the the Blue Mountains.

Larkspurs

Delphinium spp. (del-**fin**-ium: the Greek term, from "dolphin"). Flowers deep blue to violet, ¾–1¼" diam; sepals 5, petal-like, spreading, the upper one with a long nectar-bearing spur behind; petals 4, the upper 2 spurred (within the sepal spur), often much paler; leaves 2–5" diam, narrowly palmately lobed and/or compound. Ranunculaceae (Buttercup family).

Menzies larkspur, *D. menziesii* (men-**zee**-zee-eye: after A. Menzies, p 97). 6–20" tall; root tuberlike. Low W-side clearings. Color p 134.

Rockslide larkspur, *D. glareosum* (glare-ee-**oh**-sum: on gravel). 6–12"; leaves mostly basal, ± fleshy. Alp/subalpine rock crevices. Illustrated at right.

Other Northwest Larkspur species may be much taller and may have smaller, narrower, or paler flowers, but all share the structure—a long-spurred upper sepal and two unlike pairs of petals at the flower's center. All are poisonous if grazed in quantity. The seeds have for millennia been ground up to poison lice.

Herbs: irregular dicots

These typically have 5 sepals and 5, 10, 15 or more stamens in addition to their 5 petals or corolla lobes (fused petals); the female parts aren't in fives. Also included, on pages 220–25, are flowers with just one set of conspicuous flower parts in fives—either petals or sepals but not both, and not the stamens. These variables tend to reveal family relations. The rose family mostly has 15 or 20 stamens; the phlox family has 5; primroses have 2 sepals and parsleys have none.

If you have a 5-petaled flower that you can't locate here, try these leads: shrubs include many 5-petaled genera; if they're very low and barely recognizable as subshrubs, they'll be with the shrubs on pages 106–14 if the genus as a whole is evergreen. Irregular dicots, pages 192–201, mostly have 5 corolla lobes, but these lobes are very unlike each other. Composites, p 182–89, have tight heads of tiny florets which are technically 5-parted, and sometimes visibly so; wall lettuce, p 189, has 5 rays per flower head. Gentian and starflower, p 233, have 5 petals in many of their blossoms, but usually have 6 or 7 on at least as many others in the vicinity.

Herbs: 5 fused petals, 5 stamens

Large-Flowered Collomia

Collomia grandiflora (col-**oh**-mia: glue—; **grand**-if-lor-a: large flower). Corolla trumpet-shaped, ¾–1¼", light salmon-orange to ± white; stamens sometimes blue-tipped, often very unequal in length (split the corolla to see); flowers subtended by green bracts, in a single head, plus sometimes a few flowers in lower leaf axils; seeds gluey when moistened; leaves linear, 1–3"; plants annual, 8–40" tall. Dry, ± sunny spots at low to mid elevs. Polemoniaceae (Phlox family). Illustrated at right.

Alpine Collomia

Collomia debilis (**deb**-il-iss: weak). Corolla trumpet-shaped, ½–1", lavender-streaked or white to pink; stamens sometimes blue-tipped; each flower subtended by a green bract; leaves of our varieties 3–7-lobed; typically forming dense cushions 2–3" deep. Alpine. Polemoniaceae (Phlox family). Color p 137.

Spreading Phlox

Phlox diffusa (flocks: a Greek flower, meaning "flame"; dif-**you**-sa: spreading). Corolla white, pink, pale blue, or variously violet, ¾" diam, with 4–6 flat-spreading lobes at the end of a straight tube; pistil 3-tipped; flowers single on numerous leafy stems; leaves linear, pointed, ¾"; compact mats 2–4" thick. Dry ground, esp alpine but also at all elevs E Cas. Polemoniaceae (Phlox family). Color p 137.

High ridges colonized by phlox fail to retain much soil or snow; both blow away. Without a snow blanket through winter, plants there are exposed to ferocious drying winds, and to hundreds of freezing/thawing cycles; the plants withstand frost action whose powers of pulverization are amply displayed on nearby rocks. Though the rocks continually break up, their particles tend to blow away as they reach soil size, preventing soil from accumulating.

Spreading phlox exemplifies the "cushion" form adapted to this extreme environment. The smooth convex surface eases the wind on over with a minimum of resistance, and even more so when the plant contours itself in the lee of a large rock or a crevice between rocks. The tiny, crammed leaves live in a pocket of calm partly of their own making, and there they trap windblown particles that will slowly become a mound of soil. Mt. St. Helens provided a million little exhibits of this phenomenon. Miles downwind, an inch-thick blanket of ash was largely incorporated into the top soil layer within five years, but from the alpine ridges it was completely removed by wind except for what lay in deep crevices — or in sharply contrasting gray aureoles around the cushion plants.

Cushion plants also need very long (8–15') taproots. Though the ridgetops receive at least their share of our mountains' heavy snowfall, sweeping winds and a coarse rock substrate allow little of it to stay there. In effect, alpine habitats are arid.

Skyrocket

Ipomopsis aggregata* (ip-a-**mop**-sis: like morning-glory; ag-reg-**ay**-ta: clustered). Also **scarlet gilia**. Corolla scarlet, trumpet-shaped, the slightly flaring tube twice as long (½–1¼") as the slightly recurved, pointed lobes; stamens borne near mouth of tube; leaves much-dissected, lobes linear; stems to 3', many-flowered, or dwarfed (4") at high elevs. Dry clearings near and E of Cas Cr. Polemoniaceae (Phlox family). Color p 138.

---

*Ipomopsis was formerly included in genus *Gilia.*

The long tubular corolla and bright red color are both clues that this flower evolved with hummingbirds as pollinators. Most insects cannot see red, but hummers crave it.

Sky-Pilots

Polemonium (pol-em-**oh**-nium: the Greek term. Also **Jacob's-ladders**. Corolla light blue with yellow center, ½" long; leaves pinnately compound, mostly basal; leaflets 21–27; stems several, few-flowered, 4–10" (subalpine) or 10–20" (mid-elev); plants often skunky-smelling. Common around subalpine tree clumps and outcrops. Polemoniaceae (Phlox family).

P. pulcherrimum (pool-**ker**-im-um: most beautiful). Flowers wider than long, not tightly clustered; leaflets at least ¼". Also at mid elevs. Illustrated.

P. elegans (**el**-eg-anz: elegant). Flowers longer than wide, in a round cluster; leaflets crowded, scarcely ¼" (smaller than petals). WA. Color p 137.

Like most flowers, sky-pilots produce a sweet flowery fragrance in their nectaries to attract nectar-feeding insects as pollinators. In many individuals, however, this is drowned out by a skunky aroma on sepals and bracts below the flowers. A researcher of a Rocky-Mountain sky-pilot thinks the foul smell serves to repel ants; she smells it only in plants at elevations where ants abound. Unlike bees and hover flies (good pollinators) nectar-feeding ants slip right past the pollen-bearing stamens on their way to robbing the nectary, and often also destroy the pistil in the process. See if you can find both skunky and sweet-smelling sky-pilots in our mountains, and any pattern of either ant presence or elevation separating them.

Douglasia

Douglasia laevigata (da-**glass**-ia: after David Douglas, p 18; lee-vig-**ay**-ta: smooth). Corolla crimson to deep pink; ½" diam, lobes round-tipped, stamens barely appearing at the narrow throat where the lobes spread at right angles from the narrow tube; flowers mostly 2–4 on leafless branched stalks; leaves ± linear, ½"; in compact mats 2–3" thick. Alpine, esp in Olys; or on Columbia Gorge bluffs. Primulaceae (Primrose Family). Color p 137.

Douglasia resembles and often associates with a commoner cushion plant, spreading phlox (page 203). To distinguish them, note that Douglasia's deeper-red flowers are on branched, leafless stalks, and each have a single, unparted stigma.

Shooting Stars

Dodecatheon spp. (doh-de-**cayth**-ee-on: twelve gods). Corolla and calyx bent sharply back (e.g., upward), ½–1" long, fused "collar" portion very short; stamens tightly clasping the pistil, or just slightly spreading; flowers several, many facing down (i.e., the petals up) but all erect in fruit (a capsule); leaves basal on ± long leafstalks; stem 8–20". Subalpine streamsides and wet meadows. Primulaceae (Primrose family).

D. pulchellum (pool-**kel**-um: beautiful). Petals 5, pink with yellow collar and dark stamens. Illustrated above.

D. jeffreyi (jef-ree-eye: after John Jeffrey, below). Petals usually 5, deep pink with white collar. Locally abundant. Color p 138.

D. dentatum (den-**tay**-tum: toothed). Petals white with magenta collar and stamen base; leaves broadly oval, ± toothed. Wet cliffs. Uncommon. Illustrated at right.

D. alpinum (al-**pie**-num: alpine). Petals 4, pink. OR Cas, commoner S. Illustrated left.

The kind of flower shape we call "shooting stars" and botanists call "reflexed" is also common in the nightshade family, which includes tomato and potato plants. Functionally, these flowers are all "buzz pollinated." That means the stamens are designed to spew pollen only in response to furious vibration. Bumble bees visiting the flowers stay in place for a moment, vibrate their wings, and are rewarded with a shower of pollen. For the plant, there is efficiency in attracting faithful bumblebees, which on any given day visit one species of flower over and over again, and thus don't waste the flower's pollen by losing it on another kind of flower—even though the bumble bee is also smart enough to eat all the pollen she can. Some other flowers (page 198) accomplish the same thing with robust, irregular flower shapes that only a bumble bee can unlock.

John Jeffrey was hired for plant hunting on the far edge of the New World by a club of Scottish gentlemen called the Oregon Association. He explored the Okanogan, Similkameen, Fraser, Willamette, and Umpqua drainages in 1851-53, arriving overland from Hudson's Bay. He sent his last shipment of plants from San Francisco at the height of the Gold Rush, and disappeared.

Phacelias

Phacelia spp. (fa-**see**-lia: bundle, referring to the dense inflorescence). Flowers crowded, bristling with stamens about twice as long as corollas; calyx hairy; leaves gray-silky-coated. Hydrophyllaceae (Waterleaf family).

Silky phacelia, *P. sericea sericea* (ser-**iss**-ia: silky). Flowers purple (to blue or white) in a dense round spike; stamens pale-tipped; leaves deeply pinnately lobed, mostly basal, cushion-forming; stem 4–10". In WA, mainly alpine. Color p 137.

Silverleaf phacelia, *P. hastata compacta* (hass-**tay**-ta: halberd-shaped, referring to the pair of leaf lobes). Flowers drab whitish (rarely lavender); leaves narrow elliptical, often with a pair of small lobes or leaflets at the base; this variety rarely over 5" tall. Dry rocky alpine sites, OR and S WA Cas. Color p 137.

Each of our several *Phacelia* species has alpine (compact) and mid-elevation (leggy) varieties. The silky is most striking, with ornate leaves and a compact, colorful inflorescence. The unrelated but remarkably similar-looking cutleaf kittentails (page 227) grows on alpine gravels in the Olympics.

Waterleaves

Hydrophyllum spp. (hydro-**fill**-um: water leaf). Flowers in compact heads bristling with black-tipped stamens twice as long as the ⅜" corollas; calyx hairy; leaves pinnate, leaflets 5–11. Hydrophyllaceae (Waterleaf family).

H. fendleri (**fend**-ler-eye: after August Fendler). Flowers white, occasionally purple-tinged; leaflets toothed and often cleft, leaves up to 12 × 6", with soft white hair underneath; plant 1–2". Lush thickets, avalanche basins, mid elevs to subalpine.

H. capitatum (cap-it-**ay**-tum: flowers in heads). Flowers lavender to white, in spherical head; leaflets ± lobed, leaves basal, much taller (4–10") than the flower stalk (1–3") exc in a Columbia Gorge variety with 2–8" stalks and short leaves. Widespread E of Cas Crest. Color p 138.

Dogbanes

Apocynum spp. (a-**pos**-in-um: away dog!). Flowers bell-shaped, clustered; leaves opposite; stems milky-juiced, smooth, often reddish, much branched (resembling a shrub); seeds cottony-tufted, in paired long, slender pods. Scattered, commoner at low elevs. Apocynaceae (Dogbane family).

Spreading dogbane, *A. androsaemifolium* (an-dro-**see**-mif-**oh**-lium: leaves resembling *Androsaemum*). Flowers pink, fragrant, ¼–⅜", with flaring lobes; seed pods 3–6"; leaves oval, ± glossy above, pale beneath, spreading flat or drooping; plants 1–2'. Dry but often ± shady sites. Color p 138.

Indian-hemp, *A. cannabinum* (can-a-**by**-num: hemp—). Flowers tiny, whitish, with nearly straight lobes; seed pods 5–7"; leaves narrow elliptical, yellow-green, ascending; plants 1½–4½'. Usually in sun; weedy on disturbed ground.

Indian-hemp was one of the best sources of plant fiber available to the Indians. Where none could be found, spreading dogbane was sometimes substituted. Dogbane attracts a wide assortment of butterflies and bees. To humans and perhaps also to dogs, both species are purgative, diuretic, and may cause heart irregularities.

Bluebells

Mertensia paniculata (mer-**ten**-zia: after Franz K. Mertens, p 111; pa-nic-you-**lay**-ta: flowers in panicles). Also **lungwort**. Corolla blue, pink-tinged at first, short-lobed, narrowly bell-shaped, pendent, ½–¾": stem leaves pointed-elliptical, basal leaves oval on long leafstalks, both often with bluish bloom; plants many-flowered, robust, 1½–5'. Streamsides or moist clearings, mainly E-sides. Boraginaceae (Borage family). Color p 138.

Bellflower

Campanula rotundifolia (cam-**pan**-you-la: small bell; rotund-if-**oh**-lia: round leaf). Also **Scottish-bluebells, harebell**. Corolla pale blue, bell-shaped, ± pendent by maturity, ¾–1¼"; pistil 3-forked; stem leaves linear; basal leaves round to heart-shaped on long leafstalks, often withering by maturity; plants slender, 6–30". Open woods to alpine. Campanulaceae (Harebell family). Color p 138.

Buckbean

Menyanthes trifoliata (men-**yanth**-eez: monthly flower; try-fo-lee-**ay**-ta: 3-leaved). Corolla white (often purple-tinged) with hairy-faced flat-spreading lobes (¼–½") on a straight tube (¼–½"); stamens purple-tipped; flowers in a ± erect, columnar raceme; three leaflets elliptical, 2–5"; stems and leafstalks usually ± prostrate and submerged; from rhizomes. Bogs and ponds. Menyanthaceae (Buckbean family). Color p 139.

Herbs: 5 fused petals, 5 stamens *207*

Sibbaldia

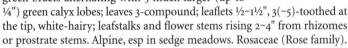

Sibbaldia procumbens (sib-
ahl-dia: after Sir Robert Sib-
bald; pro-**cum**-benz: prostrate).
Petals tiny, yellow, sitting on top of 5 slightly longer
green bracts alternating with 5 much larger (up to
¼") green calyx lobes; leaves 3-compound; leaflets ½–1½", 3(–5)-toothed at
the tip, white-hairy; leafstalks and flower stems rising 2–4" from rhizomes
or prostrate stems. Alpine, esp in sedge meadows. Rosaceae (Rose family).

Grass-of-Parnassus

Parnassia fimbriata (par-**nas**-ia: after Mt. Parnassus, a poetic allusion to
mountains in general; fim-bree-**ay**-ta: fringed). Petals white, ¼–½", long-
fringed near the base; flower in late summer, single on a 6–16" stalk; leaves
heart-shaped, basal on long leafstalks, plus one much smaller leaf sessile halfway up stem. Subalpine wet meadows and streambanks.
Parnassiaceae (Parnassia family, which was recently split
out from the saxifrage family). Color p 140.

Mitreworts

Mitella spp. (my-**tel**-a: mitre). Also **bishop's caps.** Petals
branched, threadlike, sticking out between the
white calyx lobes; flowers 10–20 along a 6–14"
stalk; leaves ± kidney-shaped, scalloped to
toothed, basal, on long hairy leafstalks. Moist
subalpine forest or meadow. Saxifragaceae
(Saxifrage family).

M. breweri (**brew**-er-eye: after Wm. Brewer).
Petals ± yellow-green, 5–9-branched;
calyx saucer-shaped. Illustrated above.

M. trifida (**trif**-id-a; 3-forked). Petals
white or purplish, 3-branched; calyx bell-
shaped. Illustrated at right.

It's the seed capsule that looks like a mitre—
a bishop's tall, deeply cleft hat.

Fringecup

Tellima grandiflora (**tel**-im-a: anagram of *Mitella*; grand-if-**lor**-a: large flower). Petals white, often aging deep pink, slender with many threadlike branches, reflexed around the lip of the jar-shaped, greenish white calyx; flowers 12–25 along one side of a 16–40" stalk; leaves ± kidney-shaped, shallowly lobed and toothed, mostly basal, on long hairy leafstalks. Moist forest or sometimes meadow. Saxifragaceae. Color p 140.

The Saxifrage family resemblance is so strong that it seems the same few features are just reshuffled from genus to genus. Some members, like *Mitella* and *Tellima*, have reshuffled names. *Tiarella* and *Tolmiea* are also typical, with racemes of small whitish flowers above toothed, roundish basal leaves in shady damp habitats.

Tiarella

Tiarella trifoliata (tee-ar-**el**-a: crownlet; try-fo-lee-**ay**-ta: 3-leaved). Flowers tiny, white, many, in a sparse raceme on an 8–16" stalk; petals threadlike, unbranched, less visible than the stamens; ovary and subsequent capsule of 2 very unequal sides; leaves mostly basal on short leafstalks, hairy, toothed, from 3-lobed to 3-compound and incised, 2–4". Abundant in dense forest. Saxifragaceae. Color p 140.

This inconspicuous but abundant forest flower has been saddled with more than its share of fluffy names—foamflower, laceflower, coolwort, false-mitrewort—without the consensus that would make any one name truly common. Why not stick with tiarella? It's a diminutive of "tiara"—more a household word than "mitre" or "wort." The original tiara was a mini-turban in ancient Persia.

For their part, taxonomists until recently saddled the plant with three different species names, distinguished by whether the leaves are lobed, compound, or both. Field research on the three types failed to turn up any clear genetic, geographic, or ecological boundaries among them, so they were reduced to varieties. Scientific Latin is an imperfect antidote to confusion over synonymous names, since Latin names frequently changed with new research.

By midsummer, many tiarella leaves display pale curlicues, the tracks of leaf-miner larvae (actually quite a few unrelated insects). Look closely and you'll see the larva at the front end of the track.

Brook Saxifrage

*Saxifraga nelsoniana** (sac-**sif**-ra-ga: rock breaker).
Petals white, elliptical; stamens almost as long as petals;
flowers ⅜" diam, several, in a loose round-topped
raceme; stem 6–12", with fine wool near the top;
leaves kidney-shaped, 1–3", with large, even
teeth, slightly fleshy, basal on 4–8" leafstalks. Wet
places, esp subalpine. Saxifragaceae. Color p 140.

Alpine Saxifrage

Saxifraga tolmiei (**tole**-me-eye: after William Tolmie,
p 197). Petals white; stamens white, flattened, red-
tipped; flowers ⅜" diam, 1–4, on nearly leafless 2–4"
stems; leaves fleshy (about as thick as wide), linear,
¼–½" long, many, densely matted. Among rocks,
alp/subalpine. Saxifragaceae. Color p 140.

This cute little plant has tubby, succulent leaves resembling stonecrop. It earns its name "rock-breaker," pioneering in rock crevices
of alpine talus where release from snow is too brief (annually) and
too recent (geologically) for a mycorrhizal fungus community to
have developed. It may be virtually the only plant on a nearly
barren gravel bed, or it may join other scarcely mycorrhizal organisms like woodrushes, sedges,
mosses, and lichens.

Leatherleaf Saxifrage

Leptarrhena pyrolifolia (lep-ta-
ree-na: slender anthers; pyro-lif-**oh**-lia:
pyrola leaf). Petals white, minute; flowers in a tight cluster; seed
pods red, paired within flattish clusters; stem dark red, 8–18"; leaves
toothed, rounded-elliptic, thick, crinkly-leathery, shiny bright
green, 1–3", basal, plus one to three much smaller ones clasping
stem. Alp/subalpine streambanks and wet gravels. Saxifragaceae.

When massed along rocky streambanks, the maroon
seed-heads and stems can be recognized from hundreds of yards away.

---

*The first edition followed *Flora of the PNW* in calling this Dotted Saxifrage,
S. punctata. Both names stand corrected. *Not* having dots is one of the key
ways to distinguish this species from the similar *S. odontoloma*.

Stonecrop

Sedum spp. (**see**-dum: the Roman term, derived from "sitting"). Petals yellow, pointed, ¼–⅜"; flowers several, in ± compact broad-topped clusters; seedpod 5-celled, starlike; leaves thick, fleshy, crammed together, often turning red; plants low (3–8"), spreading by rhizomes and/or runners. Dry rocky places. Crassulaceae (Stonecrop family).

Spreading stonecrop, *S. divergens* (di-**ver**-jenz: spreading) Leaves opposite; star-shaped seed head has spreading points. Illustrated at right.

Lanceleaf stonecrop, *S. lanceolatum* (lan-see-o-**lay**-tum: lance—). Leaves alternate, ± tubular. Color p 141.

Oregon stonecrop, *S. oreganum.* Leaves alternate, flattened oval, up to 1". Mainly W-side.

Creamy stonecrop, *S. oregonense.* Flowers cream yellow; leaves bluish, alternate, flattened, some notch-tipped, most in basal rosettes, many over 1" long and ½" wide. Mid elevs, OR. Illustrated at left.

Fat succulent leaves, like cactus stems, maximize the volume to surface-area ratio, and hence the ratio of water capacity to water loss through transpiration. Even with leaves for storage tanks, stonecrops grow only while water is available, and store water mainly to subsidize flowering and fruiting. Water-filled leaves might be vulnerable to frost damage, but stonecrops (and the succulent alpine saxifrage, facing page) resist freezing and do very well in the alpine zone. You can squeeze liquid water out of stonecrop leaves at temperatures that will freeze it immediately.

Roseroot

*Sedum integrifolium** (in-teg-rif-**oh**-lium: untoothed leaf). Also **king's crown, midsummer-men.** Petals deep red, ⅛"; stamens protruding; seed capsules five per flower, deep red; flowers several, crowded, male and female flowers on separate plants; leaves pale green, rubbery; stems 2–8", unbranched, in clumps, from rhizomes. Alp/subalpine. Crassulaceae (Stonecrop family). Color p 141.

---

*Formerly *S. roseum*; some authors separate it as *Rhodiola integrifolia.* If not split, genus *Sedum* has over 400 species.

Wood-Sorrel

Oxalis oregana (ox-**al**-iss: the Greek term, from "sharp"; or-eg-**ay**-na; of Oregon). Petals white, usually with fine red veins; flowers single, ¾–1½" diam; leaves cloverlike, of 3 leaflets, folding down at night and some other times; stems and leafstalks 4–7", from rhizomes. W-side up to 4,000,' typically in moist forests. Oxalidaceae (Wood-sorrel family). Color p 141.

Forest-floor herbs typically hold their leaves horizontal to maximize absorption of scarce sunlight. Wood-sorrel does this, but then at times creases them sharply downward, taking about six minutes to fold up and thirty minutes to flatten again. It responds this way to a puzzling variety of stimuli. When a patch of intense sunlight comes along, folding up conserves moisture and avoids sunscorch. At night the reason may be similar; there is no photosynthesis to be lost by closing up shop, and there is at least a small amount of evaporation to be curtailed. However, folding in the rain has to have a different reason—perhaps to reduce raindrop impact.

Wood-sorrel makes good mouth-entertainment. Though unrelated to European garden sorrels, genus *Rumex*, it tastes like them. All get their tartness from mildly toxic oxalic acid. Don't overdose.

Sandworts

Arenaria and *Minuartia* spp. (air-en-**air**-ee-a: sand—; min-oo-**art**-ia: after Juan Minuart.). Petals white, ¼–½"; sepals scarcely ¼", blunt (pointed in some other sandworts); styles usually 3; leaves linear, mat-forming; stem 2–6". Alp/subalpine gravels and crevices. Caryophyllaceae (Pink family).

Three-leaved sandwort, *A. capillaris* (cap-il-**air**-iss: hairleaved). Basal leaves ¾–1¼", dense; stem leaves ⅜–¾", opposite, 4–10 per stem; capsule splits six ways. Also in steppes E of Cas. Illustrated at right.

Arctic sandwort, *M. obtusiloba** (ob-too-si-**lo**-ba: blunt-lobed). Leaves ¼", dense, on prostrate stems; capsule splits three ways. Illustrated below.

Arenaria capillaris of the mountains doesn't look much like *Arenaria melanocephala* of the seashore—a bird. The Rules prohibit duplicating genus names only within the same kingdom.

---

*Formerly included in *Arenaria*.

Field Chickweed

Cerastium arvense (ser-**ast**-ium: horn—; ar-**ven**-see: of fields). Petals white, each with two round lobes; styles usually 5; calyx 5-lobed; flowers 3–8 per stem; leaves ± linear, ½–1¼", opposite or basal; entire plant downy. Various habitats; ours mostly alp/subalpine with low compact foliage and stems shorter than 8". Caryophyllaceae (Pink family). Color p 140.

White Catchfly

Silene parryi (sigh-**lee**-nee: a Greek elf?; **pair**-ee-eye: after Chas. Parry). Petals white or lavender-tinged, each deeply 4-lobed, with 2 more small lobes on the throat—a seeming inner whorl of 10 petals; calyx 5-lobed, hairy; leaves narrowly elliptical, 1–3", 2 or 3 pairs opposite, the rest basal; stem 6–15". Mainly subalpine, Olys and N Cas. Caryophyllaceae. Color p 139. Illus. at right.

Moss-Campion

Silene acaulis (ay-**caw**-lis: stalkless). Also **moss pink, cushion pink, carpet pink**. Petals pink (occasionally to white), separate though they form an apparent tube, bent 90° to spread flat; styles and/or stamens often protruding; styles usually 3; calyx shallowly 5-lobed; leaves linear, pointed, thick, crowded, to ½"; mosslike mats 2" thick. Alpine. Caryophyllaceae. Color p 139.

This genus and the two preceding are in the Pink family, so called not because the petals are pink but because they are pinked, or notched at the tip. Pinked petals do run in the family, but other family traits such as ten stamens and unfused petals are more reliable, and they distinguish moss-campion from phlox and douglasia. (See page 203 on cushion plants.)

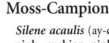

Yerba de Selva

Whipplea modesta (**whip**-lia: after A. W. Whipple). Also **whipplevine**. Flowers tiny (¼"), in a fluffy head; petals white, becoming greenish, sticking out flat between the calyx lobes; leaves opposite, often persistent, ½–1", elliptical, vaguely toothed, 3-veined; stem rising 1–6" from leafy woody runners. Locally abundant in dry W-side forest, C and S OR, and disjunct in Olys. Hydrangeaceae (Hydrangea family). Color p 141.

Yerba de selva means "forest herb" in Spanish.

Stinky Bob

Geranium robertianum (jer-**ay**-nium: crane—; robber-tee-**ay**-num: obscure reference to some damned Robert). Also **herb robert**. Flowers ½" diam; pink petals spread flat; from a tubular base enclosed in sepals; usually 2 flowers per stem; sepals and stems have straight white hairs; stems ± red-tinged; whole plant reddens after going to seed; leaves twice dissected, parsleylike, with rank peanut butter odor (varying from slight to strong) when crushed. Annual. W-side forest up to 2,000', esp Olympics and Col Gorge. Geraniaceae.

The name Stinky Bob may not have seen print until now, but all the botanists I know use it for this weed. They hate it. Some suspect it of poisoning the soil against its competitors (a strategy used by some geraniums). Don't be taken in by its demure, even charming, appearance. It invades deeper into wilderness, and into deeper shade, than its superweed forebears—Scotch broom, gorse, English ivy, English holly, and Himalayan and evergreen blackberries. Like them (with the possible exception of blackberry) it is of Northern European origin. Even though it dies off every winter and seeds itself from scratch every spring, Bob is the one weed (so far) that can take over an undisturbed Northwest forest herb layer.

Weeds

We are very lucky that the plant communities in our mountain wilderness are better than 99% native. Few areas in the world are so pure. Non-native weeds have devastated huge portions of the West's open rangeland. But once we leave roads and clearcuts behind in our mountains, the non-natives we see—wall lettuce, stinky Bob, clover, thistles, buttercups, several grasses—are concentrated along major trails and in old horse pastures, and usually outnumbered even there. Even on the wide open field of the St. Helens blast zone, non-natives didn't colonize as strongly as natives, though they certainly made a showing. Strictly nonscientifically, I would venture to say that our plant communities, as long as they aren't cleared, are pretty robust at resisting unfriendly takeovers. But new arrivals may wear their resistance down.

Animals and fungi can be weeds, too. Northwesterners know nutria, starlings, and garden slugs, but these macrofauna rarely reach our mountain fastnesses either. Insect pests and fungal diseases are

St.-John's-Wort

Hypericum formosum* (hi-**per**-ic-um: the Greek term, meaning "under heath"; for-**mo**-sum: beautiful). Flowers deep yellow, orange in bud, many; stamens showy, as long (¾–1½") as the petals; capsule 3-celled; leaves opposite, oval, ± clasping-based; stems many, 4–30". Uncommon; wet thickets, esp low subalp. Hypericaceae (St. John's wort family). Color p 141.

The Old-World St.-John's-wort, *H. perforatum*, was gathered as a spell for St. John's Eve, June 23. It's now an abundant roadside weed in dry parts of the Northwest, and a popular herbal treatment for temporary depression. It has been proven effective, but as with other herbals the dosage is poorly known and side effects are a concern. (After all, most prescription drugs originated as herbal medicines; the main difference between the two as classes of medicines is that prescription medicines have been rigorously tested.) *H. formosum* seems to have lesser amounts of similar active ingredients, but please don't pick it, since *H. perforatum* is less beautiful and more available as well as more potent.

---

*PLANTS separates our varieties as a species, *H. scouleri*.

---

scarier; many wouldn't pause even a minute at a wilderness boundary.

Competition from non-natives is a factor in the majority of species extinctions. On the whole, invasives may sound less dramatically apocalyptic than global warming, but they rank among the biosphere's five most daunting problems, and may be the least recognized. For example, it would be hard to convince many senators of the fact that free trade in unprocessed logs and wood chips is a deranged policy, risking introduction of pests or diseases whose potential for economic devastation alone makes the near-term profits look like chump change.

Since they are by definition opportunistic, weeds are expected to take advantage of any openings created by rapid climate change. Since they tend to be heavy nitrogen consumers (whereas natives are more efficient and conservative) the weed problem is expected to worsen with continued global nitrogen deposition—the airborne and waterborne spread of agriculture fertilizers.

Goatsbeard

Aruncus dioicus* (a-**runk**-us: beard of goat; die-**oy**-cus: "two houses," i.e., with male and female flowers on different plants). Flowers cream white, minute, in large (to 14") stringy panicles, the males (on separate plants) much fluffier than the females, since the 15–20 stamens are the largest flower part; leaves twice- or thrice-compound, to 20", leaflets fine-toothed, long-pointed oval, 3–6"; plant 3–6', easily mistaken for a shrub. Moist thickets up to low subalpine. Rosaceae (Rose family). Color p 142.

Goatsbeard roots and leaves made medicine for sores and sore throats among the Northwest tribes.

Partridgefoot

Luetkea pectinata (**loot**-key-a: after Count Lütke, p 111; pec-tin-**ay**-ta: cockscomb—, referring to leaf shape). Flowers white to cream, ¼" diam, in a compact raceme on a± woody 3–6" stem; leaves ± persistent, finely dissected into around 9 narrow lobes, mostly basal from runners or rhizomes; often carpet-forming. Abundant, subalpine and lower alpine. Rosaceae. Color p 140.

Partridgefoot surrounds many of the sunken beds of black alpine sedge that emerge from late-melting snowbeds, indicating a need for a slightly longer snow-free season than the sedge, or an intolerance for standing in water for a few days as the sedge does, or both. Similarly, on raw deglaciated gravel, it needs a slightly longer season than alpine saxifrage.

Purple Avens

Geum triflorum (**jee**-um: the Roman term; try-**flor**-um: three-flowered). Also **prairie smoke, old-man's-whiskers**. Flowers usually pendent, in threes, dull reddish, 1" long, vase-shaped, scarcely opening; petals yellow to pink, mostly hidden by the 5 reddish sepals and 5 bracts; seeds long-plumed; leaves mostly basal, finely cut (fernlike), hairy. Various habitats, esp alpine ridge gravels, where 4–8" tall. Rosaceae. Color p 141.

---

* Formerly *A. sylvester*.

Dwarf Raspberries

Rubus spp. (**roo**-bus: the Roman term). Petals ⅜" long, narrow; fruit of one to five glossy red one-seeded drupelets ¼" long; flower stems and toothed leaves rise 1–2" from ± woody runners. W-side forest, esp mid elevs. Rosaceae.

Strawberry bramble, *R. pedatus* (ped-**ay**-tus: 5-leafleted). Petals white; leaves 5-compound (rarely 3-compound, the lateral 2 not quite fully divided); runners smooth. Abundant in N Cas. Color p 139.

Dwarf bramble, *R. lasiococcus* (lazy-o-**coc**-us: shaggy berry). Leaves 3-lobed (sometimes 3-compound); runners smooth; ovary hairy.

Snow bramble, *R. nivalis* (niv-**ay**-lis: of snow). Petals usually pink; leaves ± heart-shaped, shallowly lobed (rarely 3-compound); runners fine-prickled. More common in OR, and at lower elevs.

At their best, these berries miniaturize the essence of raspberry flavor as perfectly as wild strawberries do the essence of strawberry. More often, the ones we sample are flat-tasting and hard, perhaps because small rodents beat us to the draw when they ripen. It's hard to see them as raspberries at all, though they're the right color, flavor, and type of fruit—an "aggregate" of "drupelets"—because the big drupelets are simply too few to form the cup shape we expect of a raspberry.

Wild Strawberries

Fragaria spp. (fra-**gair**-ia: the Roman term). Petals white to pinkish, nearly circular, ¼–½"; sepals apparently 10; stamens 20–25; berry up to ½" long; leaves 3-compound, toothed coarsely and ± evenly, on hairy leafstalks; 3–8" tall, from stolons. Forest openings up to 4,000'. Rosaceae.

F. vesca (**ves**-ca: thin). Most leaves minutely hairy on top, ± bulging between veins. Color p 139.

F. virginiana (vir-gin-ee-**ay**-na: of Virginia). Most leaves smooth and flat on top. Illustrated at left.

Close kin of these morsels are served in the most famous restaurants in France.

Cinquefoils

Potentilla spp. (po-ten-**til**-a: small but mighty).
Petals yellow, usually notch-tipped; 5 true sepals
alternating with 5 shorter bracts; leaves compound, leaflets 1–1½"; stem 4–12". Rosaceae.

Fanleaf cinquefoil, *P. flabellifolia* (fla-bel-if-**oh**-
lia: fan leaf). Leaves 3-compound, thin, coarse-
toothed. Subalpine meadow. Illustrated at right.

Varied-leaf cinquefoil, *P.
diversifolia* (div-er-sif-**oh**-lia:
varied leaf). Leaves 5-compound,
deeply toothed. Alpine.

One cinquefoil is easily overlooked, but a few thousand of them in the high-country ultraviolet can
take your breath away. Fanleaf cinquefoils are among
the earliest subalpine meadow flowers to bloom in
quantity, following close upon springbeauties and
glacier lilies, and preceding the lupine, valerian, and
bistort that typically swamp them a few weeks later.
Varied-leaf cinquefoil, equally common in the alpine
zone, is the common cinquefoil of the northeast Cascades and northern Rockies. Both *cinquefoil* (French for
"five-leaf") and *Potentilla* (medicinally potent) were
names cut out to fit European species, and don't fit ours.

Subalpine Buttercup

Ranunculus eschscholtzii * (ra-**nun**-cue-lus: froglet; ess-
sholt-zee-eye: after J. F. von Eschscholtz, p 174). Petals
glossy yellow; seeds in a tight conical head; leaves generally 3-lobed to compound, but extremely variable; stem
3–8", smooth. Subalpine meadow or scree, esp where
wet. Ranunculaceae (Buttercup family). Color p 138.

Buttercups are called *Ranunculi* ("littlest frogs")
for being small and green around the edges of ponds.
They are called buttercups for the peculiar waxy (cutinous) sheen
of their yellow petals—your first clue for telling buttercups from
cinquefoils (above). The surer clue is that buttercups lack the five
sepallike bracts (two, flanking sepal, illustrated at top of page).

---

* Our variety, *suksdorfii*, is treated as a full species by PLANTS but not FNA.

Columbine

Aquilegia formosa (ak-wil-ee-jia: the Roman term, debatably referring to water-bearing or to eagle claws; for-**mo**-sa: beautiful). Flowers nodding, several, the petal spurs and spreading ¾–1¼" petal-like sepals red, while the stamens and short, cuplike petal blades are yellow; leaves 9-compound with round-lobed leaflets, most basal on tall leafstalks; stems branching, 1–3'. Lush subalpine meadows to lower clearings. Ranunculaceae (Buttercup family). Color p 141.

The shape of columbine flowers is unmistakable, while the colors vary from species to species. The Colorado state flower is blue and white. A pale yellow Rocky Mountain columbine, *A. flavescens*, enters the northeast fringe of our range, where it is sometimes flushed with pink after messing around with our red species. Different columbines are interfertile and often grow together; they owe their separate identities to the fact that pollinators that go for red flowers are uninterested in blue flowers, and so forth. The red/yellow combination is preferred by hummingbirds, some bees, and this writer. Bees nip the bulbous spur-tip to get the nectar, and may also go around to the front door for pollen.

Herbs: 5 petals, 2 sepals

Springbeauty

Claytonia lanceolata (clay-**toe**-nia: after John Clayton; lan-see-o-**lay**-ta: narrowleaved). Petals ¼–½", white (rarely yellow, in N Cas) usually with fine pink stripes; stamens 5; stem leaves 2, opposite, ½–3", narrow-elliptical; stems 3–6", ± succulent, hollow, weak, several-flowered, often with one to four basal leaves; from a bulbous root. Meadows at all elevs, esp subalpine. Portulacaceae (Purslane family). Color p 142.

Springbeauty is a success story based on timing rather than brute size. It begins growing at its bulb tip in September, just when its neighbors are dying back. While snow insulates it for the next eight months, holding the soil close to freezing, the shoot inches up to the soil surface. Very few plants are active at such low temperatures; all are arctic/alpine specialists. Without the snow blanket it would be even colder, and growth would be impossible.

As soon as the snow melts away from the shoot in spring, springbeauty bursts to its full height of three or four inches,

---

expending in a few days its disproportionately large reserve of starches. It can even push through the last inch or two of snow by combusting some of the starch to melt itself a hole. It has two to four weeks to complete its life cycle—blooming, setting seed, and photosynthesizing like mad to store up starches for the next spring. Then it withers, existing only underground for late July and August, the peak growing season for its associates.

Plants on this sort of schedule are called "spring ephemerals." Many, such as blue-eyed-grass, are common on semiarid land with just a few weeks of wet soil following snowmelt. Springbeauty does well on such sites on the lower East slope, but in subalpine meadows its timing has a different purpose—jumping the gun on bigger, leafier plants that will monopolize the light later in the season.

A remarkable adaptation in this and many early-blooming high-country plants is a thin-fleshed hollow stem used as an internal greenhouse. When stored carbohydrates are burned off during the quick burst of growth, some of the heat produced is retained in the stem, making the internal air temperature warm enough for photosynthesis even when the outside air is not. Waste carbon dioxide from respiration also stays inside, available for synthesis into new carbohydrates.

With their concentrated starches, springbeauty bulbs are good survival forage. They taste radishy. Unfortunately, they're depleted when in bloom and hard to locate at other times, so leave them in peace unless starvation impends.

Miner's-Lettuce

Claytonia sibirica* (sib-ee-ric-a: Siberian). Also **candyflower**. Petals ¼–½", notch-tipped, white with fine pink veins; sepals 2; stamens 5; stem leaves 2, opposite, pointed/oval, 2–4", ± clasping-based; basal leaves at least as large, several, on long leafstalks; stem 5–16", ± succulent, several-flowered. Moist forests; sometimes on moss mats on trees. Portulacaceae (Purslane family). Color p 142.

Miner's-lettuce is one of our few common annuals—plants that grow from seed and die within a single growing season. Where it grows, you may find it germinating and blooming at any time of spring or summer. To try miner cuisine, find young unbloomed ones. They're mildest and tenderest.

---

* Formerly in genus *Montia.*

The definition of petals and sepals states that if they're in just one whorl, they're sepals, no matter how colorful or tender. Technically, then, there are no flowers with 5 petals and no sepals, but in appearance there are quite a few. Parsley family flowers have a vestigial whorl or fleshy ring barely perceptible below the 5 petals. This ring is a calyx, but its lobes are so reduced ("obsolete") as to be indetectable. Another apparent instance is valerian: sepals unfurl only as the flower goes to seed, so they are not visible on the fresh flower.

Sitka Valerian

Valeriana sitchensis
(va-lee-ree-**ay**-na: strong—;
sit-**ken**-sis: of Sitka, AK). Corolla white (pink-edged at first),
⅜" long, with short lobes on a slightly asymmetrical tube; calyx appearing only as a "parachute" of plumes on the maturing seed; stamens 3, protruding; inflorescences round-topped, one at top, 2–8 smaller ones in opposite pairs below; leaves opposite, compound; leaflets usually 3 or 5, elliptical, pointed, vaguely toothed; plant 2–4', rankly fragrant. Abundant in subalpine meadows; also widely scattered. Valerianaceae (Valerian family). Color p 142.

As subalpine meadows are released by spring snowmelt (in June or July), deep reddish shoots of Sitka valerian soon shoot up abundantly. The redness disappears as the foliage matures, lingering longest in the budding flowers but disappearing as they mature to white. Most redness in plants comes from anthocyanin (meaning "flower blue"), a complex carbohydrate pigment that may be red, blue, or anywhere in between; it shifts between red and blue like litmus paper, depending on acidity and other factors.

Anthocyanin is suspected of several functions in high elevation plants. First, it filters out ultraviolet radiation, which can be at least as hard on plant tissue as on human skin. Ultraviolet is more intense at high altitude, where there is less atmosphere to screen it, and around the solstice in June, when sunlight is at its peak. In June the high country is still snowbank-chilled, and plant tissues young and tender, so that's where and when anthocyanin is brought out.

Second, while reflecting ultraviolet radiation, it also seems to absorb and concentrate infrared radiation, heating the plant.

Third, anthocyanin is an interim form for carbohydrates on their way up from winter storage. To bloom and fruit early in their short growing season, high-country plants must store huge quantities of carbohydrates in their roots, and then move them up fast after snowmelt, or even before (see springbeauty, page 219). In de-reddening, valerian stuffs itself with preserves from the root cellar.

Valerian root recently regained its ancient reputation as an herbal medicine. Sitka valerian fetches some of the highest prices paid to commercial foragers, and has been overpicked in some areas. Used as a sedative, "it is most effective," writes herbalist Michael Moore, "when you have been nervous, stressed, or become an adrenalin basket case, with muscular twitches, shaky hands, palpitations, and indigestion." I'll be sure to remember that.

American Bistort

Polygonum bistortoides * (pa-**lig**-o-num: many "knees" or stem joints; bis-tor-**toy**-deez: resembling European bistort). Flowers white, small, chaffy, in a dense head about 1" × ½"; calyx lobes 5, unequal; petals lacking; stamens 8; stem leaves few, ± linear, sheathing; basal leaves much larger (3–6", on 3–6" leafstalks), elliptical; stem unbranched, 10–30". Subalpine. Polygonaceae (Buckwheat family). Color p 142.

Bistort typifies lush subalpine meadows, associating with lupine, fescue, or showy sedge.

Newberry's Fleeceflower

Polygonum newberryi * (new-**bear**-ee-eye: after John Strong Newberry of Newberry Crater fame). Also **Newberry's knotweed**. Flowers greenish, in inconspicuous spikes wedged in leaf axils; calyx lobes 5, unequal; petals lacking; stamens 8; leaves gray-green, oval, ½–2"; stems to 16"; often partly prostrate, with flaring papery sheaths above each leaf. Alpine gravels. Polygonaceae (Buckwheat family).

Few congeners look less alike than fleeceflower and bistort (above). This one comes up in spring—often from semi-barren pumice or serpentine gravel—as rich red buds and shoots. The redness may disappear, and return in late summer (page 221).

---

*Proposed partitioning the huge and diverse genus *Polygonum* would put *newberryi* in genus *Aconogonon*, perhaps as *A. davisiae*, and *bistortoides* in genus *Bistorta*. (Even binomials can be navel-gazers: we also have *Elymus elymoides* and *Icaricia icarioides*).

Fleeceflower and its cousin, dirty socks (p 230), colonized the Mt. St. Helens blast area, and typify "pumice desert" habitats, which look desertlike, even though they get lots of precipitation, because pumice retains moisture poorly. The plants don't so much tolerate drought as win a race with it by growing and flowering early.

Anemones

Anemone spp. (a-**nem**-a-nee: wind—). Also **windflower**. Sepals 5 (sometimes 6), petal-like; petals lacking; stamens many; stem leaves 3, in a whorl ¾ of the way up; basal leaves 1 to many; stems 3–12", from rhizomes. Ranunculaceae (Buttercup family).

A. oregana (or-eg-**ay**-na: of Oregon). Flowers blue-violet (occasionally pink or white), 1–2" diam; stem leaves 3–5-compound and lobed, on leafstalks. Columbia Gorge and E-side, Lake Chelan to C OR. Illustrated at left.

A. deltoidea (del-**toy**-dia: triangular). Flowers white (occasionally pinkish), 1–2" diam; stem leaves coarsely toothed, oval, attached directly to the stem without leafstalks. Common, W-side forest, OR and S WA Cas. Color p 139.

A. lyallii (lye-**ah**-lee-eye: after David Lyall, p 53). Flowers white to pink or bluish, ¾" diam; stem leaves 3-compound and toothed, on leafstalks; stem 3–4". Uncommon, W-side up to timberline. Illustrated at left.

These woodland anemones bear a close resemblance to each other, but not to our subalpine anemones (page 231).

Sweet Cicely

Osmorhiza spp. (os-mo-**rye**-za: odor root). Inflorescence loose; seeds slender, bristly; leaflets usually 9, oval, toothed; plant leggy, 1–3', licorice-fragrant. Apiaceae (Parsley family).

O. purpurea (pur-**pew**-ria: purple). Flowers pink to purple, tiny. Scattered, moist mid-elev openings.

*O. berteroi** (bare-**tare**-oh-eye: after ? Bertero). Flowers greenish white, tiny. Scattered, lower forests.

---

*The name *berteroi* was recently found to have been published before the familiar name *O. chilensis*.

Herbs: petals/sepals total 5   **223**

Gray's Lovage

Ligusticum grayi (lig-**us**-tic-um: the Roman term, referring to Liguria; **gray**-eye: after Asa Gray). Also **licorice-root**. Flowers white (sometimes purple-tinged), in 1–3 slightly rounded inflorescences 2–4" diam; leaves like Italian parsley, nearly all basal; stem 8–24", from a thick fragrant taproot. Lush subalpine meadows. Apiaceae (Parsley family).

Lovage is the "Queen Anne's lace" lookalike common in subalpine meadows in late summer.

Desert-Parsleys

Lomatium spp. (lo-**may**-shum: hemmed seeds). Apiaceae (Parsley family). Also **hog-fennel**.

Martindale's desert-parsley, *L. martindalei* (martin-**day**-lye: after I. C. Martindale). Flowers yellow, tiny, in several ½" broad-topped clusters on raylike stems from the root crown; leaves basal, pinnately twice-compound, in a nearly flat rosette. Dry rocky (often pumice) ground, esp subalpine. Color p 142.

Chocolate-tips, *L. dissectum* (dis-**ec**-tum: finely cut). Flowers usually purple-brown, tiny, in many ½" balls on rays (like fireworks) from a common point on a 20–60", hollow, often purple stalk; leaves lacy, finely cut and twice-pinnate. In sun, esp lower E-side and Columbia Gorge. Color p 142.

These are two striking species of desert-parsley, a large and tricky genus in a large and tricky family. The Apiaceae or parsley family includes carrots (called "Queen Anne's lace" when growing wild), parsnips, celery, fennel, and dill. Strong family traits make it easy to recognize but it's a hard family to identify to species.

The family is characterized by "umbels," umbrella-shaped inflorescences in which many flower-stalks branch from one point subtended by bracts; in most genera (including this one) these stalks in turn bear "umbellets" subtended by "bractlets." Leaves are often filigreelike (twice- or thrice-dissected). The family's robust taproots range in edibility from parsnips and carrots to deadly poison hemlock. Roots of "cous," a desert-parsley, were the chief vegetable of some Columbia Basin tribes. Some tribes reportedly ate young chocolate-tips roots, but others poisoned fish and lice with them. The risk of deadly mistakes forbids my recommending them.

Water
Hemlock

Poison
Hemlock

Cow-Parsnip

Heracleum lanatum * (hair-a-**clee**-um: the Greek term, after Hercules; lan-**ay**-tum: woolly). Flowers white; one to several inflorescences nearly flat, 5–10" diam, petals near edge of inflorescence much enlarged and 2-lobed; stamens 5; leaflets only 3, huge (6–16"), palmately lobed and toothed; stems juicy, aromatic, hollow, 3–10". Moist thickets up to low subalpine elevs. Apiaceae (Parsley family). Illustrated at center.

Cow-parsnips, avidly eaten and widely eradicated by cows, are also browsed by wild herbivores. Northwest tribes ate the young stems, either raw or cooked but always peeled first to remove a weak toxin which causes skin irritations in reaction to sunlight. The stems taste milder and sweeter than the rank fragrance leads you to expect.

Careless plant foragers in the Northwest have died from eating water-hemlock, *Cicuta douglasii*, and poison-hemlock, *Conium maculatum*, after mistaking these intensely toxic plants for cow-parsnips. Stature, habitat, inflorescence and purple-spotted stems contribute to these fatal errors; yet the poisonous parsleys have lacy leaves (pinnately twice- or thrice-compound) utterly unlike the three huge palmately lobed leaflets of a cow-parsnip. To be safe, never eat any part of any wild "carrot-topped" plant with dissected or compounded leaves.

---

* PLANTS uses the name *H. maximum*, which was published earlier than *lanatum*, but not validly, according to *Intermountain Flora*. Some taxonomists think our form belongs in the European species, *H. sphondylium*.

Herbs: petals/sepals total 5   **225**

There are also 4-merous monocots: skunk-cabbage and may lily, pp 160–61. Stonecrop and roseroot, p 211, occasionally have flower parts in fours, but usually in fives in our region.

Willow-Herbs

Epilobium (ep-il-**oh**-bium: pod on top). 4 petals, 4 sepals and 4 stamens borne at the tip of an extremely slender ovary 1–5 times as long as the petals; the ovary matures into a seedpod that splits into 4 spirally curling thin strips, releasing tiny downy seeds; leaves narrowly elliptical, all on stem, often opposite; from rhizomes. Onagraceae (Evening-primrose family).

Alpine willow-herb, *E. anagallidifolium** (ana-gal-id-if-**oh**-lium: with leaves like *Anagallis*). Flowers deep or pale pink to white, nearly flat, ¼–¾" diam, usually 2–4 per stem; petals 2-lobed; leaves ¾–2"; plant 2–12". Alp/sub-alpine, esp in and along streams and seeps. Color p 143.

Yellow willow-herb, *E. luteum* (**loot**-ium: yellow). Flowers pale yellow, bell-shaped, ± erect; petals ½–¾", deeply 2-lobed, crinkly; leaves 1–3", fine-toothed; 8–24". Streambanks and wet meadows. Color p 143.

Fireweeds

Chamerion* spp. (ca-**me**-ree-on: contraction from *Chamaenerion*, dwarf oleander). Flower/seed structures as in *Epilobium*. Onagraceae.

Fireweed, *C. angustifolium* (ang-gus-tif-**oh**-lium: narrow leaf). Flowers pink to purple, nearly flat, 1¼–2" diam, blooming progressively upward in a tall conical raceme; leaves 3–6" × ¾"; plant 3–8' tall. Abundant in avalanche tracks and basins, recent burns, clearcuts, etc.

Dwarf Fireweed, *C. latifolium* (lat-if-**oh**-lium: wide leaf). Also **river beauty, red willow-herb.** Flowers deep pink to purple, nearly flat, 1–1½" diam; leaves 1–2" × ½–¾"; 3–16" tall. Mtn river bars to alpine talus. Color p 143.

With its copious plumed seeds that fly in the wind, fireweed is a major invader of burns, from Northwest clearcuts to bombed urban rubble in Europe. If that makes it a "weed," so be it, but it is native, beautiful, nutritious, and not a pernicious competitor.

---

*Genus *Epilobium* was split with the support of DNA analysis, with these larger-flowered species going into *Chamerion*. This split is not yet recognized in PLANTS or many other texts. Species *alpinum* was also split, with the majority of our *alpinum* becoming *anagallidifolium*.

Unlike many pioneer herbs, it is a perennial, and seems to require mycorrhizal partners: lacking them, fireweed seedlings on deep Mt. St. Helens ash in 1981 weakened and died without flowering.

Fireweed is more abundant northward, beautifying vast areas of Alaska where trees don't grow. It was mainly northerly tribes that ate its inner stems as a staple food in spring. (Caution: may prove laxative.) Its dwarfed (but large-flowered) version earns the name "river beauty" in the Canadian Rockies, covering miles and miles of river bars, but here its elevational range is generally too high for sizable rivers.

Farewell-to-Spring

Clarkia amoena (**clar**-kia: after William Clark, p 234; a-**me**-na: delightful). 4 petals intense lavender to violet, with white streaking and often a carmine splotch at center; calyx shallowly 4-lobed, seemingly only 1 sepal; 8 yellow stamens; 4 cream stigmas; stem several-flowered, 4–32", wiry, fuzzy, often reddish near base; leaves 1–2" long, narrow. Sunny, well-drained slopes, low W-side; uncommon. Onagraceae (Evening-primrose family). Color p 144.

Growing annually from seeds, this striking flower blooms while the other herbs on its summer-dry slope die back.

Kittentails

Synthyris spp. (**synth**-er-iss: fused doors). Corolla pale blue to lavender, unequally 4-lobed, ⅜"; in small racemes; leaves basal, 1–2". Scrophulariaceae (Figwort family).

Snow queen, *S. reniformis* (ren-if-**or**-mis: round). Stems and leaves sprawling; leaves ± heart-shaped, with coarse blunt teeth. Warmer lowland forests, W OR and SW WA. Illustrated above.

Mountain kittentails, *S. missuricus* (miz-**oo**-ric-us: of the Missouri River). Stems erect, up to 12"; leaves round to kidney-shaped, with coarse blunt teeth. Disjunct in Columbia Gorge; otherwise E of our range. Color p 143.

Featherleaf kittentails, *S. pinnatifida* (pin-a-**tif**-id-a: with finely cut leaves). Stems erect, to 8"; leaves white-woolly, finely pinnate-lobed. Alpine, rare, disjunct in Olys; otherwise well E of our range. Illustrated at left.

Snow queen has been known to bloom as early as December in mild winters.

Toothwort

Cardamine nuttallii * (car-**dam**-in-ee: the Greek term; after Thomas Nuttall, p 74). Flowers pink or lavender to white, ½–1" diam, several; stem leaves 1–3, with 3 or 5 ± uneven, narrow lobes, purplish underneath; roundish basal leaves rising from the rhizomes separately; 4–14" tall. W-side lowlands. Brassicaceae (Mustard family). Color p 143.

Along with springbeauty, this is one of our earliest-blooming flowers. Toothwort is called springbeauty in some books, and the two are often confused; springbeauty (page 219) has five petals and grows in sunnier spots than toothwort.

Wallflowers

Erysimum spp. (er-**iss**-im-um: the Greek term). Petals brilliant yellow, round, ½–¾"; flowers many, in a round-topped cluster; seedpods very narrow, splitting in 2; leaves 2–5", narrow, often shallowly toothed, most in a basal rosette, a few on the stem. Brassicaceae (Mustard family).

E. arenicola (air-en-**ic**-a-la: sand dweller). Plant 10–20" tall. Mostly alpine. Color p 144.

E. capitatum * (cap-it-**ay**-tum: flowers in heads). Plant grayish-hairy, 16–32". Columbia Gorge and lower E slopes, in sun.

Maybe some "wallflowers" are modest, but not these beauties.

Bunchberry

Cornus unalaschkensis * (**cor**-nus: horn; oona-lash-**ken**-sis: of Unalaska , AK). Also **ground-dogwood**. Inflorescence subtended by four showy (½–1") white bracts often mistaken for petals; true flowers tiny, 4-merous, in a dense head ½–¾" diam; berries red-orange, several, 1-seeded, ¼" diam; leaves pointed, oval, 1–3", in whorls of six beneath the inflorescence, and in whorls of four on flowerless stems (technically 4-leafleted compound basal leaves) nearby; stems 2–8", from rhizomes. Dense mid-elev forests. Cornaceae (Dogwood family). Color p 143.

Why does this flower—a mere six-inch subshrub—look so much like a dogwood flower? Because the dogwood tree is the bunchberry's closest relative.

---

*Formerly *C. pulcherrima.*

*Formerly included in the Great Plains species, *E. asperum.*

*Western bunchberries were formerly included in the Eastern species, *C. canadensis.*

Smelowskias

Smelowskia spp. (smel-**ow**-skia: after Timotheus Smelowsky). Flowers cream white or purple-tinged, ⅜–¾" diam, several, in roundish clusters; leaves crowded, basal, 1–4", pinnately compound or -lobed, gray-fuzzy; low mat or cushion plants. Alpine. Brassicaceae (Mustard family).

S. calycina (cay-lis-**eye**-na: cuplet). Sepals falling off when flower opens. Color p 144.

S. ovalis (o-**vay**-lis: oval seedpod). Sepals remaining on opened flowers.

Bedstraw

Galium triflorum (**gay**-lium: milk—; try-**flor**-um: three flowered). Corolla white, 4-lobed, flat, up to ¼" diam; sepals lacking; flowers usually in sparse threes branching from leaf axils; leaves in whorls of 5 or 6, narrow-elliptical; stems minutely barbed, four-angled, generally sprawling or clambering, dense. Widespread in forest and thickets. Rubiaceae (Madder family).

Bedstraw grows clinging tangles of weak stems that are irresistibly easy to uproot by the fistful. This is the plant's way of attaching its seeds to passing animals. Where other plants have barbed fruits for this purpose, bedstraw barbs its entire stem, and breaks off at the roots. Several less common *Galium* species here differ in having four-leaved whorls, fuller inflorescences and a more erect stature.

Meadowrue

Thalictrum occidentale (tha-**lic**-trum: the Greek term; ox-i-den-**tay**-lee: western). Sepals 4 (or 5), greenish, ¼"; petals lacking; flowers many, in sparse racemes, male (illustrated above) and female (below) on separate plants, the males with numerous stamens of long yellow anthers dangling loosely by purple filaments; females less droopy, with several reddish pistils that mature into a starlike rosette of capsules; leaves twice- or thrice-compound, leaflets ¾–1½", round-lobed (similar to columbine); plants 20–40". Low subalpine lush meadows or open forest. Ranunculaceae (Buttercup family). Color p 144.

Veronicas

Veronica spp. (ver-**on**-ic-a: from a Greek term). Also **speedwell**. Corolla blue-violet with yellow center, unequally 4-lobed, nearly flat, ⅜" diam; in a small raceme; leaves opposite, elliptical; stem 2–6". Alp/subalpine, in drier meadows or with heather, or krummholz. Scrophulariaceae (Figwort family).

V. wormskjoldii (vormsk-**yol**-dee-eye: after Morten Wormskjold). Style and stamens shorter than petals; leaves scattered. Color p 143.

V. cusickii (cue-**zik**-ee-eye: after William Cusick). Style and stamens longer than petals; leaves ± crowded.

These flowers closely resemble the European veronica, *V. filiformis*, a weed in Northwest lawns.

Herbs: dicots, 3, 6, or several petals or sepals

Most 3- or 6-petaled flowers are monocots (pp 161–77) with 6 or fewer stamens and a total of 6 petals and sepals; most monocot leaves have conspicuous parallel veins. The dicot plants that follow don't share those characteristics. "Several" petals means a variable number between 5 and 9. Most *apparently* several-petaled flowers are composites (pp 181–89); their seeming petals are ray flowers.

Buckwheats

Eriogonum spp. (airy-**og**-a-num: woolly joints). Calyx 6-lobed; petals lacking; stamens 9; flowers small, many, above ± fused whorls of usually hairy bracts; leaves basal, oval, on short leafstalks, often woolly underneath. Rocky dryish places, alpine to steppes. Polygonaceae (Buckwheat family).

Dirty socks, *E. pyrolifolium* (pi-roe-lif-**oh**-lium: pyrola leaf). Flowers dull pinkish or off-white, reddish-fuzzy, foul-smelling; only two bracts below inflorescence; stems often red, 2–5". Commonest on pumice. Color p 144.

Oval-leaf buckwheat, *E. ovalifolium nivale* (oh-val-if-**oh**-lium: oval leaf; niv-**ay**-lee: of snow). Flowers dull cream yellow to rose-tinged; leaves silvery white (scarcely at all green), tiny, densely matted; 1½–4" tall. Alpine. Color p 145.

Sulphur-flower, *E. umbellatum* (um-bel-**ay**-tum: flowers in umbels). Flowers cream or reddish to (occasionally) bright yellow; stems 2–12". Compact alpine variety illustrated at right.

Wild-Ginger

Asarum caudatum (**ass**-a-rum: the Greek term; caw-**day**-tum: tailed). Calyx brownish purple, with three long-tailed lobes 1–3"; petals lacking; stamens 12, ± fused to the pistil; flower single on a prostrate short stalk between paired leafstalks; leaves heart-shaped, 2–5", finely hairy, spicy-aromatic, rather firm and often persistent, on hairy 2–8" leafstalks. Moist forests. Aristolochiaceae (Birthwort family). Color p 144.

This odd plant is unrelated to ginger, and even the tangy fragrance isn't really close, yet its stems as a seasoning won approval from cooks of trapping, pioneering, and wild-food stalking eras alike. The earthbound, camouflaged flowers are less fragrant. They attract creeping and crawling pollinators.

Inside-Out Flower

Vancouveria hexandra (van-coo-**vee**-ria: after George Vancouver, p 97; hex-**an**-dra: six stamen). Also **duckfoot**. Apparent petals and sepals each 6, white, sharply reflexed, ¼"; another 6–9 outer bracts fall off as the flower opens; stamens 6; flowers many, in a very sparse panicle; leaves 9- (to 27-) compound, the leaflets ¾–2", vaguely 3-lobed; plant 8–20" tall. Moist forests in W OR and SW WA. Berberidaceae (Barberry family). Color p 145.

Marshmarigold

Caltha leptosepala* (**cal**-tha: goblet; by-**flor**-a: two flower). Sepals 6–11, a few often 2-lobed, white, petal-like, ½–¾"; petals lacking; stamens and pistils many; flowers usually 2 on a forked 3–10" stem; leaves basal on 2–3" leafstalks, kidney-shaped, 2–4" across, ± fleshy, edges ± scalloped, often curling. Wet places (often in streams) esp subalpine. Ranunculaceae (Buttercup family). Color p 146.

Towhead Baby

Anemone occidentalis* (a-**nem**-a-nee: wind—; ox-i-den-**tay**-lis: western). Also **western pasqueflower**. Sepals 5–8, white, petal-like, ½–1" petals lacking; stamens and pistils many, styles growing to 1–2" and feathery as seeds mature; stem 1–2', hairy, 1-flowered, with a whorl of three leaves at mid height, plus larger basal leaves, all intricately twice- or thrice-compound, fernlike. Subalpine meadows. Ranunculaceae (Buttercup family). Color p 145.

---

* *C. leptosepala* includes the former *C. biflora.*

*PLANTS, but not FNA, splits *Anemone* and put both *occidentalis* and *drummondii* in genus *Pulsatilla.* Our woodland anemones (p 223) are unaffected.

The most strangely lovely of subalpine "flowers" is actually the seed head of this Anemone. It looks like something Dr. Seuss would have dreamed up—or more traditionally, "the old man of the mountains," or a hirsute towhead. The flower attracts less attention, blooming early when the plant is only 2–6" tall and lingering snow is keeping most hikers away. After the petals fall, growth of the stem, leaves, and styles takes off; the styles become plumes on the seeds to catch wind. Drummond's pasqueflower, *A. drummondii*, (after Thomas Drummond, page 473) has similar leaves and flowers (sometimes bluish), but straight rather than plumey styles; it grows at higher elevations.

Baneberry

Actaea rubra (ac-**tee**-a: elder, for the similar leaves; **roob**-ra: red). Numerous ¼" white stamens are the showy part of the flower; 5–10 petals (occasionally lacking) white, smaller than the stamens; 3–5 sepals petal-like but falling off as the flower opens; flowers (and berries) in a ± conical raceme; berries ⅜" diam, glossy bright red (or occasionally pure white); leaves 9 to 27-compound, leaflets pointed-oval, toothed and lobed, 1–3"; stem 16–40". Lower forests. Ranunculaceae (Buttercup family). Color p 146.

These, our most poisonous native berries, are less than deadly. A handful could render you violently ill, but even a small taste should start you spitting fast enough to save your stomach the trouble.

Goldthread

Coptis spp. (**cop**-tiss: cut—). Petals and sepals similar, each 5–8, greenish white, threadlike, ⅛–⅜" long; petals shorter than sepals, with a tiny gland on a broad spot near the base; stamens many; leaves shiny, persistent, very fernlike, at least 3-compound, toothed, incised; roots bright yellow beneath their bark; stems 2–6". Ranunculaceae (Buttercup family).

C. aspleniifolia (a-splee-nee-if-**oh**-lia: spleenwort-fern leaf). Wet forest and bogs, from Stillaguamish drainage N.

C. laciniata (la-sin-ee-**ay**-ta: cutleaf). Forests, lower W-side from Columbia Gorge S.

Goldthread solutions were long used for mouth sores in both Anglo and native cultures. There do seem to be promising antibiotics present—carrying a threat of overexploitation.

Starflowers

Trientalis spp. (try-en-**tay**-lis: 1/3, implying 4" height?). Flowers white to pink, 1 to few, ½" diam; petals, sepals and stamens each 5–8 (most often 6); leaves pointed-oval; capsule spherical; 3–8" tall. Primulaceae (Primrose family).

T. latifolia* (lat-if-**oh**-lia: broad leaf). Leaves 1½–4", in a single whorl. Widespread, in forests. Color p 144.

T. arctica.* Leaves up to 2", smaller downward along the stem. Bogs. Illustrated at right.

Yellow Pond-Lily

Nuphar polysepala* (**new**-fer: from the Arabic term; poly-**see**-pa-la: many sepals). Also **wokas**. Bright yellow, heavy, roundish 1½–3" petal-like sepals 4–8; smaller green outer sepals 4; true petals and stamens numerous, much alike, crowded together around the large parasol-shaped pistil; leaves heavy, waxy, elongated heart-shaped, 6–18" long, usually floating. Widespread in ponds and slow streams up to about 6' deep. Nymphaeaceae (Water-lily family). Color p 145.

Oregon and California tribes gather pond-lily seeds to eat. Northerly tribes reported broad-spectrum prescriptions using the roots; a sick person was steamed over them.

Mountain Bog Gentian

Gentiana calycosa* (jen-she-**ay**-na: Greek term, honoring King Gentius; cay-lic-**oh**-sa: cuplike). Also **explorer gentian**, God knows why. Corolla deep indigo blue, 1½" tall, with 4–7 shallow lobes, and fine teeth on the "pleats" between lobes; same number (4–7) calyx lobes and stamens; leaves opposite, oval, ½–1½"; stems 3–16", crowded. Subalpine, esp in wet meadows. Gentianaceae (Gentian family). Color p 146.

Thanks to the gentian's profound indigo—among the latest of late bloomers—September hikers don't entirely miss the subalpine wildflower season.

---

*Several authors, including PLANTS, demote *polysepala* to a subspecies of *N. lutea*, but FNA does not.

* Some texts, including PLANTS, treat both starflowers as subspecies of their Eurasian relatives—*T. borealis latifolia* and *T. europaea arctica*, respectively.

*Some authors split *Gentiana* and treat this as *Pneumonanthe calycosa*.

Bitterroot

Lewisia rediviva (lew-**iss**-ia: after Meriwether Lewis, below; red-i-**vie**-va: reborn). Flowers pink, apricot, or white, 2–2¼" diam, borne very low to ground, 1 per stem in small clumps; 10–18 petals and 5–9 sepals both showy; leaves basal, linear, initially fleshy but withering often by time of flowering. Arid gravels E of Cas. Color p 146. Portulacaceae (Purslane family).

It is easy to imagine this dramatic dry-ground bloom becoming an instant favorite of Meriwether Lewis, who found it in the Bitterroot Mountains. It barely enters our range.

Columbia Lewisia

Lewisia columbiana. Petals 6–11, pink with red veins, ¼–½"; sepals 2; stamens 5–6, red-tipped; leaves in a basal rosette, fleshy, linear, to 4" long; stem 4–8". Rock crevices, alp/subalpine gravels, in WA. Color p 145.

Tweedy's Lewisia

Lewisia tweedyi (**twee**-dee-eye: after Frank Tweedy). Petals 6–11, apricot pink to cream, 1–1¾"; sepals 2; stamens many; leaves in a basal rosette, rather heavy, 4–8" × 1–4"; stem 4–8". Rocky slopes, limited to E-side Cas of C WA and disjunct at Manning Park, BC. Color p 145.

Tweedy's lewisia is the most gorgeous rare species in our mountains. If you should be lucky enough to see one, **don't touch it!** Excuse my touchiness. The only specimens I've seen did well for two years between my visits there, only to be torn out by some !%*?& wretch while I was farther up the trail.

Meriwether Lewis and William Clark's voyage of 1804–06 needs no lengthy description here; what you may not know is that biological discovery was its greatest distinction. After all, Alexander Mackenzie had crashed on through to the Pacific at Bella Coola in 1789, but he and others in the Northwest were interested in little but fur. Though not scientists by profession, Lewis and Clark were briefed intensively on natural history and cartography, respectively, before they set out. And they did natural history well. Lewis ranks with Douglas and Menzies in the number of first collections of important Northwest plants credited to him. The trip's high point, both literally and figuratively, came in Idaho and Montana; here on the lower Columbia they were in previously visited territory, and they spent a miserably wet winter.

5

Ferns, Clubmosses, and Horsetails

The old term "vascular cryptogams" defines this informal group of plants. "Vascular" means having vessels, or veins — tiny tubes for conducting water and the vital materials that water can dissolve. Vessels are tiny, but their effects are conspicuous. Without them, a plant can't raise its vital fluids more than a few inches from its moisture supply. *Non*vascular cryptogams (mostly mosses and liverworts) are necessarily diminutive, while ferns and horsetails are taller, typically 6" to 48". Modern clubmosses are short enough to confuse with mosses, but they are closer to ferns. In the Mesozoic era, before seed plants took over, tall forests of fern and clubmoss "trees" covered much of the earth.

"Cryptogam" ("hidden mating") means that the sexual reproductive process in these plants is tiny and brief compared to the showy flowering and fruiting of seed plants, and doesn't produce seeds capable of extended dormancy or travel. The traveling function is left up to an asexual stage in the cryptogam life cycle — a one-celled spore. (Genetically, plant spores are more analogous to the one-celled pollen of seed plants than to seeds.)

In ferns, the dustlike spores are borne in and released from "sori" — tiny clusters appearing as dark spots, lines, or crescents in patterns on the leaf underside. In some ferns each sorus is shielded by a tiny membrane, in some others by a length of rolled-under leaf margin. Each fern frond and its stalk from the rhizome is one leaf; it is pinnately compounded or divided into "pinnae." The pinnae may be compounded an additional one to three times, but the word pinna(e) is reserved for those units branching directly from the central leaf stalk.

Ferns: evergreen

Sword Fern

Polystichum munitum (pa-**lis**-tic-um: many rows; mew-**nigh**-tum: armed). Leaves 20–60", dark, leathery, once-compound, in huge clumps; each pinna asymmetrical at base, with an up-ward-pointing coarse tooth; stalks densely chaffy; sori round. Abundant on moist W-side forest sites; less so in drier forest, incl cool shady E-side spots. Dryopteridaceae (Wood Fern family).

Sword ferns are not favored for food or forage, but florists prefer their fronds for funerals, gathering them in great numbers without apparent threat to their abundance. Indians sometimes bundled them up as mattresses. Makah children made a game of peeling off as many sword fern pinnae as they could on one breath, saying *"pila"* ("sword fern" in Makah tongue) once for each pinna.

Deer Fern

Blechnum spicant (**blek**-num: the Greek term; **spik**-ent: spiky). Leaves 12–50", dark, in clumps; pinnae slender, broadening to-ward the base and not separated all the way to the stalk; stalks dark brown, smooth. Common in moist W-side old-growth, esp in WA. Blechnaceae.

Deer fern leaves are plainly of two types—fertile (spore-bearing) leaves, and sterile, strictly vegeta-tive leaves. The fertile leaves are taller, and stand segregated at the center of each clump; their pinnae are narrower and more widely sepa-rated than the sterile pinnae, rolling tightly in near-tubes around sori crowded on

---

their undersides. The sterile leaves lack sori; they rise obliquely in a thick circle around the fertile centerpiece. They are important winter forage for deer, elk, and cattle. The rhizomes were eaten, but not highly prized, by people.

Licorice Ferns

Polypodium spp. (poly-**poe**-dium: many foot). Leaves green through winter, dark, smooth; pinnae broadening toward the base and not separated all the way to the stalk; sori exposed. Polypodiaceae.

P. glycyrrhiza (gly-sir-**eye**-za: licorice, from "sweet root"). Leaves 4–30"; spores in late fall and winter; stalk green, tastes licorice-sweet at least initially. Typically among mosses upon rocks or trees; W-side lowlands. Illustrated.

*P. amorphum** (ay-**mor**-fum: misshapen). Leaves 4–12"; spores in summer and early fall; stalk often white-coated, tastes bitter. Rock crevices, not usually in moss mats; montane, up to 6,000', W of Cas Cr.

The flavor we call licorice occurs in several unrelated plants scattered around the globe, including star anise, fennel or sweet anise, this fern, and licorice, *Glycyrrhiza glabra.* The shared chemistry is called "glycyrrhizin." People worldwide have found it good for the appetite, the digestion, the spirits, the breath, and the dreams. In the Northwest, licorice fern rhizomes were sucked by hungry hunters or berry-pickers along the trail, or fed before meals to finicky young eaters. In quantity they may prove laxative, but most people find them too bitter to eat in quantity anyway.

Licorice ferns grow on rocks, logs, and tree trunks like maples and alders, preferably in a good bed of mosses to keep their roots moist. On all but the moistest sites here the leaves are usually less than six inches tall, and die back in summer when the moss mat dries out. New leaves sprout with the fall rains. We may think of these summer-deciduous leaves as evergreen, since they're dark and more or less leathery and last all winter, but actually they fall several weeks short.

Amorphum was separated from *glycyrrhiza* on DNA grounds, though it was first named in 1927, and seems distinct on field characters alone.

Lace Fern

Cheilanthes gracillima (kye-**lanth**-eez: margin flower; gra-**sil**-im-a: slenderest). Also **lip fern.** Leaves 3–10" tall, slender, evergreen, pale, at least twice-compound, in clumps; leaflets tiny, reddish-woolly underneath, with margins rolled under; upper part of stalk hairy. Rocky sites in sun. Pteridaceae.

Not all ferns are particularly moisture-demanding. The little lace fern and parsley fern (below) are drought-tolerant, living almost exclusively in crevices of cliffs and rockpiles. Lace fern is partial to igneous rocks.

Ferns: deciduous

Parsley Ferns

Cryptogramma spp. (crypto-**gram**-a: hidden lines) Vegetative leaves 3–8" × 2–4" broad, firm, pale yellow-green, at least twice-compound, in clumps; fertile leaflets (on 7–12" tall central stalks) long, slender, tightly rolled. Rocky sites in sun. Pteridaceae.

C. acrostichoides (across-tic-**oy**-deez: top row—). Leaves rather leathery, evergreen. Dry sites, all elevs, but mainly low. Fertile pinna and whole plant illustrated.

C. cascadensis. Leaves thin, withering in fall. Dry to fairly moist sites in mountains.

Parsley fern, like deer fern, has spore-bearing leaves utterly different from its vegetative leaves—often twice as tall, but fewer, and not fine-toothed and parsleylike as the sterile vegetative leaves are.

All North American parsley ferns were formerly included with their European relatives in *C. crispa. C. cascadensis* was named and described in 1989.

Western Maidenhair Fern

*Adiantum aleuticum*** (ay-dee-**an**-tum:
not wetted; a-**lew**-tic-um: of the Aleutian
Islands). Leaf blades 4–16", fan-shaped, broader
than long, twice-compound; sori under rolled
edges; stalks black, shiny, wiry. Saturated soil or
rocks in shade. Pteridaceae.

This is our easiest fern to identify. Its striking shiny black
stalks are our only ones that split
into two slightly unequal branches,
the pinnae spreading fanlike. The stalks kept
their dark shine well in decorative patterns in Makah and Quinault
basketry, and infusions of this fern were used to enhance the black
sheen of maidens' hair, yet Anglo sources contend it was the masses
of fine dark root hairs that suggested the common name.

Bracken

Pteridium aquilinum (teh-**rid**-ium: from the Greek term for fern, derived
from "feather"; ak-wil-**eye**-num: eagle—). Also **brake fern**. Leaves 24–80"
tall, ± triangular, twice to thrice compound, undersides fuzzy; sori under
rolled edges. Widespread on ± sunny sites. Dennstaedtiaceae.

Among Northwestern wild food gourmets, the fern "fiddleheads"
picked for steaming or eating raw in salads are usually young
bracken shoots. They taste like
asparagus with a dash of
almond extract and an unnerv-
ingly mucuslike interior. Most
Northwest tribes ate bracken
fiddleheads or rhizomes, or both.
Stockmen, however, list bracken as
a poisonous plant. It's true: 600 dry
pounds of bracken consumed within a
six-week period are enough to kill a
horse. Cows are less sensitive, their lethal
dose around a ton. They don't graze it

*Formerly included in *A. pedatum*, which is now restricted to
eastern North America.

eagerly, but if their winter hay is weedy with bracken it can slowly do them in. The toxin, thiaminase, is an enzyme that breaks down vitamin B1, and vitamin B1 is the antidote. Thiaminase is equally toxic to humans, i.e., not very toxic; there is no record of a human stuffing down enough bracken to induce vitamin deficiency.

Unfortunately, deadlier flavonoids lurk here. Bracken has been found to damage chromosomes, and a certain rare stomach cancer has a relatively high incidence in Japan and Wales, two far-flung lands where bracken is eaten traditionally. Consume bracken fiddleheads, if at all, only occasionally, as mouth entertainment, not a whole salad; and watch out for the vaguely similar unfurling shoots of monkshood, a very poisonous plant.

Bracken is doubtless the world's most widespread fern. Here, only sword ferns are more abundant, and no fern grows as tall or as fast; bracken has been measured at 16' in Washington, and clocked at several inches a day. Its best Cascade habitats are lower subalpine slope meadows annually scoured by avalanches or by snow creep. It owes its success partly to "allelopathy," or secretion of chemical compounds that are somewhat toxic to other kinds of plants, and partly to vegetative reproduction, sending numerous new shoots up from the rhizomes. In some burns and clearcuts it seems able to hold off conifer reproduction for years.

Lady Fern

Athyrium filix-femina (ath-**ee**-rium: no shield; fie-lix **fem**-in-a: fern-woman). Leaves 16–80" tall, narrowing toward both ends, twice or thrice compound; sori exposed, or initially shielded on one edge; stalk base scaly. Wet ground, often with skunk-cabbage and devil's club. Dryopteridaceae.

Medieval herbalists associated the female principle with a very large fern—larger than the male fern, *Dryopteris filix-mas*. They prescribed powdered roots and leaf infusions of lady fern for such diverse ailments as jaundice, gallstones, sores, hiccups, and worms; only since 1950 have male fern rhizomes fallen from pharmaceutical favor as a dewormer. Northwest tribes used lady and male ferns medicinally, and baked the rhizomes of these and other ferns for dinner.

The alpine lady fern, *A. alpestre** is similar, but smaller (8–32" tall) and more finely incised. Common in open subalpine country, it can monopolize patches of wet talus.

Wood Fern

Dryopteris expansa† (dry-**op**-ter-iss: oak fern; ex-**pan**-sa: broad spreading). Also **shield fern**. Leaves 8–36" tall, broadly triangular, thrice compound, in small clumps; sori round-shielded; stalk bases scaly. W-side forest. Dryopteridaceae.

Indians said that eating wood fern rhizomes cleans the system—after eating poisonous plants or red-tide shellfish, for example. Pharmacognosies call them laxative.

Oak Fern

Gymnocarpium disjunctum‡ (gym-no-**car**-pium: naked fruit). Leaves 6–18" tall, broadly triangular, thrice compound, rising singly from runners; sori exposed; stalks pale, slightly scaly. W-side forest. Dryopteridaceae.

Oak fern appears to have three similar leaves on each stalk. Technically, this is a single leaf with two basal pinnae, left and right, each nearly as big and as dissected as all the remaining pinnae put together.

---

*Formerly *A. distentifolium;* PLANTS splits *alpestre*, the American ones becoming *A. americanum.*

†Formerly included in *D. austriaca.*

‡Recently separated from *G. dryopteris*, which is also found here, mainly in WA.

Clubmosses

Clubmosses, *Lycopodium* and *Diphasiastrum* spp. (lye-co-**poe**-dium: wolf foot; di-fay-zee-**ass**-trum: two-sided —). Also

ground-pines. Spore-bearing "cones" straw-colored, usually erect, often separated from green leafy stems by a slender stalk. Family Lycopodiaceae.

L. *clavatum* (cla-**vay**-tum: club-shaped). Cones ¾–3" tall, on long, often branched stalks. Forest. Illustrated at right.

D. *alpinum* (al-**pie**-num). Cones ⅜–1", arising directly without a stalk from the leafy stem; lateral leaves curled and larger than the minute dorsal and ventral leaves. Alp/subalpine. Illustrated at left

D. *complanatum* (com-pla-**nay**-tum: flattened). Cones ⅝–1¼", on branched stalks; foliage flattened, cedarlike, leaves in the dorsal, ventral, and 2 lateral ranks of 3 distinct shapes. Forest. Illustrated at left.

D. *sitchense* (sit-**ken**-zee: of Sitka, Alaska). Cones ⅜–1", arising without a stalk; 4 ranks of leaves much alike; in dense clumps. Alp/subalpine.

These little fern relatives behave much like mosses, including their ability to seemingly resurrect, when wetted, from a dead-looking dried-up state. Their vessels (which mosses lack) enable their leaves to be thicker and more evergreen than moss leaves, however, so their closest semblance might be to heather or juniper: high elevation clubmosses may go unnoticed among heathers. They bear spores at their leaf bases, but not on all their leaves: most species have visibly distinct, erect fertile portions loosely termed "cones" terminating some of their branchlets. In clubmosses these are more distinct than in spikemosses.

Of all plant and fungal spores, only clubmoss spores entered commerce, partly because they're easiest to collect. The cones were

---

*Some taxonomists have recently split *Lycopodium* into six genera including *Diphasiastrum*. The PLANTS database demurs, retaining all these clubmosses in *Lycopodium*.

cut off, dried, pounded, rubbed, and finally sifted to collect the spores, used for centuries to dust wounds, pills, and babies' bottoms (no joke) and also as flash powder. Spores are extremely fine, smooth, slippery, nonreactive (except in the noses of allergy victims), water-repellent, and nonclumping. You may have noticed these qualities in pollen, which descended from spores through evolution. Pollen and spores need to be water-repellent and nonclumping to maximize air travel, their *raison d'etre*, in the rain.

Spikemosses

Selaginella spp. (sel-adge-in-**el**-a: from a Roman term). Spore-bearing portions of stems just as green and leafy as sterile portions, but ± distinguishable from them by being more neatly four-ranked and closer-packed, and often turning erect. Family Selaginellaceae.

S. oregana (or-eg-**ay**-na: of Oregon). Pendent up to 6' long from trees; spores yellowish white. Low elevs, esp rain forest river bottoms. Illustrated at left.

S. douglasii (da-**glass**-ee-eye: after David Douglas, p 18). Foliage flattened, resembling a more robust leafy liverwort, leaves in the dorsal/ventral and two lateral ranks differ in shape. Talus slopes, low in Columbia Gorge. Illustrated at right.

S. densa. In dense clumps; spores ± orange. Rocky sites, often alpine.

S. wallacei (**wall**-a-sigh: after ? Wallace). Loosely branched; spores orange. Rocky sites, lower elevs.

Horsetails and Scouring-Rushes

Equisetum spp. (ek-wis-**ee**-tum: horse tail). Thickets of hollow vertical stems with many sheathed joints; from blackish rhizomes. Family Equisetaceae.

Common horsetail, *E. arvense* (ar-**ven**-see: of fields). Reddish tan to almost white spore-bearing stems (illustrated left) come up in early spring, soon wither; 1–3' green stems of summer (right) have jointed, wiry, whorled branches which you might mistake for leaves, and have 8–10 shallow vertical ridges. Widespread, moist ground at all elevs; weedy on roadsides.

Giant horsetail, *E. telmateia* (tel-ma-**tie**-a: of marshes). Like common horsetail, but 2–10' tall; stems have 15–40 shallow ridges. Colony-forming on marshy ground or also sometimes roadsides, low W-side.

Marsh horsetail, *E. palustre* (pa-**lus**-tree: of marshes). All stems branched and green (but die back in winter), with 6–10 strong vertical ridges; producing blunt-tipped spore-bearing cones in summer. Typically emergent from shallow water, low to subalpine elevs. Illustrated at right.

Scouring-rush, *E. hyemale* (hi-em-**ay**-lee: of winter). Stems evergreen, unbranched, ⅛–½" diam × 1–5' tall, with 18–40 fine vertical ridges; cones sharp-pointed. Wet ground, low to mid-elevs. (A smaller sp in WA, *E. variegatum*, reaches alpine elevs.) Illustrated at left.

Long ignored for being too primitive, common, and monochromatic, horsetails won their hour of media glory for sending the first green shoots up through Mt. St. Helens' debris of May, 1980. They can crack their way up through an inch of asphalt on highway shoulders. No wonder Quileute swimmers felt strong after scrubbing themselves with horsetails! And some Northwest gardeners feel weak after weeding them.

Leaves on *Equisetum* are reduced to sheaths made up of fused whorls of leaves, often straw-colored, growing from nodes at regular intervals along the stem. On horsetails, whorls of slender green branches grow just below the leaf sheaths, from the same nodes, producing a bottlebrush shape. The branches themselves have little nodes and sometimes little branchlets.

Northwest Indians ate the new fertile shoots and heads of common and giant horsetail eagerly. They were spring's first fresh vegetable—succulent beneath the fibrous skins which were peeled or spat out. (But like bracken, page 239, horsetails cause thiaminase poisoning in cattle.)

Scouring-rushes (and some horsetails) have been picked worldwide for scouring and sanding—polishing arrow shafts, canoes, and fingernails, for example—thanks to silica-hardened gritty bumps on their skins.

6

Mosses and Liverworts

The nonvascular spore-bearing plants have little ability to conduct water and dissolved nutrients from the substrate up into their tissues; in many of them conduction takes place mainly along the outside of their stems, aided by surface tension. They compensate with an ability to pass water through their leaf surfaces almost instantly, both absorbing it and giving it up easily. After a few dry days in the sun, a bed of moss may be grayish, shriveled and brittle, and look quite dead. But let a little dew or drizzle fall on it, or a little water from your bottle, and see how the leaves revive before your very eyes, softening, stretching out and turning bright green. Again, when the temperature drops below freezing they give up their free moisture to crystallize on their surface rather than inside, where it would rupture cells.

Lichens share many of these characteristics with mosses and liverworts (though unrelated to them) and may lead similar lives. All three grow abundantly on trees and rocks in our area, undergoing countless alternations between their dried-out and their moist, photosynthetically active states. When they grow on trees or other plants they are called "epiphytes" ("upon-plants") meaning that they use the support plant to hold them up off the ground, but draw little or no material out of it.

Mosses that grow on the forest floor stake out a seasonal niche as much as a spatial one, living their active season in spring and—where there is no snowpack—winter. Quick recovery from nighttime frost is essential. By late spring these mosses are shaded out by perennial herbs and deciduous shrubs, and go largely dormant until fall.

The sexual life cycles of spore-bearing plants evolved before those of seed plants, and are more primitive but emphatically not simpler; they're so complex and varied that I won't even attempt to describe them. Many mosses and liverwort species propagate vegetatively from fragments much more often than from spores. Some produce multicelled asexual propagules called "gemmae," just for this purpose. In mosses and seed plants both (see page 186) adaptation to arctic and alpine climates often entails virtually abandoning sexual reproduction in favor of cloning, either vegetative or by unfertilized spore or seed formation.

The "fruits" of mosses are spore capsules, usually borne on slender vertical fruiting stalks. To release spores, most open at the tip after shedding first an outer cap, the "calyptra," and later an inner lid, the "operculum." Most keys to the mosses first separate two primitive families (Sphagnaceae and Andreaeaceae) with spore capsules that don't fit that description at all, and then divide the remainder into two growth forms based on where on the stem the fruiting stalks sprout:

fruiting from the tip of the leafy shoot, and typically **growing upright** in crowded masses or small tufts; or

fruiting from midpoint(s) along the year's new leafy shoot, which is typically **arching, trailing or pendent**.

Season of fruiting varies with species, but usually lasts several months. Positive identification of most mosses requires not only fruiting specimens but also a microscope and a highly technical key. The following pages offer tentative identifications of a few common species, with or without the help of a 10× or 12× handlens or monocular. A basic handlens is cheap, and fun to have along if you like plant forms.

Haircap Mosses

Polytrichum spp. (pa-**lit**-ric-um: many hairs). Stems wiry, rarely branched, vertical, in dense colonies; leaves ⅜" average, narrow, in-rolling when dry (exc *lyallii*); sheathing the stem at their bases; stem and stalk (or sometimes entire plant) rich reddish; capsule single, initially cloaked (exc *lyallii*) in a densely long-hairy cap. Polytrichaceae.

P. juniperinum (jew-nip-er-**eye**-num). Leaves often bluish-coated, ending in a short reddish hair tip (with 10× lens); leafy shoots 1–4" + 1–2½" fruiting stalk; capsule (after dropping the hairy cap) 4-angled. Sunnier sites, esp. on disturbed soil, at all elevs. Illustrated at right.

> *P. piliferum* (pil-**if**-er-um: hair-bearing). Leaves end in a whitish translucent hair tip; shoots ¼–1¼" + ¾–1¼" stalk; capsule 4-angled. In sun, esp alpine. Illustrated at left.

> *P. sexangulare* (sex-ang-you-**lair**-ee: six angled). Leaves tapered gradually (not to a hair-thin tip); shoots ½–¾" + ¾" stalk; capsule (underneath the hairy cap) 6- (or rarely 5-) angled. Mainly subalpine, in extreme late-snowbed sites.

> *P. lyallii* * (lye-**ah**-lee-eye: after David Lyall, p 53). Leaves tapered gradually, ± toothed near the tip (under 10× lens); shoots ½–2" + 1½–2½" stalk; capsule 4-angled, held horizontal, cap only sparsely short-hairy. Subalpine, abundant, near black alpine sedge or alpine saxifrage; also in lowland forest.

Haircap mosses are palpably more substantial than other mosses, almost resembling small evergreen shrubs like heather or juniper. Their stems contain some woody tissue and primitive water vessels. They can even store carbohydrates in underground rhizomes, like higher plants. The leaves, too, are more complex and thicker than the translucent, one-cell-thick leaves of most mosses. Several species of haircaps have translucent leaf margins that, in drying, curl inward to protect the chlorophyllous cells. These traits generally adapt the haircaps to sunny sites, as well as to human use—the tough stems were plaited for baskets or twine, and the whole plants used for bedding. Linnaeus reported sleeping well on a haircap moss mattress on a trip to arctic Scandinavia.

---

* Some older texts have *lyallii* in a separate genus *Polytrichadelphus*.

Bearded Moss

Polytrichastrum * *alpinum* (pa-lit-ric-**ast**-rum: somewhat like *Polytrichum*). Stems wiry, reddish, ¾–4" tall + ¾–2" stalk, unbranched or slightly branched, vertical, in dense colonies; leaves heavy but fairly soft, narrow, tapering gradually, fine-toothed their entire length, the bases sheathing the stem; capsule cylindrical (not angled) underneath a densely hairy cap. All elevs W-side, esp subalpine near partridgefoot and black alpine sedge. Polytrichaceae.

To distinguish this from haircap mosses, which it often grows near, look for the nonangular capsules and, if you have a handlens, the teeth all along the leaf margins.

Menzies' Tree Moss

Leucolepis acanthoneuron * (lew-**col**-ep-iss: white scale; ay-can-tho-**new**-ron: thorn vein). Main stem 1½–3" tall, dark brown, lower portion with scattered large translucent white leaf-scales, upper portion with dense fine branches and branchlets bearing minute deep green leaves; fruiting stalks usually 2 or 3, 1½–2" tall, reddish, not twisted when dry; capsules nodding, ± pear-shaped, smooth, sometimes colorful; male plants terminating in conspicuous flowerlike green rosettes (in place of fruiting stalks). Common on soil, less so on maple bark, W-side below 3,000'. Mniaceae.

This is the commonest moss here that has a treelike growth form—vertical stems bearing leafy horizontal branches. It yields a yellow dye once used in Salish basketry. A slightly more northerly-distributed tree moss is *Climacium dendroides;* it's a little more robust (up to 4") and tufty, with upswept branches, and its capsules stand erect.

---

*This genus was split out first from *Polytrichum* and then from *Pogonatum*.
*Formerly *L. menziesii*, after Archibald Menzies, p 97.

Badge Moss

Plagiomnium insigne (play-gee-ohm-**nye**-um: slant moss; in-**sig**-nee: badge). Leafy shoots 1¼–3" tall, unbranched; leaves bright green, large (up to ⅜") and broad, sheathing the stem at their bases, edges minutely toothed (under 10× lens), drastically shriveling when dry; fruiting stalks usually 3 to 5, 1–1¾" tall, reddish grading upward to yellowish; capsules nodding, yellow, smooth; male plant terminating in a green rosette around a fuzzy disk (the "badge"). Logs or soil; sometimes forms ± pure colonies under lowland maple and alder. Mniaceae.

These are about the largest leaves you'll see on moss. At 12× magnification, held up against light, their cells can be just discerned.

Alpine Schistidium

Schistidium apocarpum* (shis-**tid**-ium: split—; ap-o-**car**-pum: fruiting at the top). Tiny cushions in rock crevices, deep green when wet, drying almost black, with a silvery surface sheen from whitish translucent hair tips on the leaves; stems about ½"; spore capsules usually numerous, much less than ⅛" tall, rarely protruding above the leaf tips. On high-elev rocks. Grimmiaceae.

Reflective whitish hair tips on moss leaves, like the silvery hairs all over some higher plants, conserve water on sunny sites by reducing heat absorption. An experiment found them to be 35% effective on a similar *Grimmia*; clumps with all their hair tips clipped off lost half again as much moisture in a day as the unclipped controls. Alpine rock surfaces are ferociously hot habitats—they pass 150° on some summer afternoons.

Frayed-cap Moss

Racomitrium canescens (ray-co-**mit**-rium: ragged hat; cay-**ness**-enz: grayish-white) and *R. elongatum*. Stems 1–3", sprawling in large mats but typically erect near the tips, ± flattened because most of the leaves are on two opposite ranks of short branchlets; spore capsules vertical, on ½" stalks that twist counterclockwise when dry; leaves taper to whitish translucent hair tips that give the whole mat an ash-gray color when dry. On rocks in sun, abundant at lower elevs. Grimmiaceae.

---

*Formerly included in *Grimmia alpestris*, a species now restricted to Europe.

Peat Mosses

Sphagnum spp. (**sfag**-num: the Greek term). Robust mosses typically in massive spongy mats, the stems crowded, supporting each other; the usual color here is pale glaucous green, paler and less yellowish than other mosses, but some species can be bright red with anthocyanins where growing in full sun; leaves tiny, mostly crowded on ¼–¾" branches, the branches either in groups of 2–5 along the stem or in a big tuft at the top; fruiting stalks short, several per shoot tip, each bearing one ± spherical blackish capsule which releases spores all at once, explosively. Typically floating in slow-moving water; or terrestrial in rain forest; all elevs. Sphagnaceae.

Peat mosses are the most primitive mosses, and at the same time the most important mosses both ecologically and economically. Estimates have them covering 1% of the earth's continents—making them one of the most extensive of all dominant plant types. They owe their success to their ability to change their environment to suit themselves and discourage others. Growing in slow-moving cold water, they draw oxygen and nutrients out of the water and replace them with hydrogen ions mainly in the form of uronic acids. The water, being too slow to replace itself frequently, is eventually too acidic and too poor in oxygen and nutrients to support the other plants growing there. At this point a whole new set of plants takes over, with peat moss the dominant. The new community is a "mire" or "peat bog" as opposed to a nonacid "marsh" or "fen." (Though peat mosses thrive in the acids they themselves create, they die in the sulphuric acids resulting from acid rain.)

Also suppressed—by cold, lack of oxygen, and certain antibiotics produced by peat mosses—are the bacteria that normally perform decomposition duties underwater. Very little decomposition takes place in a mire. The floating mass of peat moss lives and grows at the top, in the air, and dies bit by bit just below. The dead part, failing to decompose, gets thicker and thicker beneath the waterline. In some places (like western Ireland and northern Minnesota) this can go on indefinitely, the dead peat compressing and becoming a concentrated deposit of biomass suitable for fuel—the chief economic use of peat moss.

Other successions from peat moss are also well known. The peat moss surface may rise high enough above waterline—either by flotation or by thickening to rest on the bottom—to become a seedbed for dry-land plants including conifers. This is a common pathway by which glacial cirque tarns (small lakes in high basins) are converted to forests. More typically in our mountains, though, tarns have plenty of streamflow to prevent their ever turning into mires. They silt up and turn into glorious meadows after a marshy (not boggy) transitional phase. Still, peat mires are not uncommon in Oregon's High Cascades, where there is gentle subalpine topography; and peat mosses are fairly common here as minority members of marsh communities, and even as terrestrial mosses.

Peat moss was an invaluable material to some Northwest tribes, especially upcoast, where *Sphagnum* "muskeg" bogs abound. Its phenomenal water-absorbing capacity made it perfect for diapers, cradle lining, and sanitary napkins. Expectant mothers gathered quantities of peat moss, sometimes lining the entire lodge where the baby was to be born. Other mosses were sometimes given sponging, padding, and wiping tasks, mainly where peat moss was unavailable; most tribes' languages didn't distinguish types of moss other than peat moss.

Granite Moss

Andreaea rupestris (ahn-dray-ee-a: after G. R. Andreae; rue-**pes**-tris: on rocks). Plants brownish black even when wet (unlike schistidium, below; check with a few drops of water), in tight tufts usually less than 1" high; leaves minute; capsule hardly raised above the foliage, black, much less than ⅛" tall, opening by four lateral slits rather than at the tip. On rock (esp igneous) in full sun. Andreaeaceae.

The sooty pigmentation of this odd moss consists mainly of red anthocyanins on top of green chlorophylls; the former are there to protect the latter from the intense ultraviolet radiation that blasts exposed high-altitude sites.

The granite mosses are a primitive family set apart by capsule structure and leaf cells very different from other mosses.

What word consists of four Es, four As, and four consonants? Hint:

Find it on this page.

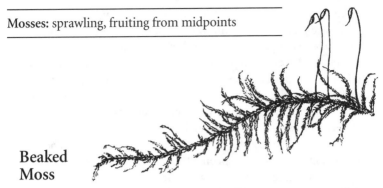

Beaked Moss

Eurhynchium spp.* (yew-**rink**-ium: true beak). Leaves green to gold, in featherlike strands often 12" or longer, with closely spaced branchlets most-ly on one plane; fruiting stalks ½–1" tall appearing in late fall, the lower por-tion minutely roughened under 10× lens. Brachytheciaceae.

E. oreganum (or-eg-**ay**-num: of OR). Branchlets hardly ever subbranched; forms luxuriant mats on ground, logs and tree bases below 4,000' on the W-side; the most abundant forest-floor moss in wetter W-side valley bottoms.

E. praelongum (pre-**long**-gum: elongated). Typically with short sub-branches on some branchlets; thinner mats; common only on streamside rocks, all elevs.

Abundance in general, and on accessible low maple branches in particular, makes these target species among moss collectors for the florist trade. Forest service regulations require permits for all "spe-cial forest products" harvesters, and permit moss removal only from branches, not from logs or the ground.

Rope Moss

Rhytidiopsis robusta (rye-tiddy-**op**-sis: wrinkled like, i.e., related to genus *Rhytidium*). Yellow-green to brownish moss in loose mats, the strands looking thick and ropy due to close-packed leaves and sparse branching; stems yellow-green; leaves ¼", irregularly deeply wrinkled (under lens), tending to curve all to one side of stem; fruiting stalks 1", red-brown; capsules often sharply crooked downward. The most abundant for-est-floor moss of higher W-side elevs (rare below 2,000'). Hylocomiaceae.

---

*This genus has been bounced around between this name and either *Stokes-iella* or *Kindbergia*.

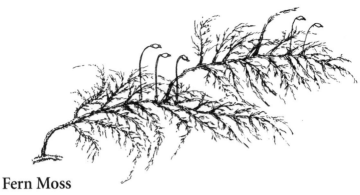

Fern Moss

Hylocomium splendens (hi-lo-**coe**-mium: forest hair; **splen**-denz: lustrous). Glossy gold to brownish green mosses in a distinctive stepwise growth form—each year's growth, shaped like a tiny (1½") fern with subbranched branchlets, rises from a midpoint on the previous year's stem, growing vertically at first and then arching into a horizontal position; a stem may show 10 or more such steps, but only the upper 1-3 look very alive; fruiting stalks few, ½–1" tall, red, not twisted; capsules ⅛", horizontal; leaves minute. Forms luxuriant mats on rocks, logs, and earth. W-side low and (less often) middle elevs. Hylocomiaceae.

Wavy-leaved Cotton Moss

Plagiothecium undulatum (play-joe-**theece**-ium: slanted capsule). Whitish-green moss in loose mats, the strands ropy but, on close examination, flat: about ¼" wide by less than ⅛" thick; leaves spreading in two planes, shiny, crinkled in crosswise waves (at 10×); fruiting stalks 2", reddish; capsules sloping, slender, grooved. On soil, well-rotted wood, or alder bark; moist forest, usually old growth. Plagiotheciaceae.

The distinctive almost bluish white cast makes this one of our easiest mosses to spot. Combine that color with the flattish strands, in suitable habitat, and you almost certainly have wavy-leaved cotton moss. It is frequent under western hemlock, apparently tolerating the deep shade and greater acidity there.

Short Pendent Moss

Antitrichia curtipendula (ant-i-**trick**-ia: opposing hairs; curti-**pend**-you-la: short pendent). Robust, rotund orange-green growths on rain-forest branches; some strands pendent, to 6"; side branches sparse, some with whiplike tips with minute root-hairs; leaves ⅛"; fruiting stalks scarce, ⅜–½", reddish brown; capsules maturing in winter. On bark in moistest W-side old-growth forests. Leucodontaceae.

This moss builds up huge biomass in the oldest, moistest forests, but most of that is up on canopy limbs. We don't know exactly why it waits for the forest's second century to thrive, and for the third to sixth century to really take off. We can guess that it has something to do with light coming into the middle canopy, thanks to the death of some of the taller trees, while the epiphytes themselves are making their own microclimate moister by intercepting and holding on to cloud moisture. Red tree voles and marbled murrelets both burrow into these luxuriant pillows to make their nests, which is probably the main reason those two species are old-growth dependent.

You're most likely to see short-pendulous moss as fragments that litter the forest floor, sometimes taking hold and growing there, but rarely flourishing. It often mixes with icicle moss; tell them apart by this one's bigger leaves, coarser branching, and less dramatically pendulous form.

Big Shaggy Moss

Rhytidiadelphus triquetrus (rye-tiddy-a-**del**-fus: wrinkled brother, i.e., related to genus *Rhytidium*; try-**kweet**-rus: 3-cornered). Light green moss in coarse mats; stems red-brown, often partly upright; leaves triangular, ¼ × ⅛", faintly but neatly pleated (under 12× lens), sticking out all ways from the stem; fruiting stalks few, 1"; capsule ± bent, maturing in autumn. Widespread on humus, logs, rocks, or trees (esp deciduous), esp. in semiopen W-side lowlands. Hylocomiaceae.

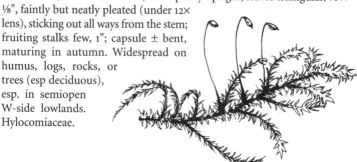

Yellow Shaggy Moss

Rhytidiadelphus loreus (**lor**-ee-us: strap). Light green, fine moss in luxuriant mats, irregularly branched or featherlike (but not as finely so as beaked moss); stems red-brown; leaves about ⅛", pleated near their bases (under 12× lens), neatly tapering toward shoot tips or curving to one side of shoot; fruiting stalks 1½", capsule very short and tubby, ± horizontal, maturing in spring. Abundant W-side in moist forests on logs (esp. where bark has fallen off), trees or sometimes ground. Hylocomiaceae.

Icicle Moss

Isothecium stoloniferum spiculiferum * (eye-so-**theece**-ium: equal capsules; sto-la-**nif**-er-um: bearing many stems; spic-you-**lif**-er-um: bearing spikelets). Glossy yellow-green festoons; strands plumelike with close branchlets, typically pendent, often 8" or longer; stems greenish brown; leaves minute, straight; fruiting stalks ¼–½", dark red; capsules maturing in winter. Moist forests, on all substrates; esp. abundant on branches. Brachytheciaceae.

This is one of the plants you might think of as the "Spanish moss" in our rain forests, but beware of popular misconceptions. Louisiana's Spanish moss is unrelated, being a seed plant in the pineapple family; and Olympic rain forest festoons also include abundant spikemoss (a fern-relative) and old-man's-beard (a lichen). These four organisms could hardly be more unrelated, but all live as epiphytes. They rarely suck anything from their host trees (a lichen exception was found recently; see page 64) though they do utilize nutrients leached by dripwater from the tree's surface, and some trees actually compete with them for this resource by extending rootlets among the epiphytes on their own bark.

*Most 1990s texts, following the 1990 *Checklist*, treat this as *I. myosuroides*. Dr. David Wagner's unpublished OR Checklist uses the time-honored *I. stoloniferum* in accord with a new genus revision that's in preparation.

Curly-leaf Moss

Hypnum circinale (**hip**-num: the Greek term; sir-sin-**ay**-lee: coiled). Very fine, delicate mosses in thin waterfall-like mats most often on conifers; stems reddish; leaves minute, narrowing (under 12× lens) to slender points in long arcs (to nearly complete circles) all to one side of stem, giving the shoot a braided look; fruiting stalks ¼–½", not twisted when dry; capsules very short (much less than ⅛"), maturing in winter. The most abundant moss low on W-side conifer trunks below 4,000'; also on other surfaces in forest. Hypnaceae.

Aspects of Tree Trunks

According to the old saw, mosses grow on the north sides of trees. Actually they grow on the wet sides. These might well be north sides due to shade, all other things being equal—on flat terrain with trees straight as plumb lines, for example. But trees around here mostly grow on slopes, and lean downslope. Their upper sides (e.g., south sides of trees on a north-facing slope) catch most of the rain and grow most of the moss.

Moist bark also favors lichens. In our wet Westside forests, however, the moistest sites often foster such heavy moss growth that only a few big lichens, such as the green dog lichen which thrives in the midst of thick moss mats, can hold their own. The most prolific lichen growth on these trees will likely be adjacent—higher on the wet side of the trunk, and in a fringe bordering the moss carpet on both edges. The dry side may appear bare, but often it is covered by crust lichens which, being easily shaded out, are at the bottom of the pecking order for good microhabitats.

The very moistest microsites are flaring tree bases and the tops of larger limbs. Both accumulate litter, which breaks down into humus and eventually forms soil.

Up on the tree trunks and branches, these sorts of differences determine a whole set of zones for different epiphytes; see page 290.

Thallose Liverworts

Order Marchantiales. Bright green, ± leathery flat lobes textured with close regular rows of bubblelike pale bumps; lobes regularly branching in 2-way equal splits; tall (¾–4") fruiting stalks present only briefly, in spring.

Marchantia polymorpha (mar-**shahn**-tia: after Nicolas Marchant; poly-**mor**-fa: many forms). Surface often bearing conspicuous cups holding a few gemmae (vegetative propagules); fruiting stalks umbrellalike, the female ones 9-lobed; on streambanks or burned or disturbed earth.

Conocephalum conica (co-no-**sef**-a-lum: cone head). No gemmae; surface bumps very large and close-packed; fruiting stalks mushroomlike, the conical head fringed with spherical spore-capsules; aromatic when crushed; widespread on moist earth, esp streambanks. Color p 489.

This type of liverwort bears no obvious resemblance to either leafy liverworts or mosses. It's more likely to be confused with foliose lichens, but the "liverlike" textural pattern distinguish it from the "lunglike" branching ridges of lungwort or the patternless black speckles on green dog lichens (page 291). Coincidentally, liverwort, lungwort, and dog lichen are all names bestowed by medieval herbalists who looked for images of body parts—God's drug pre-scriptions—in the plant world. The bumps that give liverworts their alleged liver texture are air chambers, each opening to the outside by a tiny pore. They offer a favorable environment for photo-synthesis.

Conocephalum is named for a female "cone head" that rests on the liverwort's surface for several weeks in spring, waiting for liver-wort sperms to swim to it through a film of rain or dew or in the splash of a raindrop. When the spores are ripe and weather permits, the head is raised a few inches into the air in the space of a few hours by a stem of special cells that don't grow or multiply; they simply balloon lengthwise upward. This unorthodox manner of growing a stalk offers speed but not durability. You'll be lucky if you ever catch one of these cute but short-lived fruitings.

Rarely are ecologists able to pinpoint the site requirements of a plant so confidently as in Alsie Campbell's description of where *Marchantia* grows on Oregon Cascade streamsides: "Occasionally a semiporous barrier will be deposited upon a slightly sloping, nonporous surface across which water seeps all year, such as a small log impeding drainage from an almost flat rock. If there is no disturbance, organic matter and extremely fine inorganic particles build up and form an aqueous muck." Campbell concluded that the *Marchantia* has "practical" importance in treacherously hiding slick footing.

Leafy Liverworts

Order Jungermanniales. Mosslike growths of branched, flattened ribbonlike strips (⅛" wide, ±) of leaves neatly overlapping in 2, 4 or 5 ranks.

Scapania bolanderi (sca-**pay**-nia: shovel; bo-**lan**-der-eye: after Henry Bolander). Leaves minutely toothed all around, (just visible under 10× lens), in four ranks all visible on top side (illustrated above left), but only two apparent from underneath (above right). Abundant on logs and wet sides of W-side conifers.

Porella navicularis (por-**el**-a: pore—; nav-ik-you-**lair**-iss: boatlet, referring to leaf shape). Leaves glossy olive green, smooth-margined, appear 2-ranked in top view but 5-ranked as seen from underneath. Abundant on lowland hardwoods and conifers, up to mid-canopy, esp in OR. Illustrated below.

Leafy liverworts are easily mistaken for mosses at first glance. The most dramatic difference is in the spore-bearing stalks. Those of mosses are sturdy and conspicuous several months out of the year, but the watery, insubstantial stalks of liverworts are rarely seen, since they last only for a few spring or summer days.

The foliage is just as distinctive, at least from close up; contrasted with moss foliage, it reminds me of small plants flattened by winter snows. (A few leafy liverworts, some of them common on Westside conifers, have leaves so thoroughly fringed or lobed as to obscure any neat flattened ranks.)

7

Fungi

The mushroom is not the fungus—at least not by itself. Neither is a puffball, or a shelf fungus on a tree. Each is a fruiting body (what we might loosely call a fruit) of a fungus organism which is many times larger and longer-lived. As an apple tree produces apples to carry its seeds, the fungus produces mushrooms or other fruiting bodies to disseminate its spores.

A graphic illustration is provided by a "fairy ring"—a circle or partial circle of mushrooms that comes up year after year. These mushrooms are fruits of one continuous fungus body whose perimeter they mark; it expands year by year as the fungus grows within the soil. In some years the mushrooms may fail to appear, but the fungus is still alive and growing; it merely didn't get the moisture or other conditions for fruiting, that year. The largest fairy rings on record are over 600' in diameter. Divided by the observed rate of growth, that yields a likely age of five to seven centuries. Still larger rings made by honey mushrooms (page 268) are visible from airplanes over forests: they are circular dents in the canopy, consisting of sick and dying trees attacked by the fungus. Certain map lichens (page 287) are calculated, extrapolating from diameter, to be 4,000 years old, rivaling the oldest trees. Each of these fungal circles is a genetic individual, but can't exactly be compared with an individual as we understand the term for animals and most plants. In any case most mushrooms are not individuals. (But see Morels, page 282.) The living, growing body of a fungus is a network of tiny tubes called "hyphae" (singular: "hypha"). Except when they aggregate in bundles or in fruiting bodies, hyphae are too fine to see or handle; they range from 2–10 microns thick.

A fungus is also not a plant. It's more closely related to an animal. (See the Five-Kingdom System, page 577.) Fungal cell walls get their strength from a material called chitin (also found in insect skeletons), but contain no cellulose, the characteristic fiber of the plant kingdom. Also like animals, fungi obtain their carbohydrates from photosynthetic (green) organisms. Animals get them by eating, whereas fungi employ any of four nutritional modes:

Mycorrhizal: linking up with plant roots for exchange of nutrients and water.

Lichenized: enclosing and "farming" algae and cyanobacteria.

Saprophytic: decomposing (i.e., rotting) dead organic matter.

Parasitic: drawing nutrition from living plant or animal matter.

The Fungus/Root Symbiosis

Let's set the record straight: the Web of Life is not a metaphor, it's literal truth, and it's made of fungi. Call it the wood-wide web if you will. The word "mycorrhiza," coined in 1885 from Greek words meaning "fungus" and "root," names a special growth that connects fungi with plant roots. Simply put, the job of root hairs in plants is actually performed mostly by symbiotic fungi. Soon after a plant germinates from seed, its rootlet is likely to meet up with a fungal hypha. Each contains hormones that stimulate and alter the growth of the other, forming a joint fungus/root organ (the mycorrhiza) that immediately goes into use as a nutrient loading dock. Some plants start even earlier: most orchid seeds must be penetrated by a hypha before they will germinate.

The hyphae in some classes of mycorrhizae grow into a net around the root tip. In others they digest root cell walls, penetrate and inhabit the cells, and eventually are digested back by the cells. In any case the hyphae hormonally suppress the formation of plant root hairs; at the same time they provide a preestablished network of root hair surrogates vastly finer and more efficient than the plant roots themselves. (Do the math: since an absorptive plant root is about 1 mm in diameter, and a hypha is about .003 mm, the hypha can provide about 300 times as much absorptive surface area for a given investment in molecular materials.) In addition to conveying water efficiently, mycorrhizal

The first two modes, which cover a majority of the multicelled fungi, are "mutualistic" symbioses, meaning that they may benefit both the fungal and the green partners in the relationship. The third and fourth modes do not benefit the plant hosts as individuals, but they certainly benefit plant communities. Rotting is necessary for clearing away dead material, recycling nutrients and, on a grander scale, for keeping the world from bursting into flame due to excess plant-produced oxygen in the air. Even parasitic fungi, though usually thought of as diseases, are often beneficial when viewed from a whole-systems point of view. (See page 268.)

Recent research suggests renaming the saprophytic fungi omnivorous fungi. Many of them supplement their diet of dead things by actively catching lots of very live microscopic animals and bacteria. (Page 273)

The most important thing to understand about fungi and plants is that, with only minor exceptions, symbiosis between them

---

fungi have means of making both nitrogen and phosphorus available which plants do not have. They can also bore right into solid rock, extracting nutrients, according to one recent paper. In exchange, the fungus receives the carbohydrates it needs from the host plant.

Fungi cannot produce carbohydrates, so most mycorrhizal fungi are totally dependent on their plant partners. Few plants are equally dependent on fungi, since most plants have the genetic information for making root hairs to obtain water and minerals. Planted in a rich, moist, nutritious substrate, a seedling may do just that, resisting mycorrhizal infection of its roots. But in real-world situations, nonmycorrhizal seedlings may not survive. Appreciating this fact, the timber industry inoculates conifer seeds in nurseries with suitable fungi. On a hot logged-over slope, Douglas-fir seedlings proved more likely to survive if planted right next to heath-family shrubs, because suitable mycorrhizae partner heath shrubs; in a similar study, seedlings survived only if they were inoculated with a teaspoonful of forest soil. The active ingredients in this elixir of life are poorly known, but mites, nematodes, bacteria, and other microorganisms are present in great numbers and variety, and surely share credit with the 100 miles or so of hyphal tubes per teaspoon of soil. Yes, you read 100 miles/teaspoon.

Most plants have have many mycorrhizal species as potential partners. Our conifers each have hundreds. A tree forms mycorrhizae

---

is what makes the world go 'round. When life first moved from the sea onto the land, it did so by means of partnerships between primitive fungi and algae. Soon the algae evolved into the first plants, and the plants coevolved with fungi up to the present day. About 90% of plant species are known to form mycorrhizae, and other mutualisms prevail among the remaining 10%. Mosses are the broadest plant group not yet known to be heavily mycorrhizal, and mosses are often colonized by cyanobacteria which make nitrogen available to the mosses, as they do to lichenized fungi. Sedges are a big group with few mycorrhizae, and sedges are infested by microscopic internal fungi called endophytes, which protect them from pathogenic microorganisms. (One study found that only a single

with several species at a time, and grows best if it has a range available for changing conditions. Each fungus has its own special abilities.

While the typical barter is carbohydrates from the plant in return for water and minerals from the fungus, other exchanges are common. During dry seasons the water flow is likely to reverse, with deep-rooted trees supplying most of the network's water. Small plants can receive carbohydrates from overstory plants via shared fungal partners. Suzanne Simard measured transfer of carbohydrates to Douglas-fir seedlings from birches above them; the nurture increased when the seedlings were made needier by shading them. Trees, of course, switch from receiving to donating carbohydrates once they are big enough, but non-green plants (page 177) stay on welfare lifelong.

Mycorrhizae exude some of the carbohydrate into the soil, making the soil at once more cohesive, more porous, and better aerated. They also help protect plants from disease. Root rots (parasitic fungi) have a harder time attacking roots mantled in healthy mycorrhizae, which form both a physical and a chemical barrier. Fungi regularly compete with other fungi by secreting selective toxins, and they secrete antibiotics to suppress some bacteria pathogenic to plants.

Mycorrhizae may soon lead to a new picture of the all-important nitrogen cycle. Mycorrhizal plants have been shown to meet their nitrogen needs in substrates where the old model would have said all the nitrogen was organically "bound up" and unavailable. Apparently some fungi have a unique ability to break proteins into amino acids and make these available to their plant partners.

gene mutation is required to turn a pathogenic microfungus into a beneficial one; such an adaptation could benefit the fungus, which would presumably be able to live longer in a healthy host than a dying one. No wonder fungal endophytes are proving to be extremely common in leaves.) Conifers, the group that forms the backbone of Cascade/Olympic ecosystems, are 100% mycorrhizal, *and* generally infested with needle endophytes which help protect them from grazers and pathogens, *and* copiously festooned (here) with lichens, many of which fix nitrogen.

Higher taxonomy of fungi is in a state of upheaval; it would serve little purpose to name families or orders in this book. This small chapter can only hint at the hundreds of kinds of fungi that grow here. (Even the greatest of mycologists can only hint: one estimates there are 1,500,000 species of fungi in the world, of which 5% have been named.) A huge and important group omitted due to its low visibility is the microfungi, including yeasts and molds.

Fungi: unsafe to eat

Fly Amanita and Panther Amanita

Amanita spp. (am-a-**night**-a: Greek term for some fungus on Mt. Amanus). Cap usually sprinkled with whitish warts; stem white, with skirtlike ring near the top and a bulbous (not quite cuplike) base; gills and spores white.

Fly amanita, *A. muscaria* (mus-**cair**-ia: of flies). Also **fly agaric.** Cap typically bright red (here); less often orange, yellow, or nearly white; stem base has a few slight rings, diminishing upward, just above bulb. Widespread, on the ground, mainly in fall. Color p 483.

Panther amanita, *A. pantherina* (panther-eye-na: panther—). Cap brown, tan, or nearly white; bulbous base has a single heavy, rolled upper edge which may or may not pull away from stalk. Typically under Douglas-fir; spring, fall or rarely winter.

Long famous in Europe as the archetype of malevolently alluring toadstools,* the fly amanita also has a reputation as a recreational

---

*A toadstool, in British usage, is any poisonous or unsavory mushroom. Few Americans infer any real difference between "toadstool" and "mushroom," which is a good thing. Old sayings about "how to tell a mushroom from a toadstool" were dangerous. There is no across-the-board difference, so you always have to identify the particular species.

---

or spiritual drug. Siberian tribes and, according to some scholars of the Vedas, ancient Hindus used amanitas that way. Some people in the Northwest have used them repeatedly, taking precautions that apparently work for them. I suspect the variable reactions have less to do with technique than with luck (including genetics). A wild-eyed and euphoric stranger on the trail once handed a fly amanita cap to two friends of mine, who were impressed enough to down it on the spot. One friend had an enhanced afternoon while the other, from the other half of the same cap, was in abject misery. Cramps, spasms, sweating, vomiting, lethargy, stupefied sleep, manic behavior, and subsequent amnesia are symptoms often reported, with death very unlikely, though that also has been recorded. It's a gamble I can't recommend.

The problem of identification within this freely hybridizing genus is even more unsettling. The panther amanita is considered deadly, even though its toxins are essentially just higher concentrations of those (muscimol, ibotenic acid and a little muscarine) found in the fly amanita, as opposed to the liver-destroying cyclopeptides of the destroying angels. Panther and fly are distinguished in the field mainly by color, but in fact they can range to an identical shade of off-white. In any case, they do look fine. Trailside specimens are a scenic resource **to be left untouched**.

Panther amanitas have little to do with panthers (i.e., leopards) other than being tannish and spotted, but fly amanitas have centuries of experience poisoning flies. They were traditionally left around the house broken up in saucers of sugared milk—children beware! Dogs and cats also seem to find dried Amanitas fatally irresistible.

Death Cap and Destroying Angel

Amanita spp. Flesh, gills, and stem white; stem cylindrical or slightly smaller upward, slender, with a tattered skirtlike ring (sometimes missing) and a ± bulbous base in a thin white cup (requires careful excavation to see; the cap often barely emerges from ground, and may have dirty surface); spores white. Becomes fetid with age. **Do not taste.**

Death Cap, *A. phalloides* (fal-**oy**-deez: phallus-like).Cap light yellow-green to tan, rarely almost white. Late summer and fall. Introduced from Europe, found so far mostly near cultivated filberts, chestnuts, and oaks, but may continue its spread into new habitats.

Destroying Angel, *Amanita ocreata** (oc-ree-ay-ta: sheathed). Cap white. In spring. Color p 483.

Lovely but monstrously poisonous, these are our most dangerous fungi, and they seem to be on the increase, especially in the suburbs. It's worth knowing their characteristics even though they're still uncommon here. All amanitas have white spores and more or less white gills. Most have a definite ring around the stem, the remnant of a "partial veil" that extended from the edges of the cap, sealing off the immature spores to keep them moist. More distinctively, most also emerge from a "universal veil," an additional moisture barrier that wraps the entire young mushroom, from under its base to all over its cap. As a young "button," each amanita fruiting-body in its universal veil is egg- to pear-shaped, resembling a puffball but with the outline of cap and gills visible in cross-section. Remnants of this veil *usually* persist as a cup or lip around the base of the stem, and/or on top of the cap in the form of warts, crumbs or broad patches. But absence of these remnants doesn't disprove any amanita, since the stem easily breaks off above the cup, and the cap crumbs can wash off.

All white-spored, white-gilled mushrooms should be collected with great care and examined for ring and cup. The genus *Amanita* contains many good edible species, some of them long popular in Europe, but the chance of misidentifying a deadly one leads American guidebooks to caution against all amanitas. (By the same reasoning, this book doesn't recommend any stemmed, gilled mushrooms. You need a complete mushroom book for them.)

These amanitas and the little-brown-mushroom genus *Galerina* share one of the most insidious poisons found in nature. It attacks the liver within minutes of ingestion, but symptoms don't appear for ten to fourteen hours (or possibly up to four days) by which time the liver is seriously—often lethally—damaged. Over half of the poisonings recorded in America by these species have been fatal, though hospitals have techniques to improve the odds if they know they're dealing with amanita cyclopeptides before symptoms are too advanced.

---

*Specimens from the PNW previously identified as *A. verna*, *virosa*, and *bisporigera* belong to *A. ocreata*; the other three spp. have not been confirmed from the PNW. The name Destroying Angel covers all pure white spp. with cyclopeptide toxins.

Autumn Galerina

Galerina autumnalis (gal-er-**eye**-na: helmeted; autumn-**nay**-lis: a some-what misleading name for this species). Caps mostly ¾–1¾" diam, slightly tacky and deep yellow-brown when wet, dull tan when dry, radially striped near the edge; gills pale, becoming brown with spores; stem thin, brown, darkening toward base, with a thin whitish ring; spores rusty brown. Typi-cally clustered on rotting (sometimes ± buried) wood, often among moss-es, in late fall or sometimes spring. Color p 483.

This unprepossessing "little brown mushroom," or "LBM," contains the same cyclopeptide poisons as the deadly amanitas, is just as deadly, and is far commoner here. It is considered less of a danger simply because people don't normally bother with LBMs—unless they happen to be hunting psilocybin mushrooms. *Galerina* has a few traits in common with our native *Psilocybe* species, so you'd damn well better know what you're doing if you hunt *Psilocybe*. Galerinas have also occasionally been mistaken for the edible honey mushroom.

Woolly Chanterelle

Gomphus floccosus (**gom**-fus: peg; flock-**oh**-sus: woolly-tufted). Also **scaly vase chanterelle**. Orange trumpet-shaped fungus; cap undifferentiated from stem; often deeply hollow down the center; inside surface roughened with big soft scales; outside surface paler and irregularly, shallowly wrinkled (no paper-thin gills); spores ochre. On ground, late summer and fall. Color p 483.

Mushroom guides, over the years, batted this species back and forth between the "Edible" and "Poisonous" lists. A recent verdict is "hard to digest"—and not so dangerous as to drag the true chanterelles down from the "Safe for Beginners" list on grounds of possible con-fusion. This one is more common than edible chanterelles in old-growth forest, while the Pacific golden chanterelle seems to prefer second-growth. The mechanism of these preferences is obscure, since both species accept Douglas-fir and other trees as mycorrhizal partners.

Short-stemmed Russula and Lobster Mushroom

Russula brevipes (**russ**-you-la: red—; **brev**-ip-eez: short foot). All-white mushroom, cap often bruised brown or yellowish, dry, quite concave, margins usually rolled under; 3–10" diam; gills fine, crowded; spores white to cream; flesh odorless, bland to slightly peppery; stem cylindrical, rigid, brittle, can be snapped, leaving rough, chalklike, fiberless broken surfaces. Mycorrhizal with conifers; scattered, usually ± buried in forest duff; fall.

These two species tell an irresistible Frog Prince story. Well, not exactly. As the mushroom magically morphs into the object of our desire, it turns from virginal white to enflamed and pimply. Anyway, our story begins with a rather attractive mushroom which, due to its abundance and blah flavor, was voted "most boring mushroom" at one mycophagist convention. It likes to sturdily push thick duff up from underneath, and usually has a great many crumbs on its face. It belongs to a huge and abundant genus that David Arora dubbed JARs (for "just another Russula"); many are even more attractive, their pure white, brittle flesh and gills contrasting with a peelable cap skin that may be carmine, green, or black. There are so many Russulas, so few are tasty, and identification is so difficult, that mushroom hunters rarely identify them.

Sometimes Russula mushrooms come up with a parasitic fungus, *Hypomyces lactifluorum*, inside them. Think of it as a bright orange mold. The mold prevents paper-thin gills from developing, alters the graceful form to a crude knob and the delicate, brittle flesh to spudlike firmness, and wraps the whole thing in a scurfy deep orange skin. And *Voilá*, it's delicious, a marketable delicacy. It's called a lobster mushroom.

One mystery: is it safe? Once heavily parasitized, the host mushroom is no longer identifiable to species. The few high-tech identifications to date have been only to genus: *Russula* or *Lactarius*. A few members of those genera are poisonous. And yet lobster mushrooms have a safer gastrointestinal record than lobster. (I have not heard of any poisonings.) They also keep longer than any normal mushroom. Does the parasite avoid toxic species? Do you want to take the chance? Or could it possibly neutralize toxins, the way it apparently kills or repels bugs and rot? Drug companies, are you paying attention?

Short-stemmed russula, one of the likeliest pre-lobsters in our area, is actually edible, but not at all recommended.

Shoestring Root Rot / Honey Mushroom

Armillaria ostoyae* (ar-mil-**air**-ia: banded; os-**toy**-ee: after Paul Ostoya). Cap yellow-brown to brown, with coarse fibrous scales radiating from the center; gills white, stained rusty in age; stalk has stringy white pith, and a substantial, up-flaring, brown-edged ring; clustered on wood or ground, caps often coated with spores where overlapped; spores white; coarse black threadlike rhizomorphs often visible around base, or netting across nearby wood, often under bark. Fall. Color p 483.

Mushroom-hunters know this as a long-popular, albeit unreliable, edible. Tree farmers know it as a pest, a killing pathogen on trees, and have devoted much study to eradicating it. Apparently it lives saprophytically in fertile mature forests, but often becomes a deadly parasite where the trees are stressed—in highly competitive stands, and especially in logged and roaded regions. It is a leading cause of white rot in wood. In ecological terms, that makes it a valuable recycler of nutrients and facilitator of animal habitats.

---

* Honey mushrooms used to all be *A. mellea,* but were split into many species. The splitting is still very much a work in progress. *Ostoyae* is common on NW conifers. The newly-named *nabsnona,* on alder and maple, has orange-brown cap without scales, stem brown fading upward to white.

Laminated Root Rot

The other worst root disease in the Northwest is laminated root rot, Phellinus weirii. Phellinus *species are shelf fungi related to the sulphur shelf on page 278, but don't look for identification traits on that page, or at all, because you aren't going to see this abundant fungus. It virtually never produces any shelves on trees, or any spores, but merely grows in tree roots, slowly, inexorably, passing from tree to tree when the roots touch each other. After many decades, the infested tree always dies, often with a bark beetle attack as the proximate cause. The easy way to see laminated root rot is from an airplane. Look for patches where the continuous conifer canopy is broken by many smaller trees and shrubs, their colors indicating a conifer/hardwood mix.*

Laminated root rot infests about 5% of westside forest soils. It is so incurable and so inexorable in its growth that we can reasonably ask, "why isn't it everywhere?" For one thing, it has preferences. Douglas-fir is the chief victim. Mountain hemlock and silver fir are also susceptible; western hemlock less so, and pines still less; cedars quite resistant;

(White rot breaks down both cellulose and lignin, as opposed to brown cubical rot, which breaks down only cellulose, leaving very long-lasting cubes of lignin in the soil.) Quoting an unusually sensual sentence from the Forest Service tome on the disease, "the crunch of collapsing compartments of pseudosclerotial tissue when one walks on logs decayed by the fungus adds an audible dimension to its saprophytic activities."

The media gave the honey mushroom its fifteen minutes of fame in 1992, calling it the World's Largest Living Thing. Michigan mycologists made headlines first, with a honey mushroom that spread over 37 acres. Not to be outdone, researchers here mapped one underlying 1500 acres near Mt. Adams. We aren't talking about a Godzilla mushroom cap, now, but about networks of tiny hyphal tubes. The researchers matched the genes of hyphae at widespread spots in their forest, and found that a single mushroom clone had branched out over 1500 acres. All the hyphae in the clone had grown vegetatively from a single spore, starting hundreds of years ago, but there is no reason to think that all these hyphae are still interconnected. If a clone can be World's Largest Living Thing, there are doubtless larger mushroom clones in the world, and even they could not tip the scales against a 6,000-ton aspen clone.

---

hardwoods immune; and red alder downright toxic to it. So it advances fastest where there are a lot of mature Douglas-firs, but even there it's slow. Every time a fire comes along it comes to a standstill, or even retreats if the post-fire stand is mostly hardwoods or pines. Then, remember that the climate that let Doug-fir take over the Northwest arrived only 14,000 years ago (page 20), and you can begin to see why laminated root rot has taken over only five percent.

Though about as popular as Ebola virus within the timber industry, root rot is respected by forest ecologists as an agent of biodiversity. It provides refugia where species that tend to disappear from dense conifer forest can persist, and be ready to spread out again after disturbances come along. Such species include not only broadleaf trees and shrubs, and western redcedar, but also many animals. Root rot patches are ideal deer and moose habitat, richly mixing shrubs with a few tall trees, and they have plenty of snags for cavity nesters. That's good for the surrounding forests: they need lots of cavity-nesting insectivorous birds around when pest insects start their outbreaks.

Violet Cortinarius

Cortinarius violaceus* (cor-tin-**air**-ius: curtained; vye-o-**lay**-see-us: violet).
Cap and stem ± uniformly blackish purple; cap 2–5", shiny even when dry,
covered with fine fibrous scales; cinnamon-brown spores soon color the
gills. On ground in old-growth, esp Olys, late summer and fall. Color p 483.

I admire this mushroom's amazing deep color, but I can't recommend it for eating because positive identifications in this huge and
risky genus are beyond the scope of this book. Many of the 600+
species of *Cortinarius* have rusty spores and varying shades of
lavender caps. The genus is named for its veil or "cortina," which
stretches out like a filmy curtain as the cap expands, and later leaves
cobwebby remnants rather than any substantial ring on the stem.

---

*There is a proposal to separate the species on conifers as *C. hercynicus*.

Cautious Mushroom-Eating

*Only a tiny minority of mushrooms are seriously poisonous. A greater
number may make you sick in the stomach, or uncomfortable somewhere else. Still more are considered edible by most who have tried
them, but even among "good edibles," many reputations are tainted by
a few reports—allergic reactions, really. Even the supermarket mushroom,* Agaricus bisporus, *upsets some tummies. Many other mushrooms go unrecommended on the grounds of flavor or texture; again,
one person's "edible and choice" is another person's "Bleccch!"*

*All in all, the odds favor mushroom eaters, but the risks are too ex-
treme to forgive haphazard identifications. There are old mushroom
hunters, the saying goes, and there are bold mushroom hunters, but
there are no old bold mushroom hunters. Actually, there was at least
one old, bold mycologist: Captain Charles McIlvaine lived into his
dotage despite routinely tasting mushroom species on first encounter.
He claimed to have tried well over 1,000 and liked most of them.*

*Mushroom identification is more subtle and technical than most
plant identification, often requiring chemical reagents and a microscope. There's much to be said for the rule that nontechnical guides not
entirely devoted to mushrooms should forego labeling edibles. But fungal dinners have been such treasured wilderness experiences for this
writer that I will share some favorable advice. For eating typical mushrooms—those with a gilled cap on a stem—I refer you to mushroom
books (page 600); but I can recommend certain fleshy fungi that either*

Chanterelles

Cantharellus spp. (canth-a-**rel**-us: small vase). Vase-shaped mushroom (cap undifferentiated from stem), margin often wavy or irregular when mature; spore-bearing surface of rounded ridges (not paper-thin gills) sometimes with slight cross-wrinkles to make a netlike texture; slight peppery aftertaste when raw. On ground, in fall; mycorrhizal usually with Douglas-fir.

White chanterelle, *C. subalbidus* (sub-**al**-bid-us: almost white). Cap white, bruising yellow to (eventually) rusty orange; often very stout and short; spores white.

---

lack paper-thin gills or lack a distinct stem. Each of these species can be separated from poisonous species on the basis of a careful look at field characters alone. All the same, you must assume responsibility for your own results, gastronomic and gastrointestinal.

*A **spore print** for observing spore color, used in mushroom identification, is made simply by laying a cap, without stem, flat on a piece of paper for an hour or so. If you put part of the mushroom over inked or colored paper, then white spores will show up as well as dark ones.*

***Nibbling by mammals** or lower creatures is not evidence of safety.*

***Try a nibble** before eating a quantity; give your stomach at least two hours to test it. Each person should test their own stomach. (Test only after identifying. Deadly amanitas and galerinas, pages 263–66, must be absolutely ruled out first, since even a nibble would be dangerous. No morels of any kind, page 282–83, should be eaten raw.)*

***Small children** are much more susceptible to mushroom poisoning and allergies, and should not eat wild mushrooms.*

***Eat modest quantities,** of only one species, when first trying species.*

*Excessive **bugginess or worminess** occasionally causes stomach upset. If the stems but not the caps show larval bore holes, leave the stems behind so they won't infect the caps.*

*Carry in **paper bags,** not plastic. Keep mushrooms as cool as possible.*

*Don't forget to take **plenty of butter,** especially on fall trips. Gentle , thorough sauteing, without a lid, is rarely a bad way to cook a fungus. Scrambled eggs, toast, or crackers rarely fail to compliment.*

Pacific golden chanterelle, *C. formosus* * (for-**mo**-sus: beautiful). Cap yellow-orange, smooth, underside paler; spores ochre. Color p 484.

The golden chanterelle leads the Northwest's wild mushroom trade in pounds; in dollar value only matsutake and morels surpass it. Its popularity stems not from exceptional flavor but from its rich color, easy and safe identification, profuse local abundance, resistance to bugs, and the established place in French cuisine of its smaller, brighter cousin, *C. cibarius.* Though popular among mushroom-eating forest mammals, our golden chanterelle is less rich in flavor than *C. cibarius* or our own white chanterelle.

The only poisonous mushroom sometimes mistaken for a chanterelle (aside from the questionable woolly chanterelle, above) has true paper-thin gills. Thin gills, with their higher surface-to-volume ratio, are more efficient, and evolutionarily more advanced, than chanterelle-style wrinkles.

Here's good news. Chanterelles were found to fruit slightly *more* abundantly where they're harvested year after year, at least as of thirteen years into a study by the Oregon Mycological Society in the Bull Run watershed. In the very long term, who knows? The fungus might suffer if it never got to reproduce from spores.

Oyster Mushroom and Angel-Wings

Pleurotus and *Pleurocybella* spp. Fan-shaped, usually stemless mushrooms growing in clusters or groups from the side of fallen, dead, or merely wounded trees; mildly fragrant and pleasant-tasting (edible raw).

Oyster mushroom, *Pleurotus ostreatus*[†] (ploor-**oh**-tus: side ear; os-tree-**ay**-tus: oyster). On broadleaf wood, typically cottonwood or alder in our region; cap tan, cream or oyster-gray; spore print dries pale lilac. Fall, or occasionally spring (even midwinter in warmer climates). Color p 485.

Angel-wings, *Pleurocybella porrigens*[‡] (ploor-oh-si-**bell**-a: a compound of two other genera; **por**-i-jenz: spreading). On conifer wood, typically hemlock; all white; flesh thin; spores white. Color p 485.

Pleurotus may also grow with a short, semihorizontal stem from one edge of the cap—never the center. But it's the stemlessness that

---

* A 1997 paper by S. Redhead, L. Norvell, and E. Danell confirmed the 1966 separation of our NW chanterelles from *C. cibarius* of Europe and E NA.

[†] Our western oysters probably don't belong in *ostreatus.* Different taxonomists argue for *P. sapidus* or *P. pulmonarius* as the correct name. Stay tuned.

[‡] *Porrigens* was formerly included in genus *Pleurotus.*

makes this pair the only gilled mushrooms that I can recommend for eating without more technical identification. Several undesirable species share the stemless or offcenter-stemmed habit, but each can be excluded by at least one of these traits:

tough, leathery, thin flesh;

saw-toothed gills;

yellow gills or **brown spores** or a dark, drab cap;

intense bitter or peppery taste (take small nibbles, don't swallow).

If you find oysters or angel-wings, search the log for more; the fungus inhabits the entire tree and tends to fruit here and there all over it. Slice them off rather than ripping them out, and they may produce another crop in a few weeks. Tiny beetles between the gills can be knocked loose by tapping briskly. Some people say oyster mushrooms can pass for oysters. Angel-wings are so delicately tasty that much of the flavor is the butter they're cooked in.

Carnivorous plants like Venus' flytrap may be notorious, but carnivorous fungi are news. Tiny nematode worms have long been observed tunneling in mushrooms for dinner. Many saprophytic fungi, it now turns out, turn the tables and "eat" their nematodes. The oyster has specialized cells that splash poison onto nematodes that touch them; hyphae then seek, invade, and digest the immobilized worm. Since a saprophytic diet is nitrogen-poor, saprophytes have evolved to ingest nitrogen-rich organisms such as animals and nitrogen-fixing soil bacteria.

Hedgehog Mushroom

Hydnum repandum * (hid-num: truffle; rep-**and**-um: wavy-edged). Also **sweet tooth mushroom.** Cap yellow-orange to buff or nearly white, only vaguely differentiated from stem; underside covered with fine pale teeth of mixed lengths (average ¼") in lieu of gills; spores white. Mycorrhizal with Douglas-fir; on ground, summer through fall and even winter. Color p 484.

Eyes scouring the ground for the soft gold of chanterelles may jump at this similar cap; fingers will be in for a surprise when they reach underneath to pluck it and find a curious soft, spiny texture. Don't be disappointed—this mushroom is edible, and even harder to confuse with anything poisonous. Some soil-growing toothed relatives, however, are bitter. Even the tiniest taste-test will tell you.

---

* This mushroom has gone back and forth between *Hydnum* and *Dentinum.*

King Boletus

Boletus edulis (ed-you-lis: edible). Also **porcini, cepe, steinpilz**. Cap 3-12" diam, skin tan to red-brown, often redder just under surface, ± bumpy but not fibrous, often sticky; flesh ± white, firm; pores white, becoming olive to tawny yellow with age or bruising, but never blue; stem often very bulbous, white with ± brown skin, upper part finely net-surfaced; spores olive-brown. Mycorrhizal with various conifers. Late spring to early fall. Color p 484.

Admirable Boletus

Boletus mirabilis (bo-**lee**-tus: clod; mir-**ah**-bi-lis: admirable). Cap 2–6" diam, with dark red-brown skin minutely fibrous-roughened, and cream-white flesh red-stained just under the skin; tubes yellow, bruising darker yellow (rarely bluish); stem streaked with same red-brown shade as cap; spores olive-brown. Usually on rotting wood, under hemlocks; in fall. Color p 484.

Boletes are generally mycorrhizal. Some serve as the normal host of non-green plants in the heath family, while also partnering with trees. The admirable forms mycorrhizae with hemlock roots in rotting wood, but it doesn't do the rotting itself. An abundance of potentially mycorrhizal hyphae in rotten logs may help explain the

Cautious Bolete-Eating

Many of our better edible mushrooms are boletes, or members of the family Boletaceae. They look like regular gilled mushrooms from above, but when picked reveal a spore-bearing undersurface consisting of a spongy mass of vertical tubes. If you tear the cap, you will see that the tubes are distinct from the smooth-textured flesh above them, and can usually be peeled away. Most boletes range between choice and merely edible, and none are commonly deadly. The relatively few nonrecommended species can be ruled out rather simply, so the rest can be eaten without necessarily identifying them to species. Boletes begin fruiting in midsummer, earlier than most edibles, and they are often large, supplying hearty eatings from few pickings. Their main drawback, as a group, is rapid susceptibility to insects, decay and moldy growths.

Here are the cautionary rules:

*Never eat a bolete with **red-orange or pinkish-tinged** tube openings; this trait characterizes all the moderately toxic species.*

*Try a nibble of the cap for the **bitter, burning or peppery tastes** that make some other boletes undesirable.*

nurse logs as the main seedbed for hemlocks here. (See page 22.)

A choice edible bolete—but don't eat specimens that have been attacked by white or mustard-colored mold.

Suillus

Suillus spp. (sue-**ill**-us: piglet). Also **slippery jack** (some have slimy-caps).

S. lakei (**lake**-eye: after E. R. Lake). Cap rough with red-brown flat scales, yellow and ± sticky under the scales; flesh and tubes ± yellow, maturing orange, may bruise reddish; tubes angular and radially stretched when mature; stem has whitish ring when young; base bruises blue-green; spores brown to cinnamon. Always near Douglas-fir. Edible, tasty to some. Color p 484.

S. cavipes (**cav**-i-peez: hollow foot). Cap dry, with reddish to brown scales; flesh and tubes ± pale yellow, not bruising blue; tube mouths angular, strongly radial-arranged when mature; stem reddish-scaly below ring, smooth white and slightly narrower above ring, while the white-fibrous ring itself may disappear; stem becoming hollow; spores dark brown. Always near larches. Ranges from a good edible to mediocre or bitter.

S. granulatus (gran-you-**lay**-tus: granular, a misleading name). Cap with a tacky to slimy skin, tan to cinnamon; faintly mottled; flesh white to cream;

---

*Avoid boletes whose tubes **turn deep blue** (or "bruise") within a minute or two, where handled. While a few species mildly toxic to some people show this sharp reaction, as do some of the red-tubed toxics, many of the best edibles may also bruise bluish, at least slowly, at least sometimes or in some of their parts. Many mushroom eaters in this region are undeterred by the blue bruising unless it is intense and quick, or the tube-mouths are at all reddish.*

*If the cap has a **gelatinous or sticky skin**, remove this. It upsets some people's bowels. Most people also prefer to peel off and discard the tubes from mature specimens.*

*Look closely for **larval pinholes** by slicing or snapping the stem from the cap; if there are few or none, the cap is in good condition. Then slice through the stem at mid height, and look again. If you still find few or no holes or discolorations, the stem can be eaten along with the cap flesh, especially if there is a shortage of good caps. If the stem is buggy, discard it immediately rather than giving the larvae a chance to spread.*

Don't expect boletes to keep longer than overnight in any case, except very clean young specimens in chilly weather or a refrigerator. Carry in paper bags, out of direct sun.

---

tubes tan to yellow, very small, "dewy" in youth, staining or speckling brown with age; no veil or ring; stem white, developing brown dots or smears with age; spores cinnamon to ochre. Usually under lodgepole or ponderosa pines, often abundant. Good edible.

S. brevipes (brev-i-peez: short foot). Like *S. granulatus*, but cap starts deep red-brown and pales to ochre with age, and the short stem remains pure white except, rarely, for faint dots in great age; and pores don't stain. Choice edible.

Most boletes are currently in either of two enormous genera, *Boletus* and *Suillus*. Both words were used by the Romans for certain mushrooms; one derives from the Greek for "a lump of earth," which boletes sometimes resemble, and the other from the Latin for "pigs," who are fond of eating them. Italians still name boletes *porcini*, after pigs. *Suillus* species almost all live mycorrhizally with conifers; many require pines or larches as partners, and are common east of the Cascades.

No American *Suillus* is reported as poisonous aside from warnings about numerous allergic reactions often blamed on the skin, which can be peeled before cooking. However, no single field trait distinguishes *Suillus* from *Boletus*, which includes poisonous species. Many *Suillus* have, in addition to an association with conifers, at least two of the following traits:

Tube-mouths stretched out and aligned in a direction radial from the center.

A partial veil that persists as a ring, at least for a while.

A glutinous skin on the cap, slimy when wet, tacky when dry.

Glandular dots on at least the upper part of the stem, at maturity.

Purple-Tipped Coral

Ramaria botrytis (ra-**mair**-ia: branched; bo-**try**-tiss: bunch of grapes). Cauliflowerlike structure, the fat white bases (often clustered) much more massive than the branchings on top; the blunt branch tips brownish rose to red, dulling with age; base typically submerged in duff or moss, leaving only the tips exposed; delicately fragrant; spores ochre. Under mature conifers in early fall. Color p 485.

Like many worthwhile finds among the fungi, this species makes itself hard to spot, but once you have seen one and attuned your eyes to it you may find many more. It has provided me with fine camp dinners; the literature, however, reports an intensely bitter look-alike, *R. botrytoides*. The entire group of corallike branching fungi that grow on the ground or rotten wood is relatively harmless, but includes one stomach-upsetting species, *R. formosa* ("beautiful"); it has the slim vertical branches (not thick like cauliflower) typical of the family, and is peachy-pink when fresh except for yellowish tips. Also not recommended are species that show translucent, gelatinous cores in cross-section. The remaining corals are nonpoisonous, but few are good eating.

Cauliflower Mushroom

Sparassis crispa* (spar-**ass**-iss: lacerated). Large (typically 5–24" diam) fragrant cream-white leafy structure resembling a bowlful of ribbon noodles; spores white. Saprophytic, on conifer stumps or trunks quite near the ground, usually in late fall. Color p 486.

This looks less like cauliflower than the preceding species, and more like a great heap of fettucine. An Alfredo sauce (garlic, pepper and cream) would be perfect. Long slow cooking is recommended. Beauty, fragrance, size, and moderate rarity make this a great prize for the mushroom hunter. Smart ones carefully note the location and return a year or two later.

Bear's Head Tooth Fungus

Hericium abietis† (her-**ish**-ium: hedgehog; ay-bih-**ee**-tiss: of fir trees). Also **coral hydnum**. Large (6–12", or rarely up to 30" high × 16") white to cream fungus consisting of many branches and sub-branches ending in fine teeth all pointing down; rounded overall, with crowded short branches from a massive, solid base; spores white. Saprophytic, on dead conifer wood or tree wounds, esp true firs; late summer, early fall. Color p 486.

Spectacular appearance puts this in both the "Safe for Beginners" and the "Scenic Resource" categories unless you find one well away from a trail; trailside specimens should be left alone as visual treasures. Though popular with small mammals, it gets mixed reviews from people: fragrance and flavor are lovely, but the texture bothers

---

*Older texts list this species as *S. radicata*.

† Nomenclature in this genus is Byzantine. *H. abietis* is in older guides as *H. coralloides*, but that species was split, with *H. coralloides* confined to hardwoods in E NA. Then that eastern species was renamed *H. americanum* when *H. coralloides* was shown to be exclusively Eurasian. The species on western cottonwoods may prove to be either *H. americanum* or *H. ramosum*.

---

some. The larger branches can be tough and hard to digest. Cut into the mass discreetly, removing only modest quantities of such parts as are pure white and have few or no bore holes from insect larvae. Soak them in a pot of water to float any beetles out from the crevices. Then mince and saute gently.

Sulphur Shelf Fungus

Laetiporus sulphureus* (lee-**tip**-or-us: bright pores; sul-**few**-rius: sulphur yellow). Also **chicken-of-the-woods**. Thick, fleshy shelflike growths 2-12" wide, typically in large overlapping clusters; orange above, yellow below. On conifers, summer through fall (long-lasting). Color p 485.

The shelf fungus family, Polyporaceae, is characterized by simple fruiting bodies that release spores through tiny pores on their smooth undersides. The pores are never separable from the cap flesh. Dense, rather woody flesh makes these fungi much longer-lasting than mushrooms and hence more often seen than numbers alone warrant; but it doesn't do a thing for their edibility. The one relatively tender exception is the sulphur shelf, a good edible when young. To some tastes it's just like chicken; I find it lemony.

---

* *Laetiporus* was split out from the large genus *Polyporus*. Further splitting of *sulphureus* seems likely, in time, to separate eastern populations that grow on hardwoods from western ones on conifers.

Mycocuisines of the World

Moira Savonius of England attributes to the sulphur shelf fungus "an unpleasant sour smell as well as a nasty taste," while American Vincent Marteka rates it the first choice in a poll of American mushroom hunters, and writes of traditional use of it by Indians. There are many transoceanic differences of opinion over which mushrooms are delicious, and over which are poisonous. Some are based on the chemistry of geographic races that may some day be seen as distinct species. Flavor and toxicity also vary with different soils and plant hosts.

And culture plays a large role. The English have a mycophobic tradition that regards only species of Agaricus (like the supermarket button mushroom) as deserving either the term "mushroom" or a place on the table. In sharp contrast, Italians have a mania for amanitas and boletes; French go for truffles, morels, chanterelles and boletes; and Slavs, the most eclectic in their tastes, are intimate with species in dicey

No serious toxins have been found in the shelf fungus family; occasional adverse reactions to this species have been blamed variously on eucalyptus as the host tree (no problem in the Northwest) or on allergies, excessive consumption, or overly mature specimens. To make sure of eating it young enough, take only the outer edges, and only if your knife finds them butter-tender, lemon-yellow rather than deep orange, and fat and wavy rather than thin and corrugated. New tender margins may grow in their place. Since this is both a gastronomic and a scenic resource to be shared with other hikers, limit yourself to a quantity you can easily eat, and don't even think about cutting up growths right next to a trail.

Most shelf fungi live as heart rot in either dead or living trees; in either case the cells they attack are dead cells (only the thin outer layers of a tree are alive) so they are technically saprophytes, but they kill trees indirectly by weakening them to wind breakage, and they spoil the lumber, making themselves economic pests in timber country. From an ecological point of view, killing a tree here and there in the forest is beneficial: it provides habitat, lets in light, and altogether enhances plant and animal diversity. (See page 268.)

A shelf fungus called turkey-tail, with a long and worldwide record as a folk remedy, has now shown activity in lab tests against tumors *and* viruses *and* cholesterol levels. Hey, take turkey-tail for what ails ya.

---

genera like Russula *and* Lactarius. *Chinese and Japanese traditions are bringing stranger fungal flavors and textures to American palates—leathery "tree-ears," resiny "pine mushrooms," "straw mushrooms" grown in bottles for legginess, and "black fungus" cured in brine.*

Japanese prices have exceeded $200 a pound for northwest matsutakes, Tricholoma magnivelare. *Lorelei Norvell assures us we can identify matsutakes by their "delicious" fragrance, but* Mushrooms of Northeast North America *mutters that the emperor has no clothes: "odor like dirty gym socks but usually described as spicy-sweet, aromatic, fruity, or fragrant." My take on this brouhaha, expressed as delicately as possible, is that there may be a chance convergence between matsutake vapors and human pheromones, somewhat analagous to the one between French truffles and pig pheromones, page 281. And yes, they do smell kind of like delicious dirty gym socks.*

Warted Giant Puffball

Calbovista subsculpta (cal-bo-**vis**-ta: bald foxfart;* sub-**sculpt**-a: somewhat sculptured). Stalkless, slightly flattened ball 3–6" diam, white patterned with brownish raised polygons. (Positive identification is technical, but the similar *Calvatia* species are all equally edible.) Typically subalpine among grass, or sometimes under conifers; in midsummer. Color p 484.

Most puffballs are smaller than golf balls, but *Calbovista* is baseball-sized, and some *Calvatia* species can grow to basketball size. Puffballs are a family of fungi whose round or pear-shaped fruiting bodies have neither cap nor stem nor gills. The maturing skin either splits open or opens a small hole at the top, and spores come puffing out by the millions, mostly when the puffball is struck by raindrops. Spores, like pollen, are "hydrophobic" or resistant to wetting, so their flight is undamped by rain or fog. Puffball spores, a hundred times smaller than most spores and pollen grains, are barely even subject to gravity; squeeze a ripe puffball on a breezy day, and you may truly be sending a few spores around the world.

Puffballs have been used medicinally in many cultures. Some are thought to contain anticarcinogens. No true puffballs (family Lycoperdaceae) are poisonous, but young "buttons" of deadly amanitas can be mistaken for them, so you must **slice every puffball you pick through its center vertically,** and eat only those that are pure undifferentiated white inside, from tip to toe. Amanita buttons in cross-section reveal at least a faint outline of developing stem and gills. Other telltales for the discard pile include a green-, brown-, or yellow-stained center, or a punky center distinct from a smooth ⅛" outer rind. The former indicates a maturing puffball, the latter a *Scleroderma* ("hard skin") fungus; both are unpleasant but not dangerous. Puffballs take a couple of weeks to mature, so you stand a sporting chance of catching them young enough.

If it's your first taste of puffball, just pick a small sample. You may hate it. The flavor is mild, pleasantly fungal, but the texture is slippery where sliced, a bit rubbery within. Frying in batter, if you have the means, can mask the oddness. My own proudest trailside effort was a lunch of warted giant puffball sandwiches—half-inch

---

*This name is a compound of two other genera: *Calvatia* is latin for "baldhead," while *Bovista* is old German vernacular for a puffball, with a literal meaning of "fox-fart." The same origin myth, Latinized, names our common puffball genus *Lycoperdon*.

slices fried in butter with garlic, on crackers thinly layered with anchovy paste and cheese.

Oregon White Truffle

Tuber gibbosum (**too**-ber: Latin for truffle; jib-**oh**-sum: swollen). Knobby firm lumps ¾-2½" (rarely 5") diam, with cheesy, garlicky, or eventually metallic odor; skin pale brown, bruising reddish and darkening in age; interior marbled shades of white, aging to brown with white veins. Below soil surface, usually in groups, under Douglas-fir, Oct.–Jan..

Truffles live mycorrhizally just like many mushrooms, but instead of giving their spores to the wind to carry, they use distinctive aromas to entice mammals to eat them. (See page 328.) Some of them also get by with tiny fruits that get moved around accidentally by burrowing animals.

Hundreds of truffle-like (i.e., aromatic underground-fruiting) species abound in our mature and old-growth forests. Oregon white truffle, a relatively large and uncommon one, is one of two that have widely found their way into restaurants. Its genus, *Tuber*, includes the famous white truffle of Italy and black truffle of France. I confess I've tried it in dishes in good restaurants and scarcely detected it. Perhaps my nose is color blind, or the cooks weren't quite on top of the truffle's notoriously finicky timing.

One problem is that whereas European truffles are harvested with the help of dogs or pigs that sniff them out, and hence are found at their aromatic peak, Oregon harvesters haven't succeeded in training dogs. (French pigs don't need any training; the French white truffle produces a fragrance chemically identical to one in a boar's pheromones, and it's always a sow that roots for truffles). Instead, they rake (with the help, some claim, of their own noses) in appropriate habitat, and dig up a mixed bag of ripe to unripe truffles. Raking—also practiced in the matsutake trade—is bad for forests. The ideal scenario for a Northwest truffle crop might be Italian truffles cultivated in filbert orchards and harvested with fourlegged help. You can actually order inoculated filbert trees today, after more than a century of efforts at truffle cultivation.

A certain Professor Frank, commissioned to cultivate truffles in Prussia in the 1880s, failed to grow any, but he looked at them so closely that he serendipitously made one of the great advances in mycology: discovering and naming the mycorrhiza.

Morels

Morchella spp. (mor-**kel**-a: from Old High German word for morel). 2–8"+ tall. Cap conical or rod-shaped to egg-shaped or round, the exterior honey-combed with strong ridges with deep pits in between; flesh brittle. Interior hollow, the single long hollow shared by cap and stalk; cap, attached very near its bottom to the stalk, has no underside and no gills. Stalk smooth or wrinkled; ± white. Odor slight or pleasant. Abundance peaks in late spring.

Black morel, *M. elata* (ee-**lay**-ta: tall) or *M. angusticeps* (ang-**goose**-ti-seps: narrow cap) or *M. conica.* Typically in burned areas in the mountains.

Yellow morel, *M. esculenta* (es-cue-**len**-ta: good to eat). 2–6"+ tall. Commonest at low elevs with hardwoods.

Like the Phoenix, black morels rise from the ashes of burned areas where morels have been in the soil without fruiting for many decades. It's a mystery whether these "phoenicoid" mushrooms are responding to heated dirt or to the sudden plethora of their food, dead trees. They also fruit abundantly in forests attacked by bark beetles (not heat-treated), and in deep Mt. St. Helens tephra (heat-treated). At St. Helens they proved their value to succession, popping up on barren ash; where they rotted back into the ash, algae and mosses soon flourished. Commercial morel pickers flock to burned areas in the spring after a fire; predictability helps make black morels the most harvested mushroom in the greater Northwest. (That's Oregon to Montana, with greatest harvests in the Blue Mtns. and Northern Rockies. In our mountains they rank well below chanterelles in poundage and matsutakes in cash value.)

Yellow morels are at least as tasty, and reasonably abundant, but harder to find. They seem camouflaged among old leaves, just as black morels are camouflaged amid scorched vegetation and pine cones. Two traditional tips are to follow the sweet smell of cottonwoods in spring, or to look in old apple orchards. Though primarily saprophytic, morels occasionally form mycorrhizae.

You can eat morels safely as long as you cook them and slice them lengthwise to confirm the key traits: honeycombed cap attached at its bottom (i.e. it has no underside, only the full-length hollow interior shared with the stem); and pleasant odor.

Morels recently succumbed to decades of efforts at cultivation, and you can order cultivated ones by mail. Though slightly inferior to wild ones and scarcely cheaper, they are available year-round.

Taxonomy within *Morchella* is in chaos. Better species concepts may be needed to resolve it. The old ideas of black and white morel species may get jettisoned: there are too many perfect in-betweens, and in the greenhouse "blacks" seem to beget "whites." Unlike most mushrooms, in which you find identical DNA in many fruiting bodies and year after year on a site, morels behave more like annual plants, or at least they don't tend to grown in extensive clones: adjacent fruiting bodies typically have unique DNA.

Snowbank False-Morel

Gyromitra gigas (jye-ro-**my**-tra: round hat; jye-gus: giant). Also **snow morel**. Cap dull yellow-brown, convoluted, lacking gills, flesh in cross-section thin, white, brittle; stem white, often ± concealed by cap, nearly as big around as the cap and with similarly convoluted, thin, brittle flesh enclosing many irregular hollow spaces. Under high-elev conifers immediately after snowmelt. Color p 486.

This bizarre-looking fungus is a decent edible, but unusual precautions must be observed. First, eat only specimens whose identity is corroborated by patches of melting snowpack nearby. Second, boil the material after cleaning and chopping it; avoid breathing the steam; throw out the water; and rinse the fungus again before beginning your final cooking of it.

Gyromitra toxicity was long a mystery. Countless people, over centuries, happily ate the so-called edible false-morel, *G. esculenta*, yet there were occasional fatalities. The toxin was isolated and found to be the same chemical as a rocket fuel manufactured for Apollo missions, so it is now a well-studied chemical—a deadly poison and suspected carcinogen. However, it is volatile enough to be removed by either drying or boiling, and it produces no symptoms until a victim exceeds a threshold level, presumably by eating lots of inadequately boiled *Gyromitra* over a period of a few days.

Now that the explanation is known, mushroom guides say "POISONOUS" right under the name *esculenta*, meaning "good to eat." Some mushroom buffs still eat *esculenta* after scrupulous parboilings. Some guides extend the prohibition to the entire genus: a few other *Gyromitra* species do contain the toxin, but only trace quantities have been found in *gigas*. The several distinct, irregular hollows within the broad stem, together with time of fruiting immediately after snowmelt are considered sufficient to distinguish this from any toxic species. Parboil it as an added precaution.

Lichens consist of fungi specialized to meet their carbohydrate needs from algae or bacteria they enclose. This symbiotic association is highly developed, producing organs, tissues and chemicals found only in lichens. Lichens differ conspicuously from other fungi in that they grow in the open and are tough, durable, and able to dry out and revive again. (Contrast this not with the mushroom but with the fungus' "body," which lives all year long in soil or wood beneath the mushroom site). The lichen symbiosis seems to have evolved separately in eighteen or twenty different branches of the fungus family tree. About forty algal and bacterial genera partner the several hundred genera of lichen fungi, comprising about one-fourth of all named fungi.

Whether or not the symbiosis is mutually beneficial has been debated. A leading lichenonogist once called it "controlled parasitism" in which the fungi slowly kill their green partners. At about 7% of the tissue mass of a typical lichen, lichen "photobionts"—either algae or cyanobacteria—are in a minority, cultivated role not unlike that of intestinal flora that live symbiotically in mammals. (A few invertebrate animals also incorporate symbiotic algae.)

A farm may offer the closest metaphor for a lichen. Just as irrigation enables plants to grow in climates to dry for them, and barns and hay let cattle live in climates too snowy, lichen fungi benefit algae in allowing them to grow on sites far too severe for free-living algae. They offer both physical shelter and chemical protection: the best-known functions of special lichen chemicals are to repel herbivores, microbes, and competing plants. You could say we have here counterparts to a farmer's greenhouse, pesticides, herbicides, and deer repellent. So at this point most lichenologists view the symbiosis as mutualistic.

It was formerly assumed that lichen algae must also be able to thrive on their own in order for lichen spores to function: spores would have to land near a free alga in order to begin the farming life. However, the commonest genus of lichen alga, *Trebouxia*, has never been found outside of a lichen, and it turns out that lichen spores appropriate *Trebouxia* from other lichens. On the other hand, the second commonest alga, *Trentepohlia*, and most lichen cyanobacteria are reasonably common as free-living organisms.

Most lichens do produce spores in fruiting bodies analogous to those of other fungi. Sexual propagation via spores is important in maintaining their genetic diversity, but is far less common a route than propagation from fragments that include both partners together. These may be just any old fragment that happens to break off, or they may be specially evolved propagative bundles ("propagules") in the form of powders, grains or tiny protuberances.

Lichens are loosely (not taxonomically) sorted by growth form. Three forms did the trick for over a century, but recent books may have five or six. We'll use four:

Crust lichens are thin coatings or stains on or in rock or bark surfaces—so thin that you could not pry them up.

Leaf lichens are also thin, ranging from closely adhering, paintlike sheets with distinct, thick, more or less priable margins, to saladlike heaps attached to their substrate in only a few spots.

Shrub lichens are made of fine branches, either erect or pendent.

Twig lichens stand up, with little or no branching; often above a mat of scales.

Of all familiar, visible organisms, lichens have perhaps the most modest requirements—a little moisture, sunlight either minimal or excessive, and solid materials carried in even the cleanest air. From minimal input comes meager output; growth rates measured in lichen species range from .0012" to about 4" per year.

Lichens spend much of their lives dried out, all activity suspended. In this state they can survive temperatures from 150° (typical of soil surfaces in the summer sun) down to near absolute zero (in laboratories). They have to dry out and suspend respiration to get through hot days in the sun, yet at 32° or a bit colder they remain active and unfrozen, thanks to complex chemistry including alcohols. Our alpine lichens get some of their photosynthesizing done while buried in snow, which keeps them moist and lets sunlight in. Lichens on rocks can sustain activity as long as they are supplied with atmospheric moisture—rain, snow, dew, fog, or mere humidity. As with mosses only more so, success in lichen niches is a matter of making hay while the rain falls, and then drying up. Perhaps the best-known lichen habitats are alpine and recently deglaciated rocks. Far greater lichen biomass, in our region, grows in a seemingly opposite environment with moderate temperatures, low light levels and high rainfall: the bark of rain forest trees. There, too, the lichens dry out every time rain and fog stop for a few days. Most lichens will actually die if they don't get to dry out periodically.

Lichens that colonize bare rock may, after centuries of life, death and decomposition, alter the rock enough for plants to grow, initiating the long slow succession of biotic communities. Countless naturalists from Linnaeus to our high school biology teachers have been enamored of this scenario, but in fact it is not a common path of "primary succession" on barren, newly-exposed ground. One thing the first pioneer plants do need is some usable nitrogen, so associations with either free-living or root-nodule bacteria are typical. Mosses loosely coated with cyanobacteria pioneer on rock, and nodulated trees and shrubs like alders pioneer in crevices that hold a bit of fine gravel or dust. On barren ash at Mt. St. Helens, lupines and other subalpine perennials were the chief pioneers; the small lichen patches that did make an appearance were judged more likely to inhibit than to nurture subsequent plant growth.

The ability of lichens to break down rock has been overrated; it is negligible compared to the effects of frost. Lichens secrete acids that dissolve minerals from rock, but this chemical etching is one of nature's slower tools for disintegrating rocks. Slightly faster is lichens' physical crumbling of rock—effective on soft limestone and shale, and also on old stained-glass of cathedrals. Lichens' gelatinous gripping surfaces expand and contract as they moisten and dry out: this effect, powerful enough to crumble tiny bits of rock, has been experimentally replicated using plain gelatin.

A second appealing myth inspired by lichens' minimal needs proposes them as candidates for restarting succession, or even evolution, after a global ecocatastrophe. During the period of atmospheric H-bomb tests, and again after Chernobyl, arctic lichens accumulated radioactive fallout without apparent harm to themselves, while they passed on dangerous amounts of it into the bones of lichen-eating caribou and caribou-eating Inuit and Lapps. Lichens might be comparative survivors of radioactive contamination—but only in the unlikely event that it is not preceded by other air pollution. Lichens' diet of airborne solids makes them extremely sensitive to airborne sulphur dioxide and other pollutants. Since some lichens are more tolerant than others, scientists devise scales of increasingly tolerant species of a region, and then monitor an airshed's pollution over the years by checking which species are present. No lichens survive in the worst urban air.

Map Lichen

Rhizocarpon geographicum (rye-zo-**car**-pon: root fruit). Chartreuse yellow patches broken by fine black lines and surrounded by a wider black margin. On rocks; abundant in exposed situations. Color p 487.

Lichens grow at extremely slow but steady rates. Because of its ubiquity on arctic and alpine rocks, map lichen is an outstanding indicator of the number of centuries elapsed since glacial retreat from the rocks. Radial growth rates of 3 and 3⅓ millimeters per century—after a slightly faster initial "spurt"—were found for map lichens in Colorado and Wyoming; 3,000-year-old lichens were 4–4½" in diameter.

Clot Lichen

Mycoblastus sanguinarius (my-co-**blas**-tus: fungus bud; sang-gwin-**air**-ius: blood red). Gray patches without sharp edges, on bark, texture grainy to warty, with clusters of ± shiny blackish fruiting disks .05-.1" diam.; under each black disk, if it's sliced off, is a bright red spot in the lichen cortex. Dry tree bark microsites (see p 290).

Cryptobiotic Crusts

In severe environments—both alpine and semidesert—soil surfaces are often mixed together with small bits of lichens, cyanobacteria, mosses, and fungi. The resulting crust, ranging from one-eighth of an inch to over an inch thick, often goes unnoticed, but is vitally beneficial. It stays relatively cool and moist in the sun, resists erosion, and (when it includes cyanobacteria either free-living or in lichens) fixes nitrogen. (On the other hand, in favorable climates, including on fresh Cascade mudflows, a flourishing carpet of lichens can hinder plant establishment.)

Cryptobiotic crust (the word means "hidden life") is easy to damage and slow to repair itself. A footprint in it can last for decades. If you hike off-trail above treeline, watch for nubbly, crusted sandy earth and avoid walking on it. Detour onto snow or bare rock; in a pinch, even raw gravels or dense sedge turf are more durable than crusted soils.

Corkir

Ochrolechia spp.* (oh-kro-**lek**-ia: ochre bed?). Also **pumpkin pie lichen**. Light gray patches without sharp edges, on bark, with clusters of small ± orange to salmon-pink fruiting disks, avg ⅛" diam.

O. laevigata (lee-vig-**ay**-ta: smooth). Crust very thin, often smooth; disc rims thin, white. Abundant on alder and maple.

O. oregonensis (oregon-**en**-sis: of Oregon). Crust thicker, finely warty; discs abundant, with a double outer ring which matures orange. Abundant on conifers. Color p 487.

This lichen's main significance to us is in lending its ghostly whiteness to the bark in young forests. Other whitish crustose lichens also grow on bark, especially of red alder, but corkir is the easy genus to recognize thanks to its distinctive white-rimmed discs, which look a bit like tiny pumpkin pies.

Historically, not whiteness but brilliant shades of purple and red and rich browns have made corkir valuable. Mainly in Scotland, *O. tartarea* was scraped from rocks for use as a dye, going into international trade in such forms as Harris Tweeds and litmus paper. Dye-lichen gathering has rarely flourished for long in any given locale, since lichens grow so slowly that they are quickly depleted. "Corkir" was an archaic Celtic word for this lichen, and "cudbear" was a more recent dialect name derived from "Cuthbert," a trade name. Neither term is common parlance in America, but then, few lichen names are. Corkir grows on trees here, and is inseparable from the bark, whose tannin would ruin any attempt to use it as a dye. *O. laevigata*, in particular, permeates the bark, with only its spore-bearing disks sitting upon the surface. It looks more like a stain than a crust; you might think there is nothing there but bark.

A great many lichens yield yellow, olive or brown dyes when boiled in water. The transformation to purple and red comes when lichens containing gyrophoric acid, such as these three species and the rock tripes, are cured for several weeks in warm ammonia. Stale human urine was the form of ammonia used from the beginning (probably B.C. around the Mediterranean) through the nineteenth century. Yet the dyed fabric came out with a fine fragrance longer-lasting than the color.

---

*A revision of the genus found that *pallescens* and *tartarea* don't occur here.

Dust Lichens

Also **imperfect lichens, powdery paint lichens.**

Lepraria spp. (lep-**rair**-ia: leprous, i.e., scurfy). Color p 487.

Chrysothrix chlorina (clor-**eye**-na: greenish yellow). Color p 487.

C. candelaris (**cris**-o-thrix: gold thread; candle-**air**-iss: luminous).

This degenerate form of lichen growth is just a granular layer of fungi and algae bundled together in little clumps called "soredia." Many lichens have soredia as their vegetative propagules. Apparently dust lichens came about when some soredia—in several unrelated lines of lichens—learned the trick of propagating more soredia without bothering to propagate the rest of the lichen. Lacking the tough cortex layer of more complete lichens, dust lichens are more vulnerable to drying out, but better able to absorb moisture from the air. Indeed, they live by absorbing humidity from the air, but actually repel raindrops and drips, and are unable to absorb liquid water. Therefore they specialize in deprived substrates like the undersides of limbs, and rock overhangs. Naturally, they like foggy climates, and go absolutely wild in waterfall spray zones.

"With only the slightest exaggeration," wrote lichenologist Trevor Goward, "dust lichens may be said to drink without water, photosynthesize without sunshine, and reproduce, so far as we know, without sex." Early naturalists filed them under *Lichenes Imperfecti* within Deuteromycetes, two taxonomic dustbins indicating the naturalists' inability to categorize fungi that had never been seen with sexual organs. Modern molecular techniques allow transferring former members of these dustbins into their rightful places all over the great family tree. Genus *Chrysothrix* was created to hold some species formerly in *Lepraria.*

Lepraria seems to fill in bare spaces in almost any sort of alpine community, frosting old dead moss turf or bare soil with white, and typically producing a nubbly texture of 2" mounds. It also abounds on bark, specializing in twigs and in dry sides of trees. It looks simply like a powdery white coating with indistinct, fading margins and no specialized organs.

C. chlorina is less extensive but much more noticeable; it's the brilliant chartreuse green coating on wet cliffs such as the basalt beside Columbia Gorge waterfalls.

C. candelaris is golden yellow on bark.

Oregon Lungwort

Lobaria oregana (lo-**bair**-ia: lobed; or-eg-**ay**-na: of Oregon). Also **lettuce lichen**. Big "leaves" very pale green above when dry, bright green when wet, ridged in a branching pattern (on underside, these ridges are valleys, as opposed to the ridged veins under dog lichens); cream-colored underneath when dry, mottled with brown in the furrows; margins deeply lobed, curling; fruiting organs rare. On W-side trees or sometimes rocks. Color p 488.

Massive proliferations of lungwort grow in thick saladlike beds up on top of limbs in the conifer canopy. Lungwort litter on the forest floor gives a hint of the abundance above, but the true quantity went unappreciated until rock climbing hardware was brought to bear on forest science. It was then calculated that this species supplies up to half the nitrogen input in the oldest westside forests. (Lungwort mass is substantially higher on 700-year-old trees than on 400-year-old trees, and higher in very cool moist valleys than in average westside forests; see Canopy Zones, below.) Cyanobacteria in the lichen pull nitrogen out of the air; their fungal cosymbionts appropriate it; and it moves on in the nutrient cycle when it leaches

Canopy Zones

Canopy scientists find that old-growth trees offer epiphytes just as wide a range of habitats as the contrasting moisture regimes east and west of the Cascades. Upper canopy branches receive the most moisture, but lose it quickly and totally in the intense wind and sun. They support thick beards of pendulous lichens, which excel at intercepting fog and dew and taking advantage of the few moist/bright minutes per day that result. At the other end, jungles of thick moss thrive on the north sides of tree bases, where the sun never shines and the wind scarcely blows.

Other mosses (chiefly short-pendent and heron's-bill moss) gradually take over the tops of large branches at all heights. They need a moist microclimate and are very good at creating it for themselves, intercepting and condensing far more fog and rain moisture than the barer branch was able to, and sponging it up, releasing it slowly after the foggy or rainy weather passes. Eventually an actual soil results. Red tree voles live out their lives on this lofty earth; fireweed, devil's-club, out in rainwater, or when the lichen is eaten by insects, red tree voles, or decomposing bacteria. To intercept nutrients before they wash away, alders, maples, and cottonwoods may extend rootlets among the lichens and mosses on their own bark.

The word "lungwort" derives from the medieval Doctrine of Signatures, which prescribed this lichen for lung ailments because of its textural resemblance to lung tissue. At least seven unrelated green plants have also been called lungwort.

Dog Lichens

Peltigera spp. (pel-**tidge**-er-a: shield bearer). Also **veined lichens, pelts.** Big sheets with lobed and curled-up margins; conspicuous tan to dark red, ± tooth-shaped fruiting bodies on lobe edges; underside netted with branching veins, raised from surface, bearing coarse hairlike rhizines.

P. canina (ca-**nye**-na: of dogs). Gray or brownish, covered with minute hair visible with handlens; lobe edges often downcurled; rhizines tufted; on forest floor, esp E-side.

P. rufescens (roo-**fes**-enz: reddening, a misleading name). Gray or brownish, covered with minute hair visible with handlens; lobes only 1–4⅜" wide, upturned, often whitish; rhizines densely matted; on dry exposed sites, incl alpine crusts.

---

hemlock, and salal have been seen taking root and growing in it; and the host tree itself, if it is an alder or maple, may extend aerial roots into it for a share of its fertility.

Bruce McCune hypothesizes that a single epiphyte gradient works in three dimensions at once: from the top to the bottom of a forest, from drier to wetter forest locations, and through time as the forest matures. Evidence suggests this succession continues well past 400 years of stand age, giving truly ancient forests ecological traits they don't share with the mere 200-year-old forests usually defined as "old growth."

The sequence, starting at the high/dry/young end, is:

1. Witches'-hair, horsehair, and beard lichens

2. Puffed and rag lichens

3. Lungwort, green dog lichen, and other lichens with cyanobacteria; also globe lichen.

4. Mosses and leafy liverworts.

P. membranacea (mem-bra-**nay**-cia: thin). Gray or brownish, covered (at least near edges and on underside veins) with minute hair visible with hand-lens; rhizines separate, long (often ⅜"); forest floor, W-side lowlands.

P. neopolydactylon (neo-polly-**dac**-til-on: new many-fingers). Upper surface olive gray to brownish, hairless; fruiting bodies long and narrow, ± tan; rhizines long (often ⅜"); moist forest floor.

P. britannica. Bright green above when wet, with many dark bumps; pale green to tan when dry; abundant in moss mats on high limbs of old conifers and on rock, soil, or tree bases. Color p 488.

Dark gray colors in lichens reveal the presence of cyanobacteria. (These used to be known as "blue-green algae.") *Nostoc*, a nitrogen-fixing blue-green genus, is the chief blue-green partner in gray dog lichens. In green dog lichens like *P. britannica*, which mainly employ green algae, *Nostoc* appears only here and there in dark superficial bumps cultivated where *Nostoc* colonies have fallen. These characters can be erratic: colonies of *britannica* often include gray individuals that lack the green alga, but those individuals may later catch some green algae and sprout green lobes. The Northwest has at least 25 gray and 4 green species of *Peltigera*, more than any other part of the world.

The Gitxsan tribe had a charming name for these lichens: "frog's blankets." The European name dates from the medieval Doctrine of Signatures, which looked in nature for semblances of body parts and read them as drug prescriptions in God's own handwriting. In the dog lichen's erect fruiting bodies they saw dog teeth, so they prescribed dog lichen for dogbite disease: the decoction for rabies, right up until the last century, was ground dog lichen and black pepper in milk. The Doctrine was a wrong turn in the history of herbal medicine. Lichens do have medicinal value, and they were used more appropriately in pre-Christian Europe.

Rag Lichen

Platismatia glauca (plat-iss-**may**-sha: broad—; **glaw**-ca: pale). Also **ragbag**. Fluffy wads of small sheets (up to 1" wide) with strongly ruffled edges; pale greenish gray above; underside patchy with white, greenish brown, and black; surface often granular-coated.

Rag lichen abounds on some small urban trees, since it tolerates pollution well. Native to six continents, it is one of the most cosmopolitan lichens. Along with several puffed lichens (page 294), it grows throughout young forest conifers, but shifts into the mid-canopy as the forest ages; in ancient forests you will see them mainly where they have fallen the ground.

Rock Tripe

Umbilicaria spp. (um-bil-ic-**air**-ia: navel—). Dark gray-brown leafy lichen attached to a rock by a single, central "umbilical" holdfast; tough and leathery wet, hard and brittle when dry; ± lobed and curling at the edges; ± smooth above, often with coarse black or pinkish tan hairs ("rhizines") beneath. Abundant on dry, exposed rock at all elevs. (*U. virginis*, recognizable by extra-dense long rhizines underneath, is strictly limited to high elevations; indeed, its first record was from "8,200 feet" on 7,965-foot Mt. Olympus!) Color p 487.

Indians boiled rock tripe for a fish roe adulterant—Indian hamburger helper, so to speak. Chinese and Japanese fry it up to eat like potato chips, or relish it tender in salad or soup, always drying and boiling it first to leach out dark and bitter flavors. *Trappeurs* in nineteenth-century Canada credited *tripes-des-roches* with saving them from starvation—but never with tasting good.

Jewel Lichen

Xanthoria elegans (zan-**thor**-ia: yellow; el-eg-enz: elegant). Also **elegant orange lichen.** Bright orange patches adhering tightly to rocks, thus easily mistaken for a crustlike lichen, but with slightly raised flakes and distinct, lobed edges; fruiting discs deeper orange, small, concentrated near center of patch. Widely scattered, esp alpine; also spectacularly abundant mingled with chartreuse *Acarospora* spp. on basalt cliffs in E WA. Color p 487.

This lichen often marks habitual perches of rockpile-dwelling animals like pikas and marmots, where it is fertilized by the nitrogen in urine. More conspicuous than the pika itself, this orange splash may help us spot the source of the "eeeenk."

Puffed Lichens

Hypogymnia spp. (hypo-**jim**-nia: naked underneath). Also **bone lichens**, **tube lichens**. Tufts of hollow branches, sharply two-toned, pale greenish gray above with black specks, blackish brown beneath, lighter brown at the tips; numerous yellowish brown fruiting cups on upper sides average ⅛" diam. Common on small limbs.

H. enteromorpha (enter-o-**mor**-fa: intestine shaped). Branches alternately puffed and constricted; often crowded in a flattened cluster; tubes interior surfaces dark.

H. imshaugii (imz-**how**-ghee-eye: after Henry Imshaug). Tufts relatively airy, erect, with tubular branches forking dichotomously; interior surfaces white.Color p 487.

Wolf Lichens

Letharia spp. (leth-**air**-ia: death—). Brilliant sulphur-yellow stiff tufts, the profuse branches cylindrical or ± flattened, often pitted, black-dotted. Drier tree-bark sites; abundant on pine and juniper.

L. columbiana (co-lum-be-**ay**-na: of the Columbia R.). With conspicuous fruiting cups with brownish disks average ¼" diam (up to ¾"). Color p 488.

L. vulpina (vul-**pie**-na: of foxes). Fruiting cups absent or rare. Color p 489.

Somewhere there was a tradition of collecting this intense-colored lichen to make a poison for wolves and foxes; my American sources say this used to be done in Europe, while a British source writes it off as an American barbarism.

Wolf lichen imparts to fabrics a chartreuse dye close to its own color. Before they had cloth, Northwest tribes used the dye on moccasins, fur, feathers, wood, porcupine quills for basketry, and their own faces.

Reindeer Lichens

Cladina mitis (cla-**dye**-na: branchlet; **my**-tis: mild). Profusely fine-branched lichens 2–4" tall, in dense patches, on soil but barely attached to it. Color yellowish when moist, sometimes with bluish bloom. Widespread; fairly common in n WA among alpine sedges and heathers. Color p 489.

C. rangiferina (ran-ji-fer-**eye**-na: of reindeer). As above, but ash-gray; rare.

Though found at all elevations here, reindeer lichens are best known for covering vast areas of arctic tundra, where they are the winter staple food of caribou (known in Europe as reindeer). They aren't really very digestible or nutritious; even caribou prefer green leaves when they can get them, but to occupy that particular range they adapted to wintering on lichens. This requires ceaseless migration, since the slow-growing lichens are eliminated where grazed for long. Lapps even harvest lichens for their reindeer herds. Some Inuit relish a "saladlike" delicacy consisting of half-digested lichens from the stomachs of caribou killed in winter.

Closer to home we encounter them, dyed green and softened in glycerine, as fake trees and shrubs in architectural models. They also supply extracts for commercial uses including perfume bases and antibiotics. They are the chief source of the antibiotic "usnic acid" for German, Finnish, and Russian salves applied to ailments ranging from severe burns and plastic surgery scars to *Trichomonas* and bovine mastitis.

Iceland-Moss

Cetraria ericetorum (set-**rair**-ia: shield—; er-iss-e-**tor**-um: among heaths). Shrublike clumps 1–3" tall by 2–8" wide, brown to olive when dry, consisting of narrow flattened lobes with sparsely fringed edges rolled nearly into tubes, with white specks (visible with 10× handlens) aligned under edges. On soil, mostly alpine.

C .islandica (iss-**land**-ica: of Iceland). As above, but with white specks scattered across backsides, and lobes scarcely rolled up.

C. nivalis*(niv-**ay**-lis: of snow). Pale yellow; some white specks beneath; lobes scarcely rolled up. Color p 488.

The misleading but time-honored common name "Iceland-moss" comes from Europe, where this is the best-known lichen eaten by people. It is sold as an herbal medicine in Sweden, and manufactured into teas and throat lozenges in Switzerland. Scandinavian sailors used to bake Iceland-moss flour into their bread to extend its shelf life at sea. The lichen had to be parboiled with soda before milling, or it would have been unspeakably bitter. In North America it was popular among the Inuit.

---

* The 6th Lichen Checklist has *nivalis* in a separate genus *Flavocetraria*, but our authority thinks the split is unsupported.

Witches'-Hair

Alectoria sarmentosa (alec-**tor**-ia: rooster[?]; sar-men-**toe**-sa: twiggy). Pale gray-green festoons on trees; wispily pendulous, 3–30" long; when pulled, strands snap straight across. Abundant on trees, mid elevs to timberline. Color p 489.

In heavily browsed areas like Olympic valleys, witches'-hair* may show a browse line at the maximum height elk can reach. Deer and elk browse lichens in winter, mainly because they help them absorb nutrients from the green plants of their winter diet.

What may look like a similar "browse line" of witches'-hair in higher forests is actually a marker of spring snowpack depth. With daylength and temperatures rising, and rain plentiful, spring is the prime growing season for high-elevation lichens, so they disfavor the part of the trunk that is buried at that time.

Horsehair Lichen

Bryoria spp.[†] (bry-**or**-ia: moss—). Also **tree hair, black tree lichen.** Blackish 2–16" festoons of extremely fine (less than .02" diam), weak, ± matted fibers, often speckled with pale, powdery propagules; on high-elev trees, krummholz, and rarely rock surfaces. Color p 489.

These fibrous tendrils look ominously parasitic but, like other lichens, are actually as likely to contribute to the trees' nutrition as to steal from it. Black visual accents add drama to eccentric tree shapes, whose chief sculptor is the weather. An uglier, somewhat pathogenic fungus is snow mold, *Herpotrichia nigra*, ("black creeping hair"), which turns mountain hemlock and silver fir branches into mats of smutty needles, mainly during late-snowmelt years.

Indians ate horsehair lichen, especially in cold interior areas where carbohydrate foods were scarce. Reports vary as to whether it was delicious or starvation fare, bitter or soapy or sweet or bland.

---

* Few lichens' names are household words, but we who attempt popular writing on them like to provide common names, at least at the genus level, to encourage interest in lichens. In picking names, we try to balance what makes subjective sense with what has a toehold in usage, either in regional speech, in other guide books, or in antiquity. Witches'-hair and dust lichens are two names I changed since 1988 simply because another guide book came along with names that made sense. Thanks, Trevor Goward.

[†] Genus *Bryoria* was created out of part of *Alectoria* in 1977.

No doubt the lichens do vary a lot, either within a species or be-tween species that are hard to tell apart visually, even for Indians. Some Indians, too poor for leather footwear, bundled the lichen up to make well-padded shoes.

Old-Man's-Beard

Usnea spp. (**us**-nee-a: Arabic term for a lichen). Pale greenish gray tufts on trees; our species range from densely bushy, 1¼–3", to pendent strands 20" long; when stretched gently, the thicker branches (unless extremely dry) reveal an elastic, pure white inner cord inside the brittle, pulpier skin—like wire in old cracked insulation. All elevs, but commoner low.

Beard lichens of this genus are abundant throughout boreal regions, and have figured in industrial schemes to convert lichen starches into glucose for food, or alcohol for fuel or drink. Even abundant lichens are quickly depleted, due to their extremely slow growth; not enough can be gathered to sustain a starch industry.

Globe Lichen

Sphaerophorus globosus (sphere-**ah**-for-us: sphere bearer; glo-**bo**-sus: round). Robust (not hairlike), brittle, stiffly bushy tufts 1–3" diam., light red-brown to gray when dry, greenish wet; fruiting bodies, if present, are tiny (.08") globes filled with sooty black spores, on branch tips. On trees, from base well up into canopy. Color p 488.

Fungi: twig lichens

Worm Lichen

Thamnolia subuliformis (tham-**no**-lia: bushy, a misleading name; sub-you-li-**for**-mis: awl shaped) and *T. vermicularis* (ver-mic-you-**lair**-iss: worm-like). White tapering tubes 1-2½" tall, without fruiting cups, typically in lack-adaisical clumps of standing tubes with some reclining tubes and a few branched tubes. Alpine. Color p 487.

These two species are chemical variants, being distinguished at the species level solely on the basis of different "lichen acids" they con-tain. As a genus, worm lichens are distinctive. Several variable *Cladonia* species may be wormlike or awllike when they fail to fruit, but are gray-green or tan-brown in contrast to the bone white of worm lichens.

Matchstick Lichen

Pilophorus aciculare (pil-**ah**-for-us: hair bearing; a-sic-you-**lair**-ee: needle-like). Pale gray stalks ⅜–1" long, rarely branched, with fat rounded black fruiting tips; standing or reclining in dense clumps, on rocks in forest. Color p 488.

British Soldiers

Cladonia spp. (cla-**doe**-nia: branched).

Cladonia bellidiflora (bel-id-if-**lor**-a: martial flower). Greenish gray stalks, heavily flaky-coated, ½–2" tall, bearing large, often lobed, scarlet fruiting heads; often from a flaky mat. On rocks, soil or logs. Color p 489.

C. transcendens. Greenish gray 1–2" stalks, granular-coated and/or with small flakes, bearing small, ± round scarlet heads. On rotting wood or tree bases.

The huge genus *Cladonia* has a two-part growth form. The primary growth is a mat of flakes, or "squamules," resembling some leaf lichens only finer. After a while, fruiting "twigs" may rise from this mat. Sometimes the mats of squamules just persist and spread without fruiting; at the other extreme, in species like *bellidiflora* the mat of primary squamules may die and disappear, while the stalks themselves grow thick coats of squamules. Several species fruit bright red; the name "British Soldiers" is borrowed from *C. cristatella*, the common red-capped species of the northeast states.

Pixie Goblets

Cladonia fimbriata (fim-bree-**ay**-ta: fringed). Clustered greenish gray golf-tee-like fruiting stalks ½–1¼" tall, from a thick flaky mat; "baby tees" may sprout from rims of main ones. On soil, stumps, fenceposts, etc. Color p 489.

Though golf tees are more obvious, the image of goblets for pixies is suggested by a the name of a relative (uncommon here), *C. pyxidata,* which actually refers to *pyxis,* a Greek goblet-shaped container with a lid. Many *Cladonia* species produce "golf tees."

8

Mammals

We scarcely need to be introduced to mammals. We *are* mammals. We're well schooled in the salient characteristics of mammals, most definitive being the mammary glands which, on females, produce milk to nurse the young. Live birth is typical, though neither universal (egg-laying platypuses are mammals) nor unique (live-bearing snakes are not). Warm-bloodedness (maintaining an elevated body temperature) is universal among both mammals and birds, and has also been found in some other animals and plants. (See pages 220, 454).

In mammals only, a coat of keratinous hairs serves to insulate body temperature: perhaps even more than breasts, hair is the definitive mammalian body part. Whales, armadillos, and other mammals even less hairy than we are all have at least a few hairs at some developmental stage. Mammal coats come mainly in shades of brown and gray. No fur is bright blue or green, as some feathers are, even on the exceptional mammals, like skunks, whose coloring is "showy" rather than camouflaging. Most mammals need to be inconspicuous. They achieve that by wearing camouflage colors, by being quiet and elusive, and by being nocturnal. That explains why mammalwatching is a pastime less popular than birdwatching, and why knowing mammal tracks, scats, and other signs is key to being woodswise to mammals. The mammals we see most often here each have reasons to be unafraid: porcupines have their defenses, tree-climbing squirrels and burrowing marmots and pikas have their alarm networks and refuges, and National Park-dwelling deer, elk, bears, and goats have big brains that have adapted to their legally protected status. Watch out for them!

Small mammals are especially limited to the murky corner of the spectrum. Experienced field naturalists can sometimes recognize the species they study, using color differences they have learned in a particular locale. They may report these shades as "dusky" or "buffy," "tawny" or "ochraceous"—terms somewhat less useful to nonscientists. Photos can be a big help, but their colors vary with lighting and printing. And the animals themselves vary. In a given species, there may be different shades for different seasons, for juveniles versus adults, for infraspecific varieties and color phases, for the paler underside and darker back, and between the hair tips, underfur, and guard hairs. Among closely related mammals, populations of dry regions are often paler than their wet-side relatives, each tending to match the color of the ground so as to be less visible to predators (especially owls) that hunt from above in dim light. Dry-country (e.g., Eastside) creatures run around on pale dry dirt, whereas moist forests have dark floors of humus and vegetation.

Positive identification of small mammals utilizes the number and shape of molar teeth and caliper measurements of skulls and penis bones (a feature of most male mammals) for which the creature must first be reduced to a skeleton. But don't worry—this book will not go into molar design or the meaning of "dusky," but will offer size, tail/body length ratio, form, habitat, and sometimes color, to facilitate educated guesses as to small mammal identities. Often our glimpses of shrews, mice and voles, unless we trap them or find them dead, are so fleeting and dark that we can make only a downright wild guess, based mainly on habits and habitat.

Charles Bendire (born Karl Emil Bender in Germany) watched birds and other creatures while stationed near Harney Lake in 1874-1877, and reported what he saw in copious letters to eminent Eastern naturalists. To them he was a diamond in the rough, an army Major previously noted only as the intrepid Indian-fighter who dissuaded Cochise from returning to the warpath. His reports were published as Birds of Southeastern Oregon *and later as a thick* Life Histories of North American Birds. *He was first to unmask the kokanee salmon as a landlocked form of sockeye.*

Shrews

Sorex spp. (**sor**-ex: the Roman term). Mouselike creatures with very long, pointed, wiggly, long-whiskered snouts, red-tipped teeth, and ± naked tails. Order Insectivora (Shrews and moles). (Color p 490).

Trowbridge shrew, *S. trowbridgii* (tro-**bridge**-ee-eye: after W. P. Trowbridge). 2½" + 2¼" tail; gray-black exc white underside of tail. Abundant in W-side forests. Illustrated.

Dusky shrew, *S. monticolus* (mon-**tic**-o-lus: mountain-dweller). 2¾" + 1¾" tail; dark brown. Forests, WA and N OR.

Wandering shrew, *S. vagrans* (**vay**-grenz: wandering). 2½" + 1½" tail; fur dark gray frosted brown on back, pinkish on sides, and pale on belly. Meadows both low and high.

Masked shrew, *S. cinerea* (sin-**ee**-ria: ashen). 2¼" + 1¾" tail; brown with ± tan underside. Drier mtn forests in WA.

Water shrew, *S. palustris* (pa-**lus**-tris: of swamps). 3" + 3" tail; blackish above, paler beneath; tail sharply bicolored. In and near high-elev marshes and lakes.

Marsh shrew, *S. bendirii* (ben-**dear**-ee-eye: after Charles Bendire, see facing page). 3½" + 3" tail; blackish all over. W-side lowlands, often in water.

Shrews, our smallest and most primitive mammals, lead hyperactive but very simple lives. As shrew expert Leslie Carraway writes, "*S. vagrans* exhibits some behavior that tends to indicate it does not perceive much that transpires in its microcosm." Day in and night out, shrews rush around groping with their little whiskers, sniffing, and eating most everything they can find. This goes on from weaning, between April and July of one year, until death, generally by August of the next.

Of course that's an oversimplification. They eat insects and other arthropods (often as larvae), earthworms, and a few conifer seeds and underground-fruiting fungi; they have been known to kill and eat other shrews, and mice. They have 24-hour cycles of greater and lesser activity based largely on when certain types of prey are easiest to get, but as a rule they can't go longer than three hours without eating, and the smaller species must eat their own weight equivalent daily. As with bats and hummingbirds, such a high caloric demand is dictated by the high rate of heat loss from small bodies: at two grams, masked shrews approximate the lower size limit for warm-blooded bodies. Baby shrews nurse their way up to this threshold while huddling together so that the combined mass of the litter of four to ten easily exceeds two grams. Whereas bats and hummingbirds take half of every day off for deep, torpid sleep (page 314), shrews never do. Nor do they hibernate. It's hard to imagine how our shrews meet their caloric needs during the long snowy season when insect populations are dormant, and heat loss all the more rapid. But they do—or at least enough of them do to maintain the population.

One cause of mortality seems to be a sort of Shrew Shock Syndrome triggered, for example, by capture or a sudden loud noise. Some scientists relate it to the shrew's extreme heart rate (1,200 beats per minute have been recorded) and others to low blood sugar caused by even the briefest shortage of food. At any rate, perhaps the most frequent sign of our abundant shrew population is their little corpses on the ground. Shrews are ill adapted to evade predators; their eyesight and hearing are poor. Their only defense is unsophisticated but effective: they are simply unappetizing. Owls, Steller's jays, and trout are among the small minority of predators known to have acquired a taste for shrews.

Marsh and water shrews, the types most likely to tempt trout, spend much of their time in the water, going after tadpoles, snails, leeches, etc. They have such terrific buoyancy, thanks to fur that traps an insulating air layer next to the skin, that they can literally run across the water surface for several seconds. When they dive and swim, they must paddle even more frenetically to stay under; as soon as they stop, they bob to the surface. Yet marsh shrews can stay down for three minutes and more. They have stiff, hairy fringes on the side of their hind feet for more efficient paddling.

Our more terrestrial shrews may run on the surface or even climb trees, but most of the time they are subsurface. Dusky specializes in the duff layer; the bigger, stronger Trowbridge's gets down into the mineral soil; and Vagrant tunnels *through* the duff *upon* the mineral soil.

Shrews are ferociously solitary. In order to mate, they calm their usual mutual hostility with elaborate courtship displays and pheromonal exchanges—a real-life "taming of the shrews."

Shrew-mole

Neurotrichus gibbsii, (new-ro-**try**-kus: hairy wire, i.e. tail; **gib**-zee-eye: after George Gibbs, p 53). 3" + 1½" tail; gray-black; tail hairy—unlike any other shrew or mole; teeth not red-tipped; eyes tiny; no visible ears; forefeet and claws larger than rear ones, but less so than in moles; snout long, whiskered. Mainly in W-side forest. Insectivora (Shrews and moles).

The shrew-mole certainly appears to be the odd half-breed its name suggests, though it's officially in the mole family. (Shrews and moles are the two big families in the order Insectivora, or "insect-eaters"). It burrows so much less effectively than other moles that it is largely confined to the leaf-mold and loose-humus layer. On the other hand, it is the one mole that sometimes forages aboveground, even climbing bushes in search of bugs.

Moles

Scapanus spp. (**scap**-an-us: digger). Burrowing animals, blackish with pink, ± naked tail and snout; eyes and ears barely visible; forefeet huge, turned-out, heavily clawed. Order Insectivora (Shrews and moles).

Coast mole, *S. orarius* (or-**air**-ius: coastal). 5" + 1¼" tail. Sporadic, all elevs.

Townsend mole, *S. townsendii* (town-**send**-ee-eye: after J. K. Townsend, page 313). 7" + 1½" tail. W-side meadows, rarely up to subalpine.

Of all our mammals, moles are most specialized for burrowing. They sort of swim through loose soil. The forelimbs are heavily developed, while the pelvis and hindlimbs are small and weak. Eyes and ears are both almost entirely overgrown with skin and fur so as not to clog up with dirt. While the eyes barely function at all, the ears are quite sharp at receiving earthborn sounds, enabling the mole to detect and hunt earthworms (its main food) by sound.

These true moles are commonest in lowland pastures, but the coast mole also inhabits forests in most parts of our range, and both species are sometimes found in subalpine meadows. Each individual defends its own network of tunnels, which lack entrance holes. Coast moles usually tunnel just below the surface, pushing up sinuous ridges of soil. Townsend's moles tunnel several inches down, and get rid of the dirt by pushing it up to form numerous mole hills, larger and more perfectly hemispherical than hills made by gophers or boomers. (Compare "gopher eskers," page 320).

Bats

Order Chiroptera (kye-**rop**-ter-a: hand wing).

As evening gets too dark for swifts and nighthawks to continue their feeding flights, bats and owls begin to come out for theirs. Though the largest bats and smallest owls overlap in size, 5½" with a 16" wingspread, bats are easy to tell from owls by their fluttering, indirect flight. You are unlikely to see one well, since our species never venture out in the daytime. I won't discuss our ten or twelve species individually, but this doesn't mean bats are unimportant or uninteresting. They are extremely abundant (exceeded among mammalian orders only by the rodents) and probably

Animal Sonar

You have probably heard that bats use a sort of ultrasonic radar to find their way around and to locate and catch prey. This is surprisingly recent information. In 1794 it was first observed that bats get around fine with their eyes blocked, but become helplessly "blind" with their ears blocked. The obvious deduction—that bats literally hear their way around as competently as other animals see theirs—was too strange to win acceptance for more than a century. Not until 1938 were instruments able to detect bats' high-frequency squeaks, whose echoes bats hear in a sonarlike perceptual capacity called "echolocation."

A typical bat "blip" lasts a thousandth of a second, during which time it drops an octave and spreads out from a focussed sound to a nearly omnidirectional one. These precise shifts, and the very short wavelength, give the echoes such fine tuning that the bat not only locates objects but perceives their texture and their exact motion. It's strictly fast-food for a bat to nab a mosquito, for example, distinguishing it from a shower of cottonwood fluff amid an obstacle course of branches.

From a casual blip rate of several per second in the open air, the bat steps up to over fifty per second when objects of interest come within a yard or so. That's as far as a bat can echolocate, since high-pitched sounds don't carry far. (Contrast with the great carrying power of a grouse's low "booming.") To compensate for such "nearsightedness," the bat's reactions must be extremely quick, and its blip extremely loud;

take a bigger slice out of the insect population than any other type of predator. Most bats, including all of ours, are insect-eaters, like their closest relatives the shrews, so calling them flying mice or flitter-mice (two colloquial terms probably descended from the German *fledermaus*) is a near miss—these are "flying shrews."

Bats catch flying prey either in the mouth or in a tuck of the small membrane stretched between the hind legs, from which the mouth then plucks it while the bat tumbles momentarily in mid-flight. Each wing is a much larger, transparently thin membrane stretched from the hindleg up to the forelimb and all around the four long "fingers." Since the wing has no thickness to speak of, it is less effective than a bird or airplane wing at turning forward motion into lift. To compensate, bats generally have much greater wing area per weight than birds, and use a complex stroke resembling a

---

the decibel level an inch from a bat's mouth is several times that of a pneumatic drill at 20 feet. Those God-awful earsplitting nights in the country! (Well, they would be, if our hearing were sensitive to 80,000 cycles per second instead of its mere 15,000. "Concert A," the note orchestras tune by, is 440 cycles, roughly at the middle of our audible sound spectrum.) To protect the bat's own hearing from damage, its auditory canals vibrate open and shut alternately with the blips, admitting only the echoes. Bats also have lower-pitched (humanly audible) squeaks for communication.

The nocturnal aerial hunting made possible by echolocation must be a key to bats' success, since in the daytime they are at an overall competitive disadvantage to birds, who can fly much faster, thanks to feathers. Styles of echolocation in bats are highly diversified and specialized. (A few kinds of bats, though none in this part of the world, see pretty well, echolocate poorly, and shun nighttime activity.)

Aspects of echolocation have been found in many unrelated animals. Some moths evade bats by emitting batlike blips to scramble the bats' radar. Porpoises and toothed whales echolocate as sophisticatedly as bats. Some shrews echolocate, crudely. Cave-dwelling birds have learned to do it. The ability may be latent in most mammals; blind humans often learn to echolocate impressively, though rarely developing special calls for the purpose. The human auditory system, according to one theory, also vibrates shut to save us from the racket of our own voices.

---

human breast-stroke to pull themselves continually upward. Bats achieve only modest airspeeds, compared to birds, but they are much more maneuverable at close quarters. They actually chase flying insects rather than simply intercepting them.

Bats roost upside down, hanging from one or both feet. In this position, often in large groups, they sleep all day and hibernate all winter, except for a few winter-migrating species. Though our bats prefer to roost in caves—especially in winter, for insulation—they typically settle for tree cavities and well-shaded branches. After mating in autumn, most species females store sperm to delay fertilization, and bear a single young in spring. Except while out hunting, the mothers nurse the young almost constantly the first few weeks, hanging upside down in the roost.

Bats may carry rabies, but even rabid ones rarely bite people.

Pika

Ochotona princeps (ock-o-**toe**-na: the Mongolian term; **prin**-seps: a chief). Also **cony.** 8" long if stretched out, but appearing a thickset 5–6" long in typical postures; tailless; brown; ears round, 1/2" diam. On talus, in Cas. Order Lagomorpha (Rabbits). Color p 490.

A cryptoventriloquistic nasal "eeeenk" in the vicinity of coarse talus (rockpile) identifies the pika for you. Look carefully for it on the rocks. You would think of it as a rodent, but there's something definitely rabbitlike in its posture—perhaps the sharply nose-down head angle, the neck drawn back in an S curve. Pikas are in fact more rabbit than rodent;* they comprise a family in the rabbit order.

Pikas are thought of as subalpine creatures, and most of them do live up high, but others are just as happy on talus slopes down at the lowest elevations in our range—just above the highway in the Columbia Gorge. On the other hand, they haven't migrated

---

*Rabbits and pikas were once classified as rodents, but are now a separate order, Lagomorpha. They are thought to have diverged early in mammal evolution. Rodents and lagomorphs share incisor teeth that grow throughout life as fast as they wear down. Rodents have four such incisors; lagomorphs have eight—a second upper and lower pair are right behind the first. Lagomorphs are also unusual in having the testes in front of the penis.

across the broad lowlands to reach the Olympics. They depend on talus crevices for refuge; they make quick forays into surrounding vegetation to harvest some, and run back carrying big mouthfuls crosswise. Each year, each little haymaker stores several bushels of mixed greens for winter. Visible haypiles are often under rock overhangs, but others are deep in the rockpile. Haypiles are prone to rotting, and pikas try to include some toxic plants to inhibit rot; the toxins may degrade with age, allowing the plant to be eaten. Pikas graze on grasses in summer, but turn to broadleaved perennials and even a few woody plants for haymaking.

The young stake out their own territory (usually toward the center of a rockpile, since choice outer sites near the meadow are taken by dominant individuals) and make their own hay their first summer, even if they're only about half grown at the time. The rockpile may appear to unite a colony, but pikas live in it solitarily except while mating.

The "eeeenk" call—amazingly loud for such a tiny creature—seems to serve as both territorial assertion and alarm. While no crevice large enough to admit a pika can keep out a weasel, the

Coprophagy

An exclusive diet of vegetative parts of plants presents a severe challenge to mammalian digestive systems because of the high fiber content (and other disproportions: see page 332). As we learned in childhood, the large grazing mammals meet the challenge with cud-chewing and multiple stomachs, enabling them to take in lots of greens in a hurry, out in the open, and then retire to chew in a relatively safe hideout.

Pikas, most rabbits, packrats, and some other herbivorous rodents are able to digest food twice without having to squeeze extra stomachs into their tiny frames; they cycle their food through the whole digestive canal twice, eating their own (and sometimes others') "soft pellets" of partly digested material, and later excreting "hard pellets" of hardcore waste. Different things may be going on in different animals. In some, the food is cultured with a bacterium that requires sunlight to complete its digestive work; other animals eat their pellets immediately, before they can get a tan. Apparently, a longish spell in the caecum (a pocket between the stomach and the large intestine) releases vitamins which rockpile offers a maze where the pika may lose the weasel and lay low. The pika knows its rockpile, is superbly surefooted on it and, according to more than one report, may be aided by other pikas coming out from refuge to distract the weasel by running around like crazy. This kind of report sets some naturalists to arguing over whether it's proof of altruism (evolved traits endangering individual lives for the benefit of the genetic group) or merely foolish nervous agitation.

The name "pika" derives from the way Siberian Tungus tribespeople say "eeeenk," so it should be pronounced "peeeeka." That's the accepted pronunciation in Canada, but south of the 49th I've mostly heard "pike-a," perhaps due to confusion with "pica" or "piker." Others say "cony," but that name refers originally to unrelated Old-World beasts.

Snowshoe Hare

Lepus americanus (**lep**-us: the Roman term). Also **varying hare**. 16" when stretched out, + 1½" tail; gray-brown to deep chestnut brown (incl tail) in summer; in winter, high Cas and E-slope race turns white, with dark ear-tips; W-slope race stays brown; ears slightly shorter than head. Nocturnal and secretive; widespread in forest. Order Lagomorpha (Rabbits). Color p 490.

Thanks to their "snowshoes"—large hindfeet with dense growth of stiff hair between the toes—these hares can be just as active in the winter, on the snow, as in summer. They neither hoard nor hibernate, but molt from brown to white fur, and go from a diet of greens to one of conifer buds and shrub bark made all the more accessible by the rising platform of snow. They make the animal tracks we see most often while skiing. They also become the crucial staple in the winter diet of several predators—foxes, great horned owls, golden eagles, bobcats, and especially lynxes. Though the hares' defenses (camouflage, speed and alertness) are good, the predator pressure on them becomes ferocious when the other small prey have retired beneath the ground or the snow. Hares can support their huge winter losses only with even greater summer prodigies of reproduction, the proverbial "breeding like rabbits." Several times a year, a mother hare can produce two to four young. She mates immediately after each litter, and gestates 36 to 40 days.

Drastic population swings in 8 to 11-year cycles are well known in northerly parts of showshoe hare range, but not here.

The other kind of "varying" the hare is named for—from summer brown to winter white pelage—is true of some hares here. The semiannual molt is triggered by changing day length. In years when autumn snowfall or spring snowmelt come abnormally early or late, the hares find themselves horribly conspicuous and have to lay low for a few weeks. Permanently brown races have evolved in lowland areas that fail, year after year, to develop a prolonged snowpack, e.g., our Westside foothills and mid-elevations. These brown hares stand out during the occasional snows. The rest of the year they make the most of their camouflage, foraging when they can best see without being seen—by dawn and dusk, and sometimes on cloudy days in deep forest. Snowshoe hares don't use burrows, but retire to shallow depressions called "forms," under shrubs.

Though infrequently vocal, snowshoe hares have a fairly loud aggressive/defensive growl, a powerful scream perhaps expressing pain or shock, and ways of drumming their feet as their chief mating call. A legendary courtship dance, in which they may literally somersault over each other for awhile, appears to crescendo out of an ecstatic access of foot-drumming.

Hares (genus *Lepus*) are born fully furred and ready to run. and eat green leaves within hours of birth. Rabbits are born naked and blind, and must be nursed for 10–12 days before leaving the nest. Physical differences between the two are quite arcane. Northwest rabbits include several species of *Sylvilagus* (sil-**vil**-a-gus: forest rabbit). The mountain cottontail, *S. nuttallii,* a smallish rabbit with pure white tail, may be seen along the forest-steppe margin east of the Cascades, and the brush rabbit, *S. bachmani,* in Westside valleys in Oregon. True to its name (and to legend), the brush rabbit lives in the briar patch and rarely comes out. It loves blackberries. The mountain cottontail ventures out to graze on grasses from its refuge under sagebrush, bitterbrush, or rabbitbrush. As steppe animals go, it is only marginally adapted to drought, and has learned to climb juniper trees at night to nibble foliage, largely for their dew. Few lagomorphs climb trees.

Boomer

Aplodontia rufa (ap-lo-**don**-sha: simple teeth; **roo**-fa: red). Also **mountain-beaver, sewellel, chehalis.** 12–14" rotund body; tail vestigial, inconspicuous, 1–2"; dark brown above, slightly paler beneath; with blunt snout, long whiskers, small eyes and ears, long front claws. Scrubby moist W-side habitats. Order Rodentia (Rodents). Color p 490.

Boomers are big, slow, nearly tailless, partly arboreal, mostly burrowing rodents. They achieve several distinctions, all rather ludicrous. They host the world's largest (⅜") species of flea. They are the only surviving species in the most primitive living family of rodents, having changed little since they first appeared, very early on in the evolution of rodents. Naturalists never quite know what to call them, apart from "living fossils." Most manuals list them under Mountain-beaver, but then immediately fall back on Aplodontia, apologizing that this is neither a beaver nor especially a mountain-dweller. Everyone in my end of the county that has boomers calls them "boomers," so I guess that's good enough for

John Kirk Townsend came to Oregon with Nathaniel Wyeth and Thomas Nuttall (page 71) in 1834. Young (24) and enthusiastic, he wrote a charming popular account of their shared travels. Though best remembered among birders, he collected and described several new plants and animals (Townsend's mole, vole, chipmunk, etc.). He filled in as Fort Vancouver's physician between Gairdner's and Tolmie's (page 198) tenures there, no mean feat during the epidemics that were slaughtering Northwest Indians at the time. Of portaging around the Cascades of the Columbia in heavy rain, Townsend wrote: "It was by far the most fatiguing, cheerless, and uncomfortable business in which I was ever engaged, and truly glad was I to lie down at night on the cold, wet ground, wrapped in my blankets, out of which I had just wrung the water.... I could not but recollect ... the last injunction of my dear old grandmother, not to sleep in damp beds!!!"

Occupational hazards brought him to an untimely end, as they did several other explorer-naturalists. He devised his own formula to keep pests from eating his stuffed specimens; it contained arsenic; he died at age 42 of chronic arsenic poisoning.

me. Their vocalization, by the way, is hardly explosive, but it might be transcribed as "moom." Sort of a low moan, repeated.

Boomers prefer wet, scrubby thickets and forests at all elevations. They are doubtless thriving in this century, with the proliferation of second-growth timber; Northwestern "stump farmers" know them well. They honeycomb their half-acre home ranges with shallow burrow systems, making many molehill-like dirt heaps. Mainly nocturnal, they are active year round, eating sword ferns and bracken, vine maple and salal bark, and Douglas-fir seedlings. The latter makes them unpopular with foresters, of course, but their digging does a lot for soil drainage and friability, and disseminates spores of certain desirable underground-fruiting fungi that have no other means of spore travel.

Chipmunks

Tamias spp.* (**tay**-me-us: storer). Rich brown with four pale and three dark stripes conspicuous down the back and from nose through eyes to ears. Order Rodentia.

Townsend's chipmunk, *T. townsendii* (town-**send**-ee-eye: after J. K. Townsend, facing page). 6" + bushy tail 5"; pale stripes ± gray. Dense forest.

Yellow-pine chipmunk, *T. amoenus* (a-**me**-nus: delightful). 5" + bushy tail 4"; pale stripes yellowish brown. Open conifer forest and timberline areas. Illustrated at right, and color p 492.

Along with Douglas' squirrel, these small chipmunks are our most conspicuous forest mammals — diurnal, noisy, and abundant. They have a diverse vocabulary of chips, chirps, and tisks easily mistaken for bird calls. Townsend's is often heard without being seen, since it is shy, in keeping with its predilection for heavy forest cover. Though sometimes seen together, the two species are more often separated by habitat if not by range; yellow-pine chipmunks require open forest, and tend to be either higher or farther east than Townsend's.

Our chipmunks are semi-arboreal, nesting either in burrows or up in trees. They forage terrestrially for seeds, berries, a few

*Many older texts have Western chipmunks in a separate genus *Eutamias*. Our authority finds this segregation poorly supported.

insects and, increasingly toward winter, lots of underground fungi. To facilitate food-handling, they have an upright stance (like other squirrels and gophers) that frees the handlike forefeet. They store huge quantities of food, carrying it to their burrows in cheek pouches. Their winter strategy varies with climate and genetics, but commonly they rely on stored food alone, without fattening up. They pass the winter with a series of torpid bouts at only moderately depressed body temperatures; every four or five days they get up to excrete and eat from stores in the burrow. You may hear their chatter even in midwinter, and on milder days at lower elevations they are likely to go out and forage. The young, though born naked, blind and helpless, mature fast enough to disperse and make their own nests for their first winter.

Marmots

Marmota spp. (mar-**moe**-ta: the French term). Also **rockchuck**, **whistle-pig**, **whistler**. Heavy-bodied, thick-furred, large rodents of mountain meadows and talus, known for their piercing "whistles." Order Rodentia.

Hoary marmot, *M. caligata* (cali-**gay**-ta: booted). 20" long + 9" tail; grizzled gray-brown, with black feet and ± white belly and bridge of nose. alp/subalpine in WA Cas.

Olympic marmot, *M. olympus*. Similar to hoary marmot (considered a subspecies by some) but face and feet markings less contrasty; back often yellowish by late summer, possibly bleached by urine-soaked burrow walls. Alp/subalpine in Olys. Color p 491.

Yellow-bellied marmot, *M. flaviventris* (flay-vi-**ven**-tris: yellow belly). 16" long + 6½" tail; yellowish brown, often gray-grizzled, with ± yellow throat and belly; feet darker brown. From Cas Cr E, mainly on basalt lowlands, but sometimes subalpine (as it is in Rockies and Sierra Nevada).

It's hard to feel you're really in the high country until you've been announced by a marmot, with a sudden shrill shriek. Sadly, subalpine habitat often lacks marmots for no apparent reason. The shriek (not a whistle, in that it's made with the vocal chords) is a warning that may send several other marmots lumping along to their various burrows. On the way they pause, perhaps standing up like big milk bottles, to look around and see how threatening you actually appear. A more fearsome predator than yourself, such as a red-tailed hawk, would have elicited a shorter, descending whistle conveying greater urgency. In your case, they easily become nearly oblivious to you, or even quite forward and interested in your goods. Or you may get to watch them scuffle, box, and tumble, or hear more of their vocabulary of grunts, growls and chirps.

Marmots need their early warning system because they're slower than many other prey, and count all the large predators as enemies. They are rarely hunted by people any more, though Indians and Inuit used to think them worth hunting for both fur and flavor. To protect themselves from the phenomenal digging prowess of badgers, our yellow-bellied marmots locate their burrows in rockpiles. Olympic marmots, with no badgers to worry about, often burrow in loose meadow soils, but occasionally a whole hibernating family is dug out and eaten by a bear.

As befits the largest members of the squirrel family, marmots take their hibernating seriously. They put on enough fat to constitute as much as half their body weight, and then they bed down for more than half the year, the colony snuggling together to conserve heat. Resist the temptation to think of seven-month hibernation as a desperate response required by an extreme environment. It is just one of several strategies that work here; other small subalpine grazers like the pika and the water vole stay active beneath the snow at a comfortable constant 32°, while long-legged browsers forage above the snow, a few staying subalpine, most migrating downslope. These different wintering strategies go with tastes for different plants, so the grazing species rarely compete directly for one food resource.

Marmots concentrate a year's worth of eating into a brief green season. The season doesn't have to be summer. Olympic and hoary marmots keep a winter schedule (hibernating late September to early May) similar to that of yellow-bellied marmots of the high Rockies; but our yellow-bellies, low on the Cascades' east slope, fatten in April and May and go down for their seven-month slumber in midsummer when the heat dries up spring's herbs and grasses. Summer torpor is termed "aestivation" as opposed to "hibernation," but these marmots perform the two consecutively without noting the distinction.

Young yellow-bellies mature fast enough to disperse (leave their maternal care and burrow) at the end of their first or, more often, second summer. Hoary and Olympic marmots, with an even shorter, colder active season, mature very slowly for rodents, dispersing only in their third summer when their mother's subsequent

---

Mammals

litter arrives. Young and yearling marmots suffer heavy casualties to both predation and winter starvation. Even more than a mother bear, a marmot mother is hard put to fatten enough for her nursing litter's hibernation as well as her own; in alternate years she is infertile, restoring her metabolic reserves while casually tending her yearlings. A dominant male may thus keep two mates, impregnating the fertile one and leaving her to run a nursery burrow while he shares a burrow with the infertile one and her yearlings—a

Torpor and Hibernation

Most warm-blooded species have normal body temperatures about as warm as our 98.6°, but many of them spend much of their time at sharply reduced metabolic levels, which we lump together under the word "torpor." Torpor is a condition of deep sleep, with very slow breathing (one per minute) and heartbeat (four to eight per minute) at body temperatures close to the ambient temperature, down to a limit a few degrees above freezing. Its purpose is to conserve calories at times when they are hard to come by. There are several patterns of torpor:

Daily torpor, *such as the daily sleep of bats and the nightly sleep of hummingbirds; ordinary sleep would waste too many calories through heat loss from tiny bodies like these, in temperate climates.*

Seasonal torpor, *usually called either hibernation (from the Latin for "winter") or aestivation (from the Latin for "summer"); the animal may waken occasionally to excrete, stretch, eat stored food, or perhaps even go out and forage a bit.*

Occasional torpor, *a last-ditch response to food shortage, or even to a momentary shock, as in "playing possum."*

Animals adapt to various habitats in their use of torpor. Some species of jerboas include subarctic races that hibernate, desert races that aestivate, and in-between races active year round. Some chipmunks vary from year to year, as well as with elevation and latitude, as to whether they will hibernate or forage through the winter, and they may dehibernate if the weather turns better in midwinter. They also seem to include, within hibernating races, genetic minorities that never hibernate. Some ground squirrels and marmots go into aestivation in the summer and don't come out until they dehibernate in early spring. Most temperate-zone bats hibernate in addition to sleeping torpidly every day of their active season.

social structure common to both hoary and Olympic marmot colonies. The colony resembles an extended family; the "aunts and uncles" are subordinate adults who surround the dominant "alpha *ménage à trois*" with their this-year's and last-year's litters. As summer wears on, parents increasingly work at chasing their grown yearlings away from the colony. Most of the marmot tussles you see are simply play between youngsters, but those that end in a one-sided chase are more likely adults making yearlings unwelcome.

Hibernation is a strategy with great advantages, but also with severe costs and problems. First, the animal must put on a lot of weight—33% to 67% on top of its midsummer weight. Most species can't gain much weight on greens and fungi, so they have to do it all late in the season, after the carbohydrate-rich seeds and berries ripen. Much of the gain is in form of brown fat, which can be oxidized to produce heat directly, without muscular contractions. But burning off fat draws water out of the bloodstream, whereas burning off muscle adds water, and dehydration is one of the worst problems hibernators deal with; so considerable muscle tissue is also put on, and burned off. Hibernation requires pituitary hormones to suppress urine formation in order to conserve water, and it requires special chemistry to ameliorate the toxicity of urea that accumulates when it isn't eliminated in urine.

Exactly what triggers hibernation and dehibernation is a challenging scientific problem. There is evidence that scarcity of food, abundance of fat, outside temperature, day length, and absolute internal calendars are among the triggers for various species. Most hibernators gradually decrease their food consumption for some weeks in anticipation. Once it's hibernating, a rodent is hard to rouse. To wake up, most species spend several hours raising their body temperature by violent shivering. Marmots hibernate in heaps, and the shivering of one will trigger the others to join in a group shiver.

Bears are sometimes said not to be "true hibernators," but a fairer statement might be that bear and squirrel hibernation are physiologically different. Bears lower their body temperature only a little, and rouse into full activity quickly, when they rouse at all. However, some other changes in their bodily functions are as extreme as those of squirrels, and certainly as effective. Perhaps bears are simply so much bigger and better-insulated that to lower their body temperature while still sustaining life would be downright difficult, and serve no purpose.

Douglas' Squirrel

Tamiasciurus douglasii, (tay-me-a-sigh-**oo**-rus: chipmunk squirrel; da-**glass**-ee-eye: after David Douglas, p 18). Also **chickaree, pine squirrel.** 7" + bushy 5" tail; gray-brown above, with reddish tinge; orange, variably grayed, below; the two color areas separated by a slight black line conspicuous only in summer. Dense conifer forest. Order Rodentia. Color p 491.

Noisy sputterings and scoldings from the tree canopy call our attention to this creature which, like other tree squirrels, can afford to be less shy and nocturnal than most mammals thanks to the easy escape offered by trees. Scolding lets all the neighborhood squirrels know there's a possibly dangerous animal nearby, but once they know about you they don't seem to consider you much of a threat. There *are* predators that take squirrels quite easily—martens, goshawks, and large owls—but apparently they were never common enough to put a dent in the squirrel population, and are scarcer than ever today, in retreat from civilization. Unlike squirrels.

Sometimes in late summer and fall we know Douglas' squirrel by the repeated thud of green cones hitting the ground. Since cones are designed to open and drop their seeds while still on the tree, closed cones you see on the ground are likely a squirrel's harvest. The squirrel runs around in the branches nipping off cones, twelve per minute on Douglas-fir or up to thirty per minute for some smaller cones; then it runs around on the ground carrying them off to cold storage. True-fir cones are too heavy to drag or carry, so it gnaws away just enough of the outside of the cone to lighten it to a draggable weight, while leaving the seeds still well sealed in. Some day, it will carry the cones back up to a habitual feeding-limb and tear them apart, eating the seeds and dropping the cone scales and cores, which form a heap we call a "midden." Either the center of a midden or a hole dug in a streambank may be used to store cones for one to three years. The cool, dark, moist conditions keep the cone from opening and losing its seeds and also, incidentally, keep the seeds viable. Foresters learned to rob middens, and squirrels became the chief suppliers of conifer seed to Northwest nurseries by 1965. This scam is in decline now that nurseries are choosier about their genetic stock.

Mushrooms, which must be dried to keep well, are festooned

in twig crotches all over a conifer, and later moved to a dry cache such as a tree hollow. With such an ambitious food-storage industry, this squirrel has no need to hibernate. For the winter, it moves from a twig and cedar-bark nest on a limb to a better-insulated spot, usually an old woodpecker hole. This-year's young winter in their parents' nest (unlike smaller rodents such as mice and chipmunks) since they need most of a year to mature.

The proportion of all conifer seeds that are consumed by rodents, birds, and insects is huge, exceeding 99% in some poor conecrop years; foresters have long regarded seed eaters as enemies. But the proportion of conifer seeds that germinate and grow is infinitesimal anyway, and of those, the percentage that were able to succeed *because* they were harvested, moved, buried, and then neglected is significant. Trees coevolved with seed eaters in this relationship, and may depend on it (see page 49). Additionally, all conifers are dependent on mycorrhizal fungi, many of which depend in turn on these same rodents to disseminate their spores. Conifers limit squirrel populations by synchronizing their heavy cone crop years. A couple of poor cone crop years bring the number of squirrels way down, and then the trees produce a bumper crop, with way too many seeds for the reduced population to harvest.

Western Gray Squirrel

Sciurus griseus (sigh-**oo**-rus: the Greek term, derived from "shade tail;" **gris**-ee-us: gray). 12" + very bushy tail 10½"; gray frosted with silver-white hair tips; belly white; ears ± reddish. Mainly E-side pine forest in OR; rare in WA (Chelan and Klickitat Counties). Order Rodentia. Color p 492.

Scarcer than Douglas squirrels and rarely vocal or bold, these gray beauties are infrequently seen or heard. With their huge tails, they are gracefully athletic to watch. Large size and good meat make them popular game. They are protected, as a threatened species, in Washington, but still hunted in Oregon, perhaps explaining their shyness. Truffles contribute the bulk of their diets, but pine nuts and acorns provide crucial richer fare in late summer and fall, so the species is more or less confined to woodland with pines or oaks.

Northern Flying Squirrel

Glaucomys sabrinus (**glawk**-amiss: silvery-gray mouse; sa-**bry**-nus: of the Severn*). 7" + 5½" tail (broad and flat); large flap of skin stretching from foreleg to hindleg on each side; eyes large; red-brown above, pale gray beneath. Widespread in ± open forest. Order Rodentia. Color p 490.

You aren't likely to see these pretty squirrels; they are active in the hours just after dark and before dawn. On a quiet night in the forest, you might hear a soft birdlike chirp and an occasional thump as they land low on a tree trunk. They can't really fly, but they glide far and very accurately, and land gently, by means of the lateral skin flaps which triple their undersurface. They can maneuver to dodge branches, and almost always land on a trunk and immediately run to the opposite side—a predator-evading dodge that includes a feint of the tail in the opposite direction. Large owls preying on them often pick off and drop the tail, so one flying squirrel part you have a better chance of seeing is a jettisoned tail.

Flying squirrels usually nest in old woodpecker holes, and have their young gliding at two months of age, around midsummer. They don't hibernate, nor do they store great quantities of food for winter as Douglas' squirrel does. They eat truffles (undergroundfruiting fungi) almost exclusively in parts of our range. They get through winter on horsehair lichens, which also insulate their nests, in areas where truffles are seasonal. (Exclusive fungivory seems unique to the Northwest: in the East, northern flying squirrels have extremely varied diets.) The truffle/flying squirrel/spotted owl food chain may be a key to spotted owls' dependence on old growth forest, since truffles abound only in old-growth. By far the highest truffle production is in thoroughly rotted fallen trees. If future logging plans could leave both the coarse woody debris and some patches of old trees, that would benefit flying squirrels, red-backed voles, and ecological health overall.

---

*Sabrinus is often identified as a river nymph from Roman mythology without saying why the nymph's name was given to this species. The clearest reason is that the type, or first-described specimen, of the species came from near the Severn River in Ontario. That river is named after England's Severn River, originally named Sabrinus by the Romans.

Golden-Mantled Ground Squirrels

Spermophilus spp. (sper-**mah**-fil-us: seed lover). Also **copperhead**. 7" + 4" bushy tail; medium gray-brown with 2 dark and 1 light stripe down each flank; no stripes on face, head or neck, unlike chipmunks; head and chest (the "mantle") rich yellow-brown; "milk-bottle" posture typical while looking around. E-side and subalpine. Order Rodentia. Color p 492.

S. lateralis (lat-er-**ay**-lis: sides, referring to stripes). In OR.

S. saturatus (satch-er-**ay**-tus: dark). In WA.

These ground squirrels occupy about the same open-forest range as the yellow-pine chipmunk, but seem to sidestep out-and-out competition by being more arboreal and by hibernating for months, fattening grossly in the fall. To car campers they may appear more common than chipmunks, since they are campground scavengers. But if you're an Easterner exploring the West, forget what the ranger told you in Colorado or Wyoming about all the stripy critters being ground squirrels, not chipmunks; here, we have more chipmunks. Ground squirrels' cheek pouches—the mucus-lined mouth interior extending nearly to the shoulders, with a capacity of several hundred seeds—are similar to those of many squirrels and some mice.

Pocket Gophers

Thomomys spp. (**tho**-mo-miss: heap mouse). 5½" + small ± naked 2½" tail; highly variable gray-brown tending to match the local soil; front claws very long, eyes and ears very small, incisors large and always showing. Open areas with loose soil; abundant on E-side steppes; also subalpine. Order Rodentia.

T. mazama (ma-**za**-ma: the Crater Lake volcano). In Olys and OR Cas.

T. talpoides (tal-po-**eye**-deez: mole-like). In WA Cas and E WA and OR.

Pocket gophers spend their lives underground, and have much in common with moles—powerful front claws, heavy shoulders, small weak eyes, small hips for turning around in tight spaces, and short hair with reversible "grain" for backing up. But moles are predators of worms and grubs, and gophers are herbivores. They can suck a plant underground before your very eyes, making hardly a dent on the surface. They get enough moisture from their food that they don't even go to water to drink. In fact, only two occasions

---

always draw them into the open air. One is mating, in spring. That takes only a few minutes, and draws out only the males. Afterward, they return to mutually hostile solitude, plugging up burrow openings behind them. The other is the eviction of young gophers from their mothers' burrows. Though badgers and gopher snakes are well equipped to take gophers, the underground life is so safe overall that gophers limit themselves to one small litter per year.

Our *T. mazama* does go out on occasion, mainly at night. Also, any gopher that lives where it gets snowy may, without exactly going out, eat aboveground foods like bark and twigs by tunneling around through the snow. In spring (July or so in the high country) you find "gopher eskers"—sinuous ridgelets about 3" wide of dirt and gravel that came to rest on the ground during snowmelt. (Color p 490). Shortly before snowmelt, the gopher resumed earth burrowing, and used the snow tunnels it was abandoning as dumps for newly excavated dirt. Summer "tailings" heaps are fan-shaped.

When Mt. St. Helens blew, some gophers survived in their burrows while their plant communities got buried. When they dug out to the surface afterward, they churned old soil into the new ash, enabling new plant seedlings to contact mycorrhizal spores which were essential to plant survival in the nitrogen-poor ash.

A pocket gopher's "pocket" is a cheek pouch used, like a squirrel's, to carry food. Unlike a squirrel's, it opens to the outside. Furlined and dry, it turns inside out for emptying and cleaning. "Gopher teeth," big protruding incisors, are used (at least by gophers) for digging. The lips close behind them to keep out the dirt.

Beaver

Castor canadensis (castor: the Greek term). 25–32" + 10–16" tail; tail flat, naked, scaly; hind feet webbed; fur dark reddish brown. In and near slow-moving streams. Order Rodentia. Color p 491.

The beaver is by far the largest North American rodent today, and was all the more so 10,000 years ago, when there was a giant beaver species the size of a black bear. Of all historical animals, the beaver has had the most spectacular effects on North American landforms, vegetation patterns, and Anglo-American settlement. If that's not enough, it's also Oregon's State Animal.

Though beavers themselves are infrequently seen by hikers, they leave conspicuous signs—beaver dams, ponds, and especially beaver-chewed trees and saplings.

The sound of running water triggers a dam-building reflex in beavers. They cut down poles with their teeth and drag them into place to form, with mud, a messy but very solid structure as large as a few yards wide and several hundred yards long. Rather inconspicuous dams are more common in our range. A beaver colony may maintain its dam and pond for years, adding new poles and puddling fresh mud (by foot agitation) into the interstices.

Most beaver foods are on land, so the adaptation to water is for safety's sake. The pond is a large foraging base on which few predators are nimble. Over most beaver range (though rarely here), pond ice in winter walls them off from predators. Living quarters, in streambank burrows or mid-pond lodge constructions, are above the waterline, but their entrances are all below it, as are the winter food stores—hundreds of poles cut and hauled into the pond during summer, now submerged by waterlogging. Cottonwood, willows and aspen are favorites. Beavers can chew bark off the poles underwater without drowning thanks to watertight closures right behind their incisors and at their epiglottis. They maintain breathing space just under the ice by letting a little water out through the dam. They are well insulated by a thick fat layer just under the skin, plus an air layer just above it, deadened by fine underfur and sealed in by a well-greased outer layer of guard hairs.

The typical beaver lodge or burrow houses a pair, their young and their yearlings. Two-year-olds must disperse in search of new watersheds, where they pair up, typically for life, and found new lodges. While searching, they may be found far from suitable streams. Territories are observed with little apparent aggression.

When beavers dammed most of the small streams in a watershed, as they once did throughout much of the West, they stabilized river flow more thoroughly, subtly, and effectively than concrete dams are able to do today. Beaver ponds also have dramatic local effects. First off, they drown a lot of trees. Eventually, if maintained by successive generations, they may fill up with silt, becoming first a marsh and later a level meadow or "park" with a stream meandering through it. Such parks well below treeline are abundant and much appreciated in the Rockies, but less common in our range.

Beavers were originally almost ubiquitous in the U.S. and Canada, aside from desert and tundra. Many Indian tribes felt kinship with beavers, showing them respect in lore and ritual, while also hunting them for fur and meat. Europeans, in contrast, trapped beavers just to obtain a musky glandular secretion ("castoreum") for use as a perfume base. There was a busy castoreum trade for centuries, before, in the late 1700s, the beaver hat craze hit Europe, and the demand for dead beavers skyrocketed, not letting up until the supply became scarce in the mid-1800s. Strange as it seems today, the beaver-pelt economy provided virtually the sole impetus for explorations of the American West during that period, including the Lewis and Clark Expedition and the Louisiana Purchase itself. Beaver pelts are still on the market today, though changing fashion has allowed their value to fall far below that of many carnivore furs. Populations have recovered about as much as they can, reaching even into central Seattle and Portland, but will never foreseeably regain their natural level because so much beaver habitat has been lost, and the beaver's considerable ability to reconstruct it is not easily tolerated by an agricultural economy.

Jumping Mice

Zapus spp. (**zay**-pus: big foot). 4" + 5–6" tail (longer than body); back has broad stripe dark brown to black; sides paler; belly buff-white; hindfeet several times longer than forefeet; ears small. Thickets and meadows near streams, May to Sept. Order Rodentia.

*Z. trinotatus** (try-no-**tay**-tus: 3-striped back). Sides ± washed with deep orange. Mainly W-side. Illustrated at right, and color p 492.

*Z. princeps** (**prin**-seps: a chief). Sides ± washed with dull lemon yellow. Mainly E-side.

The jumping mouse normally runs on all fours, or hops along in tiny hops, or swims, but if you flush one it's likely to zigzag off in great bounding leaps of 3 to 5 feet. This unique gait gives you a good chance of recognizing them, even though they're mainly nocturnal and not all that common. The oversized feet are for power, and the long tail for stability: jumping mice that have lost or broken their tails tumble head-over-heels when they land from long jumps. While none of our other mice or voles hibernate at all, this one hibernates deeply for more than half the year. It eats relatively rich food—grains, berries, and tiny (¼" or less) underground fungi that grow on maple roots.

Deer Mouse

Peromyscus maniculatus (per-o-miss-cus: boot mouse; ma-nic-you-lay-tus: tiny-handed). 3½" + 3-4" tail (length ratio near 1:1); brown to (juveniles) blue-gray above, pure white below incl white feet and bicolored, often white-tipped tail; ears large, thin, fully exposed; eyes large. Ubiquitous. Order Rodentia.

The deer mouse could be called the North American Mouse; it is far and away the most widespread and numerous mammal on the continent. Not shy of people, it makes itself at home in forest cabins, farmhouses, and many city houses in the Northwest. It is not as urbanized as the house mouse, which originated in Europe and is now in cities worldwide.

The deer mouse builds a cute but soon putrid nest out of whatever material is handiest—kleenex, insulation, underwear, moss, or lichens—in a protected place such as a drawer or hollow log. In winter it is active on top of the snow. It is omnivorous, with an emphasis on larvae in the spring and seeds and berries in the fall. Such a diverse diet adapts it well to recent burns and clearcuts; as the forest matures, deer mice are gradually displaced by the more specialized fungus-eating voles. Deer mice displayed an astonishingly stable response to the greatest disturbance our region has seen in this century—Mt. St. Helens' 1980 eruption. They were common in the blast zone so soon after the eruption that they are presumed to have survived the blast in their homes, and to have found sufficient food under the ash.

Dear mice carry the hantavirus, whose flulike symptoms can turn deadly if untreated for a few days. The greatest danger to humans is in dry, dusty cabins with deer mice; people can become infected by breathing mouse-contaminated dust. It would also be a good idea to minimize handling deer mice, and to wash your hands promptly and thoroughly if you do handle one

---

Packrat

Neotoma cinerea (nee-ah-ta-ma: new cutter; sin-ee-ria: ashen). Properly **bushy-tailed woodrat**. 8–9" + 7" tail covered with inch-long fur, hence more squirrel- than ratlike; brown to (juveniles) gray above, whitish below; whiskers very long; ears large, thin. Can either run or, if chased, hop like a rabbit. Widely but patchily distributed in non-alpine sites with rock outcrops or talus. Order Rodentia.

For some strange reason, packrats love to incorporate man-made objects, shiny ones especially, into their nests. Possibly some predators are spooked by old gumwrappers or gold watches, or perhaps the packrat's craving is purely aesthetic or spiritual. She is likely to be on her way home with a mud pie or a fir cone when she comes across your Swiss Army knife, and she obviously can't carry both at once, so there may be the appearance of a trade, though hardly a fair one from your point of view. Packrats have other habits even worse than trading, often driving cabin dwellers to take up arms. They spend all night in the attic, the woodshed, or in the walls noisily dragging materials around—shreds of fiberglass insulation, for example. Or they may mark unoccupied cabins copiously with foul-smelling musk. The males mark rock surfaces with two kinds of smears, one dark and tarry, one calcareous white and crusty.

Our common species, the bushy-tailed, is an active trader, but

---

Mice or Voles?

Out of the 4,000-plus species of mammals living today, almost 1,700 are rodents, and of those, almost 1,300, or 32% of all mammalian species, are myomorphs, or mouselike rodents. As with insects, songbirds, grasses, and composite flowers, such disproportionate diversification bespeaks competitive success in recent geologic times.

The three large groups within the Myomorpha are the Old World rats and mice; the New World rats and mice; and the voles or "field mice." Jumping mice are one of several smaller families. Mickey, Minnie and Mighty Mouse, with their huge ears, are based on the house mouse, Mus musculus, *which is in the Old World group along with the black rat and Norway rat. This notorious scaly-tailed, un-American* it has evolved away from the use of stickpiles as dwellings, more often nesting in crevices of trees, talus, cliff, mine or cabin. (Other kinds of packrats build 2–8' stickpiles with water-shedding roofs and several rooms — storerooms, nests and latrines. In Nevada caves these last for millenia, and enable paleobotanists to calculate vegetational changes going back to the last glacial stage.) The bushy-tailed builds only modest stickpiles and uses them to cache food. If it does nest in one, it's likely to be in a tree.

Unlike its relatives, this species has a harem mating system; some reports claim the overall sex ratio is skewed, with two to three females for each male. Each female can bear several litters per year. Diet includes a great variety of plants and fungi.

Long-Tailed Vole

Microtus longicaudus (my-**cro**-tus: small ear; lon-ji-**caw**-dus: long tail). 4¾" + 3" tail (length ratio 3:2); ears barely protruding; fur gray-grizzled, feet pale, tail bicolored. Brushy streamsides, clearcuts, etc. Order Rodentia.

Voles of this large genus, related to arctic lemmings, are known for drastic population swings on a 3- or 4-year cycle, with each species synchronized over much or all of its range. Mysterious hormonal/ behavioral mechanisms, rather than either starvation nor preda-

tion, seem to curb the population explosions somewhat short of mass starvation— though not always in time to prevent serious damage to seed or grain

trio is adapted to life around humans, and has spread to every urban area in the world. In the Northwest, our native mice apparently some-how confine the house mouse, true to its name, to indoor habitats.

Our native myomorphs all have more or less furred tails. Aside from the abundant deer mouse and woodrat (both New World types) most myomorphs here are voles, distinguishable to the layman by their blunter snouts and smaller tails, eyes and (often nearly invisible) ears. Voles are herbivores, whereas many rats and mice are omnivores.

Our authority ranks the three big mouse groups as subfamilies (Murinae, Sigmodontinae, Arvicolinae) in one big mouse family. The Arvicolinae (voles) were formerly named Microtinae, and "microtine" remains a common term for voles among field biologists.

crops. The Northwest's most notorious vole "plagues" have been of *Microtus montanus* in Klamath and Deschutes Counties.

Creeping Vole

Microtus oregoni (or-eh-**go**-nigh). 4½" + 1⅜" tail (length ratio 3:1); gray-brown fur exceptionally short, dense. W-side forests and esp clearcuts, dry meadows, and deciduous woods. Order Rodentia.

Our smallest vole stays within an inch one way or the other of the ground surface, either burrowing shallowly in loose dirt or plowing little runways through turf, under logs, or inside rotten logs. This offers some protection from hawks, but not from weasels. Creeping voles maintain sparse populations in forests, ready to multiply rapidly, along with grasses and herbs, after a disturbance.

Townsend's Vole

Microtus townsendii (town-**send**-ee-eye: after J. K. Townsend, p 313). 5½" + 2¼" tail (ratio a little over 2:1); ears distinctly protruding. Moist to marshy meadows at all elevs W of Cas Cr. Order Rodentia.

This large vole feeds on the succulent stem-bases and root-crowns of lush sedge and grass meadows—a habitat also favored by northern harriers, which feed heavily on the succulent Townsend's vole. The voles make extensive runway complexes through the grass, swim well, and burrow to make their homes, often with underwater entrances.

Water Vole

Microtus richardsoni (richard-**so**-nigh: after Sir John Richardson, p 473). Also **water rat**. 6½" + 3" tail (length ratio 2:1); fur long and coarse, ± reddish dark brown above, paler beneath. In and near high bogs, streams and lakes. Order Rodentia.

Our largest vole might be thought of as a small muskrat, except that it goes into the water for refuge, rarely for forage. It dines on our favorite lush wildflowers—lupine, valerian, glacier lilies, and such—eschewing grasses and sedges. In winter it digs up bulbs and root crowns of the same flowers, or eats buds and bark of willows and heathers, while tunneling around under the snow. Look for mud runways running straight to the water's edge from its burrow entrances, which are up to 5" in diameter.

Muskrat

Ondatra zibethicus (ahn-**dat**-ra: Huron tribe's term for muskrat; zi-**beth**-ic-us: civet- or musk-bearing). 9–13" + 7–12" tail; tail scaly, pointed, flattened vertically; fur dark glossy brown, paler on belly, nearly white on throat; eyes and ears small; toes long, clawed, slightly webbed; voice an infrequent squeak. Largely nocturnal; scattered, in or near slow-moving water up to mid elevs. Order Rodentia.

We are tempted to think of the muskrat as an undersized beaver, and with good reason, even though its anatomy reveals instead an oversized vole, or "field mouse." Leading similar aquatic lives, beavers and muskrats grow similar fur, which was historically trapped, traded, marketed, and worn in similar ways. (The guard hairs are removed, leaving the dense, glossy underfur.) Several million muskrats are still trapped annually—more individuals and more dollar value than any other U.S. furbearer. In the South, the meat also finds a market as "marsh rabbit."

Like beavers, muskrats build either mudbank burrows or domed lodges with several underwater entrances. They are smaller than beavers—half the length and rarely a tenth the weight—and their teeth and jaws aren't up to cutting wood, so they build no dams or ponds. Soft vegetation like cattails, rushes, and water lilies makes up the bulk of their diets, their lodges, and the rafts they build for picnicking on. They deviate from the vegetarianism typical of the vole family, eating tadpoles, mussels, snails, or crayfish. Their interesting mouths remain shut to water while the incisors, out front, munch away at succulent underwater stems. They can take a big enough breath in a few seconds to last them 15 minutes underwater. Both sexes, especially when breeding, secrete musk on scent posts made of small grass cuttings. Neatly clipped sedge and cattail stems floating at marsh edges are a sign of muskrats.

The South American coypu or nutria, *Myocastor* ("mouse beaver") *coypus*, a similar rodent but about twice as big, may be seen at the Willamette Valley foot of the Cascades. Nutria fur farms were established in the early 1930s in response to an aggressive, deceptive promotion campaign. When profits failed to materialize, most of the hard-up farmers just turned their rodent herds loose,

---

despite laws prohibiting this. Coypus have since multiplied to where they threaten some crops and native competitors, particularly muskrats. Today, their fur fetches a high enough price to warrant trapping and skinning them, but not enough to compensate for the ecological havoc they wreak.

Red-Backed Voles

Clethrionomys spp. (cleth-ri-**ah**-no-mis: keyhole mouse). 4" + 1¾" tail; gray-brown with distinct rust-red band down length of back; tail ± bi-colored similarly; active day or night. Coniferous forests. Order Rodentia.

C. gapperi (**gap**-per-eye: after Gapper). In WA.

C. occidentalis (ox-i-den-**tay**-lis: western). In OR or rarely SW WA.

Red-backed voles should be respected as gourmets, since they dine largely on underground-fruiting fungi—which few of us are aware of except when, as "truffles," they are imported from France or Italy at $300 a pound. It's no accident that truffles are uniquely fragrant, delicious, and nutritious. These fungi have no way of disseminating their spores other than by attracting animals to dig them up, eat them, excrete the undigested spores elsewhere, and preferably thrive on them over countless generations. Many of our forest

---

Rodents and Fungi

Underground-fruiting fungi—"truffles," loosely speaking—are the mainstay of rodent diets in Western conifer forests.

Rating the nutrition in these morsels has proven tricky. Laboratory analysis finds them very high in protein, very low in fats, moderate in carbohydrates, and very high in some vitamins and minerals. But digestibility turns out to be abysmal. After all, the principal contents are spores, and passage of spores through the rodent's digestive tract intact and viable is the whole point of the relationship, from the fungus' point of view, so spores have to be pretty indigestible. After adjusting for digestibility, truffles seem barely worth eating. Two factors tip the scales in their favor: they fruit in late fall and winter, when green foods are least nutritious; and finding them consumes fewer calories than finding plant foods because it's done with the nose, a small mammal's most effective sense organ.

rodents evolved as avid participants in this scheme, but none are more dependent than red-backed voles. Since the fungi stop fruiting if their conifer associates die (see page 260), red-backed voles disappear after a clearcut or destructive burn. They can't switch from fungi to fibrous vegetation because their molars have lost the ability to keep growing throughout life to replace unlimited wear and tear. Lifelong growth characterizes rodent incisors, and also the molars in some species such as the creeping vole, enabling the latter to switch to grasses and flourish in clearcuts.

Heather Vole

Phenacomys intermedius (fen-ack-o-mis: impostor mouse). 4¼" + 1⅜" tail (length ratio 3:1); gray-brown above, paler beneath; tail distinctly bicolored; feet ± white, even on top. Sporadic, mainly subalpine. Order Rodentia.

The heather vole lives around the low heath shrub community— heathers, subalpine blueberries, kinnickinnick and manzanita. You may spot a heather vole's nest shortly after snowmelt: a 6–8" ball of shredded lichens, moss, and grass, typically with a big heap of dung nearby. (Color page 490). This winter nest was built in a snow burrow on the earth surface; the summer nest will be underground.

High moisture content dilutes the nutrition, too, but is valuable in itself; eating it is often safer from predators and less taxing than making the trip to a stream or puddle to drink. To put that another way, moist fungi enlarge the fungivores' habitat by freeing them from having to live near creeks. (On the other hand, some rodents like Douglas squirrels hang fungi up to dry, preserving them for winter when, as is widely observed, moisture tends to be in good supply around here.)

Fungal spores aren't the only potent stowaways in vole and squirrel droppings. Nitrogen-fixing bacteria, which live in the truffles, also pass unharmed through the rodents' bowels, as do yeasts which contribute nutrients the bacteria need in order to fix nitrogen. Since nitrogen fertility is often a limiting factor on conifer growth, the conifers may be as dependent on the bacteria and yeasts as on their mycorrhizal partners the truffles. It adds up to a five-way symbiosis, including the rodents that disseminate all four other partners.

Red Tree Vole

*Phenacomys longicaudus** (lon-ji-**caw**-dus: long tail). 4¼" + 3" tail (ratio of lengths much less than 2:1); back light cinnamon, belly white with gray underfur; ears ± concealed, hairless; claws sharp, strongly curved. On conifers, in OR. Order Rodentia. Color p 490.

Relatively uncommon and rarely seen, the tree vole is one of the strikingly few animals that subsist on our most plentiful "green vegetable," conifer needles. It is not an easy life. Tree vole populations are limited and sporadically distributed, despite the ubiquity of the resource and the lack of competition for it. The hardship of eking nutrition out of needles is evidenced by prolonged gestation (28 to 48 days), small litters (of one to three) and slow infant development in tree voles, compared to similar-sized rodents.

Branchlets (Douglas-fir preferred) are cut at night and carried to the nest for painstaking nibbling. The vole can eat only the needle margins, leaving the two resin ducts whose pitchy contents would overwhelm its digestive system. A fraction of the resulting debris (100 needles may be consumed per hour) is used to line the nest, an airy edifice enlarged over the generations to include several rooms and escape tunnels. One escape tactic appears to consist of a leap and free fall from the conifer canopy, with legs spread wide like a flying squirrel prototype. Experienced tree voles almost always land on their feet.

Researchers find tree voles hard to get to and impossible to count; you can't bait them into a trap because the only thing they want to eat is always copiously available. Still, there is little disagreement over their likely dependence on old-growth, and their consequent precarious status. Young forests don't have fat enough limbs for tree vole nests; don't retain a limb long; may not intercept enough fog to slake a tree vole's thirst; and may not retain liquid water through the dry spells, mainly because short pendent moss doesn't proliferate until the trees are several hundred years old.

Porcupine

Erethizon dorsatum (er-a-**thigh**-zon: angering; dor-**say**-tum: back). 28–35" long, incl 9" tapered tail; large girth; blackish with long coarse yellow-tinged guard-hairs and long whitish quills visible mainly on the rear half; incisors orange. Widespread, commoner E-side. Order Rodentia. Color p 491.

---

*Some authorities consider tree voles a separate genus, *Arborimus*.

Porcupines' bristling defenses permit them to be slow and unwary. This is both good and bad news, for you. Though they're mainly nocturnal, you stand a good chance of seeing one some morning or evening, and possibly of hearing its low murmuring song. And you stand a good chance of having your equipment eaten by one during the night. Porcupines crave the salts in sweat and animal fat, and don't mind eating boot-leather, rubber, wood, nylon, or for that matter brake hoses, tires, or electrical insulation, to get them. (Car parts have also been consumed by marmots at Hurricane Ridge.) **When camping in E-side valleys, always sleep by your boots**, and make your packstraps hard to get at, too. Fair warning.

Quills and spines are modified hairs that have evolved separately in many kinds of rodents, including two separate families both called Porcupines. On American porcupines they reach their very most effective form: hollow, very loosely attached at the base, and minutely, multiply barbed at the tip. The barbs engage instantly with enough grab to detach the quill from the porcupine, quickly swell in the heat and moisture of flesh, and work their way farther in (as fast as one inch per hour) with the unavoidable twitchings of the victim's muscles. Though strictly a defensive weapon, quills can eventually kill, either by perforating vital organs or, more often, by starving the poor beast that gets a noseful. But if you can keep your dog and your boots away from porcupines, don't worry too much about your own skin: just maintain a modest safe distance while the porky, most likely, retreats up a tree. A white-people's myth holds that porcupines throw their quills, but in fact the thrashing tail has only a slightly greater range than you would expect.

Since they have evolved no defenses other than their quills, porcupines have to be born fully quilled and active in order to survive infancy in adequate numbers. This requires very long gestation (seven months) and small litters (one or rarely two). But still...how to get the little spikers out of the womb? Answer: the newborn's soggy quills are soft, but harden in about half an hour as they air-dry. And then again...how to get mama and papa close enough to mate? Or baby close enough to nurse? Solving these problems has given porcupines their

---

Achilles' heel, or rather, soft underbelly. With a quill-less underside including the tail, porcupines can safely mate in the same position as other mammals, provided she draws her tail scrupulously up over her back. (They mate in late autumn, but are otherwise solitary.) If it weren't for that unarmed belly, predators would have no place to begin eating.

And predators there are, mainly fishers and cougars; rarely coyotes, bobcats, and even great horned owls. The soft underbelly is well protected as long as the porky is alive enough to stay rightside up. Fishers attack via the head—and so should you, with a heavy stick, if you ever find yourself lost and starving and near a porcupine. Some states protect porcupines on the grounds that they are easy edible prey for unarmed humans lost in the woods. They are not choice fare. They were eaten, though, by Indians, who turned the quills into an elegant art medium on clothing and baskets.

Porcupines eat leaves, new twigs and catkins in the summer, and tree cambium, preferably of pines, in winter. They select cambium near the top of the tree, where it is sweetest. Bright patches of stripped bark high up in pines are a sign of porcupine use. Occasionally they kill a tree by girdling it, but more often they kill only the top. The tree responds by turning a branch upward to form a new main trunk, but this puts a permanent kink in the tree, a fate worse than death according to timber economics. Killing the tree would at least release its neighbors to grow faster, but kinking it doesn't, while greatly devaluing it at the sawmill. So foresters are alarmed at the increasing porcupine populations of this century, which resulted mainly from human persecution of predators.

Like the red tree vole and the blue grouse, the porcupine reveals the nutritional stress of subsisting on this all-you-can-eat cafeteria. Porcupines inexorably lose weight in winter, even while keeping their grossly overdeveloped guts stuffed with bark. In summer, trees can't avoid providing more fattening fare in their new foliage, but defend themselves with toxically high levels of potassium. For the porcupine kidney to keep up with the task of eliminating potassium, the porcupine is driven to find low-acid, low-potassium sources of sodium. Your sweaty boots and packstraps fit the bill, and some of the coolant hoses and wire insulation it can find in the hikers' parking lot are even better. For similar reasons deer and elk eat the mud around soda springs, and mountain goats go after human urine.

Red Fox

Vulpes vulpes (**vul**-peez: the Roman term). 24" + 15" tail; shoulder height 16" (terrier size); usually red-orange with black legs and ears, white belly and tip of tail (the red phase). Mainly alp/subalpine and E-side. Order Carnivora, Canidae (Dog family).

Foxes are little-seen here. They are nocturnal, shy, elusive, and alert, and though they can bark and "squall," they rarely make a concert of it. Their tracks and scats are hard to tell from small coyote ones, and their dens are most often other animals' work taken over without distinctive remodeling. Rocky areas are preferred.

If you have the luck to see this fox, you'll recognize it easily if it's a typical red one. Other color phases are rare in the Northwest, but do not strictly follow geographic rules. Even littermates may differ, like blonde, dark, and redheaded human siblings. The "silver phase"(when, rarely, it occurs at all in the NW) is actually all black except for the white tail-tip and some grizzling on the back and shoulders. A gray-colored fox without the telltale white tip would be a Gray Fox, *Urocyon cinereoargenteus* (you-**rah**-see-on: burnt dog; sin-ee-rio-ar-**jen**-tee-us: ashy silver). Gray foxes have been seen in Central Oregon but not, as far as I know, in Washington.

Red foxes mate in midwinter, bear their litters (of four to seven) in early spring, and commonly stay mated. In contrast to the cat and bear families, canids make good fathers. Foxes eat insects, earthworms, fruit and seeds, and some birds eggs in addition to the preferred mice, hares, frogs and squirrels. They hunt with devious opportunism and stealth, often culminating in a spectacular aerial pounce. The huge plumey tail offers balance, and also keeps the face warm when they curl up. They prefer habitat with mixed meadow and trees, and rarely venture into dense Westside forest.

As wolf range shrank over the last century, coyote and red fox range expanded; red foxes took wolves' place as the world's most widely-distributed wild mammal. It is often said that foxes moving into hitherto foxless habitat (including the Olympic Peninsula and the Willamette Valley) are fur farm escapees, but this has been neither proven nor disproven. Fur farm stock might have Eastern and/or European genes, but all are *V. vulpes* anyway. Certainly red foxes have adapted and spread in the Northwest. In California, and probably now on SW Oregon beaches, they expanded into range where they threaten certain endangered ground-nesting birds.

Coyote

Canis latrans (can-iss: dog; lay-trenz: barking). 32" + bushy tail 14"; shoulder height 16–20"; medium sized, pointy-faced, erect-eared gray to tawny dog, grayer and thicker-furred in winter; runs with tail down or horizontal. Ubiquitous. Order Carnivora, Canidae (Dog family). Color p 492.

In pioneer days, wolves and coyotes were called "timber wolves" and "prairie wolves," respectively. Wolves ruled the forests, leaving coyotes to range over steppes, brushy mountains, and prairies. But during the nineteenth century, guns and traps tipped the scales in favor of the coyote by aiming at the bigger predators—cougar and grizzly bear as well as the wolf. Greater size made these animals more vulnerable than coyotes for at least three reasons: more fearless and unwary; more feared and hated by people; and fewer, because higher on the "food chain" pyramid. After the big predators were nearly extirpated from the lower 48, smaller "varmints"—coyotes, bobcats, and eagles—inherited the brunt of predator-hatred, even though they are too small to significantly limit deer or sheep numbers. (They prey mainly on rodents, hares and insects.)

Coyotes are America's most bountied, poisoned, and targeted predator; yet they have proven uncannily adept at surviving and even increasing. Predator control appears to have done them more good than harm; they have stepped in wherever the wolf disappeared, including most of our range.

Considering how abundant they are, we rarely see coyotes, thanks to the same wariness that enables them to survive human persecution. You may hear them howling at night, and can guess that hair-filled scats in the middle of the trail are likely theirs, especially when placed smack dab on a stump, hummock, footlog over a creek, in an intersection, on a ridgetop, or any combination of the above. Coyote feces and urine are not mere "waste," like yours, but more like graffiti signatures full of olfactory data which later canine passers-by, even other species, can read. In Chinook myth, Coyote consulted his dung as an oracle! The male canine habit of fiercely scratching the ground after defecating probably deposits still more scents from glands between the toes. The long noses in the dog family really are "the better to smell you with, my dear"; the large olfactory chamber is arrayed with scent receptors. Coyotes can detect the passage of other animals a mile or two away, or days earlier. No less important (in ways we puny-nosed ones have a hard time either imagining or measuring) is the ability to read "scent posts" for data on the condition and activities of fellow coyotes. "Asserting territory" does not well describe scent-marking by coyotes; that they are territorial at all is increasingly doubted.

As for their lovely coloratura howling at night, most people hearing it feel that it, too, conveys something above and beyond mere location—though helping a family group relocate each other is its best-understood function. Often it's hard to tell how many coyotes we are listening to; the Modoc used to say it's always just one, sounding like many. Coyote choruses intersperse long howls with numerous yips; wolves howl without yipping.

Though preferring small mammals and birds, coyotes are prepared to subsist through hard times on grasshoppers, or on fruit, on winter-killed deer and elk, or occasionally on fawns. Stalking mice, they patiently "point" like a bird-dog, then pounce like a fox. Against hares they use the fastest running speed of any American predator. To run down weakened deer, they work as a pack, like wolves, but this is very rare. Usually they hunt alone or pair up cleverly, one partner either decoying or flushing prey to where the other lurks. An unwitting badger, eagle, or raven, may be briefly employed as a partner, but most often it's the coyote's own mate.

The female tends to pick the same mate year after year, and the pair displays apparent affection as well as loyalty. To say they mate for life would be about as euphemistic as saying that Americans do. In years when coyotes are abundant and/or rodents are unusually scarce in a given area, as many as 85% of the mature females there may fail to go into heat, and those who do so will bear smaller litters than usual . On the other hand, they reproduce like crazy wherever their own populations have been depleted, such as where predator control men have been at work. Again, this helps make them impossible to get rid of—but exemplifies the population control innate in many mammal species. Currently-infertile females and the corresponding unattached males often spend the year with their parents, helping to raise the new litter. This extended family displays loyalty, but not of the ferocious sort typical of wolf packs, nor does it grow large enough to be called a pack.

Curiously, the fierce antagonism of wolf packs toward outsiders (including coyotes) may be crucial in maintaining wolves and coyotes as distinct species. Wolves, coyotes, jackals, and domestic dogs are all interfertile and beget fertile offspring. Yet they are dramatically different, physically and behaviorally, despite having long occupied overlapping ranges, so the frequency of their interbreeding must be very low. Wild "coy-dog" hybrids do occur, yet seem unable to establish reproducing populations, perhaps partly due to the dog half's maladaptation to the wilds and partly to a badly confused sense of a mating season: coyotes have one, domestic dogs don't.

Coyote the Trickster is a ubiquitous, complicated figure in all western Indian mythologies, possessing an unsurpassed, if devious, intelligence undermined by downright humanoid carelessness, greed, conniving lust, and vulgarity. In some myths, Coyote exemplifies the bad, greedy ways of hunting that destroyed a long-gone

---

Coyote and the Cedar

Coyote was traveling. He passed the mountains. He followed the trail through the deep woods. As he was traveling along, he saw an immense cedar. The inside was hollow. He could see it through a big gap which opened and closed. The gap opened and closed as the tree swayed in the wind. Coyote cried, "Open, Cedar Tree!" Then the tree opened. Coyote jumped inside. He said, "Shut, Cedar Tree!" Then the tree closed. Coyote was shut inside the tree.

Inside the tree, Coyote said, "Open, Cedar Tree!" The tree did not answer. Coyote was angry. He called to the tree. He kicked the tree. The tree did not answer. Then Coyote remembered that he was Coyote, the wisest and cunningest of all animals. Coyote began to think.

After he thought, Coyote called the birds to help him. He told them to peck a hole through Cedar Tree. The first was Wren. Wren pecked and pecked at the great cedar until her bill was blunted. But Wren could not even make a dent. Therefore Coyote called her Wren.

Then Coyote called the other birds. Sparrow came, Robin came, Finch came, but they could not even break the heavy bark. So Coyote gave each a name and sent them away. Then Owl came, and Raven, and Hawk, and Eagle. They could not make even a little hole. So Coyote gave each a name and sent them away. Then he called Downy Woodpecker. Finally Downy Woodpecker made a tiny hole. Then Pileated Woodpecker came and pecked a large hole. But the hole was too small for Coyote. So he saw there was no help from the birds.

Then Coyote remembered again that he was Coyote, the wisest and cunningest of all the animals. Then Coyote began to think.

Edenlike abundance. In others, he brought the poor starving people rituals and techniques they needed for catching salmon. Each of those tells half the story that anthropologists now reconstruct: the first people that migrated into North America found an Eden-like abundance; eventually the population reached a saturation point for simple hunting and foraging, and the people had to learn to store salmon and roots. Some tribes, on learning about Jesus, saw Him as the white man's Coyote since He came to Earth to improve people's lot. And then again, in many origin myths Coyote is the Creator—which suggests the mythmakers fostered no illusions that the world always works perfectly.

After he thought, Coyote began to take himself apart. He took himself apart and slipped each piece through Woodpecker's hole. First he slipped a leg through, then a paw, then his tail, then his ears, and his eyes, until he was through the hole, and outside the cedar tree.

Then Coyote began to put himself together. He put his legs and paws together, then his tail, his nose, his ears, then his body. At last Coyote put himself together again except his eyes. He could not find his eyes. Raven had seen them on the ground. Raven had stolen them. So Coyote, the wisest and cunningest of all animals, was blind.

But Coyote did not want the animals to know he was blind. He smelled a wild rose. He found the bush and picked two rose leaves. He put the rose leaves in place of his eyes. Then Coyote traveled on, feeling his way along the trail.

Soon he met a squaw. Squaw began to jeer, "Oh ho, you seem to be very blind!"

"Oh no," said Coyote, "I am measuring the ground. I can see better than you can. I can see spirit rays." Squaw was greatly astonished. Coyote pretended to see wonderful things at a great distance.

Squaw said, "I wish I could see spirit rays!"

Coyote said, "Change eyes with me. Then you can see spirit rays."

So Coyote and Squaw traded eyes. Coyote took Squaw's eyes and gave her the rose leaves. Then Coyote could see as well as ever. Squaw could see nothing. Coyote said, "For your folly you must always be a snail. You must creep. You must feel your way on the ground."

Ever since that time snails have been blind. They creep.

—Cladsap tale, slightly abridged from Katherine Berry Judson

Gray Wolf

Canis lupus (**loop**-us: the Roman term). 52" + bushy tail 18"; shoulder height 26–34"; large, erect-eared gray to tan dog with massive (not pointy) muzzle, long legs; grayer and thicker-furred in winter; runs with tail down or horizontal. Vanishingly rare; listed as endangered in both states. Order Carnivora, Canidae (Dog family).

Whether or not our range supports wolves today is controversial. Several areas in the North Cascades—the east shore of Ross Lake, the upper Twisp River, and the Crest south of White Pass—have each produced series of sightings and howlings lasting several years. Many of the observations have been by experienced Forest or Park personnel. So I, for one, am convinced that the North Cascades have a few small resident packs that are just barely hanging in there.

Olympic National Park is studying reintroducing wolves. I hope in my lifetime to see their effects on the park's hooved populations. These effects would cascade down through the plant communities. Northwest ecosystems evolved with wolves as a vital component, and should benefit from getting them back again. There was never a fact-based reason to persecute them.

Captive wolves and hybrid wolf/dogs are turned loose from time to time, usually because their "owners" tire of dealing with them, and have usually been behind sightings that recur near human habitation. Some hybrids are so nearly wolf that behavior, not DNA, is the sure way to tell them apart. (Dogs were bred from wolves starting about 12,000 years ago; most taxonomists reject Linnaeus' name for them, *Canis familiaris,* in favor of *C. lupus.*) Released captives are dangerous to humans and livestock, they confuse public policy about wolves, and they threaten the purity of the gene pool of any wild wolf population we may have.

Wolves are closely related to coyotes. What differentiates the two (and isolates them reproductively, maintaining them as distinct species) is wolves' remarkable, intense social structure. Thanks to pack hunting, they're alone in the Americas in being able to take on prey as large as elk and moose or, on occasion, as fierce as black bears and cougars. Second, they don't hurt people. I'm not saying never ever, but let's just say we could have fun listing household conveniences that pose more danger. Um, bobby pins...

Black Bear

Ursus americanus. 4–6" long (4" tail inconspicuous) 3–3½" at shoulder; jet
black with a tan nose. (May be brown E
of the Cas, or red-brown, "blue" gray, even
white elsewhere in the West; but most of ours stand
out as very black even at a distance.) Facial profile ±
straight; no hump over shoulder; claws dark, 1–1½".
Ubiquitous; esp in Olys. Order Carnivora, Ursidae.

Perhaps even more than sneaky Coyote, smart
Raven, and industrious Beaver, Bear has always been seen by
humans as somehow kindred. Though Bear's reflection of human
nature is at once darker and grander than Coyote's or Beaver's, it
is hard to pin down the essential quality. Mammalogists would concede that bears are among the most humanlike of animals in terms
of their feet and their diet. The feet are five-toed, plantigrade
(putting weight on the heel as well as the ball and toes) and about
as big as ours, so that the prints—especially the hind print—look
disturbingly familiar. The diet includes almost anything, and varies
enormously by season, region and individual. Plant foods predominate, starting in spring with tree sapwood or cambium, horsetails, grass, bulbs, and all kinds of new shoots, and working up to
enormous berry gluttony in fall, the fattening-up season. The typical prey are small mammals, and insects or larvae where they can
be lapped up in quantity, as from anthills, grubby old logs, wasp
nests, or bee hives—preferably dripping with honey. An adult bear
can chase virtually any predator from its kill, but is less adept at
hunting for itself, so large animals are most often eaten as carrion.
Many bears are skilled at snatching fish from streams. Some develop predilections for robbing woodpecker nests, grain crops, fallen
orchard fruit, garbage dumps, or hiker camps.

During heavy berry-eating, bear scats become semiliquid like
cow pies, and show lots of fruit seeds, leaves (blueberry), or skins
(apple). Earlier in the season, they are thick, untapered cylindrical
chunks, perhaps showing animal hair, but often closely resembling
horse manure. Fresh, they are usually as jet-black as the beast itself.
Bears leave distinctive marks on trees from three activities. When
they eat cambium, they strip away large swaths of bark with irregular incisor gashes, at 3–6' off the ground; this may kill the tree. Second, they sometimes assert territory by marking selected trees with

several long, parallel, often diagonal claw-slashes 5–9" from the ground. Third, during the spring molt, a tree may show vague abrasion and lots of bear hair 2–4' up, from several bears rubbing their itchy backs against it. (Compare with cat scratch-marks, page 493).

Once the ripe fruits are all gone in the fall, there is little a bear can do to fatten up; if it isn't fat enough by then, it will likely die before spring, but that rarely happens. Activity begins to slow down even before hibernating; bears appear listless while preparing their dens. This may include building a substantial nest of fluffy stuff—ideally cedar bark, which stays resilient under the prolonged burden. The bear sleeps curled up in a ball with the crown of its head down. Between the insulative nest and the superlatively thick fur, the bear loses little heat to the air of its den, and maintains a body temperature of about 88°, in contrast to the 40° hibernating temperature of many squirrels. But its heart rate may reach an astonishing low of just eight very weak beats per minute. And, unlike

Hang Your Food!

In the past decade, the "problem bear" syndrome, long known from the Rockies and Sierra Nevada, has infected the Olympics. (Meanwhile, in Yosemite it got so bad that bears were ripping doors off of two or three parked cars a night...) I'm referring to black bears that learn to look for their dinner in campers' gear.

Whenever you handle food in the mountains, remember two objectives: to protect your body and equipment from serious accidental damage by bears going after your food, and to prevent innocent bears from becoming problem bears. Don't tempt them.

Never: **Discard** *food or "leave it for the chipmunks."*
Cook *more than you will eat.*

Always: **Pack** *your food in airtight, smelltight containers.*
Hang *your food and garbage during day hikes and at night.*
Burn *out your empty cans on your stove or in your fire.*
Pack out *all your empty packets, bags, and burnt cans.*

You owe it to the bears, and to the hikers who will follow you here.

The techniques needed today are more laborious than they used to be when we hardly had problem bears, and we could just toss our food bags over a tree branch on a cord, and tie it down. Smart bears may learn to sever or pull the cord. Starting at the beginning:

squirrels, it may go the full six or seven months without eating, urinating, defecating or, presumably, waking up. (In other cases, it may wake easily and dehibernate briefly at any time of winter.) The urea waste that would ordinarily be excreted in urine is somehow recycled into new proteins, alleviating the problem of muscle atrophy during hibernation. Fecal accumulation is so reduced that the winter's worth can be saved until spring dehibernation.

Two or three cubs are born around January. The mother wakes up to give birth, then nurses them mostly in her sleep for the next few months. A den of cubs nursing emits a hum like a beehive, only much deeper. Cubs are smaller at birth, in ratio to their adult weight, than almost any mammals short of marsupials. In nursing them to viable size for the real world, the mother may lose 40% of her weight during hibernation, as opposed to 15–30% for adult males. Rather than taking on this stress in consecutive winters, she just hibernates with her yearling cubs in alternate years.

---

*Set up an eating camp and a sleeping camp 150' apart. In the former, you cook and eat, hang your food **and** garbage in big plastic bags, wash your dishes and store them **and** the clothes you ate dinner in **and** the shorts you spilled sardine oil on, day before yesterday. In the latter, you sleep peacefully away from previous campers' food smells as well as your own. Overnight food bags should not double as stuffsacks, because then your sleeping gear will smell like food.*

To hang the food, find a long, strong limb 12-15' above ground. (If you're in a Park campsite you may find the crews have strung up a wire for this purpose.) Put roughly equal amounts of food into two bags or groups of bags. Tie the first bag to the cord end, throw the cord over a point in the limb at least 5' from the tree trunk, and pull the bag right up to the limb. At a point on your cord that's about as high as you can reach, tie on the second bag. Coil the loose cordage and tuck it into this bag. With a stick, push the second bag up until the two bags are counterbalanced equally high—and out of reach of beasts incapable of grasping a stick to push the first bag back up again.

If the trees are too small to offer suitable limbs, you'll have to climb two trees and draw your foodbags up 12' off the ground midway between them. And if you want to camp where there aren't trees for that either, you'll have to buy and use bearproof plastic canisters, which may put a severe crimp in your haute route *cuisine.*

Some speculate that the tree-climbing skills of black bears evolved as protection from the only other animals on this continent big and mean enough to prey on them regularly—grizzly bears. The well-known ferocity of black bear mothers in the company of their cubs more likely evolved to protect cubs from grown-up males of their own species; subadult bears may also wind up cannibalized if they are foolish enough to stand up to a big boar.

Consider bears dangerous even though black bears (not grizzlies) normally withdraw from any contact with people. Bears encountered by hikers often fit one of the two "abnormal" types—sows with cubs, and "problem bears" familiar with campers and camper food. Human injuries from black bears have been extremely rare historically, but are bound to increase if more and more naive campers leave more and more food around.

Don't go backpacking in terror of bears, but go in knowledge-able wariness of them. If you follow game paths into thickets (where bears like to sleep through the day) make lots of cheerful noise as you approach. If a bear moseys into your camp vicinity, stand and bang pots and pans or blow whistles. If it still seems ntent on approaching, distance yourself from your food. If you meet one in the open, observe and let your intuition tell you if the bear is threatening. If so, retreat discreetly. Sometimes you can slowly and straightforwardly circle widely around a black bear, if it hasn't already run off. If a bear actually charges you, simply stand still; you have no chance of outrunning it. (Bears are slow only in comparison with deer and cougar.) The charge will probably be abandoned as soon as the bear can see you're a person. (Bears are very nearsighted.) If you're attacked, curl up face-down in the fetal position and play dead. That's the very very last, unlikely resort; don't worry about it, worry about your ounce of prevention—for you and everyone else to hang your food.

Grizzly Bear

Ursus arctos horribilis (**ur**-sus: Roman term for 'bear'; **arc**-toce: Greek for 'bear"; hor-**rib**-il-iss: horrible). 6–8" long (3" tail invisible); shoulder height 4½"; brown (rarely black) ± grizzled with light tan; hump over front shoulder; facial profile is concave; claws pale, foreclaws typically 3"+ long. WA Cas. Listed as endangered in both states. Order Carnivora, Ursidae.

An interagency study to verify presence of grizzly bears in Washington failed to come up with verifiable DNA, but it did produce photos and plaster casts of tracks with amply long claws, as well as reasonably certain reports of sightings ranging as far south as Mt. St. Helens. Biologist John Almack feels that there are likely around ten grizzlies, resident but highly mobile and elusive.

The largest animal in Order Carnivora, a grizzly is big and fierce enough to take any hooved mammal, but isn't fast enough to hunt healthy deer regularly. So its diet is much like a black bear's, with roots, berries, insect grubs, pine nuts, spawning salmonids, small mammals, and large mammal carrion each important.

Grizzlies avoid contact with people. Most scientists believe they do not normally view people as food; on the other hand, they show little fear of people in close encounters. The ways to avoid trouble with black bears, on pages 342–3, are also good for grizzlies.

Subspecies *horribilis*, the grizzly bear of the Western states and provinces, was once considered a full species. Other *U. arctos* subspecies include the even larger Kodiak brown bear and the much smaller brown bears of Eurasia. The polar bear, *U. maritimis*, must be a close relative, as captive polar bears and grizzlies have produced fertile offspring together.

Raccoon

Procyon lotor (**pro**-see-on: a star near the Dog Star; **low**-tor: washer, a misnomer). 22" + 12" tail; gray with black mask across eyes and rings around tail; thickset and bushy-furred; all toes long and clawed. Lower elevs. Order Carnivora, Procyonidae.

Northern outliers of a generally tropical family, raccoons, like bears, belong to order Carnivora but resemble Primates, our own order, in two ways. First, they are omnivorous not merely by habit but by tooth structure, with plenty of blunt molars for grinding plants rather than cutting meat. Second, they are plantigrade—resting the heel down on the ground. With long toes on all four feet, raccoons rival primates in dexterity; they can turn doorknobs. They raid garbage cans in Portland, and are actually commoner around civilization than in our mountains, where they concentrate around lowland lakes and streams. Their food includes berries, acorns, small mammals, frogs, bugs, fish, and crayfish. They climb trees for refuge, and are fond of large hollow trees for their dens, either at the base or in a crotch. Though not strictly territorial, they are generally solitary and mutually hostile except when mating.

Weasels

Mustela spp. (mus-**tee**-la: the Roman term). Very fast, slinky, slender, short-legged, long-necked animals; in characteristic running gait, the back is arched; ears inconspicuous; rich medium brown above, white to orange-yellow beneath, incl feet and insides of legs and (long-tailed only) some of tail; most E-side and high-elev weasels turn pure white in winter, exc tip of tail always black; males almost twice as heavy as females. Ubiquitous. Order Carnivora, Mustelidae (Weasel family).

Long-tailed weasel, *M. frenata* (fren-**ay**-ta: bridled). 9–11" + 5–6½" tail (larger dimensions are male average; smaller are female); deep cream to yellow underneath (in summer). Illustrated at right.

Short-tailed weasel, *M. erminea* (er-**min**-ee-a: the Roman term). 7–8" + 2½–3½" tail; white to light cream underneath. Color p 494.

Narrow, linear shapes like the weasel's are rare among the smaller warm-blooded animals because they are so costly to heat, but, for weasels, there's no question of the shape being worth the price—a caloric intake requirement averaging perhaps 40% of body weight per day. Other small mammals share a roughly common shape, one that during sleep or torpor can be rolled up into an approximate sphere, the most efficient of all shapes for retaining heat. Weasels and their streamlined relatives roll up into, at best, a lumpy sort of disk, which takes 50–100% more calories to maintain at a temperature than a spherically rolled rodent of similar weight. But when it needs to eat, the weasel can chase that rodent down any hole or through any crevice; a weasel is much thinner, faster, and fiercer of tooth and claw than any animal anywhere near its own weight.

Though mouse-sized prey are their staple, weasels can also run down squirrels in trees and snowshoe hares on snow—prey several times their own weight. Like the smallest members of many other predatory families, they make a relatively easy living: they go after the most abundant prey, and are the surest of catching it. The food chain is really an extremely broad pyramid; very few individuals can fit at the top as large predators. Perhaps the greatest wonder is that weasels aren't far more abundant than they are.

Reports of weasel "killing sprees" in which they kill far more than they can eat are numerous and confirmed. It should be allowed, though, that human observation may have inhibited or overlooked the weasel's efforts to cache the leftovers for later use.

There are also clear cases of weasel cannibalism, including juveniles eating their own litter-mates, once they get carried away with the taste or smell of blood. They are undeniably among the most ferociously aggressive of predators. They may themselves fall prey to owls, foxes, bobcats, or occasionally snakes. They nest in burrows of chipmunks, ground squirrels, moles, etc., often lining these with fur plucked from the body of the former occupant.

The term "ermine' is applied by naturalists to the short-tailed weasel only, but by furriers and the general public to the fur of both species interchangeably, so long as it's in the white, winter pelage. In fact, most ermine coats are made from long-tailed weasels because there are more of them out there to catch, and it takes fewer of them to make a coat. It still takes hundreds of them, though, so a single pelt commands a surprisingly low price. It has been proposed that the black tail-tip on the otherwise white winter fur serves as a decoy; the weasel can usually escape hawk or owl talons that strike this one body part that's conspicuous against snow.

Mink

Mustela vison (vice-un: an archaic French term). 13–16" + 6–8" tail; long, narrow and short-legged; dark glossy brown except variable white patches on chin, chest, belly; ears inconspicuous. In and near streams, marshes, and sometimes lakes. Order Carnivora, Mustelidae (Weasel family).

The mink is an aquatic weasel, preying on fish, frogs, crayfish, ducks, water voles, and muskrats. Some populations become fully terrestrial for a while, subsisting on hares and voles, while others line the B.C. and Alaska coast, subsisting on crabs. The muskrat, a preferred prey, is also a mink's "most dangerous game" because it is much larger; a muskrat can drown a mink by dragging it under. In deep water, muskrats even attack minks fearlessly. On the other hand, a duck that thinks it can shake a mink by taking to the air may be in for a fatal surprise: cases are on record of minks hanging on for the flight until the duck weakens and drops. But whenever they can, minks, like weasels, kill quickly with a bite into the back of the neck or skull.

The foul discharges from under the tail that we associate with

---

skunks are characteristic of the whole weasel family. Skunks alone have developed their marksmanship and range, maximizing the anal gland's potential as a defensive weapon, but minks have an even worse smell. They spray when angered, alarmed, or captured, when fighting each other (they are viciously antisocial) and to mark territory or repel raiders of their meat caches. It may seem ironic that there is so much blood, gore, and stench in the pedigree of a mink coat; but anyone lucky enough to watch a mink in its habitat is likely to admire it. Most mink coats these days come from commercial mink ranches. Newfangled colors of mink are bred just to keep fur fashions hopping.

Marten

Martes americana[*] (**mar**-teez: the Roman term). Also **pine marten**. 16–18" + 8" tail; body narrow, legs short, tail fluffy, nose pointy; variably buff to cinnamon-brown to nearly black; (looks ± like a smaller red fox on shorter legs). In trees, in remote wilderness. Order Carnivora, Mustelidae (Weasel family). Color p 494.

Martens have evolved a striking resemblance in form, color, and habits, to their favorite prey—tree squirrels. They even eat conifer seeds sometimes, like Douglas squirrels, or a few berries, and occasionally raid birds' nests. Like weasels, they excel as predators because their prey is abundant and has only meager defenses against them. But unlike weasels, their populations, already self-limiting, have been further reduced by trapping and probably by a strong aversion to civilization. Today they are common only in mountain wilderness with conifers. Even there, we rarely see them because they are usually up in the branches, where they are fast, well camouflaged, and active mainly at dawn, dusk, or under heavy overcast. Still, curiosity and appetite sometimes lure one right into a hiker's camp. Winter forces them to forage on the ground more—often under the snow—hunting voles and hares.

Their musk secretions are milder than those of most weasel family kin, and are used mainly to mark tree branches to ward off other martens. Except of course during a brief season when about 50% of other martens find the smell not repellent but, on the contrary, quite attractive.

Fisher

Martes pennanti (**pen**-an-tie: after Thomas Pennant). Also **wejack**, **pekan**. 20–25" + 13–15" tail; long, thin, and short-legged; glossy black-brown, occasionally with small white throat patch; ears slightly protruding. Rare; dense forest. Order Carnivora, Mustelidae. Color p 494.

Fishers don't fish. The name may derive from the Dutch *visse*, meaning nasty. Fishers eat mainly porcupines and snowshoe hares. In fact, they are the only predator that hunts porcupines (which outweigh them about 2 to 1) by preference. Though fishers may eat porcupines via their soft underbellies, the myth that they attack there, by means of a flip with the paw or a fast burrow under the snow, is dubious. After all, those floppy quills lie on the ground and don't really leave space for paw insertion. Darting, dodging attacks to the face, with both tooth and claw, have been observed, repeated for maybe half an hour, until the porcupine is too weak to flail. Fishers end up with quill bits scattered throughout their organs and musculature like shrapnel, though the majority soften in the stomach and pass safely through; scats containing pieces of quills are a sign of either fisher or cougar.

Fishers can rotate their hind feet almost 180° for running down tree trunks. They're fast enough to run down and kill martens.

The only predators tough enough to overcome fishers rarely find it worth the fight, and are too slow to chase them. The only animals that threaten the fisher are people. Fisher pelts, ringers for Siberian sable, usually rank as the highest-priced North American pelt. Trapping virtually eliminated fishers from the lower 48 states by 1940, but since then, foresters have been bringing them back to reduce the runaway porcupine populations that resulted largely from the lack of fishers. Oregon reintroduced several dozen since 1961, but there is little evidence of any subsequent increase. Washington hasn't reintroduced any, but probably had more to start with. The Olympics never had porcupines, but did have fishers. Whether they have any today is uncertain.

Reproduction in the weasel family usually involves delayed implantation: the fertilized ovum undergoes its first few cell divisions and then goes dormant for weeks or months before implanting in the uterus and resuming its growth in time for springtime

---

births. Increasing day length triggers implantation. The delay is extra long in the fisher, producing a total gestation of up to 370 days, only around 60 of them active. Thus, the female often goes into heat just a few days before or after giving birth, and mates before weaning her two or three helpless newborns.

Otter

Lutra canadensis (**loo**-tra: the Roman term). Also **river otter**. 27–29" + thick, tapering, muscular tail 17–19"; dark brown with silvery belly, pale whiskers, very small ears, webbed feet. In or near rivers, lakes or ocean. Order Carnivora, Mustelidae .

Otters are among the unlucky species for whom people are belatedly discovering fondness and admiration—only after reducing them to near rarity. In both Europe and America they were trapped for fur or shot on sight as vermin, largely because anglers accused them of more predation on trout than they actually inflict. Ancient Chinese fishermen, in contrast, trained them to herd fish into nets; a few European hunters trained them to retrieve waterfowl.

Today, otters are mentioned in arguments over the existence of nonhuman play. Many reputable observers report them running up snowy hills again and again just to body-sled down, or body-surfing in river rapids for no apparent reason. Others claim these behaviors are mere transportation. Otters would rather slide on their bellies than walk anytime, even on level ground but preferably down a steep otter slide with a big splash in the river at the bottom. They frolic and tumble in the water, often in family groups after the pups are six months old; up to that age the mother scrupulously keeps them away from the father. Oddly, the pups seem afraid of the water and have to be taught to swim. Otters have a low, mumbly "chuckle" while nuzzling or mating.

Fishermen here see otters regularly. Look on riverbanks and lakeshores for otters' easily recognized slides, tracks or "spraints." The latter are fecal scent-markers placed just out of the water on rocks, mud banks or floating logs, and usually showing fish bones, scales, or crayfish shell bits under a greenish, slimy (when fresh) coating which smells distinctive but not unpleasant. Otter staples are crayfish and slow-moving fish; they rarely compete for game fish. Amphibians and voles round out their diet.

Wolverine

Gulo gulo (**goo**-low: gullet or glutton). Also **skunk-bear**. 26–30" + 8–9" tail; somewhat like a small bear but with ± distinct gray-brown to yellowish striping across the brow and down the sides to the tail; fur thick and long. Near timberline; very rare—sighted here only in N Cas and Three Sisters areas. Listed as threatened in OR. Order Carnivora, Mustelidae. Color p 493.

Wolverines reached the verge of extinction from the lower 48 states, but since 1965 seem to be coming back. They have raided a few campgrounds in Northern Idaho, so you may possibly have them to worry about in North Cascades camps before long. As they're the largest members of the weasel family, their reputation as the scrappiest, nastiest fighters on the continent should come as no surprise. Even cougars and bears will usually yield their kills to wolverines, who like nothing better than to polish off another predator's dinner. They're also known for raiding trappers' cabins and caches up North, trashing them thoroughly and spraying them up with truly execrable musk. The powerful scent repels other carnivores from the wolverine's meat caches, and is also crucial, along with a summer-long mating season, when wolverines seek compatible wolverines. ("SWF, attractive, into winter sports, for nonconfining relationship...") They have always been extremely sparse and solitary, roaming continually over vast home ranges.

Badger

Taxidea taxus (tax-**eye**-dee-a **tax**-us: both from the Roman term). 25" + 5" tail; very broad, low, flat animal with thick fur grizzled gray-brown, while ± yellowish, esp the tail; white stripe down face; forefeet heavily clawed for digging. Visitor on E slope, up to Cas Cr in OR. Order Carnivora, Mustelidae (Weasel family). Color p 494.

This squat, ungainly, but fantastically powerful burrowing creature lives mainly by digging ground squirrels, gophers, and snakes out of their holes. It is common in the drier country just east and south of our range.

Skunks

Spotted skunk, *Spilogale putorius* (spil-**og**-a-lee: spot weasel; pew-**tor**-ius: putrid). 10–11" + 5" tail (kitten-sized); glossy black with many ± lengthwise intermittent white stripes; tail ends in a rosette of long white hairs.

Striped skunk, *Mephitis mephitis* (mef-it-iss: pestilential vapor). 18" + 11" tail (cat-sized); glossy black with 2 broad white stripes diverging at nape to run down sides of back, plus thin white stripe on forehead. Both skunks widespread but much commoner in farmlands than in mtns here, and rare at high elevs. Order Carnivora, Mephitidae (Skunk family).* Color p 493.

Skunk coloration is the opposite of camouflage; it's to a skunk's advantage to be conspicuous and recognized, since its defenses are so good. The rare animal that fails to stay clear may receive additional warnings such as forefoot stamping, tail raising, or a handstand with tail displayed forward like a big white pom-pom. (The handstand, rare among striped skunks but well described among spotteds, has been explained as tempting an attacker to bite the tail, doing little damage to the skunk while fixing the attacker's face in the line of fire.) Only as a last resort does the skunk turn around and fire its notorious defensive weapon—up to six well-aimed rounds of N-butyl mercaptan in a musky vehicle secreted just above the anus. This substance burns the eyes, chokes the throat, and of course stinks like hell. It can be shot either in an atomizer-style mist or, more typically, in a water-pistol-style stream fanned across a 30–45° arc for greater coverage. Range is well over 12'. The skunk scrupulously avoids fouling its own tail. Traditional antidotes to skunk spray include tomato juice, ammonia, gasoline, and incinerating the affected clothes; juice is the least unpleasant, fire the most effective. Soap and water don't do much. The musk is extracted, chemically stripped of scent, and used commercially as a vehicle for perfumes. Now, *there's* a silk purse from a sow's ear!

Only great horned owls seem to prey on skunks regularly. They may sometimes hit hard and stealthily enough to forestall the spray defense, but more likely they're just thick-skinned, with their built-in protective goggles and weak sense of smell. Many big owls smell skunky and have skunk-bitten feet. As far as the odds-makers of natural selection are concerned, skunk defenses are superlative. But like porcupines, skunks seem to be as prone to little parasitic animals as they are well-defended against big predatory ones.

Of our two skunks, the spotted is slimmer, speedier, and more carnivorous, though both species eat some vegetation. Foods include insects and grubs, mice, shrews, and occasionally ground-nesting birds and their eggs. Skunk dens are most often burrows

---

*A 1997 revision takes skunks, for the first time, out of the weasel family.

dug by other animals. Skunks fatten up for winter and sleep in their dens—not torpidly—for days at a time during the coldest spells.

Cougar

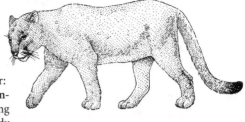

Puma concolor *
(**poo**-ma: name for it in the Quechua language of Peru; **con**-color: all one color). Also **mountain lion, puma**. 4–5' long + 2½' tail; ours ± ruddy brown (deerlike), but species ranges in color from nearly black or slate gray to pale sand; no spots or ear tufts exc on kittens; our only cat with long thick tail. Vocalizations varied (purrs, chirps, yowls) but infrequent. Uncommon and elusive; widespread. Order Carnivora, Felidae (Cat family). Color p 495.

Cougars take many kinds of prey from grasshoppers and mice on up through porcupines and coyotes to elk—but their staple is deer. A male (the larger sex) can eat about one deer every 10–14 days, up to 20 pounds at a time, burying the remains to come back to later. Buried meat, which may assault your nose, is a sign of cougar. He (or she) locates deer by smell or sound, stalks it slowly, crouching, freezing for periods in a position a deer might mistake for a log, then pounces the last 30 feet or so in a few bounding leaps. He bites the prey in the nape, and may either bite through the spinal cord or snap it by twisting the head back. If that fails, he tries to hang on until the prey suffocates. Our cougars are lighter than our deer, on average, and much lighter than elk, so their hunt is risky. They are sometimes trampled or thrown hard enough to kill them, and one was found pinned until it starved under an elk it had killed.

---

* Many texts include this and most cats in genus *Felis*. The number of genera in the cat family is a notoriously long-running taxonomic tempest. The current checklist of the Am. Soc. of Mammalogists (Wilson and Reeder, 1993) divides Felidae into eighteen genera, where the previous version saw only four. I'm sure Wilson had convincing grounds; the checklist as a whole doesn't seem given to radical splitting. Still, genus splitting of this type is usually a question of taste: there is little disagreement over the shape of the family tree, but only over the proper taxonomic level for the branchings. Having to change familiar names for reasons of taste (fashion, some would say) sets some non-taxonomists to grumbling.

Most game managers agree on the value of cougars as the only remaining major predator of deer. Their chief benefit to deer and elk may lie in keeping them moving on their winter range, which helps avoid overgrazing of particular areas. Cougars select young, old, or diseased herd members—the easiest and safest to attack—minimizing their impact on deer and elk numbers.

Voters in both NW states banned the use of dogs to hunt cougars. Wildlife managers responded by sharply dropping the price of cougar hunting permits. Initial results in Oregon show this sustaining hunting pressure, which should help keep cougars suitably wary of people. Cougar numbers continue a slow increase.

Cougars sometimes follow solitary hikers, unseen, for days. They hardly ever let hikers catch a glimpse of them, and you can consider yourself lucky if you run across a clear set of cougar tracks. On the other hand, I have to revise my 1988 statement that they "attack people so rarely that the danger isn't worth worrying about." In the intervening decade there have been a few attacks on people, some fatal. Most were on children or solitary small adults. (Also many dogs and cats have been snatched, sometimes from large campgrounds.) It seems cougars are now habitat-limited rather than hunting-limited. Subdominant and dispersing individuals are pushed into more marginal habitat, closer to more humans and with a poorer supply of prey; they are hungrier more of the time. So they are forced to stretch their idea of appropriate prey.

The first cougar safety rule is never to leave small children unattended. If you see a cougar, pick up any children immediately, stand tall and confident, and maintain eye contact. Move you arms and pack in any way that will make you look bigger. Act unlike prey. Do not run or turn your back. Retreat slowly. If the cougar still seems aggressive, throw sticks or rocks at it if you can without having to crouch. If attacked, fight back aggressively with any weapon you can grab, and try to stay on your feet; it may give up in favor of easier prey.

Cougars are solitary, with large home ranges, the males' overlapping those of females. Males respect established home areas, rarely fighting over them. They mark their presence by scraping piles of dirt together with their urine or scats. After seeing a cougar, I found scats on the trail in several piles a few feet apart, and each had claw marks in the dirt radiating out from it. The same scent markers help the sexes find each other when a female is in heat, which may be at any time of year. A male roams with and sleeps near the female for about two weeks, and no longer: if she let him approach the kittens, he might eat them. She rears the young for well over a year. After they are fully grown she may consort with a male again, breeding only every other year. She has a loud, eerie mating "scream" that sounds strangely human.

Lynx

Lynx canadensis. * 31" long + 4" tail; gray cat ± tawny-tinged, never clearly spotted or barred exc the black tip of stubby tail; ears tufted, and cheeks ruffed, with long hairs. To confirm a lynx sighting, you would need to measure several footprints well over 2" long, and/or see a tail-tip black underneath as well as on top. Remote mtns with deep winter snowpack—mainly the N Cas. Order Carnivora, Felidae (Cat family).

The lynx is often thought of as a larger version of the bobcat. In fact, it weighs about the same as a bobcat but looks larger with its longer fur and legs and bigger feet—adaptations to deep snow and cold. Preying almost exclusively on the snowshoe hare, the lynx is perhaps the most single-minded of our predators.

The lynx is listed as threatened in the lower 48 states. It is still fairly numerous, though declining, in Canada. Lynxes may be able to hold on in Washington's NE Cascades and Okanogan Mtns. if the current area of little-visited roadless habitat can be maintained. They are very shy of people. In Oregon, a handful of lynxes have shown up in the Cascades in recent decades, and a few more in the Blue Mountains, but Oregon's lynxes have probably always been refugees from overblown population cycles up north rather than true self-maintaining populations. Lynx populations in Canada cyclically rise and plummet in response to fluctuations in the hare population. Snowshoe hare populations in our area do not cycle much, perhaps because the cycles are a lynx/hare feedback loop and we're lacking in lynxes.

---

* Some texts lump this lynx with Eurasian ones, and/or the genus as a whole with the mewing cats, making our lynx *Lynx lynx* or *Felis lynx,* and our bobcat *Felis rufus.* (Note the grammatical use of "lynx Lynx lynx" in a sentence.)

'Lynxes' and 'lynx' are about equally accepted as the plural form. Both Maser (1998) and Verts and Carraway (1998) say "lynxes." Given a choice, I always favor an 's.' Almost any animal name is used as a plural without 's' in some circles, as in "We saw three sow bear." To my ear, that style is disrespectful.

Bobcat

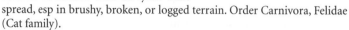

Lynx rufus* (links: the Greek term; **roo**-fus: red). Also **wildcat**. 28" long + 6" tail; tawny to gray cat, generally with visible darker spots, and bars on outside of legs and top (only) of tail; ears may show tufts, and cheeks ruffs, but these tend to be shorter than on lynx. Widespread, esp in brushy, broken, or logged terrain. Order Carnivora, Felidae (Cat family).

The bobcat is another lovely creature we have all too little chance of seeing even though it inhabits every part of our range, and is thought to be as abundant here as it ever was. You just might surprise one if you travel quietly, but generally they keep out of sight.

Wild cats all like to work out their claws and clawing muscles on tree trunks, just like house cats scratching furniture. Bobcat or lynx scratchings (color page 493) will be 2' to 5' up the trunk, cougar scratchings 5' to 8' up. These gashes may be deep, but rarely take off much bark; tree-clawing that strips big patches of bark is more likely bear work. Wild cats also often scratch dirt or leaves to cover their scats, at least partly. These scratchings may be accurately aimed at the scats, unlike the random pawings of male dogs next to their fecal markers. Bobcat and cougar scats also tend to me more segmented than coyote scats.

To preserve their sharpness for slashing or gripping prey, cat claws are kept retracted most of the time, and rarely show in cat tracks. One toe (the first, or "thumb") has been lost from the hind foot, but on the forefoot has only moved a short way up the paw, enlarging the grip. The hind legs are powerful, for long leaping pounces, but cats other than the cheetah aren't especially fast runners. The cat jaw is shorter and "lower-geared" than most carnivore jaws, and has fewer teeth. (Since mammals evolved from reptiles with many teeth, having fewer teeth is a sign of further evolution; typically they're also more efficiently specialized. Humans are evolving toward fewer teeth by losing the four wisdom teeth.) Cats have relatively small and unimportant incisors, huge canines for gripping and tearing, and a quartet of enlarged, pointed molars

---

*Sometimes known as *Felis rufus*. See footnote, p 355.

---

called carnassials which, rather than meeting, shear past each other like scissor blades for cutting up meat. Cat tongues are raspy with tiny recurved horny papillae, which can clean meat from a bone or hair from a hide. The cat nose is short, suggesting less reliance on smell than in the dog family. As in owls, the eyes are large, far apart, and aimed strictly forward to maximize three-dimensionality. Their eyes, like an owl's, reflect fire or flashlight beams in the dark. A reflective layer right behind the receptor cells on the retina redoubles light intensity at night. Except in cougars, which have round pupils, cat pupils narrow to vertical slits for maximum differentiation between night and day openness.

In most bobcat diet studies, hares and rodents predominate, in that order, but in the Oregon Coast Range boomers were by far the preeminent prey. In winter they may turn to deer somewhat, occasionally hunting fawns, but more often finding carrion.

Bobcat	Lynx	Cougar	Domestic dog

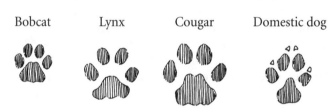

Cat Tracks

Claws: cat claws are normally retracted while walking, and hardly ever print. In contrast, claws show up clearly in full footprints of dogs and wild canids, not to mention otter, wolverine, badger, and bear prints which all have five clawed toes rather than four.

Pad: the wide, central sole (behind the toes) of a cougar or bobcat print is indented or scalloped once in front and twice in back; dog pads are convex (not indented) in front, as are lynx pads though the fur often obscures this feature in a lynx print.

Proportion: the two outside toes on a cat print are more nearly along-side the two central toes; on a dog print they're more nearly behind the front two.

Size: cougar's are 3-3½" long and wide, bobcat's are 1¾-2". Otherwise the two are much alike.

Look near the tracks for scats and scratchings, described above.

Mule Deer

Odocoileus hemionus (oh-doe-coe-ill-ee-us: hollow teeth; hem-ee-**oh**-nus: half ass, i.e. mule). 4¼' long + 6–8" tail (goat-sized or a bit larger); medium tawny brown or in winter grayish, with white patches on throat, inside of legs, and rump just under the tail; belly paler; males have antlers (see page 362); fawns are white-spotted; large (8–9") ears rotate independently of each other. Ubiquitous. Order Artiodactyla (Cloven-hooved mammals).

Mule deer, subspecies *hemionus*. Tail pale with black tip. Cas Cr and E-side.

Blacktail deer, ssp *columbianus*. Tail dark brown to black. W-side. Color p 495.

The blacktail deer of our Westside and the mule deer of our Eastside and the Rockies and Plains were once considered two distinct species, and now that they've been lumped there's a dilemma over which common name to use for the whole species. Both have tails black at least at the tip, and both have mulishly large ears in comparison to the Eastern whitetail deer.*

When fleeing, mule deer (unlike whitetails) break into a peculiar high-bounding gait called "stotting." This isn't as fast as a flat-out run, but it enables them to react to rough terrain with abrupt, unpredictable changes of direction— a hard act to follow for any predator giving chase, who has to respond at once both to the obstacles under its own feet and to the deer's changing course. Presumably, stotting evolved as advantageous in rough terrain, while sprinting is better on Eastern prairies and deciduous woods. In the dense vegetation west of the Cascades, stillness and concealment tend to work better than either running or stotting.

Wolves and cougars were the chief nonhuman predators of American deer, but since we've nearly eliminated wolves and reduced the number of cougars, domestic dogs are a more frequent cause of death—along with hunters, cars, and trains. Even dogs that wouldn't know what to do with a deer if they caught up with one will often run it to its eventual death by barbed wire entanglement or a broken leg. Deer are transfixed by a strong beam of light

---

*The endangered Columbian whitetail deer, *Odocoileus virginianus leucurus*, was once widespread in the Puget-Willamette Trough, is are now reduced to small populations, one on the Umpqua and one on the lower Columbia. Oddly, while this NW subspecies dwindled (in conflict with agriculture) the main subspecies, from an original range in eastern NA, thrived thanks to deforestation and spread westward as far as NE Washington.

at night, making them frequent victims of cars and trains. Coyotes, bears and bobcats rank as infrequent predators of deer, taking mainly fawns, or adults already close to death from other causes.

Though the last twenty years have seen some decline in the Northwest, we still have a lot more deer than we did two hundred years ago. Anglo civilization has been very good for deer, thanks more to its war on forests than to its war on predators: old-growth conifer forest supports few deer, but brushy clearcuts are deer heaven. In the absence of wolves, deer tend to increase beyond the carrying capacity of their habitat; then, during severe winters, huge numbers are so malnourished that they fall prey to parasites and/or coyotes. Degraded deer habitat doesn't look denuded, but it's short on the particular browse species that supply adequate fats, proteins, and trace minerals.

Browsing is a sophisticated, serious business. Spend a while sitting quietly near some deer and see exactly what they eat.(They are fairly approachable in Olympic National Park, where they've been protected for generations.) They often show an intense preference for a particular bush, which must contain good levels of some nutrient. They lap up springwater—no matter how muddy it has become from trampling hooves—that contains mineral salts they crave. They chomp mushrooms, "nature's salt licks," for other hard-to-find minerals. They strip horsehair lichen from tree limbs; it has little nutritive value on its own, but offers minerals that enhance utilization of the austere winter diet of twigs, evergreen needles and leaves. Like other cud chewers, deer can live on a high-roughage diet thanks to cellulose-digesting bacteria in their first (pre-cudchewing) stomach. They have to browse for the nutritional demands of these bacteria; inadequate protein can kill the bacteria, leaving the browser dangerously malnourished with its belly full.

Steep south slopes just above river-bottoms are ideal winter range. The low elevation and the insulating tree canopy offer warmer temperature and much shallower snow, while the south aspect lets in a little of the low-angle sunlight, and tends to have more shrubs. In summer, our deer move upslope to meadows, clearcuts, and open woods, where they fatten up on herbaceous plants.

The only close social tie among deer is between a doe and her fawns and yearlings. Males are solitary or form loose small groups, except during rutting when the sufficiently dominant ones follow single does in heat for a few days each. A doe seeks seclusion even from her yearlings before and after giving birth; it's up to the year-lings to reunite with her afterward. For their first few weeks she hides the new fawns—separately, if there are two or three—in nestlike depressions under brush. She browses in the vicinity, strives to repel other does, and comes back to nurse mainly at night. If a threatening large animal like you approaches, she will resolutely ignore the fawns, acting nonchalant. (She will meet a fox or bobcat, however, with a bold counterattack.) Occasionally people come across the hidden fawn and not the foraging doe, and make the cruel mistake of "rescuing" the "abandoned" fawn. Unless you ac-tually find the mother dead, assume a fawn is being properly cared for, and leave it in peace, untainted by human contact.

Deer are outstanding subjects for the study of pheromones—chemical messages sensed by smell—usually among members of one species. Mule deer are rather antisocial: they use several pheromones apparently to repel each other (a function akin to territoriality, though mule deer are not territorial). Tarsal glands, for ex-ample, are buried in patches of dark hair on the inside of the ankle joints, midway up the rear legs; to activate tarsal phero-mones, deer of any age and sex urinate on these patches and rub them together. While most pheromones are secreted in sweat or sebum (skin oil), deer urine is itself pheromonal—its chemistry reveals the animal's health and strength. A subordinate deer will sniff the tarsal patch-es of a dominant deer and then retreat to a respectful distance, showing that it got the message.

Glands on the forehead are rubbed on shrub twigs to advertise the presence and condition of a dominant buck, or to mark pos-session of a sleeping bed. Interdigitate glands, between the two toes of the hoof, secrete a more attractive pheromone, marking a deer's trail for other deer to follow. Metatarsal glands, on the outside of the lower hind leg, secrete a garlicky odor to signal fear or alarm.

The bacterium *E. coli* 0157, which has proven deadly in under-cooked hamburgers, is common in American deer. Hunter-bagged venison, including jerky, should be cooked to 165°. (Venison sold commercially is imported, and has not been implicated.) Windfall apples are suspect since they may have contacted deer scats.

Elk

Cervus elaphus (**sir**-vus: the Roman term for deer; **el**-a-fus: the Greek term for deer). Also **wapiti**. 7–8' long + 4–6" tail (large cow-sized); brown (in Olys) or tan (in Cas) with large, sharply defined tawny-pale patch on rump, and extensive darker tinges on neck, face, legs and belly; males have antlers; fawns are white-spotted. Widespread; abundant in Olys. Order Artiodactyla (Cloven-hooved mammals). Color p 496.

In this century, elk inhabit coniferous forests and high mountains of the West. Before white settlement they were common all the way East to the Appalachians, even Vermont and South Carolina. Great herds of them on the Plains were second only to buffalo both in sheer biomass and as a food and material resource for humans. Like the buffalo (properly "bison") they were shot in huge numbers, especially by ranchers wanting to eliminate grazing competition. They were able to hold on in the mountains and deep forests until an alarmed public, rallying around a famous hunter named Teddy Roosevelt, got refuges and hunting restrictions enacted to allow their population to recover. The very idea of conserving species was essentially new to (white) America at the end of the last century. Even then, the point, as popularly understood, was to conserve them for future generations of people to hunt.

The Olympic National Park has native Roosevelt elk, the westside subspecies. The Cascades have sparser elk populations descended largely from Rocky Mountain elk, which were introduced here in the 1920s when elk seemed nearly extirpated from the Cascades. We don't know exactly where the two subspecies natural ranges met, or exactly what the native elk of the Cascades were like.

Indeed, there have been intense politicized controversies over the "natural" population levels and locations of elk in general. The most reliable appraisal is that they are native to most parts of the U.S. and Canada that supported either forest or grassland; and that they have always been sensitive to hunting pressure. Their numbers were suppressed by Indian hunting beginning a few thousand years

---

ago, and rebounded a few hundred years ago when Indians were decimated by introduced diseases. They were high (would that be "naturally" or "unnaturally" high?) when white settlement began, and plummeted due to hunting in the nineteenth century. They've done pretty well in this century with regulated hunting, but have become unnaturally high in National Parks with no hunting, no wolves, and somewhat reduced cougar numbers.

After Mt. St. Helens erupted, elk provided great photos nonchalantly browsing on some of the first plants to emerge in the devastated blast zone. They were quicker to move back in than anyone expected, and they sped the revegetation process by bringing spores of mycorrhizal fungi back many miles at a time. Most plants would have had a hard time establishing themselves in sterile ash.

In Europe, a smaller, darker subspecies (*C. elaphus elaphus*) is the red deer or stag that Robin Hood hunted and commercial hunters still sell as venison. If you're thinking that the species known to the English as a "deer" ought, in English, to be a deer, you're right. A different genus exists which we ought to call "elk," as Europeans do and had done for centuries before Americans ever dubbed it a "moose." American races of both *Cervus* and *Alces* are much larger than their European counterparts, and the confusion must have begun when English colonists first met the American whitetail, about the size of a European red deer, and called it a deer. When a later generation, pushing Westward, met a race of *C. elaphus* about twice as big, they understandably thought it must be an "elk"—the larger European cervid whose flattened antlers and huge loose-fleshed muzzle they had doubtless never seen. The misnomer stuck, even through generations of texts trying to replace it with the Shawnee name "Wapiti." American elk and American moose were each formerly recognized at the species level (*Cervus canadensis* and *Alces americana*), but today taxonomists insist that our moose is merely a subspecies of European elk, our elk a subspecies of European red deer, and our deer something else again.

The best routes for viewing elk are around timberline in the Olympics in early fall; spring trips to Olympic river bottoms are also good. Most of the year, elk travel in herds segregated by sex, the mature bulls in bands of ten or fifteen, and the females and young males in larger herds. In late summer, the bulls become mutually hostile, and the largest, most aggressive of them (called "primary bulls") divide out harems from the cow herds. They tolerate yearlings, but drive away two- and three-year-old males. The harem's movements, like those of the cow herd in winter, are subtly directed by a matriarch apparently respected for her maturity rather than her size or strength. The bull seems to tag along rather than to lead, and he may lose part or all of his harem if he lets himself be distracted. Other bulls will surely be distracting him, hoping to take over the harem by overcoming him in a clash of antlers staged at dusk or dawn. This is the rutting season.

Bulls have evolved many curious behaviors for challenging each other and working up their sexual or combative frenzies:

Bugling. This unique call includes a deep bellow and a farther-carrying whistle. Elk cows also bugle, though less commonly, when calving in spring.

Antler-thrashing. These attacks on small trees and brush (common also among deer bucks) were formerly described as "polishing the antlers" or "rubbing off the itchy velvet" but they are now interpreted as making visual challenges or markers, as warm-up or practice for sparring, or as autoerotic stimulation.

Pit-wallowing. Shallow wallowing pits are dug and trampled out and lined with urine and feces. Bulls also use their antlers to toss urine-soaked sod onto their backs. Water may collect in a wallow the next winter, turning it into a pool lasting several years.

The reek of urine advertises the bull's physical condition, helping him avoid injuries by intimidating a challenger before combat begins. Elk can smell the degree to which a bull has been metabolizing fat as opposed to fresh food or, worse yet, muscle. A bull metabolizing only fat is one so well fed that he can devote all of his energy to the rut without being weakened by hunger.

Keeping track of a harem, defending it from other bulls, and reaping the sexual rewards is not only hard work, but so time-consuming that this well-fed bull can no longer eat or rest. Almost inevitably, primary bulls succumb in the same season to lesser but better-rested rivals, and often these "secondary bulls" yield in turn to "tertiary bulls." After defeat, they wander off alone, catch up on sleep, and show no further interest in sex that year. They may be weakened enough to reduce their chance of surviving winter. Large, sexually successful bulls have several years shorter life expectancy than bulls who never grow large enough to compete. The latter are "opportunistic bulls;" while spending the rutting season alone, they

---

stand at least a chance of mating with a stray cow. All in all, elk have an unusually extravagant courtship system.

While Rocky-Mountain elk cows may bear young every year, starting at age two, Roosevelt elk only go into estrus every other year, and also have poorer calf survival rates. This suggests that Westside vegetation is of low overall forage quality for elk and deer, no matter how luxuriant it may seem to us. Browsing techniques and care of the young among elk are much like those described for deer (page 357) except that to an elk cow, humans are puny med-

Antlers

True horns are sheaths of keratin, like fingernails; they form from epidermal tissue at their bases, and slowly slide outward over small bone cores, growing throughout life; they never branch. They are found, generally on both sexes, in the cattle family, including sheep, goats, and antelope. Antlers, on the other hand, made of solid bone and usually branched, are a defining characteristic of the deer family. (The deer and cattle families are the two largest families of ruminants, or cud-chewers; ruminants plus the pig family make up the cloven-hooved order.) Antlers form inside living skin—complete with hair and blood vessels—and stretch the skin outward as they grow. This skin, or "velvet," must die and slough off before the antlers come into use in the fall. In late winter the antlers weaken at their bases and are soon knocked off. On the forest floor, tiny incisors set to work converting them to mouse bones. A new pair will begin to grow by early summer.

Cumbersome and easily entangled in brush, antlers probably affect survival negatively. Not they, but hooves, are a deer's defensive weapon. (Caribou, or reindeer, are the one exception: most females have small antlers and use them defensively.) Antlers exist to help establish dominance among males during the rut. Big antlers, like bright plumages on small male birds, are an example of "fitness" evolved through sexual selection: the survival of the fittest is as a genetic line, not as long-lived individuals. In other words, highly competitive large-antlered elk bulls tend to die younger than weaker ones who rarely fight over cows, but the latter, leaving few offspring, are unfit. Some scholars think antlers' primary value is visual—to attract females and/or to intimidate rival males, decreasing risk to life and limb. Much of the sparring that goes on appears to be for "sport" or release of rutting energy; much takes place in the absence of females.

dlers to be chased from the nursery. Biologists who tag elk calves have to be quick tree-climbers. Barbed wire elk exclosures in the Hoh valley have shown that selective browsing substantially affects the vegetation of Westside bottoms where elk herds winter. Elk increase the amount of Sitka spruce, which is too prickly to eat; thin the vine maples and especially the salmonberries, which they love; and clear the understory in general. The down side is that opening up the understory, in combination with lots of human visitation, has sped the invasion of weedy clover, dandelions, and buttercups.

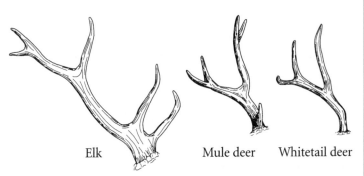

Elk   Mule deer   Whitetail deer

*Certainly, antlers are less than ideal deadly weapons; like boxing gloves, they may regulate and extend combat, and they may be less deadly than smaller sharper headgear would be. But don't think antlers don't really mean it; the case against them has been overstated. Closer observation has failed to demonstrate a major role for antlers in either erotic stimulation or intimidation displays, while it **has** traced a substantial proportion of male mortality to combat injuries.*

Each antler on elk and whitetail deer has one main beam from which all the other points branch. On mule and blacktail deer, both branches off the first Y *may be again branched. Average sexually mature elk have five-pointed antlers; older bulls may grow six, seven, or rarely eight. Mature mule deer typically have four or five points; their record is seven. Most yearling bucks east of the Cascades grow "forks" of two points, while the less well-fed yearlings on the Westside, where the profuse greenery makes surprisingly poor deer browse, usually grow unbranched "spikes." The number tends to increase year by year, but also responds to nutrition, and thus serves to advertise physical condition. Rich feeding in captivity has produced five-point antlers on yearlings, while meager range can limit even dominant bucks to forks.*

Moose

Alces alces (al-sees: Latin form of the originally Norse word that became, in English, 'elk'). 9' long + 7" tail; females much smaller. Dark gray-brown; long horselike head with loose overhanging upper lip; antlers have broad flat blades and many points; long dewlap hangs from throat, esp on males; pronounced shoulder hump. Tracks of adults 5"+ long, more pointed than elk; typical scats oval, 1½–1⅞" long; willow thickets with numerous broken, chewed, and bent-over tops are a sign of moose. Mainly in river bottoms, E-side in N Cas. Order Artiodactyla (Cloven-hooved mammals).

Moose have gone from rare to abundant in British Columbia during this century, and Washington has been getting moose overflow. Cascades moose are mainly in undisturbed mountain habitat, though that may change. The continent-wide population explosion is credited to the conversion of old forests to second-growth and brush (especially willows, their staple food) and, in some areas (not BC) the elimination of wolves.

Moose tolerate human proximity. Usually described as docile, they're unlikely to run away if you view them from a respectful distance. Close up, a degree of unpredictable skittishness combines with sheer weight to produce the surprising statistic that more people are killed by moose than by grizzly bears. (They're the one common species of roadkill weighty enough for mutual assured destruction.)

Mountain Goat

Oreamnos americanus (or-ee-**am**-nos: mountain lamb). 58" long + 6" tail, 36" shoulder height; all white, with "beard," shoulder "hump," and "pantaloons" formed of longer hair; hooves and sharp, curved horns black. Alp/subalpine in Olys and WA Cas. Order Artiodactyla (Cloven-hooved mammals). Color p 496.

The mountain goat is a deservedly legendary creature that ought to be among our most desired wildlife encounters. Unfortunately, many hiker-to-goat encounters take place in the Northeast Olympics, where the goats are not native and are now pests. To alleviate damage to subalpine plant communities, the Park braved tourist sentimentality and flew more than 300 goats out during the 1980s. By 1990, these removals in combination with several harsh winters reduced the goats, and in places the vegetation is coming back.

In the 1920s, before the Park was established, mountain goats were introduced for hunting, and they quickly overpopulated much of the range. They radiated from the north corner where they were introduced, but seem reluctant to push west of the Bailey Range climatic crest except during very light snowpack years. Cold wind may not penetrate their insulation, but floundering through wet snow all day and night is a problem. Unlike goats in the Rockies, which seek bare windswept ridges in winter, Olympic goats move down to closed forests where they can find thinner snow to paw through. They eat enough huckleberry twigs, lichens, and subalpine fir needles to keep their stomachs busy, but extract so little nutrition from this winter fare that they must live mainly on stored fat. They eat snow rather than seeking running water.

Apparently, mountain goats are nowhere limited primarily by predation. Eagles have been known to take kids and yearlings, dive-bombing to knock them off ledges, and cougars occasionally take even adults, but overall goats are fairly predator-proof with their proverbial evasive skills on precipitous terrain, as well as hooves and horns as defensive weapons. The hooves have strong, sharp outer edges and a hard, rubbery corrugated sole for superlative grip. Forage and climate seem to be the limiting factors on goat populations. Winter starvation and disease are ranking causes of death, along with the inevitable attrition from falling. It's possible that reintroducing wolves to the Olympics could reduce goat numbers indirectly by preventing them from carrying out their downslope winter migration. They have been decimated wherever they were freely hunted, but they lose their fear of people after a few generations in a national park. Be careful to suspend your stashed gear and bestow your urine only on the rocks.*

The ridgecrest paths they beat are a help on hikers' high-routes in the Olympics, though they often betray us by leading out onto rock faces that we hikers may see as requiring climbing technique or hardware. Tufts of white floss on branch tips remind us these are not paths for mere Vibram.

---

* Mountain goats in the NW get too little sodium in their diets, so they crave the sodium in our urine, as well as in mineral springs. Many are brazen enough to enter camps to eat freshly urine-soaked earth. In the process they demolish precious alpine turf, which is slow to heal. To prevent this, urinate only on bare rock or gravel when in goat country—anywhere above tree line in the Olympics or the Goat Rocks Wilderness.

Mountain goats are classified in a tribe with chamois, which lead a similar life in the Alps. Both differ from true goats and sheep in several respects, though all are in the cattle family. Mountain goat horns and skulls are not massive enough to sustain bouts of butting. Male mountain goats are thickened at the other end instead; the skin of their rumps, where they are likely to be gored in their flank-to-flank style of fighting, has been known to reach ⅞" thick, and was used by Alaskan tribes for chest armor. More important, the males evolved a powerful inhibition against any real fighting or sparring at all; the occasional pair who get carried away and actually fight are usually both retired from further rutting competition, with broken horns if not severe wounds. The effective breeding males are those who manage to intimidate the others with visual and olfactory displays, without ever coming to blows. Pit wallowing is indulged in, as among elk, and males often spend the winter in filthy coats, looking rattier still in spring while these molt in big sheets, revealing immaculate new white.

Males in most populations let themselves be chased around by the females and immature males, who aren't as inhibited from using their horns. Females may viciously charge males who come too close, except during a brief sexually receptive period in fall when they allow the male a creeping, submissive-looking courtship. A single kid is normally born in May or June. Mothers are legendarily protective, walking, for example, against a kid's downslope flank to prevent a fall in steep terrain.

Bighorn or mountain sheep, *Ovis canadensis*, were widespread until this century on the steppes of Eastern Washington and Oregon. The sheepherding industry disagreed with them—domestic sheep competed with them for the grass on steep slopes, and brought a disease which killed many bighorns—and they died out from the Cascades in the 1920s. They have been reintroduced in a few places on the eastern fringe of the Washington Cascades. Survival is dicey for these small bands. If they do survive and thrive, they are not likely to spread far into our mountains, since their natural habitat is arid grasslands.

9

Birds

Birds are winged, warm-blooded vertebrates with feathers. Wings first developed in some dinosaurs; whether or not birds are simply direct descendents of dinosaurs is hotly debated. One fossil found recently appears to show primitive feathers on a winged dinosaur. DNA evidence shows that birds and crocodilians are each other's closest living relatives—closer than crocodiles to lizards or birds to mammals.

In one conspicuous way, birds and mammals (which diverged from reptiles much earlier) evolved in parallel: both bird and mammal lines produced keratinous skin growths to serve as insulation and make warm-bloodedness possible. While mammals got hair, birds got feathers, whose extreme light weight is well suited for flying. As you know from the sales pitch on down sleeping bags, bird plumage is still unequaled among resilient, deformable, durable substances, in insulation value per weight.

In addition to insulating, feathers do much for the bird's shape, size, and color: plucked, a duck, a crow, a hawk, and a gull would look surprisingly alike in form, as well as pathetically small. Body plumage as much as doubles a bird's girth. The "fat" gray jays you see while skiing aren't fat, they're just fluffing out their plumage to maximize its insulation value, like what you are trying to do, unwittingly and ineffectually, when you raise goosebumps. Less fluffed out in flight (an intense activity that supplies heat in excess) body plumage serves the equally crucial function of streamlining.

The long outer feathers of wings and tail, meanwhile, provide most of the bird's airfoil surface at very little cost in weight. They constitute typically 35% to 60% of a bird's wingspread and 10% to 40% of its length. Feathers make the bird.

Color in most plumages—nearly all female and juvenile plumages and a great many fall and winter male plumages—emphasizes camouflage. Since pale colors make good camouflage against the sky, and darker colors against foliage or earth, most birds are paler underneath than on top. A mother and young in the nest need to be especially well camouflaged, since they can do little but sit tight when predators pass overhead. (The mother could fly, of course, but she stays to protect the flightless young.) Males are freer from the need for camouflage than females, and much freer than earthbound mammals. In them (and in the females of a very few species) sexual selection has been free to evolve gaudy plumage.

A showy plumage doesn't look equally good to all female birds; it looks best to females of the same species. For efficient pairing up, conspecifics need to recognize each other quickly and accurately; but no efficiency is lost if only females have this ability.

The same goes for bird songs, the main courtship display for many species. Some females sing, but far less often than males. ("Songs" are distinguished from "calls" as being longer and more complex, and characteristic of Order Passeriformes, often called "songbirds." Experienced birders can identify many species by song alone; but females and juveniles in many genera are nearly impossible to identify when no males or songs are present.).

Birds molt, or replace all of their feathers, at least once a year even if they don't have different seasonal plumages. The latter are mostly a matter of making the male alternately showy for courtship and camouflaged for the nonbreeding seasons. Ptarmigan, however, simply alter their camouflages to suit the season; they may go through two or three seasonal plumages (to match snow, no snow, or patchy snow) and the females and juveniles go through them along with the males. With a few exceptions like the mallard and the dipper, the large feathers of the wing and tail molt just a few at a time, making the bird look tattered but still permitting flight.

Another feather maintenance procedure is preening with the toes or beak, aided in most birds by oil from a preen gland. Much time is devoted to this crucial task of aligning and oiling plumage to keep it intact as an airfoil, as insulation and as waterproofing.

Along with wings and feathers, the evolution of bird flight entailed radically larger and more efficient respiratory systems. The stamina needed for a single day of flying, let alone for migrating across oceans, would be inconceivable in a mammal. It demands a lavish supply of oxygen to the blood, and of blood to the muscles. Cooling—direly needed during flight—is also done through the breath. Breathing capacity is augmented by several air sacs and, in many birds, by hollow interiors of the large upper leg and wing bones, all interconnected with little air tubes. Each breath passing through the lungs to the sacs and bones and back out through the lungs is efficiently scoured of its oxygen.

Hollow bones, their interiors crisscrossed with tiny strutlike bone fibers in accord with the best engineering principles, doubtless evolved to save weight, yet some birds lack them. Loons, for example, have solid bones—perfectly serviceable in a bird that dives for a living and doesn't fly much. But some diving birds have hollow bones, and a few soaring birds manage with solid bones.

The other large bone in a bird is the sternum, or breastbone, projecting keellike in front of the rib cage to provide a mechanically advantaged point of attachment for the flight muscles. These muscles, known on the dinner table as "breast meat," are the largest organs in flying birds. They power the flapping wings, and also guide flight by controlling the orientation of each and every feather along the wing edge through a system of tendons like ropes and pulleys. There is scant muscle in the wing and none in the foot, which is moved via tendons from muscles along the upper leg bone, held against the body. A flying animal ideally concentrates all its weight in a single aerodynamic "fuselage" close to its center of gravity.

The wing is analogous at once to both wing and propeller of an airplane. This is no accident; pioneers of mechanical flight studied and tried to copy bird flight for centuries before Wilbur and Orville finally, albeit crudely, got it right, using a design that separated the propelling and lifting functions of the bird wing. Like a propeller, wings provide forward thrust by slicing vertically through the air while held at a diagonal—the rear edge angled upward on the downstroke and vice versa.

Once there is enough forward motion and/or headwind to provide strong airflow across the wings (bird or airplane), their shape provides vertical lift by creating a low-pressure pocket in the air curving over their convex upper surface, while the lower surface is effectively flat. This upperside-convex principle is common to all flying birds except perhaps hummingbirds; but wing outlines have diverged in many specializations. See water wings (loon, page 371, and dipper, page 409), soaring wings (page 374), speed wings (page 382), little-used wings (grouse, page 384–86), and hovering wings (hummingbirds, page 394).

Highly mobile and often migratory, birds wander from their usual ranges more than plants or mammals do. The 88 species described in this book are fewer than half of those reported for our range. Among those excluded is the American robin, which is common here but much commoner in cities. The great blue heron, on the other hand, though more characteristic of lowlands and even cities than of mountains, is included because it is sure to draw attention, admiration, and curiosity. I have mainly tried to include the birds most characteristic of our mountains, conspicuous or not.

Nomenclature of species in this book follow the American Ornithologists' Union *Checklist*. Birds are the only group for which decisions on names, both scientific and common, are made by a committee and then accepted as "official" by just about everyone on the continent. I note well-known common names that were once official with the word "formerly," and vernacular names that were never official with "also." The *Checklist* added the modifiers "Northern," "American," and "Common" in several cases to distinguish American species from Eurasian ones, so these words don't need to be repeated with every mention of the bird. I don't follow the A.O.U.'s. indiosyncrasy of capitalizing all common names.

The size figure that begins each description is the length from tip of bill to tip of tail of an average adult male; females are the same or more often a little smaller, except among raptors, where they are considerably bigger. The *Golden Guide*'s figures are used—measurements of "live birds hand-held in natural positions." These run about 10% shorter than those in other bird manuals which, following taxonomic tradition, are measurements of long-dead specimens or skins forcibly hand-stretched. Novice birders would do well to fix in their minds images of sparrow size (4–6"), robin size (8–1/2"), jay size (9–12"), crow size (17"), and raven size (21") as a mental yardstick. Unfortunately, size isn't always helpful in the absence of other identifying characters; it's difficult, for example, to tell a goshawk from the smaller Cooper's hawk against the open sky.

Habitat and behavior are useful clues, especially if you're

content with a smart guess as opposed to a positive identification. Many small birds are faithful to plant communities they have adapted to for forage and/or cover. Certain species of deciduous streamside thickets on the Westside, for example, are rarely seen in the surrounding conifer forest, and vice versa. Within a forest, one species prefers the canopy, another the tall shrubs, and another the low shrub layer. After the nesting season, birds that don't migrate away may shift to different habitats for forage and cover, as their caloric needs, the weather, and the foods available all change.

Common Loon

Gavia immer (**gay**-via: the Roman term; **im**-er: sooty). 24", ws 58" (variable size, generally much larger than ducks); bill heavy, tapered, ± ravenlike; breeding-season adults (both sexes) with iridescent green/black head, white collar, black/white checked back, white belly; winter plumage dark gray-brown above, white below; in flight, head is held lower than body, and feet trail behind tail. Lakes; rare. Gaviidae (Loon family).

The varied nocturnal "laughs" and "yodels" of loons have been called beautiful, horrible, hair-raising, bloodcurdling, magical, and maniacal. Unequivocally they are loud.

Loons resemble diving ducks in their feeding and locomotion skills. They eat mainly fish, plus some frogs, reptiles, leeches, insects, and aquatic plants. Like ducks they use both wings and webbed feet to swim underwater. Diving either headfirst or submerging submarinewise, they can go deeper than any other birds (300 feet down!) thanks largely to their heavier bodies—only slightly less dense than water. Their heavy bones are a primitive trait that doubtless remains advantageous for diving. It is disadvantageous for flying; though loons can fly fast and far, they land gracelessly, with a big plop, and take off with great effort and splashing. Loons can become trapped for days or weeks on forest-lined lakes too small for their low-angle takeoff pattern—waiting to take off into a gale, when one arises. On their feet they're still more inept and cumbersome; the extreme rear placement of their legs is great for swimming but awful for walking. They go ashore (on an island) only to breed, and nest in soggy plant debris at the water's edge. She and he take turns on the eggs.

After wintering near the coast, some loons move to mountain lakes, arriving soon after the ice breaks up. Loons are sensitive to human disturbance during the breeding season, and have nearly disappeared from the Cascades as a breeding species. Ross Lake is our only lake known to have them still.

Pied-Billed Grebe

Podilymbus podiceps (pod-i-**lim**-bus: from the Greek term; **pod**-i-seps: rump feet). 9" long, stocky; bill high, very stout, with downcurved ridge, pale with a black band across it (on summer adults); both sexes drab brown mottled white, white under tail; summer adults marked with black on face and throat; in flight (rarely seen), head is slightly lower than body, and feet trail behind the very short tail. Lakes, marshes, uncommon. Podicipedidae (Grebe Family). Color p 497.

Like loons, grebes are a primitive order of birds poorly adapted for flying and worse for walking, but superlatively built for diving. Grebe toes—fat scaly lobes—paddle even more efficiently than webbed feet; they use a side by side stroke resembling the human butterfly stroke but without any help from the forelimbs. (Diving ducks, in contrast, paddle their feet alternately, and also use their wings.) By exhaling deeply to decrease their buoyancy, grebes can quietly submerge and skulk with only head or nostrils above water. Grebe hatchlings take up the submersible life before they can even swim, by clinging to a diving parent's back. The widespread pied-billed grebe is timid and rather antisocial, but capable of remarkable vocalizations sometimes compared to a braying donkey or a squealing pig. Crayfish are a favorite food.

Great Blue Heron

Ardea herodias (**ar**-dia her-**oh**-dias: Roman and Greek words for heron). 38", ws 70"; gray (± bluish) with some white, black, and dark red markings; bill, neck, and legs extremely long; neck held "goosenecked" in flight; huge birds seen in slow-flapping low flight over rivers and lakes are generally this species. Various loud, gutteral croaks. Order Ciconiiformes, Ardeidae (Heron family). Color p 498.

The heron's way of life is to stand perfectly still in shallow water until some oblivious frog or small fish happens by, and then pluck or spear it with a quick thrust of the beak. The prey see little of the heron but its legs and shadow, and perhaps mistake it for an odd reed or cattail. A heron can nail prey even at night, as members of this order have excellent night vision.

Turkey Vulture

Cathartes aura (cath-**ar**-teez: purifier; aura: breeze). Also **turkey buzzard.**
25"; ws 72"; plumage black exc whitish rear half of wing underside; head
naked, wrinkled, pink (exc black when young); soars with wings in a shallow V, often tipping left or right, rarely flapping. Open country. Migratory: here late Feb through Oct. Order Ciconiiformes, Cathartidae (New
World vulture family).

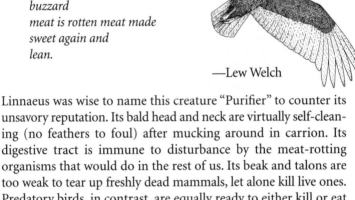

bird of rebirth
buzzard
meat is rotten meat made
sweet again and
lean.

—Lew Welch

Linnaeus was wise to name this creature "Purifier" to counter its
unsavory reputation. Its bald head and neck are virtually self-clean-
ing (no feathers to foul) after mucking around in carrion. Its
digestive tract is immune to disturbance by the meat-rotting
organisms that would do in the rest of us. Its beak and talons are
too weak to tear up freshly dead mammals, let alone kill live ones.
Predatory birds, in contrast, are equally ready to either kill or eat
carrion. Vultures go long periods without food, and when they find
it they gorge themselves, perhaps accounting for their apparent
lethargy on foot and difficulty in taking flight. (If hungry enough,
they'll fill their stomachs with plant foods.) Once on the wing, they
are the best soarers of all land birds, rarely needing to flap.

A congregation of vultures wheeling usually means carrion
below, and other vultures seem able to read this sign, slowly gathering from miles around. Vultures locate their food by both sight
and smell. Birds generally have little sense of smell, but vultures
have a sharp sense at least for certain carrion smells. Natural gas
pipeline companies found that by perfuming their gas with ethyl
mercaptan they could get vultures to lead them to pipeline leaks.

Several turkey vultures may gather around a carcase, but they
eat one at a time, in order of dominance yielding occasionally to

---

desperation. Dominant individuals have redder heads, and seem to flush even redder as a dominance display.

"Buzzard," an old word tracing from the Roman *buteo*, was always applied broadly by the English to include hawks (genus *Buteo*) as well as Old World vultures, which are in the hawk family. When we Americans say "buzzard," we mean a vulture, not a hawk. American vultures and condors resemble Old World vultures due to convergent evolution (see page 390), but are distantly related. (Since 1873, some scientists have argued that they are closer to storks than hawks. The Seventh *Checklist* made that view official, but it is still controversial; even DNA evidence has been unable to resolve the dispute.) New World vultures include the largest U.S. bird: the endangered California condor, *Gymnogyps californianus* (**jim**-no-jips: naked vulture). Condors were common here in Lewis and Clark's day, but their range shrank inexorably until they survived only in captivity. Rerelease into the wild began recently—a nip and tuck battle against extinction.

Soaring Wings

Vultures share with the large Falconiformes—eagles, vultures, ospreys, and buteo hawks—a broad, spread-tipped wing and tail design specialized for soaring over land. These contrast with the short wings of accipiter hawks, the narrow wings of falcons, and the clean, linear wings of gulls and albatrosses which also soar superlatively, but on entirely different air currents, over the ocean.

Falconiform soarers stay aloft largely by seeking out "thermals," or columnar upwellings of warm air—the daytime convection pattern of low, warm air rising to trade places with higher, cooler air. They don't try to cross large lakes, or travel at night or in the early morning, since thermal air is warmed by land absorbing and reradiating sunlight. Dry, sparsely vegetated land does it best, so steppes and prairies are especially popular with soaring birds. To travel, they may climb one thermal spirally, then glide obliquely downward to the next thermal, and climb again. To migrate, they often wait for a low-pressure weather trough, or follow long north-south mountain ridges that produce wavelike updrafts by deflecting westerly winds. Tightly packed mountain topography, like ours, produces oblique thermals along creek headwaters. Soarers can use these just as well.

Mallard

Anas platyrhynchos (ay-nus: the Roman term; plat-i-**rink**-os: broad nose). 16"; males (Sept-June) have iridescent dark green head separated from red-brown breast and brown back by white neckband; bill yellow on males, black/orange on females; both sexes have a band of bright blue with black/white trim on upper rear edge of wing, and much white under wings; females, juveniles, and summer males speckled drab. Loud quack. Marshy lakes, as in the C OR Cas. Anatidae (Waterfowl family). Color p 497.

The mallard is a good example the numerous surface-feeding, or "dabbling" or "puddle" ducks. It is conspicuous over much of the Northern Hemisphere—except during duck hunting season, when it makes itself perplexingly scarce. Tasty flesh contributes to its renown. Domestic ducks were bred largely from mallards, centuries ago, and breed with them when given the chance; city park ducks often include mallards and hybrids together.

Dabbling ducks feed by upending themselves in shallow water and plucking vegetation from the bottom. They also eat a few molluscs and insects, and a very few small fish. They take flight abruptly and steeply, unlike diving ducks which splash along the surface.

Mallards are among the birds that molt their flight feathers all at once, rendering them flightless; to escape predators they hide out for the duration in large groups in marshes. You may then see mallard mothers with chicks trailing behind, but no fathers. After the young are independent, it's the mothers' turn to molt. While flightless, they are "sitting ducks," but the rest of the time they can practice "sleeping with one eye open." If four mallards are asleep in a row, the two in the middle close both eyes while the two on the ends tend to keep the end-of-the-line eye open for predators. A scientist ran brain scans on mallards in this condition, and found that the brain hemisphere connected to the open eye remained semi-wakeful and capable of rousing the bird upon sighting a predator, while the other hemisphere experienced normal sleep.

Common Merganser

Mergus merganser (**mer**-gus: diver; mer-**gan**-ser: diving goose). 18"; breeding males mostly white beneath with black back and head, and red bill, the head showing greenish iridescence in strong light, and becoming brown in non-breeding season; females with red-brown head sometimes showing slight crest on nape, and red bill, otherwise grayish, with darker back and ± white throat and breast. Lakes and streams. Anatidae. Color p 497.

Mergansers are carnivorous "diving ducks" as opposed to the more numerous "dabbling ducks" who don't dive, but merely dip, for their mostly vegetable foods. Instead of a Donald Duck-type broad bill, mergansers have a long, narrow bill with a hooked tip and serrated edges for gripping their slippery aquatic prey—amphibians, insects and other invertebrates, and fish. Of our three merganser species, the common is the largest, most montane, and certainly the commonest. Those who don't fly north to breed generally move up to mountain lakes, finding woodpecker holes or other cavities to nest in.

Harlequin Duck

Histrionicus histrionicus (hiss-tree-**ah**-nic-us: actor or jester, referring to clownlike facial markings). 12"; breeding males plumed in a clownlike patchwork of slaty blue-gray, rich brown on the flanks, and white splotches with black trim—but may appear merely dark from a distance; others dark brown with several small white patches on head, and whitish belly. Rough water. Order Anseriformes, Anatidae (Waterfowl family . Color p 497.

Whether in whitewater rivers or heavy surf, harlequins display phenomenal pluck and strength as swimmers. They spend most of their time on rocky coastlines, where they dive for shellfish. After courting and pair-bonding, they move inland to nest along mountain streams, where they feed largely on insects. The grass-lined nest is built under streamside brush, or among boulders. The females stay to incubate and raise the chicks alone, the males returning to sea. Populations wintering on the Olympic Coast include some that nest on the Hoh in May along with others that nest in Alberta in July. Unlike most ducks, they rarely mix with other species.

Wags have compared harlequin plumage to unfinished paint-by-number art. The feathers were once used to adorn ladies' hats.

Osprey

Pandion haliaetus (pan-**die**-un: a mythic king; hal-ee-**ay**-et-us: sea eagle, the Greek term for osprey). Also **fish hawk**. Males 22", ws 54", females larger; blackish above, exc white crown; white beneath, with black markings most concentrated at wing tips and "elbows"; the "elbow" break is sharper both rearward and downward than on similar birds, suggesting a shallow **M** while soaring. Frequent calls include loud whistles and squeals. Near rivers and lakes. Order Falconiformes, Pandionidae (Osprey family). Color p 498.

In a hunting technique that wins respect if not utter astonishment, the osprey dives into water from fifty to a hundred feet up, plucks a fish from a depth of one to three feet, and bursts immediately back into flight, gripping a squirming fish sometimes as heavy as itself. The soles of its feet are toughened with minute barbules that help grasp wet fish. The osprey is a nearly worldwide species comprising a genus and subfamily by itself.

Ospreys are among several birds of prey that suffered heavy losses in some areas from toxic chemicals like DDT. Toxins from prey concentrate in the tissues of predators; birds are especially sensitive to them. But in the Northwest, so far, ospreys coexist with civilization, perhaps even benefitting where rivers are dammed.

Bald Eagle

Haliaeetus leucocephalus (hal-ee-ee-et-us: sea eagle; lew-co-**sef**-a-lus: white head). Males 32", ws 80", females larger; adults blackish with entire head and tail white; immatures (1–3+ years) brown; wings held flat while soaring. May be seen anywhere in our range, but common only on C OR High Cascade lakes, the Nooksack and Skagit valleys, the Klamath Basin and the Olympic seacoast. Calls: various weak chips and squawks, or louder ± gull-like shrieks. Order Falconiformes, Accipitridae (Hawk family). Color p 498.

The national symbol, bald eagles have been considered vermin to be shot on sight for most of America's history. Alaska even offered a bounty for shooting them until 1952, twelve years after it became illegal in the lower 48 states. Some Westerners still fear and hate eagles enough to break the law.

The Northwest is lucky to have fairly plentiful bald eagles along the coast from the Aleutians to the Columbia, spilling inland along salmon streams and to high lakes where waterfowl concentrate. The areas listed above hold the largest breeding populations of bald eagles south of Canada. Fondness for fish and waterfowl tends to keep them near water, but they are sometimes sighted in our mountains, and seem less averse to deep forest than the other big soarers.

Despite a public image as a fearsome predator, the bald eagle far more often scavenges carrion or robs other birds—ospreys, gulls, kingfishers, and smaller bald eagles—of their prey. Most salmon it eats are spawned-out carcasses. At lambing time on sheep ranches, bald eagles eat afterbirths and stillborn lambs. Grossly

---

exaggerated fears of lamb and salmon predation fueled America's animosity toward eagles for the last two centuries.

Our bald eagles breed in mid to late winter. That way the young, after an extraordinarily long time in the nest (six weeks incubating under both parents taking turns, and ten to twelve weeks from hatching to flying) will be ready to fly up the coast in time for the summer coho salmon runs in Alaska. Those that migrate work their way back down the coast in conjunction with salmon runs that follow heavy fall rains. They reach Washington in November, and peak there in January. Many of our birds, especially those in Oregon, seem to be resident rather than migratory.

A spectacular courtship "dance" of bald eagles has been described many times: the male dive-bombs the female in midair, she rolls over to meet him, they lock talons and plummet earthward, breaking out of their death-taunting embrace at the last possible instant. Juvenile bald eagles engage in every kind of courtship behavior short of mating, which waits for the fifth or sixth winter.

North American tribes associated the bald eagle with sickness, death, and healing, and hence as an ally or guardian of shamans. Eagle feathers were used in healing rituals, and it was variously said that an eagle would fly over a sick person, would eat a dead person, or would scream to a person soon to be killed by an arrow.

Northern Harrier

Circus cyaneus (circus: Greek term for a circling hawk; sigh-**ay**-nee-us: blue). Formerly **marsh hawk**. Males 16¼", ws 42", females much larger; conspicuous white rump patch on both sexes; males ash gray above, whitish underneath with black wing tips and tail bars; females speckled reddish brown, paler beneath; tail long and narrow; wings held well above horizontal while gliding. Marshes and lush meadows. Accipitridae (Hawk family).

The harrier cruises dry grasslands and wet meadows alike. It nests among tall grass, and spends several hours a day cruising just inches above the tops of the reeds, grasses, or low shrubs. When a vole takes off running underneath it, the agile hawk may harry it through many dashes and turns before dropping on it. It is an unusual hawk in hunting primarily by sound; in experiments, harriers precisely locate and attack tiny tape players concealed in meadow grass peeping and rustling like voles. In this respect harriers evolved convergently with owls, developing an owllike facial ruff of feathers, which enhances hearing.

The harrier is also a unique hawk in mating polygamously. Some males manage to feed two or even three nests of about five young each. The mothers often leave the nest momentarily to take midair delivery of morsels from their harried breadwinners. A female, having paired and begun a nest, may dump that mate if he is turning out to be a poor provider, and join the harem of a better one. A male courts by means of a "sky dance" in a grand U pattern, culminating by landing on the nest site he proposes. More vigorous dancers get more mates.

Red-Tailed Hawk

Buteo jamaicensis (bew-tee-o: the Roman term; ja-may-ik-**en**-sis: of Jamaica). Males 18", ws 48", females larger; tail (adults) red-brown above, pink below, broadly fanned out; brown above, highly variable beneath, from dark brown to (most often) white with delicate red-brown patterning. Usually seen soaring. Call a short hoarse descending scream. Order Falconiformes, Accipitridae (Hawk family). Color p 499.

The red-tail is easily America's oftenest-seen large bird of prey. It is comfortable around freeways, often perching on roadside fenceposts. Its preferred natural habitat is grassland mixed with some trees, such as our Eastside ponderosa pine timberline. On a continental scale it has been on the increase, doubtless aided by the conversion of forest and tallgrass prairie to more transparent habitats.

Adaptability, opportunism, and economy are the keys to the red-tail's success. Lacking the speed that makes falcons and accipiters perfect specialists, it adopts a variety of hunting ploys based on acute vision and effortless soaring. Hares and ground squirrels, the preferred prey, may get an aerial swoop after a patient, stealthy approach. Or the hawk may brazenly land between a rodent and its refuge, forcing the rodent into an end run; the hawk tries to snatch it. Band-tailed pigeons may be swooped upon while feeding in brush. Lizards, snakes, and slugs are easy, and form a large part of the diet in some seasons. Red-tails are also pirates, robbing hawks and even eagles or great horned owls of their kills. In winter, individuals that remain in the snowy North show a remarkable ability to conserve calories and subsist on a skimpy, irregular diet.

Accipiters

Accipiter spp. (ak-**sip**-it-er: Roman term meaning a fast flier). Tell these from other hawks by behavior, and by proportionately short, broad wings and long tails; the tail is often narrow (not fanned out), is broadly barred (± black/white) its full length, and has a pure white tuft under its base; three species hard to tell from one another—size ranges overlap, females being about as big as next bigger species' males; both sexes slaty gray above, or ± brownish; yearlings brown above, pale beneath with red-brown streaking. Calls cackling, infrequent. Order Falconiformes, Accipitridae (Hawk family).

Sharp-shinned hawk, *A. striatus* (stry-**ay**-tus: striped). Males 10½", ws 21" (jay-sized); tail square-cornered, dark-tipped; underside pale with fine brownish barring. Often at forest/clearing edges, or alpine. Illustrated above.

Cooper's hawk, *A. cooperii* (coo-**per**-ee-eye: after William Cooper). Males 15½", ws 28" (crow-sized); tail rounded, with slight white tip; underside pale with red-brown barring. Forest understory, edges, or streamside brush.

Goshawk, *A. gentilis* (jen-**tie**-lis: aristocratic). Males 21", ws 42" (red-tailed hawk size) tail rounded, with slight white tip; underside pale with fine blue-gray barring. Deep wilderness forests. Color p 498.

These hawks evolved in the forests. Their long tails lend maneuverability while the short wings avoid branches. Cooper's typically bursts out from a concealed perch; the sharp-shinned flies around more or less constantly and randomly, and chases the birds it happens to surprise; the goshawk also cruises, flushing grouse and ptarmigan, its chief prey, and also taking some squirrels and hares.

Each day while young are in the nest, a sharp-shinned father brings home about two sparrow-sized birds apiece for his family of seven or so. That's a lot of hunting. He seems to stay in shape with playful harassment of larger birds, even ravens. Accipiter males select a limb not far from the nest and take prey there to pluck it before eating it or delivering it to the nest. An indiscriminate scattering of thousands of small feathers may be a sign of one such pluckery in the branches above. Either parent may make a nasty fuss over an animal, such as yourself, happening near the nest.

Accipiters are often described as nonsoarers, with a flight rhythm of five flaps and a short glide—sometimes a useful identifying trait. But in the strong sustained updrafts of rugged mountains they appear perfectly capable of soaring till hell freezes over.

Golden Eagle

Aquila chrysaetos (ak-will-a: Roman term for eagle; cris-ay-et-os: gold eagle). Males 32", ws 78", females larger (up to twice as heavy); adults dark brown all over; juveniles have white bases to their main wing and tail feathers (but never an all-white tail, as in bald eagle, nor a white rear edge of wing, as in turkey vulture); wings held flat while soaring. Call (rarely used) is rapid chipping. Open country; wary of humans. Accipitridae (Hawk family); order Falconiformes. Color p 499.

Golden eagles inhabit any North American terrain that has plenty of vertical relief, few trees, and populations of both hares and large diurnal rodents like marmots or ground squirrels; the hares provide winter fare while the rodents hibernate. Winter may impel an eagle to attempt larger prey such as fox, or rarely coyote or deer. This is reportedly accomplished with a plummeting, falconlike dive; momentum multiplies the eagle's ten pounds into enough force to overpower heavier prey.

Normally, the golden eagle hunts from a low, fast-soaring cruise, using angular topography both for visual cover and for updrafts. It also robs hawks and falcons of their kills; hawks rarely venture, let alone nest, within half a mile of an eagle's aerie. The latter is a stick structure 4' to 6' in diameter, and growing from 1' deep to as much as 5' with many years of reuse—yet somehow hard to spot against its cliff.

American Kestrel

Falco sparverius (fahl-co: the Roman term; spar-ver-ius: sparrow). Formerly **sparrow hawk**. Males 9", ws 21", females slightly larger; red-brown above, exc wings blue-gray on adult males only, and tail tipped with heavy black band and slight white fringe; brown-flecked white beneath (exc dark tail). Call a sharp, fast "killy-killy-killy." ± open country. Order Falconiformes, Falconidae (Falcon family). Color p 498.

The kestrel is one of the smallest, most successful, least shy, and most often seen raptors. When not perched on a limb or telephone wire, it often hovers in place, wings fluttering, body tipped about 45°, facing upwind, 10-20' above a field or roadside. From this vantage it can drop and strike prey quickly, as a larger, broader-winged hawk might do from a low soar. Grasshoppers and other big insects are staples; mice are also taken. If all these are scarce, the kestrel may fly down sparrow-sized birds.

Prairie Falcon

Prairie falcon, *Falco mexicanus.*
Males 16", ws 40", females larger; wings pointed, tail narrow. Dusty to (less often) slaty brown above, strongly mottled cream white beneath, with blackish wingpit (analogous to armpit) patches; may have a vertical streak below eye, but narrower and less distinct than on peregrine. E-side steppe year-round, wandering in summer to timberline meadows near Cas Cr. Color p 497.

The prairie falcon can take birds, as other falcons do, but its chief prey are ground squirrels. When it hunts them around Cascade timberline after its spring nesting season in the Eastside dry country, it is our most conspicuous falcon. A parent with a fledgling may defend it by means of dive-bombing attacks at the heads of intruders, veering away at the last instant—and provide a lucky hiker with one of the great adrenalin-stimulating wildlife encounters.

Prairie falcons favor alpine areas less than the larger falcons—merlin, peregrine, and gyrfalcon—but the latter are all rare here.

Speed Wings

Falcons in flight are told from other hawks by their pointed, swept-back wings and straight, or even slightly tapering, tails. (They also soar, though infrequently, with tail fanned out like other hawks.) This must be the optimal wing design for sustained speed, since so many of the fastest flyers—falcons, swifts, swallows, and nighthawks—evolved it independently.

The fastest of all falcons in level flight is said to be the largest falcon, the gyrfalcon, Falco rusticolus, *of the Arctic (rarely reported seen here). In ancient falconry, the gyr was so highly esteemed that kings reserved it for their exclusive use.*

Almost as highly rated was the slightly smaller peregrine, which earns the title of world's fastest animal with its "stoop"—not exactly flight but more like skydiving targeted at airborne prey. The wings are held close to the sides to provide control with a minimum of drag. Most hawks and eagles will stoop occasionally, when presented with an irresistible target, but only the peregrine virtually limits itself to midair prey, and has perfected the stoop. The figure 180 miles per hour was

Peregrine Falcon

Peregrine falcon, *F. peregrinus* (pair-eg-**rye**-nus: wandering). Also **duck hawk**. Males 15", ws 40", females larger; wings pointed, tail narrow. Color variable, ours most likely slate blue to (immatures) dark brown above, white beneath with dark mottling and ± reddish wash except on pure white throat and upper breast; face has a distinctive high-contrast rounded dark bar descending across and below eye. Rare; reintroduction habitats are Crater Lake and the both sides of the Columbia Gorge. Falconidae (Falcon family).

During the 1960s, use of DDT (as well as the capture of peregrines for falconry) was banned in the U.S. after it was shown that the severe worldwide decline of peregrines was caused chiefly by breakage of thin-shelled eggs from falcons contaminated with DDT and related insecticides. Programs for captive breeding and release of peregrines were funded and a recovery process begun. Success is coming slowly, hindered partly by poaching (peregrines fetch astronomical prices from falconers, especially in the Middle East). Also it is likely that other pollutants cause some eggshell thinning.

Aside from the reintroduced pairs, peregrines have been successfully exploiting a new habitat—large cities—where two of their favorite things abound: high ledges to perch and nest on, and pigeons to eat. A different subspecies has always commonly wintered at points on the Northwest Coast, preying on shorebirds.

---

heard for years, based on a 1930 report by a small plane pilot who said he was passed by a stooping peregrine while he was diving at 175 mph. He was disbelieved by some who felt sure that the race must belong to the swifts. Ornithologist Vance Tucker, who is at work on settling the argument with optical measurements, retorts that swifts are probably no swifter than pigeons. He expects this year to report measurements of a peregrine stooping at 157 mph, but he also thinks, based on theoretical analysis of the peregrine as a falling body, that they can do over 220. "Searching for the top speed is something like trying to measure the top speed of a Porsche by watching cars on a freeway. The longer you watch, the higher the record, but you are unlikely to measure the top speed that the car is capable of, because that speed is seldom practical on a freeway."

Ken Franklin of Friday Harbor takes a different tack: he sky-dives with a peregrine. He says that the falcon kept up with him on dives whose free-fall portion he calculated as faster than 200 mph.

Spruce Grouse

Dendragapus canadensis (den-**drag**-a-pus: tree lover; can-a-**den**-sis: of Canada). Also **Franklin's grouse, fool-hen**. 13"; males slaty to brownish black above, with red-orange eyebrow-comb, black beneath, with white bars or large flecks on flanks and upperside of tail; others mottled red-brown (darker than ruffed grouse, redder than sooty grouse); tails of both sexes dark with ± distinct reddish tip. Very quiet vocally; courting males drum, in a series of low thumps, and can produce a pair of sharp "wing-claps" in defense of territory. Near timberline, uncommon, mainly E-side of N Cas. Order Galliformes, Phasianidae (Pheasant family).

The spruce grouse earns its nickname "fool hen" by being preposterously fearless around humans—vulnerable even to sticks and stones. Combine that unfortunate naiveté with tender, juicy, tasty flesh (at least in summer when the bird hasn't been eating conifer needles) and you get severely reduced numbers of spruce grouse, concentrated today where protected in National Parks.

Birds of the chickenlike order, Galliformes, feed and nest on the ground, and fly only in infrequent short bursts. They have undersized wings and pale breast meat, indicating a scanty supply of blood to the flying muscles. After the fowl has been flushed a few times in quick succession, these muscles are too oxygen-short to fly again until they are rested. Tirelessness in flight is more the norm among other kinds of birds which, being infrequent walkers, have dark breast meat and pale and scanty leg meat. Even in winter, when the spruce grouse spends most of its time in trees, it mainly walks along the branches, getting added grip from special comblike tissue that grows along its feet in fall and falls off in spring.

In winter, spruce and blue grouse subsist entirely on conifer needles, a very poor diet but a plentiful one. Spruce grouse seem to prefer pines. To adapt, their intestine lengthens by about 40% each fall; they pack their digestive tracts full each evening and spend all night digesting, and still some 75% of the fibrous matter passes through undigested, creating a thick buildup under roost trees. They lose muscle mass inexorably on this diet, but are able to make it up on insects and berries in summer.

---

* Whether or not Spruce and Blue Grouse belong together as a genus is a long-running issue. *Birds of North America* asserts that they do not (because DNA shows Blue's closest relative is Sage Grouse, a different genus) and that Spruce Grouse should be in either *Falcipennis* or *Canachites*.

Blue Grouse

Dendragapus obscurus (ob-**skew**-rus: dark). Also **hooter;** our variety the **sooty grouse**, . 17"; adult males mottled dark gray above, pale gray beneath, with yellow eyebrow-comb; others mottled gray-brown; both sexes have blackish tail. Male's courtship call a series of 5 or 6 low hoots; hen with chicks clucks. Fairly common and frequently seen; all elevs in montane forest. Order Galliformes, Phasianidae (Pheasant family). Color p 499.

Blue grouse spend the breeding season in relatively open habitats, enriching their diets with caterpillars, plant shoots, berries, and even mushrooms. For winter they move into dense conifer stands, which offer better thermal cover, visual cover, and plenty of needles, which are all they'll find to eat in winter anyway. In some populations this pattern means they actually migrate upslope for winter, but that isn't likely in our range. They prefer Douglas-fir needles, and in experiments have been able to maintain their body weight on 100% Douglas-fir needles, but not on needles of other species. (See spruce grouse, facing page; digestibility rates and adaptations are probably pretty similar for the two species.)

Both the courting "hoot" and the chief visual display of the males—bare yellow patches on the neck—are performed by inflating a pair of air sacs in the throat.

Ruffed Grouse

Bonasa umbellus (bo-**nay**-sa: bull; um-**bel**-us: umbrella). Also **drummer**. 14"; mottled gray-buff; tail red-brown or gray (two color phases) with heavy black band at tip and faint ones above; males have slight crest; black neck "ruff" is erected only in courtship display. Distinctive "drumming" in lieu of a vocal mating call is common in late spring, occasional (territorial?) at other seasons; also an owllike hoot is sometimes heard. Lower forests. Order Galliformes, Phasianidae (Pheasant family).

The male ruffed grouse makes a mysterious noise. Even Press Expedition men—seasoned frontiersmen who made the first recorded trip across the Olympics—seem to have mistaken it for, of all things, unseen geysers bubbling. It's an accelerating series of muffled thumps, known as drumming or booming, made with sharp downstrokes of his wings while perched on a log. You can't tell what direction or distance it's coming from. Very low-pitched sounds carry farthest in forests, but they sound nondirectional. An attracted female must have a tantalizing search in store for her.

Birds

At the end of it, she can watch his fantailed, ruff-necked dance, and then mate with him, but that's all he has to offer her; she will incubate and raise the young by herself. She nests on the ground, like other grouse, and trusts her excellent camouflage up until the last second, when you're about to step on her unaware. Then she flushes explosively, right under your nose. She may actually try to scare you away, if there are young to protect, or to draw you away from them with her famous broken wing routine. You are touched. She knows a thing or two about psychology.

Though their a range is congruent with conifer-dominated forests, ruffed grouse are usually found near deciduous trees.

White-tailed Ptarmigan

Lagopus leucurus (la-**go**-pus: hare foot; loo-**cue**-rus: white tail). Also **snow grouse**. 10"; underparts white; upper parts white in winter, mottled brown in summer, patchwork of brown and white in spring and fall; feet feathered; bright red eyebrow-comb on males in spring. Soft clucks and hoots. Alp/subalpine, sometimes much lower in heavy snow seasons; WA Cas. Order Galliformes, Phasianidae (Pheasant family). Color p 499.

Though smaller than their grouse relatives, ptarmigan are the largest creatures that make our alpine zone their exclusive home. Dwarf willows are their staple in winter, crowberries in fall. Like other grouse, they rely on camouflage to protect them from predators. Considering the visual acuity of hawks, this seems an especially risky strategy above tree line. In winter they switch to pure white plumage and stay on pure white snow as much as possible, digging into it for shelter and to reach willow buds. Once their summer plumage grows in, they stay off the snowfields.

The "p" in ptarmigan is not only silent but silly. It must have found its way into print long ago in the work of some pedant who assumed "ptarmigan" to be Greek. It's Gaelic.

Spotted Sandpiper

Actitis macularia (ak-**tie**-tiss: shore dweller; mac-you-**lair**-ia: spotted). Also **teeter-tail**. 6¼"; light brown above with white eye stripe and wing bars, white below; summer adults dark-spotted white below, with ± yellowish legs and bill; dips and teeters constantly when on the ground; flies with wings stiffly downcurved. Call a high clear "peep-peep," usually in flight or when landing. Single or in pairs, along streams and lakes, esp subalpine. Scolapacidae (Sandpiper family). Color p 500.

Like the dipper, which also feeds in frothy streams, the spotted sandpiper dips from the knees; it distinguishes itself in tipping forward and back, hence its nickname "teeter-tail." When threatened by a hawk it can dive like a dipper as well. In feeding it doesn't dive, but plucks prey from shallow water or the bank nearby, or sometimes from midair. Prey range in size up to trout fry, though insects predominate. No plant foods are eaten. Spotted sandpipers are widespread, breeding in almost any mountains north of Mexico and then wintering on seacoasts where they can count on mild weather. That just barely includes the Washington Coast.

Sex roles are reversed in this and a few other sandpipers. The females are larger, more aggressive, and more dominant; they migrate to the breeding grounds first; establish and defend territories; court the males; initiate sex; do less than their share of sitting on the eggs; and do very little raising of the young brood aside from serving as a sentinel. They have less prolactin than the males, prolactin being a hormone that promotes parental caregiving. Many females are monogamous, but the fittest are serially polyandrous: a pair courts, bonds, builds a nest, and provisions it with four fertile eggs, and then she leaves that family and goes off to do it all over again with a second, a third, and even a fourth male in one season. It's different, but it makes sense. But......why sandpipers?

Band-tailed Pigeon

Columba fasciata (co-**lum**-ba: the Roman term; fas-ee-**ay**-ta: banded). 13½"; gray with purplish and whitish hues, broadly fanned gray tail, yellow legs and black-tipped yellow bill, thin white band across nape (adults only). Call a low, owllike "whoo-whoo." Columbidae (Pigeon family).

Flocks of band-tailed pigeons rove our Westside forests, and timberline and croplands as well, from April through October, then winter far to the south. Here they gorge on our tasty berries (salal, madroño, elder-, salmon- and blackberries, etc.) and, not coincidentally, become tasty and desirable game themselves. A federal ban was placed on hunting them in 1916, perhaps in fear of repeating the passenger pigeon tragedy, but their numbers recovered somewhat and a short season was reinstated. Their habit of laying only one egg per nest kept recovery slow. As many as 50 pairs may nest in one large conifer, with as many again in the next tree over.

Owls

Order Strigiformes, Strigidae (Typical owl family).

Great horned owl, *Bubo virginianus* (bew-bo: the Roman term; vir-jin-ee-**ay**-nus: of Virginia). Males 20", ws 55", females larger; large "ear" tufts or "horns," yellow eyes, and reddish tan facial ruff; white throat patch, otherwise finely barred and mottled gray-brown. Identifiable by long, low hoots (four to eight in series) heard year-round, but oftenest in Jan–Feb breeding season. Nocturnal; widespread and common in forests.

Spotted owl, *Strix occidentalis* (strix: as in "strident," Greek term imitating screech owl; ox-i-den-**tay**-lis: western). Males 16", ws 42", females larger; no "ear" tufts; dark eyes, yellow bill; dull brown, white-spotted above and barred beneath. Strident hoots in series of three to four. Nocturnal; uncommon, in mature dense conifers.

Barred owl, *Strix varia* (**vair**-ia: variegated). Males 17", ws 44", females larger; like spotted owl, but white flecking on back is ± horizontal bars, and on chest is more a white field with vertical brown flecks. Strident hoots in series of six to nine, like a dog yelping at the moon. Nocturnal; in forest.

Northern saw-whet owl, *Aegolius acadicus* (ee-jo-lius: a Greek term for owl; a-**kay**-di-cus: of E Canada). Males 7", ws 17", females larger; reddish brown above, white/brown smeared (adults) or golden (juveniles) beneath; yellow eyes, V-shaped white eyebrows. Rarely-heard call is short, monotonous squeaks, like filing on (whetting) saw teeth. Nocturnal, rarely seen; in conifers.

Northern pygmy owl, *Glaucidium gnoma* (glaw-**sid**-ium: small owl, derived from "gleaming"; **no**-ma: gnome). Males 6"; ws 15" females larger (i.e. barely robin-sized, but clearly owl-shaped); brown with slight pale barring, dark eyelike pair of spots on nape; eyes yellow; longish tail often held cocked; flight swift, darting, audible, with rapid beats—qualities atypical of owl flight. Call like whistling over a bottle (somewhat like a squirrel). Primarily diurnal; ±open forest.

Owls have universally evoked human dread, superstition, and tall tales with their ghostly voices and silent, nocturnal predatory flight. Various parts of their anatomies found their way into talismans and potions both medical and magical. Owl pellets seem almost ready-made talismans, while they provide naturalists with clear information on owl diets and distribution. Pellets are strikingly neat oblong bundles coughed up by owls to rid them of indigestible parts of small prey (and anything else) they swallow. Hard, angular parts are smoothly coated with fur. A spot with many pellets suggests an owl's roost on a limb above. (Hawks make similar but smaller and fewer pellets, eating their prey in smaller pieces and digesting it more completely.)

While all owls are formidable hunters, evolution has specialized them for a broad spectrum of habitats and roles, roughly paralleling the specializations of hawks and eagles. The ferocious little pygmy owl darts about catching insects and also birds up to and greater than its own size. Like some 40% of owl species, it hunts mainly by day. The nocturnal great horned owl can hunt mammals much heavier than itself, such as porcupines and large skunks, as well as almost any sort of creature down to beetles and worms. Where common, cottontails are its chief prey.

The most striking things about owls are their sensory adaptations. They have the broadest skulls of any birds, separating their eyes and their ears as widely as possible to maximize three-dimensionality of vision and directionality of hearing; an asymmetry of their skulls enables their ears to pinpoint prey along the vertical axis as well as the horizontal. In experiments, barn owls locate and catch mice by hearing alone, in absolute darkness. The facial ruff of feathers, plus ear flaps hidden under its outer rim, funnel sound to the highly developed inner ears. (The "ear tufts" or "horns" on top of some species' heads are unconnected with hearing, but serve expressive and decorative functions.) Owls' eyes are the most frontally directed of any bird's; this narrows the field of vision but makes nearly all of it three-dimensional. The bill is squashed down out of the way for the same reason. (Try straining your eyes left, then right, to see the translucent profile of your nose on either side; only that portion—about a third—of your field of view lying between the "two noses" is seen in 3-D, by both eyes.) The owl's adaptive tradeoff—narrower field of view than other birds', but all of it three-dimensional—favors zeroing in on prey, not watching out for predators. To look around, an owl can twist its neck in a split second to anywhere within a 270° arc. The eyeballs, which don't rotate in their sockets (the neck does it all), evolved an optimal light-gathering shape: somewhat conical, like a deep television tube, with a thick powerful lens. The retina has a reflective backing (the kind that makes nocturnal mammals' eyes gleam in your headlights) behind the photoreceptor cells. These are almost all rods (high-sensitivity vision) and few cones (color vision).

Owls' light perception threshold is between a thirty-fifth and a hundredth of ours. They have much sharper acuity for detail than we do, even by day, and a modicum of color perception as well.

Most owls practice utterly silent flight, a magical thing to witness. Their feathers are literally muffled, or damped, with a velvety surface and soft-fringed edges, incurring a tradeoff in efficiency and speed. Their flapping is slow and easy, thanks to low body weight per wing area. (With extra fluffy body plumage, owls are far slimmer and lighter than they look.) Silent flight enables owls in flight to hear the movements of small rodents, while in turn it keeps the sharp-eared prey in the dark over someone coming for dinner. This tempts one to fancy that mice live in utter ignorance of owls except as invisible agents of disappearances from the family.

Saw-whet and spotted owls depend on camouflage rather than

Raptors

Once long ago, the hawks, eagles, owls, and vultures comprised a single order, Raptores, from the Latin for "snatcher." When scientists learned that hawks and owls are not related, but merely resemble each other due to convergent evolution, they put owls in their own order, but "raptor" persevered as a casual term. Recently, New World vultures were moved to the stork order because they, too, may be unrelated birds with convergent similarities. Today the word "raptor" isn't very useful: some people include owls as raptors, and some don't, and who knows about vultures if they are neither predators nor hawk relatives?

The one good thing about it is that it highlights classic convergent evolution. The dramatic convergent traits of raptors are heavy, hooked bills; large, heavily muscled feet; and females larger than males. The connection of the first two to predatory life is clear, but that of the third is puzzling. The female-to-male weight ratio averages as high as 3:2 in northern harriers and can reach 2:1 in golden eagles. The fact that hawks and owls separately evolved larger females, while equal or larger males are almost universal in the other bird orders, argues that the trait must offer a significant advantage to birds of prey. (But: see Sandpiper, p 387.) It does not prevail among mammals, which have larger males with the exception of hyenas (predators), nor among lower animals which, predatory or not, more often have larger females.

Traits that Old World and New World vultures share include featherless heads, weak talons, hooked beaks, and soaring wings.

escape when approached by large creatures; people alert enough to spot them can approach quite close. Spotted and great horned owlets seem to attempt flight from the nest before they are ready; landing on the forest floor, there they must reside until fully fledged. The parents continue to feed and guard them—aggressively in the case of the great horned. If you find an adorable, fluffy owlet on the ground, **back off**.

The spotted owl, though never commonly seen anywhere, became a media star and a pawn in political chess because it needs extensive old-growth forest for habitat. (This is true of many species, but was first proven of this one.) The subspecies will almost certainly die out if all old-growth forests outside of present parks and Wilderness Areas are cut before others mature to replace them. The Endangered Species Act enables environmentalists to use the spotted owl as a legal tool to protect old-growth. The acreage of old-growth needed for the species to survive may even be greater than what now exists. High government officials once replied that, at $300,000 a year per bird in lumber value forgone, the Forest Service cannot afford spotted owls. A wide range of estimates are quoted by partisans of one side or the other as to how many spotted owls survive today, how many are needed for the species to survive, how many hundreds of acres each pair requires, how much use they can make of second-growth as part of their habitat, how widely separated their parcels of old-growth can be, and so on.

While enviros and loggers argued over the spotted owl, its closest relative, the barred owl, upended the playing field in ways we barely grasp yet. Barred owls were virtually unknown in our range until the 1980s, but are spreading with astonishing speed. Both species require forest, so the treeless Great Plains separated eastern from western *Strix* populations, presumably allowing them to evolve into separate species in the first place. It may have been global warming that enabled barred owls to expand their range northward into the boreal forests, enabling a Saskatchewan end-run around the Great Plains by 1912. As of 1996 they were as numerous as spotted owls in the never-logged Mt. Rainier N. P., with a slight tendency to occupy younger, more broken forests. They bear larger broods, are more aggressive, less dependent on old-growth, less picky about their diet, and require less territory per pair. It's hard to name a strong reason why they wouldn't completely replace spotted owls and drive them to extinction, but that's a great unknown: it's not unlikely that spotted owls have some advantage we haven't figured out yet. I would hate to lose them.

Further research may provide better data on these issues and, more important, better establish that *it's not just spotted owls*, but a whole, almost inconceivably intricate ecosystem, and the productivity of the lumber and fishery industries themselves, that are endangered by disregard for the value of extensive old-growth.

Common Nighthawk

Chordeiles minor (cor-**die**-leez: evening dance; minor: lesser, a false name since this is now the larger species of nighthawk). 9", ws 23"; wings long, bent backward, pointed, falconlike; mottled brown/black, with white wing-bar; males also have white throat and a narrow white bar across tail. Marshes and ± open areas, all elevs. Caprimulgidae (Nightjar family). Color p 500.

Nighthawks are most often seen at dusk: no self-respecting nighthawk would be on the ground at that hour, when insects are on the wing. Like swifts and swallows, they prey on insects by flying around with their mouths open. Their flight is wild and erratic like a bat's, but swift like a falcon's—though they aren't really any kind of hawk at all. Males may interrupt their erratic feeding flights with long steep dives that bottom out abruptly with a terrific raspy, farting noise of air rushing through the wing feathers. This is their courtship. The vocal call is a softer, nasal beep repeated while feeding. Nighthawks are our briefest breeding visitors, here only from June through early September. They nest on gravelly ground with very little construction work, and they have an odd style of perching, lying lengthwise along a branch. A population decline related to the general use of insecticides is suspected.

Swifts

Order Apodiformes, Apodidae (Swift family).

Vaux's swift ("Voh's"), *Chaetura vauxi* (key-**too**-ra: hair-thin tail; **voh**-zigh: after William S. Vaux). 4½"; slaty to brownish gray, somewhat paler beneath; wings long, pointed, gently curved; tail short, rounded. Rapid chipping. Widespread. Color p 499.

Black swift, *Cypseloides niger* (sip-sel-**oy**-deez: like *Cypselus*, the Old World swift; **nye**-jer: black). 7"; black all over; wings long, pointed, gently curved; tail slightly forked. Call rarely heard. Subalpine; uncommon (only one breeding site known in OR Cas, a handful in WA, the Newhalem vicinity being best known).

Swifts may not be among the swiftest after all, but they sure are impressive flyers. They do all their hunting, eating, drinking, and apparently even their mating aloft: they stop flying to mate, so they do it in free fall, then safely disengage after several seconds. They often fly 600 miles in a day—and make it look playful, interspersing short glides between spurts of flapping, and creating their famous optical illusion of flapping left and right wings alternately. Unfortunately they do most of this, especially in fair weather, too high up for us to see in detail.

Swifts—"strainers of aerial plankton," as Evelyn Bull so felicitously puts it—can only maintain their high metabolisms on a steady supply of flying insects. Few insects fly during cold weather, so when it's cold and gray, swifts may fly off for a few days, as far as they need to to find sun, or else stay home but go cold and torpid (see page 314). Nestlings remain torpid while Mom and Dad vacation in the sun. People sometimes mistake torpid swifts and nighthawks for dead, and pick them up, only to be startled when they fly off in perfect health as soon as they're warmed up.

Swifts' stiff, spine-tipped tail-feathers help them perch on sheer surfaces. Black swifts nest on cliffs, often behind waterfalls. Vaux's swifts glue their nests to the insides of hollow trees or chimneys. In Southeast Asia, swift nests are gathered for the famous curative delicacy "birdsnest soup," featuring filmy masses like boiled egg whites—actually the special saliva swifts work up for gluing nests. Groups of Vaux's swifts numbering in the thousands congregate at a hollow tree or chimney over a period of a few weeks in fall, building up for massed migration. After sundown, they create a tornado-like vortex as they all fly into the roost. Their numbers are in a severe decline reflecting the shrinking supply of large trees allowed to remain in the forests to become hollow.

Hummingbirds

Order Apodiformes, Trochilidae
(Hummingbird family).

Calliope hummingbird, *Stellula calliope* (**stell**-you-la:
starlet; ca-**lie**-o-pee: a Muse). 2¾"; bronze-green above,
white below with reddish tinges; throat has long deep purple streaks on
adult males, small dark speckles on others. Uncommon; timberline and
E-side. Illustrated.

Rufous hummingbird, *Selasphorus rufus* (se-**lass**-for-us: lightbearer; **roo**-
fus: red). 3½"; males red-brown with iridescent red throat patch, and some
white on belly and green on wings and crown; females and juveniles mostly
green with some reddish near base of tail. Flight produces a deep dragon-
flylike hum. Our common hummingbird.

The redeeming virtue, for me, of the garish reds and yellows the
camping suppliers sell us is their attractiveness to hummingbirds.
My red bootlaces alone draw several hummers a day in the alpine
country in July; they pause only an instant to discover my boots are
no bed of columbine. I can only hope the pleasure they bring me
doesn't cost them much.

Most bright red flowers that bear nectar at the base of tubes
1–2" long are adapted to pollination by hummingbirds. Columbine
and skyrocket are stereotypical, and are certainly beloved of hummers, but various pinkish to red flowers are also important nectar
sources: currants, fireweed, paintbrush, lilies, fool's-huckleberry.
Rufous males may reach Washington as early as late February, and
under these nectar-deprived circumstances they get by gleaning
aphids, hawking midges, and sucking sap from sapsucker wells.

The Rufous ranges farther north than any other hummer—
Valdez, Alaska—and the Calliope migrates farther per gram of flesh
than any other warm-blooded creature; at one tenth of an ounce,
it is the smallest U.S. hummer. Both of these species migrate in a
counterclockwise loop, north along the Pacific, then inland in summer, and south along the Rockies to central Mexico.

The age-old mystery of exactly how birds navigate on long migrations is finally beginning to yield. By day, they orient themselves
by the polarization of sunlight (which they can somehow see) and
use that to recalibrate their sense of the earth's magnetic field
(which they can somehow feel). By night, which is when small birds
tend to migrate, they use both the stars and the magnetic field.

The smallest of all birds, hummers have frantic metabolisms in common with shrews, the smallest mammals.Ounce for ounce, a hummingbird flying has ten times the caloric requirement of a person running—and we don't have to spend all day running, while hummingbirds do spend most of their waking hours flying around in search of nectar for those calories. Daily, they consume up to half their body weight in sugar. Before migrating, they need lots of extra carbohydrates to convert into fats. Their whirring flight, suggestive of a huge dragonfly, does in fact work more like insect flight than like that of other birds, and allows stationary and backward hovering, but no gliding. The wings beat many times faster than other birds' thanks to an extremely shortened wing with long feathers; there's very little mass to flap. Hummers' hyperkinetic days are complemented by torpid (no, not torrid) nights, with temperature and metabolism sharply lowered (see page 314).

Hummingbirds are belligerent toward their own and larger species: calliopes have been seen dive-bombing red-tailed hawks. Harassment of large birds by small ones is called "mobbing." There are records of predators actually being killed by mobs of smaller birds, but single hummingbirds don't seem like a threat. Still, studies have shown that small birds that mob—even when it's two or three little birds harassing a predator twenty times their size—are preyed upon less than those that don't. Possibly the predator conserves energy by saving its killer moves for unwary prey.

Rufous hummingbirds' territoriality seems to concern food rather than sex. (Hummers don't pair up anyway, but mate freely.) Both sexes stake out their patch of the nectar resource even during two-week refueling stops during migration, and defend it with the same tall elliptical flights they use for courtship: a courting rufous male swoops around and around in an ellipse hundreds of feet high, at the lowest point passing at high speed only inches from the demure object of his attentions, simultaneously eliciting a shrieking noise from his wings. Males flash their "gorgets" (iridescent, erectile throat patches) both in courtship and in aggression.

---

*The smaller the warm-blooded body, the more energy is required to keep it warm. Heat is produced in proportion to size (i.e., volume) but is dissipated into the air in proportion to surface area. Reducing the length and width of a body by half, for example, divides its surface area by four (2×2) and its volume by eight ($2 \times 2 \times 2$), thus doubling the rate of heat loss.

Belted Kingfisher

Ceryle alcyon (**ser**-i-lee **al**-see-on: two Greek terms for kingfishers). 12"; head looks oversized because of large bill and extensive crest of feathers; blue-gray with white neck and underparts and (females only) reddish breast band. Call a long, peculiar rattle. Along streams, year-round. Alcedinidae (Kingfisher family).

The Greeks had a myth that the Halcyon, a kind of bird we presume was a kingfisher, floated its nest on the waves of the sea while incubating and hatching the young. Hence "halcyon days" are a fortuitous respite from the storms of life.

Our kingfishers, in real life, raise their young amid a heap of regurgitated fish bones at the end of a hole in a mud bank. Is "nest" too sweet a term for such debris? They look for their prey—fish, crayfish, waterbugs and larvae—from a perch over a stream or occasionally a lake. (They can also hunt from a hover where branches are in short supply, as is rarely the case on our streams.) After diving and catching a fish, they often return to thrash it to death against their branch before swallowing it headfirst. Fishermen have long resented kingfishers' success rate, but statistically the birds are unlikely to reduce trout numbers significantly. The kingfisher population has plummeted during the advance of civilization; there was once a pair of kingfishers for virtually every creek in the U.S.

Woodpeckers

Order Piciformes, family Picidae.

Pileated woodpecker, *Dryocopus pileatus* (dry-**oc**-o-pus: tree sword; pie-lee-**ay**-tus: crested). 15"; all black exc bright red, large, pointed crest, black/white-streaked head with (males only) red moustache, and white underwing markings visible only in flight; drumming very loud, slow, irregular; call a loud rattling shriek with a slight initial rise in pitch. Deep forest with many standing dead trees or snags. Illustrated at right.

Northern flicker, *Colaptes auratus* (co-**lap**-teez: pecker; aw-**ray**-tus: golden). 11"; gray-brown with black-spotted paler belly, black-barred back, black "bib," and reddish crown, moustache (males only) and underside of wings and tail. Varied calls include a flat-pitched rattle. Semiopen habitats. Color p 500.

Hairy woodpecker, *Picoides villosus* (pic-**oy**-deez: like genus *Pica*; vil-**oh**-sus: woolly). 7½"; black and white exc (males only) a small red patch on peak of head; wings strongly barred. Widespread.

Downy woodpecker, *Picoides pubescens* (pew-**bes**-enz: fuzzy). 5¾"; like Hairy only smaller. Less common: restricted to lowlands with some deciduous trees. Color p 499.

White-headed woodpecker, *Picoides albolarvatus* (al-bo-lar-**vay**-tus: white mask). 7¾"; black all over exc white head, throat, and patches near tip of wings; male has small red patch on nape. Ponderosa pine forest, where locally common though inconspicuous; walks head-down or sideways on tree trunks.

Woodpeckers are the one kind of non-songbird that often flocks with songbirds (Passeriformes). Woodpeckers resemble songbirds, but differ in several specialized traits. Most have two front and two rear toes, rather than the 3-and-1 arrangement of perching-bird toes. Strong sharp claws on 2-and-2-toed feet, plus short stiff tail feathers, give them the grip and the bracing they need for hammering the full force of their bodies into a tree. Naturally, they also have adamantine chisel-like beaks, and thick shock-absorbing skulls to prevent boxers' dementia. Before diving into work on a tree, they listen for the minute rustlings of their insect prey boring around under the bark. Insect larvae and adults provide the bulk of their diets, seeds and berries the rest. Females are smaller and thinner-billed than males. They excavate less than males, foraging often by prying bark up, and so exploit a slightly different resource than their mates. For snatching grubs out of their tunnels, the woodpecker has a barb-tipped tongue much longer than its head. The tongue shoots out and then pulls back into a tiny tubular cavity looping around the circumference of the skull.

Though jackhammering for food is the woodpecker norm, and was likely the first task woodpecking evolved for, not all woodpeckers forage that way. The flicker pecks for insects in the soil or catches them in midair, and the white-headed relies heavily on pine seeds, also foraging for insects by prying the bark.

But all woodpeckers (or at least all of these woodpeckers) do use woodpecking for two other vital tasks. First, they chop large squarish holes for their nests, padding them with a few of the chips. Such nests are dry and easy to defend, allowing prolonged rearing—advantages that have led several other species to depend on abandoned woodpecker holes for their nests. Second, they drum—the classic woodpecker drumroll—on resonant trees to assert territory or to point out a nest site to a prospective mate. (When you hear slower, irregular tapping on trees, that's either foraging or spousal communication.) Not that either sex lacks a voice—flickers vocalize diversely and often; downies and white-headeds rarely. The pileated, our largest woodpecker, has an especially strident and impressive call like a harsh, maniacal laugh, which it seems to use when disturbed—such as whenever you or I come around. Once you know the pileated's "laugh" you'll know, when you hear it, to pause and look for a glimpse of one of our flashiest birds.

Pileateds eat ants almost exclusively, and often chop many inches deep into rotten wood to dig out carpenter ant nests. Each bird requires lots of dead trees, so the species dwindled as old-growth forests vanished from most of the continent. It was also hunted. More recently it has recovered, and is quite willing to brave urban woods if they have enough snags. A few pileateds have become pests, chopping away at house and phone-pole timbers.

Red-Breasted Sapsucker

Sphyrapicus ruber*(sfie-ra-**pie**-cus: hammer woodpecker; **roo**-ber: red). 7¾"; sexes alike; entire head and breast has a scarlet overlay; white mustache extends from top of bill ± to below eye; back and wings black and white; belly pale, ± yellow-tinged. Taps in a syncopated rhythm, but does not jackhammer, on trees. Calls are catlike mews and "cherrrrs." Forests including some hardwoods, mainly W-side; year-round, moving lower in winter. Picidae (Woodpecker family).

Neat horizontal rings of ¼" holes drilled through tree bark are the work of this deviant woodpecker, which drills these "wells," leaves, and comes back another day. Time allows sap not only to flow, but also sometimes to ferment, and certainly to go to work as bait for adult insects, which figure even more than sap in the sapsucker's diet. Butterflies and moths in experiments prefer their foods fermented, and inebriated behavior has been observed in butterflies and sapsuckers alike.

Damage to the bark is insufficient to kill the tree by girdling it,

---

* Recently separated from the Yellow-bellied Sapsucker, *S. varius*, and the Red-naped Sapsucker, *S. nuchalis* (which is fairly common on the Cas E slope). The three hybridize where ranges overlap.

but any breaching of the bark increases the odds for fungal diseases to invade. On balance, though, sapsuckers are good for trees, because they're leading predators of spruce budworm moths, which are major pests. They can nab insects in midair, glean ants from bark crevices, and vary their diets with berries.

Other birds also dine at these sap wells, which are especially critical to the rufous hummingbird when it finds itself too early, during northward migration, for adequate nectar supplies.

Olive-sided Flycatcher

Contopus cooperi * (**cont**-o-pus: short foot; **coo**-per-eye: after Jas. or Wm. Cooper). 6¼"; olive-gray with pearly white smear down throat and breast; white downy tufts on lower back visible esp in flight. Order Passeriformes, Tyrannidae.

The olive-sided's song, usually asserted from some conifer pinnacle, is always a treat: it has been written down as "THREE cheers," "Quick!...FREE beer," or "Tuck...THREE bears." These flycatchers summer throughout our forests, clearcuts, and timberlines. They eat winged insects, spotting individuals from their perch and darting out to snatch them. In contrast to the constantly flying grab-bag method of swifts and swallows, which nets small insects, flycatchers eat medium-sized insects. They are reportedly fond of bees.

Pacific Slope Flycatcher

Empidonax difficilis † (em-**pid**-o-nax: gnat king; dif-**iss**-il-iss: difficult). 5"; olive brown above with 2 whitish wing-bars; pale yellowish olive beneath; white eye-ring, two-toned bill. Abundant but inconspicuous; usually in deciduous understory. Tyrannidae (Tyrant flycatcher family). Color p 501.

The specific name *difficilis* means that it's next to impossible to identify *Empidonax* birds in the bush. They are hard to see, staying camouflaged among foliage. This one has a fairly recognizable call, though: a very high, rising "pseeeet." The song is similar to the call, but much repeated, in threes, with slight variations.

---

* The 7th *Checklist* changed this species from *borealis* to *cooperi* after someone found that *cooperi* was originally published three months earlier.

† The 7th *Checklist* split *difficilis*, formerly the Western Flycatcher, into 2 spp.

Vireos

Hutton's vireo, *Vireo huttoni* (veer-ee-oh: green; **hut**-un-eye: after William Hutton). 4"; greenish-gray above with two white wing-bars, slight eye-ring and white area in front of eye; underside pale olive; two-note call repeated metronomically, the second note higher and accented. Year-round, W-side part-deciduous forest. Vireonidae (Vireo family).

Cassin's vireo, *V. cassinii** (cas-**in**-ee-eye: after John Cassin). 4¾"; greenish gray above; heavy white eye-ring and line in front of eye; flanks yellowish, belly white. Varied, low 2–3-note phrases at 2–4-second intervals, second note accented. Forest understory, in summer. Color p 500.

Female and male vireos take turns warming the eggs, and won't leave them even if approached and handled; they're oddly sluggish birds. The nest is a small cup of grasses lined with lichens, moss, or feathers, often decorated outside with bark, petals or catkins held on with spiderwebbing. It dangles from a fork in horizontal branches not too high up in a conifer.

Swallows

Order Passeriformes, family Hirundinidae.

Violet-green swallow, *Tachycineta thalassina* (tacky-sin-ee-ta: fast moving; tha-**lass**-in-a: sea green). 4¾"; dark with green/violet iridescence above; white below, extending around eyes and up sides of rump to show as two white spots when seen from above; wings backswept and pointed, tail shallowly forked. Various high tweets. Open areas; in flocks; spring and summer.

Tree swallow, *T. bicolor* (by-color: 2-colored). 5"; iridescent blue-black above, white below (not extending above eye or rump); otherwise like violet-green swallow. Color p 501.

Cliff swallow, *Petrochelidon pyrrhonota*† (pet-ro-**kel**-id-on: rock swallow; per-o-**no**-ta: red back). 5"; blackish wings and tail, whitish below, with cinnamon red cheeks and paler rust-red rump and forehead; wings backswept and pointed, tail square to barely notched.

A swallow's flight is graceful, slick, and fast, though perhaps less swift than a swift's. A swallow's swallow, or more precisely its gape, is striking. The wide, weak jaws are held open almost 180° while the swallow knifes back and forth through the air intercepting insects. People who rise before daylight may hear a twittering flock of

---

* In 1998 the Solitary Vireo was split into three species, one of them Cassin's.
† *Pyrrhonota* was lumped into *Hirundo* in 1983, then reseparated in 1998.

violet-green swallows already up and feeding. I guess this tells us that small flying insects also get up early, and that swallows don't hunt by eyesight. (They intercept more or less randomly once they've located a concentration of prey.)

Swallows generally nest in large colonies. Cliff swallows build striking gourd-shaped mud nests on cliffs or under bridges or eaves. *Tachycineta* swallows use ready-made crevices and tree holes.

Steller's Jay

Cyanocitta stelleri (sigh-an-o-sit-a: blue jay; **stell**-er-eye: after Georg Steller, below). 11"; deep ultramarine blue with ± black shoulders and dramatically crested head. Widespread near conifers. Corvidae (Crow family).

Birds of North America describes the following repertoire of vocalizations documented by students of the Steller's jay: creak; squawk; growl; rattle; song; Ut; Ow; Wah; Wek; Aap; Tjar; Tee-ar; gutteral notes; and mimicry. Mimicry includes an uncanny imitation of a red-tailed hawk's scream. This presumably deceives other birds into clearing out while the jay feeds, but perhaps it sometimes warns of an actual hawk. Jays and crows are the birds most often seen harassing or "mobbing" birds of prey—a defense of smaller birds against larger ones (see page 395). This jay is omnivorous, smart, and aggressive—traits that run in the crow family. It will commonly rob the caches of its cousin, Clark's nutcracker.

The smaller, paler Blue Jay proper, *C. cristata*, is a rare visitor here from the East. Westerners sometimes say "blue jay" either for Steller's or for the western scrub jay, *Aphelocoma californica*, a

---

Georg Steller was the first European naturalist-explorer on northeast Pacific shores. A German, he crossed Siberia to accompany Danish Captain Vitus Bering on a Russian ship built and launched from Kamchatka in 1741. They were just east of Cordova, Alaska when they turned around late that year, and they didn't quite make it back to Kamchatka. Marooned for a terrible scurvy-ridden winter on small, rocky Bering Island, the Captain and many of the crew died. Steller survived, but took to drink and died in Siberia without ever reaching Europe again.

---

crestless jay, blue above and white beneath, seen increasingly on dry slopes in and near the Willamette Valley.

Clark's Nutcracker

Nucifraga columbiana (new-**sif**-ra-ga: nut breaker; co-lum-be-**ay**-na: of the Columbia river). 11"; pale gray (incl crown and back) with white-marked black wings and tail (white outer tail-feathers and rear wing-patch); long thin grayish bill. Call a harsh "kraaa, kraaa." Mostly in subalpine habitats with whitebark or lodgepole pines. Order Passeriformes, Corvidae (Crow family).

Flashy black/white wings and tail distinguish Clark's nutcracker from the more numerous gray jay. Like the jay, the nutcracker has been known as the "camp-robber," but mainly in California where there are none of the nervy jays that better deserve the name.

Clark's nutcrackers and whitebark pines (page 48) provide a charming example of coevolution. While many conifers hide or protect their seeds from seed-eaters as long as possible, the whitebark pine exposes them early and conspicuously, and makes them all the more tempting with extra oils and proteins. It also fails to provide them with membranous wings such as most pine seeds have to help the wind carry them. Clark's nutcracker obliges by collecting the seeds compulsively, selecting the high-quality ones (most nutritious and most viable), eating some on the spot and burying all the rest, a few at a time, for retrieval in winter.

Though canny enough to remember cache locations for up to nine months, the birds are so industrious that they store two or three times as many as they can consume. The remainder have thus been planted, often many miles from their source—a great advantage to the pines, especially in recolonizing large severe burns, or in recovering range given up during the Ice Age. The strong-flying nutcrackers have a typical foraging range of 14 miles from their caches, and can carry over 150 whitebark pine seeds in sublingual pouches that bulge conspicuously at the throat. Lodgepole pine seeds are eaten, too. Poor pine seed crop years cause irruptions of nutcrackers into far-flung lowlands in search of substitute fare, and the decline in whitebark pines due to white pine blister rust has caused a great decline in the number of nutcrackers.

Gray Jay

Perisoreus canadensis (pair-i-**sor**-ee-us: "I-heap-up"). Also
Canada jay, **camp-robber**, **whiskey-jack**. 10"; fluffy pale
gray with dark brownish gray wings, tail, rump
and (variably) nape and crown; short, ±
black bill; juveniles all dark gray exc pale
cheek-streak. Calls a whistled "Whee-oh,"
and various others. Deep forest and
timberline, often with spruces. Order
Passeriformes, Corvidae (Crow family).

Like their close relatives the crows, jays seem coarse and vulgar but
are intelligent, versatile and successful. Their voices are harsh and
noisy, but capable of extreme variety and accurate mimicry of other
birds. Equally versatile in feeding, ours eat mainly conifer seeds,
berries and insects, but also relish meat when they can scrounge
some up or kill a small bird or rodent. Gray jays, or "camp-
robbers," were known for thronging around logging-camp mess
halls; a trapper would sometimes find them nipping at a carcass
while he was still skinning it. You will find them just as interested
in your lunch, and bold enough to snatch proffered food from your
fingertips. Their nonchalance reminds skiers that winter here is
perfectly livable for the well-adapted. Gray jays and Clark's nutcrackers are so comfortable in the cold that they nest and incubate
their young with plenty of snow still on the ground—or even on
their heads. To store food for winter, the jays glue little seed bundles with sticky saliva, and leave them in bark crevices or foliage.

American Crow

Corvus brachyrhynchos (**cor**-vus: raven; brak-i-**rink**-os: short beak). 17";
black with blue-purple-green iridescence; tail squared-off; rarely glides more
than 2–3 seconds at a time. Lowlands. Corvidae (Crow family).

Most of the crowlike birds you see in our mountain wilderness are
ravens; crows characteristically inhabit farmlands, and avoid both
deep forest and cliffy terrain. You are most likely to see them here
along lowland streams and meadows, or in part-deciduous forest.
They scavenge carrion, garbage, fruit, snails, grubs, insects, frogs,
and eggs and nestlings from birds' nests. Species as large as ducks,
gulls, and falcons may be victims, and some songbirds count crows
among their major enemies.

Common Raven

Corvus corax (**cor**-vus: the Roman term, from **cor**-ax: the Greek term, imitating raven's voice). 21", ws 48"; black with purple-green iridescence, and shaggy grayish ruff at throat; bill heavy; tail long, flared then tapered; alternates periods of flapping and flat-winged soaring. Call a throaty croak. Timberlines (subalpine and E-side). Corvidae (Crow family).

You can tell Raven from little sibling Crow by Raven's greater size, heavier bill, ruffed throat, more prolonged soaring, and by its voice: an outrageously hoarse guttural croak rather than a nasal "caw." At timberline in our mountains and near the Eastside steppes you are more likely to see ravens. Their courtship flights in spring are a sight to remember: they do barrel rolls or chaotic tumbles while plummeting, then swoop, hang motionless, all the while exercising their vocabularies. The ensuing family group — four or five young are typically flying by June — often stays together through the following winter, and may flock with other families. Ravens mate for life (but see page 412 before you get sentimental) and live as long as thirty years. The nest is high, solid, and cozy, perhaps lined with deer hair, but filthy and smelly by our standards, and often flea-ridden. Ravens eat anything crows eat and then some; by grouping up they can take live prey as large as hares.

Ravens were once abundant throughout the West, but westward settlement pushed them back to remote deserts and mountains. Just as the wolf was more vulnerable than the smaller coyote, the raven was more vulnerable than the crow. In raven's case there were especially feeble grounds for seeing a conflict with agriculture.

Ravens were accepted members of tribal life in Northwest Coast villages. Raven was seen as at once a trickster and a powerful, aggressive, chiefly figure — much the equivalent of Coyote among intermountain tribes. He was a Creator in origin myths. His croaks were prophetic, and a person who could interpret them would become a great seer. To inculcate prophetic powers in a chosen newborn, the Kwakiutl would feed its afterbirth to the ravens. A mythic view of ravens and crows as powerful, knowing, and somewhat sinister is virtually universal worldwide. French peasants thought that bad priests became ravens, and bad nuns, crows.

The raven is the largest of all Perching birds* (Passeriformes). They are the most recently evolved avian order, with by far the greatest number of species, which indicates success and rapid evolution. The evolution of seed plants was accompanied by the specialization of seed eaters—songbirds and rodents, mainly—and a wave of predators specializing in eating seed-eaters. The raven rides the crest of both waves: it eats rodents, nestlings, and eggs, as well as seeds. By some accounts it is the most advanced bird.

Bernd Heinrich, who writes so interestingly about bumblebees, has also taken up ravens. He casts doubt on one well-known anecdote that's often said to prove raven intelligence—their teaming up to heist meat from coyotes—but believes (as do many native tribes) that ravens will lead a wolf or a human hunter to prey, on the odds that they will end up with the scraps. Heinrich devises ingenious tests of raven intelligence. For example, he found that they remember where they cached seeds under snow, rather than smelling them out; moreover, they keep a corner of their eye open for where other ravens are caching seeds, and try to rob those caches first. To avoid being robbed, they fly much farther before caching when other ravens are within view.

Chickadees

Poecile spp.[†] (**pee**-sil-ee: many-colored). Order Passeriformes, Paridae (Chickadee family).

Mountain chickadee, *P. gambeli* (**gam**-bel-eye: after William Gambel). 4¼"; black crown, eye-streak and throat; white eyebrow and cheeks, grayish belly, gray-brown upperparts. Subalpine and E Cas slope.

Black-capped chickadee, *P. atricapillus* (ay-tri-ca-**pill**-us: black cap). 4½"; black crown and throat, white cheeks; grayish belly, gray-brown upper parts. Lower thickets, streamsides.

---

* Perching birds are also known as "songbirds." Both perching and singing are characteristic of this order but are also done, depending on how you define them, by many other birds as well. The advantage of the more cumbersome term "perching bird" is that it refers to an easily defined anatomical structure, the foot with one long rear toe opposing three front toes.

[†] The Seventh *Checklist* took New World chickadees out of genus *Parus*, and gave them their own genus.

Chestnut-backed chickadee, *P. rufescens* (roo-fes-enz: reddish). 4¼"; black crown and throat, white cheeks and belly, rich red-brown back and sides. Abundant year-round in W-side forests.

The various chickadees, gleaners of caterpillars and other insects from the branches, reside here year-round, nesting in fur-lined holes dug rather low in tree trunks either by woodpeckers or by themselves, in soft punky wood. They tend to partition the habitat vertically—chestnut-backed feeding in the canopy, black-capped in the shrubs. They also eat seeds to varying degrees, and store seeds for winter. "Chick-a dee-dee-dee" transcribes the most characteristic of their calls; their song (mountain and black-capped only) is more relaxed, on two notes descending. Chickadees seem to epitomize the chipper dispositions people want to see in songbirds, and they let us see it, being tamer than most.

Recycling for Bird Brains

To the long list of remarkable weight-saving adaptations in birds, recent studies of chickadees add the ability to grow new brain cells. You may have heard that you lose brain cells throughout adulthood (especially during episodes of overindulgence) but never grow new ones. Now, the discovery of newly-formed neurons in chickadees foreshadowed a similar discovery in humans. In both cases, the location is the hippocampus, a part of the brain involved with learning and memory.

Chickadees were found to grow new neurons in the hippocampus in a big burst each fall, when they store seeds in caches they will have to find again through winter; an even bigger hippocampal growth spurt hits juveniles when they disperse from their natal territory, and have to learn the ins and outs of the new environment they will inhabit for the rest of their lives. But their number of hippocampal cells does not grow through life, as it does in small mammals. The hypothesis is that each hippocampal neuron can store only one memory; and that birds recycle neurons whose memories are no longer needed (like a RAM Cache). In a tiny flying animal, a brain big enough for a lifetime of memories might never get off the ground.

Male warblers recognize the song of each neighbor male. As long as each singer is known to the other, and stays on his own territory, both are spared a fight. They remember each other's songs from year to year, as they return from Central America to reclaim their old haunts.

Brown Creeper

Certhia americana (**serth**-ia: the Greek term). 4¾"; mottled brown above, white beneath; long downcurved bill. Call a single very high, soft sibilant note. On tree trunks, year-round, widespread and common but very inconspicuous. Order Passeriformes, Certhiidae (Creeper family). Color p 502.

You probably won't see a brown creeper unless you happen to catch its faint, high call, and then patiently let your eyes scour nearby bark. (Many of us are literally deaf to it's call, if our hearing is high-frequency-challenged—a defect associated with males and with rock and roll.) This well camouflaged full-time bark dweller gleans its insect prey from bark crevices, and nests behind loose bark. In contrast to nuthatches, which usually walk down tree trunks, the creeper spirals up them, propping itself with stiff tail feathers like a woodpecker's. Crevices approached from above and below would present different types of prey, putting creepers and nuthatches in different ecological niches.

Nuthatches

Sitta spp. (**sit**-a: the Roman term). Order Passeriformes, Sittidae (Nuthatch family).

Red-breasted nuthatch, *S. canadensis*. 4"; blue-gray above, pale reddish below, with white throat and eyebrow, black (males) or dark gray crown and eye-streak. Widespread in forest, esp W-side. Illustrated at left, and color p 501.

White-breasted nuthatch, *S. carolinensis* (carol-in-**en**-sis: of the Carolinas). 5"; blue-gray above, white below (may have a little red under tail), with black (males) or gray crown, but all-white face. Subalpine and E-side pine (or esp oak) woodland.

Nuthatches are known for walking headfirst down tree trunks, apparently finding that way just as rightside up as the other. They glean insects from the bark, and eat seeds in fall through spring. They nest in dead snags, quite inconspicuous but identifiable by their odd habit of smearing pitch around their hole. Even in deep wilderness they aren't shy, and draw our attention with their penetrating little call, a tinny "ank" or "nyank." They are year-round residents, but may move to different elevations or subregions in response to poor cone crops or other conditions.

Winter Wren

Troglodytes troglodytes (tra-**glod**-i-teez: cave dweller, a misleading name). 3¼"; finely barred reddish-brown all over; tail rounded, very short, often (as in all wrens) held upturned at 90° to line of back. Near the ground in forest with dense herb or low shrub layer; year-round. Order Passeriformes, Troglodytidae (Wren family).

The winter wren is conspicuous mainly by its song, a prolonged, varied, often-repeated, virtuoso sequence of high trills and chatters. It moves in a darting, mouselike manner, eats insects, maintains a low profile among the brush, and goes to great lengths to keep its nest a secret. Several extra nests are often built just as decoys, and the real occupied nest has a decoy entrance, much larger than the real entrance but strictly dead-end. Real and decoy nests are camouflaged to boot.

In Europe, this species (the only native wren) has long been familiar around cities and towns, whereas on this continent it favors undisturbed habitat. Apparently, adaptation to civilization is possible even for a species that has resisted it for dozens of generations.

Kinglets

Regulus spp.* (**reg**-you-lus: small king). Regulidae (Kinglet family).

Golden-crowned kinglet, *R. satrapa* (sat-ra-pa: ruler). 3½"; gray-green above, whitish below, with 2 white wing-bars; central yellow (female) or orange (male) stripe on head is flanked by black and then white stripes at eyebrow. Very high, lisping "chee, chee" call. Widespread, year-round, in conifer canopy. Illustrated at left.

Ruby-crowned kinglet, *R. calendula* (ca-**lend**-you-la: larklet). 3¾"; gray-green above, whitish below, with white eye-ring and two white wing-bars; rarely-visible scarlet spot on crown is displayed only by excited males, leaving the species almost indistinguishable from Hutton's vireo. Scolding "jit-it" calls, and long, variable song of chatters, warbles, and rising triplets. Mainly winter and spring, in brush and lower canopy of W-side clearings.

Constant movement—wings twitching even when perched—characterizes kinglets. They catch insects, sometimes in flight but mostly on bark and foliage, where their tiny size enables them to forage on twigs too weak to support other gleaning birds. Gleaning is a full-time job; insects are a less concentrated energy source than seeds, and occur less predictably. Kinglets supplement with some seeds. Traveling in flocks seems to help gleaners locate insect populations. Mixed flocks of golden-crowned kinglets, chickadees and woodpeckers are often seen in winter. Flocking birds with small bodies that stay through winter here are thought to stay warm some nights by huddling together as big balls of birds.

DNA studies suggest the two kinglets are more distantly related than most congeneric bird pairs; there may be a genus split and/or a family switch in their future.

American Dipper

Cinclus mexicanus (sink-lus: the Greek term). Also **water ouzel**. 5¾"; slate gray all over, scarcely paler beneath, often with white eye-ring; tail short; feet yellow. In or very close to cold mtn streams. Order Passeriformes, Cinclidae (Dipper family). Color p 500.

It's no wonder that dippers make such an impression on campers throughout America's Western mountains, considering how much trouble campers have keeping warm. Winter and summer, snow, rain, or shine, dippers spend most of their time plunging in and out of frigid, frothing torrents, plucking out invisible objects—actually aquatic insects such as dragonfly and caddis fly larvae, and sometimes tiny fish. Somehow they walk on the bottom, gripping with their big feet. They can also swim with their wings, quickly reverting to flight if they get swept out of control downstream. They can dive to considerable depths in mountain lakes, and occasionally they forage on snowfields. They show little interest in drying off. Even in flight they are usually in the spray zone over a stream, and they often nest behind waterfalls. In August they have a flightless molt period when swimming becomes their only escape from predators. They never really get soaked to the skin, thanks to extremely dense body plumage and extra glands to keep it well oiled.

No, "dipper" implies no shyness toward water, not in these birds. The name refers to their odd, jerky genuflections repeated as often as once a second while standing, and accompanied by blinking of their flashy white eyelids. Their call, "dipit dipit," is forceful enough to carry over the din of the creek. Even in midwinter they occasionally break into song. Both sexes are virtuosi, with long, loud, lyrical, bell-like, and extremely varied songs.

Birds

Bluebirds

Sialia spp. (sigh-**ay**-lia: the Greek term). Turdidae (Thrush family).

Mountain bluebird, *S. currucoides* (cue-roo-**coy**-deez: warbler-like). 6";
summer males turquoise above, shading through pale blue beneath to
whitish on throat; females and winter males gray-brown with varying
amounts of blue on tail, rump, and wings. Soft warbling song at dawn;
"phew" call. Alp/subalpine in summer, and in OR pine forests year-round.
Color p 502.

Western bluebird, *S. mexicana.* 5½"; summer males deep blue above, rich
red-brown breast and backband, whitish belly; females similar but much
duller, with dark bluish-gray head. Single, soft "phew" calls. Semiopen lowlands; uncommon.

Bluebirds drop on insect prey from a low hover or perch. In fall
they fatten up on berries. They nest in woodpecker holes; the severe
decline of the Western bluebird is partly due to competition for
these holes from introduced sparrows, starlings, etc. The mountain
bluebird, meanwhile, prospers from clearcutting, ranching, and
nestbox construction.

Townsend's Solitaire

Myadestes townsendi (my-a-**des**-teez: fly eater; **town**-send-eye: after J. K.
Townsend, p 313). 6¾"; gray with white eye-ring; dark tail has white feathers on sides (like the more abundant junco, p 415; solitaire is longer, slenderer, more upright, more arboreal); dark wings have buff patches, visible
underneath in flight. Call a high, ringing "eep"; song a long melodious
warble heard at any season. Conifer forest and timberline. Order Passeriformes, Turdidae (Thrush family). Color p 500.

The solitaire returns to the mountains early, searching the first
snow-free areas for a nesting cavity in a stump or rotting log. It likes
the edges of clearings, and seems to be on the increase in the Cascades as this habitat type proliferates in the form of patch clearcuts.
After the breeding season it may gather in large flocks, belying its
name. Most populations seek out juniper woodlands east of the
Cascades for winter, and subsist almost exclusively on juniper
berries; a few individuals manage on the West side, finding good
supplies of some other winter-persistent berry. They defend their
berry territories with fierce attacks on intruders of various species.
In summer they mainly eat insects.

Varied Thrush

Ixoreus naevius (ix-**or**-ius: mistletoe mountain, referring to food and habitat; **neev**-ius: spotted). 8"; breast, throat, eyebrow and wing-bars rich rusty-orange (males) or yellow-buff (female), contrasting with slate-gray breastband, cheeks, crown, back, etc; whitish belly; perches or walks with body more horizontal than the similar robin. W-side forest. Turdidae (Thrush family).

The varied thrush sings a single note with odd, rough overtones, like two slightly dissonant notes at once; after several seconds' rest, it sings another tone, similar but higher or lower by some irrational interval. Prolonged early or late in the day, in deep forest or fog, this minimal music acquires powers of enchantment over people.

The thrush itself is close cousin to a robin, living mainly on insects and berries. The American robin, *Turdus migratorius*, is also common in our mountains; it is less shy and less flashy, lacking the white wingbars or the gray breastband.

Varied thrushes migrate into the mountains in early spring, and back to the lowlands in fall. Foraging on the ground, they can't last through many days of snow cover.

Swainson's Thrush and Hermit Thrush

Catharus spp. (**cath**-a-rus: pure). 6¼"; gray-brown above; pale eye-ring; belly white, breast spotted. Turdidae (Thrush family).

Swainson's thrush, *C. ustulatus* (ust-you-**lay**-tus: singed). Back and head ± reddish; tail less so. Various partly open lowland habitats; winters in Central America. Illustrated at left.

Hermit thrush, *C. guttatus* (ga-**tay**-tus: spotted). Tail, but not back, is rusty red; tail is "nervously" raised and lowered every few seconds, while wings may twitch. Mainly subalpine; winters in W-side lowlands. Color p 501.

Thrushes of this genus have some of the most lyrical and virtuosic of songs. Hermit prefaces a fast phrase with a single long clear note, then performs variations at different pitches. Swainson's begins with a slow phrase of two to four notes, then spirals upward, flute-like, and also may repeat at different pitches. Both species forage on the ground for earthworms, insects, and berries.

Warblers

Yellow-rumped warbler, *Dendroica coronata* (den-**droy**-ca: tree house; cor-o-**nay**-ta: crowned). Includes **Audubon's** and **myrtle warblers**. 4¾"; yellow in 5 small patches (mere tinges on females): crown, rump, throat, sides; mostly gray/black (breeding males) to soft gray-brown (others), with white eye-ring and one ± vague wing bar. Song a long trill. Widespread. Color p 501.

Townsend's warbler, *D. townsendi* (**town**-send-eye: after J. K. Townsend, p 310). 4¼"; whitish beneath, greenish gray above, with two white wing-bars; crown black ; sides of face (exc dark cheek patch) and breast bright yellow. Song a series of wheezes rising to 1–2 clear notes. Mid-elev to high forest.

Hermit warbler, *D. occidentalis* (ox-i-den-**tay**-lis: western). 4¼"; bright yellow over almost entire head; black throat bib on breeding males; very white beneath, ± greenish gray above with two white wing bars. Song of 5–7 slurred notes, wheezy but bright. Low to mid-elev forest. Illustrated at right.

MacGillivray's warbler, *Oporornis tolmiei* (op-or-**or**-nis: autumn bird; **tole**-me-eye: after William Tolmie, p 197). 4½"; yellow beneath, grayish olive above; solid gray "hood" (head and throat) with incomplete white eye-ring. Short song of about three rising and two falling notes. All elevs, typically in shrubs growing in forest gaps. Parulidae (Wood Warbler family).

Extra-Pair Goings-On

> *"Birds don't do it,*
> *bees don't do it,*
> *WE are the only ones*
> *that fall in love."*

Sly and Robbie, in the above lyric, got it more nearly right than Frank Sinatra's original version. The DNA police have been looking into avian paternity, and they've demolished the faithful chirping couples stereotype which inspired centuries of bad verse. In many bird species a male may help build the nest, sit on the eggs, defend the territory, and/or bring food to the young, but that species' "social monogamy" rating bears little correlation with that male's likelihood of being the sire of all the young in that nest. There's a whole lot going on on the sly.

Even more interesting than the rate of EPCs (extra-pair copulations) is the diversity of patterns among closely related species, or even between populations of the same species. For example, the extant study of cliff swallows found that 2% of fertilizations were extra-pair, whereas the study of tree swallows found 44%. The EPC picture in swallow

Most sparrow-sized birds around here with some yellow on them are some kind of warbler. This large family is known for long winter migrations to the tropics and for distinctive (but not always warbling) songs. Most warblers also have "chip chip" calls. Birders concentrate on learning the songs, since there are so many kinds of warblers and they all tend to keep themselves inconspicuous among foliage. Most are gleaners of insects; many also hawk at larger insects; some vary their diets with fruits and seeds.

The closely related Townsend's and hermit warblers have distinct ranges, and hybridize where they meet. Though the hermit is by far the commonest warbler in many Cascade forests, Townsend's apparently out-competes it, and is expanding. The current front lines, or hybrid zones, are in the southern WA Cascades and the central OR Cascades, with Townsend's advancing southwestward from the North Cascades and from the Ochocos.

---

colonies is further complicated by a great deal of "intraspecific brood parasitism," in which a female waits for a neighboring nest to be momentarily unattended, and then slips in and lays an egg. Her victims will feed her young along with their own. This gets worse: a male slips into an unattended nest and rolls an egg out, to its doom, perhaps to make room for his mate to lay an egg there, or perhaps to keep his female neighbor receptive to his seductions. Either way, it's his genes.

Diverse strategies are being pursued here, and there are ongoing academic imbroglios—replete with anthropomorphic terms like "divorce," "harem," and "cuckold"—over how to interpret them. There are male strategies and female strategies, but the latter are more likely the key, since females apparently control the fertilization success of copulations. One scientist who watched black-capped chickadees in a small area over a 20-year period witnessed thirteen extra-pair trysts; in each case the female actively sought out a male of higher social rank than her own mate. A later study using DNA fingerprinting corroborated his observations. A study in one warbler species found that males with larger song repertoires were able to seduce more females, and that the females were getting what they were looking for: fitter genes, as measured by the likelihood of offspring returning to breed a year later.

American Pipit

*Anthus rubescens**(**anth**-us: Greek term for some bird; roo-**bes**-enz: reddish). Formerly **Water Pipit**. 5½"; sexes alike: gray-brown above, buff below, with white outer tail feathers and dark legs; bill slenderer than sparrows. Alpine/subalpine in summer. Order Passeriformes, Motacillidae (Pipit family).

Distinguish the pipit from our other common species with white outer tail feathers (junco and solitaire) by its habit of regularly jerking its tail down as it walks along foraging for invertebrate prey, sometimes in shallow water or on snow. To attract a mate and, once he has one, to assert territory, the male flies straight up and then drifts down on spread wings, singing a thin, high "cheee" or "chewee" all the while. Often the song or the call can identify the bird while it flies too high to be spotted. The call note suggests "pipit."

Western Tanager

Piranga ludoviciana (pir-**ang**-ga: name for it in the Tupi language, of Brazil; loo-do-viss-i-**ay**-na: of the Louisiana Purchase area). 6¼"; summer males have bright red to orange head, yellow breast, belly and rump, black backband, tail and wings, and white wing-bars; others yellowish to greenish gray above, yellow beneath. Generally near treetops in ± open forest, in summer. Order Passeriformes, Thraupidae (Tanager family).

Lewis and Clark described many new plant species, but only three new birds: Lewis' woodpecker, Clark's nutcracker, and the western tanager, whose scientific name refers to the tract they explored, the so-called Louisiana Purchase. "Tanager" and "Piranga" are native names for the birds from deep in the Amazon rain forest, where some tanagers winter. This particular species travels only as far as Central America. Its breeding plumage here rivals that of gaudy jungle birds, but when in the jungle it wears dull winter plumage.

Tanager beaks are intermediate between the insect-picking thin

---

*In the 1998 Checklist American Pipits were separated from (European) Water Pipits, *A spinoletta* .

beaks of the preceding birds (pages 406–14) and the heavy, seed-crushing beaks of birds to follow; tanagers switch from an insectivorous diet to one of ripe berries in late summer.

Song Sparrow

Melospiza melodia (mel-o-**spy**-za: song finch). 5½"; brown with blackish streaking above, white below with brown streaking convergent at throat, above a mid-breast brown spot; pumps its tail in flight. Widespread year-round, esp in thickets. Emberizidae (New World sparrow family). Color p 501.

"Sparrow" is a catchall term for a lot of common, drab brown birds which few beginners care to identify. They aren't really a taxonomic group—less so with each new revision of bird taxonomy. This species, as its name suggests, is a melodious sparrow, and is one of the most widely distributed birds in America. Its typical song—heard on spring and early summer mornings—is a few clear piping notes, then a lower, raspy buzz or series, ending with around three quick, clear but unemphatic notes.

Dark-eyed Junco

Junco hyemalis (**junk**-oh: rush, a plant with no obvious connection; hi-em-**ay**-lis: of winter). Formerly **Oregon junco.*** 5¼"; tail dark gray-brown except for white feathers at sides; belly white, throat and above variably gray and brown. Song a simple, hard trill. Ground-foraging and -nesting; probably the most abundant bird in our mtns. Order Passeriformes, Emberizidae (New World sparrow family). Color p 501.

Though juncos migrate, we have them year-round: many migrate upslope from northwest cities and farms in early summer while others arrive from California, and still others, having wintered here, leave for the Yukon to breed. They are primarily seed-eaters, turning to insects in summer and feeding insects and larvae to their young. After the young leave the nest, juncos travel in loose flocks until the next summer.

---

*The 1983 Sixth *Checklist* lumped our common form, hitherto *J. oreganus*, with the Slate-colored Junco, *J. hyemalis*, to comprise the Dark-eyed Junco. The varieties look quite different.

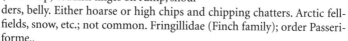

Gray-Crowned Rosy Finch

Leucosticte tephrocotis (lew-co-**stick**-tee: white patch; tef-**roc**-o-tiss: ashen head). Formerly **rosy finch.*** 6¼"; brown with blackish face, gray crown or entire head, and (males esp) reddish tinges on rump, shoulders, belly. Either hoarse or high chips and chipping chatters. Arctic fellfields, snow, etc.; not common. Fringillidae (Finch family); order Passeriforme..

The finch family name, Fringillidae, comes from the same Latin root as "frigid." Rosy finches are the most purely alpine birds of the West, at least in summer; they have been seen as high as 11,000' on Mt. Rainier. They nest in high rock crevices, reportedly even in ice crevasses, and often forage on glaciers, utilizing a resource all climbers have noticed—insects that collapse on the snow, numbed by cold after being carried astray by diurnal upvalley winds. The bulk of their diet is vegetable, including seeds, white heather flowers, and succulent alpine saxifrage leaves. Most of our rosy finches winter east of the Cascades, where they prove congenial with such lowland conveniences as window feeding-boxes, grain elevator yards, railroad beds where grain has spilled, and the company of dozens of other rosy finches. Sometimes you see whole flocks of males; for unknown reasons there are far more male than female rosy finches.

Purple Finch and Cassin's Finch

Carpodacus spp. (car-**pod**-a-cus: fruit eater). Older males ± reddish, esp toward late summer, with dark gray wings and white belly; females (and males up to breeding yearlings) a sparrowlike gray-brown with streaked to spotted white breast and belly, white eyebrow-streak. Order Passeriformes, Fringillidae (Finch family).

Purple finch, *C. purpureus* (pur-**pew**-rius: purple). 5½"; older males broadly dusky rose to wine red; undertail feathers white. Song a long rolling

---

*Several species of rosy finch were combined into one (*L. arctoa*) by the 1983 Sixth *Checklist*, only to be reseparated in 1998 by the Seventh *Checklist*.

warble. W-side forests, esp where broken.

Cassin's finch, *C. cassinii* (cas-in-ee-eye: after John Cassin). 6"; males' red limited to crimson crown and pale red breast; females' eyebrow streak scarcely visible; undertail feathers dark-streaked white. Varied warble full of breaks and squeaks. Subalpine and E-side. Color p 501.

When the red-flowering currant blooms, the purple finch is sometimes seen eating the flowers for their nectar-rich ovaries. Cassin's finch is more likely eating conifer buds. Both are primarily seedeaters later in the year.

Red Crossbill

Loxia curvirostra (**lox**-ia: oblique; cur-vi-**ros**-tra: curve bill). 5½"; older males red; females yellowish beneath, greenish gray above; young mature males often orange while grading from yellowish to red; wings (all) solid dark gray. "Chip, chip" call; warbling song. In flocks, in the coniferous canopy. Order Passeriformes, Fringillidae (Finch family). Color p 502.

A small shower of conifer seed coats and seed wings often means a crossbill flock is above. You have to be close to see the crossed bill: the lower mandible hooks upward almost as much as the upper one hooks downward. These odd bills can move sideways to efficiently pry cone scales apart. Evolution has specialized crossbills to clean up conifer seed crops when the remaining seeds are too sparse for larger seed-eaters like squirrels and woodpeckers, and too tightly encased in the cone for siskins and finches. They can keep cleaning up the leftovers from the fall crop well through winter and usually spring, depending on tree species; then in summer their jaws open wide to glean insects.

The catch to crossbill specialization is that one size and style of crossed bill can only be really efficient at one size of cone, which in any given region means one species of conifer—a species that retains many of its seeds through winter and keeps many of them out of the tiny bills of siskins. To pass their bill size on to their offspring, the birds must find mates of similar bill size. They do so with slight differences in their call notes, which enable different-billed populations to share range without interbreeding. And not interbreeding means—you guessed it!—the red crossbill is really eight different species, distinguishable by bill size and call note but

---

not by plumage. Our region has at least four. (They aren't named yet, let alone officially recognized. One scientist wants to compromise and call them "cryptospecies." Most birders aren't happy with the idea of species that can't be distinguished by plumage, but others are already trying to learn the different calls.) The Douglas-fir or ponderosa pine eaters migrate sweepingly, because these trees produce a good cone crop in one area one year, then somewhere else next year. Specialists in western hemlock and lodgepole pine, which are consistent producers, get to stay put.

Pine Siskin

Carduelis pinus (card-you-**ee**-lis: from "thistle"; **pie**-nus: pine). 4¼"; gray-brown with subtle lengthwise streaking; yellow in wings and tail may show in flight. Various distinctive scratchy twitters and sucking wheezes. In large flocks in treetops; abundant subalpine year-round. Order Passeriformes, Fringillidae (Finch family). Color p 501.

Siskins' narrow, sharp bills (in contrast to the heavy conical ones typical of their family) limit them to lighter seeds—thistle, foxglove, and birch seeds, for example—along with insects and buds. Siskins hang upside down from catkins while extracting the seeds. The populations move around sweepingly, tending to be locally abundant in alternate years.

Pine siskins look nondescript, but call and fly quite distinctively. Often a flock's twitterings seem to match its breathtaking undulations and pulselike contractions and expansions in flight. I once saw one of these aerial ballets soon after a display by the Navy's Blue Angel jets, and thought, "Why do people bother to watch those clumsy novices?"

10

Reptiles

We may habitually say "reptiles and amphibians" in one breath, or even lump them together as "herptiles," but they are quite different. Amphibians evolved from fish; they pioneered on land with the use of two key innovations: air-breathing organs (lungs or skin) and legs. Certain lunged amphibians later developed two innovative moisture barriers—scaly skin and hard eggshells—and could then exploit sunny and arid terrain. That evolutionary step eventually led to birds, mammals, and the groups traditionally called reptiles. However, today's scaly-skinned groups—tortoises, crocodilians, and snakes/lizards—turn out not to be each other's closest kin. Once the dust settles on this taxonomic debate, the class Reptilia will either include birds or no longer exist. The Squamata, or snake-and-lizard group, should still exist, and could give this chapter a title with a greater shelf life.

Western Fence Lizard

Sceloporus occidentalis (skel-**op**-or-us: leg pores; ox-i-den-**tay**-lis: western). Also **bluebelly**. 6–8½" long; belly relatively wide, legs big, with very long toes on rear; scales spiny, abrasive; back olive brownish; belly pale, with many light blue flecks and patches; yellow-orange under legs; males have two blue throat patches. Diurnal; in warm sunny habitats from C WA South. Iguanidae (Iguana family).

With their long toe-claws, fence lizards are agile climbers, fond of fenceposts. In winter they hibernate, perhaps in an old log. In spring, females lay clutches of five to fifteen eggs in loose dirt. For courtship, territory assertion, and other communication they have a precise gestural language including pushups, headbobbing, teeth-baring, throat-puffing, and side-flattening, much of it tailored to display their blue patches. (Each iguanid species seems to have its own language.) Contact with you may alarm one enough to provoke several of these gestures or a quick scurry to the far side of the tree or rock.

Northern Alligator Lizard

Elgaria coeruleus* (el-gar-ia: after ? Elgar; see-**rue**-lius: blue). 8½–10" long; body thick, legs and toes slender; scales heavy, rough; dark olive back with light stripe; belly gray to bluish. Diurnal; mainly W-side to subalpine. Anguidae (Anguid lizard family).

Scaly skin distinguishes lizards from salamanders. The scales on alligator lizards are heavy enough to serve as armor, but at considerable cost to flexibility; breathing is facilitated by a pair of large pleats along the lizard's sides. If you pick up an alligator lizard you may encounter its other defenses — it can bite quickly and hard, albeit harmlessly, defecate all over your hand, or snap off its tail. Many lizards share this famous trait of fracture planes in the tail. It lets a lizard escape while a predator holds and likely consumes the still-writhing tail. The lizard grows a new tail within weeks. Northern alligator lizards are themselves predators of millipedes, snails, and other crawling things. They walk stiffly, somewhat snakewise, on legs too weak to get their bellies off the ground. The young are born live, fully formed, in litters of two to thirteen in late summer.

Northwestern Garter Snake

Thamnophis ordinoides (**tham**-no-fis: shrub snake; or-din-**oy**-deez: patterned). 15–24" long; black, brown, tan, gray or greenish, usually with 1 or 3 yellow, orange or red stripes down back; belly yellow to gray, sometimes red-spotted. Common in ± open areas, W-side below 4,000'. Family Colubridae.

---

* Genus *Elgaria* was separated from *Gerrhonotus* in 1988.

Our range is not prime snake country; these pretty little snakes are easily our commonest, and even they avoid deep forest. They like to bask in the sun, sometimes intertwined in groups. They eat worms, slugs, and small amphibians. They give birth in summer to three to fifteen live, worm-sized snakelets. (Most reptiles lay eggs.)

Our other two commonest snake species are larger (18–50") garter snakes, the western terrestrial, *T. elegans,* and the common, *T. sirtalis.* Unlike the northwestern, these two species try to stay near water, which they use for refuge.

Gopher Snake

Pituophis catenifer* (pih-**too**-o-fis: pine snake; ca-ten-if-er: chain-bearer, referring to the pattern.) 3–6' long, heavy-bodied, relatively small-headed; tan with blackish blotches, largest ones along the back, flanked by two nearly solid narrow stripes. Low E-side. Family Colubridae.

The only snake you would likely mistake for a rattler around here is the gopher snake. The resemblance may be a case of adaptive mimicry for fright value; it even includes a threatening vibration of the tail which, when it rustles dry leaves, can sound much like a rattler. This snake is nonvenomous, killing its prey, including gophers, by constriction. It can also climb trees and prey on nestling birds.

Constricting characterizes one small branch of the huge family Colubridae, which contains some 68% of all snakes.

---

* Formerly combined with more easterly relatives in genus *melanoleucus.*

Racer

Coluber constrictor mormon (col-ub-er: Roman term for some snake). Our subspecies the **western yellowbellied racer**. Grayish olive above, yellowish beneath; adults plain, but juveniles patterned with brown for all or part of their length; 22–36+" long. Any open lowlands. Family Colubridae.

This agile, slender snake is true to its name "racer," but not to its name *constrictor* since it kills its prey—mostly insects and some small rodents and reptiles—with its mouth, not with its coils. Though nonvenomous, it may bite and thrash when captured.

Western Rattlesnake

Crotalus viridis oreganus (crot-a-lus: rattle; **veer**-id-iss: green; or-eg-**ay**-nus: of Oregon). Our subspecies the **northern Pacific rattlesnake**. 16–60" long, heavily built, with large triangular head; tail terminates in rattle segments; variable brown, black, gray, and tan colors in a pattern of regularly spaced large ± geometric dark blotches against paler crossbars. Lowest E-side and S Willamette Valley elevs, typically on talus or rock outcrops. Viperidae (Pit viper family).

We're lucky in having no poisonous snakes except along the eastern and southern low fringes of our range, where the rattler may be found. Avoid it. This species can inject a dose of venom lethal to small children and many mammals, though almost always merely painful to adult humans. (A solitary victim might possibly be incapacitated long enough to die of hypothermia if warm clothes and food are far away.) Rattlesnakes hunt at dusk, dawn, and night. A light, dry rustling sound from their rattles is the typical warning to large intruders. Far from being aggressive toward humans, they will almost always flee if given the chance.

11

Amphibians

Though considered terrestrial vertebrates, amphibians are only marginally terrestrial; they lack an effective moisture barrier in either their skins or their eggs, so to avoid deadly drying they must return to water frequently, venturing from it mainly at night or in the shade, and never far. Most of them hatch in water as gilled, water-breathing, legless, swimming larvae (e.g., tadpoles), later metamorphose into terrestrial adults, and return to water to breed. Hence the word "amphibious," from "life on both sides." A few amphibians manage to be completely terrestrial in moist habitats; several others have regressed to a fully aquatic life. Western Oregon and Washington, abounding as they do in moist habitats, may be weak on reptiles, but have historically supported ungodly numbers of unnoticed (quiet, nocturnal, largely subterranean) amphibians.

Today, amphibians are in decline worldwide. The causes are poorly. Permeable skin makes amphibians vulnerable to environmental contaminants, which are certainly one of the leading causes of decline, along with draining of wetlands and deforestation. One study in the Northwest implicates ozone depletion. (See page 430.) Another finds tiny parasitic worms causing treefrogs to grow extra legs, but fails to show or explain any recent increase.

Among vertebrate animals, mammals and birds are "warm-blooded," whereas reptiles, amphibians and fish are "cold-blooded." This doesn't mean they're self-refrigerating, but they're never a lot warmer than their environment. They need some ambient heat to help them be active, yet they can sustain activity in astonishing cold—long-toed salamanders in our high country typically breed in sub-40° water with winter's ice still on it. Nevertheless they hibernate through most of the freezing season. At the other extreme, amphibians rarely survive heat over 100°. Ironically, their intolerance of heat won salamanders and newts a superstitious reputation as fireproof. No doubt that's because they know how to survive a ground fire; they take refuge in a familiar wet crevice or burrow, just as they do from the midday sun. When Mt. St. Helens blew up, amphibian species likely to be swimming in mid-May survived very well in the blast zone, but those more likely to be in shallow burrows died. Their false reputation as heatproof may historically have put some newts into hot water of the black magic variety.

> *Fire burn, and cauldron bubble.*
> *Fillet of a fenny snake,*
> *In the cauldron boil and bake*
> *Eye of newt and toe of frog ...*

Rough-Skinned Newt

Taricha granulosa (**tair**-ic-a: mummy; gran-you-**low**-sa: grainy). 6–7" long; back warty-textured (exc on breeding-season males) greenish black to almost translucent brown; underside orange to yellow; ribs not visible. W-side. Salamandridae (Newt family). Color p 503.

Newts are a family of salamanders with relatively bright colors and toxic skin secretions. Salamanders in general protect themselves with both skin toxins and nocturnality, but this newt is so toxic it doesn't need to be nocturnal. That makes it our most often-seen salamander, commonly foraging on gray summer days in forest not far from its retreat in a pond or marsh. When threatened, it goes into a rigid reflexive posture for two or three minutes. displaying its bright underside by curling up until its tail is near its upturned chin. This presumably deters predators by reminding them of the newt's poisonous skin. Newt toxicity varies from one population to another; for some reason Willamette Valley newts are intense, while Vancouver Island newts are innocuous. Correspondingly, Vancouver Island garter snakes have failed to develop the resistance to newt toxins that generally enables garter snakes to prey on newts. Most small predators, in experiments, die quickly when force-fed bits of newt skin. Living newts rarely release much of their toxin, and it's only toxic when consumed anyway, so handling a newt is not too risky, but I still recommend a thorough hand-washing afterward.

At breeding time (winter or spring) the male's skin smooths out, his tail flattens, his genital region swells, and his underside turns a brighter orange. Newts migrate accurately back to their natal pond. Some have proven sadly faithful to drained pond sites.

Torrent Salamanders

Rhyacotriton (rye-a-co-**try**-ton: brook sea-god). 3–4½" long, slender, bug-eyed; olive to chocolate brown above, ± yellow-flecked beneath; 14–15 rib grooves; males have squarish anal lobes behind rear legs. Dicamptodontidae.

Olympic Salamander, *R. olympicus.* In the Olympics.

Cascade torrent Salamander, *R. cascadae.* W-side Cascades between Tout-le and Mackenzie R. drainages. Color p 503.

This delicate, pretty little salamander generally stays in mountain creeks or within splash range of them.

Pacific Giant Salamander

Dicamptodon tenebrosus*
(die-**camp**-ta-don: twice-curved
teeth; ten-eb-**roe**-sus: dark). 7–12" long, stocky; brown to purplish with black splotches; belly light brown; ribs indistinct. W-side forest. Family Dicamptodontidae. Color p 503.

While other salamanders are limited to eating insects and other small invertebrates as food, this one—the largest terrestrial sala-mander—can catch and eat mice, garter snakes, and small sala-manders. In small mountain streams it is the dominant predator, outweighing all salmon and trout put together.

It is the only salamander with a real voice, variously described as a "yelp" and a "rattle." Salamanders have no eardrums or exter-nal openings to receive communications, but they do have inner ear organs which are presumed sensitive to vibrations transmitted up through the legs. Larvae have intricate plumelike red (blood-filled) structures where we might expect ears; these are external gills that "breathe" or absorb oxygen suspended in water. Some Pacific giant larvae metamorphose into terrestrial adults at about 3", in their sec-ond summer. Others never do metamorphose, but instead mature

---

* Formerly known as *D. ensatus.*

---

sexually as aquatic larvae and may grow as long as 12". This latter life-cycle ("neoteny") is common in both the mole salamanders and this family. Dicamptodontids, found only in the Northwest, hole up in crevices between streambed rocks; they are decimated in logged watersheds where erosion fills the streams with mud.

Ensatina

Ensatina eschscholtzii * (en-sa-tee-na: small sword; es-**sholt**-zee-eye: after J. F. Eschscholtz, p 174). 3–4½" long; typically mottled dark brown over orange; variable in color but always mottled and rather translucent; 5 toes on rear feet; tail constricted at base. W-side forest, usually under litter, in rotten logs, burrows, etc. Plethodontidae (Lungless salamander family).

Ensatinas are the most numerous amphibians in most Westside forest regions. They choose drier habitats than our other salamanders. Reportedly, they can hiss like snakes. When threatened, an ensatina stands as high as it can on its legs and raises and/or thrashes its tail, exuding (and sometimes throwing) a mildly toxic, sticky white mucus from glands on the tail. If the threat escalates or the tail is bitten, the tail snaps off right at its constricted base, giving the ensatina time to escape while the predator is distracted; a jettisoned tail can thrash for several minutes. The blood vessels have tiny muscles to shut them off, and the tail regenerates over a year or two— still, it isn't a sacrifice to take lightly.

Western Red-Backed Salamander

Plethodon vehiculum (**pleth**-o-don: many teeth; ve-**hic**-you-lum: carrier). 3–5" long, slender; brown or black exc for a ± full-length broad, even-edged back stripe red to orange or yellow, tan or even greenish; 16 rib grooves, or 15 in C OR. W-side forest. Plethodontidae. Color p 502.

Salamanders of this family lack lungs or gills, and breathe through their skins exclusively. Lungless salamanders of the West hatch into miniature "adults," having breezed through the larval stage within the egg; they are completely terrestrial. The mother lays her eggs on the ground and guards them. This species lives (by the millions) under moss and logs in the forest, or under stones in wet talus.

---

* The Northwest's variety of ensatina, *E. e. oregonensis*, would become a full species alongside up to ten more southerly varieties, under one opinion.

Larch Mountain Salamander

Plethodon larselli (lar-**sel**-eye: of Larch Mtn). 3–4" long, slender; gold-flecked blackish above, with a ± broken reddish tan back stripe; red to pink-orange beneath. Columbia Gorge (both states) and very local in S WA Cascades. Plethondontidae (Lungless salamander family). Color p 503.

This salamander does not stick to streams and seepage, but finds cool, moist refuges in basalt talus. It employs a curious defense against large creatures, coiling and uncoiling its body so rapidly as to fling itself about, perhaps in mimicry of poisonous millipedes.

Oregon Slender Salamander

Batrachoseps wrighti (ba-**tray**-co-seps: frog lizard; **right**-eye: after Margaret and A. H. Wright). 3¼–4" long, extremely slender; dark brown above, with a ± vague, reddish to greenish back stripe; white-blotched black beneath; 16 or 17 rib grooves. OR only, W-side below 4500'. Plethodontidae. Color p 502.

Salamanders of wormlike slenderness crawl around in termite or beetle tunnels in rotten wood, preying on springtails, mites, beetle larvae, and worms. They depend on big, old logs for refuge from summer heat. Slender salamanders reportedly employ both the coiling defense (above) and the tail-breaking defense.

Long-Toed Salamander

Ambystoma macrodactylum (am-**bis**-ta-ma: blunt mouth; macro-**dac**-til-um: big toes). 4–6" long; wide, blunt head; long legs; dark gray-brown with a thin, irregular, full-length back stripe bright yellow to greenish or tan; 12–13 rib grooves. Ambystomatidae (Mole salamander family). Color p 503.

Our widest-ranging salamander inhabits both alpine meadows and sagebrush country. Like other amphibians it stays close to water, especially in arid terrain. In the high country it breeds even before the ice is gone, to make the most of its brief, frigid active season, and still the larvae need two summers before metamorphosing. Laying eggs in shallow water makes it vulnerable to UV-B (seepage 431).

Artificially stocked trout displaced the long-toed salamander from the top of the food chain in most high-subalpine and alpine lakes, and the Northwest salamander (*A. gracile*) in slightly lower or deeper lakes. Finding themselves prey for the first time in untold generations, the salamanders became scarce and very secretive, but generally survived. They multiply quickly if the fish are removed.

Lungless and mole salamanders have elaborate mating rituals

ending, in many species, with a procession: he walks along dropping gelatinous sperm cases and she follows, picking them up with her cloacal lips for internal fertilization. A long-toed male may literally interlope: he slips in between the romantic duo, mimics a female walk to escape notice, and places his sperm cases on top of each of the first male's, assuring himself of paternity.

Western Toad

Bufo boreas boreas (bew-foe: the Greek term; **bor**-ius: northern). Also (our subspecies) **boreal toad**. 2–5" long; thick; sluggish; skin has large bumps, the largest being two oval glands behind the eyes; olive to grayish, with a narrow pale stripe down back, and blotches on belly. Widespread. Bufonidae (Toad family). Color p 502.

Toads are distinguished from frogs by their warty skin, toothless upper jaw, sluggish movement (generally walking rather than hopping), and parotoid glands behind the eyes. These bulbous protrusions exude a thick, white, nauseating, burning poison related to digitalin, effectively deterring predators. (It does not cause warts.) Toads' slow pace limits them to slow, creeping invertebrate prey.

Toads resist drying better than most frogs and salamanders. Our only toad, the western, inhabits animal burrows and rock crevices, and is often seen in mountain meadows and woodlands well away from watercourses. It is less strictly nocturnal than most toads, especially at elevations where nights are too cold for much toad activity. Lacking the inflatable vocal sac many of its relatives boast, it has a weak, peeping voice.

In 1995, a team of O.S.U. zoologists made headlines worldwide with a study investigating western toads' disappearance from seemingly pristine Cascade lakes. They found most eggs in some high ponds killed by a fungal disease common among hatchery trout. If they shielded the eggs with mylar that blocked ultraviolet-B rays, a healthy number of eggs resisted infection, and hatched. The problem, in other words, was a combination of two human interventions: stocking high lakes with trout, and depleting atmospheric ozone, with resultant dramatic increases in UV-B. This was the first demonstrated case of ozone depletion threatening a species. It drove home the point that even the most remote or protected wilderness paradise is vulnerable to global change.

The team found Cascades frogs suffering in exactly the same way, and found long-toed salamanders hatching with debilitating deformities unless they were shielded from UV-B. In contrast, the Pacific treefrog was able to repair UV-B damage. Most amphibians lay eggs in UV-safe environments such as shady pools or deeper water, so the ozone connection can explain only a fraction of worldwide amphibian declines.

Pacific Treefrog

Pseudacris regilla * (sue-**day**-cris: false cricket-frog; ra-**jil**-a: queenlet). Also **Pacific chorus frog.** 1–2¾" long; skin bumpy; toes bulbous-tipped; color extremely variable, and may include green or red; in Cascades usually gray-brown with large irregular black splotches; males' throats gray. Ubiquitous. Hylidae (Treefrog family). Color p 503.

Voiced frogs employ a variety of calls, including alarm, warning, territorial, and male and female release calls. The familiar pond frog choruses are likely (at least around here in spring) to be mating-call duets and trios of male treefrogs. The male amplifies his voice with a resonating throat sac he blows up to three times the size of his head. Active and vocal day and night,he has a rather musical, high-pitched call. Tree frogs are distinguished by their bulbous toe pads, which offer amazingly good grip on vertical surfaces such as trees. Our species probably spends more time in water and on the ground than on shrubs and trees. It has a sticky tongue for catching insects.

Red-Legged Frog

Rana aurora (**ray**-na: the Roman term; aurora: dawn, referring to redness). 2–4" long; grayish to reddish brown with small dark blotches; yellow underneath, ± reddish on rear legs and lower belly, toes only slightly webbed. Lower W-side forest. Ranidae (True frog family). Color p 503.

These diurnal frogs are sometimes seen well away from the ponds and stream backwaters they require for breeding. They prefer low elevations, but range farther north than the Cascades frog. They are almost gone from the Puget-Willamette Trough part of their range; predation by introduced bullfrogs (*R. catesbeiana*) is a big threat to them, along with stream pollution and habitat alteration.

Their croak is feeble, rough, and prolonged.

---

*Also known, in a long-running taxonomic controversy, as *Hyla regilla.*.

Cascades Frog

Rana cascadae (cas-**cay**-dee). 1¾–2¼" long; brown to yellow-olive with black spots above, yellow underneath; yellow jawline; toes only slightly webbed. In Cascades, mid-elev to timberline, always near water. Ranidae (True frog family). Color p 502.

The diurnal Cascades frog is often seen basking on high-country shores and marsh meadows. It croaks in a rapid, raspy chuckling manner, several blips per second. Escaping into water, it swims off across the surface rather than diving as its relatives do. Countless tadpoles (the larval stage) of this species inhabit shallow seasonal ponds. Both the shallowness of the water and the high elevations expose the eggs to more intense ultraviolet radiation than other frogs' eggs, and in this time of damaged stratospheric ozone there is reason to fear this could threaten the species. See pages 426–27.

Northwest tribes associated frogs with wisdom. Certain barbaric cultures make them into good luck amulets or sacrificial victims to bring rain.

Tailed Frog

Ascaphus truei (**ask**-a-fus: not digging; **true**-eye: after F.W.True). 1–2" long; skin has sparse small warts; olive to dark brown with large irregular black splotches and black eye-stripe. Abundant (up to five per square yard) in undisturbed mtn streams. Ascaphidae (Tailed frog family).

Tailed frogs spend most of their time in fast, cold creeks. They attach their eggs like strings of beads to the downstream side of rocks. The tadpoles suck firmly onto rocks, or perhaps to your leg or boot when you wade a creek, but don't worry, they aren't bloodsuckers. The silent, nocturnal adults are less easily encountered. They don't have real tails; those little soft protuberances are male cloacas, and they fertilize the females internally. You might think a seeming penis prototype to be an advanced item on an amphibian, but sorry, guys: this is considered the most primitive family of frogs. Its other members are in New Zealand.

12

Fishes

Fish have not fully returned to our mountains since the last Ice Age. Where glaciers advanced, aquatic life necessarily retreated before them; when the glaciers retreated, fish were able to return only so far as they could swim, so each stream is generally fishless above a certain impassable waterfall. Only strong-swimming, cold-loving species, mostly salmon and trout, make it into our mountains at all, and many of these fight their way to their upper distributional limit just once in their lives, when at their peak, and at a cost of total and terminal exhaustion. They may be phenomenal waterfall leapers, but still, there are limits. Above the critical waterfall live healthy aquatic communities whose animal members—invertebrates, amphibians, and small mammals—all got there overland or airborne.

Higher still, in mountain lakes, aquatic communities have recently been joined (and much altered) by trout who rode up the trail in saddlebags or flew there in airplanes. Fish population of our high lakes is a product of human management—again favoring salmon and trout. Sometimes trout competitors have been introduced accidentally (as escaped bait) and lakes have had to be poisoned with rotenone, and then restocked with trout. Amphibians are selected very differently in high lakes with and without finny predators. Effects of the change in amphibians cascade down through the food chain. North Cascades National Park spent a decade studying these effects, and must soon decide what to do about them. A relatively pristine and little-visited park, it takes ecosystem preservation seriously as its mission, and may consider turning at least several high lakesheds back over to the amphibians.

Some of the most accessible fishing lakes are stocked with catchable-size trout before and during the fishing season; such trout are made of fishfood flakes, like supermarket trout, and only freshness makes them taste any better. More often stocking is done with fingerlings soon after the fishing season. Still, the lake may get nearly fished out each season, so that almost all the catch is two-year-old hatchery trout. Remote high lakes may be stocked only occasionally and have near-natural, self-sustaining populations. Or they may support healthy trout for years at a time but lack reproducing populations for want of a proper spawning bed. The bed must be clean gravel of the right size, at the right depth, with a moderate current to keep it aerated and silt-free, since silt suffocation is the chief cause of egg and infant mortality.

Check a lakeshore near an inlet or outlet stream and follow the stream to its first waterfall and if you find a shallow gravelly spot in early summer, you may see a trout busy swimming back and forth over it. A logjam at the outlet stream, or slabby shallows nearby, tend to be good places to spot fish at any time of year. Polarizing sunglasses (or a camera polarizer) can help you see fish. Trout don't feed all day—only when the insects are most active. When the lake is first ice-free, feeding may go on from midmorning to midday. By October they may feed all afternoon. If luck brings you a calm feeding period after an extended blow, look for frenzied feeding where floating insects are concentrated against the downwind shore.

Another limiting factor on fish in high lakes, strange as it may sound, is high temperature. Except in tiny pools, the water is never

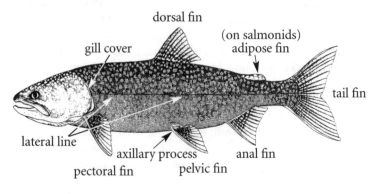

dorsal fin

(on salmonids) adipose fin

gill cover

tail fin

lateral line

axillary process

pectoral fin

pelvic fin

anal fin

what we would call warm, but trout may suffer or die of heat in water that could chill and "freeze" a person in short order. Since they are "cold-blooded," their body temperatures drop with that of the water, but their health isn't at risk; only their activity and growth rates are reduced. Under ice for nine months, high country trout spend a very slow winter without danger or discomfort, but also without growing. In the smallest and/or highest bodies of water that support trout, they never grow very big, maturing and spawning at three to six years of age while only 3–5" long and still displaying the parr marks typical of juvenile trout elsewhere.

Some lakes are too clean to make good fish habitat. The aquatic food pyramid rests upon algae, which in turn depend on minerals not present in rain or snow; water has to pick these up in its passage over or through the earth. Small drainage basins, high snowfall, barren or impermeable terrain, and rapid turnover of lake water often combine, in our region, to severely limit nutrients. Stocked trout grow poorly in such lakes, and may not reproduce.

All the fishes in this chapter are carnivores. Each species in its tiny "fry" stage eats zooplankton until it grows large enough to subsist on larger crustaceans and insects of all life stages. The young fish soon add snails, worms, isopods, freshwater shrimp, amphibian larvae, and fish eggs and fry to their diets. Any fish species, even their own when at a smaller stage, may be fair game.

Salmon and trout that reach large size in fresh water even eat waterfowl chicks, adult amphibians, and water shrews. In salt water they become voracious predators on fish after first growing up on a diet of tiny krill. On their return to freshwater for spawning, most eat little or nothing, but metabolize stored fat and muscle tissue. (There are exceptions. Sockeyes will feed en route to spawning during a last summer vacation in a lake. Some steelhead and sea-run cutthroat individuals not only eat a healthy diet while swimming upstream, but return to sea and spawn again the following year.) Spawning, they may look like they're at death's door, and they are. With pale, crumbling flesh, they make poor eating. (Bald eagles don't seem to mind). Fungus-aided decomposition during and after spawning may have evolved because its residues nourish the food chain that will feed the young after they hatch. Sea runs of fish transferred huge quantities of nutrients from the ocean into the stream ecosystems. Those must be sorely missed today, with the runs down to small vestiges of their former selves.

Pacific Salmon

Oncorhyncus spp. (onk-o-**rink**-us: swollen snout). These three species have more than twelve rays in the anal fin. Salmonidae (Salmon family). Spawning males illustrated.

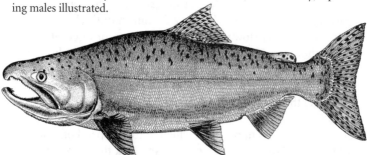

Chinook salmon, *0. tshawytscha* (cha-**witch**-a: a Kamchatkan native term). Also **tyee, king salmon.** Black spots on back and both lobes of tail fin; black gums on lower jaw; spawning adults dark, rarely red; juveniles at 4" have tall parr marks bisected by the lateral line, and a dark-margined but clear-centered adipose fin.

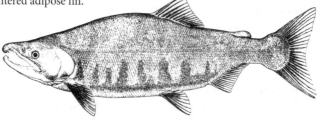

Sockeye salmon/Kokanee salmon, *0. nerka* (ner-ka: the Russian term). No dark spots on back or tailfin; 28–40 long thin rough gill-rakers in first gill arch; spawning adult has greenish dark head, crimson body; male is slightly humpbacked; 4" juveniles have small, oval parr marks almost entirely above lateral line. WA; hatchery population in Deschutes R. system in OR.

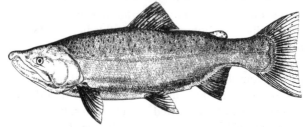

Coho salmon, *0. kisutch* (**kiss**-utch: Kamchatkan native term). Also **silver salmon.** Black spots on back and upper half of tail fin; white lower gums; spawning males have brilliant red sides; 4" juveniles have tall parr marks bisecting lateral line, all-dark adipose fin and dark leading edge of anal fin.

Pacific salmon range the Pacific Rim from California to Korea, and some also range the Arctic from the Mackenzie to the Lena. First described to science by Steller (page 401) in Siberia, they were given species names from Russian and Kamchatkan languages. They are called salmon after the Atlantic salmon, *Salmo salar*.

Salmon are "anadromous" ("up-running") fishes; they migrate upstream from the sea to spawn. They require clear, cold, well-aerated gravelly creeks to nurse them in infancy, and larger bodies of water richer in animal life to rear them to maturity. It may be no surprise that they find the ocean ideal for the latter phase, but it's remarkable that they're perfectly adapted, as water-breathing creatures, to handle the chemical shock between salt and fresh water. Some species can revert to a purely freshwater life cycle if they become landlocked by new dams or natural topographic changes.

When they reach the sea, our chinook and steelhead travel far north, even to the Aleutians, and stay out there from one to several years. Their ability to home back to their natal stream is a wonder of animal navigation. Once they get close to the right river, they zero in on the mineral "recipe" of the precise tributary of their birth by means of smell, a sense located in fish in two shallow nostrils unconnected to their mouths. Some go only a few miles upriver, but chinook and chum navigate the Yukon more than 2,000 miles.

Once back at the spawning grounds where she was born (and here I describe a generalized salmon-family life cycle) the female chooses a gravelly spot, usually in a riffle, and begins digging a trough, or "redd," by turning on her side and beating with her tail. A dominant male moves in to attend her, and becomes aggressive to outsiders, attacking any who come too close. He may nudge her repeatedly. When she signals her readiness by lowering a fin into the redd, he swims up alongside her, they open their jaws, arch their backs, quiver, and simultaneously drop her eggs and his milt. Other males hitherto kept at bay now dash in and try to eject some of their own milt onto the eggs. Hundreds to thousands of orange-red eggs come out tiny, then quickly swell, absorbing water along with the fertilizing milt. The female's last maternal act is to cover them under several inches (up to 2 feet) of gravel as she extends her redd, digging the next trench immediately upstream from the last, with intermittent resting spells. Different males may attend her subsequent efforts. Pacific salmon die soon after spawning, as do a majority of steelhead and eulachons.

The eggs take a few months to hatch; the colder the water, the longer they take. The newly hatched "alevin" remains in the gravel layer several weeks, still nutritionally dependent on the yolk-sac suspended from its belly. As the yolk is depleted, the fish adapts to a diet of zooplankton and emerges from the gravel as a "fry." In a year or two they grow to "parr" size, displaying the "parr marks" that make them easier to identify. We call them "smolts" at whatever age they go to sea—from month-old, ¾" pink salmon fry to ten-year-old, 12" cutthroat trout in severe Alaskan habitats.

Salmon were incalculably important to all the Northwest Coast and Columbia River nations. The Indians' expressed their gratitude in countless ceremonies and stories of dreadful times before someone (like Coyote or Raven) gave salmon to the people. Archaeologists confirm that people were in the Northwest for millenia before developing a regionwide economy based on storing salmon through winter. And at around that time, about 3,500 years ago, Northwest culture blossomed.

The people sure did learn how to catch salmon: with hook and line, with spears, from platforms over waterfalls, with one- or two-man dipnets of spruce-root twine, with larger basketry nets or long seine nets or wicker traps or wooden weirs. People fished during the spawning runs. Smoking and drying kept the bounty in season as long as possible, long past what we might consider palatable. Myths also reflect a painful awareness that the runs couldn't be counted on. Elaborate taboos were observed to prevent any offense to the Salmon and assure his return. Yet overall, salmon so astronomically outnumbered people that there was no need for restraint in harvesting them. Salmon fishing-and-trading camp was Fat City—particularly at Celilo Falls on the Columbia, which, for one month a year for thousands of years, became the biggest city west of the Mississippi. (Today it lies drowned under a reservoir.)

Nineteenth century white men who promoted a worldwide market for canned Pacific salmon liked to reassure each other that they were developing an inexhaustible resource and sparing scarcer resources on land. By the end of the century they had to face the fact that the salmon were seriously overfished. Salmon populations today are a small fraction of what they once were. It's unlikely that even a halt to fishing could restore them. Loss of spawning habitat is a more intractable problem than overfishing.

Another genie which cannot be fully rebottled is the hatchery programs, which began, ironically, with high hopes of mitigating harm from overfishing and dams. Since wild salmon each spawn in the stream where they were born, each stream's stock is genetically isolated; we can presume that by now each stock is the stock best adapted to its particular stream. Similarly, the spring, summer, and fall runs of chinook are genetically isolated even from their compatriots of the same stream. (That's why the Endangered Species Act treats stocks and runs, rather than species, of anadromous fish.) Over the first decades of hatcheries, millions of smolts with genes from just a handful of rivers were released without spending time in those rivers, so they spawned everywhere they could get to, spreading their poorly adapted genes and hatchery-bred diseases to nearly every wild stock. Hatchery programs today are more sophisticated and less harmful. For example, some rivers receive no new hatchery stock, allowing fishermen to fish (catch and release only) for "wild" steelhead; on others, hatchery releases all have a clipped fin, so fishermen know they can keep those but must release the notchless ones. Still, the most cost-effective salmon recovery plan would likely delete most hatcheries.

Chinook, the largest salmon, swim the greatest distances up river, and spawn in larger streams than their kin. Chinook runs are called "spring," "summer," or "fall," but arrival dates in Northwest freshwater occur sporadically from April through December, with a few even in the other months. A Montana-sized patch of chinook habitat was written off in one stroke when Grand Coulee Dam was drawn up. A landlocked population of chinook survives above Cushman Dam in the Olympics. Two small dams on the Elwha wiped out a small run with famously huge individuals, some over 100 pounds. Destroying the two dams (an idea being worked over in Congress as we go to press) would provide a great opportunity to see if such a run could re-evolve.

Sockeye when spawning typically turn deep red both inside and out. Their spectacularly dense crimson spawning runs are famous in both B.C. and Alaska, but the ones in disturbed watersheds are fast diminishing. The small, landlocked form (Kokanee salmon) rivals trout as a sport fish in many lakes of Northeast Washington and the Rockies. The sea-run form (unlike other salmon) always seeks a lake for part of its life cycle—one or two juvenile years, and then a final summer before spawning. They go to higher tributaries than chinook, and may swim nearly as far.

Two other species, chum (*O. keta*) and pink salmon (*O. gorbuscha*), forgo the upstream heroics, limiting their efforts to a few weeks within a few miles of saltwater (or at least of very large lowland rivers in the case of chum), and the fry float back to sea immediately upon emerging. So they are not fish of our mountains. Chum were called "dog salmon" by Alaskan tribes who fed them to their dogs, favoring the richer chinook for themselves. (Never let your dog eat salmon or trout raw. Many dogs are lethally susceptible to a bacterium in some salmon; wild canids and bears acquire immunity from a sublethal infection in youth.) Pinks spawn and die as they approach their second birthday, so they remain the smallest anadromous salmon. On any given river they run mainly in odd- or mainly in even-numbered years. Washington and Oregon runs are in odd years.

Coho spawn in slow, low-gradient lowland streams—even

Fish Habitat Destruction

As we learn more about why salmon and trout have declined, it seems that almost everything people have done that makes the Northwest less natural makes life harder for fish.

Siltation *ruins the clean gravel salmonids need for spawning. Streambed gravel gets muddy when livestock tromp around in it, or when erosion brings silt down from hillsides where heavy equipment is used for logging, roadbuilding, or any other construction.*

Loss of shade *makes some small streams too warm for salmon after either logging or livestock activities remove streamside plants.*

Snags and logs *used to have huge effects on streamflow, slowing it down and creating pools and meanders, which are essential fish habitat. Some big logjams were semipermanent, accumulating new logs as fast as old ones rotted out. For over a century after white people settled here, they went to great expense to get rid of logjams and snags. The main purpose was to improve navigation, or to let sawlogs and log rafts float down to the mill. (There was an egregiously destructive technique called a splash dam—a temporary dam built just to be breached, creating a flash flood to move logs down to a mill on streams otherwise too small to carry them.) Logs were also taken out of small streams just to mill them, and of course a future of endless fifty-year logging rotations in a watershed will end the supply of really big linchpin logs for* urban ones. Beaver ponds make ideal rearing pools for the fry. Coho historically made up in numbers what they lacked in size, enough to rank them high in both sport and commercial catches, at least for Oregon. But today the upper-Columbia runs are extinct, the mid-Columbia runs are in danger, and the coastal and Willamette runs are down to less than 5% of historical numbers despite infusions of enough hatchery stock to outnumber naturally-spawned coho for decades now.

Recent coho declines are blamed largely on warming of offshore waters with consequent loss of overall fertility and increase in warmwater predators, especially mackerel. Coho don't swim very far north during their ocean phase, leaving them the salmon most vulnerable to global warming. But to some degree, this sea change is part of a natural fifty-year cycle (page 567) that makes salmon alternately abundant and scarce off our shores, and the reverse off

future logjams. As recently as 1980, some logs were still being removed in the mistaken belief that it would help fish get upstream.

Seasonal fluctuation *is aggravated when a watershed has a high proportion of its forest logged. Rain and snowmelt runs off much faster because less is absorbed by soil and plants, and snow melts sooner, especially when rain falls on it. This creates floods during winter rains and reduced, warmer streamflow in summer.*

Pollution *comes from mines, factories, farms, sewage, and lawn and pavement runoff.*

Draining *of marshes and beaver ponds has eliminated habitat.*

Irrigation *of farms reduces some inland streams to warm, muddy trickles in summer.*

Dams *are the problem we've known about longest, but we keep learning of more ways that dams kill fish. Some dams are too high to have fish ladders; even on moderate ones many fish get lost or exhausted at fish ladders. Electric turbines cut up smolts on the way down. Smolts die of bubbles that form in their blood due to pressure changes during the drop. Big reservoirs above dams warm the water up in the sun; harbor non-native warmwater predators; lack enough current to move smolts downstream on schedule; and dilute the chemistry of small tributaries, making it hard for adults to locate their natal stream.*

Alaska. In the early 1990s, salmon thrived off Alaska, with plenty of cold water, but in 1997 the Bering Sea abruptly warmed by 6°, and Alaska's runs dropped sharply.

Cutthroat Trout

Oncorhynchus clarki* (**clark**-ee: after William Clark, p 234). Jaw lines streaked red or orange underneath; jaw longer than other trout, opening to well behind the eye; base of tongue has tiny teeth,[†] usually palpable; dorsal fin has 9–11 rays, pelvic rays usually 9, anal rays 9 (range 8–12); adults generally dark-speckled, but sometimes (esp on introduced fish from Rocky-Mtn stock) only near the tail; juveniles develop the throat streaks quite early, and have many small spots above and between the lateral parr marks but none or few (1–5) in a median line ahead of the dorsal fin. Salmonidae.

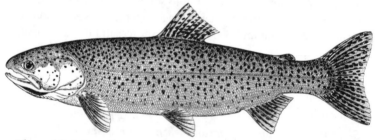

The reddish "cuts" on a cutthroat's throat serve to emphasize gestures and displays. They're a much more reliable i.d. character than the red rainbows on rainbow trout; occasionally they're obscure on cutthroats when very young, newly returned to freshwater, or dead. Coloring is notoriously variable in salmon and trout. Like chameleons only much slower, trout alter their camouflage in response to colors they see; experimentally blinded trout eventually contrasted sharply with their associates.

Cutthroats include the full range of migratory patterns. Sea-run and freshwater populations cohabit in many coastal streams. Some populations are nonmigrating residents of small streams, and tend to be small and short-lived fish; that can happen above a

---

* Formerly *Salmo clarki*, when it was thought to be more closely related to Atlantic salmon than to Pacific salmon

[†] Teeth on fish are used not for chewing but for gripping prey prior to swallowing it. They aren't confined to the jawbone area. Feeling for teeth inside the mouth can help i.d. trout; but don't try it on one you're going to release.

waterfall barrier. (How can there be trout above barriers? Artificial stocking, of course, but also trout populations may have predated barriers, especially in Oregon where glaciers never extended far down the rivers.) Sea-run cutthroats may run to sea twice before maturing to spawn. They rarely spend as much as a year there per trip, nor do they go very far; many stay right in the estuary. Hence they don't grow as large as steelhead. For their size they are formidable predators, with their big mouths and extra teeth.

Cutthroat trout were probably as abundant here as rainbow trout originally, but are far rarer today since they are hard to raise in hatcheries. The freshwater populations, though much diminished, seem reasonably stable. Many anadromous runs are extinct, or endangered by the same habitat and climate problems as our other salmonids.

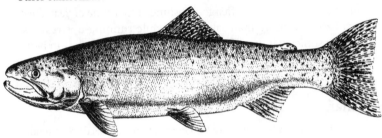

Rainbow Trout / Steelhead

Oncorhyncus mykiss * (me-kiss: a Kamchatkan tribal term) Coloring extremely variable; flesh bright red to white; spawning adults usually have a red to pink streak (the "rainbow") full length on each side, much deeper on males; returning sea-run fish (steelhead) are silvery all over with guanine (a protein coating on all salmonids fresh from the sea) which obscures any coloring underneath; dorsal fin rays typically 11–12, pelvic fin rays 10, anal fin rays 10 (range 8–12); juveniles have a distinct row of 5–10 small dark spots along the back straight in front of the dorsal fin, plus 8–13 oval parr marks along the lateral line. Rainbows common in high lakes and streams. Salmonidae.

The sea-run form of this species has unparalleled mystique among fishermen who, with good reason, think of it as an altogether

---

* Formerly *Salmo gairdneri*. Moved from genus *Salmo* because it's closer-related to Pacific than to Atlantic salmon. Put into species *mykiss* because it's the same species as the trout of Kamchatka, which were named earlier.

different fish—steelhead. At sea the trout grow faster and reach larger sizes than those who stay in fresh water. Big and strong, steelheads are notoriously hard to land, and harder still to locate. A favorite riffle for steelhead is a fiercely guarded secret.

Its freshwater form is rainbow trout, the West's best-known sport fish. It is native up and down the Pacific Slope from Mexico to the Alaska Peninsula and inland throughout the Columbia River system. (And in its totally domesticated form, the common trout of dinner tables, it is raised today anywhere in the world with a temperate climate.)

Wild steelhead usually swim to sea when two years old, and feed for one to four "salt years" before their first spawning run. Their runs vary as to timing; the main spawning run is in midwinter—another reason for the popularity of steelhead fishing, since few other species offer good fishing at that time of year. Steelhead also eat more than salmon do while running upstream, so they're somewhat more inclined to bite, and their flesh is in better condition. Summer-run steelhead usually spend all fall and winter in the streams, waiting to spawn in early spring.

Char

Salvelinus spp. (sal-vel-**eye**-nus: the German term Latinized). Salmonidae.

Bull trout, *S. confluentus* (con-flu-**en**-tus: of rivers). Adults broadly built, the head and midsection typically as high as they are wide. Olive-greenish back and sides regularly pink- to yellow-dotted; juvenile parr marks wider than the light spaces between; dorsal fin unmarked, with 10 or 11 rays, anal fin usually with 9. Mainly E of Cas Crest.

Flyfishing as we nonhunting nongathering catch-and-release nerds practice it isn't even fishing, really. It links us not to the Food Chain but to the Idiot Joy Chain, which differs from a Food Chain in that it has no top or bottom. Rod in hand on the Idiot Joy Chain, I find myself no more worthy or wise or deserving or in touch with I.Q. points than the stone-, water-, insect-, fish-, and sunlight-links in the same Chain… I fish in fall to feel the slow tilt of planet and weakening solar rays abandon every waterbug, wildflower, mating dance, and tree leaf summer gave us. I fish in spring to feel the same planetary tilt resurrect every creature and joy that autumn killed…

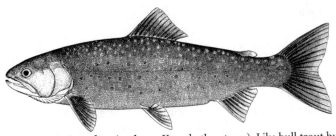

Dolly Varden, *S. malma* (mal-ma: Kamchatkan term). Like bull trout but slenderer: head height greater than width. Rivers in nw WA.

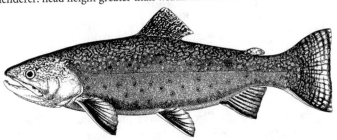

Brook trout, *S. fontinalis* (fon-tin-ay-lis: of springs). Dark green back and sides with "wormy" patterns and red spots surrounded by blue haloes; dorsal fin dark-spotted, with 8–10 rays, anal fin with 7–9; juveniles' broad parr marks overlaid with lighter red and yellow dots. Native to eastern NA.

Commonly called trout, fish of this genus are more properly char, or charr, or charrr (in the American, English, and quasi-Scottish spellings). Mature char are distinguishable from true trout by having light spots against a darker background, rather than vice versa. They are described as smarter than salmon in W.F.W.D. literature: "Log jams, cascades and falls that are barriers to the chinook's brute

It leaps again…and I suddenly know a litany of things I can't possibly know: that the souls of trout too leap, becoming birds; that trout take a fly made of plumage out of yearning as well as hunger; that an immaterial thread carries a trout's yearning through death and into a bird's egg; that the olive-sided flycatcher, using this thread, is as much trout as bird as it rises to snatch the mayfly from its chosen pool of air; that the flycatcher that was the trout was the mayfly that was the river that was the creeks that were last year's snowpack that was last year's skies…

— David James Duncan

strength and the steelhead's acrobatic abilities may be only minor obstacles to the cunning and guile of [char]…Some go as far as to stick their heads out of the water to peek and find the easiest route." But when it comes to fishhooks they are seen as more naive and less feisty, making them less popular with anglers out for sport, and more popular with ones out for meat. Flavor is fine.

The bull trout, once an abundant Western trout with huge catch limits and even bounties (because it eats salmon fry) is now in dicey condition, extinct in many watersheds and endangered in others. It requires even colder, cleaner gravelly streams for spawning than our other salmonids. After logging high in a watershed muddies the gravel and warms the water by reducing shade, it may take decades before the stream is again good enough for a bull. This information has helped scientists' idea of a healthy streamside buffer to stretch to at least 300 feet. Also, reproduction has suffered where introduced brook trout have crossbred with bull trout to produce sterile hybrids. (Brookies were, after rainbows, the second most commonly stocked trout; they are no longer stocked in watersheds with bull trout.) Looking ahead, further global warming could make even a perfectly pristine stream too warm.

While our native char all spawn in mountain stream headwaters, populations vary in how far they migrate: they may live the bulk of their lives in small streams (nonmigrating) or bigger ones, or in lakes or the ocean (anadromous). They migrate far for trout, exceeding 115 miles on the Skagit and in the Rockies, where they reached a record 32 pounds. The Cascades record is 22½ pounds.

Dolly Varden and bull trout, long a single species, were separated in a 1978 paper. Though no technical argument against the change turned up, agencies and fishermen (and Yours Truly) dragged our heels at first, partly because the two are very hard to tell apart. Dollies are almost always anadromous; bulls rarely so. Dollies were named—allegedly by the first pioneer woman to see them—for their resemblance to a polkadot print fabric of the day, which was named after a gaudy character in Dickens' *Barnaby Rudge*. It was probably a bull trout that she first called Dolly V., but when the species was split, the polkadot name went, along with the Latin name, to the coastal species on which the Dolly dots are often not apparent, due to a silvery coating. Fishermen had long called the big lunkers with the really broad heads "bull trout," so at least that name fits the new species.

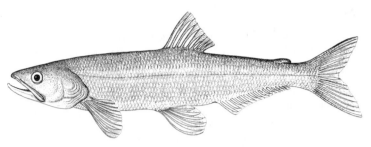

Eulachon

Thaleichthys pacificus (thay-lee-**ic**-thiss: plentiful fish). Pronounced "**you**-la-kon." Also **candlefish**. 5–8" fish, blue-gray above, silvery below; distinguished from salmon and trout by pelvic fin attached forward of dorsal fin and lacking an "axillary process," a small flap or scale just above the base of each pelvic fin. Sporadically abundant on lower W-side rivers in brief February or March spawning runs. Osmeridae (Smelt family).

Our common smelt, the eulachon or candlefish is so oily that it can be burned like a candle, once dried and threaded with wick. Its oil was the universal condiment in the cuisine of Coastal tribes and of many inland tribes who went to the Coast to trade for it. The name "eulachon" is from the Chinook trading jargon. It fetched a handsome price in British Columbia well into this century. The bitter froth of whipped soapberries suffused with eulachon oil was so popular it was nicknamed "Indian ice cream"; in later times, whopping doses of sugar were added.

In this century, dipnetting for "smelts" has been popular on lower Columbia tributaries. During heavy smelt runs it required so little skill or patience that bucketsful of smelt were wasted by people whose enthusiasm for hauling them in exceeded their enthusiasm for cooking them or giving them away. Those cornucopia days may or may not be gone forever. Smelt runs are mysteriously sporadic and variable on each river; the Sandy had no smelt at all for sixteen years, then had several good runs in the 1970s and 1985, but none since. Washington considers the species a candidate for listing, and sharply restricts netting.

Eulachon eggs have an outer membrane that bursts and sticks to the bottom on contact, leaving the egg in its inner membrane attached by a thread. The larvae drift to sea immediately on hatching, so the species is seen here only as spawning adults—about 95% three-year-olds, and 5% making a second run as four-year-olds.

Sculpins

Cottus spp. (**cot**-us: Greek term for some river fish). Also **muddler minnows, bullheads**. Scaleless, sometimes ± prickly, minnow-sized fishes with wide mouths, thick lips, depressed foreheads, very large pectoral fins, a ¾-length dorsal fin in 2 parts, and unforked tail fin. Widespread in streams. Cottidae (Sculpin family).
Torrent sculpin, *C. rhotheus* (**rowth**-ius: of noisy waters).
Slimy sculpin, *C. cognatus* (cog-**nay**-tus: related).
Shorthead sculpin, *C. confusus* (con-**few**-sus: clouded).

These funny-looking little fish are adapted to life on the bottom: wide, depressed mouths for bottom-feeding; motley drab colors for camouflage against the bottom; eyes directed upward, the only direction there is to look; and huge pectoral fins to anchor them with little effort in strong current. The eggs, laid in spring, adhere to the underside of stones, and are guarded by the father.

As eaters of eggs and competitors of fry, sculpins are enemies of young salmonids, but larger salmon and trout find sculpins to be a fine food resource. Turn about is fair play, no? Trout are so fond of them that they have inspired a trout fly pattern, the "muddler minnow." In all likelihood, nearly all the salmon eggs ending up in sculpin bellies were those not adequately buried in gravel by their mothers, and would have perished one way or another. In the balance, sculpins are not a threat to game fish.

Sculpins are found above impassable waterfalls on some of our rivers. They probably got there via waterways that crossed present-day drainage divides during unique geologic moments as the ice sheet retreated.

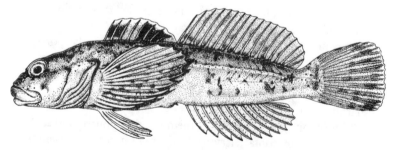

We are all in the gutter, but some of us are looking at the stars.
— Oscar Wilde

13

Insects

Insects—six-legged animals with jointed external skeletons made of chitin—are far and away the most diverse and successful kind of animals on earth. Over half a million species have been named, and at least as many remain to be discovered and described. Only a tiny sample of our insects can be discussed in this space: some of the ever charming butterflies, the invaluable pollinators—bumble bees and hover flies—and a rogues' gallery of unloved insects.

A majority of insect life cycles entail metamorphosis from a wingless larva, which does most or all of the eating and growing, to a pupa or resting stage, and finally to a winged, sexual adult.

Mosquitoes

Order Diptera (Flies), family **Culicidae.**

A female mosquito has a most elaborate mouth. What we see as a mere proboscis is a tiny set of surgical tools—six "stylets" wrapped in the groove of a heavier "labium" flanked by two "palps." The operation begins with the two palps exploring your skin for a weakness or pore. There the labium sets down. Delicately and precisely, two pairs of stylets—one for piercing, one for slicing—set to work. They quickly locate and pierce a capillary, then bend and travel a short way within it. The remaining two stylets are tubes; one sucks blood out while the other pumps saliva in, stimulating bloodflow to the vicinity and perhaps inhibiting coagulation. Up to the point of blood stimulation, to which you may be allergic, you probably feel nothing. (Mosquito detection is the chief remaining "usefulness of hair on the legs," or so mused Gary Snyder in his 1951 journal from a North Cascades fire lookout.)

Unlike bee stings, whose function is to inflict pain or injury, a mosquito bite raises its bump and itch—an allergic reaction to mosquito saliva—only incidentally. The sensitivity is acquired. The first few times a given species of mosquito bites you, there's no pain or welt. As you develop sensitivity to that species, your response speeds up from a day or so, at first, to one or two minutes. Eventually you may become again desensitized to that species. We never notice this cycle because we fail to distinguish among the species.

The females need at least one big blood meal (greater than their own weight) for nourishment to lay eggs. It takes human-feeding species about two minutes to draw enough. Aside from that meal, they eat pollen and nectar; some plants may depend on them as pollinators. Male mosquitoes eat nectar only, but contribute to our discomfort all the same: they hover around warm bodies in the reasonable expectation that that's where the girls are. If we wanted, we could get males to fly down our throats by singing the pitch hummed by female wings. Male antennae have evolved into plumes that vibrate sympathetically with conspecific female wing beats, and the males home in toward any steady source of this pitch.

Each mosquito species has its own wing beat frequencies, one for the males and a slightly lower one for the females; young adults speed up their wing beats as they reach sexual maturity. Wing beats range up to 600 per second in mosquitoes, and peak at over 1,000 in their relatives, the midges. Anything over 50 beats per second is too fast to be triggered by individual nerve impulses. Instead, the thoracic muscles are in two groups, each stretched by the contraction of the other, and contracting in a twitchlike reflex. The thorax shell snaps back and forth between two stable shapes, like the lid of a shoe polish tin, one shape holding the wings up and the other down. The nervous system need supply only a slow, unsteady pulse of signals to keep this snapping vibration going. (Flies and many other insects fly similarly.)

Most mosquitoes are active only a short period each day. The time varies from species to species, but just before and after sunset and just before dawn are most popular.

The choice of victim, or "host," is also specialized. Certain varieties of the familiar domestic species *Culex pipiens* never bite people, but others rank among the peskiest. (**cue**-lex: the Roman term; **pip**-ee-enz: piping.) Most of our mountain mosquitoes are of genus *Aedes* (ay-**ee**-deez: repugnant). While other genera set their eggs afloat on bodies of still water, *Aedes* cannot; they lay eggs in the fall on spots of bare ground likely to be briefly submerged in the spring, when the larvae hatch and take off swimming. Alternatively, some boreal *Aedes* overwinter as already-mated females, and lay eggs on the melting snowpack in spring. In any case, the larvae, or "wigglers," feed by filtering algae and bacteria out of water.

Gruesome concentrations of mosquitoes typify the Far North, where musk-oxen and nesting ducks make ideal hosts. One stoical researcher counted 189 bites on a forearm exposed for one minute. From that he extrapolated 9,000 bites per minute for one entire naked person, who could lose one-fourth of his blood in an hour.

Mosquitoes are probably the best studied of all insect families, largely because, as vectors of two tropical diseases, they wrought major effects on economic and military history. Malaria, introduced here in 1830, within four years killed a majority of the Indians on the lower Columbia, shattering tribal culture and leaving the Willamette Valley wide open to unimpeded white settlement. The carrier, mosquito genus *Anopheles* (an-**ah**-fel-eez: worthless), still lives here, but since most sloughs and lakes were drained in the last century its numbers have been too small to sustain a reservoir of the disease in this climate. In 1803, yellow fever also entered our history, from a safe distance: it killed nine-tenths of a French army sent to conquer Haiti and the Mississippi Valley, leaving Napoleon in much more of a mood to sell "Louisiana" to Thomas Jefferson at a price Congress couldn't refuse. This purchase led directly to Lewis and Clark, and ultimately to the Oregon Territory ending up as part of the U.S. rather than of Mexico, Canada, or Russia.

No-see-ums

Culicoides spp. (cue-lic-**oy**-deez: gnat-like). Also **punkies, biting midges**. Order Diptera (Flies).

The name "no-see-ums" suffices to identify these pests. At up to ⅛" long, they are just big enough to see, but small enough to invade screened cabins. They are hard to make out in the waning light of dusk, when they do most of their biting. Surprise and defenselessness irritate us more than the bites really hurt. No-see-ums are so localized around their breeding grounds that we can usually escape by walking fifty feet. Breeding habitats include puddles, intertidal sands, and humus.

The chief victims of this bloodsucking family are other insects ranging from their own size on up to dragonflies. In some species the females prey on the males, and one pirate species sucks mammal blood from mosquito abdomens.

Deer Flies

Chrysops spp. (**cry**-sops: appearing golden). Order Diptera (Flies).

About the size of house flies but much slower and softer, deer flies are maddeningly easy to kill—maddening because it's an irresistible exercise in utter futility. Where there's one deer fly, there are a thousand. On a hot July day in a North Cascades basin, the only respites may be nightfall, tent netting, your fastest stride, or rain, none of which are what you had in mind for this otherwise lovely afternoon. Travel sometimes helps, since most deer flies stay within half a mile of the marsh or pond where they overwintered as larvae. Ranging from dull gray-brown to nearly black, the dozens of species of deer flies are distinguished partly by the patterns of pale brown blotches on their clear wings.

Horse Flies

Tabanus spp. (ta-**bay**-nus: the Roman term). Order Diptera (Flies).

Horse flies are our biggest, fastest, strongest biting flies, so we're lucky they're sparse enough to view as individuals: when you manage to swat one, you may actually be ahead of the game for awhile. They also obsess about the tops of our heads, often diverting them from our more vulnerable parts. Even so, they're hard to catch up with. With black coloring and iridescent eyes, they resemble very large house flies.

Horse flies are commonest near large-mammal habitat. The

nectar- and pollen-eating males are seen less often than the blood-sucking females. With larvae going through two winters before metamorphosing into adults, horse flies are long-lived, as flies go. Both horse and deer flies are also known as gad flies. Dictionaries may spell them "horsefly" and "gadfly," but entomologists prefer to keep "fly" separate in the names of true flies (order Diptera) to distinguish them from non-flies such as dragonflies and butterflies.

Black Flies

Simulium spp. (sim-**you**-lium: simulator).
Order Diptera. (Flies). Also **buffalo gnats.**

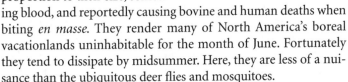

These vicious biters raise a welt way out of proportion to their size, sometimes draw-

ing blood, and reportedly causing bovine and human deaths when biting *en masse.* They render many of North America's boreal vacationlands uninhabitable for the month of June. Fortunately they tend to dissipate by midsummer. Here, they are less of a nuisance than the ubiquitous deer flies and mosquitoes.

"Black" flies are medium to dark gray, and stocky for their length (about ⅛"). They look humpbacked, and tilt steeply forward while biting. Only the females bite. Once fed, they dive in and out of cold, fast streams attaching eggs singly to submerged stones. The larvae stay underwater, straining plankton, moving around and then reanchoring themselves with a suction disk. After emerging from pupation, the adults burst up through the water in a bubble.

Hover Flies

Order Diptera, family **Syrphidae**. Also **flower flies.**

Hummingbirds, kestrels, and many insects achieve midair stasis, but only certain hover flies adopt it as their normal stance. They are more stationary than hovering bees or other insects, which inevitably bob and weave.

Hover flies in the woods, seemingly transfixed by an afternoon shaft of sunlight, are males maintaining territory near a good spot (such as a rotting tree hole) for a female to lay eggs. The female's last mating before laying eggs confers the best odds of prolific fatherhood. The sunbeam helps the fly maintain his required thoracic temperature, quite close to our own 98.6°. Watch a stationary male, and you may see him abruptly chase an approaching male or an unreceptive female, then reclaim his post.

In the mornings, both males and females visit flowers in meadows, the females gorging on proteins they require to develop their eggs, the males snacking lightly but mostly patrolling territory in hopes of a chance at a receptive female. Unlike bees, which use their long tongues to draw nectar out of deep flowers, flies have short tongues, visit shallower flowers, and primarily eat pollen. Pollen grains are encased in extremely durable, acid-resistant shells. (That's what makes 50,000-year-old pollen deposits so useful for studying prehistory.) But they release their protein-rich contents after soaking in the plants' own nectar; so the fly takes a sip of nectar after stuffing its gut with pollen.

Only bees are more valuable than hover flies as pollinators worldwide, and in high mountain meadows, where bumblebees are the only common bees, flies do more pollinating than bees. They also carry pollen farther (an advantage in terms of plant genetic diversity) but are slightly less faithful to a plant species on any given day. The maggotlike larvae of many hover flies perform another huge service to plants; they are the leading predators of aphids.

However dreadful the larva may appear to an aphid, hover flies are perfectly charming from our point of view, once we outsmart the adults' mimicry of black-and-yellow-banded bees and wasps. Hover flies even sound like bees, employing similar wingbeat frequencies. Mimicry is excellent protection against any predator that ever made the mistake of attacking a bee or wasp. The simplest way for us to tell hover flies from bees and wasps ought to be counting the wings; flies (Order Diptera, "two wings") have two, other flying insects have four. Unfortunately, the very narrow hindwings of bees and wasps (Order Hymenoptera, "membrane wings") are translucent and hard to see in a live insect. Long antennae, clubshaped ones especially, are a more useful stinger warning; most hover flies have antennae shorter than their heads, and a thick, probing proboscis. Yellowjackets at rest fold their wings straight down their backs; hover flies and bees make a V shape. Hover flies and bumble bees are far more abundant here, especially in high meadows, than all other bees and wasps. If it looks like a yellowjacket (slender, not furry) but seems to like you and flowers, trust it.

Bumble Bees

Bombus spp. (**bom**-bus: "buzz"). Large, rotund, furry, yellow-and-black bees; queens in most species are ¼–⅞" long, and fly in the spring; workers ¼–¾" long, appearing late spring to fall. Ubiquitous. Order Hymenoptera (Ants, wasps, bees).

Much "common knowledge" about bees is actually about honey bees, which aren't even native to the Americas. (The European honey bee, *Apis mellifera*, invaded America along with European culture, but is not abundant in our wilderness. A honey bee worker stings only once, losing her stinger and often her life, but other bees have repeat-use stingers. Honey bees have an elaborate social order and communication rituals, but most native bees are so-called "solitary bees"—they may live gregariously, but they don't organize societies with a division of labor. In the 1990s, wild honey bees in America are being decimated by a newly arrived parasite, the Varroa mite. It will be interesting to see how well the native bees reclaim the pollinator roles that honey bees long ago displaced them from.)

Bumble bees, our commonest bees, are in the honey bee family, and do have a strong social order though their colonies are relatively small and short-lived. Each colony begins with a queen who comes out from hibernating among dead leaves, having mated with several males the previous fall. Typically choosing a mouse or vole burrow for her nest, she secretes beeswax to make "pots." In some she lays eggs on a liner of pollen and nectar, sealing them over with more wax. Others she fills with honey (nectar concentrated within her body, chiefly by evaporation) which she sips for energy while working her muscles and pressing her abdomen onto her eggs—incubating them with body heat, like a warm-blooded bird. The first brood is all workers, or small, nonmating females. Maturing in three or four weeks, they take over the nectar and pollen gathering chores while the queen retires to the nest to incubate eggs and feed larvae. Protein-rich pollen nourishes the growing larvae, while pure carbohydrate nectar and honey are all that's needed by the energetic adults. Bumble bee honey is as delicious as honey bee honey but can't be exploited by large omnivores like people and bears because

---

bumble bees don't store much for the future; the queen keeps producing just as many broods of larvae as the growing population of workers can feed. As the food supply allows, late broods will include increasing numbers of sexuals—male drones from unfertilized eggs, and new queens produced simply by more generous and prolonged feeding of female larvae. Only the queens eat well enough to survive the onset of winter. The rest die in the fall, after the drones and queens have mated. By feeding only a small minority for hibernation, bumble bees conserve nectar and pollen resources which are scarce in cool climates.

Other key adaptations include the use of ready-made insulated nests; the relatively large, furry bodies; and the skill of raising a near-constant body temperature for flight in a wide range of weather conditions. Bernd Heinrich has cataloged such varied, extensive, and sophisticated forms of thermoregulation in insects, especially bumblebees, that he calls them "Thermal Warriors," and completely rejects the description of insects as cold-blooded. Arctic bumble bees have been seen in flight in a snowstorm at 6° below freezing. Generally, bumble bees are the most valuable plant pollinators at high latitudes and altitudes.

Some apparent bumble bee queens are false bumble bees, genus *Psithyrus* (**sith**-ir-us: whisper). These nest parasites murder queen bees and usurp their colonies. *Bombus* queens may also usurp each other's colonies if they can, but *Psithyrus* queens are genetically committed to it; they produce no *Psithyrus* workers, and their legs carry no pollen. Worker bees on guard duty may be able to get enough stingers through an invader's armor to kill her, but once a false queen has established herself, the workers keep bringing home the bacon obliviously. It is not unusual to find several dead queens in a nest, or to find colonies of mixed species.

Ant Lion

Myrmeleon immaculatus (mer-**me**-lee-on: ant lion; im-ac-you-**lay**tus: unspotted). Also **doodle bug**. Larvae found underneath ¼–⅝" diam (rarely up to 1½"), perfect conical pits in fine dry sand, up to ½" long, sand-coated, pinkish gray with six black spots on stout body, two long heavy mandibles longer than the rest of the head; adults like frail, feeble damselflies, 1½" long, with four 1"-long, narrow, little-used wings. Commoner E of Cas Cr. Order Neuroptera (Vein-winged insects).

Ant lion eggs are laid in the sand. As soon as they hatch, the larvae dig pits to trap ants and other crawling insects. Try dropping an ant into one if you go for life-or-death entertainment, and you may catch some action—the ant lion's pit-digging motions. It flips its head and mandibles violently, tosses sand up the slopes of the pit, and rotates its body, keeping the prey trapped. As the larva grows, it moves on to bigger and better traps. Both common names refer to the ferocious predatory larvae. The adults, though large, are delicate, slow, innocuous, and rarely encountered.

Cooley Spruce Gall Aphid

Adelges cooleyi (a-**del**-jeez: unseen; **coo**-lee-eye: after R. A. Cooley). Soft hemispherical bodies .04" long, covered at most stages with waxy, cottony white fluff; wings (if present) folded rooflike over body; on Douglas-fir needles (related species also on true firs or pines); more conspicuous are their conelike galls (illustrated) on branch tips of spruces, esp Engelmann. Widespread on and near spruces. Order Homoptera (Aphids etc.).

Many spruces seem to have an odd, spiky sort of cone in addition to their larger papery-scaled ones. Looking closer, we can see these aren't really cones because they are at branchlet tips, rather than several inches back, and because they are fused wholes, not a set of wiggleable scales. The "spikes" turn out to be simply spruce needles with a hard brownish or greenish skin drawn tight like shrinkwrap. This is a "gall," material secreted by the tree in response to chemical stimulation by an insect. Other examples of aphid galls include bright red marginal swellings on shrub leaves; the light, tan orbs on oak limbs are galls of tiny gall wasps.

Though each spruce gall ends one branchlet's growth, galls in themselves are hardly ever a serious drain on their host plants. Living aphids sometimes are. They suck plant juices through minute piercing tubes nearly as long as their own bodies. They seem to suck in far more plant sugar than they can consume, since they pass copious sticky "honeydew" excretions. Some aphids are "herded" by ants or other insects that feed on aphid honeydew, but on our fir trees honeydew is more likely to end up consumed by a dreadful-looking black smut fungus. Our forest trees are not much hurt, though, by either the feeding or the housing activities of this aphid.

Spruce gall aphids actually feed mostly on fir trees. Their life cycle includes no larvae, pupae, or males as those terms are

---

normally defined. Instead it is divided into five forms or castes, each egg-laying. One wingless form overwinters on spruce, then lays the eggs of the gall-making form, which emerges from the gall in late summer and flies to a Douglas-fir to lay eggs. These eggs produce the fir-overwintering form which in turn engenders two forms, one wingless and firbound, the other flying to spruce to beget either the spruce-overwintering form or a short-lived intermediary sexual generation. But sexuals are unknown, or at least very rare, in our region. The various female forms are perfectly able to perpetuate their clone "parthenogenetically," (without fertilization).

Balsam Woolly Aphid

Adelges piceae (pie-**see**-ee: of spruces). Soft hemispherical bodies ½–5" long, covered at most stages with waxy white "wool"; rarely found in winged stage. Sporadically epidemic on true firs. Order Homoptera (Aphids etc.).

The balsam woolly aphid coevolved in an unthreatening relation-ship with the fir species of Europe, but when accidentally intro-duced into North America, where it has no natural enemies, it proved deadly to several American firs. Subalpine firs have been devastated by it in many areas below 5,500', while grand and silver firs are moderately susceptible. The tree's leader may droop and break off early in an attack, then all the foliage may turn red-brown from the top downward and the trunk hemorrhage with resin.

This aphid resembles the innocuous Cooley spruce gall aphid (above) but feeds on true fir stems or twigs, which swell up in "gouty" knobs. Dispersing mainly on wind currents, this species rarely grows wings and never migrates to spruces or makes galls. Reproduction is asexual and males are unknown.

Ten-lined June Beetle

Polyphylla decemlineata (poly-**fil**-a: many leaves; des-em-lin-ee-**ay**-ta: ten lined). ⅞–1¼" long, brown, with broad white stripes lengthwise on back; hairy under-neath; males have large, thick, twisting antennae; adults found feeding on conifer foliage, or flying into lights at night. Order Coleoptera (Beetles).

The white, usually C-curved larvae (typical of the Scarab fam-ily) feed on plant roots, becoming occasional pests in conifer nurs-eries. The handsome adults huff and puff audibly through their breathing holes when disturbed.

Golden Buprestid

Buprestis aurulenta (bew-**pres**-tiss: Greek term, meaning "cow-swelling," for some beetle; or-you-**len**-ta: golden). ½–¾" beetle; metallic emerald green, coppery iridescent down center, edges, and underneath; back ridged lengthwise. Widespread but shy, adults may be found feeding on foliage, esp Douglas-fir. Order Coleoptera (Beetles).

This beetle beauty rivals our most glamorous butterflies. Foresters count it among our pests. Because it attacks trees in relatively small numbers it rarely does more than cosmetic damage, but that can add up to a lot of dollars. The larvae bore deep into seasoned heartwood, and may continue to do so as long as fifty years after the wood is milled and built into houses. Such records make the buprestid a contender for the title of longest-lived insect, though the larvae mature in less than a decade in natural habitats.

Rose chafers, genus *Dichelonyx* (die-kel-**oh**-nix), are also metal-green to coppery-purple beetles, but are rarely even ½" long.

Ponderous Borer

Ergates spiculatus (er-ga-teez: worker; spic-you-**lay**-tus: with little spikes). Also **pine sawyer, spiny longhorn beetle**. Large beetles 1¾–2½" long; back minutely pebbled, dark reddish brown to black; thorax ("neck" area) may bear many small spines; antennae long, jointed, curved outward. Order Coleoptera (Beetles).

Attracted to light, these clumsy nocturnal giants startle us when they come crashing into camp. The equally ponderous larvae take several years to grow to a mature size of up to 3", chewing 1" to 2" diameter holes through pine or Douglas-fir heartwood. Loggers call the larvae "timber worms." One logger was inspired by their mandibles in inventing the modern saw chain design.

The ability of adult beetles to both fly and bore may be a key to their great success. They comprise easily the largest and most diverse order, not only among insects but among all living things. Their name, Coleoptera, means "sheath wings" in Greek. The two forewings are modified into a hard sheath that encloses and protects the two hindwings when they are folded up, enabling beetles to bore into hard materials without jeopardizing their wings.

Pine Beetles

Dendroctonus spp. (den-droc-ton-us: tree murder). Very small (⅛–¼") black to pale brown or red beetles with tiny, elbowed, clubtipped antennae; adults and larvae both live in inner bark layer, hence are little seen, but their excavation patterns in the bark and cortex are distinctive. Ubiquitous. Order Coleoptera (Beetles).

Mountain pine beetle, *D. ponderosae* (ponder-oh-see: of ponderosa pine, though in fact this beetle is commoner on lodgepole while the following species is almost exclusive to ponderosa).

Western pine beetle, *D. brevicomis* (brev-ic-**oh**-mis: short hair).

Douglas-fir beetle, *D. pseudotsugae* (soo-doe-**tsoo**-ghee: of Doug-fir).

Spruce beetle, *D. rufipennis* (roo-fip-**en**-iss: red wing).

Mtn. Pine Beetle

Western Pine Beetle

Pine beetles are among the most devastating insect killers of western trees, especially lodgepole and ponderosa pines. The first signs of their attack are small round entrance holes exuding pitch and/or boring-dust. The pitch is the tree's counterattack, an attempt to incapacitate the beetles. The many exit holes, a generation later, look as if they were made by a blast of buckshot.

After the bark falls away you can see dramatic branched engravings underneath. The beetles, though less than ⅛" wide, chew much wider egg "galleries" through the tender inner bark layer, just barely cutting into the sapwood. The hatched larvae set off at right angles to the gallery—often in neat, closely spaced left/right alternation—growing as they proceed, and then pupating at the ends of their tunnels. From there they bore straight out through the bark upon emerging as adults. The tunnels are left packed with "frass" of excreted wood dust. In most species, the egg gallery runs from several inches to a yard, straight up and down the wood grain, and the tunnels of the larvae run straight to the sides or fan out slightly. However, western pine beetle galleries curl and

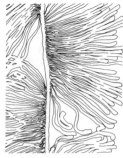

Douglas-Fir Beetle

Spruce Beetle

crisscross all over the place like spaghetti, and the larvae leave little impression on the inner bark, preferring the outer bark. The related engraver beetles (next page) reveal their identities with further variations on the theme.

These beetles are all native here. In most years they benefit the forest by culling the damaged, diseased, or slower-growing trees. Vigorously growing trees are unpalatable and unnutritious; the beetles must overpower the tree's health or it will overpower them. They do so by attacking *en masse* and by bringing pathogenic fungi along for assistance. Single females scout, and then release scented pheromones to attract others to a vulnerable tree. Each female is followed into her entrance hole by a male, and they work as a pair.

Mountain and western pine beetles have occasional population outbreaks—typically after drought has stressed the region's forests for several years—when they kill trees regardless of health. They kill entire stands. At these times their economic equation shifts, making it advantageous to them to go for the biggest and healthiest trees. The best preventive may be thinning pine forests to keep them vigorous, and also to put each tree out of range of beetle pheromonal communication—about 20'—from the next tree. Unfortunately, the stumps left after thinning may foster the spread of serious fungal diseases. Ponderosa pine stands used to be kept thin by frequent fires, and pine beetle outbreaks were less common. But as foresters seek ways to heal the "sick forests" left by decades of fire suppression and high-grade logging in the ponderosa pine region they meet frustration after frustration, as a fix for one problem often exacerbates another. "Once the straw has broken the camel's back, simply removing the straw does not allow the camel to rise again." *

---

* This aphorism on ecological threshold effects is David Perry's wording, in *Forest Ecosystems,* paraphrasing D. L. Knowlton.

Engraver Beetles

Scolytus spp. (sco-**lie**-tus: truncated) ⅛" long, shiny blackish beetles; abdomen appearing "sawed off" a bit shorter than the end of the wing covers; known mainly by their egg galleries in the inner bark of dead and dying trees. Ubiquitous. Order Coleoptera (Beetles).

Douglas-fir engraver, *S. unispinosus* (you-ni-spy-**no**-sus: one-spined).

Fir engraver, *S. ventralis* (ven-**tray**-lis: on the belly).

Fir branch engraver, *S. subscaber* (sub-**scay**-ber: somewhat rough).

The Douglas-fir engraver leaves its signature on a high proportion of fallen Doug-firs that lie in full or partial sunlight—a deep but rather short (4–6") egg gallery carved along the grain of the inner bark and sapwood, from which issue an array of larval tunnels that start out perpendicular but soon curve up or down, finally running with the grain. (If the tree falls into heavy shade, the related Douglas-fir pole beetle, *Pseudohylesinus nebulosus,* may cut nearly identical marks in it.)

The fir engraver carves true firs, and its signature is 90° different: the main gallery runs straight across the grain, the larval tunnels with the grain. Still more distinctive is the mark of the fir branch engraver, which looks like a rounded **E** branded into the inner bark of dead lower (or fallen) branches of true firs. This species rarely attacks the main trunk; you could think of it as aiding the tree's self-pruning efforts.

In the Northwest alone, dozens of species in the Scolytidae family of beetles take on specialized roles in recycling woody waste, a process crucial to the forest's vitality. Many of them have special organs ("mycangia") for holding and disseminating spores of fungi which, along with bacteria, are essential partners in this great symbiosis. A majority of them, like the Douglas-fir engraver, rarely attack trees or branches that aren't already done for. And then again, some are killers. Dutch elm disease is a fungus inadvertently introduced to America

Douglas-Fir
Engraver

Fir Engraver

on its *Scolytus* beetle host, with disastrous results; the disease never threatened European elms, which are genetically resistant to it. With native pests like the western pine beetle and the fir engraver, it isn't clear to what extent the occasional disastrous infestations depart from the natural order. Even the killer species are, in normal years, cullers of infirm individuals, benefitting the health of their victim population like wolves culling an elk herd.

If not for its attackers, a tree would be virtually immortal— just as long as it could keep growing — since trees do not get old in the sense that animals do. Without beetles and fungi, would the forest stop growing short of impenetrability? It's hard to imagine such a world.

Striped Ambrosia Beetle

Trypodendron lineatum (try-po-**den**-dron: bore tree; lin-ee-**ay**-tum: lined). ⅛" long, shiny black to brown beetles with faint paler stripes lengthwise on wing covers; head hidden from above by thorax, so body appears to have only two sections; antennae shaped like very fat clubs; known mainly by their heavily black-stained pinholes deep in wood. In all major W-side conifers. Order Coleoptera (Beetles).

Ambrosia beetles are named for their cultivation of "ambrosia" fungi for food. They carry the fungus with them and inoculate it into holes they bore in downed or dying trees. If moisture and other conditions are perfect, the fungus will grow just fast enough to feed the beetles and their larval brood without smothering them.

Though bark beetles (previous pages) also bring fungal allies to their attacks on trees, their food is still the tree cambium itself. Only ambrosia beetles get their nourishment directly from the fungus, which in turn gets it from the tree; since the fungus can break down the hardest of heartwood, ambrosia beetles are not confined to the thin tender layers under the bark, but burrow straight into the sapwood and sometimes even the heartwood. The fungus stains the wood around each bore hole black, wreaking economic havoc on logs that are cut in the autumn and left out through winter.

Large fallen trees take several centuries to decompose, and would take longer still if the decomposers (fungi and bacteria) didn't have borers to make a rapid initial penetration of the protective bark. The forest ecosystem needs the logs to decompose in order to make both space and nutrients available for new plants.

Tent Caterpillar Moths

Malacosoma spp. (ma-la-co-**so**-ma: soft body). Moths ws ¼–1½", variably brown, forewing (the one in view when wings are folded) divided in thirds by two parallel fine lines; larvae (caterpillars) 2" when fully grown, bristling with tufted long hairs, generally dark brown with blue, orange and reddish markings; egg masses on small twigs, esp at crotches, covered with a gray to dark brown foam that hardens to a ± waterproof coating. Widespread on broadleaf trees and shrubs; occasionally on conifers. Order Lepidoptera (Moths and butterflies), Lasiocampidae (Lappet moth family).

Western tent caterpillar moth, *M. californicum.* Egg masses plastered against twigs.

Forest tent caterpillar moth, *M. disstria* (dis-**try**-a: variously striped). Egg masses evenly encircling twigs.

Our region has an outbreak of tent caterpillars on red alder every ten years or so. Many trees are defoliated and achieve little growth for a year or two, but few are killed. The "tent" is a big erratic web of silk that affords caterpillar groups protection and insulation during resting periods between feeding sprees. Our abundant forest tent caterpillar is the only kind that doesn't build tents, though the resting colony may spin (and lie on) a rudimentary silken web.

Tent caterpillars pupate within silken cocoons, coated with a skin-irritating dust, under curled leaves. Adult tent caterpillar moths have no working mouthparts; they survive purely on what they ate as caterpillars, living just a few days to mate and lay eggs.

Moths vs. Butterflies

Moths and butterflies together comprise the order Lepidoptera ("scaly wings"). Some generalizations can be made about differences between the two, though there are exceptions to all except antenna shape:

Moths

are mostly nocturnal;

have slender-tipped, or else fernlike, antennae;

have bigger bodies for their wing size;

may pupate in a chrysalis with an outer "cocoon" of silk;

raise their body temperatures before flying by vibrating their wings;

perch with wings spread to the sides, either flat or angled rooflike, forewings covering hindwings.

Cascade-Olympic Natural History

(It could be said of insects generally, to varying degrees, that adults are ephemeral bridges from one larval generation to the next.) In tent caterpillars, larvae do most of the traveling as well as all the eating and growing; they have long bristles to help the wind carry them. Tiny larvae are already formed within the egg cases by winter, ready to chew their way out when the leaf buds burst in spring.

Trees are far from defenseless against foliage grazers. They need only slow the caterpillars' growth by a few percent to increase dramatically the number taken by predators and parasites. They can do this by loading their leaves with tannin and other hard-to-assimilate chemicals. However, producing the tannin requires an investment of energy that the trees do well to avoid, so they may load only some of their leaves with tannin, forcing the caterpillars to expose themselves to predatory birds while searching for palatable leaves. Or they may wait until attacked, and only then step up tannin production. Remarkably, trees may increase their tannin in response to an insect attack on a nearby tree of the same species, sensing chemicals analagous to distress pheromones cast upon the breeze by the attacked tree. This is among the clearest evidence to date of communication among plants. In the words of one enthusiastic scientist, "plants, after all, are really just very slow animals."

White-lined Sphinx Moth

Hyles lineata (hi-leez: of woods; lin-ee-ay-ta: lined). Ws 2¼–3½"; large heavy-bodied moths with rapid, buzzing wingbeats suggestive of hummingbirds; forewings dark olive brown with a broad pale stripe to the tip, and white-lined veins; hindwings pink and black, much smaller. Most often seen seeking nectar at dusk or by day. Order Lepidoptera, Sphingidae (Hawk moth family). Color p 504. (Comments on following page.)

Butterflies

are diurnal;

have club-tipped antennae;

have smaller bodies relative to wings;

pupate in a naked, more or less rigid shell, or "chrysalis;"

warm their muscles before flying by basking;

perch with left and right wings pressed together vertically, except when basking in sunlight .

Moths of this family are unusual in being active both day and night in their search for nectar. Their deep-pitched buzzing flight enables them to hover, and they seem on first acquaintance to resemble other nectar feeders—bumble bees or, in the case of this species, hummingbirds—rather than other moths. The bee-like species have hairy bodies and mostly clear wings.

Swallowtails

Papilio spp* (pa-**pil**-ee-o: butterfly). Large butterflies with "tail" lobe trailing each hindwing (four tails on these species, but none on some others), dramatically black-patterned, often with blue or orange spots near tail. Order Lepidoptera, Papilionidae (Swallowtail family).

Anise swallowtail, *P. zelicaon* (zel-ic-**ay**-on: a name from *The Iliad*). Ws 2½–3½", yellow with black markings ± along veins. Widespread near desert-parsley, cow-parsnip and related plants, the larval host. March–Sept. (has one or two broods each year). Color p 504.

Western tiger swallowtail, *P. rutulus* (**root**-you-lus: shining, red-orange, or gilded). Ws 3½–5", yellow with black "tiger" stripes across veins back from leading edge of wing, and along body. often abundant, usually near water; eats willow and cottonwood. April–Aug. Color p 504.

Pale tiger swallowtail, *P. eurymedon* (you-**rim**-e-don: Agamemnon's charioteer in *The Iliad*). Ws 3½–4½", cream yellow (females) to ± white (males) with heavy black "tiger" stripes. Sporadic, often near snowbrush. May–Aug. Color p 504.

Anise and pale swallowtails are often seen "hilltopping" on Hurricane Ridge and elsewhere; certain butterfly species use tall landmarks (trees, buildings and even TV towers where hills are lacking) to help locate mates. The males arrive first, staking out sections of ridgeline and defending them against conspecific males while waiting for the females. Similarly, western tiger swallowtails use riverbanks, canyons, or other lineations of trees as their singles bars.

The larvae (caterpillars) flourish by late summer, and pupate over winter. Caterpillars of the anise swallowtail have striking black/yellow back bands against green, and are found on parsley-family plants such as garden fennel or anise. Caterpillars of both tigers have eyespots; these mock eyes function defensively, as do the antlerlike scent glands (on all swallowtail caterpillars) which they stick out when disturbed.

---

*Some texts split this genus, placing *rutulus* and *eurymedon* in *Pterourus*.

Parnassians

Parnassius spp. (par-**nas**-ius: of Mt Parnassus, referring to mtn habitat). Ws 2–3"; white butterflies with gray to black markings and small red, often black-rimmed eyespots. Papilionidae (Swallowtail family).

P. smintheus* (**sminth**-ius: Mouse God, a name of Apollo). Fore- and hind-wings usually with several red spots; antennae ringed black/white. WA, above timberline, typically on or near stonecrop, the larval food. June–Aug. Color p 504.

P. clodius (**cloh**-dius: a Roman politician). Eyespots (usually four) on hind-wings only, antennae black. Pupates in a cocoon. Widespread near forest edges; larvae feed on bleeding-heart. May–Aug. Color p 504.

The gray patches on parnassian wings actually just lack the minute scales that otherwise cover butterfly wings, leaving them trans-lucent like the wings of bees or flies. Scales give butterfly and moth wings their opacity, color, and softness. Hundreds of scales dust your fingertips if you attempt to grasp a butterfly.

Female parnassians are usually seen with a waxy object on the rear end, which hardens from a liquid extruded by the male during mating, and blocks other males from mating with that female. It is largest on *clodius*, whose mating style is scientifically described as rape. In butterflies with more evolved courtship behavior, already-mated females can and often do decline; but *clodius* uses this chas-tity belt instead.

Western White

Pontia occidentalis † (**pon**-sha: a name of Aphrodite; ox-i-den-**tay**-lis: west-ern). Ws 1¼–2", white with variable degrees of gray checking, esp on top of forewing, and pastel gray-green to yellow-brown vein linings, esp beneath hindwing. Abundant on mountaintops; occasional in other open habitats. April–Sept. Order Lepidoptera, Pieridae (Sulphur family). Color p 504.

Pairs of butterflies, especially whites and sulphurs, are often seen following each other upward in tall spirals. It is pleasing to think of these spiral flights as prenuptial stairways to heaven, but some observers see a countererotic situation—an already-mated female's last-ditch effort to escape an unwanted suitor by wearing him out in flight, or agonistic behavior between two males.

---

* Until recently, *smintheus* was included in the Eurasian *P. phoebus.*

† Some texts include *Pontia* in a broad genus *Pieris.*

Mustard White

Pieris napi * (**pie**-er-iss: a Greek Muse; **nap**-eye: of rape, a host plant). Also **veined white**. Ws 1½–1⅞", white with veins ± darkened, esp beneath; dark-stained near body; underside sometimes yellowish. Widespread in forest; feeds on mustard family, incl toothwort. March–Sept. (has two broods each year). Order Lepidoptera, Pieridae (Sulphur family). Color p 504.

Western Sulphur

Colias occidentalis (**coh**-lius: another name of Aphrodite). Ws 1¼–2", yellow (rarely orange or albino) usually with a dark dot in center of forewing and a white, ± dark-ringed dot on hindwing; male has a heavy black border above and a faint pink fringe all around wings. Widespread, esp streambanks and roadsides; larvae feed on legumes, e.g., lupine, sweet-pea. May–Sept. Pieridae (Sulphur family). Color p 505.

Sara Orange-Tip

Anthocharis sara (an-**thoc**-a-ris: flower grace: **sah**-ra: Sarah, Latinized). Ws 1¼–1¾", white to (females only) ± yellow with deep orange forewing tips, gray-green marbling under hindwing. Widespread in sunny habitats; larvae feed on mustard family plants. Among the earliest butterflies: late March (at low elevs) to August (high). Pieridae (Sulphur family). Color p 505.

Ochre Ringlet

Coenonympha tullia ampelos † (see-no-**nim**-fa: common nymph; **too**-lia: the daughter of Cicero; **am**-pelos: Wine, a youth loved by Dionysus). Ws 1¼–1¾", white-streaked rich ochre all over exc under hindwing, where ± gray-green; sometimes with eyespots near margins underneath. Cascades; abundant around grasses, the larval food. April–Oct. Satyridae. Color p 505.

Wood Nymphs

Cercyonis spp. (ser-**sigh**-o-nis: a legendary thief?). Drab black-brown above, barklike brown beneath; two black eyespots (sometimes indistinct) on each forewing; spots ± yellow-rimmed beneath and sometimes above; up to six tiny eyespots on hindwings. Cascades; abundant in ponderosa pine zone; larvae eat grasses, adults various flowers. Satyridae .

---

* *Pieris* is sometimes split, placing *napi* in genus *Artogeia*.

† Some authorities regard *ampelos* as a full species.

Large wood nymph, *C. pegala* (peg-a-la: a mythic name). Ws 1¾–2¾", much paler beneath (esp females). June–Sept. Color p 505.

Dark wood nymph, *C. oetus* (ee-tus: doom, i.e., blackness). Also **least wood nymph.** Ws 1½", almost as dark beneath as above; second forewing eyespot small and often inconspicuous. June–Aug.

Alpines

Erebia spp. (er-ee-bia: underworld, i.e., darkness). Ws 1½–2", dark brown with marginal rows of orange-haloed, yellow-pupilled black eyespots on all four wings, the haloes coalescing into an orange band on the forewings, esp in Vidler's. Order Lepidoptera, Satyridae (Satyr family).

Common alpine, *E. epipsodea* (ep-ip-**so**-dia: upon itself?). Alpine to low E-side marshes and meadows, Cas only. May–Aug. Color p 505.

Vidler's alpine, *E. vidleri* (vid-ler-eye: after Vidler). Strictly alp/subalpine, in N WA and BC only. Late June–Aug. Color p 505.

Caterpillars of alpines and arctics feed on grasses. The adults bask in preparation for flight, augmenting their metabolic energy with solar energy collected in their spread wings.

Eyespots

The pale dots ringed with dark, and often again with pale, that decorate many butterfly wings actually offer valuable protection from predators. Birds are fooled into pecking at the fake eyes, thinking them vital targets when the opposite is the case. Butterflies have little trouble flying with somewhat tattered hindwings—where most eyespots and all "tails" (similar diversionary ornaments) are located.

The eyespot ruse can also be effective in an even braver use. Newly emerged butterflies go through a few flightless hours when their wings are soft and useless. Wings first take form all wadded up inside the pupal shell, or "chrysalis," and as soon as the adult butterfly emerges it pumps fluids in through the veins to extend the wings to their proper shape. Then they need several hours to dry into rigidity. Apparently, large eyespots on the upper wing surface save many butterflies by actually frightening birds away during those vulnerable hours. The butterfly responds to an exploratory first peck by abruptly opening its folded wings; between the two "eyes" suddenly revealed, the bird imagines a larger face than it had meant to take on.

Arctics

Oeneis spp. (ee-**nee**-iss: a mythic king). Orange- or gray-brown exc silvery gray-brown under hindwing (for camouflage against bark or soil); 1 to 3 smallish black eyespots; forewing long and angular. Satyridae.

Sierra Nevada arctic, *O. nevadensis* (nev-a-**den**-sis: of the Sierra Nevada). Also **great arctic.** Ws 2–2½"; in Cas, esp E-slope. May–Sept of even-numbered years only, with rare exceptions. Color p 505.

Chryxus arctic, *O. chryxus* (**crix**-us: gold—). Ws 1¾–2"; sporadic at mid to high elevs in WA and BC. June–Aug. Color p 505.

Arctics, like anise swallowtails (page 464) are "hilltoppers" with a powerful drive to travel uphill. Ridgelines acquire dense, evenly spaced populations of hilltopping males, with scattered cameo appearances by eligible maidens foraging up from the more benign meadow environment. The male (lacking sharp eyesight) will rush out from his perch to greet any lepidopteran, and if it's a conspecific he engages it in a spiral duet flight. Somehow while spiralling upward he learns the visitor's gender, and the spiral ritual becomes either a courtship flight or a duel to defend his territory.

On each forewing's front edge a male has a dark stainlike patch of "scent scales" which emit attractive pheromones.

Painted Lady

Vanessa cardui (va-**nes**-a: derivation moot; **car**-dew-eye: of thistles). Ws 2–2¼", salmon to orange above with short white bar and black mottling near forewing tip, row of 4–5 tiny eyespots near hindwing margin; larvae are spiny, lilac with yellow lines and black dots, and typically spin nets around thistle tops. Occasionally ubiquitous. April–Sept. Order Lepidoptera, Nymphalidae (Brush-footed butterfly family). Color p 505.

The painted lady normally resides in climates warmer than ours. Occasionally the population irrupts thousands of miles in all directions, making painted ladies the most nearly worldwide of all insects. (The irruption requires several generations, with individuals migrating "only" a few hundred miles.) They don't survive winter here, and few make the trip up from Mexico in non-outbreak years, so they have been rare here except (most recently) in 1966, 1973, and 1992. In recent years they have been bred for commercial butterfly releases, which are not as benign as they seem. Preferred foods are thistles and other composites, but when overcrowded the larvae become omnivorous.

Lorquin's Admiral

Limenitis lorquini * (lim-en-**eye**-tiss: harbor goddess, **lor**-kwin-eye: after Pierre J. M. Lorquin). Ws 2¼–2¾", black above exc red-orange forewing tips and a heavy white band (broken by black veins) across both wings parallel to margin; dramatically striped beneath, mostly russet and white; flies with twitchlike beats alternating with gliding. Widespread, notably on stream-sides, the larvae feeding on willow and cottonwood leaves. May–Oct. Order Lepidoptera, Nymphalidae (Brush-footed butterfly family). Color p 505.

The handsome admiral male is a scavenger of dung and dead things, as well as a nectar-feeder. In the large and colorful family Nymphalidae, or brush-footed butterflies, the front two legs are short, brushlike appendages useless for walking or perching.

Milbert's Tortoiseshell

Aglais milberti (a-**glay**-iss: Brightness, one of the Graces; **mil**-bert-eye: after Milbert, a friend of the namer). Ws 1½–2", dark brown above with two ± distinct orange blotches on each leading edge and a broad orange and yellow (to white) band just inside the narrow dark brown margins; gray-brown beneath with ± light/dark patterns mirroring the upperside. Widespread, common in high meadows; larvae eat nettles, adults often visit daisies. Feb.– Oct. Nymphalidae (Brush-footed butterfly family). Color p 506.

Pale green egg clusters—or bristly small black web-spinning cater-pillars—on nettles are likely those of Milbert's Tortoiseshell.

California Tortoiseshell

Nymphalis californica. (nim-**fay**-lis: nymph—). Ws 1¾–2¼"; mostly yellow-orange above with a continuous dark margin and several large dark blotches on leading edge; mottled gray-brown beneath for camouflage against bark—much like anglewings (below) but with smoother wing out-line. Widespread, occasionally abundant; larvae eat snowbrush. Feb.–Nov. Nymphalidae (Brush-footed butterfly family). Color p 506.

In cold regions, tortoiseshell and anglewing adults hibernate, often in tree hollows. Getting an early start in spring, California tortoiseshells may breed two or even three generations a year here. Their populations are volatile, going through wild boom-and-bust cycles for unclear reasons. During boom years, thousands of them are smashed by cars as they stream through mountain passes, while the larvae defoliate snowbrush far and wide.

Limenitis is sometimes split, placing *lorquini* in genus *Basilarchia.*

Mourning Cloak

Nymphalis antiopa (an-**tie**-o-pa: a leader of Amazons). Ws 2–3¼"; ± iridescent deep red-brown above with full-length cream yellow border lined with bright blue spots; drab beneath, barklike gray-brown with dirty white border; margins ragged. Widely scattered on streamsides with cottonwood and willow. March–Oct. Order Lepidoptera, Nymphalidae (Brush-footed butterfly family). Color p 506.

The mourning cloak is known throughout the Northern Hemisphere. The adults hibernate—occasionally coming out to fly on sunny winter days—and sometimes aestivate through late summer. They breed during both spring and fall active seasons.

Anglewings

Polygonia spp. (poly-**go**-nia: many angles). Also **commas**. Ws 1¾–2¼", wing margins lobed fancifully, as if tattered; burnt orange above with dark margins and scattered black blotches; silvery gray-brown beneath. Ubiquitous; larvae eat currants, willows, rhododendron, nettles, etc. March–Sept. Nymphalidae (Brush-footed butterfly family). Color p 506.

Anglewings are amazingly well camouflaged against bark: one moment they flit about almost too fast to follow, and in the next they disappear by abruptly alighting with wings folded. A tiny but distinct pale mark centered beneath the hindwing is variously boomerang, comma, C, or V-shaped on different species of anglewing.

Greater Fritillaries

Speyeria spp. (spy-**ee**-ria: after Adolph Speyer). Ws 1½–3", orange with ± checkerlike black markings above; hindwing gray to golden tan beneath, with many round silvery-white to cream spots; forewing pale ochre to golden brown beneath, with blackish checks sometimes giving way to a few marginal white spots. Ubiquitous; larvae eat violets, adults suck nectar from composites, penstemons, dogbane, stonecrop, etc. May–Sept. Order Lepidoptera, Nymphalidae (Brush-footed butterfly family). Color p 506.

This gorgeous genus is behind many supposed monarch butterfly sightings in our region. Real monarchs, *Danaus plexippus*, depend on milkweed as a larval host, and hence are rather rare here.

Speyeria is a difficult genus even for specialists. The great spangled fritillary, *S. cybele*, is sexually dimorphic, with females black and pale yellow quite unlike the males, and unlike most other fritillaries. The name fritillary (in both lilies and butterflies) refers to a Roman dice-box with checkered markings.

Checkerspots

*Euphydryas** (you-**fid**-rius: shapely nymph) and *Charidryas** spp. (ca-**rid**-rius: grace nymph). Ws 1¼–2", generally 3-colored above—blackish, red-orange and pale yellow in a fine check pattern (sometimes just black and cream in *E. anicia* but never just black and orange as in fritillaries, and black rather than orange tends to predominate); mostly brick-red beneath with yellow to white checks and black veins. Abundant in sunny dry and rocky habitats; larvae feed on penstemon, paintbrush, other figwort-family plants, and snowberry (*E. anicia*) or on asters (*C. hoffmanni*). April–Aug. Order Lepidoptera, Nymphalidae (Brush-footed butterfly family). Color p 506.

Identifying these notoriously variable species often requires studying their genitalia under a microscope. If it's mainly black above, with red-orange traces near the tips and front edge, and it's near snowberry, it's likely a snowberry checkerspot, *E. anicia colon.*

Field Crescentspot

Phyciodes pratensis† (fis-**eye**-o-deez: seaweed-red; pra-**ten**-sis: of fields). Ws 1¼", largely black above with rows of red-orange and yellow-orange spots, the outermost spots crescent-shaped; patterns similar beneath but much paler, orange and yellow-brown with little or no dark brown. Common in sun at mid to high elevs. May–Sept. Nymphalidae. Color p 506.

Sooty Hairstreak

Satyrium fuliginosum (sa-**tee**-rium: satyr—; foo-li-jin-**oh**-sum: sooty). Also **sooty gossamer wing**. Ws 1" uniformly dark gray above, ashy gray beneath with faintly lighter and darker speckles. E slope of Cascades, where locally abundant in high meadows with lupine, the larval food plant. June–Aug. Lycaenidae (Copper family). Color p 507.

This species lacks the "hair" that hairstreaks are named for—a pair or quartet of hair-thin wing "tails"—but it sure has the "streak." Notoriously hard to keep track of when streaking around, it can sometimes be seen when flowers hold its attention. The sooty resembles females of the large group known as blues (and like them it likes lupines). While male blues are indeed usually blue, the un-blue female blues tend to be a bit browner than the sooty hairstreak on top, a bit whiter and more strongly speckled underneath.

---

* *Charidryas* was previously within genus *Chlosyne*; *E. anicia colon* was previously within genus *Occidryas*, as species *O. colon.*

† Formerly *P. campestris*, which has almost the exact same meaning.

Purplish Copper

Lycaena helloides * (lie-**see**-na:: she-wolf; hel-**oy**-deez: like species *helle*).
Ws 1", males dark brown above with purplish iridescence sometimes catching light, and an orange zigzag along hindwing margin; females yellow-
orange above with brown speckles and borders; both yellow-orange-brown
beneath with dark speckles and an orange zigzag on hindwing. Widespread.
May–Sept. Order Lepidoptera, Lycaenidae (Copper family). Color p 507.

Mariposa Copper

Lycaena mariposa * (mair-ip-**oh**-sa: butterfly in Spanish). Ws 1", males
dark brown above, with purplish iridescence and orange zigzag (see above)
often obscure or not evident; females lighter brown to orange, with dark
speckles and borders; hindwings ashy gray beneath, forewings orange with
speckles. often abundant in mid- to high-elev meadows, bogs, and clearings.
June–Sept. Color p 507.

Iridescence is common among tropical butterflies; here we find it
in coppers, a large group of small, mostly orange-brown butterflies.
Iridescent butterfly scales may have microscopic ridges that reflect
light prismatically, or they may be of two types on one butterfly,
regularly interspersed on the wing surface and held at different
angles—not unlike the way fabric designers combine contrasting
warp and weft threads to make an iridescent satin weave.

Arctic Blue

Agriades franklinii † (a-**gry**-a-deez: wild— ?; **frank**-lin-ee-eye: after Sir
John Franklin, facing page). Ws ¾", males silvery blue above, females rusty
gray-brown with white-haloed dark spots; both sexes ± white-fringed; light
gray-brown beneath with white-haloed spots. Strictly high-elev (6,500'+)
here; larvae eat shooting stars. Late June–Aug. Lycaenidae (Copper family).
Color p 507.

Scarce and drab, this doughty blue is nonetheless conspicuous from
time to time as the only butterfly flying in gray weather on high
windswept ridges. It ranges around the Arctic Circle in the lowlands, and ventures southward along the Cordilleran summits.

---

* The large genus *Lycaena* is sometimes split, putting both *helloides* and
mariposa in *Epidemia*.

† In various texts, the arctic (or "high mountain") blue is species *glandon* or
aquilo or *rusticus* in genus *Plebejus* or *Agriades*. Relationships with Eurasian
relatives are the issue.

Common Blues

*Lycaeides** spp. (lie-**see**-id-eez: like genus *Lycaena*) and *Icaricia** spp. (ic-a-**ree**-sha: after Icarus and genus *Aricia*) Ws 1"; males blue above, females brown, darkening at margins but white-fringed; grayish white beneath, dark-speckled esp on forewing. Lycaenidae (Copper family).

Northern blue, *L. idas* † (**eye**-duss: a hero, one of Jason's Argonauts). May have rows of orange crescents parallel to margin; these are on underside of blue males, both sides of brown females. Abundant at mid to high elevs; larvae eat lupine and other legumes. July–Sept. Color p 507.

Boisduval's blue, *I. icarioides* (ic-airy-**oy**-deez: like Icarus, who flew too close to the sun). Widespread, always near lupine, the larval food. May–Aug.

Male blues congregate to sip water from mud. Caterpillars of many species are attended by ants who eat "honeydew" secreted by the caterpillars. In this mutualistic symbiosis, the "stock-herding" ants sometimes attack and repulse beetles that parasitize caterpillars.

---

* These genera were separated out from a large genus *Plebejus*.

† A recent revision took American populations out of the Eurasian species *argyrognomon* and placed them in the Eurasian species *idas*.

Sir John Richardson and *Thomas Drummond* went on *Sir John Franklin's* second expedition into Arctic Canada. Richardson had also been on the first, barely returning alive and certainly without his specimens, so it was game of him to try again. Twice was enough, though; rather than perishing on Franklin's ill-fated third expedition, he lived on as an eminent naturalist and author of a fauna of boreal America.

Young Drummond, meanwhile, soon separated from the party and spent the winter alone—two months without seeing a soul, six months without a person he shared a language with—in an improvised brush hut in Alberta, relying on game for food. The doughty Scot summed up his relations with grizzly bears thus: "The best way of getting rid of the bears, when attacked by them, was to rattle my vasculum or specimen-box, when they immediately decamp." He had known David Douglas (page 18) in Scotland; chance brought them together again in the Rockies in 1827, and they took the same ship back to England. They had a great time talking botany. Before his unexplained death in Cuba in 1835, Drummond spent two years on the first extensive botanical exploration of Texas.

Dotted Blue and Square-Spotted Blue

Euphilotes * spp. (you-fill-**oh**-teez: after genus *Philotes*). Ws ½–¾", males blue above, females brown, both with a row of ± distinct orange spots near hindwing margin; marginal fringes of alternate black/white dashes; bluish white beneath, with dark speckles. Mainly E slope of Cas; larvae feed on sulphur (and other) buckwheat. May–Aug. Lycaenidae (Copper family).

Dotted blue, *E. enoptes* (ee-**nop**-teez: mirror).

Square-spotted blue, *E. battoides* (bat-**oy**-deez: like sp. *baton*). Color p 507.

The square-spotted breeds once a year and flies in May and June; the dotted has two annual generations, one flying in April and May and the second in July. other than that, specialists have found little to separate these two species behaviorally, geographically, or physically, except for microscopic differences in their genitalia.

Elfins

Incisalia spp. (in-sis-**ay**-lia: cut—). Lycaenidae (Copper family).

Brown elfin, *I. augustinus* (august-**eye**-nus: majestic—, a perverse name for this species). Ws ¾–1", plain brown above; no white fringe; reddish brown beneath with vaguely-defined dark inner portion of hindwings. Widespread; larvae feed on buds and flowers of shrubs incl salal and sagebrush. March–July. Color p 507.

Western pine elfin, *I. eryphon* (er-if-un). Ws ¾–1", light brown above with black/white-dashed marginal fringe usually visible; sharply zigzag-patterned beneath, light and dark reddish brown with black; older larvae pine-needle green, with paired whitish lengthwise stripes. Often abundant near pines, the larval food plant; adults visit willows, spiraea, buckwheats, etc. April–July. Color p 507.

Moss's elfin, *I. mossi*. † Ws ¾", all brown (females ± reddish) with black/white-dashed marginal fringe ± visible; two-toned beneath, the paler gray-brown outer sections sharply, irregularly divided from the darker inner sections. Sporadic in ± low rocky, sunny habitats with stonecrop, the larval food plant. March–early May. Color p 507.

Moss's elfin is the first butterfly to emerge from a pupa in spring, sometimes while snow still covers much of the ground. Any other butterflies flying then (anglewings or tortoiseshells, most likely) have almost surely hibernated as adults.

---

* *Euphilotes* was separated out from a large genus *Philotes*.

† Formerly considered a subspecies of the early elfin, *I. fotis*.

14

Other Creatures

Western Black-Legged Tick

Ixodes pacificus (ick-so-deez: like birdlime, i.e., sticky). Also **deer tick**. Small tick: adults about the size of this symbol: ϙ (less than half the size of the much more common wood tick and dog tick). With a 12× handlens, you should be able to see eight legs from near the head end, and a flat oval abdomen with a dark central oval and paler red perimeter.

Ticks are related to mites, and more distantly to spiders. The entire group differs from insects in having eight legs and two main body sections, rather than six and three, respectively. Ticks live on blood they suck from warm-blooded animals. They climb to the tips of grasses or shrubs (not trees) and wait for a chance to brush off onto a good host. Western black-legged ticks typically parasitize deer, deer mice, lizards, and birds.

Hikers in the Cascades and Olympics don't often pick up ticks, and even less often these tiny ticks that can carry Lyme disease. The tick would have to have picked up the germ from a previous host: deer mice, though asymptomatic, are thought to be a common reservoir. Since the chance is there, it pays to know the drill.

If you find a tick on you, and can brush it off easily, you haven't been bitten yet, so don't worry. If it has taken hold, pluck it carefully: using tweezers if available, grab the tick firmly by the head, not the abdomen, and tug gently and repeatedly until it releases its grasp. The point is to avoid leaving the tick's mouthparts imbedded in your skin, since they can continue to convey infection. Some claim that it helps to first soak the tick in alcohol or stove fuel.

Deer ticks have a two-year life cycle, and are most likely to transmit Lyme disease in the spring. Only a minority of deer ticks (3% in Oregon, in the one published study) harbor the Lyme spirochete (a bacterium), and even those that do rarely transmit it in the first day or two of sucking your blood, so antibiotics are not recommended unless an antibody test confirms the disease. Watch the area where the tick bit for a rash over the next 3 to 30 days. It would be a red rash that becomes warm and continues to spread for several days (not just an immediate small red bump around the bite, which would be an ordinary bite reaction). If you get the rash, see a doctor, who should prescribe an antibody test after the antibodies have had time to build up. (The "Western blot" test is more accurate than the "Elisa" test, which produces significant numbers of false positives.) If you test positive, a long dose of strong antibiotics will almost certainly stop Lyme disease in its tracks.

Unfortunately, some victims go straight to the disease without ever getting the rash, and some are never aware of their tick bite. In fact, one study found that people are most likely to get the disease from nymph-stage ticks, which are only half as big (φ) as the adults, and paler, so that they are rarely noticed and removed before they get the two days they may need to transmit the germ. So have your doctor test for Lyme if you develop the following symptoms without an alternative explanation for them, within a month after any rural outing: flu-like neck stiffness, fever and chills, jaw discomfort, painful muscle or joint stiffness, swollen glands, red eyes. Even at this stage, treatment with strong antibiotics usually works well. If untreated for a few years, Lyme disease can cause irreversible neurological problems, or a type of arthritis.

A vaccine for Lyme disease became available in 1999. However, it was only 76% effective in tests of a series of three vaccinations over the course of a full year, and much less effective after only one or two; further, its long-term safety is still unknown, and there is a rationale for concern over hypothetical autoimmune effects. It is not recommended for anyone under age 15, over 70, or pregnant, and even for the rest of us it is recommended only for people who work or frequently recreate outdoors in regions with moderate or high Lyme disease risk. The recent "wave" of cases in the Northwest was only enough to raise the risk here from none to low.

Banana Slug

Ariolimax columbianus (airy-o-lie-max: compound of two Greek-derived slug genera; co-lum-be-**ay**-nus: of the Columbia River). Very large slugs (commonly 4–6", up to 10¼", when crawling); back netted with fine, dark, mostly lengthwise grooves, exc for the smooth mantle capping about ¼ of its length, near the front; large breathing hole near right-hand edge of mantle; color variable, typically olive, with blackish blotches varying from covering nearly the entire (hence blackish) slug, to merely a single spot on the mantle or no spots at all. W-side forest floor. Arionidae. Color p 503.

Snails are not slugs that acquire shells; slugs are snails that lost them, in whole or in part. (Banana slugs retain a small vestigial shell, buried in the mantle or "cap.") Shell atrophy occurred repeatedly in snails of regions short on both the chief raw material (calcium) and the chief need (drought) for snail shells. The primary function of a land-snail shell is to provide a handy moisture-conserving shelter when it gets a bit warm and dry outside. Slugs are found almost exclusively in moist, heavily shaded regions, often with calcium-poor volcanic soils. When they need to conserve water they retreat under vegetation or earth in lieu of a shell, and shrink to a fraction of their crawling length. Slug activity is restricted to nighttime and dim, humid daytime conditions, because only then can enough humidity be absorbed to replenish the water expended in slime. Water loss in slime for crawling is far greater than water loss by evaporation through the skin, even on wet days. Slime varies from slippery to tacky, and is used for traction and for lubrication of the slug's smooth, tender sole.

Protection from predators is only a secondary function of snail shells. Many slugs make up for that loss by loading their slime with bitter or caustic chemicals. (Fried banana slugs are sometimes eaten, after a vinegar bath to remove the slime, by Northwesterners of French and German extraction. They aren't all that different from escargots.) Some are also brightly colored to advertise their repulsiveness; "banana slug" refers to the chrome yellow color of the southernmost races (if the word is not too strong) of this species and its close kin, *A. californicus*. Other Northwest slugs, in genus *Prophysaon*, have a lizardlike ability to self-amputate their tails to decoy predators.

Slugs are hermaphrodites. In some types, each individual produces its sperm and its eggs asynchronously, making self-mating impossible. In others fertility is synchronous, and two slugs may fertilize each other in one 12- to 30-hour entwining. Banana slugs are notorious for chewing off their penises to conclude mating (both partners chew), probably because their unusually large organs are more difficult for them to withdraw than to regenerate later. Since touch is the only well-developed sense in snails and slugs, by touch they must identify potential mates. To make themselves recognizable, the species have evolved a bizarre assortment of palpable structures—sharp little jabbing darts, delicately branched sperm packets, and overdeveloped penises, all with dimensions peculiar to the species. (Banana slug penises are large, but nothing like those of one rare race in the Alps—32½" tumescences dangling from 6" slugs.) The darts were recently found to have, at least in one species, functions more sophisticated than mere species recognition: they inject a mucus with hormones that alter the female tract to make sperm passage easier.

A slug eats a wide variety of fungi and plants, rasping away at them with a tongue covered with several thousand minute teeth.

Snow Worms

*Mesenchytraeus** spp. (mez-en-kye-tree-us: after genus *Enchytraeus*). Also **glacier worms**. Slender worms, average 1" long, body segmented or ringed by fine constricted bands. In late-lying snowfields or glacier surfaces, spring and summer. Enchytraeidae

Snow worms are "segmented worms" (oligochaete annelid worms) related to earthworms and, more closely, to the enchytrae cultured and sold as aquarium food. They eat snow algae including watermelon snow (page 482), and may be eaten by birds like dippers and rosy finches. Some kinds of spiders, insects, and nematodes (more primitive worms) are also adapted for life in snow. All are active at temperatures close to 32°, and able to survive even colder temperatures either by dehydrating to prevent tissue freezing, or by restricting freezing to their intercellular spaces. Both strategies require synthesis of special proteins to lower the protoplasmic freezing point to well below 32°.

---

*A 1971 taxonomic revision of the oligochaete worms declared the widely used name *Mesenchytraeus* invalid, replacing it with *Analycus*, but this change hasn't been widely adopted.

Giardia

*Giardia duodenalis** (jar-dia: after Alfred Giard; du-od-en-ay-lis: of the digestive tract).

One single-celled "animal" of intense interest to hikers is this intestinal parasite. Much remains to be learned about giardia, but two points seem clear: first, it can cause extremely unpleasant symptoms, colorfully described by the Oregon State Health Division as "sudden onset of explosive, watery, foulsmelling diarrhea with nausea and anorexia and marked abdominal distention with flatulence" perhaps accompanied by "chills and low-grade fever, vomiting, headache and malaise"; second, those who wish to incur no risk of picking it up in the mountains must treat all drinking and toothbrushing water.

An Australian parasitologist couple rhapsodized over Giardia—"the only microorganism we know to smile"—in a paper titled, "My Favorite Cell: *Giardia*." Their affection is inspired less by the smile than by Giardia's unusual combination of primitive traits bridging the realm of protozoa with that of bacteria.

Of the many mysteries of giardia, the burning issue for non-scientists is how to avoid it. There are ways, but all of them sacrifice the immediacy, flavor, and spiritual fulfillment of prostrating ourselves to the mountain stream goddess and drinking deeply. (If there is a safe place to do that still, it must be at the foot of a glacier or snowfield—almost as pure as the driven snow. Springwater isn't necessarily safe, since neither passage through earth nor freezing are any problem for giardia cysts, a communicable dormant phase of the creature.) Bringing water to a full boil, even for an instant, is 100% effective at any elevation in our range, and should also be adequate for *Cryptosporidium*, another water-borne digestive-system pathogen. Disinfectant tablets of tetraglycine hydroperiodide are quite effective, but only if given enough time to work; the colder the water, the more time they need. The better filter pumps on the market are effective, albeit tedious and expensive.

Symptoms usually appear, when they appear at all, one to three weeks after exposure. They typically last three or four days at a time, but may recur *ad nauseam*. If you think you've got them, see a doctor, who will probably send a stool sample to the lab. If it comes back negative, try again and again, since the cysts pass out of your system only at cyclic intervals. The three medications currently used in the U.S. for giardiasis each have nasty side effects and many contraindications, including pregnancy; some are also carcinogen suspects. Atabrine is the most effective, Flagyl the close second and a bit less nasty. A cure often requires more than one weeklong course. Some people (pregnant ones especially) may prefer giving their own systems time to bring the giardia into balance.

The deeper puzzle about giardia is why we weren't hearing about it twenty or fifty years ago. Many people think giardia arrived recently in the back country, brought by the hordes of backpackers and their dogs (both species often negligent of burying their scats) but this is impossible to prove. The journals of Northwest explorers like Meriwether Lewis and David Douglas are rife with bowel complaints sounding not unlike giardiasis. Giardia are distributed worldwide, in both underdeveloped and industrialized lands, and abound within feces of dogs, cats, cows, horses, moose, coyotes, beaver, muskrats, water voles, birds, etc. Some giardia strains appear highly host-specific, while others are thought by most specialists to be transmissible from one mammal species to another, including humans. Beavers are the wild species most likely to be a problem for us, hence the ailment's nickname, "beaver fever." Water voles, which (like beavers) normally defecate in the water, and are much more numerous in our subalpine waters, have been named as suspects, but in fact *G. muris*, the species in small rodents, does not infect humans.

Tolerance of particular strains of giardia is part of the explanation. Human populations *not* reporting giardiasis turn up many giardia carriers in random samples; an estimated ten to twenty percent of Americans are now hosting giardia asymptomatically, never experiencing symptoms. I'll bet I am, for one, along with most of you who drank from as many mountain streams as I did in years past. In one study in Colorado, odds of coming down with symptoms were inversely correlated with length of residency there. (Children are also more susceptible than adults; however, infants, who might otherwise be at greatest risk, seem to be protected by a giardicidal toxin in normal human milk—an argument against the use of infant formula in the Third World, where diarrheal dehydration is a leading cause of infant mortality.) The mix of Cascade backcountry sheepherders, loggers, hunters and other recreationists of twenty to fifty years ago presumably included a much higher percentage of long-term area residents than today's backpackers, and a higher proportion of "rugged types" unlikely to report or seek treatment for giardiasis. Uneven reporting and scarce records hinder appraisal of the alleged increase in the disease.

It is still possible that we rarely catch giardia from other mammals, after all, and mainly have human slobs to blame. If this proves true, we can at least have the satisfaction of feeling a little bit safer in very remote areas and earlier in the season, since the cysts are not thought to live more than a few months outside of hosts. In the meantime, don't count on it. And since it is known that humans can transmit the parasites to other humans, always defecate well away from any body of water, and cover up with six inches of dirt.

---

*Species-level taxonomy of *Giardia* is a moot point awaiting new species concepts. (The biological species concept defines a species as a group of interfertile individuals, but that doesn't work for the one-celled organisms that reproduce asexually.) The mass media usually say *G. lamblia* for the human form, but scientists prefer *duodenalis*. Another synonym is *G. intestinalis*. The five-kingdom system outlined on p 577 puts *Giardia* in the (non-Animal) Kingdom Protoctista. In two-kingdom systems it was a protozoan animal.

Watermelon Snow

Chlamydomonas nivalis (clam-id-o-**mo**-nus: mantled unit; ni-**vay**-lis: of snow).

Pinkness in late-lying snowfields consists of pigments in living algae. These algae are the producers in an entire food cycle that operates in snow. Snow worms, protozoans, spiders and insects are grazers on the algae, and are eaten in turn by predators like the rosy finch. Droppings from the predators, bodies of producers and grazers, and pollen and spiders blown from downslope provide food for decomposers (bacteria and fungi) that complete the cycle. The algae live on decomposition products and on minerals that fall on the snow.

Most of the pinkness is in energy-storing oils within "resting spores" that sit out the winter wherever they happen to end up in the fall. In spring, under many feet of new snow, they respond to increasing light and moisture by releasing four "daughter cells" that swim up to the surface. The year's crop becomes visibly pink only where concentrated by the melting of the snowpack surface. Your footstep concentrates algae into visibility by compressing the top inch of snow to a thin film. The algae also gravitate into random depressions in the surface. Once concentrated, they melt their depressions deeper by absorbing more infrared radiation than the surrounding white. By late summer, this circular process (wind-blown dirt also contributing color) contributes to the texture we call "sun cups." Notice how footprints across a snowfield are incorporated into the sun-cup pattern.

Some say watermelon snow smells or tastes like watermelon; others warn of diarrhea.

Over one hundred species of snow algae have been named. *C. nivalis* is our most abundant by far, but the watermelon snow you see may include other red species. Yellow, green, and purple snow algae are also known. Taxonomically, *Chlamydomonas* is a green alga. Its chlorophyll and celluloselike cell wall would seem to make it a sort of plant, but its swimming ability and well-developed eyespot are more animal-like—an example of why protoctists are neither plants nor animals (see page 577).

Autumn galerina, p 266. Destroying angel, p 265.

Fly amanita, p 263. Honey mushroom, p 268.

Violet cortinarius, p 269. Woolly chanterelle, p 266.

Hedgehog mushroom, p 273.

Pacific golden chanterelle, p 271.

Admirable boletus, p 274.

King boletus, p 274.

Suillus, p 275.

Warted giant puffball, p 280.

Oyster mushroom, p 272.

Angel-wings, p 272.

Sulphur shelf fungus, p 278.

Purple-tipped coral, p 276.

Snowbank false-morel, p 283.

Bear's-head tooth fungus, p 277.

Cauliflower mushroom, p 277.

Map lichen, p 287.

Jewel lichen, p 293, and Rock tripe, p 293.

Worm lichen, p 297.

Corkir, p 288, and Puffed lichen, p 294.

Dust lichens: *Lepraria* and *Chrysothrix candelaris*, p 289.

Wolf lichen, p 294.

Globe lichen, p 297.

Iceland-moss, p 295.

Matchstick lichen, p 298.

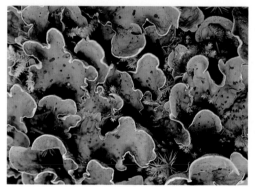

Dog lichen, *P. britannica*, p 291.

Oregon lungwort
underside, p 290.

Reindeer lichen, p 294. British soldiers, p 298.

Pixie goblets, p 298.

Thallose liverwort,
p 257.

Wolf lichen, p 294, Witches-hair, p 296, and
Horsehair lichen (obscure), p 296.

Shrew, p 301.

Boomer, p 310.

Pika, p 306.

Snowshoe hare, p 308.

Red tree vole, p 330.

Northern flying squirrel, p 318.

Heather vole winter nest, p 329.

Gopher core, p 319.

Olympic marmot, p 312.

Beaver, p 320.

Douglas squirrel, p 316.

Porcupine, p 330.

Mammals

Golden-mantled ground squirrel, p 319.

Jumping mouse, p 322.

Western gray squirrel, p 317.

Yellow pine chipmunk, p 311.

Coyote, p 334.

Bear scratchings, p 339.

Otter, p 348.

Striped skunk, p 350.

Bobcat scratchings,
p 354.

Wolverine, p 349.

Mammals

Marten, p 346.

Fisher, p 347.

Short-tailed weasel, p 308.

Badger, p 349.

Cougar, p 351.

Blacktail deer buck "in velvet," p 356.

Elk, p 359.

Mountain-goat, p 364.

Mammals

Mallard, p 375.

Harlequin duck, p 376.

Common merganser, p 375.

Pied-billed grebe, p 372.

Prairie falcon, p 382.

Osprey, p 376.

Great blue heron, p 372.

Goshawk, p 380.

Bald eagle, p 377.

American kestrel, p 381.

Red-tailed hawk,
(immature), p 379.

Golden eagle, p 381.

Vaux's swift, p 392.

White-tailed ptarmigan, p 386.

Downy woodpecker,
p 397.

Blue grouse, 385.

Northern flicker, p 396.

Common nighthawk, p 392.

Spotted sandpiper, p 386.

Rufous hummingbird, p 394.

American dipper, 409.

Townsend's solitaire, p 410.

Pacific slope flycatcher, p 399.

Cassin's vireo, p 400.

Tree swallow, p 400.

Yellow-rumped warbler, p 412.

Red-breasted nuthatch, p 407.

Cassin's finch, p 416.

Hermit thrush, p 411.

Song sparrow, p415.

Pine siskin, p 418.

Dark-eyed junco, p 415.

Red crossbill, p 417.

Western red-backed salamander, p 426.

Mtn. bluebird, p 410.

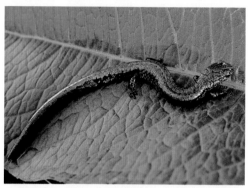

Oregon slender salamander, p 427.

Brown creeper, p 407.

Western toads, p 428, and Cascades frog, p 430.

Rough-skinned newt, p 424.

Long-toed salamander, p 427.

Pacific giant salamander, p 425.

Larch Mountain salamander, p 427.

Pacific treefrog, p 429.

Olympic salamander, p 425.

Red-legged frog metamorphosing from tadpole to adult, p 429.

Banana slug, p 477.

Butterfly photos are male uppersides unless noted otherwise.

Anise swallowtail, p 464.
Western tiger swallowtail, p 464.
Pale tiger swallowtail, p 464.

White-lined sphinx moth, p 463.
Parnassian, *P, smintheus*, p 465.
Parnassian, *P, clodius*, p 465.
Western white, p 465.
Mustard white, p 466.

Western sulphur, p 466.
Sara orange-tip, male, p 466.
Sara orange-tip, female, p 466.
Common alpine, p 467.
Vidler's alpine, p 467.
Ochre ringlet, p 466.

Chryxus arctic, p 468.
Sierra Nevada Arctic, p 468.
Large wood nymph underside, p 467.
Lorquin's admiral, p 468.
Painted lady, p 468.

Mourning cloak, p 470.
California tortoiseshell, p 469.
Milbert's tortoiseshell, p 469.
Anglewing, *P. faunus*, p 470:
    male upperside
    male underside

Greater fritillary, *C. cybele*, p 470:
    male upperside
    male underside
    female underside
Checkerspot, *E. anicia colon*, p 471.
Field crescentspot, p 471.

Purplish copper, p 472.
Mariposa copper, 472:
    male upperside
    female underside
Sooty hairstreak,
p 471.

Northern blue, p 473:
    male upperside
    female upperside
    male underside
Arctic blue, p 472.
Square-spotted blue,
p 474.

Brown elfin, p 474.
Western pine elfin,
p 474.
    male upperside
    female underside
Moss's elfin, p 474.

Basalt cinder.   Basalt, p 533.
Andesite with horneblende crystals.   Andesite, p 536.
Dacite, p 538.   Rhyolite, p 538.

Pumice, p 539.
Tuff, p 539.

Obsidian, p 541.
Tuff, p 539.

Granite, p 541.
Gabbro, p 543.

Granodiorite, p 541.
Peridotite, p 543.

Mudstone, p 544.
Arkose sandstone, p 545.

Shale, p 544.
Graywacke, p 545.

Limestone, p 546.
Quart-rich vein rock.
Conglomerate, p 548.

Chert, p 547.
Quartz crystal, p 547.
Breccia, p 549.
Breccia, p 549.

Rocks: sedimentary

Slate, p 551.
Hornfels, p 554.

Phyllite, 551.
Greenstone, 552.

Gneiss.
Gneiss, p 555.

Greenschist, p 552.
Schist with garnet and black mica,
p 551.

15

Geology

Cascade Volcanoes

Few Northwesterners in the first three quarters of the twentieth century thought of the Cascade volcanoes as active. Even the Encyclopedia Britannica, contradicting itself, told us that they were "considered extinct, but must have been active within historical time." Indeed, nineteenth-century settlers left many reports of eruptions, some factual and others fanciful, but most sounding curiously blase. That attitude passed, over the generations, into inexplicable obliviousness, even among some geologists and engineers. Rivers were dammed close to Mt. Baker and Mt. St. Helens— known to have erupted 120 years ago—and papers were published asserting that Mt. Hood, Mt. Rainier, and Glacier Peak show no sign of activity for thousands of years past.

Then in 1975, Mt. Baker heated up, melting some of its crater ice into a lake, and emitting steam and traces of ash. Geologists, suddenly finding an attentive audience, saw no strong evidence of imminent eruption, but pointed out the obvious—Mt. Baker is not extinct. Taking a fresh look, they found new signs of many ash and/or dome eruptions, and many mudflows with and without eruptive activity, within the last 600 years on each of the five above-named cones. In his U.S. Geological Survey hazard evaluations, Dwight Crandell singled out mudflows as a hazard and Mt. St.

Helens as the likeliest site of hazardous eruptions in the near term.

It was a good call. St. Helens burst into activity in 1980, and persisted in more or less activity for several years. The climactic eruption of May 18 did not involve a great amount of magma (by world standards or even Mt. St. Helens' own) but it was the most violent and destructive eruption yet beheld in an admitted State of the Union. (Alaska's 1912 eruption of Mt. Katmai was far bigger).

The eruptive mechanism had five main steps:

1. Over two months prior to May 18, dacite magma ascended into the mountain. An old plug dome filling the central vent diverted the magma toward a point on the north slope between and above two more recent lateral plug domes, the Goat Rocks and the Dog's Head. The upper north slope gradually bulged outward over the intruding magma, weakening the rock and oversteepening the slope.

2. At 8:32:10 a.m. on May 18, a minor quake triggered the oversteepened bulge into an enormous landslide. This took the lid off the underlying gas pressure.

3. Seconds later, a mixture of volcanic gas, steam, a little fresh magma, and a lot of old rock exploded horizontally northward with tremendous force, scouring and leveling forests as far as 15 miles (the Blast Area). Though early reports assumed this blast to be a "glowing avalanche" (a rapid gravitational flow of incandescently hot new ash suspended in magmatic gases), in fact it was merely "warm." Toutle River mudflows were of this blasted rock mixed with melted glacier ice. Glaciers on St. Helens' other three sides didn't melt, but disappeared under a heavy coat of ash.

4. An eruption of purer dacite fragments and gas ensued. It lasted nine hours. Its convective (vertical) force raised an ash column 15 miles high, which the wind carried eastward around the globe. At least one small glowing avalanche descended the south slope.

5. A dacite lava dome began to extrude, terminating the eruption.

On May 25, new gassy magma exploded the May 18 dome into ash and formed a new dome. This cycle repeated four times in 1980.

Activity diminished slowly over the next two decades, but that is not a long time for a volcano. Recent estimates of the life expectancy of Cascade-type stratovolcanoes put it in the range of half a million years of serious mountain-building. Most, including St. Helens, shifted their main vent at least once. St. Helens could rekindle soon, or it could lapse into dormancy before growing again in a later century, perhaps from a new vent outside the present crater.

If all eruptions were like the May 18 one, then volcanoes would be holes, not mountains. And yet, a close look at St. Helens' fresh mess helped geologists to see that neither lateral blasts nor sector collapse are uncommon. Our cones are prone to collapse because they get dissolved from the inside out by sulfuric acid that forms when upward-percolating volcanic gases meet groundwater. Mt. Rainier's Osceola event (already recognized for one of the world s biggest mudflows) left an amphitheater-shaped crater after removing a St. Helens-like quantity of rock from the top of a Rainier significantly taller than the one we know and love.

Mudflows

Mudflows may be the worst hazard we face from our volcanoes, because they are more common, hard to predict, and fast-moving than eruptions proper. Clocked at over 16 miles per hour on the upper reaches of the Toutle River on May 18, a St. Helens mudflow was doubtless slower than many, yet you could not have outrun it on rough terrain.

A mudflow can be described as a cross between a flash flood and a landslide of volcanic ash mud, typically having a mortarlike consistency. The mud is so dense that boulders float on it rather than tumbling along. Our volcanoes are susceptible to mudflows because much of their slopes is made of loose (or merely frozen solid) ash and glacial rubble covered with snow or ice. A classic cause of large mudflows is an eruption of very hot ash melting a glacier; the mud is then a mix of new ash, glacier ice and water, and underlying old ash and rocks.

Similar flows can originate without eruptive activity. Mudflows are usually considered distinct from ordinary (unheated) floods and avalanches, but it can be hard to determine whether fluctuating volcanic heat is a factor in glacial "outburst floods" on volcanoes. Unheated flash floods in the presence of copious loose ash act much like a typical mudflow, though they rarely get quite as big. Mudflow-type deposits from recent outburst floods can be seen on Dusty and Kennedy Creeks of Glacier Peak and on Kautz and South Tahoma Creeks and the Nisqually River of Mt. Rainier.

Mudflows are slow to revegetate because of their great depth and chemical uniformity. Alders are valuable pioneers on mudflows here; their nitrogen-fixing ability is crucial in the pure mineral mud.

Plate Tectonics

Beneath all the erupting and intruding and folding and faulting that produces our mountains there is a Grand Design or mechanism. The upheavals (tectonics) that raise mountains are caused by collisions between segments (plates) of the Earth's crust, which grind along at speeds up to two or three inches a year. New plate material is generated out of fresh basalt lava at mid-ocean ridges, where two plates move apart; material plunges back into the depths at "subduction zones," where plates collide. Geologists recognize about ten big plates covering the Earth, the largest one underlying most of the Pacific.

Most freshly generated plate material is "oceanic crust," a sheet of basalt two to five miles thick. Under an ocean for millions of years, the sheet accumulates thick beds of marine sediments on top that gradually become sedimentary rocks. "Continental crust" is a thicker but less dense (i.e., lighter weight) crust of many kinds of rock, but with a predominant composition of granite rather than basalt. Due to its thickness and low density, continental crust rides high upon the semifluid subcrustal base; very little of it is covered with sea water, at least in this day and age. Conversely, most oceanic crust does lie under the oceans.

Since no one can ever see the earth's mantle layer *in situ*, geologists' speculations regarding the force that drives the plates are a bit like the proverbial descriptions of an elephant by several seeing-impaired persons. Nearly all theories have something to do with hotter materials rising and cooler ones sinking.

Each of the continents is built around a "craton" area of very old crust that has existed for a good part of the Earth's 4.7 billion years. When continental crust collides with oceanic crust, the former usually stays on top while the heavier oceanic basalt plunges underneath ("subducts"), to be resorbed into the mantle. Some marine sediments, being relatively lightweight, get scraped off on the continental edge and become a part of it. Islands also ride on the oceanic plate until they raft ashore, typically jamming onto the continent's edge while the plate they rode on subducts. (Picture a big pot of thick broth not quite boiling, with bits of foam appearing out of the rising part, floating off to the side, coalescing along the way with other bits of foam, and finally accreting to a large stable mass of foam along one edge, where the roiling broth passes under them and convects to the bottom of the pot.) In this fashion the continents have grown for some three billion years. North America, for example, has only the Canadian Shield for its ancient craton, while the West Coast states and most of British Columbia seem to be a collage of small "terranes" accreted within the last 4% of the earth's history.

Subduction produces mountains in several ways:

1. The scraped-off marine sediments can pile up and produce a Coast Range like California's. The Oregon and Washington Coast Ranges are somewhat like California's, but retain great slabs of un-subducted basalt as well as marine sediments.

2. Inland from a coast range or other style of subduction complex there typically lies a line of volcanoes. It's called an arc, because several subduction arcs in the eastern Pacific, like the Aleutians, are conspicuously arc-shaped; but straight ones like the Cascades are also common. The oceanic plate descends at a 20°–60° angle, putting it well underneath the edge of the continental plate, where heat and pressure on it cause partial melting. (This is less deep than where the Earth's mantle is generally molten.) Only some of the minerals, or rock-composing chemicals, melt; the mineral mixtures that melt are usually light enough to rise toward the surface as fluid magma in pulses. The chemical proportions in the magma determine what kind of rocks it will produce. Andesitic and basaltic magmas—typical of arc volcanism—reach the surface to erupt as stratovolcanoes, shield volcanoes, or cinder cones. Remnants of the same magma are left behind down in the plumbing, where they slowly crystallize as dioritic, gabbroic, or other dark intrusions.

Sometimes chemical evolution of the rising magma raises the silica content enough to make a dacite or rhyolite. These magmas—lighter in both color and weight—are extremely viscous, like cold peanut butter, and reach the surface relatively rarely. When they do, the event may be explosive, as at Mt. St. Helens on May 18, 1980, producing copious ash and tuff; or it may be the gentler growth of a lava dome.

3. More often, pale magmas as they near the surface solidify as "batholiths" or smaller "plutons" of granitic or other pale intrusive rock. A mountain range may still result eventually, due to the thickening or deepening of continental crust along the line of magma formation. The thickened line floats higher than the other areas of

continental crust. Any overlying volcanoes and surrounding materials erode off the top, exposing the intrusions, which persist for millions of years as a granitic mountain range.

The volcanic Cascades fit the volcanic arc model quite well. Different phases of Cascade volcanism have been active over the last 35 million years, sometimes more effusively so than our present cones which date from the last million years. Shifts in the direction, speed, and downward angle of subduction may have caused the change from Western Cascades to High Cascades volcanism.

The Columbia Basalt Floods are a greater mystery, and may not be directly related to the Cascade arc. The hypothesis that could perhaps be called most mainstream is that they are a preliminary stage of an incipient rift, which might some day break the continental plate apart along a north-south line in the Great Basin area. Another hypothesis views the Columbia Basalts, Idaho's Craters of the Moon and Snake River volcanics, and the Yellowstone caldera as sequential locations of a hot spot—a locus of upwelling magma that is independent of both oceanic and continental crustal locations because it rises from beneath the crust. The classic example is Hawaii: look on a globe at the long chain of Hawaiian Islands and seamounts, which are sequential volcanoes of the Hawaii Hot Spot.

The most far-out hypothesis starts from the perception of a close correspondence in time between the world's great basalt floods and the great extinction events. One objection to the current asteroid or comet impact theory of extinctions is that fossil evidence indicates rather gradual great extinctions, taking perhaps a million years for all the species to die off, whereas the postulated climate or atmospheric effects of an impact would have done their work in an instant of geologic time. But basalt floods peak for a few million years; if they were somehow set off by impacts of extraterrestrial objects, then they could have caused extinctions over a million-year period. Three of the biggest extinction events (Permian, Triassic, and Cretaceous) correlate with the three biggest basalt floods (Siberian, Central Atlantic, and Deccan). However, there was no major extinction when the Columbia Basalts erupted.

Getting back down to earth, so to speak, western North America's terranes don't simply raft straight ashore and stick: they come onboard at an oblique angle and then slide, or smear, or roll northward. This started with the most inland accreted terranes, the ones in eastern British Columbia that buckled the continental edge 180 million years ago. They piled up offshore sediment beds as big overlapping sheets which we see today in the Canadian Rockies. Today, similar forces are thrusting up sheets of basalt flows and off-shore continental sediments to make the Olympic Mountains.

Picture the West Coast as a series of bricklike blocks. At the south end, the Sierra Nevada and Klamaths are now combined in one long, solid, deep brick sliding north-northwest. To the north of us, British Columbia has very solid, deep bricks side by side, which used to move northwest but are now "sutured" to the continent. Under BC's Coast Mountains lies a vast, little-understood complex of batholiths interfingered with a few small terranes. Our North Cascades seem to be the southern corner of this Coast Belt. The Coast Belt is the more eastern belt of the Insular (island) Super-terrane. A more western part is Wrangellia, the terrane that first established the idea of terranes breaking up and "smearing out" along the continental edge as they arrive. Wrangellia's other pieces are Alaska's Wrangell Mountains, probably the Queen Charlotte Islands, and perhaps the area around Hell's Canyon on the Snake River. The rock formations of the Wrangell Mtns. and of Vancouver Island are clearly the same, and they originated as an island arc close to the Equator.

The bricks of the Washington and Oregon coast seem to absorb the compression between the Insular and Coast bricks to the north and the Klamath and Sierra bricks to the south. The W Oregon/ SW Washington brick absorbs it by rotating clockwise. The Olympic Mtns. brick absorbs it by scrunching up with many underthrust faults all cramming into a horseshoe shape (see map, page 550) reflecting the corner the Olympics are being pushed into.

The North Cascades are a beautifully messy tectonic story. Rowland Tabor and colleagues described fourteen terranes within the North Cascades alone—an extreme case of small terranes, as well as of distance travelled. (A certain fossil sea creature from the North Cascades lived in the tropics in the Mesozoic era; it is also found in a few East Asian terranes, and nowhere else. So these terranes—some here, some in SE Asia—presumably started out close together but are now on opposite sides of the earth from each other.) In various remote locations, most North Cascades rocks were laid down, contorted, metamorphically squeezed, and in places remelted at depth. By 100 million years ago the fourteen terranes were grouped together and close to the North American continent at Baja California. See page 554 for more of this story.

For as long as there have been world globes to display the fit of the continents on opposite sides of the Atlantic, there have been theories of "continental drift." But these were considered fanciful by most scientists until 1915, when Alfred Wegener elaborated them with enough supporting evidence to spark several decades of gradually intensifying debate. In the 1950s and 60s, technology for dating rocks and locating deep earthquakes, deep-sea contours, magnetic polarity of sea-floor basalts, etc., escalated the sophistication of the debate and turned it in Wegener's favor.

The science of plate tectonics (the term that supplanted "continental drift") is still in constant ferment. Expect the number of terranes to shrink as further study finds that some pairs of terranes share common origins: a terrane is a provisional thing, always reflecting the limits of the current state of the science. Several hypotheses mentioned in this chapter may face harsh re-evaluation as geology continues to develop. One thing is clear: even as issues boil and bubble, the basic picture of subducting plates is ever more firmly corroborated. Radiotelemetry now measures distances accurately enough to actually measure the speed of plates—two to three inches a year, roughly as Wegener predicted.

Earthquakes

Geology has been an exciting science for the last forty years thanks to plate tectonics, and for the last twenty the Northwest has been one of the more catastrophically exciting regions. First we had St. Helens, and now we're one-upping California with our own rumors of The Big One.

In an eerie parallel to the erstwhile complacency about allegedly extinct Cascade volcanoes, the belief that the Northwest lacks big earthquakes survived the first several decades of plate tectonics theory. It became clear that we are in a subduction zone, and that other subduction zones make big earthquakes, so geologists for a while worked on figuring out what makes Cascadia different. It turns out the main difference is our lack of a written history before 1790. The last Big One came in the night, at 9:00 p.m. on January 26, 1700. It may have been a magnitude 9—about as big as they get. The tale is told in Indian legends, and it is written down as the record of tsunamis at points along the coast of Japan. Kenji Satake's team of geologic sleuths compared the timing and size of the waves with those of recent tsunamis, whose causative earthquakes along North and South America are known, to come up with the date, hour, and magnitude. They knew what decade to look at thanks to years of dogged sleuthing by Brian Atwater and other Northwest geologists who were increasingly certain that the Cascadia subduction zone has a regular history of major quakes, with the most recent around 300 years ago. All up and down the coast, they had found tsunami-deposited sediments way above any historic surf level, and trees killed by changes in sea level. The trees had rings; the rings could be compared to rings in living trees; and the rest, as they say, is history.

Big Ones hit us about 400 to 500 years apart, on average. But earthquakes do not come like clockwork. No one knows how to predict them. A 1997 consensus found that during the past 3500 years there had been a few intervals of 3–400 years between great subduction quakes, but also at least one interval of over 800 years. (If there was ever an interval shorter than a century, it probably wouldn't show up in the kinds of evidence that have been studied.)

Actually the Northwest, and especially Oregon, is seismically quieter than many subduction zones, and the reason still needs to be figured out. One explanation, if correct, suggests that Northwest offshore quakes are no greater than magnitude 8—still big, but not as bad as a 9. Most papers on the subject say "at least 8."

But don't relax yet. Not if you live near Seattle. About a thousand years ago, Seattle had a magnitude 7.5 on its very own Seattle Fault. The Bainbridge Island shore next to the fault was raised 21 feet. Major rockslides came down in Seattle and in the southeastern Olympics, where several new lakes were created by rock avalanche dams. Not to be outdone, Portland stands right on the Portland Fault Zone. A magnitude 7.5 quake on a fault under one of these cities would likely wreak more havoc in the city than a magnitude 9 at the offshore subduction trench. It was a 6.9 quake that levelled much of Kobe, Japan, in 1995. Historically, western Washington has had enough quakes to rate as moderately active; in 1949, a magnitude 7.1 quake hit south of Tacoma, and in 1872 a quake near Lake Chelan was around 7.4.

Geologic Time

4.7 billion years ago, Earth formed.

3.9 billion — *Oldest rocks yet dated solidified from magma.*

3.4 billion — *Oldest fossilized life forms—bacterial mats.*

2 billion — *Cyanobacteria began making a breathable atmosphere.*

1.6 billion — *Oldest rock crystals in our region formed from magma.*

590 million — *Oldest multicelled animal fossils. Oldest North Cascades rock formation, the Swakane gneiss.*

440 million — *Life moved onto land. First plants evolved.*

225 million — *Dinosaurs became dominant land animal. Much of N Cas Core Complex crystallized or metamorphosed.*

100 million — *Flowering plants became predominant. Terranes of N Cas and W BC reached the edge of NA continent off Baja CA, piled up, erupted, metamorphosed, began sliding north.*

65 million — *Dinosaurs went extinct. Mammals took over.*

60 million — *Uplift of Rocky Mtns was at its most intense.*

55 million — *Crescent basalts of Olympic Peninsula erupted.*

45 million — *N Cascade terranes all ± in place, sutured to continent.*

37 million — *Cascade arc volcanism began.*

17 million — *Cascade volcanism quieted down; Columbia River Basalt Floods began erupting.*

14 million — *Flood basalts waned; W Cascades volcanism resurgent.*

7.4 million — *Cascades volcanism shifted from Western to High arc.*

2.5 million — *Goat Rocks volcano started to build*

2 million — *Pleistocene Ice Age began.*

1.8 million — *Ancestral hominids shaped stone tools.*

1,150,000 — *Kulshan Caldera blew at Austin Pass—as big a blast as Mazama, but never built a mountain, just a caldera.*

730,000 — *Earliest eruptions of today's High Cas stratovolcanoes.*

500,000 — *Mt. Adams built itself. First* Homo Sapiens, *in Africa.*

115,000 — *Last glacial stage of the Ice Age began.*

40,000 — *Mt. St. Helens started to build.*

30,000 — *Likely first human migration from Asia to NA.*

4.7 billion	3.9 billion	2.5 billion	1.6 billion	590 million	225 million 100 million Ice Age & recent

Recent Time

15,000 BCE	Last Ice Age glacial maximum in PNW. 100 Bretz (or Missoula) floods began, continued 2,000+ years.
14,000	Puget and Okanogan Ice Sheet lobes gone from WA.
12-10,000	Alpine glaciers readvanced; 1,000-year cold snap in Europe, but the degree of cooling in PNW is not known.
11,000	Huge eruption(s) of Glacier Peak shot pumice far and wide. Hunters made Clovis-style spear points found near Wenatchee. Many large mammals went extinct.
8,000	Salmon fishing common in the Columbia Gorge.
7,300	Kennewick Man lived.
7,000	Warmer than the 20th century; 4,000-year "climatic optimum" began.
6,200	Big Lava Beds poured out, S of Mt. Adams.
5,700	Mt. Mazama erupted, shot pumice far and wide, then collapsed, forming Crater Lake Caldera.
3,600	Osceola mudflow (Mt. Rainier) buried Puyallup area.
2,000	NW Coast people began relying on stored salmon as a food and cedar as a material—a major culture shift.
0	Mt. Rainier built its present summit. Mt. St. Helens built its present flanks.
500 ACE	Belknap lava flows at Mackenzie Pass. Mt. Hood erupted, producing Crater Rock and large debris fan below it.
1500	Landslide dammed Columbia R., forming first a lake, then the Cascades the mountains were named after.
1700	Last major earthquake on Cascadia Subduction Zone.
1785	Fur trade began between coast peoples and Europeans.
1800	Mt. Hood erupted, producing Old Maid Flat mudflow.
1820	Greatest post–Glacial stage glaciation ("Little Ice Age").
1830-80	Minor activity on Mts. Baker, Rainier, St. Helens.
1914-17	Major eruption of Mt. Lassen.
1980	Major eruption of Mt. St. Helens
today	Glaciers retreating. Mountains rising.

Glacial max. Bretz Floods — Glacier Peak — Mazama — Osceola mud — 0 — A Big quake today

Glaciers

Wherever an average year brings more new snow than can melt, snow accumulates and slowly compacts into ice. Eventually, the ice gets so thick and heavy it flows slowly downhill until it reaches an elevation warm enough to melt it as fast as it arrives. This flowing ice is a glacier, a mechanism that balances the snow's "mass budget." Mt. Olympus' Blue Glacier has the fattest mass budget—most snow, and most melt—of all glaciers measured in the U.S.

Ideally, the rate of flow is equal to both the excess snow accumulation in the upper part of the glacier and the excess melting in the lower part; this ideal glacier would neither advance nor retreat. Few glaciers are so stable. Instead, the elevation where the glacier terminates in a melting "snout" advances and retreats (drops and rises) in response to climatic trends. (Retreating glaciers don't turn around and flow back uphill, of course, but simply melt away at the bottom faster than their rate of arrival there.) A global warming trend of the last 100 years is causing widespread glacial retreat. In our region this intensified in the warm/dry 1930s and '40s, then paused in the 1950s and '60s, when many glaciers advanced.

The formula for advance or retreat is complex. Even neighboring glaciers vary greatly in the time lag from climatic trends to glacial ones. On Glacier Peak, for example, the Chocolate and Dusty glaciers advanced during the cool 1950s and '60s while the Whitechuck, a low-angle and relatively low-altitude glacier, inexorably wasted away, approaching stagnation. A glacier "stagnates" after shrinking so much that it no longer has enough mass and slope to keep flowing.

You can see the difference between advancing and retreating glacier snouts. Ideally, the former have high, bulging fronts that advance upon fields or forests like giant bulldozers, while the latter are thin, perhaps even concave, and surrounded by barren bouldery expanses from which they just retreated. Around here, unfortunately, both types of glaciers terminate in barrens, since even our advancing glaciers haven't yet made up the ground they lost 50 to 130 years ago, too recently for much revegetation. Still, a retreating snout typically tapers off, and is dirty and rocky with surface debris concentrated over recent decades; it may even be hard to tell where the glacier leaves off and the rock rubble or "till" ensues. An advancing snout, in contrast, may present a clifflike face where ice blocks come crashing down, or a chaotic expanse of towering ice chunks called seracs.

Paralleling the sides of a glacier or the arc of its snout, you often find low, rather smooth ridgelines of sand, gravel, and rock rubble, perhaps in parallel series. These are recessional moraines. They mark lines where the retreating glacier advanced or held a line for a few years before receding again. Many of these, located near the present terminus, were created during the last 200 years' retreat. Older ones obscured by vegetation reveal to the practiced eye a map of the end of the latest Ice Age, 21 to 17 thousand years ago.

Small glaciers in pockets on the steep faces of North Cascade peaks seem to be nearly vertical. Gnarly blue wrinkles show that they are glaciers. Often they terminate over bands of vertical rock. Ice blocks that break off and avalanche down the rock band may re-coalesce into a lower glacier, if the basin where they collect is high and/or shaded enough for them to stay frozen. Some basin glaciers, with or without hanging glaciers above them, are supplied far more by avalanches than by direct snowfall.

Regardless of whether it forms from fresh snow, avalanches, or huge blocks of older ice, a glacier's ice has a consistency utterly un-like a snowbank. Underneath perhaps a "firn" of last year's snow, what was once snow is now recrystallized into coarse, nubbly gran-ules with hardly any air space. Eventually even the granular texture will grade into massive blue ice, though a microscope will still re-veal a texture more granular than that of, say, frozen lake ice.

Our temperate-zone glaciers are "warm" glaciers at close to 32° throughout, in contrast with "cold" arctic glaciers. Warm glaciers,

Crevasses

As flow accelerates in a glacier, the semisolid mass stretches, leaving stretch marks in the form of deep cracks or crevasses. Other crevasses open where glaciers bend or compress. Crevasses are often bridged by masses of recent snow which may or may not be solid enough to walk across. Crossing glaciers is reasonably safe for parties of three or more that follow these rules:

First rehearse self-arrest *and belaying technique with ice axes;*

Rope up *properly;*

Include *at least one member experienced on glaciers.*

like ice skaters, glide on a film of pressure-melted water. They pour around bedrock outcrops by melting under pressure against the upstream side of the knob and refreezing against the downstream side (repaying the heat debt incurred by the first change of state). They erode rock ferociously, not because either the water layer or the ice itself is abrasive, but because sand, pebbles, and boulders are gripped and ground along over the substrate. It's the rock sediment load that does the grinding in both glacier and river erosion; the difference between the two is a little like that between a power belt-sander and a sandstorm. The glacier's grit leaves parallel grooves or "striations" across bedrock convexities. Look for these at the lip of any high basin or "cirque" carved by an alpine glacier. In the area east of Ross Lake, there are even striations crossing high divides—proof that the Cordilleran Ice Sheet crossed here, since alpine glaciers necessarily originate below the high ridges.

Rock Flour

A milky-white color betrays streams that originate from the snouts of glaciers. At least three White Rivers and a Whitechuck in the Cascades are all named for their "rock flour"—silt-sized sediment pulverized by the sole of a glacier and carried in the meltwater. Ice preserves the rock from alteration into darker mud. Streams get milkier as summer progresses; clear runoff from rain and snowmelt reaches a peak during the warm rains of spring, then dwindles while glacial melting increases in summer heat.

In lakes, rock flour gives a chalky green hue. This is conspicuous in tarns near glaciers, and also in Lake Diablo as contrasted with Ross Lake. Ross Lake drains a large basin east of the climatic Cascade Crest, where glaciers are relatively few and small. Lake Diablo, despite dilution by all of Ross Lake's clear outflow, is chalky green with Thunder Creek's rock flour from the huge North-face glaciers of Mts. Logan, Boston and Eldorado.

In the Olympics, most rock flour is in the Hoh and Queets Rivers, and Silt Creek. You can also find it in some Elwha tributaries. The snowfinger at the source of the Elwha was described as a glacier at the turn of the century, and the stream is still a bit milky.

Some writers find straight milky meltwater unpalatable, but I like it just fine. I figure it comes with a mineral supplement, and an exceptionally remote risk of giardia.

Ice Ages

If you love dramatic high-relief scenery in the style of the North Cascades or the Alps, count yourself lucky to have been born in an interglacial stage of an ice age. Mountain erosion without ice usually results in tame, monotonous slope angles and ridge patterns.

The occurrence of an Ice Age in geologic history, obvious as it seems today, was controversial 150 years ago; later geologists looked for signs of earlier Ice Ages in the 4,700,000,000 years of earth history and decided there might have been two or three. Recent thinking is that the regular, rhythmic banding of many kinds of ancient sedimentary beds may record climatic flipflops—hundreds of Ice Ages, or something like. The Pleistocene Ice Age has been going on for two million years, encompassing the evolution of *Homo sapiens* and most of the growth of today's Northwest volcanoes. It has cycled many times between glacial stages averaging 100,000 years and interglacial stages averaging 20,000. (The latter are usually not full returns to pre–Ice Age conditions, which included neither large Polar ice caps nor alpine glaciers at temperate latitudes.) Within the interglacial stage the ice caps and glaciers advance and retreat in accord with subtler climatic cycles (page 566).

During a typical glacial stage, about half of North America was covered by two huge ice sheets, one on either side of the Canadian Rockies, similar to those blanketing Greenland and Antarctica today. The western one (the Cordilleran Ice Sheet) covered parts of Alaska, the Yukon and British Columbia and entered our range briefly at its most recent maximum, 17,000 years ago. At that point it shoved up against the Olympics, extended long tongues down the Puget Trough to just past Olympia, and ground across North Cascade ridges. The North Cascades must have looked the way southeast Alaska's mountains do today—great banded riverlike glaciers with branching tributaries filling the valleys, and marginal peaks protruding as "nunatak" islands.

Not the vast ice sheet, but the hundreds of alpine valley glaciers, gave our region its dramatic facelift. Wherever you see a U-shaped valley cross-section today, picture a thick glacier flowing for at least 1,000 years. The glaciers marked their farthest advance about 17,000 years ago, when the climatic cycle must have reversed. By 14,000 years ago all ice was in full rout, the glacial stage over.

Front-line tongues of the Cordilleran Ice Sheet entered many

North Cascades valleys that held north-flowing rivers. The ice dammed these rivers, creating lakes that rose until they spilled over a more southerly pass. Some of these overflow streams were temporary (though each probably happened more than once, with the Ice Age's repeated glacial stages) and the main signs they left of their passage were sharp gorges that had to have been cut by fiercer streams than we see today. (E.g., Canyon Creek.) Others cut so deeply that when the Ice Sheet melted away, the old northward outlet was no longer as low as the new southward defile, so the river kept its new course. Geologists call that a drainage reversal.

The grand specimen of a reversal may be the Skagit itself. The Gorge below Diablo has long been a puzzle, because it is narrow and V-shaped, while the Skagit Valley both above and below there is glacially U-shaped. Geologists Ralph Haugerud and Jon Riedel believe that before the Pleistocene ice the Ross Lake part of the Skagit flowed north to the Fraser, through either the Silverhope or the Nicolum valley. Probably one of the glacial stages before the last

The Bretz Floods

The basalt cliffs of the Columbia Gorge are strikingly clean of loose rock rubble. They got this way by scouring action from river floods 400' to 1,000' deep. That's right—the Columbia ran 1,000' deep at The Dalles where it backed up against the Cascade Range, and was still over 400' deep where it broke out from the confining gorge at Chanticleer Point near Corbett. This represents 200 times as much water as in any Columbia River floods in the historic record, and doubtless more than any other river flood interpreted from the geologic record anywhere. There were between forty and one hundred of these deluges, in Richard Waitt's interpretation: a series of fifteen of them at 35- to 55-year intervals shows in a single pile of sediments.

The last flood was perhaps 16,000 years ago; there could conceivably have been people living in the area. Source of the flood water was Lake Missoula, an ice-dammed lake in western Montana with about half the volume of modern Lake Michigan. The lake filled several long mountain valleys of the Clark Fork drainage when that river's route north to the Columbia was blocked by a south-flowing lobe of the Cordilleran Ice Sheet. (Such lakes were common in the Ice Age; see top of this page on the Skagit Gorge.) At Lake Missoula, the ice dam either floated or burst each time the lake rose high enough, and then the one brought about a drainage reversal as described above, with the old divide being breached around where Gorge Lake and Diablo Dam are today. (This would explain the Skagit crossing the clear "backbone" and climatic crest of the North Cascades.) Later, the Puget Lobe of the Ice Sheet sent a distributary tongue *up* the Skagit Valley, U-shaping it as far as Rockport and damming the river to form a large lake; the Ross Lake lobe also continued down through the Skagit Gorge, but too briefly to reshape it from its freshly cut V to a typical glacial U. The valley in between, around Marblemount, probably has its broad flat floor for reasons related to crumblier bedrock west of the Straight Creek Fault more than to glaciers.

One effect of the great ice sheets was to lower sea level as much as 300' by retaining ice that would otherwise be water in the oceans. This turned a wide area of shallow sea between Siberia and Alaska into habitable dry land, allowing many new mammals, probably including humans, to migrate to the New World. As the ice sheets melted, sea level rose worldwide; then for centuries afterward, sea

---

entire lake drained rapidly. Small-scale periodic floods due to ice-dam floating occur today in Iceland, source of the exotic term "jökulhlaups" sometimes applied to Lake Missoula's floods.

John Shaw's alternative hypothesis proposes that there was just one or a very few great floods from Lake Missoula, plus at least one even bigger flood that came down the Okanogan valley from a vast sub–Ice Sheet lake in central British Columbia.

The floods explain several previously mystifying features of the Northwest landscape, including eastern Washington's Dry Falls, Coulees, Potholes, and Channeled Scablands, and the Willamette Valley erratics. A glacial erratic is a boulder transported by glaciers and dropped far (typically 10-100 miles) from its bedrock source. The Willamette erratics were puzzling because they're found where no glaciers ever were, let alone the particular glaciers that plucked these particular boulders in Montana or British Columbia. They must have ridden the floods in icebergs that drifted out to the margins of a backwater lake filling the Willamette Valley, where they beached and melted. Other erratics indicate huge backwater lakes east of the Cascades.

The floods are named after geologist J Harlan Bretz, who first recognized the evidence and collected enough of it to convince others. Other names for them include Spokane and Missoula Floods.

---

level seemed to retreat on the Northwest coast and on other coasts near vanished ice sheets. That's because the sheer weight of ice pressing down on continental plates made them float lower on the lithosphere. When the weight was removed, the upward rebound of these tectonic plates lagged centuries behind the rise in sea level because rock flows more slowly than water. "Isostatic rebound" forces us to acknowledge that ice sheets , and even glaciers, weigh in as heavyweights—they're geology, not just weather! Ice sheets can easily contain or channel lava flows, and recent thinking holds that they can actually suppress both earthquakes and volcanism.

As for "mere" alpine glaciers, it turns out that they are responsible for leaving many Cascade lava flows perched along the crests or flanks of between-glacier ridges during the Ice Age. When hot lava meets ice, some ice melts, sure, but also some lava freezes: it forms a solidified skin which conducts heat poorly and directs the rest of the lava flow where the glacier tells it to go.

Theories of the cause of ice ages are complex and controversial. The intensity of solar radiation hitting earth varies with at least five known aspects of planetary motion, day/night and summer/winter being the quickest. At very long but calculable intervals, the three slower cycles coincide to reduce solar heating over long periods. That astronomical compound cycle ("Milankovitch Cycles") correlates well with ice ages, but it may be augmented by other causes, dozens of which have been suggested: volcanic dust; dust from meteor or comet impacts on earth; asteroid dust in vast interplanetary belts that the earth may pass through; carbon dioxide levels; methane released from methane hydrates on the sea floor; salinity-based ocean circulation; and continental drift as it affects the configuration of ocean currents, the sizes of continents and their locations relative to the poles, and the height and configuration of mountain ranges. Sunlight itself varies in at least three cycles which we are only beginning to measure. And ice sheets set up feedback loops to either sustain or reverse an ice age.

At 14,000 years old, the current interglacial has neither lasted longer nor grown warmer than previous ones of this Ice Age. Nothing in the geologic record gives cause to doubt that another glacial stage will come. However, scientists fear that the next re- or deglaciation may be triggered by human-caused excesses of greenhouse gases such as carbon dioxide and methane. (See page 568.)

Classification of the earth's materials begins with the three ways that material can be transformed into new kinds of rock:

Igneous rocks solidified from lava, which was older rocks melted by heat.

Sedimentary rocks settled as fragmentary material (such as mud) and were then compacted and/or chemically cemented.

Metamorphic rocks recrystallized (but did not melt) from other rocks under intense heat and pressure.

Igneous rocks are divided into two textural classes—fine-grained and coarse-grained—and then graded by texture and chemical (or mineral) composition. High-silica rocks tend to be "light," low-silica rocks "dark." Each "darkness" grade on the compositional scale can occur with either a fine or a coarse texture. The two textures tend to correlate (and for our purposes we will assume they always correlate) with two origins:

volcanic, from magma that erupted upon the continental surface or the ocean floor, congealing quickly to produce fine crystals; or

intrusive, from magma that solidified into rock somewhere beneath the surface, and cooled slowly, producing coarse texture.

Basalt

Color p 508.

The most abundant rock in Oregon and Washington and, though less visibly, in the Earth's crust as a whole, basalt is the darkest of our major lava mixes. We think of it as normally black, but it ranges down to light gray and is often altered to greenish or reddish. Its surface is drab and massive, usually without conspicuous crystals or other features except, frequently, bubbles, or "vesicles." These show that the lava came up from the depths full of dissolved gases. Just as uncapping a bottle of soda releases bubbles of carbon dioxide which, under pressure, had been dissolved invisibly in the liquid, so lavas often foam up as they near the surface. Abundant

Stratovolcanoes

include all the prominent Cascade volcanoes. They build up over long periods (up to one million years) by alternating lava flows (andesite, dacite, and basalt) with copious tuff flows and ashfall. Mt. Rainier—207 cubic miles of it, rising more than 10,000'—is a big one. Vents move around over the centuries; "satellite" vents may erupt cinder cones, and late-stage vents often produce lava "plug domes."

Cinder Cones

typically erupt from a single vent within a span of 100 years or far less, and rarely achieve 1,000' of relief. They erupt as fountains of small, foamy basalt or andesite "cinders," and often extrude tonguelike basalt flows from their bases. Examples abound in Central Oregon.

Lava Domes

superficially resemble cinder cones, but at heart they are massive extrusions of pasty, viscous rhyolite or dacite. The surface cracks into blocks, and some tumble down the steep sides, forming a rubbly cone. The vent plugs up within a few years, rarely producing 1,000' of relief.

Shield Volcanoes

made of multiple basalt flows produce only gentle relief. A few build for millions of years: "the world's biggest mountain," Mauna Loa, is 10,000 cubic miles rising 29,000' above the sea floor. Cascade shield volcanoes like Larch Mtn. and the Simcoes are 3,000'–5,000' high.

Flood Basalts

are not mountains; they are so fluid when molten that they pour out flat. Yet they have the greatest volumes and flow rates of any terrestrial volcanoes. The Columbia River Basalt, a ten million-year sequence of flows, contains more than 60,000 cubic miles of lava.

vesicles indicate that the rock congealed near the surface of a particular lava flow. In older basalts (e.g., those of the Olympics) vesicles may appear as solid polka-dots, the holes having filled with water-soluble minerals. Polygonal (6-, 5-, or 4-sided) basalt columns, often neatly vertical at one level and splayed-out at another, are another well-known characteristic. They result from shrinkage during cooling of large flows. Vesicles and/or columns also occur in andesite, though less commonly.

Basalt lava erupts in several styles. One of them, the basalt flood, is a volcano, but not a mountain, since the floods are so liquid that they flow out flat before solidifying. The Columbia Gorge and the smaller canyons of the Klickitat, Clackamas and Sandy Rivers all cut through multilayered, often columnar formations of Columbia River Basalt—vast outpourings that covered much of eastern Oregon and Washington and flowed down the river valley to the ocean between 17 and 12 million years ago.

Originally flat and close to sea level, the flood basalts were later arched to over 2,800' in the Gorge, 5,500' near Mt. Adams, and possibly over 7,000' near Mt. Rainier. Under Mt. Hood, however, faults dropped them to below sea level—Oregon's High Cascades stand in a trough, next to an arch raising the Western Cascades. The folding and faulting were gradual enough that rivers like the Columbia and Klickitat were able to keep pace in their downward erosion.

Two kinds of mountains usually made of basalt are shield volcanoes and cinder cones. Both are plentiful in the Cascades. Shield volcanoes, being made of basalt just slightly less fluid than the flood kind, are generally too low-relief to be dramatic peaks in themselves, but the entire High Cascades Plateau, on which the prominent volcanoes stand, is a montage of overlapping basaltic shields.

The Cascade stratovolcanoes, though generalized as andesitic, are in fact layerings of flows ranging all the way from rhyolite to basalt. A few stratovolcanoes, like Middle Sister, are largely basalt.

Yet another type of effluence—oceanic basalt—is far and away the most extensive of all. Most erupts under the ocean and remains there forever. A bit of oceanic basalt crops up in the North Cascades, most often metamorphosed into greenstone.

The entire east and north rim of the Olympics consists of a huge slab of basalt bent into a horseshoe shape and wedged up 90° from underneath, the flow-tops facing east and north. Some of the flows have glassy-rinded, blob-shaped "pillow" structures that basalt characteristically forms when it erupts underwater; others erupted upon land. For decades these Crescent basalts were described as oceanic, but more recently some geologists have reinterpreted them as continental. If so, they are unusually extensive flows—equal, say, to Hawaii (the Big Island) as a whole, and almost comparable to a flood basalt province—suggesting the influence of a mantle plume.

Mt. Constance, The Brothers, Mt. Angeles, Mt. Washington, and all the other peaks conspicuous from Puget Sound are of the Olympics' basaltic horseshoe, and Mt. Deception, the second highest Olympic peak, is of a smaller basalt arc. Crescent Basalts are among the hardest, most erosion-resistant rocks in the Olympics, and the most popular with rock climbers.

Andesite

Color p 508.

Andesite lavas make rough gray, greenish, or sometimes reddish brown rocks. Often they are speckled with crystals up to ¾" across, scattered throughout a fine matrix otherwise lacking crystals of visible size. These were already crystallized in the molten magma when it erupted. With close examination and a little practice, you can easily tell them from the shards of noncrystalline whole rock jumbled up in tuff.

The different lava rocks, however, can be hard to tell apart. Color descriptions are unavoidably vague; andesite is "medium-dark," between dark basalt and light dacite and rhyolite, but actual tints overlap, and green and reddish hues are unpredictable. The technical definitions are ranges on a graph of bulk chemistry, so positive identifications may require specimens to be pulverized and analyzed by a lab. Light color correlates with silica (SiO_2) content—around 50% in basalt, 60% in andesite, 70%+ in rhyolite. (Most magmatic SiO_2 combines with other elements to form such minerals as the feldspars; only the SiO_2 excess over about 55% crystallizes as quartz, which is SiO_2.)

Andesite is named after the world's highest volcanoes, the Andes. It is better than the other lavas at layering to form stratovolcanoes, so you see tons of it on Mt. Rainier and Mt. Hood. But studies of the total volume of various rocks in the Cascades find less andesite than either the darker or the lighter volcanic rocks.

Volcanic Cascades Geology

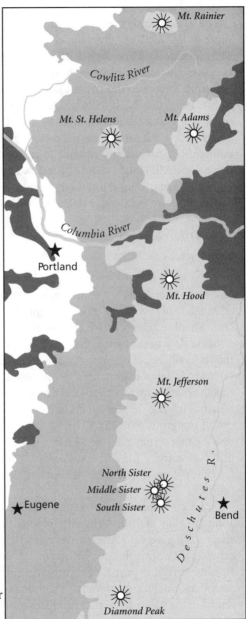

Western Cascade
volcanic rock

High Cascade
volcanic rock

Columbia River
flood basalt
(where exposed; also
underlies much of the
intervening area;
exposed cliffs in
western Columbia
Gorge are too slender
to show.)

Dacite

Color p 508.

Dacite lavas are intermediate in silica content, viscosity and color—more or less medium-gray, sometimes pinkish, brownish or buff. They include light and dark scattered crystals often, flow-streaking occasionally, and bubbles or holes rarely. They are common in Romania, known to the ancient Romans as Dacia, hence the word dacite. Here, they built most of Glacier Peak plus the plug domes on several peaks. Disappointment Peak on Glacier Peak and Crater Rock on Mt. Hood are dacite domes whose eruptions melted enough iced-up ash and pumice to create enormous debris fans downslope. Mt. Hood's debris fan below Crater Rock underlies the Palmer Glacier, Timberline Lodge, and the entire smooth south slope seen from Portland. Mt. St. Helens' lava dome is also dacite.

Rhyolite

Color p 508.

Rhyolite lavas are pale, typically pinkish tan rocks, usually easy to tell from other lavas but sometimes confused with tuff, which is often made of rhyolite magma that exploded rather than flowing as lava. Rhyolite is named for the Greek word for flow. Streaky or swirling flow patterns may help to distinguish it, especially from tuff or basalt. But it was actually one of the least fluid of lavas. Lava viscosity increases dramatically with silica content, and flowing rhyolite may be up to a thousand times more viscous than flowing basalt. "Flowing" almost seems like the wrong word—it squeezes out of the ground more like dried-up peanut butter. It so resists flowing that it may plug up a given vent forever, marking the final phase of activity for some volcanoes. The southernmost major Cascade volcano, Mt. Lassen, is about as big a dome as rhyolite can produce.

The constipating viscosity of rhyolite helps to explain the abundance of granite—rhyolite magma that never managed to erupt. (See page 541.) Alternatively, gas-rich rhyolite magma may explode, showering the area with pumice, ash and larger fragments; rhyolite tuff and pumice are superabundant in some volcanic provinces, including Nevada. Then again, sometimes rhyolite erupts in the glassy form that produces obsidian.

Pumice

Color p 509.

More often than not, magmas reach the surface bearing a gas component that expands, sometimes explosively, as it is released from subterranean pressure, blasting globs of glassy froth sky-high—a little like a well-shaken bottle of warm Guinness. In mid-air, the froth may harden into pumice, a volcanic glass so full of gas bubbles that it's light enough to travel on the wind, even in sizable chunks. Most of our recent volcanoes and much terrain downwind of them are mantled with pumice fragments. In particular, ridgelines for a good 20 miles east of Glacier Peak (including the misspelled Pomas Pass) are covered with pumice from a huge explosive eruption about 12,000 years ago. Like St. Helens' more modest ash plume of May 18, 1980, Glacier Peak's extends in only one direction; it was a single, intense event so brief that the wind made no shifts. Dust-sized ash (much of it pumice) from that eruption is recognized in soil profiles all across Montana—a layer a ways below the one from the great Crater Lake eruption of 7,700 years ago.

Pumice has unusual uses—grinding away at toes or kitchen grills, mixing into concrete as soundproofing, etc. Breaking or grinding a piece of pumice may release a sulfurous smell, the original volcanic gases (largely sulfur dioxide and carbon dioxide) still trapped in little bubbles. These are much tinier than the vesicles in basalt and andesite, and make pumice lighter than vesicular lava.

Tuff

Color p 509.

Much of the volcanic rock produced by our volcanoes was never flowing lava, but instead blasted violently into the air as pyroclastic ("fire-broken") fragments. These range from "bombs" bigger than basketballs to dustlike "ash." (Named for a rough resemblance to wood ashes, volcanic ash is no more "burnt" than any other volcanic material.) The fragments may quickly wash away or otherwise fail to cohere, but some consolidate into rocks called "tuff."

Tuff has two distinct ways of consolidating from ash. Ash*fall* is material that shot up into the air and settled back to earth at modest temperatures; decades have to pass before sufficient groundwater full of dissolved silica percolates through to cement it into an "ashfall tuff." Ashfall is typically found in graded beds, each bed coming from a single ash eruption and having coarse fragments at its base (they fall to earth fastest) and finer fragments toward its top. Ash*flow*, on the other hand, comes barreling down the slopes suspended in hot whirling volcanic gas; much of the gas exsolves out of the fragments even as they fly. These events move as fast as avalanches, and are sometimes called "glowing avalanches," or *nuees ardentes*. The ashflow is laid down fast and hard, without grading, and is quickly cemented by its own heat into a "welded tuff." Ashfall tuff is often crumbly, and vulnerable to erosion, but welded tuff is hard; ashfall tuff's closest resemblance may be to sandstone (tuff is sometimes classed as a sedimentary rock), but welded tuff resembles lava. The easiest way to tell tuff from lava is if there are inclusions; in lava these are crystals, often of a contrasting color. In tuff they are usually coarse, irregular fragments about the same color and composition as the rest of the tuff.

Between Mt. Baker and Mt. Shuksan, a very deep tuff formation underlies Table Mtn. and other lava flows. Geologist Wes Hildreth believes a volcano erupted there, blasting through both a nonvolcanic ground surface and an ice sheet; the huge vent filled with tuff, and if any mountain at all was created, the glacier soon swept it away. He named it Kulshan Caldera, after Mt. Baker.

Tuff makes up a big portion of old Western Cascades rock and newer High Cascades rock. The highest Cascade peaks are stratovolcanoes — structures of lava flows interlayered with pyroclastic deposits both loose and tuffaceous. Lava is the strong part, but lava flows alone cannot build volcanoes that combine the height, steepness, and graceful conical form of ours; tuff's contribution is needed. Particles dumped in a heap settle at their own proper "angle of repose." (Watch sand settle in an hourglass for an elegant demonstration of this.) Angle of repose varies with particle roughness, angularity, and moisture — in a word, cling. It ranges between 33° and 37° for most scree, may reach 39° for cinder cones, and even higher for welded tuffs, which cheat. Lava flows cannot create such steep angles. Pyroclastics on a stratovolcano fill in the gaps and gouges left by viscous lava flows and subsequent erosion, until the mountain approximates a 35° cone steepening a bit toward the top. Mt. St. Helens used to look like Mt. Fuji, more perfect than our other cones because it had erupted enough since the Ice Age to repair the disfigurements of glaciation. Then it blew perfection away.

Obsidian

Color p 509.

Obsidian is commonly called "volcanic glass," and that's exactly what it is. It is distinguished by breaking like glass, in a pattern of concentric arcs. It is ideal for chipping into sharp arrowheads and other tools, so it was a major trade commodity for all western tribes. The main source near here was central Oregon's Newberry Crater—actually a caldera, like Crater Lake. There are smaller obsidian flows among the Three Sisters, but there isn't much of it in the rest of our range.

Technically, glass is noncrystalline. Obsidian is lava that cooled without organizing its ions into crystalline minerals. (Many lavas lack visible crystals, but microscopically are a mix of crystals in a glassy matrix.) Even though chemically equivalent to the pale lavas, rhyolite and dacite, obsidian is usually black or dark red-brown.

Geology: intrusive igneous rocks

Diorite and Granite

Color p 510.

Granite has a high recognition factor, partly for its frequent role as the heavy in rock-climbing thrillers, and partly for its countless appearances in cemeteries and kitchen counters. The highly polished cut surfaces have taught us the texture of granitic intrusive rocks—tightly interlocked coarse crystals of varicolored minerals. Quartz is the white to buff, translucent component; feldspars are salmon to pale gray; glittering black flakes are biotite, or "black mica"; hornblende and pyroxene are darker grays.

The word *gran*itic derives from these *gran*ular crystals, and the word intrusive describes their typical origin. While some magma (molten rock) rises and *extrudes* onto the earth's surface through a volcano, other magma merely *intrudes* among subsurface rocks and solidifies there, at depth. This may be an entire magmatic pulse that fails to ever reach the surface, or it may be a remnant left behind in the "roots" or "plumbing" of a volcano. In either case, if it cools in a large mass, it changes from liquid to solid state very slowly, over hundreds of thousands of years, allowing its atoms plenty of time to precipitate out in an organized manner, forming larger and larger mineral crystals. Large (coarse) crystal size characterizes the granitic class of igneous rocks.

Since magma under pressure exploits weaknesses in the rock it intrudes, there are many narrow intrusions, called "dikes" and "sills," that were originally forced into cracks. These can be an inch wide, or many yards; narrower ones, if intruded into relatively cool surroundings, may cool nearly as fast as lava, producing a microcrystalline rock, such as andesite. Otherwise, dikes are typically granitic or coarse.

Of the several shapes of intrusions, the ones that supply the most volume of granitic rocks are large, seemingly bottomless ones called plutons, of which the very biggest (those over 38 square miles at the surface) are called batholiths ('deep rocks" in Greek). Plutons *per se* aren't visible topographic features; they're simply areas on and under the earth surface where intrusive rocks are the bedrock.

There's a reason these paragraphs have spoken often of granitic rocks and only once of granite. Rock climbers and kitchen designers may speak of any sort of coarse-grained igneous rock as granite, but geologists do not. Hedging by substituting "granitic" is loose but not incorrect. Geologists use "granitoid" to include true granite and all other intrusive rocks with at least a 1:5 quartz/feldspar ratio. Our commonest intrusives are granodiorite and tonalite; we have a fair amount of granite as well, particularly in the Golden Horn Batholith, an area on the North Cascades Highway including the headwaters of Granite Creek, the Early Winters Spires and Liberty Bell—beloved of rock climbers and photographers. Intrusive rocks are rare in our range outside of the North Cascades.

Granite is typically pinkish or yellowish white with darker speckles. Also abundant in the North Cascades is diorite, a darker salt-and-pepper speckled rock with less than 20% quartz. Geologists say that diorite is darker than granite, with granodiorite in between, but if you look at the picture (page 510) you may think that description is deceptive. The darkness difference between these two rocks lies not in their dark crystals, but in their light ones—pale feldspar versus even paler quartz. In the granite specimen, they are a mixture of pale gray feldspar with a greater portion of pinkish translucent quartz. In the granodiorite they look uniformly pale gray and are almost all feldspar. By "dark," geologists really mean "lacking much quartz."

A single quartz/feldspar chart defines the light, medium, and dark igneous rocks of both coarse or fine categories; each coarse (intrusive) type has a chemically equivalent fine (volcanic) type. Granite's equivalent is rhyolite, and the Golden Horn Batholith, when it was still molten magma, probably fed a rhyolitic volcano. Granodiorite and tonalite are equivalent to dacite, and diorite to andesite, and sure enough, those types of lava predominated in the volcanoes of the same periods and terranes as our intrusions.

Gabbro

Color p 510.

Gabbro is the intrusive counterpart of basalt: it contains the same mix of minerals, but in somewhat coarser crystals. While basalt is the most abundant volcanic rock, gabbro is a relatively rare intrusive rock. Apparently basalt doesn't tend to plug up plumbing. (Abundant granite, in contrast, cools from highly viscous rhyolite lava, which plugs up all the time.) Gabbro crops up in the North Cascades as medium-sized dikes, never as large batholiths. In places (lining Fourth-of-July Basin, for example) extensive bands of dark gray gabbro alternate dramatically with pale granitic bands. Gabbroic bands are usually well over 4" wide, considerably wider than the bands typical of schist or gneiss. The minerals within gabbro show little color contrast, making the crystals inconspicuous.

Peridotites

("Per-**id**-o-tights"). Color p 510.

Unusual intrusive rocks loosely termed peridotites are characteristically green, often flecked with black crystals, with a greasy-looking luster. They weather to produce red soils difficult for most plants to grow in. An abrupt transition to reddish soil with sparse, dwarfed plant cover may be a clue to these "serpentine" soils underlain by peridotites. They are found in a long arc around Mt. Stuart that includes Tumwater Canyon and much of Ingalls Creek; all over the Twin Sisters near Mt. Baker; and in smaller outcrops scattered through the North Cascades.

In general, peridotites are restricted to environs of deep faulting within subduction-zone mountain ranges. They are thought to be pieces brought up from the upper mantle, the subcrust layer of the earth. Peridotite is defined by a high proportion (40%+) of the yellow-green mineral olivine, which predominates in the mantle. Olivine-rich material is too heavy to reach the surface without exceptionally deep and rapid rock movement. Peridotites containing over 90% olivine are "dunite," the least adulterated mantle specimens. Geologists fascinated by dunite mostly have to content themselves with little bits and pieces. The Twin Sisters, probably the largest outcrop of dunite in the Western Hemisphere, attest to the violent crustal upheaval that produced the North Cascades.

Peridotites have no fine-grained (volcanic) equivalent because lava isn't hot enough to melt them. Their crystals must originate long before (and far below) the melting of the magma. Solid peridotite rocks occasionally shoot out of volcanoes along with molten lava, and can be seen as inclusions after the lava hardens.

Geology: sedimentary rocks

Shale

Color p 511.

Abundant throughout the Olympics, shale consists of clayey river mud carried out to sea and piled up in ocean basins to such depths that through thousands or millions of years under the weight of subsequent layers it was compacted into more or less solid rock. Most kinds of sediments have to be cemented together with water-soluble minerals to become sedimentary rocks, but clay particles are so minute and flaky that they can become shale through compaction alone, or with minor amounts of cement. Shale is still close enough to simple clay that you can breathe on it and smell clay, or break a piece in your hands, or scrape it with your knife and spit on the scrapings to mix up a batch of fresh clay mud.

Shale is generally gray, and has a strong tendency to break into flattish leaves along its bedding planes. A similar rock that doesn't break in flat leaves (due to different mineral content) is mudstone. Where we find shales and mudstones, we may also find less- and more-processed beds nearby—dense clays that lay on the ocean floor too briefly and shallowly to get compacted into rock, and others that got buried long and deeply, and metamorphosed into slate or phyllite.

Sandstones

Arkose and
Graywacke. ("**gray**-wacky"). Color p 511.

Sandstone is a broad term for sedimentary rock made up of compacted sand-size (.06-2 mm) particles cemented together with water-soluble minerals like silica or calcite. The sand grains may be largely quartz, as in the classic blond sandstone. Quartz sandstone is uncommon here, though there is some near Mt. Olympus. It's hard to figure out how beds or beaches of nearly pure quartz sand ever collect, since the waters that bring them are eroding all the diverse rocks of a watershed. The answer is that quartz is both hard and chemically stable, tending to break down to sand-size particles and then stop breaking down. In contrast, feldspars and other abundant minerals tend to end up as silt and clay mud through a process of chemical weathering with water. Eventually, the bulk of sand-size particles in a body of water are quartz, as the finer silt washes away; this takes a long time, preferably in pounding surf, and it helps to have a quartz-rich source.

The common sandstones of our mountains had neither the quartz-rich source nor the time. Geologists give them other names, reserving "sandstone" unmodified for quartz sandstone. Feldspar-rich arkose sandstone, common in the North Cascades, looks coarse, motley, and sometimes pinkish, resembling granite and diorite, from which it derives. It forms in lakes, riverbeds and shallow seas near active mountain ranges where granitic rocks are rapidly uplifting and eroding; transport and deposition is too swift to allow chemical weathering to remove the abundant feldspars.

North Cascades arkoses formed in basins nestled among the edges of ancestral mountains. The basins, lying between pairs of faults, dropped during rare intervals of crustal compression that interrupted our more usual crustal stretching. Just as fast as they dropped, they filled up with sediments carried off of the nearby mountains. Sands in the arkose around Leavenworth derive from erosion, 50-60 million years ago, of the same Mt. Stuart Batholith that still stands high above them. Extensive Eastside exposures are in the Wenatchee-Chiwawa River trough and a swath along the Methow Valley. Westside outcrops are largely among foothills, but also include a few such peaks as Gothic and Mt. Hagan, demonstrating good erosion resistance at least in some cases.

Coast ranges, including the Olympics, typically contain a lot of "dirty" sandstone called graywacke. A belt of graywacke and some paler sandstone (arkose and quartzose both) runs through the heart of the Olympics from the upper Soleduck to the North Fork Quinault, including several peaks of Mt. Olympus. Graywacke resembles shale in its dark color and clayey odor when damp, and is held together mainly by compacted clay rather than by soluble minerals. With its mixed-size, angular fragments, often of andesite, it may equally resemble volcanic tuff; but tuff is as rare in the Olympics as graywacke is in the Oregon Cascades.

Graywackes are thought to be deposited in deep ocean trenches above subduction zones, offshore from chains of volcanoes, when avalanchelike bursts of mud-and-sand slurry course down the slopes of these trenches at intervals of several hundred years, dropping many inches or feet of sediment at a time. These "turbidity currents" are the only well-accepted mechanism for laying down unsorted sediments (i.e., a range of particle sizes in each bed). Though unsorted, "turbidite" beds are more or less "graded": each single bed, or layer deposited by one turbidity avalanche, starts at its bottom with coarser sediments, which settled quickly, and grades upward to fine sediments, which may have taken weeks to settle. Of course, the original top and bottom are most likely turned some other way by the time you see them, due to radical faulting and folding in the Olympics. However that may be, the fine sediments of one bed adjoin the coarse sediments of the next.

Limestone

Color p 512.

Many marine sediments, including those that become sandstone or shale, are ground-up rocks from the continents. Others are deposits of ground-up and/or dissolved seashells. Hard-shelled marine organisms (don't picture shellfish, since the majority are microscopic, and many are plants) make shells out of various compounds, most abundant being calcite ($CaCO_3$). Sedimentary rock characterized by over 50% calcite content is limestone. (You can test for limestone with a drop of hydrochloric acid or vinegar, which will effervesce in reaction with the alkaline calcite.) Some limestones are virtually pure crystalline calcite precipitated upon the ocean floor from completely dissolved shells of dead organisms.

Others, such as chalk, form from marine algae that secrete calcite without making a substantial shell. Typically, precipitated calcite cements pulverized shell material.

Limestones underlie vast regions of the midwestern U.S. and many other parts of the globe. Here, too, they may be the commonest shelly rocks, but that's not to say they're truly common. Chowder Ridge's 150 million-year-old limestone bouillabaisse, cropping out from the much younger flanks of Mt. Baker, is one example. Another is limestone that formed in small interstices between the undersea basalt flows that are now high in the eastern Olympics; minerals from the hot lava altered much of it to deep red. Slopes above the Napeequa River have some belts of marble, which is metamorphosed limestone.

Quartz and Chert

Color p 512.

The most familiar kind of "rock crystal" is quartz—transparent (though sometimes tinted) with six generally unequal sides and a six-faceted point. It's the only stone in this chapter that forms single crystals; it's the only one that's a mineral rather than a rock. In geologists' terms, a rock is a mixture of minerals whose proportions to each other vary only within limits that define that kind of rock; the respective mineral crystals, whether visible or microscopic, are discrete. A mineral, on the other hand, is a single chemical compound or continuum of compounds with one characteristic crystal shape. Quartz is silicon dioxide (SiO_2, usually simply called silica) adulterated with too few impurities to break up its proper crystal form. It is hard, too hard to scratch with a knife, lightweight and light-colored, and very abundant as a rock ingredient; it is in nearly every light- to medium-colored rock you see, except limestone. Its abundance at the earth's surface is thought to result from its light weight—it has risen among heavier materials while powerful forces stirred the earth around for some four billion years. (Meanwhile, the heavy metals nickel and iron accumulated toward the Earth's core. They are the most abundant elements in the Earth, but aren't abundant at the surface.)

Large, free-sided quartz crystals are not abundant, but they do catch the eye. You can find them in several parts of the Olympics, including crevices in greenstone on Crystal (!) Peak and Chimney

Peak. They form in cavities in rocks (often volcanic) that spent a long time filled with moving groundwater rich in dissolved silica. The silica precipitated out as "rock crystals" on the cavity lining, just like sugar crystallizing on a string as "rock candy" (named after quartz.) Quartz veins in intrusive and metamorphic rock bodies reflected as a gleam in a prospector's eye, since precious metals occur in or near them; the same hot subterranean streams carry and deposit both silica and minerals.

Virtually pure quartz may also occur as the opaque rock chert, a cryptocrystalline or microcrystalline (i.e., not visibly crystalline) form. Chert resembles porcelain while crystalline quartz is transparent like glass, and that's no coincidence: ground-up silica rock is the main ingredient in both glass and porcelain. Both porcelain and a hard chert called Arkansas novaculite can be used to whet a fine edge on a knife. Like glass and obsidian, chert chips with an even, shallowly concave fracture; its dark form, flint, rivaled obsidian as an arrowhead and blade material among stone-tool cultures.

Cherts form in several very different ways. The commonest is similar to limestone—crumbled marine shell material settling to the ocean floor or precipitating there from solution in sea water. While most seashells are made of calcite, the main mineral in limestone, there is also a large group of one-celled organisms that make a sort of shell of silica, and these are the main source of chert.

Conglomerate

Color p 512.

Conglomerates are defined as sedimentary rocks composed at least 50% of erosion-rounded stones over 2 mm in diameter; most of them are pebble beaches and river bars turned to stone. They have to include both smaller rock particles to fill in the spaces, and soluble minerals as glue. Well-cemented conglomerates will break straight through pebbles and interstices alike—a fine sight. Weaker ones break through the cement (or "matrix") only, leaving the pebbles sticking out just like from any old gravel bank. There are good conglomerates around Devil's Dome and Holman Peak, east of Ross Lake. Ludden Peak in the Olympics is a spectacular knob of hardened "metaconglomerate"—compressed so hard during metamorphism that the pebbles were all flattened in one direction.

Breccia

("**bretch**-ia"). Color p 512.

Breccia consists of unrounded rock pieces bound up in a fine-grained matrix other than volcanic tuff. The distinction from conglomerate, in which the inclusions are erosion-rounded, may seem trifling, but on further thought it is puzzling, since only eroded rocks are normally deposited as sediments.

There are several brecciating processes, some sedimentary, some volcanic, and some more or less metamorphic, as follows. All involve breakage, from which the Italian word breccia derives.

Sedimentary breccia is often a coarser version of graywacke containing shaley shards ripped from the surface of deep-sea sediments by a turbidity current and then deposited among the turbidite sediments. Alternatively, ordinary landslides in shaley, slaty, or limestone terrain can end up compacted into breccia.

Volcanic breccia (the commonest type here) can be simply the margins of basalt flows, where chunks of crust that formed as a skin on the slowly flowing lava are still visible after being shattered and reincorporated by the continuing flow. In this case, matrix and inclusions are of the exact same rock. Alternatively, as a body of magma rises, pieces of the surrounding rock break off and fall into it. Sometimes these pieces happen to be rocks whose melting point is much hotter than the temperature of the magma, and they maintain their own integrity as the magma around them solidifies into an intrusive rock. Granitic magma, for example, has a much lower melting point than high-grade metamorphics. Breccia of dark igneous pieces, both round and angular, in a granitic matrix can be seen on the south side of Roland Point, Ross Lake.

Tectonic breccia is a mix of coarse and fine rock fragments broken by shearing forces within a fault, and then compacted under moderate pressure; sometimes you can visually match up the broken edges of adjacent fragments.

There is a lot of breccia out there, but much of it looks like an obscure mess and fails to catch anyone's eye. It usually takes rock saws and polishers to reveal the splendid breccia sections that appear in books and as architectural facings.

Olympic Mountains Geology

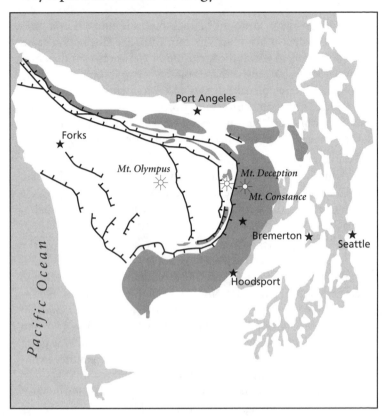

 Major thrust faults

 Basalt: the two large belts (the "basaltic horse-shoe") are part of the Crescent Formation. The small segments inside the big outer fault have been called the "inner basaltic rings."

Slate and Phyllite

Color p 513.

Slate looks like what it is: metamorphosed shale. Even the names look alike. They share dark gray colors (varying through reds and greens in slates) and platy textures that tend to break into flat pieces. Surprisingly, the flat cleavage of slate is not at all the same thing as the flat bedding plane of shale. Bedding planes started out horizontal, being simply the layers of mud or other sediments as they settle out from the water. Slaty cleavage planes, in contrast, are perpendicular to the direction of pressure that metamorphosed the rock. There may have been two or more such directions at different times, producing slate that fractures into slender "pencils." Some slates metamorphosed from mudstone, and never had distinct bedding planes; in others the bedding has faded. Commonly, though, the parent shale's bedding planes are visible as streaks or bands in slate, either happening to align with the new cleavage planes or crossing them, but no longer causing a plane of weakness.

Slate gets a slight satiny luster from microscopic crystals of mica and other minerals. Metamorphism has aligned these all parallel, creating the primary cleavage plane and making it relatively shiny. Higher-pressure metamorphism of the same rock produces larger crystals (just barely visible without a lens), a much stronger, glittery but perhaps wavy gloss, and a somewhat weaker tendency to split. Such rock is called "phyllite" by geologists, though it is sold as roofing "slate." Slate and phyllite are abundant, often together, in the Olympics, and sporadic in the North Cascades. Slate is shatter-prone and weak in landforms, and phyllite just slightly less so (unless it gets cooked; see Hornfels, page 554.)

Schist

Color p 514.

Conspicuous fine-layered texture in a rock may be of either sedimentary or metamorphic origin (see Slate, above). Metamorphic layering changes with increasing heat and pressure; the parallel layers may get tightly crimped, crumpled or curved, while the rock's strength in most cases increases. At the same time, the flaky crystals (mainly mica) first grow larger as "slaty cleavage" converts to "schistose foliation," and then are replaced altogether by coarse crystals that may show "gneissose banding." Though "schist" derives from the Greek for "split" (as in schizophrenia), schists aren't nearly as easy to split as slates. Schistose texture, which defines schists, is tricky to describe; worse, it is often dulled and obscured by weathering or rust. Unweathered specimens glimmer in the sun, showing the parallel orientation of their mica flakes.

Schists vary widely in color. A typical variety just east of Glacier Peak is garnet-biotite schist. The garnet appears as scattered, reddish, smeared crystals ¼" or larger, with schistose foliation making almond shapes around them. Black mica gives the rock an overall blackish hue. Garnet did not exist in these rocks until they reached the exact degree of heat and pressure that produces garnet schist. Metamorphism not only recrystallizes preexisting minerals, it makes new minerals by recombining atoms into new molecules. The mineral content of metamorphic rocks is determined partly by the overall proportions of elements in the parent material, and partly by the grade of heat and pressure that they went through.

Schists are widespread in the North Cascades. Olympic rocks are younger and have seen only lower-grade metamorphism, producing abundant slates and a few low-grade schists.

Greenstone and Greenschist

Color p 514.

Greenstone is an informal term for mildly metamorphosed basalt or andesite. It looks like basalt with a greenish cast. It is harder than basalt, as attested by the sheer relief of Jack Mountain, part of a belt of old metamorphosed sea-floor basalt in the North Cascades. Basalts in the Olympics are also metamorphosed in places (e.g., Mt. Ferry to Mt. Christie) but few basalts of the Oregon Cascades have been buried deep enough for metamorphism.

Mt. Shuksan and Whitechuck Mtn. are made of greenschist, a metabasalt differing from greenstone in its schistose texture, often with smeared-out lustrous crystals. This Shuksan greenschist's grade requires deep burial, then extremely rapid uplift, i.e. its metamorphism is high-pressure, low-temperature, and unusually brief. This happens only in very tempestuous subduction zones.

North Cascade Geology

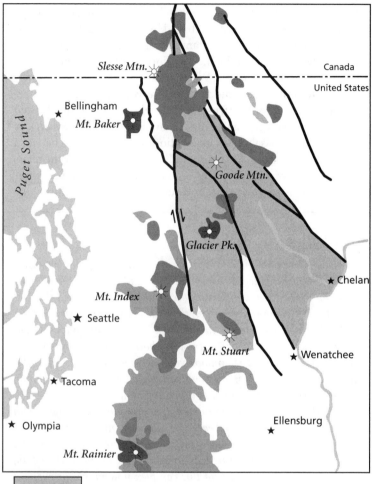

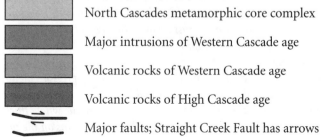

North Cascades metamorphic core complex

Major intrusions of Western Cascade age

Volcanic rocks of Western Cascade age

Volcanic rocks of High Cascade age

Major faults; Straight Creek Fault has arrows

Hornfels

If you ever notice that you have just left an area of granitic rocks, you may be in the vicinity of hornfels. It is a "contact metamorphic" rock, meaning that it was baked by close contact with hot intrusive magma, but not substantially altered by pressure at that time. It was also altered by the addition of volatile chemicals suffusing out from the magma. Where hornfels occurs in shale, it may grade into spotted slate and then shale as you walk a few yards farther from the granitic intrusion. Hornfels is a fine-grained, often dark gray to black crystalline rock resembling basalt; the easiest way to tell it from basalt is by its location near granitics. The word means "horn rock" in German, and I'm not sure whether the reference is directly to animal horns or to the many "horn" type mountains in the Alps, but in either case the idea was that this is one

The Peripatetic Baja B.C.

Gneiss predominates in the North Cascades Metamorphic Core Complex—that big two-legged wedge shape on the map (page 553), lying between the Straight Creek Fault (vertical) on the west and the Ross Lake Fault System (diagonal) on the east. The Core has been in three or four successive mountain ranges, each including magma as well as folding and faulting. The area's oldest batholiths that are still discernible formed about 220 million years ago beneath a volcanic tropical island arc, probably in the Southeast Pacific. Metamorphism began in the churning, grinding roots of that first mountain range.

Multiple batholiths and intense metamorphism happened again between 120 and 80 million years ago. At that point the Core Complex had joined an apparent welter of terranes that were smashing together at the edge of the North American continental plate, near where Baja California is today. (Much of this complex now makes up western British Columbia, which has been nicknamed "Baja BC.") Serious Crunch Time: Terranes were thrust up over the edges of other terranes and the whole pile became inordinately thick. Two effects of crustal overthickening are, first, the thick pile weighs heavily on whichever crustal rocks are on the bottom, so they undergo high-pressure metamorphism; and second, these deep-formed high-grade metamorphics are destined eventually to rise to the surface because the whole thick pile floats upon denser subcrustal rock, and the mountains on the top tough rock. Such awesome peaks as Hozomeen, Shuksan, and the ultimate North Cascades fang, Slesse, occur where metamorphic rocks were further cooked by contact metamorphism.

Gneiss

("nice"). Color p 514.

North Cascades climbers know gneiss intimately. Redoubt, Fury and Terror, Snowfield and Eldorado, Forbidden and Formidable, Boston, Buckner, Logan, Goode, Johannesberg, Magic and Mixup, Maude, Fernow, Fortress and Bonanza—peaks forming a backbone of the range are made of Mesozoic and older gneiss. Plainly, gneiss stands up to erosion every bit as well as the intruding granitics and better than nearby schists.

Gneiss is a broad field term for a texture and a metamorphic

---

of the pile keep eroding away into surrounding basins.

Meanwhile (from 100 to 45 million years ago) Baja BC swept north along the edge of California, much as the portion of California outboard of the San Andreas Fault sweeps today. By 45 million years ago, Baja BC was sutured to the continent, and an outer slice of terranes had sheared off along the Straight Creek Fault and continued northward another sixty miles or more. The period from 60 to 40 million years ago in the NW is a mystery, subject to myriad duelling hypotheses. One thing we know is that along the NE edge of the Core the gneiss was widely migmatized: it became an unbelievably chaotic hash of gneiss layers swirled with countless slender dikes of magma. (See Migmatite, below.) That part of the Core is called the Skagit Gneiss.

Having arrived, the terranes were soon perforated by yet another volcanic arc, the Cascades, beginning around 35 million years ago and continuing today. The volcanic Cascade Arc and Baja BC overlap just partially: the Baja BC part of the arc—the North Cascades—was sharply uplifted, especially in the past seven million years, so its volcanoes, unlike the old Cascade volcanoes farther south, completely eroded off the top, exposing both the Metamorphic Core rocks and the volcanoes' "roots" or "plumbing"—the batholiths on the map (Snoqualmie, Cloudy Pass, Index, Chilliwack group, etc.).

Erosion has worked fast to keep these mountains from being any higher than they are. Net uplift in places exceeded 18 vertical miles.

---

intensity grade. Gneiss is intermediate between schist and granitic rocks in appearance, in grade, and often in location. Some gneiss started out as shale or arkose and was metamorphosed by heat and pressure past the phyllite and schist stages, nearly to the point of melting. Other gneiss—the more common type here—was granitic before metamorphism; gneisses of sedimentary and igneous parentage look pretty similar in the field. Coarse gneiss may overlap fine-grained granitics in crystal size, but the grains are at least slightly flattened in gneiss, never in granite. The plane of flattening may also show lighter and darker bands, often contorted. Gneiss fragments often break along planes of glittery mica flakes. For the rock to be gneiss rather than schist (which also has minerals segregated in bands) flaky minerals must be outweighed by fatter grains overall.

Migmatite

In much of the Skagit gneiss complex, metamorphic heat and pressure were extreme; the best calculation to date was 1,330° at a depth of 19 miles. Under those conditions the rock is thought to melt partially, producing magma that swirls around with the surrounding solid rock before recrystallizing into ribbons (dikes and sills) of granitic rock. The spectacular product, called migmatite (from the Greek for "mix") makes prized facing stone for buildings. In between the granitic stripes and swirls, darker gneiss or schist remains; the edges between the two are sharp, so we know that the mass as a whole wasn't melting. Exactly how migmatites are created has been a great geologic puzzle. In some cases the granitic liquid may get injected along cracks from a nearby magma body.

Migmatites appear in roadcuts in the Skagit Gorge, near Ross Lake Overlook, and at Chelan Falls. Migmatite differs from metamorphic breccia in the coarse crystalline (granitic) texture of the matrix portion.

16

Climate

Weather may be critical to the success of your trip to the mountains, and it is at least as crucial in determining the landforms and life forms you will see. One weather fact you know already—it rains a lot here.

It rains a lot in winter, almost as much in fall and spring, and relatively little in June through September.

It rains a lot west of the Olympic and Cascade Crests, but much less on the east slopes, approaching desert conditions at the foot of the Cascades.

It rains a lot and snows even more at higher elevations.

The resulting snowpack is slow to melt due to its sheer mass rather than to really cold weather; it persists longer in summer, and produces more glaciers and permanent snowfields, than snow in other mountains with equally mild or somewhat colder climates, such as the U.S. Rockies.

When It Falls

Our summer "drought" is without equal among the world's rainy climates. Most climates with strong wet seasons and dry seasons are tropical, and lack summers and winters. Most of the Temperate Zone, on the other hand, gets precipitation all year round, or with a slight emphasis in summer. Our climate is a midpoint between California's Mediterranean type (dry summers and subtropical temperatures) and Southeast Alaska's West-Coast Marine type (copious rain, slightly reduced in the summer, and cool temperatures year-round). Our closest analogs are certain narrow locales in southern Chile, western Scotland, the northern Honshu coast on the Sea of Japan, and Norway's Fjord Country. Each of those wet West-Coast Marine climates produces 1½ times as much rain and snow in its wettest winter month as in its driest summer month. That's nothing; here, most weather stations record between 6 and 20 times as much precipitation in December as in July.

Causes for our unique weather lie in the border tension between the cold polar air mass and the warmer subtropical air mass. The front between those masses runs around the world between roughly 40° and 60° North latitude; rather than running due east it wanders in giant lobes directly under the polar front jet stream, a lofty belt of high-velocity west wind circling the globe.

Though the jet stream's lobes or loops vary somewhat unpredictably, causing year-to-year weather eccentricities, nearly every autumn brings a southward migration of the jet and expansion of the polar air mass. On average, the polar jet crosses Anchorage in September, Ketchikan in October, Bella Coola in November, Astoria (and all of our range) in December, and Eureka in January. Those are the respective wettest months when each locale is directly in line for rainy "storms"—low-pressure centers spun off from the edge of winter's great Aleutian Low.

The air in the storms, originally quite cold, travels for days across relatively warm (45°) ocean, to reach our shores modestly warmed and immodestly moistened. On a satellite photo the storms look like whorls of clouds spiraling counterclockwise. On a weather map they look like steep, eastward-drifting waves written in heavy "front" lines. The leading edge of the wave crosses us as a warm front, and the trailing edge, 8 to 48 hours later, as a cold front. The lulls in between are typically filled with partly cloudy, showery weather comprised of unstable (busily convecting) moist warm air.

Rarely, the jet stream develops a sharp northward swing offshore, dragging warm, sunny California weather into our area for days or weeks of winter. Alternatively, a strong southward swing of the jet, inland, may drag Arctic cold pressure over the midcontinent; some of this air pours gravitationally over the Cascades from the east (especially down the Columbia Gorge) sliding in under the warmer marine air to produce lowland snow and/or freezing rain.

If the southward swing is near the coast, Arctic air and high pressure can take over the whole Northwest, for a sunny cold period.

As summer approaches, the jet stream snakes its way back north, taking the frontal systems with it. Its progress is more uneven than in fall. The Aleutian Low weakens into indistinctness while a subtropical North Pacific High strengthens and stabilizes, typically with a large, benign bulge in our direction. The Polar Front continues to bring rain to the coast, but now mostly in British Columbia and Alaska. All along the West Coast, including our range, summer drought gets less and less consistent northward.

Our dominant summer air consists of NW breezes spinning clockwise out from the center of the North Pacific High. Since these travel across ocean colder (55°) than themselves, they are unable to evaporate much moisture from it. They are chilled by contact with the water, often creating vast ocean fogbanks, but on hitting the warmer land surface they warm, and the fog soon dissipates. Sometimes during high pressure, the moist marine airflow gets strong enough to blanket Olympic Westside valleys and much of the Puget-Willamette Trough with low clouds and even drizzle, while peaks and slopes above 3,000' remain crystal clear.

All this means that it's certifiably possible to enjoy summer recreation anywhere in our range, despite rumors to the contrary. It does **not** mean that you can safely go unprepared for bad weather. Several recent Julys have brought blizzards to North Cascade locales as low as 4,000'.

Where It Falls

In contrast to our precipitation's unique summer/winter split, its west/east imbalance is common in mountain ranges, typifying mountains as rainmaking devices and as barriers between moist marine air and drier continental air. When a prevailing air flow crosses mountains, the air must inevitably rise. In rising, it gets thinner (because it has less atmosphere above it to weigh down on it) and cools. Other factors being equal, clear air cools 5.5° with each 1,000' of altitude. Other factors are rarely equal, so the actual lapse rate is usually somewhat less.

The air's capacity to carry water vapor rises and falls with temperature. When air containing water vapor cools, it may sooner or later reach a point where it can no longer carry all of its moisture,

---

which will condense into clouds or fog and then may fall as precipitation. Where the air descends after crossing mountains, the effect is reversed. If there was just enough moisture to make clouds and drizzle on the windward slope, the clouds may abruptly vanish as they cross the crest. If it's wetter, heavy weather on the windward slope may turn to scattered showers on the downwind slope.

Sometimes the condensation and then re-evaporation of moist air flowing over a mountain becomes a graphic image in the sky—a lenticular ("lens-shaped") cloud. These pure white slivers or crescents hang motionless over high peaks. They may stack up two or three deep, and they may stand downwind instead of (or in addition to) directly over the peak. A lenticular cloud is that portion of a uniform layer of air which, as it flows over the mountain, is cooled enough to condense some of its water vapor into cloud droplets. After descending abruptly, the layer may bounce upward once or twice, in waves, to form downwind lenticular clouds.

Since the prevailing wind here is from the WSW in winter and the SW in spring and fall, and the Olympics are a more or less round mountain range, their downwind side, known as the "Rain Shadow," is on the NE. The Elwha and North Fork Skokomish Valleys are rain-shadowed, receiving less than a third as much precipitation as the Hoh and Quinault; the Dungeness and Dosewallips are even drier. A crooked chain of ridges, running from Sourdough Mtn. to Prospect Ridge via the Bailey and Burke Ranges, constitutes the Olympic Crest as far as climate is concerned, though the term is not in common usage.

The Cascades comprise a long north/south divide, so their wet side is their west side even though prevailing winds are southwesterly. The barrier is broken by our two biggest rivers, the Columbia and Skagit, creating two unique biogeographic locales astride the climatic fence. The Columbia Gorge cuts through the Cascades nearly at sea level, funneling wind and weather, as well as fish, plant species, and human traffic, between the Eastside and Westside lowlands. Some Westside species, like Oregon white oak, reach the Eastside in and near the Gorge. Many plant varieties are found only in the Gorge, or found there disjunctly (far from the closest similar populations.) On the other hand, the river itself is a barrier to North-South spread of some small animals, like red-backed voles; many butterfly species are also bounded by it.

In fall and winter, relatively high pressure east of the Cascades pours down the Gorge in the form of a protracted east wind strengthening toward the west; the Northwest's record windspeed was clocked at Crown Point, the funnel's mouth. When a freezing east wind slides down the Gorge under the edge of a rain-bearing warm front, it produces freezing rain, colloquially a "silver thaw." In summer, when high pressure blankets the Northwest, prevailing westerlies are focused by the Gorge into a steady west wind, strongest toward the east end, where it has made Hood River into a world-renowned windsurfing center. Evidence of both Gorge Winds takes the form of "flagged" trees; those at the east end sweep eastward, those at the west, westward.

The Skagit rises within the Cascades rather than east of them, so the Cascade Crest is customarily drawn (along with county lines and the Pacific Crest Trail) along the eastern edge of the Skagit drainage. This book does not follow that custom, because the upper Skagit Valley (above Ross Dam) is in rainfall and biotic regimes that fit the Eastside type better. To put that another way, the most pronounced divide in terms of rain shadow runs along the Picket Range and down the center of North Cascades National Park; that divide is the Cascade Crest—in terms of climate, plant and animal life, and the purposes of this book. The dramatic contrast between this true crest's glacier-mantled peaks and the drier Eastside peaks (from viewpoints like Crater Mtn.) exactly resembles that between Crest and Eastside peaks elsewhere in the North Cascades.

The Puget-Willamette Trough is moderately rain-shadowed by the Olympic and Coast Ranges. Though urbanites of Seattle, Portland, and Vancouver share a sometimes hysterical belief that they see a lot of rain, their actual recorded precipitation of 33-42" per year is precisely in a league with Peoria, Providence, Chattanooga, Calistoga, and the worldwide average. The number of gray and rainy days per year is indeed high in Northwest cities, but the bulk of the rain—60" to 250"—falls on the Cascade and Coast Range flanks. One indicator that the Trough isn't very wet is the ponderosa pines and the climax grand firs in the Willamette Valley, resembling the dry east slope of the Cascades.

The rain shadow effect can be put to use in planning outings. If the day for your trip arrives gray and showery, consider shifting to an Eastside destination. You might not find clear skies, but you will almost certainly get less wet than on the Westside. The one common exception is a summer high-pressure system with fair mornings and a line of afternoon or evening thunderheads developing along the eastern front of the Cascades; this is decent weather on either slope, producing only light rainfall. Just move away from salient trees or peaks if lightning begins to strike nearby.

If you want to reach high country in June or July, but snow still covers most of it, head for the northeast corners of the North Cascades (the Sawtooth or Pasayten Wildernesses) and Olympics. Less snow accumulates there, and it melts off weeks earlier each summer. In Oregon you have to go to the Wallowas or Strawberries, since no high Cascade ridges extend far east of the Crest.

Forecasting Rain

Instruction in do-it-yourself weather forecasting seems called for at this point. But it could be guaranteed to dissatisfy—often. All the same, there is some value in the old saws about types of clouds to watch out for:

"Mare's-tails." These are cirrus clouds—the very high, thin, wispy family—arrayed in parallel, all or most of them upturned at one end like sled runners. Especially if blowing northward, they may presage a weather front by 12 to 24 hours. Broad sheets of cirrus whiteness, if northbound and/or thickening and lowering, may have the same meaning. However, scattered shreds of cirrus resembling pulled-out cotton puffs are typical of good weather.

"Cloudcaps." Small clouds sitting all day around the heads of outstanding peaks are common, and not necessarily ominous. If they thicken steadily for hours, they may be the most visible part of an increasing cloudiness presaging rain. Portentous or not, they are already bad weather ahead if the peak they cap is your goal. Reconsider: the view will be erased, the wind strong and cold. Also watch lenticular cloud streamers above or downwind of high peaks; their arrival or increase displays an increase in wind speed and/or moisture of the air. But the moist air flow may be modest, especially in summer, and may come and go without producing heavy weather.

Cumulus clouds—the white, rounded puffy kind—increasing in the afternoon are usually a stable fair weather pattern, not a bad omen. Along a mountain range they may by evening build and darken into cumulonimbus, perhaps generating thunderstorms. Even if this pattern repeats for days, it may be followed by either better or worse weather. Morning cloudiness filling Westside valleys is not necessarily a bad sign either, even if it brings palpable moisture or if it rises rapidly and temporarily engulfs the ridges.

It takes years of familiarity with the weather patterns of a particular mountain area to develop a really good eye for weather signs. Whether you think you have such an eye or not, it is vital to carry into the high country enough insulation, shelter and food to keep you alive, and enough navigation aids and skills to get you out again, should the weather happen to turn bad.

In the short run, the most useful instruction is to catch a complete weather forecast. Weather Radios can be taken backpacking, but mountain topography blocks their wavelength, so the signal only reaches places high enough to receive a nearly straight beam. Major-network forecasts are less useful—generalized, short-range, focussed on the urban area. Try phoning the National Park or Forest Ranger Station closest to your destination; they usually have a local weather forecast, and they can always look out the window.

Forest Microclimate

All of the above climatic subjects—the ones weathermen talk about—are macroclimatic. Of equal concern to hikers and other creatures is the microclimate, or narrow climate near the ground. A microclimate may be much warmer or cooler than its surroundings for several reasons:

Hot air rises and cold air sinks. Where protected from wind, small masses of cold air may descend along stream drainages, or settle in valleys and slight depressions. Caves like Lavacicle Cave, a lava tube, collect cold air drainage intensely, retaining year-round ice at moderate elevations.

Ground and lakes heat up in the sun, even on cloudy days, and heat the air next to them. Dark surfaces heat much more than pale ones, south-facing slopes much more than north-facing ones. East slopes heat best in the morning, west slopes in the afternoon. High peaks are subject to especially intense solar radiation, including heat, by way of reradiation from surrounding clouds, snow or ice. In one extreme example, dark, dry humus soil on a high south-facing slope was found to reach 175° while the surrounding air was only 86°. For a seedling or a crawling invertebrate, 175° summer afternoons would simply be that habitat's facts of life—or death.

Vegetation insulates; the tree canopy, the shrub, herb, and moss layers, and the snowpack are all blankets, keeping everything under them warmer in cold weather, and vice versa. The combination of ground heat retention and snowpack insulation create a winterlong 30–32° environment utilized by many rodents who would otherwise either hibernate or live elsewhere. Deer and elk take "thermal cover" in deep forests during cold spells of winter. On summer days, on the other hand, the forest is cooler than clearings.

Vegetation and rough topography impede wind. This effect allows cold air collected by sinking (or air heated by warm ground) to stay put longer than they otherwise would.

A forest canopy may also make the community under it either drier or moister. You may notice that rain dripping from a forest canopy ("throughfall") starts and ends much later than individual showers in nearby clearings, and it falls as much bigger drops. Measured during a rain shower, it amounts to less; much of the rain is absorbed by the canopy and the epiphytic plants on the trunk, re-evaporating eventually without ever reaching the ground. Light drizzle around here often fails to wet the forest floor at all.

An opposite effect also works here; when fog sweeps the forest canopy, moisture condenses on foliage, and some drips to the ground as throughfall while a rain gauge in the open receives no precipitation. Since low vegetation can catch only a fraction of the the fog that a tall forest can, clearcutting a high Cascade watershed is estimated to immediately reduce its total precipitation by about half. Rain, fog throughfall, wind and sun all hit different parts of a tree differently, so that each tree offers several microclimates for small plants that would grow on it. (Page 290.)

Effects of a tree canopy on evaporation are also mixed, and even harder to measure. Trees shade the forest floor from the drying sun, but they also suck huge volumes of water up through their roots and transpire it into the air, leaving soils parched. Gravelly, underdeveloped soil and dependence in summer on residual snow-melt both exacerbate understory drought in our mountains. Small plants in competition with overstory trees may be handicapped even worse for water than for light; many of our sparsest understory communities are found under somewhat open canopies. Non-green plants (page 177), with their fungal lifelines borrowing water back from the tree roots, are at a particular advantage there.

Snowpack depth is reduced under forest cover. Though most snow that settles in the canopy does reach the forest floor, some of it melts first, and most of it, falling in big clumps, is much compacted on impact. Winter melting is greater in the forest. The dark canopy absorbs solar radiation and reradiates some heat downward into the insulated forest microclimate, while the bright white of snow-covered clearings reflects nearly all of the solar radiation that hits it, and doesn't heat up as much.

On the other hand, when warmer air masses arrive in spring and summer, the canopy insulates the forest floor from this warmth. Now melting proceeds faster in the open than in the forest, and the snowpack disappears from clearings several days sooner than from adjacent forest. Within meadows, individual trees hasten snowmelt because, while their insulative value is negligible without companions, their heat-absorbing effect is maximized.

All the above microclimatic effects on temperature and moisture determine which plants can live on a microsite.

Mountain Microclimate

Mountain and valley forms have broader effects (sometimes called "mesoclimate" when measured on a scale of a few kilometers rather than meters). Just as the sun shines hotter at noon than in morning and evening, hotter at the equator than here in the mid latitudes, and hotter in summer than in winter, it shines hotter on south-facing slopes than on other aspects. South slopes have hotter, drier plant community types than north slopes. That was long assumed to be just because of the difference in sunlight angle, but ecologist Andrea Woodward set out a transect of rain gauges and found big differences in rainfall from windward to leeward sides of a ridge. The northeast side of a ridge—the same side always seen as moist because it escapes the hot afternoon sun—is also the leeward side during typical rainstorms, and the rainfall curve peaks there—a short distance downwind of the crest—before falling off dramatically in the familiar "rain shadow" effect. This could be simply because the clouds release the most rain directly above the ridgeline or even a bit upwind, but the raindrops blow downwind as they fall. She found leeward/windward slope differences to be complex and profound. The lowest slopes on the leeward side get the least precipitation, but have the moistest soils, partly because they receive subsurface drainage from the highest leeward slopes, which get the most rainfall but have soils too coarse to hold on to it. Over time, the cool moist soils are s elf-reinforcing: they retain more organic content (which holds on to water well) because fire is less frequent and humus decomposition is slower there.

Bottoms of steep-sided valleys have cooler, moister micro-climates not only due to cold air drainage but also because the sun shines there fewer hours a day. The effect is strongest in east/west-running valleys, weakest in south-draining valleys where midday sun hits the bottom head-on. High nonforested peaks and ridges, at the other extreme, receive copious sunlight but are unable to hold its heat. High thin air tends to be chilly.

The warmest level in mountains is a a mid-elevation "thermal belt" subject to neither cold air drainage nor thin air heat loss. If you want to sleep warmer, you may gain as much as 15° by leaving a stream bottom and camping on a slightly higher bench.

Mountains' chief effects on broad prevailing winds are to deflect them from deep valleys and to strengthen them on salient peaks, major divides, and through long gorges aligned with the wind. The air flow, like a river in a narrowing gorge, is constricted, and has to speed up just to maintain a constant volume.

The air contained in valleys expands in the daytime heat and contracts again at night. Feel Gaia's breathing in the resulting "valley winds" and "slope winds," often stronger than the broader prevailing windflow. The valley wind is a main trunk flow parallel to the main creek or river of the valley, whereas the slope wind is a thin sheet of air moving up or down the valley walls. Up in the day and down at night is the basic rule for both, but the valley wind, being larger, lags behind the slope wind. In early morning, for example, the upslope wind begins while the night's downvalley wind continues in the valley's center. The winds are strongest in clear summer weather. Occasionally the flow buffets in fierce pulses lasting a few seconds each, just after sunset, when downslope and downvalley winds join forces.

Climate Oscillations

By now, most people on the West Coast are aware of the weather pattern called the El Niño Southern Oscillation. It brings us warm offshore waters and warm, relatively dry winters; years with the opposite conditions are sometimes called "La Niñas". The oscillation has different sets of effects in many other parts of the world.

There's been less media attention to research on some slower and more regular climatic cycles. In the Northwest, we seem to get alternating wetter and dryer periods averaging 25 years long. This century's cycle shifts came in 1925, 1946, 1977, and probably 1994, with 1977–1994 being a dry period. One name that has been proposed for this cycle is North Pacific Decadal Oscillation (NDO). It has been recognized especially well in the North Pacific area, but it may well be global. Trends that have been correlated so far include (taking, arbitratily, the dry phase):

El Niño years several times a decade;

few salmon in OR and WA; bumper crops of salmon in Alaska;

more warm/dry winters in the PNW (summers are affected little);

few hurricanes in the Atlantic;

drought in sub-Saharan Africa.

The cycles seem to be caused by shifts between strong and weak thermohaline circulation in the ocean. *Thermo* refers to temperature, *haline* to salt. At certain places (especially, during the present interglacial, off Greenland and Antactica) relatively cold, unsalty seawater accumulates, and sinks because it is heavier than warmer, saltier water. It flows away across the sea floor, and warmer, saltier water flows as a surface current to replace it where it sank. That's why the Gulf Stream can cover most of the far North Atlantic, making Europe much warmer than any other region at a comparable latitude: air arrives in Europe warmed after passage across this very broad warm surface. Efforts to map the cold deep currents together with the surface currents have come up with a grand loop, nicknamed the Conveyor, uniting all of the five oceans.

While strong/weak shifts of the Conveyor may cause our 50-year NDO cycles, it is thought that near-total shutdowns of the Conveyor also occur. These may be the cause of extreme climate flipflops on a 1,500-year average cycle,* which appear to have operated throughout the Ice Age/post–Ice Age period. I say "flipflops" because the transitions are rapid: average temperatures

---

*Current terminology for these is Dansgaard-Oeschger cycles (the strong ones during the latest glacial stage) or Bond cycles (weaker, interglacial). Dansgaard, Oeschger, and Bond are scientists who identified the cycles.

shift by 4–14° in a few decades. Many flipflops were strong enough to switch the earth between glacial and interglacial stages, and some of them did exactly that. Many others apparently did not last long enough for big ice sheets to either form or, if present, to melt away. The last great interglacial stage, from 140,000 to 115,000 years ago, was a bit warmer than our millenium, on the whole, yet it flipped several times into glacial-level temperatures for hundreds of years at a time. The period from 9,000 to 5,000 years ago, a bit warmer than subsequent millenia and often called the Climatic Optimum, also caught a serious chill about 8,200 years ago. But on the whole, flipflops in the last 10,000 have jumped fewer degrees than those of the preceding 140,000 years.

For as long as geologists have understood sedimentary rock strata for what they are, they have noted that for huge periods, many millions of years at a time, sedimentary formations produced sharp-edged alternating bands—coal seams alternating with shale, for example. Return intervals for those are longer still than the ones discussed above, more on the order of entire glacial and interglacial stages, or the Milankovitch earth-orbit cycles. Earlier geologists had to content themselves with unresolvable speculation as to why the bands alternated. Now that the idea of oscillations between two stable regimes is in the forefront of Pleistocene climate theory, it seems natural to see oscillation as a ruling principle of climate on Earth. I wouldn't be surprised if additional oscillating Ice Ages are recognized, as science progresses.

Future Climate

The global climate system is nothing if not complex and mysterious, full of triggers, thresholds, and feedback loops. All parties would surely agree that our understanding of it is dim. Yet it's important to realize that fossil fuels-related industries have poured huge sums of cash into the debate to foster an illusion that scientists are evenly divided on global warming, or that the science is so murky that no policy decisions should be based on it yet. Scientists are not evenly divided. As the 1980s and 90s go by, continuing a global warming trend, it is nearly certain that humans are drastically effecting climate, and that grim consequences are likely.

Several lines of reasoning, as well as computer models, suggest that continued CO_2 increases and warmer temperatures might trigger a shutdown of the Conveyer. While past shutdowns may have thrown the Earth into glacial stages, one that came on top of a future 5° or 6° of CO_2-induced warming ought to look pretty different from past ones. It might even cancel out the warming for much of the earth, returning many of us to something like the climate we knew and loved, while deep-freezing only Europe. Remember that Europe is the area most warmed by the Conveyer. No one knows how the global CO_2 experiment will turn out. There are many possibilities, but nearly all of them involve severe problems.

Global-warming optimists like to point to a potential benign feedback loop: an atmosphere richer in carbon dioxide should accelerate photosynthesis in plants, which should dampen greenhouse changes by consuming carbon dioxide and producing oxygen. Researchers are at work in our forests trying to measure both legs of that loop:

How much has tree growth accelerated due to carbon dioxide increases? A study trying to answer that question in the PNW finds an acceleration trend, but one that correlates more clearly with cyclical warmer decades than with the steady CO_2 increase trend. A broader study seems to support that conclusion, finding an overall increase since 1850 in western NA, but with the strongest acceleration in boreal and high-elevation trees.

What effect does old-growth forest have on atmospheric carbon dioxide and oxygen?

Plant photosynthesis is the big gorilla in the carbon dioxide picture. In any year, plants consume twenty times as much carbon dioxide as fossil fuels release. Sounds great, right? The plants turn around and release half of that CO_2 through respiration, leaving the other half tied up in biomass. The biomass half will also be released if and when the biomass burns or decomposes, so it's ultimately a zero-sum game. Its benign aspect is equal to the amount of carbon tied up in biomass at any given time. (All animal and fungal life owes its existence to oxygen and hydrocarbons produced by photosynthesis. The original fount of photosynthates was the bacterial kingdom; the first plants apparently evolved after animals and fungi. Plants then took the baton and ran with it in grand style, though with great ongoing support from bacteria, especially through nitrogen fixation.) Some biomass gets tied up more or less forever, after being carried out to the anaerobic bottom of the sea and/or buried deep in sediment layers, perhaps turning into a fossil fuel.

Northwest forests may tie up carbon better than any other plant communities on earth. In full old-growth flower they contain the greatest amounts of standing biomass per acre. But even more important is the below-ground biomass—the roots, down wood, fungi, and humus in the soil. Cool soil temperatures slow down decomposing bacteria and fungi, so that wood in our soils takes centuries to decompose, in dramatic contrast to tropical rain forest, where it takes a year or two. If any plant communities perform even better as carbon sinks, they would be north of here, where biomass production is slow but decomposition is still slower, sometimes coming to a dead halt due to either freezing (permafrost) or acidity (peat bogs).

Some in industry or in politics would like us to believe that cutting "stagnant" old forests and replacing them with "vigorous" 50-year rotations will help the atmosphere. They need to do the math. Forest ecologists who did the math found that even the most generous allowances for lumber tied up in buildings and paper tied up in landfills fail to outweigh the accelerated decomposition of biomass when old-growth is logged. Our forests tie up the most possible carbon when they are left alone. Equally unsound are some of the ideas about fighting global warming by planting trees all over the globe. Yes, trees should be planted; yes, new trees can consume carbon dioxide; but there is no long term gain if the plantations are shortlived single-species crops with little resemblance to natural native communities.

How will the Cascades and Olympics change if the globe warms? We don't know for sure, but the bleak truth is that severe losses in ecosystem health and diversity are likely. If the year 2050 gives us a climate much like what we see in, say, the Monterey-to-Yosemite transect today (not an unpleasant climate by any stretch) the red fir and sequoia and Jeffrey pine communities would hardly be able to migrate 600 miles north and fill all their appropriate sites in fifty years. Our dominant trees would do their best to hang on, and that's a lot. Very few of them are physically unable to survive a climate four degrees warmer than their present one, and the dominants are too big to suffer right away from weedy competition. But their resilience is compromised by forest fragmentation—the patchwork of logging-damaged communities (see pages 38–39). Non-native weeds, including new ones from the south, would be encouraged by the fast-changing conditions and by the CO_2-rich air. We would probably see vast damage from insect infestations; some of our most destructive pests are held in check, in the present century, by average-and-colder winters. And we would see much, much more fire—too much fire to keep contained, especially with large tracts of insect-killed trees available for fuel.

In the high country, glaciers would waste away except at the highest elevations. The vegetation zones would migrate upward, but forest could invade parkland meadow fifty times faster than meadow soil could develop on alpine fellfields or newly deglaciated rock rubble. No foreseeable reader of this book will see a meadow where we now have a glacier, but we may see thick stands of saplings in place of many of today's meadows. After all, that happened to many meadows within thirty-year spans in this century. So there could be a huge net loss of subalpine meadows. On the other hand, those frequent fires could work to keep the subalpine zone herbaceous, though they might create grasslands or bracken brakes rather than avalanche lily swards.

Whether the Northwest will stay rainy as it warms is not known; one model predicts drier summers and wetter-than-ever winters.

Concerns about a warming earth provide new reasons to cut back logging of mature Northwest forests, both when we look at the causes of warming and when we look at its effects. First, logging these forests contributes to greenhouse gases. Second, it makes the remaining forest ecosystem less natural, less diverse, less rich, less resilient, more vulnerable to the effects of warming. If we log too much now (and we have been logging far too much for decades) we increase the chance that the whole ecosystem will be devastated by fires and insects, leaving very little to log a hundred years from now on either timber industry or national forest land. If, on the other hand, we preserve all of our present old-growth and make ecosystem health the primary overriding rule in managing the harvestable remainder of the federal timberlands, we will be using our forests in the most effective way for the preservation of both a timber resource and a natural ecology in the Northwest.

Appendixes

Scientific Latin

For centuries, we writers of field guides have preached that you readers should learn the Latin names because they are used consistently—from one region, or nation, or book, or decade, to another—unlike common names.

You may think we were lying. Different books have different names for the same species. Nomenclature is in a state of ferment. One reason is decentralization: regional botanists are rebelling against the taxonomic tradition in which most judgements were made by a few senior taxonomists examining pressed, dried herbarium specimens; they point out that the real thing—the live plant in its native habitat—can look quite different.

Another is the inherent conflict between two of taxonomy's main roles: first, a stable, internationally agreed-upon set of names for species; and second, a hierarchical set of names that reflects the "family tree" of evolutionary descent. Molecular biology and other high technologies today offer a level of accuracy in reconstructing the family tree that Linnaeus and Darwin never dreamed of. Taxonomists have leapt to the task of overhauling old hierarchies, but the limited funding and personnel available for this very noncommercial branch of biology will make the current overhaul take decades. Many recent name changes result from new takes on family tree relations. Others are skirmishes in the age-old war between splitters and lumpers, which is a question of taste, not of absolute truth, regarding the proper size of genera and families.

In the meantime, names will be unstable, and you readers—as well as bureaucrats, politicians, and the many biologists who lack intense interest in taxonomy—may be frustrated. Taxonomists are committed to pursuit of the family tree and will not abandon it, but they are aware of their "cus-tomers'" unhappiness, and have seriously looked at changing the rules to promote name stability. The obvious modest solution is to be conservative, and insist that new ideas be debated among specialists for perhaps a few years until a degree of consensus is reached, and only then codified as a new set of names for an entire genus or family at once.

The PLANTS database list, maintained by the U.S. government, often seems to fall short on conservative attitude, accepting published changes while perhaps lacking staff time for thorough critical analysis. I follow in-stead the checklist of the Oregon Flora Project, a collaboration of Oregon botanists whose goal is to produce a volume (on paper and online) of plant descriptions, complete for the state. As we go to press, the checklist is un-finished, but I was able to obtain guidance directly from the project leaders. Also helpful was a collaborative flora of California, *The Jepson Manual*. A *Flora of North America*, by a vast and far-flung blue-ribbon panel, is much farther even from completion than the *Oregon Flora*.

In footnotes regarding plant names, "formerly" is short for "in Hitch-cock and Cronquist (1977)" since that series was the nomenclatural standard in the PNW from the 1950s until recently. Plant names noted as used by "some authorities" are generally those preferred in either PLANTS, *Flora of N.A.*, *The Jepson Manual*, *Intermountain Flora*, Pojar and McKinnon (1994), or Taylor and Douglas (1995). Texts I used for other life forms are identified in the Selected Readings with the words "Our authority" in bold type.

I still like Latin names, regardless of whether they're more stable than common names. At least they're more international. Scientists have to use them, because the codified system regulating them anchors them to partic-ular organisms—something common names can never offer.

I also like real common names—the ones that are a rich folklore. I hate to see common names coined purely for the sake of avoiding Latin names. (Come on, Latin names aren't *that* hard: five-year-olds have little trouble with *Velociraptor*.) If a name has to be coined, how common can it be? In some cases I stick to Latin at the species level, since the common-usage name refers to a genus. This is especially true among lichens. I believe any English name that's been in use for centuries, if one exists, is the common name, even if transferred from Eastern or European members of the same genus (lungwort, corkir, rock tripe, British soldiers, Iceland-moss, etc.). A lot of scientists hate the misleading implications of many common names within their own field of interest, but never hesitate to use a flagrant mis-nomer, such as Western hemlock, when it's outside their discipline.

Pronunciations of genus and species names are suggested in this book simply to keep the names from seeming too intimidating to use at all. If you want to pronounce them some other way, feel free. Biologists themselves are far from uniform in their pronunciations. There is a long-running schism between American and Continental styles. William Weber, in *Colorado Flora*, argues that Americans should adopt the Continental style so that tax-onomic Latin can be more of an international language. Unfortunately, the two styles are different enough that Americans who adopt Continental pronunciations will, I fear, find themselves frequently misunderstood during the 99% of their discussions that are with other Americans.

In brief, in Continental style the five vowels are always "ah, eh (or ay), ee, oh, oo," the *ae* dipththong is "eye," *c* is always "k," and *t* has a crisp sound even in *-atio*. The American style thoroughly Americanizes the vowel sounds, both long and short, but mostly sticks to Latin rules on consonants and syllable stressing. The consonant *x* is phonetically a "z," final *es* is "eez," *ch* is "k," *j* is "y," and *th* is always soft as in "thin," never hard as in "then."

Syllable stressing causes difficulty and variation within the American style. The Latin rule says the second-to-last syllable is stressed if its vowel is long, is a diphthong (vowel pair), or is followed by two consonants before the next vowel; otherwise the third-to-last syllable gets the stress. When uncertain of the length of the vowel, I refer to *Webster's Third New International Dictionary, Gray's Manual of Botany*, or Jepson's 1925 *Manual*.

I depart from the rule for a few names that have entered the English language. For example, we stress the third-to-last syllables in *Anemone* and *Penstemon*, though ancient Romans stressed the second-to-last.

Other exceptions are the many proper names with Latin endings tacked on. We try to pronounce them as the person whose name is being honored would have. For example, *jeffreyi* obviously starts with a "j" sound rather than a "y" sound as in Latin. But for words that end in double *-ii*, most scientists don't go so far as to violate Latin rules with, for example, "**Doug**las-eee" rather than "Da-**glass**-ee-eye." (Weber argues for "**Doug**las-eee," on both Continental-style and honoring-Douglas grounds.) Unfair though it may be, we Anglicize when the honored person's language is too tricky for Anglo tongues. For example, *Castilleja*, named after a Spanish botanist, is "cas-ti-**lay**-a" here, while in Spain it would be "cah-stee-**yeh**-ha."

For this edition I've simplified the *-oides* ending to "-**oy**-deez," which I hear more often from scientists today than the traditional "oh-**eye**-deez."

I devised no airtight phonetic system ; my attempt was simply to break each name into units that, as English, would be hard to mispronounce.

If I omit the pronunciation and translation of a genus or species, it's either the same name as the preceding entry; or obviously similar to its English translation (e.g., *americanus*). A family name with its English equivalent omitted is either the same as the preceding, visibly similar to its English version (e.g., Orchidaceae), or so obscure that the only way to come up with an English equivalent would be to fabricate one out of the Latin name.

For pronouncing names of families and orders, a few rules will suffice. Animal families end in *-idae*, with the third-to-last syllable stressed: Canidae is "**can**-i-dee." Plant families end in *-aceae* with the "a" stressed: Pinaceae is "pie-**nay**-see." (I'm simplifying again. Purists say "pie-**nay**-seh-ee.") Bird orders end in *-formes*, "**for**-meez." Insect orders end in *-ptera* with the *p* pronounced and stressed, as in "**Dip**-ter-a."

Chronology of Early Naturalists

1741	Georg Steller, sailing from Kamchatka under Captain Vitus Bering, explored islands now in Alaska. Page 401.
1778	Captain Cook visited Vancouver Island; little is known of anything William Anderson, the naturalist on board, accomplished there.
1787	Archibald Menzies visited Vancouver Island briefly. Page 97.
1791	A grand Spanish expedition under Alejandro Malaspina reached British Columbia; Bohemian botanist Thaddeus Haenke was aboard, but his important collections were from earlier in the voyage.
1792	Menzies returned to the Northwest under Captain Vancouver.
1803-06	Georg Heinrich von Langsdorf's attempts to preserve plants from Alaska and California were largely thwarted by his captain, Nicolai Petrovich von Rezanoff. Rough seas on the Columbia Bar kept them from landing in Washington.
1805-06	Lewis and Clark canoed the lower Columbia. Page 234.
1815-18	Chamisso and Eschscholtz studied Alaska and California under Russian captain Kotzebue. Page 174.
1825-27	David Douglas made his first (and more successful) exploration of the PNW for the Royal Horticultural Society. Page 18.
1825	John Scouler arrived with Douglas, then explored on his own near the Columbia and on the British Columbia coast. Page 67.
1825-27	Drummond and Richardson collected in western Canada on Franklin's second expedition. Page 473.
1826-29	Karl H. Mertens sailed around the world; his stop at Sitka yielded many new plant species. Page 111.
1830-33	David Douglas returned to the Northwest. Page 18.
1833	William F. Tolmie began a long career in the Northwest with the Hudson's Bay Co. Page 197.
1834	Nuttall and Townsend reached the Northwest with Nathaniel Wyeth. Pages 74 and 313.
1844	Karl A. Geyer crossed the Rockies. Page 150.
1851-53	John Jeffrey hunted plants for the "Oregon Association" of Scotland. Page 205.
1855	John S. Newberry studied the east flank of the Oregon Cascades. Page 222.
1858-59	David Lyall and George Gibbs studied the 49th Parallel while surveying for the Boundary Commissions. Page 53.
1874-77	Major Charles Bendire was stationed in Oregon. Page 300.

Five-Kingdom Taxonomy

The following chart's purpose is to show the relative positions in the living world of organisms discussed in *Cascade-Olympic Natural History*. These and the higher categories they belong to are in boldface type. A few undiscussed organisms are shown for comparison, in light type.

The chart follows *Five Kingdoms* (3rd Edition, 1998), by Margulis and Schwartz at the Kingdom, Phylum, and (where possible) Class levels. They have revised extensively, yet they advocate a conservative approach giving some weight to morphological variation, as opposed to pure phylogenetic approaches that reflect only the timing of family-tree branchings. The latter typically recognize three taxa at the highest tier: Bacteria; Archaea (more primitive bacteria); and then everything with cell nuclei as the third, demoting plants, animals, and fungi to the second tier or even lower. But many purists publish only unranked trees (cladograms) rather than trying to force-fit the artificial Linnaean hierarchies onto the natural family tree .

At best I can only offer a snapshot of a moving subject at one moment in time. For updates, explore http://phylogeny.arizona.edu/tree

The weakest kingdom in this particular system is the Protoctista, which can be defined only by exclusion of the other four kingdoms. Protoctists have cell nuclei. They originated as symbiotic combinations of various bacteria, which lack nuclei. They include "protozoans," single-celled algae, and large multi-celled algae such as the seaweeds.

In the Animals, a single phylum Craniata (animals with skulls) now holds the vertebrates. The 36 other phyla are loosely termed "invertebrates," a non-taxonomic term definable only as "everything else." The arthropods (animals with jointed exoskeletons) are still considered a natural taxon, i.e., a branch of the great family tree; but because they are so many and varied they are now a set of three phyla; one of these, Mandibulata (insects and myriapods) is still by far the largest animal phylum.

In the Fungi, the phylum for lichens has been deleted; closer study of lichen fungi identifies them as either Basidiomycota or (far more commonly) Ascomycota. The former Deuteromycota—fungi that have never been seen with reproductive organs—were likewise stripped of rank; they, too, are identifiable as a great many Ascomycota and a few Basidiomycota.

In the Plants, the first seven phyla are spore plants and the last five are seed plants. The first three lack vessels; they form the nonvascular group (formerly a single phylum, but now seen as having arisen separately from the algae). The next four are vascular spore-bearing plants. The next four bear seeds but do not enclose them in a thickened ovary wall, or "fruit." They are the gymosperms, often ranked as a single Division Gymnospermae with the conifers, ginkgos, cycads, and ephedras as four classes. ("Division" is another word for "phylum," among plants.) The final phylum, Anthophyta, is also called angiosperms. Many systematists today reject its traditional bifurcation into Dicots and Monocots.

Kingdom	Phylum	Class
Bacteria	Cyanobacteria Proteobacteria 12 other phyla	
Protoctista	Archaeprotista Chlorophyta 28 other phyla	
Animalia	31 primitive phyla **Annelida** **Chelicerata** Crustacea **Mandibulata** Mollusca	 **Arachnida** Malacostraca Myriapoda **Hexapoda** (= Insects) Bivalvia **Gastropoda** 5 other classes
	Craniata (= Vertebrates)	Cyclostomata Chondrichthyes **Osteichthyes** Choanichthyes **Amphibia** **Reptilia** **Aves** (= Birds)

(continued)

Order	Examples
	Blue-green bacteria in lichens *E. coli*
	Giardia, trichomonas Watermelon-snow, green algae in most lichens
	Snow worms, earthworms **Ticks,** mites, spiders Crabs, shrimp, pillbugs Centipedes, millipedes **Flies, mosquitoes, beetles, aphids, butterflies** Clams, scallops, oysters **Slugs,** snails Octopi, squids, nautilus
	Lampreys Sharks, rays **Trout, salmon, sculpins** Lungfish
Caudata	**Salamanders, newts**
Salienta	**Frogs, toads**
Testudines	Turtles, tortoises
Squamata	**Lizards, snakes**
Crocodylia	Crocodiles, alligators
Gaviiformes	**Loons**
Podicepediformes	**Grebes**
Ciconiiformes	**Herons, New world vultures,** storks, flamingos
Anseriformes	**Ducks,** geese
Falconiformes	**Hawks, eagles, osprey**
Galliformes	**Grouse, p̃tarmigan,** chickens, quail
Charadriiformes	**Sandpipers,** gulls
Columbiformes	**Pigeons,** doves
Strigiformes	**Owls**
Caprimulgiformes	**Nighthawks**
Apodiformes	**Swifts, hummingbirds**
Coraciiformes	**Kingfishers**
Piciformes	**Woodpeckers**
Passeriformes	**Jays, swallows, warblers , finches, many others**
Many other orders	

Kingdom	Phylum (Division)	Class
Animalia (continued)	Craniata	Mammalia
Fungi	Zygomycota Basidiomycota Ascomycota	
Plantae	Bryophyta	Sphagnopsida Andreaeopsida Bryopsida
	Hepatophyta	
	Anthoceratophyta	
	Lycophyta Psilophyta Sphenophyta Filicinophyta	
	Cycadophyta Ginkgophyta Coniferophyta	
	Gnetophyta	
	Anthophyta = Flowering plants	

Order	Examples
Marsupialia	Opossum, kangaroos
Insectivora	**Shrews, moles**
Chiroptera	**Bats**
Primates	Monkeys, lemurs, apes, human
Cetacea	Whales, porpoises
Carnivora	**Dog, bear, raccon, weasel, cat**, hyena, and seal families
Perissodactyla	Horse, rhinoceros
Artiodactyla	**Deer, cow/sheep**, and 7 other families
Lagomorpha	**Pika, rabbit, hare**
Rodentia	**Mice, voles, squirrels, beaver, porcupine**
	Many small underground-fruiting fungi, bread mold
	Chanterelles, boletes, all gilled mushrooms
	Most lichens, truffle, morel, snow mold, molds, yeasts
	Peat moss
	Granite moss
	Most other mosses
Jungermanniales	**Leafy liverworts**
Marchantiales	**Thallose liverworts**
	Hornworts
	Clubmosses, spikemosses
	Whisk ferns
	Horsetails
	Ferns
	Cycad "palms"
	Ginkgo
Pinales	**Pine, cypress**, sequoia, and monkey-puzzle families
Taxales	**Yew** and two other families
	Mormon-tea (*Ephedra*)
	Broadleaf trees and shrubs, flowering herbs

Abbreviations and Symbols

', "	feet, inches
°	degrees Fahrenheit
+	or more
±	more or less
×	by (as in length by width); also: lens magnification power
avg	average
C	central
Cas	Cascade(s)
Cr	Crest
diam	diameter (at breast height: 4'6" above ground)
E	east(ern)
elev(s)	elevation(s)
E-side	the area east of the Cascade Crest
esp	especially
FNA	*Flora of North America*; see pages 574, 597
exc	except
incl	including
mtn(s)	mountain(s)
N	north(ern)
NA	North America
Oly(s)	Olympic Mountains
OR	Oregon
PLANTS	the species list of the US Dept. of Agriculture; see pages 574, 609
PNW	the Northwest: OR, WA W British Columbia, and SE Alaska
S	south(ern)
spp.	species plural: any and all of the species of a genus
W	west(ern)
WA	Washington
ws	wingspread: the measurement across outspread wings
W-side	the area west of the Cascade Crest

Glossary

Abundant: present in great numbers—even more numerous, at least within some habitats, than what is implied by "common."

Alevin: a hatchling fish, especially a salmon or trout in the stage when it is still attached to and nourished by an egg yolk sac.

Alpine: of or in the elevational zone above where tree species are found growing numerously in upright tree form. Some texts define "alpine" as above the growth of tree species in any form, even **krummholz**; but in **our mountains** krummholz is found at the same elevations as most of the vegetational characteristics thought of as alpine elsewhere.

Alternate: arranged with only one leaf at any given distance along a stem. Contrast with **opposite** or **whorled**.

Anadromous: participating in a life cycle of birth and breeding in streams or lakes separated by an extended period of growth at sea.

Angle of repose: the steepest slope angle that a given loose sediment is able to hold.

Anomalous: differing from a norm, such as characteristic color or form.

Ascending: held in positions generally well above perpendicular to the stem or axis, but not nearly parallel or aligned with it; intermediate between **spreading** and **erect**.

Ash: fine particles of volcanic rock (usually glassy in structure) formed when **magma** is blasted out of a volcano in a fine spray.

Aspect: the compass direction a slope faces.

Awn: a stiff, hairlike extension of the tip of a **bract** in the **floret** of a grass.

Axil: the crotch between a stem and a leaf.

Basal: (said of leaves) attached to a plant at its root crown, not at any higher point on the stem.

Batholith: a large formation of **intrusive** igneous rock with no known bottom; i.e., a large, essentially monolithic intrusion exposed at the surface. In technical usage, a batholith must include at least 100 square km of exposed or subsoil bedrock.

Biomass: total living matter, usually expressed as a measure of dry weight (or sometimes volume) per unit area.

Bisexual: with functioning stamens and pistils in the same flower.

Bloom: a pale, powdery coating on a surface.

Boreal: of the Northern Hemisphere-wide belt dominated by coniferous forests and transitional between Arctic and **Temperate** climate.

Bract: a modified leaf or leaflike appendage, often **subtending** a flower or **inflorescence**, and generally smaller and/or more specialized than a leaf.

Broadleaf: common term for all trees and shrubs other than **conifers**; very few have leaves narrow enough to be confused with conifer needles.

Buttress: a wide flaring-out at the base of a tree.

Call: any vocal communication common to birds of a given species. Compare **song**.

Calyx: a flower's **sepals** spoken of collectively, or else a ring of sepallike lobes that would be sepals if they were separate all the way to their bases; i.e., the outermost **whorl** or circle of parts of most flowers. Plural: "calyces." Compare **corolla**.

Canopy: in forest structure, the uppermost more or less continuous mass of tree branches and foliage. All those trees of such stature that their tops form part of the canopy may be collectively called the "canopy layer."

Cap: the spreading top portion of a typical mushroom, supported by a stem and supporting **gills**, tubes, or spines on its lower surface only.

Capsule: a seed pod, technically a nonfleshy **fruit** that splits to release seeds; in mosses, the spore-containing organ.

Catkin: the form of **inflorescence** of certain trees and shrubs, consisting of a dense **spike** of minute, dry, petal-less flowers.

Cirque: a head of a mountain valley having a characteristic amphitheater shape due to glacial erosion.

Class: a **taxonomic** group broader than an **order** or **family** and narrower than a (plant) division or (animal) phylum. Examples: mammals, fishes, birds, spiders, insects, dicots.

Clastic: formed out of fragmented bits of rock (a description of most **sedimentary** rocks except those formed by chemical precipitation).

Climax: a more or less hypothetical condition of stability in which all **successional** changes resulting from plant community growth have taken place, so that further changes can only follow destructive disturbances.

Cloaca: an anal orifice (in birds, reptiles, fishes, etc.) through which the urinary, reproductive, and gastrointestinal tracts all discharge.

Clone: a group of genetically identical progeny produced by vegetative or other asexual reproduction from a single progenitor. (In nonscientific use, this term sometimes refers to the seeming individual, rather than the aggregate, as a clone.)

Clone: to reproduce asexually.

Composite: a member of the plant family Asteraceae (formerly Compositae), characterized by composite flower heads which resemble single flowers but are actually well-organized inflorescences of tiny flowers. Examples: daisies, thistles, dandelions.

Compound leaf: a structure of three or more leaflets on stalklike ribs, resembling as many leaves on a branchlet except that it terminates in a leaflet rather than a flower, a bud, a growing shoot, etc., and that it grows from a node on a stem but its leaflets do not each grow from nodes of their own.

Congener: a member of a species in the same genus.

Conifer: a tree or shrub within a large group generally characterized by needlelike or scalelike leaves and by seeds borne naked between the woody scales of a "cone," or (in the yew family) borne naked but cupped within a berrylike "aril." (Some writers do not include the yew family as conifers. See page 581 for one **taxonomic** treatment of conifers.)

Conspecific: (an individual) of the same species.

Convect: to move upward and downward due to temperature contrasting with that of other fluids in the same system—hot air rises, cold air sinks.

Cordillera: the entire mountain system comprising the western half of North America, from the Olympics to the Front Range of the Rockies, including most of Alaska, the Yukon, British Columbia, and Mexico. In Spanish, *cordillera* simply means "mountain range."

Corolla: the whorl or circle of a typical flower's parts lying second from the outside; i.e., the **petals** spoken of collectively, or else a ring of lobes that would be petals if they were separate all the way to their bases. **Compare calyx.**

Cosymbiont: a "partner" in a **symbiotic** relationship with a given organism.

Cotyledon: a seed leaf—the specialized leaf first produced by a plant after germinating from a seed, significant particularly in that the most consistent distinction between the **dicot** and **monocot** classes is whether two simultaneous seed leaves are produced, or just one.

Crevasse: a large crack in a glacier, expressing flow stresses.

Crown: the leafy (top) part of a tree.

Crust: the surface layer of the earth, averaging about six miles thick under the oceans and twenty miles thick in the continents, defined primarily by lower-density (lighter) rock than what's underneath.

Crystal: the specific structure of many chemical compounds (including all **minerals**) in which the atoms position themselves in a particular geometry that repeats indefinitely; usually visible in broken surfaces of the material.

Deciduous: (a tree or shrub) shedding its leaves annually; i.e., not **evergreen**. ("Deciduous" can also refer to any shedding part, e.g., petals that fall off before the pistil matures, or sepals that fall off as the fruit matures.)

Dicot: any member of one of the two huge groups of flowering plants; includes all of our **broadleaf** trees and shrubs and virtually all of our terrestrial **herbs** except lilies, orchids, and grasslike plants (the **monocots**). Short for "dicotyledon." Taxonomic status of the dicots is in question, since many studies suggest they arose on several different branches of the family tree.

Dike: a body of more or less homogeneous rock that is very much longer and deeper than it is thick: usually an **igneous** rock body from fluid **magma** intruded into a **fault** or crack in a contrasting rock body.

Disk flower: one of the tiny, often dry and drab-colored flowers making up a dense circle either in the center of a **composite** flower head (the "eye" of a daisy) or comprising an entire composite flower head such as a pearly-everlasting. Only in the family Compositae.

Disturbance: an external force which causes abrupt changes in a plant community. Clearing by humans, extraordinary floods, and fires are usually considered disturbances, while "normal" weather effects are not.

Disjunct: separated (said of a local population of a species separated other populations by an area lacking that species).

DNA: (deoxyribonucleic acid) the basic molecule that makes up genes, which are passed from parent to offspring and control the form taken by each living cell. DNA research uses techniques developed in recent decades to analyze the genetic make-up and lineage of any living organism.

Dominant: a plant species contributing easily the greatest percentage of cover within a given layer of a plant community. When no layer is specified, the uppermost layer is assumed, e.g., the **canopy layer** in a forest or the **herb layer** in a meadow.

Duff: matted, partly decayed litter on the forest floor.

Erect: aligned nearly parallel with the stem, if describing a leaf, a flower-stalk, etc.; or more or less vertical, if describing a main stem.

Evergreen: bearing relatively heavy leaves which normally keep their form, color, and function on the plant through at least two years' growing seasons. Opposite of **deciduous**, with **persistent** describing an in-between leaf type.

Family: a **taxonomic** group broader than a genus or species, and narrower than an **order** or **class**. Latin names for families end in -*aceae* if they are plants and -*idae* if they are animals.

Fascicle: a bundle, especially the characteristic cluster of one to five pine needles sheathed at their base in tiny dry, membranous **bracts**.

Fault: a fracture in rock or earth (or the location of that fracture) where relative earth movement on the two sides has taken place; may be of any size.

Floret: a small, inconspicuous flower within a compact inflorescence such as the **head** of a **composite** or the **spikelet** of a grass.

Fruit: among the seed plants, an **ovary** wall matured into a seed-bearing structure; also, more broadly, any seed-bearing or **spore-bearing** structure.

Fry: young fish (both singular and plural). Among salmon and trout, the fry stage can be understood to follow the **alevin** stage and precede the **parr** stage; some species migrate to sea as fry.

Fused: unseparated; fused **petals** (or **sepals**) form a single **corolla** (**calyx**) ring or tube, usually with lobes at the front edge that can be counted for identification purposes.

Gills: (1) in aquatic animals, the respiratory organs where oxygen suspended in the water passes into the animal; (2) on some mushrooms, **spore**-bearing organs consisting of paper-thin or sometimes wrinklelike radii on the underside of the **cap**.

Granitic rocks: coarse-grained **igneous** rocks; see **intrusive** rocks. (Geologists prefer the more techical term "phaneritic" to describe coarse textures, reserving "granitic" for a narrower group of high-silica igneous rocks.)

Head: a tight, compact **inflorescence**.

Herbaceous: not **woody**; the aboveground parts normally dying or withering at the end of the growing season. (Some low, soft-stemmed plants classed as herbs may persist through milder winters and into summer.)

Herb layer: all the **herbaceous** plants and low shrubs of comparable size, as a group comprising a structural element of a plant community. Typical forest communities here have a **canopy** layer, one or two shrub/small tree layers, an herb layer, and a moss layer.

Here: in our range; i.e., in the Olympic Mountains and the portion of the Cascade Range from Diamond Peak north. See page 4.

High-grade: (said of metamorphic rocks) altered by relatively high degrees of heat and pressure.

Hybrid: an offspring of parents of different species.

Hyphae: the countless, minute filaments that carry on all the normal nutritive and growth functions of a fungus. (Singular: "hypha.")

Igneous rocks: rocks that reached their present **mineral** composition and texture while cooling from a liquid into a solid state; may be either volcanic or, if they solidified underground without ever erupting, **intrusive.**

Inflorescence: a cluster of flowers from one stem, or the cluster's pattern.

Intergrade: to vary along a continuum between one well-defined type (such as a species or a rock type) and another.

Introduced: not thought to have lived in a given area (**the Northwest,** in this book) before the arrival of white people; opposed to **native.**

Intrusive rocks: **igneous** rocks that did not surface as fluid **lava** in a volcanic eruption, but solidified underground. Best-known example is granite; most intrusives are coarser-grained than most volcanic rocks and may, in nontechnical usage, be lumped under the loose term **granitic.**

Inuit: Eskimo(s).

Involucral bracts: small leaves circling a stem immediately beneath an **inflorescence** (most often a flower **head** in the **composite** family).

Irregular flower: one made of **petals** (or of **sepals**) that are conspicuously not all alike in size and/or shape; usually they make a bilateral symmetry.

Juvenile plumage: feathers (and their color pattern) of birds old enough to fly, but not yet entering their first breeding season; the two sexes are more or less alike at this stage.

Krummholz: dwarfed, ground-hugging shrubby growth, near **alpine timberline,** of **conifer** species that grow as upright trees under more moderate conditions. Translatable from German as "crooked wood"; sometimes called "elfinwood." Though this meaning is well established in English usage, a few writers object that in German scientific usage krummholz is genetically stunted growth, and the word for environmentally stunted growth is "kruppelholz" ("crippled wood").

Landlocked: (said of fish) completing their life cycle in fresh water, where some barrier (usually a dam, but sometimes natural) prevents the **anadromous** (seagoing) life cycle the species is capable of.

Larva: an insect, amphibian, or other animal when in a youthful form that differs strongly from the adult form. Caterpillars are the larvae of moths and butterflies, maggots are the larvae of flies, etc. Also "grub."

Lava: rock that is flowing, or once flowed, in a more or less liquid state across the earth in a volcanic eruption; see **magma.**

Leader: the topmost central shoot of a plant.

Leafstalk: a narrowed stalk portion of a leaf, distinguished from the leaf "blade." (Synonym of "petiole.")

Low-grade: (said of metamorphic rocks) altered by relatively mild degrees of heat and pressure.

Lumpers: scientists inclined to reduce the numbers of species, genera, etc., by recognizing any given distinction at a lower taxonomic level. Opposed to **splitters**.

Magma: subsurface rock in a melted, liquid state. If and when it reaches the surface, its name will change depending on whether it flows out in a stream or paste of **lava** or explodes into the air as **pyroclastic** fragments.

Mantle: the major portion of the earth's interior, which lies below the **crust** and above the core; it is known mainly by indirect methods like seismic studies that indicate its high density.

Margin: outer edge, as of a leaf.

Matrix: in some rocks, the fine-grained material in which much larger grains, crystals, or contrasting pieces of rock are embedded.

-merous: a suffix derived from "numerous." A 5-merous plant species is one whose **petals**, **sepals**, and **stamens** each number 5, 10, 15, or 20.

Meta-: a prefix sometimes used in naming **metamorphic** rocks in terms of the parent rock they are thought to have metamorphosed from. Examples: metaconglomerate, metaigneous.

Metamorphic rocks: rocks whose **mineral** composition and texture was established when they were "cooked" at great heat and/or pressure within the earth.

Metamorphism: the heat-and-pressure process that makes **metamorphic** rocks.

Metamorphosis: the process by which **larval** animals transform into adults.

Milt: fish semen.

Mineral: any natural ingredient of the earth having a well-defined chemical formula and a characteristic crystalline structure. Rocks and soils are largely mixtures of minerals. (The formula may express a range of compositions rather than a single uniform one.)

Monocot: any member of the group of flowering plants (the opposed group being the **dicots**) generally characterized by parallel-veined leaves and flower parts in 3s or 6s. No monocots here are **woody**, and most are either lilies, orchids, aquatic or grasslike plants. Short for "monocotyledon."

Moraine: a usually elongate heap or hill of mixed rock debris lying where it was deposited by a glacier when the glacier retreated from that point.

Mycology: the branch of biology dealing with fungi.

Mycophagy: the eating of fungi; the collecting of wild fungi for food.

Mycorrhiza: a tiny organ formed jointly by plant roots and fungi for passing nutritive substances between plant and fungus. Plural: "mycorrhizae" seems preferred in the U.S., "mycorrhizas" in Britain.

Native: (species) thought to have been living in a given area (the Northwest, for our purposes) before and independently of travel there by people. Generally this refers to travel by white people, since knowledge of pre-Columbian introductions to the New World is highly speculative. Opposed to introduced.

Nature: the universe as it was preceding or is outside of human civilization.

Nectar: a sugary liquid secreted in some kinds of flowers to attract pollinating animals.

Niche: the role of a species within an ecological community, in terms especially of how it exploits the habitat and other community members to meet its life requirements there.

Northwest, the: Oregon, Washington, Western British Columbia, and Southeast Alaska.

Nurse log: a rotting tree serving (and in many situations virtually required) as a seedbed for tree reproduction.

Offset: a short propagative shoot from the base of a plant, or a small bulb from the side of a plant's bulb.

Old-growth: late-successional natural forest. Everyone talks about old-growth, but it's very hard to define precisely. Definitions by leading scientists basically amount to lengthy descriptions of the characteristics found in 200-year-old and older NW forests. I would say NW old-growth has to have recovered with little or no human interference for at least 175 years since the last clearing **disturbance**. Note, however, that significant "older-growth" characteristics continue to develop to at least 500 years of age.

Opposite: arranged in pairs (of leaves) equally distant along a stem. The stem terminates in a bud, flower(s), or growing shoot. If it appears to terminate in a leaf or **tendril**, these are not opposite leaves, but leaflets of **compound** leaves which may be either opposite or **alternate**.

Order: a **taxonomic** group broader than a **family**, **genus** or **species**, and narrower than a **class**. Among plant taxonomists today, the orders are largely disregarded or superseded by other grouping concepts; but orders are very familiar and important groups in both birds and mammals. Examples: Rodents, carnivores, owls, woodpeckers, perching birds.

Ovary: the egg-producing organ; in flowers, this is generally the enlarged basal portion of the **pistil**, at the base of the flower.

Overstory: in plant community structure, whatever layer is highest; in a forest this would be the tree **canopy**.

Our: of or in the range explicitly covered by this book, namely, the Cascade Range from Diamond Peak North and the Olympic Mountains. See page 4.

Outwash: fragmental rock debris deposited by a glacier and subsequently carried and more or less sorted by a stream. Distinct from **till**, which is still lying, unsorted, where the glacier melted away from it.

Palmately lobed: shaped (like a maple leaf) with three or more main veins branching from one point at the leaf base, and the leaf outline indented between these veins.

Panicle: an **inflorescence** symmetrical around a main stem or axis with at least some of the side branches again branched to bear several flowers. Compare **raceme, spike**.

Parasite: an organism that draws sustenance for at least part of its life cycle out of an organism of another kind, more or less detrimentally to the latter (the "host") but without ingesting the host or any whole part of it.

Parr marks: vertical blotches that appear on the sides of **anadromous** salmon and trout of "parr" age, which comes when actively feeding in fresh water, before migrating to sea.

Pendent: attached by a downward stem from a larger stalk.

Persistent: (leaves) tending to stay on the stem through fall and winter even though functionally dead, and lacking the heavy weight and gloss characteristic of true **evergreen** leaves.

Petal: a modified leaf, typically non-green and showy, in the inner of two or more concentric **whorls** of floral leaves. If there is only one whorl, no matter how showy, its members are considered **sepals**.

Pheromone: a chemical produced by an animal that serves to stimulate some behavior in others of the same species.

Photosynthesis: the synthesis of carbohydrates out of simpler molecules as a means of converting or storing sunlight energy—the basic function of chlorophyllous or green parts of plants and algae.

Pinna: a segment of a fern or a **compound** leaf, branching directly off of the main fern stalk or leaf axis; the pinna may be additionally branched before reaching the ultimate pinnule or leaflet. Plural: "pinnae."

Pinnately compound: (said of a leaf) composed of an odd number (5 or more) of leaflets attached, except for the last one, in opposite pairs to a central leaf axis. If they are attached to mini-axes paired in turn along a central axis, the leaf is pinnately twice-compound.

Pioneer: a species growing on freshly disturbed (e.g., burned, clearcut, deglaciated or volcanically deposited) terrain.

Pistil: the female organ of a flower, including the **ovary** and ovules and any **styles** or **stigmas** that catch **pollen**.

Plate tectonics: the dynamics of the Earth's **crust** in terms of the relative motion of more or less continent-sized plates of crust "floating" on an effectively fluid layer underneath. Also, the major unifying theory that has dominated geophysical thought since the 1960's (when it was known as "Continental Drift") using those dynamics to explain much of Earth history.

Pollen: a fine dust of male reproductive cells (pollen "grains") borne on the **stamen** tips of a flower, each capable, if carried by wind, animal "pollinators" or other agents to the **pistil** of a **conspecific** flower, of fertilizing a female reproductive cell.

Pore: a minute hole; especially, one allowing passage of substances between an organism and its environment.

Propagate: to reproduce, either sexually or not.

Propagule: (in lichens and mosses) any multicelled structure more or less specialized to break off and grow into an organism independent of (but genetically identical to) the one it grew on; a means of asexual reproduction or cloning.

Prostrate: growing more or less flat upon the **substrate**.

Pupa: an insect in a generally quiescent life stage transitional from a **larva** to an adult. Plural: "pupae." Verb: "pupate."

Pyroclastic: composed of rock fragments formed by midair solidification of **lava** during a more or less explosive volcanic eruption. "Volcanic **ash**" is fine pyroclastic material; the rock "tuff" consists of consolidated pyroclastic material.

Raceme: a slender **inflorescence** with each flower borne on an unbranched **petiole** from the central axis. (Compare **panicle**, **spike**.)

Radial symmetry: an arrangement of several more or less identical elongate members (e.g., **petals**) from a central point.

Raptor: any bird of the Hawk and Owl orders. Not exactly synonymous with "bird of prey"; see page 390.

Ray flower: in a **composite** flower **head** such as a daisy or dandelion, a member which is **petallike** and strap-shaped for most of its length but tubular at its base, often enclosing a **pistil** or, in dandelion-type composites, both pistil and **stamens**. (Technically, ray flowers never have stamens—the dandelion-type flowers are "ligulate"—but the two look much alike and are both considered "rays" in this book.)

Regular: with all of its **sepals** and with all of its **petals** (if any) essentially alike in size, shape, and spatial relationship to the others.

Relief: the vertical component of distance between high and low points.

Resin blisters: horizontally elongate blisters conspicuous on the bark of younger true fir trees, initially full of liquid pitch.

Rhizine: a tough, threadlike appendage on certain lichens, serving as a hold-fast to the **substrate**, not a vessel.

Rhizome: a rootstalk, or horizontal stem just beneath the soil surface connecting several aboveground stems; sometimes thickened for storage of starches.

Rhizosphere: the layer of soil permeated and affected by roots and **hyphae**, considered as a stratum of the "biosphere."

Rut: an annual period of sexual excitement and activity in certain mammals.

Saprophyte: a fungus or bacterium that absorbs its carbohydrate nutrition from dead organisms. (Because no plants do this, and phyte means "plant," some scientists prefer to say either "saprotroph" or "saprobe.") The non-green plants, p 177, that get their carbohydrates indirectly from other plants via **mycorrhizae**, were once mistakenly thought to be saprophytes, and this mistake persists in some recent literature.

Scats: feces. (Wildlife biologists' slang derived by back-formation from "scatology.")

Schistosity: a **metamorphic** rock texture in which the **minerals** are arranged in layers of visible-sized **crystal** grains.

Scree: loose rock debris lying at or near its **angle of repose** upon or at the foot of a steeper rock face from which it broke off. (Regarded by some as synonymous with **talus**, but gravel-sized debris is more often called "scree," boulder-sized more often "talus," and debris in gullies high on a rock face usually "scree" as opposed to "talus" at the bottom.)

Sedimentary rocks: rocks formed by slow compaction and/or cementation of particles previously deposited by wind or water currents or by chemical precipitation in water.

Sepal: a modified leaf within the outermost **whorl** (the **calyx**) of a flower's parts. Typically, sepals are green and leaflike and enclose a concentric whorl of **petals**, but in many cases they are quite showy and petallike. (Sepallike leaves enclosing a **composite** flower **head** are **involucral** bracts.)

Smolt: a young salmon or sea trout when first migrating to sea, typically losing its **parr** marks and becoming silvery. (Derived from the same Old English word as "smelt.")

Softwood: any **conifer**, in industry jargon; most, but not all, conifers have softer wood than most hardwoods.

Song: a relatively long and variegated form of bird **call**, generally distinctive of a species, practiced mostly by males in the Perching Bird order (Passeriformes).

Songbirds: a popular term for the bird order Passeriformes, comprising over half of all bird species. Also known as "perching birds."

Sorus: a small clump of **spore**-bearing organs visible as a raised dot line, crescent, etc. on a fern or other leaf. Plural: "sori."

Spawn: to breed (said of fish and other aquatic animals).

Spike: an **inflorescence** of flowers attached directly (i.e., without conspicuous stems of their own) to a central stalk. Compare **raceme, panicle.**

Spikelet: in the **inflorescence** of a grass, a compact group of from one to several **florets** and associated scalelike **bracts**, on a single axis branching off of the central stem.

Splitters: scientists inclined to increase the numbers of species, genera, etc., by recognizing any given distinction at a higher taxonomic level. Opposed to **lumpers.**

Sporadic: irregularly distributed over a range, perhaps common in some locales but not reliably so for any zone or major community type.

Spore: a single cell specialized for being released and later growing and differentiating into a new multicelled individual, among the lower plants and fungi. It is thought of as corresponding functionally to the seed in higher plants, since it travels; but in ferns and mosses it is comparable morphologically and genetically to the **pollen** grain, since it is not the sexually produced stage in the life cycle of the species.

Spreading: (said of leaves, branches, etc.) tending to grow in a horizontal to slightly raised position. Compare **erect, ascending, pendent.**

Steppe: unforested arid regions or plant communities dominated by sparse bunchgrasses and/or shrubs. Instead of the common-parlance "sagebrush desert," ecologists say "sagebrush steppe," reserving "desert" for sites so barren that no plant community can be described. True deserts cover large areas of the world, but in the U.S. they persist only on such forbidding **substrates** as active dunes, or dry lakebeds too saline or alkaline for plant growth.

Stamen: a male organ of a flower; typically, several of them surround a central **pistil**, and each consist of a **pollen-covered** tip on a delicate stalk.

Stigma: the **pollen**-receptive tip of the **pistil** of a flower.

Stolon: a stem that trails along the ground, producing several upright stems and thus enabling the plant to spread vegetatively.

Stomata: minute **pores** in leaf surfaces for the **transpiration** of gases. Singular: "stoma." Plural sometimes anglicized to "stomates."

Style: the stalklike part of a flower's **pistil**, supporting the **stigma** and conveying male sexual cells from it to the **ovary.**

Subalpine: of or in the elevational zone lying below the **alpine** zone where tree species are absent, dwarfed, or **prostrate**, and above the continuous forest.

Subduction: the hypothesized process in which the edge of a "plate" of the Earth's **crust** bends and sinks underneath the edge of an adjacent plate, eventually to be reconsumed in the underlying **mantle.**

Subduction zone: an elongate region including the margins of both a subducting plate and an overriding plate. Our mountains parallel, and are indirect products of, the subduction zone of the Juan de Fuca Plate with the North American Plate, immediately off the OR/WA/BC coast.

Subshrub: a perennial plant with a persistent, somewhat **woody** base, thus intermediate between clearly an "herb" and clearly a "shrub."

Substrate: the base on which an organism lives. Examples: soil, rock, bark.

Subtend: to be immediately below and next to.

Succession: change in the species composition of a plant community that results from soil/biotic interactions internal to the community.

Symbiosis: intimate association of unlike organisms for the benefit of at least one of them. Symbioses can be **mutualistic**, where both or all partners benefit; **parasitisic** (one benefits, one suffers); **commensal** (no material is transferred, and neither partner suffers substantially), or other permutations of benefit, harm, and indifference.

Talus: rock debris lying at the foot of a rock face from which it broke off. May imply cobble- to boulder-sized fragments, in contrast to finer **scree**.

Taxon: a species, genus, or other unit of classification. Plural: "taxa."

Taxonomy: the scientific naming and classifying of organisms, particularly within the Linnaean system (species, genus, etc.) which uses Latin and Latinized names and endeavors to reflect lines of evolutionary descent.

Tectonic: related to large-scale geologic deformation such as folding, **faulting**, volcanism, and regional **metamorphism**.

Temperate: of the climatically moderate parts of the world. Opposed to Tropical on the one hand and the Arctic on the other.

Tendril: a slender organ that supports a climbing plant by coiling or twining around something.

Tepal: a **petal** or **sepal** on a flower (such as some lilies) whose petals and sepals are identical to each other.

Terminal: located at an end, such as a growing tip of a plant or the lower end of a glacier.

Terrane: in **plate tectonics** jargon, any geologically mapped area whose rock formations originated without a known relation to those of adjacent terranes, suggesting that at some time the may not have been near each other.

Till: Rock debris of mixed sizes, once transported by a glacier and still lying where the glacier deposited it while melting back. Compare **outwash**.

Tolerance: the relative ability of various plant species to thrive under a given limiting condition. In this book, as in most technical writing on Northwest forests, **understory** tolerance (of which shade tolerance is the major component) is to be understood where no other condition is specified.

Glossary

Transpiration: emission of water vapor into the air through plant surfaces.

Turf: an upper layer of soil permeated by a dense, cohesive mat of roots, especially of grasses and/or sedges.

Ubiquitous: found everywhere (within **our range** or a given part of it). This means that the species may inhabit any part of **our mountains,** with the possible exception of the **alpine** zone, at least at some time of year.

Umbel: an **inflorescence** in which several flower **pedicels** diverge from a single point atop the main stem. Example: carrot tops or "Queen Anne's Lace."

Understory: in plant community structure, any community layer except the highest one, or all such layers collectively.

Veil: a membrane extending from the edge of the **cap** to the stem, in certain mushrooms when immature, soon rupturing and often persisting as a ring around the stem; also (the "universal veil") in most *Amanita* mushrooms when they are very young "buttons," an additional, outer membrane extending from the edge of the cap to the underground base of the mushroom, soon rupturing and often visibly persisting as a more or less cup-shaped enlargement of the mushroom's base.

Vesicle: a small hole in a volcanic rock, which originated as a gas bubble in **lava**; vesicular porosity characterizes all pumice and many basalt and andesite specimens.

Whorl: an arrangement of three or more leaves (or other parts) around the same point along a stem or axis.

Widespread: More or less common (but not necessarily **abundant** or **dominant**) over a large portion of **our** range. Used in this book to imply more consistent occurrence than **sporadic**, but less so than **ubiquitous**.

Woody: reinforced with fibrous tissue so as to remain rigid and functional from one year to the next. Woody plants are trees or shrubs. Opposed to **herbaceous**.

Zooplankton: nonplant aquatic organisms that drift with the currents, lacking effective powers of either locomotion or attachment. A loose term including anything from one-celled organisms up to jellyfish and **larvae** of some insects. Pronounced "zoh-oh-**plank**-ton." Singular: "zooplankter."

Selected References

Plants (Chapters 2–6)

Arno, Stephen F. 1977. *Northwest Trees.* Seattle: The Mountaineers.

Bilderback, David E., ed. 1987. *Mt. St. Helens 1980: Botanical Consequences of the Explosive Eruptions.* Berkeley: U of CA.

Brayshaw, T. Christopher. 1996. *Trees and Shrubs of British Columbia.* Victoria: Royal B. C. Museum.

Buckingham, Nelsa M., et al. 1995. *Flora of the Olympic Peninsula.* Seattle: NW Interp. Assoc. and WA Native Plants Society. Little more than a checklist, but very expert, with useful habitat codes and taxonomic notes.

Chambers, Kenton L., and Scott Sundberg. 1998—. *Oregon Vascular Plant Checklist.* Corvallis: Oregon Flora Project (OSU). **Our authority** on scientific names of flowering plants to the extent determinations were available as of when we go to press.

Cooke, Sarah Spear, ed. 1997. *A Field Guide to the Common Wetland Plants of Western WA and Northwestern OR.* Seattle: Seattle Audubon Soc.

Cronquist, Arthur, et al. 1972—. *Intermountain Flora.* 6 volumes to date. NY: NY Botanical Garden Press. The Great Basin plus the rest of Utah.

Flora of N. A. Editorial Committee. 1993—. *Flora of North America N of Mexico.* 5 volumes to date, of 30 planned. NY: Oxford U Pr. **Our authority** on scientific names of ferns, clubmosses, spikemosses, and horsetails.

Franklin, Jerry F., and C. T. Dyrness. 1973. *Natural Vegetation of OR and WA.* USDA Forest Service GTR-PNW-8. Reprinted with additional bibliography, 1988. Corvallis: OSU Pr. Not a fun read, but a groundbreaking reference.

Gleason, Henry A. 1952. *New Britton and Brown Illustrated Flora.* 3 vols. NY: NY Botanical Garden.

Haskin, Leslie L. 1949. *Wild Flowers of the Pacific Coast.* Portland: Binford & Mort. (Reprinted 1977. NY: Dover.) A charming old-fashioned flower book; it retells reported Indian uses, some of them pretty questionable.

Hayes, Doris W., and George A. Garrison. 1960. *Key to Important Woody Plants of Eastern Oregon and Washington.* USDA Agr. Handbook No. 148.

Henderson, Jan A., et al. 1989. *Field Guide to the Forested Plant Associations of the Olympic N.F.* USDA For. Serv. Tech. Paper R6 ECOL TP 001-88.

——. 1992. *Field Guide to the Forested Plant Associations of the Mt. Baker-Snoqualmie N.F.* USDA For. Serv. Tech. Paper R6 ECOL TP 128-91.

Hickman, James C., ed. 1993. *The Jepson Manual of Higher Plants of California.* Berkeley: UC Press.

Hitchcock, C. Leo, and Arthur Cronquist. 1976. *Flora of the Pacific Northwest.* 3rd Printing, with corrections. Seattle: U of WA Press. The bible for serious plant identifiers in the Northwest, it takes some getting used to. It contains all of the species in the five-volume edition listed below, but with art and other data much abridged. Scientific names now rather outdated.

Hitchcock, C. Leo, A. Cronquist, M. Ownbey, and J. W. Thompson. 1955–69. *Vascular Plants of the PNW.* 5 volumes. Seattle: U of WA Pr. At full size, the exceptional beauty of Jeanne R. Janish's botanical illustrations is striking. They are reproduced in many other books, including the one in your hands.

Jolley, Russ. 1988. *Wildflowers of the Columbia Gorge.* Portland: OR Hist. Soc.

Little, Elbert L., Jr. 1980. *The Audubon Society Guide to North American Trees: Western Region.* NY: Knopf.

Lawton, Elva. 1971. *Moss Flora of the PNW.* Nichinan, Japan: Hattori Bot. Lab.

Moerman, Daniel E. 1998. *Native American Ethnobotany.* Portland: Timber.

Moore, Michael. 1993. *Medicinal Plants of the Pacific West.* Santa Fe: Red Crane Books.

Pojar, Jim, and Andy MacKinnon, eds. 1994. *Plants of Coastal British Columbia.* Edmonton, Alberta: Lone Pine. Published in U.S. as *Plants of the Northwest Coast.* Very thorough. Includes bryophytes and lichens (an excellent treatment by Trevor Goward) but no nonlichenized fungi.

Ross, Robert A., and Henrietta L. Chambers. 1988. *Wildflowers of the Western Cascades.* Portland: Timber.

Sudworth, George B. 1908. *Forest Trees of the Pacific Slope.* USDA Forest Service. (Reprint, 1967. NY: Dover.)

Schofield, W. B. 1969. *Some Common Mosses of B.C.* Victoria: BC Prov. Museum.

Szczawinski, Adam F. 1969. *The Orchids of B.C.*. Victoria: BC Prov. Museum.

——. 1970. *The Heather Family of British Columbia.* Victoria: BC Prov. Mus.

Taylor, Ronald J., and George W. Douglas. 1995. *Mountain Plants of the Pacific Northwest.* Missoula: Mountain Pr.

Taylor, T. M. C. 1973a. *The Ferns and Fern-allies of British Columbia.*

——. 1973b. *The Lily Family of British Columbia.*

——. 1973c. *The Rose Family of British Columbia.*

——. 1974a. *The Pea Family of British Columbia.*

——. 1974b. *The Figwort Family of British Columbia.* (All) Victoria: BC Provincial Museum.

Tilford, Gregory L. 1997. *Edible and Medicinal Plants of the West.* Missoula: Mtn. Pr.

Turner, Nancy J., and Adam f. Szczawinski. 1991. *Common Poisonous Plants and Mushrooms of N. A.* Portland: Timber.

Underhill, J. E. 1974. *Wild Berries of the PNW.* Saanichton, B.C.: Hancock.

Weber, William A., and Ronald C. Wittmann. 1996. *Colorado Flora.* Two Vols.; Rev. Ed. Boulder: Colo. Assoc. Univ. Press. Interesting extreme positions on Latin pronunciation and genus-level splitting.

Plant Articles

Alverson, Edward R. 1993. Recent taxonomic Changes for Oregon ferns and fern allies. *Kalmiopsis.* :16–23.

Am. Forestry Assoc. 1998. National register of big trees. *American Forests.*

Arno, Stephen F., and J. R. Habeck. 1972. Ecology of alpine larch in the PNW. *Ecol. Monographs* 42: 417-50.

Campbell, Alsie G., and J. F. Franklin. 1979. Riparian vegetation in OR's W. Cas. Mtns. Bull. No. 14, Coniferous Forest Biome. Seattle: U of WA Press.

Anderson, Lewis E., H. A. Crum, and Wm. R. Buck. 1990. List of the mosses of North America N of Mexico. *The Bryologist* 93: 448-71. **Our authority** on scientific names of mosses.

Braatne, J. H., and L. C. Bliss. 1999. Comparative Physiology ecology of lupines colonizing early successional habitats on Mt. St. Helens. *Ecology* 80(3): 891-907.

Cullings, K. W., T. M. Szaro and T. D. Bruns. 1996. Evolution of extreme specialization within a lineage of ectomycorrhizal epiparasites. *Nature* 379: 63–5.

Del Moral, R., and L. C. Bliss. 1993. Mechanisms of primary succession: insights resulting from the eruption of Mt. St. Helens. *Adv. in Ecol. Res.* 241-65.

Douglas, George W. 1972. Subalpine plant communities of the western North Cascades, WA. *Arctic & Alpine Research* 4: 147–66.

Douglas, George. W., and L. C. Bliss. 1977. Alpine and high subalpine communities of the N. Cas. Range, WA and BC. *Ecol. Monographs* 47: 113–50.

Dyrness, C. T., J. F. Franklin, and W. H. Moir. 1974. A preliminary classification of forest communities in the central portion of the Western Cascades in OR. Bull. No. 4, Coniferous Forest Biome. Seattle: U of WA Pr.

Evans, R. D., and R. W. Fonda. 1990. The influence of snow on subalpine meadow community pattern, N Cas., WA. *Canadian J Botany* 68: 212–20.

Fonda, R. W. 1974. Forest succession in relation to river terrace development in Olympic National Park, WA. *Ecology* 55: 927-42.

Fonda, R. W., and L. C. Bliss. 1969. Forest vegetation of the montane and subalpine zones, Olympic Mtns., WA. *Ecol. Monographs* 39: 271–301.

Hennon, Paul. E., and Chas. G. Shaw III. 1997. What is killing these long-lived defensive trees? [Alaska yellow cedars] *Journal of Forestry* Dec.: 5–10

Kuramoto, R. T., and L. C. Bliss. 1970. Ecology of subalpine meadows in the Olympic Mtns., WA. *Ecol. Monographs* 40: 317–47.

Lillybridge, Terry R., et al. 1995. *Field Guide to the Forested Plant Associations of the Wenatchee National Forest*. USDA Forest Service PNW-GTR-359.

McKee, Arthur, G. LaRoi, and J. F. Franklin. 1980. Structure, composition, and reproductive behavior of terrace forests, S Fork Hoh River, ONP. In *Proceedings of the 2nd Conf. on Sci. Research in Nat. Parks, San Francisco, 1979*.

Nadkarni, N. M. 1985. Roots that go out on a limb. *Natural Hist.* 94(5): 42–49.

Silen, Roy. R. and D. L. Olson. 1992. A pioneer exotic tree search for the Douglas-fir region. USDA Forest Service PNW-GTR-298.

Fungi (Chapter 7)

Arora, David. 1986. *Mushrooms Demystified*. 2nd Edition. Berkeley: Ten Speed Press. An excellent, very thick, mushroom guide.

Bessette, Alan E., Arleen R. Bessette, and David W. Fischer. 1997. *Mushrooms of Northeastern North America*. Syracuse, N.Y.: Syracuse U. Pr.

Lincoff, G. H. 1981. *The Aud. Soc. Field Guide to N. A. Mushrooms*. NY: Knopf.

Marteka, Vincent. 1980. *Mushrooms Wild and Edible*. NY: Norton.

McCune, Bruce, and Linda Geiser. 1997. *Macrolichens of the PNW*. Corvallis: OSU Press. Every region should have a lichen guide this good! Fine color photos by Sylvia and Stephen Sharnoff, who also illustrate *Lichens of N. A.*, by I. M. Brodo, in progress. Excludes crust lichens, considered too technical.

McKenny, Margaret, and, Daniel E. Stuntz. 1987. *The New Savory Wild Mushroom.* Seattle: U of WA Press. The best PNW-only mushroom guide.

Miller, Orson K., Jr. 1972. *Mushrooms of North America.* NY: Dutton.

Persson, Olle. 1997. *The Chanterelle Book.* (Orig. Swedish edition publ. in 1994.) Berkeley: Ten Speed Press.

Pyrozynski, K. A., and D. L. Hawksworth, eds. 1988. *Coevolution of Fungi with Plants and Animals.* London: Academic Pr.

Savonius, M. 1973. *All Color Book of Mushrooms and Fungi.* NY: Octopus Bks.

Fungi Articles

Ahmadjian, Vernon. 1982. The nature of lichens. *Natural Hist.* 91(3): 31-37.

Barron, George. 1992. Jekyll-Hyde Mushrooms. *Natural Hist.* 101(3): 47-52.

Denison, William C. 1973. Life in tall trees. *Scientific American* 228(6): 74-80.

Douglas, G. W. 1974. Lichens of the N Cas. Range, WA. *Bryologist* 77: 582-92.

Goward, Trevor. 1996. Dust to dust. *Nature Canada.* Summer 1996: 44-45.

Helgason, T., et al. 1998. Ploughing up the wood-wide web? *Nature* 394:431.

Hosford, David, et al. 1997. *Ecology and management of the commercially harvested American matsutake.* USDA Forest Service PNW-GTR-412.

Jongmans, A. G., et al. 1997. Rock-eating fungi. *Nature.* 389: 682-83.

McCune, Bruce. 1993. Gradients in epiphyte biomass in three *Pseudotsuga-Tsuga* forests of different ages in W OR and WA. *Bryologist* 96(3): 405-11.

Molina, Randy, et al. 1993. *Biology, ecology and social aspects of wild edible mushrooms in the forests of the PNW.* USDA For. Service PNW-GTR-309.

Näsholm, Torgny, et al. 1998. Boreal forest plants take up organic nitrogen. *Nature* 392: 914-16.

Selosse, M-A., and F. le Tacon. 1998. The land flora: a phototroph-fungus partnership? *Trends in Ecology and Evolution* 13(1): 15-20.

Shaw, Charles G. III, and Glen A. Kile, eds. 1991. *Armillaria Root Disease.* USDA Forest Service Agr. Handbook No. 691.

Simard, Suzanne W., et al. 1997. Net transfer of carbon between ectomycorrhizal tree species in the field. *Nature* 388: 579-82.

Thies, Walter G., and Rona N. Sturrock. 1995. *Laminated root rot in western NA.* USDA Forest Service Gen. Tech. Report PNW-GTR-349.

Trappe, James M. 1998. Lessons from Alpine Fungi. *Mycologia* 80(1): 1-10.

Trappe, J. M., and D. L. Luoma. 1992. The ties that bind. In *The Fungal Community*, 2nd Ed., ed. G. C. Carroll and D. T. Wicklow. NY: Marcell-Decker.

Mammals (Chapter 8)

Chadwick, Douglas H. 1983. *A Beast the Color of Winter: the Mountain Goat Observed.* San Francisco: Sierra Club.

Maser, Chris. 1998. *Mammals of the Pacific Northwest.* Corvallis: OSU Press. A relatively personal work on mammals, in the old "field naturalist" mode.

McKenna, Malcolm C., and Susan K. Bell. 1997. *Classification of Mammals Above the Species Level.* NY: Columbia U. Pr.

Murie, Olaus J. 1975. *A Field Guide to Animal Tracks.* Boston: Houghton.

Savage, Arthur, and, Candace Savage. 1981. *Wild Mammals of Northwest America.* Baltimore: Johns Hopkins.

Vaughan, Terry A. 1978. *Mammalogy.* Philadelphia: Saunders.

Verts, B. J., and L. N. Carraway. 1998. *Land Mammals of Oregon.* Berkeley: U of CA Pr. **Our authority** on the scientific names of mammals.

Whitaker, John O., Jr. 1998. *The Audubon Society Field Guide to North American Mammals.* Rev. Ed. NY: Knopf.

Wilson, D. E., and D. M. Reeder. 1993. *Mammal Species of the World.* 2nd Ed. Washington, DC: Smithsonian Inst. Pr.

Mammal Articles

Almack, J. A., and S. H. Fitkin. 1998. *Grizzly Bear and Gray Wolf Investigations in WA State, 1994-1995.* Olympia: WDFW.

American Society of Mammalogists. *Mammalian Species.* Series.

Barash, David P. 1974. The social behavior of the hoary marmot. *Animal Behavior* 22: 256–61.

Clutton-Brock, T. H. 1982. The functions of antlers. *Behavior* 79: 108–23.

de Vos, A., P. Brokx, and V. Geist. 1967. A review of social behavior of the NA cervids during the reproductive period. *Am Midland Nat.* 77: 390–417.

Jones, J. K., et al. 1992. *Revised Checklist of North American Mammals N of Mexico.* Occasional Papers, The Museum, Texas Tech. U., No. 146: 1–23.

Muller-Schwartz, D. 1971. Pheromones in the black-tailed deer. *Animal Behavior* 19: 141-52.

Rogers, Lynn. 1981. A bear in its lair. *Natural History* 90(10): 64–70.

Roze, U. 1985. How to select, climb, and eat a tree. *Natural Hist.* 94(5): 63–68.

Smith, Andrew. 1997. The art of making hay. *National Wildlife* 35(3): 31–35.

Woodward, Andrea, et al. 1994. Ungulate-forest relationships in Olympic N. P.: retrospective exclosure studies. *NW Science* 68(2): 98–110.

Birds (Chapter 9)

American Ornithologists Union. 1998. *Check-list of North American Birds.* 7th Edition. Lawrence: Allen Press. **Our authority** on names of birds.

Contreras, Alan. 1997. *Northwest Birds in Winter.* Corvallis: OSU Pr.

Beebe, F. L. 1974. *Field Studies of the Falconiformes of BC.* Victoria: BC Prov. Mus.

Farrand, John, Jr., ed. 1983. *The Audubon Soc. Master Guide to Birding.* NY: Knopf.

Gilligan, Jeff, et al., eds. 1994. *Birds of Oregon: status and distribution.* McMinnville: Cinclus. Out of print. One of its co-editors, Alan Contreras, is at work on a volume to take its place, forthcoming from O.S.U. Press.

Kaufmann, Kenn. 1996. *Lives of North American Birds.* Boston: Houghton.

MacRae, Diann. 1995. *Birder's Guide to Washington.* Houston: Gulf Publ. Co. Site guide; some non-avian natural history. Fine drawings by Libby Mills.

National Geographic Society. 1999. *Field Guide to the Birds of North America.* Second Edition. Washington, D.C.: Natl. Geog. Some prefer this bulkier guide for its detailed drawings, which often distinguish geographic races.

Nehls, Harry B. 1981. *Familiar Birds of the NW.* Portland: Aud. Soc. of Portland.

Peterson, Roger Tory. 1990. *A Field Guide to W Birds.* 3rd Ed. Boston: Houghton.

Robbins, Chandler S.; Bruun, B.; Zim, H. S.; and Singer, A. 1983. *Birds of North America.* NY: Golden. Compact, easy-to-use bird guide.

Stokes, Donald and Lillian. 1996. *Stokes Field Guide to Birds: Western Region.* Boston: Little, Brown.

Terres, J. K. 1980. *The Audubon Soc. Encyclopedia of NA Birds.* NY: Knopf.

Udvardy, Miklos D. F. 1977. *The Audubon Soc. Field Guide to NA Birds: Western Region.* NY: Knopf.

Bird Articles

Barnea, A., and F. Nottebohm. 1996. Recruitment and replacement of hippocampal neurons in… chickadees. *Proc. Natl. Acad. Sci. USA* 93: 714–18.

Benkman, Craig W. 1993. Adaptation to single resources and the evolution of crossbill (*Loxia*) diversity. *Ecol. Monographs* 63(3): 305–25.

Birds of North America. . Phila: Acad. of Nat. Sci.; and Washington DC: Am. Ornith. Union. Within a few years, this ambitious series of single-species issues will summarize available science on all 700+ species N of Mexico.

Brown, C. R. and M. B. 1990. The great egg scramble. *Nat. Hist.* 99(2): 34–40.

Franklin, Ken. In press. Vertical flight. *N Am. Falconry Journal.*

Griffiths, C. S. 1994. Monophyly of the Falconiformes… *Auk* 111(4): 787–805.

Otter, Ken, et al. 1998. Do female black-capped chickadees prefer high-ranking males as extra-pair partners? *Behav. Ecol. Sociobiol.* 43: 25–36.

Rattenborg, N.C., et al. 1999. Half-awake to the risk of predation. *Nature* 397: 397–98.

Reptiles and Amphibians (Chapters 10-11)

Behler, John L., and, F. Wayne King. 1979. *The Audubon Society Field Guide to North American Reptiles and Amphibians.* NY: Knopf.

Collins, J. T. 1990. *Standard common and current scientific names for N Americanamphibians and reptiles.* 3rd ed. Soc. for Study of Amph. and Rep.: Herp. Circ. No. 19. **Our authority** on scientific names of herps.

Corkran, Charlotte C., and Chris Thoms. 1996. *Amphibians of Oregon, Washington and British Columbia.* Edmonton: Lone Pine.

Hedges, S. B., and L. L. Poling. 1999. A molecular phylogeny of reptiles. *Science* 283: 998–1001.

Kiesecker, J. M., and A. R. Blaustein. 1995. Synergism between UV-B Radiation and a pathogen magnifies amphibian embryo mortality in nature. *Proc. Natl. Acad. Sci. USA.* 92: 11049–52.

Leonard, W. P., et al. 1993. *Amphibians of WA and OR.* Seattle: Sea. Aud. Soc.

Leonard, William P., and Robert M. Storm, Eds. 1995. *Reptiles of WA and OR.* Seattle: Seattle Aud. Soc.

St. John, Alan D. In press. *Reptiles of the PNW.* Edmonton: Lone Pine.

Stebbins, Robert. C. and Nathan. W. Cohen. 1995. *A Natural History of Amphibians.* Princeton, NJ: Princeton Univ. Pr.

Fishes (Chapter 12)

Wydoski, R. S., and R. R Whitney. 1979. *Inland Fishes of WA.* Seattle: UW Pr.

Insects (Chapter 13)

Arnett, Ross H. 1985. *American Insects.* NY: Van Nostrand. **Our authority** on scientific names of insects other than Lepidoptera.

Borror, Donald J., D. M.DeLong, and C. A Triplehorn. 1976. *An Introduction to the Study of Insects.* 4th Edition. NY: Holt.

Cole, Frank R. 1969. *The Flies of Western NA.* Berkeley: U of CA Pr.

Furniss, R. L., and Carolin, V. M. 1977. *Western Forest Insects.* USDA Forest Service Misc. Publ. No. 1339. Mainly about insects destructive to trees.

Gillett, J. D. 1971. *Mosquitoes*. London: Weidenfeld and Nicolson.

Heinrich, Bernd. 1979. *Bumblebee Economics*. Cambridge: Harvard U Pr.
———. 1996. *The Thermal Warriors*. Cambridge: Harvard U Pr.

Hinchliff, John. 1994. *An Atlas of OR Butterflies*. Corvallis: OSU Bookstore.
———. 1996. *An Atlas of WA Butterflies*. Corvallis: OSU Bookstore.

Hughes, Dave, and Rick Hafele. 1981, *The Complete Book of Western Hatches*. Portland: F Amato Pubns. Entomology applied to dry-fly fishing.

Milne, Lorus, and Margery Milne. 1980. *The Audubon Society Field Guide to North American Insects and Spiders*. NY: Knopf.

Pettinger, L. F., and D. W. Johnson. 1972. *A Field Guide to Important Forest Insects and Diseases of OR and WA*. USDA Forest Service PNW Region. Source of bark beetle gallery drawings on pp 458-60.

Opler, Paul A., and Amy Bartlett Wright. 1999. *Western Butterflies*. 2nd Ed. Boston: Houghton.

Pyle, Robert Michael. 1981. *The Audubon Society Field Guide to North American Butterflies*. NY: Knopf.
———. In press. *The Butterflies of Cascadia*. Seattle: Seattle Audubon Society. **Our authority** (via personal communication) on names of butterflies.

Swan, L. A., and C. S Papp. 1972. *The Common Insects of NA*. NY: Harper.

Thornhill, Randy, and John Alcock. 1983. *The Evolution of Insect Mating Systems*. Cambridge: Harvard U Pr.

Insect Articles

Deyrup, Mark. 1981. Deadwood decomposers. *Natural History* 90(3): 84–91.

Heinrich, Bernd. 1990. The antifreeze of bees. *Natural History* 99(7): 53–58.

Hubbell, Sue. 1997. Trouble with honeybees. *Natural History* 106(5): 32–43.

Raffa, K. F., and A. A. Berryman. 1983. The role of host plant resistance in the colonization behavior and ecology of bark beetles. *Ecol. Monographs* 53: 27–49.

Shaw, David C., and R. J. Taylor. 1986. Pollination ecology of an alpine fell-field community in the North Cascades. *NW Science* 60: 21–31.

Other Creatures (Chapter 14)

Garric, Richard K. 1965. The cryoflora of the PNW. *Am J of Botany* 52: 1–8.

Meyer, Ernest A. 1985. The epidemiology of giardiasis. *Parasitology Today* 1(4): 101–5.

Upcroft, Jacqui, and Peter Upcroft. 1998. My favorite cell: Giardia. *BioEssays* 20(3): 256–63.

Geology (Chapter 15)

Allen, John Eliot. 1979, *The Magnificent Gateway: a Layman's Guide to the Geology of the Columbia River Gorge.* Portland: Timber.

Allen, J. E., et al. 1987. *Cataclysms on the Columbia.* Portland: Timber.

Alt, David D., and Donald W. Hyndman. 1978. *Roadside Geology of Oregon.* Missoula: Mountain Pr.

——. 1984. *Roadside Geology of Washington* Missoula: Mountain Pr.

——. 1995. *Northwest Exposures.* Missoula: Mountain Pr. Alt and Hyndman make geology easy and fun, but play fast and loose with the hypotheses.

Dietrich, Richard V. 1980. *Stones: their Collection, Identification and Uses.* San Francisco: W. H. Freeman.

Dietrich, R. V., and B. J. Skinner. 1979. *Rocks and Rock Minerals.* NY: Wiley.

Harris, Stephen L. 1988. *Fire Mountains of the West.* Missoula: Mountain Pr.

Tabor, Rowland W. 1975. *Guide to the Geology of Olympic National Park.* Seattle: U of WA Pr. Excellent popular-level presentation of the Olympics.

Tabor, Rowland, and Ralph Haugerud. 1999. *Geology of the North Cascades.* Seattle: Mountaineers. It's medium-format and has showy photography, and it's also the real goods, by specialists in the subject.

Geology Articles

Atwater, B., and E. Hemphill-Haley. 1997. *Recurrence intervals for great earthquakes of the past 3500 years at NE Willapa Bay, WA.* USGS Prof. Paper 1576.

Babcock, R. S(cott), et al. 1992. A rifted margin origin for the Crescent Basalts and related rocks... *J of Geophysical Research* 97(B5) 6799–6821.

Bucknam, R. C., E. Hemphill-Haley, and E. B. Leopold. 1992. Abrupt uplift within the past 1700 years at S Puget Sound, WA. *Science* 258: 1611–14.

Hildreth, Wes. 1996. Kulshan Caldera: a Quaternary subglacial caldera in the N Cascades, WA. *GSA Bulletin.* 108(7): 786–93.

Hildreth, W., and M. A. Lanphere. 1994. Potassium-argon geochronology of a basalt-andesite-dacite arc system (Mt. Adams). *GSA Bull.* 106: 1413–29.

Lescinsky, D. T., and T. W. Sisson. 1998. Ridge-forming, ice-bounded lava flows at Mt. Rainier, WA. *Geology* 26(4): 351–54.

O'Connor, James E., and Richard B. Waitt. 1995. Beyond the Channeled Scabland: a field trip to Missoula Flood features... *OR Geology* 57(3-5):51–115.

Satake, Kenji, et al. 1996. Time and size of a giant earthquake in Cascadia inferred from Japanese tsunami records of January, 1700. *Nature* 379: 246.

Shaw, John, et al. 1999. The Channeled Scabland: back to Bretz? *Geology* 27(7): 605–08.

Tabor Rowland W., et al. 1989. *Accreted Terranes of the North Cascades Range, WA.* Amer. Geophys. Union Field Trip Guidebook T307.

Vallance, J. W., and K. M. Scott. 1997. The Osceola Mudflow from Mt. Rainier: sedimentology and hazard implications… *GSA Bull.* 109(2): 143–63.

Waitt, R. B., Larry G. Mastin, and James E. Begét. 1995. Volcanic-hazard zonation for Glacier Peak volcano, WA. USGS Open-file Report 95-449.

Wells, Ray E., Craig S. Weaver, and Richard J. Blakely. 1998. Fore-arc migration in Cascadia and its neotectonic significance. *Geology* 26(8): 759–62.

Climate (Chapter 16)

Bond, Gerard, et al. 1997. A pervasive millenial-scale cycle in North Atlantic Holocene and glacial climates. *Science* 278: 1257–66.

Broecker, W. S. 1999. What if the conveyor were to shut down? Reflections on a possible outcome of the great global experiment. *GSA Today* 9(1): 1–7.

Geiger, R. 1965. *The Climate Near the Ground.* (Rev.) Cambridge: Harv. U Pr.

Haq, B. U. 1998. Gas hydrates: Greenhouse nightmare? Energy panacea or pipe dream? *GSA Today* 8(11): 1–6. http://www.geosociety.org/pubs/gsatoday

Lydolph, Paul E. 1985. *The Climate of the Earth.* Totowa, NJ: Rowman.

Mantua, Nathan J., et al. A Pacific interdecadal climate oscillation with impacts on salmon production. In press. *Bulletin of Am. Meteor. Soc.*

Reifsnyder, W. E. 1980. *Weathering the Wilderness.* San Francisco: Sierra Club.

Woodward, Andrea. 1998. Relationships among environmental variables and distribution of tree species at high elev. in the Oly. Mtns. *NW Sci.* 72: 10–22.

Cross-Disciplinary and Miscellaneous

Arno, Stephen F. 1984. *Timberline:* Seattle: Mountaineers.

Beckey, Fred. 1987, 1989, 1995. *Cascade Alpine Guide: Climbing and High Routes.* 2nd Ed. 3 volumes. Seattle: Mountaineers. The climbers' route reference; also a wealth of research on history and geology; WA and BC only.

Borror, Donald J. 1960. *Dictionary of Word Roots and Combining Forms.* Mtn. View, CA: Mayfield.

Boyd, R., Ed. 1999. *Indians, Fire, and the Land in the PNW.* Corvallis: OSU Pr.

Csuti, Blair, et al. 1997. *Atlas of Oregon Wildlife.* Corvallis: OSU Pr.

Davis, James Luther. 1996. *Seasonal Guide to the Natural Year: OR, WA, and BC.* Golden, CO: Fulcrum.

Douglas, David. 1980. *Douglas of the Forests: the North American Journals of David Douglas.* Edited by John Davies. Seattle: U of WA Pr.

Dukes, Jeffrey S., and Harold A. Mooney. 1999. Does global change increase the success of biological invaders? *Trends in Ecol. and Evol.* 14(4): 135–39.

Duncan, David James. 1995. *River Teeth: Stories and Writings.* NY: Doubleday. Reissued by Bantam.

Franklin, J. F.; Hall, F. C.; Dyrness, C. T.; and Maser, C. 1972. *Federal Research Natural Areas in Oregon and Washington: a Guidebook for Scientists and Educators.* Portland: USDA Forest Service PNW Forest and Range Exp Sta.

Franklin, Jerry F., et al. 1991. Effects of global climatic change on forests in Northwestern NA. *NW Environmental Journal* 7:233–254.

Graumlich, Lisa J., and Linda B. Brubaker. 1989. Long-term trends in forest net primary productivity: Cascade Mtns., WA. *Ecology* 70(2): 405–410.

Guenther, Erna. 1973. *Ethnobotany of Western WA.* Seattle: U of WA Pr.

Judson, Katherine B. 1910. *Myths and Legends of the PNW.* Chicago: McClurg.

Kohm, Kathryn A., and Jerry F. Franklin, eds. 1997. *Creating A Forestry For The 21st Century.* Washington, D.C.: Island.

Kozloff, Eugene N. 1976. *Plants and Animals of the Pacific Northwest.* U of WA Pr. A good guide to Puget-Willamette lowland species, giving rare attention to molluscs, arthropods, mosses and liverworts.

Lewis, Meriwether, and William Clark. *The Journals of Lewis and Clark.* Edited by Bernard DeVoto. 1953. Boston: Houghton.

Luoma, Jon R. 1999. *The Hidden Forest.* NY: Holt. The story of the H. J. Andrews Experimental Forest and what's being learned there.

Maser, Chris, and Trappe, James M. 1984. *The Seen and Unseen World of the Fallen Tree.* USDA Forest Service PNW-164.

Margulis, Lynn, and Karlene V Schwartz. 1998. *Five Kingdoms.* 3rd Ed. NY: W. H. Freeman. **Our authority** on taxonomy at the kingdom and phylum levels; R. H. Whittaker's five kingdoms revised by eminent microbiologist.

McKelvey, Susan Delano. 1955. *Botanical Exploration of the Trans-Mississippi West,* 1790–1850. (Reprinted 1991. Corvallis: OSU Pr.)

Perry, David A. 1994. *Forest Ecosystems.* Baltimore: Johns Hopkins. Textbook; excels in its clarity on the interconnectedness of all the parts.

Perry, David A., et al., eds. 1989. *Maintaining the Long Term Productivity of Pacific Northwest Forests.* Portland: Timber.

Perry, David A., et al. 1991. Biological feedbacks to climate change: terrestrial ecosystems as sinks and sources of Carbon and Nitrogen. *NW Environmental Journal* 7:203–232.

Rogers, Maggie. 1996. Hello: 4,500 new species like it here: imported wood products can bring trouble. *Mushroom the Journal.* Summer 1996: 24–27.

Ruggiero, Leonard F., et al, tech. coords. 1991. *Wildlife and Management of Unmanaged Douglas-Fir Forests.* USDA Forest Serv. PNW-GTR-285.

Schoonmaker, Peter K., Bettina von Hagen, and Edw. C. Wolf. 1997. *The Rain Forests of Home.* Washington, D.C.: Island.

Snyder, Gary. 1969. *Earth House Hold.* NY: New Directions. Contains interesting journals from stints (1951–52) as a fire lookout in the N Cascades. Snyder's early poetry (*Myths and Texts; Riprap; Mountains and Rivers Without End; The Back Country.*) is rich with PNW wilderness experience.

Spring, Ira, and Byron Fish. 1981. *Lookouts: Firewatchers of the Cascades and Olympics.* Seattle: Mountaineers. Entertaining lore

Storer, T. I., and R. L. Usinger. 1963. *Sierra Nevada Natural History.* Berkeley: U of CA Pr. The inspiration for *Cascade-Olympic Natural History.*

Turner, Nancy J. 1979. *Plants in BC Indian Technology.* Victoria: BC Prov. Mus.

———. 1997. *Food Plants of Interior First Peoples.* Vancouver: UBC Pr.

———. 1995. *Food Plants of Coastal First Peoples.* Vancouver: UBC Pr. Nancy Turner's three volumes together are the most compact, authoritative, inexpensive reference on Northwest ethnobotany that we could ask for. Too bad there's nothing like them on peoples south of the 49th Parallel.

Verner, Jared, and Allen S. Boss, eds. 1980. *California Wildlife and Their Habitats: Western Sierra Nevada.* USDA Forest Service GTR-PSW-37. Source of mostof the drawings in Chapters 8, 9, and 11.

Web Sites

Most of the scientific journals referenced above have Web sites; some give abstracts or summaries of articles; some offer complete articles.

http://plants.usda.gov/plantproj/plants/index
The PLANTS database of plant and lichen names.

http://www.orst.edu/dept/botany/herbarium/
OSU Herbarium, including the Oregon Flora Project.

http://www.fna.org/
Flora of North America, the set of books in progress.

http://phylogeny.arizona.ed/tree
Pure phylogenetic family trees of higher taxonomy, with links to subtaxa.

http://www.lichen.com
Lichens of North America, Irwin Brodo's book in progress.

http://ucs.orst.edu/~mccuneb/
Bruce McCune's lichen homepage.

http://www.mycoinfo.com
"The World's First Mycological E-Journal" and Internet Bookstore.

http://www.wisc.edu/botany/fungi/volkmyco.html
Tom Volk's Fungi, with great Fungus of the Month articles, photos.

http://nmnhgoph.si.edu/msw/
Updates of the Wilson and Reeder mammal list

http://www.orst.edu/pubs/birds/
The Oregon Birds Forum—work in progress on *Birds of Oregon.*

http://www.birdsofna.org/
Birds of North America, the series.

http://www.geosociety.org/
Geol. Soc. of Am., including their monthly, *GSA Today.*

http://www.nichols.edu/departments/Glacier
Mauri Pelto's North Cascades Glacier Climate Project.

http://vulcan.wr.usgs.gov
USGS Cascade Volcano Observatory

http://www.ocs.orst.edu/
Oregon Climate Service. State Climatologist George Taylor publishes on climate cycles affecting the PNW

http://www.naturenw.org/
The Forest Service's information site, esp for recreation and publications.

http://www.dfw.state.or.us
OR Dept. of Fish and Wildlife

http://www.wa.gov/wdfw
WA Dept. of Fish and Wildlife

http://www.nps.gov/mora
Mt. Rainier National Park

http://www.nps.gov/noca
North Cascades National Park

http://www.nps.gov/olym
Olympic National Park

Index

Index 623